CONCISE COMPENDIUM OF THE WORLD'S LANGUAGES

CONCISE COMPENDIUM OF THE WORLD'S LANGUAGES

BY

GEORGE L. CAMPBELL

LONDON AND NEW YORK

First published 1995
by Routledge
11 New Fetter Lane, London EC4P 4EE

Simultaneously published in the USA and Canada
by Routledge
29 West 35th Street, New York, NY 10001

First published in paperback 1998
Reprinted 1999

Routledge is an imprint of the Taylor & Francis Group

Printed and bound in Great Britain by
T.J. International Ltd, Padstow, Cornwall

British Library Cataloguing in Publication Data
A catalogue record for this book is available from the British Library

Library of Congress Cataloguing in Publication Data
A catalogue record for this book is available from the Library of Congress

ISBN 0–415–11392–X (hbk)
ISBN 0–415–16049–9 (pbk)

CONTENTS

INTRODUCTION

The *Concise Compendium of the World's Languages* derives from the two-volume *Compendium of the World's Languages*, published by Routledge in 1991. 'Concise' in the title refers to the reduced number of languages here covered – about a hundred as compared with some 300 in the larger work. Many of the articles selected for inclusion in the present book have, in fact, been substantially amplified. In the concise edition the purpose remains the same: to provide brief descriptions, phonological, morphological, lexical snapshots, in non-technical language, of a fairly wide cross-section of contemporary natural-language systems.

Articles were selected in the light of three criteria:

1. Number of speakers: most languages spoken at present by at least 5–10 million people are included.
2. Socio-political interest and importance: under this heading, certain minor languages have been included whose speakers have, for whatever reason, acquired a heightened political profile and topical relevance: Basque, Macedonian, Kurdish, and Zulu have been chosen simply as representatives of this class, certainly not as its only members.
3. Initially, it had been hoped to illustrate most of the world's language families by at least one member, but constraints of space ruled this out. However, space has been found for four minor languages of great intrinsic interest: Navajo, Lappish, Nama, and Nivkh.

By the same rationale, dead languages have been excluded. Here, the retention of Classical Chinese (Wenli) and Sanskrit may appear anomalous. The explanation is that both of these are, in a sense, living languages. Classical Chinese on two counts: the language of the Yuan drama and the Ming/Qing novel does not differ greatly from literary Modern Standard Chinese; and by virtue of the Chinese script even Tang poetry and the Confucian classics are on visual hold, as it were, and readily accessible to literate Chinese of latter-day generations. As for Sanskrit, it has consistently acted, and continues to act, as an inexhaustible reservoir of living tissue for the new Indo-Aryan languages, by supplying them with straight implants (*tatsama* 'just as it was', scil. in Sanskrit) or its genetic progeny (*tadbhava* 'derived from that', scil. from Sanskrit).

As a result of the greatly reduced coverage, much of the Bibliography which rounded off the *Compendium* became irrelevant, and has been discarded. The remainder has been re-arranged by language. As in the *Compendium*, verses 1–8 of the first chapter of St John's Gospel have been appended as an illustrative example to most articles. Where no translation of this gospel is available, an alternative passage from the New Testament has been substituted and identified. Alone in the present book, Nivkh, which was unwritten until the 1930s, has no illustrative text.

The relevant script tables are collected at the end of the book.

In conclusion, I would like to express my gratitude to Simon Bell and Claire Trocmé for their invaluable help in the production of this book.

ABBREVIATIONS

abl.	ablative
abs.	absolute
acc.	accusative
adess.	adessive
adit.	aditive
affirm.	affirmative
Afr.	Afrikaans
anim.	animate
Ar.	Arabic
Assyr.	Assyrian
aux.	auxiliary
Av.	Avestan
Azer.	Azerbaijani
Bel.	Belorussian
BI	Bahasa Indonesia
BP	Brazilian Portuguese
Ch.	Chinese
Ch.Ap.	Chiricahua Apache
Chip.	Chipewyan
cl.	class
CL	Classical Latin
com.	comitative
comp.	comparative
conj.	conjunctive
D	Dutch
dat.	dative
def.	definite
dep.	dependent
EArm.	Eastern Armenian
EP	European Portuguese
erg.	ergative
ESlav.	Eastern Slavonic
excl.	exclusive
fam.	familiar
fem.	feminine
Fin.	Finnish
Fr.	French
fut.	future
gen.	genitive
Gk	Greek
Gm.	German
hon.	honorific
IE	Indo-European
illat.	illative
imper.	imperative
imperf.	imperfect
impers.	impersonal
inanim.	inanimate
incl.	inclusive
Ind.	Indonesian
indef.	indefinite
iness.	inessive
instr.	instrumental
It.	Italian
Jap.	Japanese
K	Kråmå (Javanese)
Lat.	Latin
lk	link
loc.	locative
masc.	masculine
ME	Middle English
MF	Middle French
MSC	Modern Standard Chinese

N	Ngoko (Javanese)	pron.	pronoun
Nav.	Navajo	prox.	proximate
neg.	negative		
neut.	neuter	refl.	reflexive
nom.	nominative	rel.	relative
		Romy	Romany
O/obj.	object	Russ.	Russian
obl.	oblique		
obv.	obviative	S/sbj.	subject
OE	Old English	SC	Serbo-Croat
OF	Old French	sing.	singular
OI	Old Irish	Skt	Sanskrit
Old Ch. Slav.	Old Church Slavonic	Sl.	Slovene
		Slav.	Slavonic
opt.	optative	Som.	Somali
Osc.	Oscan	Sp.	Spanish
		SSlav.	Southern Slavonic
p.	person	subj.	subjunctive
part.	partitive		
pass.	passive	trans.	transitive
perf.	perfective		
pl.	plural	Ukr.	Ukrainian
Pol.	Polynesian		
poss.	possessive	V	verb
pp.	past participle	Viet.	Vietnamese
prep.	preposition(al)	VN	verbal noun
pres.	present	voc.	vocative
pret.	preterite		
prog.	progressive	WArm.	Western Armenian

AFRIKAANS

INTRODUCTION

Afrikaans belongs to the West Germanic branch of Indo-European, and is derived from the same sixteenth-century Dutch dialect, Frankish in origin, which underlies modern Dutch. It took shape first in Cape Colony, where Jan van Riebeeck had arrived in 1652, and spread to the rest of South Africa, from the seventeenth century onwards. It has been a literary language for a little over a century. On both counts, it is the youngest of the Germanic languages. At present, it is spoken by about 4 million people.

The language was originally known as Kaaps-Hollands or Plat-Hollands. The designation 'Afrikaans' was adopted towards the end of the nineteenth century. From 1910 till 1925, Dutch and English were the joint official languages of the Union of South Africa; in 1925 Afrikaans replaced Dutch. The use of Afrikaans is mainly characteristic of the Cape Province, the Orange Free State, and the Transvaal.

SCRIPT

Roman, 26 letters as in English; *c*, *q*, *x*, *z*, are rarely used. The circumflex is used to mark the long open *ê*, *ô*: *lê* = /lɛː/.

PHONOLOGY

Consonants

stops: p, b, t, d, k, g, ʔ; palatalized k′;
affricates: ts, tʃ
fricatives: f, v, s, ʃ, j, x, ɦ
nasals: m, n, ɲ, ŋ
lateral and flap: l, r
/z/ occurs in a few loan-words.

[g] and [x] are allophones: cf. *berg* 'mountain', /bɛrx/, pl. *berge*, /bɛrgə/. /p, t, k/ are non-aspirate, /b, d/ in final position are unvoiced → [p, t]. Dutch /sx-/ = Afrikaans /sk-/, and Dutch final *-t* drops: e.g. *nacht* > *nag* /nax/ 'night'; *nest* > *nes*, 'nest'.

Vowels

front: i, iː, e, ɛ, ɛː, y, yː
middle: ə, əː, a, ɵ, ɪ, ɪː
back: ɑ, ɔ, ɔː, oː, u, uː, ʊ

/eː/ is realized as [e(ː)ə] or [ɪə]; /oː/ as [o(ː)ə] or [ʊə]. /a,ɛ,ɔ/ are nasalized when followed by *n* + fricative: e.g. *mense* [mɛ̃ːsə], 'people'; *aangesig* [ãːxəsɪx], 'face'.

DIPHTHONGS
Simple (short) or lengthened; all are falling.

short: əy, oʊ, œy (= Dutch /ʌy/), ɑi, ɔi, ui
long: ɑːi, oːi/ɔːi, eːu

Stress

Stress is free, associated with pitch. The main stress is normally on the root. In separable verbs, however, the stress is transferred to the prefix.

MORPHOLOGY AND SYNTAX

The division into common and neuter nouns, retained in Dutch, has been lost in Afrikaans. A single definite article – *die* – applies to all nouns, singular and plural: e.g. *die vader* 'the father' – *die moeder* 'the mother' – *die kinders* 'the children'. *'n* = [ə] is used as singular indefinite article: e.g. *'n vliegtuig* 'a plane'.

NUMBER
-e is a frequent plural marker, with phonetic adjustment, where necessary, at juncture; *-s* and *-ers* are also used: e.g. *wolf* – *wolwe*; *skip* 'ship' – *skepe*; *dag* 'day' – *dae*; *oom* 'uncle' – *ooms; kind* 'child' – *kinders*.

CASE
There is no inflection for case in Afrikaans; the genitive relationship is expressed periphrastically with the particle *se*: e.g. *sy vader se huis* 'his father's house'; *Pretoria se koerante* 'Pretoria's newspapers, the Pretoria papers'.

The indirect objective case of a personal noun is marked by the preposition *vir* 'for, to': *gee ... vir die arme kind* 'give the poor child ...'; *Sê vir oom, hy moet tuis kom* 'Tell uncle to come home.' The use of *vir* with a direct personal object seems to be possible. Mironov (1969) gives the example: *Jan slaan vir Piet* 'Jan strikes Piet.'

Adjective

As attribute, adjective precedes noun. After either article, *-e* is normally added to all polysyllabic and some monosyllabic adjectives: e.g. *die Nederlandse taal* 'the Dutch language'. The addition of *-e* may induce change in stem final: e.g. *Die kind is **goed***; but, *Dit is 'n **goeie** kind* 'This/he/she is a good child.' Many adjectives remain uninflected: e.g. *Dit is 'n donker nag* 'It's a dark night.'

COMPARATIVE
Made with *-er*: phonetic change at junctures: e.g. *donker* 'dark' – *donkerder*; *doof* 'deaf' – *dower.*

Pronoun

Some vestiges of common Germanic inflection survive in the singular forms: the third person singular forms are marked for gender:

		Singular			*Plural*	
		Subject	*Object*	*Possessive adjective*	*Subject/ object*	*Possessive adjective*
1		ek	my	my	ons	onse
2		jy	jou	jou	julle	julle se
		U	U	U	U	U
3	masc.	hy	hom	sy		
	fem.	sy	haar	haar	hulle	hulle se
	nt.	dit	dit	—		

The predicative possessive forms are *myne, joune, U sy'n/s'n,syne, haar se*; pl. *ons sy'n, julle sy'n, hulle sy'n*: e.g. *my boek – die boek is myne – die boek is julle s'n*. *U* is the polite address form.

DEMONSTRATIVE PRONOUN/ADJECTIVE
e.g. *hierdie* 'this', *daardie* 'that'.

INTERROGATIVE PRONOUN
wie 'who?'; *wat* 'what?: e.g. *In wie se naam*? 'In whose name?'

RELATIVE PRONOUN
wat is used for all referents: e.g. *die boek wat daar lê* 'the book that is lying there'; *die man/die vrou wat daar woon* 'the man/woman who lives there'. 'Whose' is rendered as *wie se: die man wie se huis verkoop sal word* 'the man whose house is to be sold'.

Numerals

As in Dutch with some changes in spelling: e.g. D *vijf* 'five' = Afr. *vyf.*

Verb

Apart from the *ge-* prefix on most past participles, all verbal inflection has been lost. The verbal base is identical with the present tense of the indicative mood: e.g. *val* 'to fall', *ek/hulle val* 'I/they fall'. Auxiliaries such as *het, is, sal, word* are used to make composite tenses. The typical Germanic past-tense forms, whether strong or weak (*see* **German**), have disappeared, leaving the composite form with *het* as the sole past tense in Afrikaans, apart from *was*, the past tense of *is* (*cf.* **Yiddish**): e.g. *ek het geval* 'I fell/have fallen'. If the verb begins with an inseparable prefix, e.g. *be-*, *er-*, *her-*, *ver-*, etc., the *ge-* of the past participle is dropped; i.e. here, the past participle coincides with the stem and the present tense.

SEPARABLE VERBS

The order of components in the tense structure of verbs with separable prefixes may be illustrated as follows, for *saambring* 'to bring along with one':

present: *ek bring my broeder saam* 'I'm bringing my brother along with me'
past: *ek het my broeder saam.ge.bring* 'I brought/I've brought ...'
future: *ek sal my broeder saam.bring* 'I shall bring ...'
split infinitive: *om saam te bring* '(so as) to bring along with one'

PASSIVE

The model auxiliary *word* is used in the present and the future:

present: *die huis word gebou* 'the house is being built'
past: *die huis is gebou* 'the house was built'
past anterior: *die huis was gebou* 'the house had been built'
future: *die huis sal gebou word* 'the house will be built'

IMPERATIVE MOOD

A simple imperative form is once again identical with stem and present tense; and, as in the present tense, a separable prefix follows: e.g. *oppas* 'to take care', *Pas op*! 'Take care!' A polite hortative form can be made with the auxiliary *moet*: e.g. *jy moet weggaan* 'you should/must go'. *Moet* + *nie* → *moenie* provides a negative imperative: e.g. *Moenie hier staan nie*! 'Don't stand here!'

NEGATIVE

The negative particle *nie* is recapitulated in composite verbal forms: e.g. *hy het nie gekom nie* 'he didn't come;' *hy het niks gedoen nie* 'he didn't do anything'.

NON-FINITE FORMS

The infinitive form is heavily eroded; e.g. *hê* (< *heb* < *hebben*) 'to have'; *sê* (< *seg* < *seggen*) 'to say'.

The present participle retains its original Germanic form: e.g. *lesende* 'reading'; *vallende* 'falling'; *Al pratende het hulle uit die kamer gestap* 'Talking, they left the room.'

Past participle: *ge-* prefix, except in verbs with an inseparable prefix; cf.

Hy het die boek gelees 'He read/has read the book'
Hy het die boek vertaal 'He translated/has translated the book'

Prepositions

Prepositions require the objective form of personal pronoun: e.g. *met haar* 'with her'; *Ek hou nie van hom nie* 'I don't like him' (lit. 'hold not with him'); *Ek wil môre graag by jou kom kuier* 'I'd like to come and visit you tomorrow' (*graag* = Gm. *gerne*)

Word order

SVO in principal clause; in subordinate clause SOV; if the subordinate clause precedes the principal clause, the word order in the latter is VSO.

Subordinate clause, past tense: OSV aux.: e.g. *die motorkar wat ek gister gekoop het* 'the car I bought yesterday'.

Subordinate clause, future tense: OS aux. V: e.g. *die brief wat ek môre sal ontvang* 'the letter which I'll get tomorrow'.

If a modal auxiliary is present, the order is SO aux. modal aux. V: e.g. (*Hy het gesê dat*) *hy ons môre sou kan help* ('He said that) he would be able to help us tomorrow.'

1 IN die begin was die Woord, en die
Woord was by God, en die Woord
was God.
2 Hy was in die begin by God.
3 Alle dinge het deur Hom ontstaan,
en sonder Hom het nie een ding ontstaan
wat ontstaan het nie.
4 In Hom was lewe, en die lewe was
die lig van die mense.
5 En die lig skyn in die duisternis, en
die duisternis het dit nie oorweldig nie.
6 Daar was 'n man van God gestuur,
wie se naam Johannes was.
7 Hy het tot 'n getuienis gekom om van
die lig te getuig, sodat almal deur hom
sou glo.
8 Hy was nie die lig nie, maar hy moes
van die lig getuig.

AKAN or TWI

INTRODUCTION

This language is spoken in two major dialects, Ashanti and Fante, by up to 8 million people in Ghana. Akan belongs to the Kwa group of the Niger-Congo family. The form described here is Ashanti, the dialect spoken by the great majority of the Akan-speaking population.

The Basler Evangelische Missionsgesellschaft undertook the task of creating a Twi literary language in the 1840s, and the next 40 years saw the appearance of a Twi Bible, a definitive grammar, and a dictionary, mostly the work of J.G. Christaller. This early literary activity was based on the minor but politically and geographically accessible Akuapem dialect. Through the first half of the twentieth century, however, Ashanti began to be recognized as the proper base for a national literary language. Though certain scholars (e.g. Danquah) continued to write in Akuapem, others like Nketia and Tabi switched to Ashanti. In 1968 A.C. Denteh launched the important literary periodical *Odawuru*.

SCRIPT

Roman plus ɛ, ɔ. In 1961 the Bureau of Ghana Languages devised a common standardized script for all forms of Akan. Tone is not normally marked, nor is nasalization. The correspondence between the script and the actual sounds of Akan is rather weak.

PHONOLOGY

Consonants

stops: p, b, t, d, k, g, ɖ
affricates: tʃ, dʒ
fricatives: f, ɸ, s, ʃ (ç), h
nasals: m, n, ɲ, ŋ
trill: r

Note: all consonants tend to be palatalized before front vowels, and stops tend to affricates.

There is a labialized series: /k°, g°, h°, n°, ŋ°/; /v/ and /l/ occur in foreign words. /ɖ/ is notated as *ḍ*; /ɸ/ as *w*.

Vowels

i, ɪ, e, ɛ, æ, å, ɔ, o, ŭ, u, y

/e/ and /å/ have no nazalised counterparts; all other vowels take nasalization.

VOWEL HARMONY

lax series: ɪ, ɛ, ɑ, o, ʊ^
tense series: i, e, a, o, u

This division is important for vowel harmony: briefly, a *lax* vowel followed by /i/, /a/, or /ʊ/ is promoted to the next-highest vowel in the *tense* series, e.g. the sequence /ɪ...ʊ/ → /i...u/.

Vowel harmony determines the vocalic structure of the possessive and subject pronouns.

Tones

Three tones, which are phonemic: high, middle, and low. The tones in Akan are characteristically 'terraced', i.e. successive highs begin on a slightly lower level. This in turn affects successive middle tones, but low pitch is not affected.

MORPHOLOGY AND SYNTAX

Noun

No grammatical gender. Nouns are uninflected, though tonal patterns vary, depending on whether the noun is isolate, in construct (e.g. preceded by possessive pronoun), or in a compound.

There are several ways of making a singular noun plural. *-nő́m* is a pluralizing suffix: *ɔyére* 'wife', pl. *ɔyérenő́m*.

Pluralizing prefixes:

m-: *ɔba* 'child', pl. ***mma***;
a-: *ɔkérãmãñ* 'dog', pl. *akérãmãñ*;
n-: *ɛdá* 'day', pl. *nná*.

Some plurals are suppletive: *osáni* 'warrior', pl. *asáfoɔ*

POSSESSION

Marked by order: X's Y = XY – *Ghánà mãñ* 'the country of Ghana'; or, a possessive pronoun may be inserted: *abofára nő nhő́mã* 'the child's (his) book'.

In compounds *ab*, *a* may retain its isolate tone, *b* takes possessive tonal pattern: *Asante.héne.fié* 'the king of Ashanti's palace' (*héne* 'king', *ofíe* 'house').

LOCATIVE

There is a locative marker in *-beá*, and the noun expressing agency adds *-fo*; thus from the root *yaré* 'to be ill', we get: *ayaresábèa* 'hospital'; *ɔyaresáfò* [ɔyar-esáfòɔ], 'doctor'.

Adjective

As attribute, adjective follows noun, and is often reduplicated: *mmára fófòro pii* 'many new laws' (*mmará* 'law', *fófòro* 'new'); *búùku kétewaa tuntum̃* 'a small black book' (*tuntum̃* 'dark in colour').

Exceptionally, some adjectives make a plural form.

Comparative is made with *sẽñ*: *eyé duru* 'it is heavy', *eyé duru sẽñ búùku nő* 'It is heavier than the book.'

Pronoun

Emphatic personal independent + subject markers (here + copula)

	Singular		*Plural*	
	Independent	*Subject marker*	*Independent*	*Subject marker*
1	mẽ	mẽyɛ	yéŋ	yɛyɛ
2	wó	wóyɛ̀	mő	mőyɛ̀
3	ɔnő	ɔyɛ	wɔ́ŋ	wɔyɛ
impersonal	ɛnő	ɛyɛ	ɛnő	ɛyɛ

The objective forms: *mẽ, wo, nõ* are reduced as verbal suffixes to *-m̀, -ẁ, -ǹ*.

DEMONSTRATIVE PRONOUN

(*ɛ*)*há* 'this/here'; (*ɛ*)*hó* 'that/there'. *Eyí* is a demonstrative adjective: *nhőmã yí* 'this book'.

INTERROGATIVE PRONOUN

ɛhẽna 'who?'

RELATIVE PRONOUN

nea, áà; *ɔyaresáfóɔ áà ɔ́ɔkɔ* 'the doctor who is going'.

Numerals

1–10: *baakő, mmienű, mmiensá̃, ɛnnã́n, enűm, ensĩá, ɛnsɔ̃́n, ɛŋwɔtwé, ɛŋkorɔ̃́ŋ, edú*. 11, *dúbàakő*; *12, dúmìenű* ... 20, *aduonũ*; 21, *aduonűbàakő* ... 30, *aduasá̃*, 40, *aduanã́ñ*. 100, *ɔhá*, 101, *ɔhá né baakő* ...

Verb

Subject markers prefixed to stem: *hu*(*nu*) 'to see', present tense:

singular	1	mĩhu	plural	yehũ
	2	wúhũ		mű̃hũ
	3	ohũ		wohũ

Negated by low-tone nasal prefixed to stem: *mẽte Twi̋i* 'I speak Twi'; *mẽnté Twi̋i* 'I don't speak Twi'.

Prefixed pronominal object: *mẽte aséɛ* 'I understand' (*aséɛ* 'meaning'), e.g.:

mẽte **wá**sè	I understand	you	ɔte **ma**se	he understands me
nasè		him	**wa**se	you
másè		you (pl.)	**wɔn** ase	them

TENSE AND MOOD MARKERS

progressive tense: the pronominal vowel is lengthened: *mẽkã́* 'I speak': /mẽekã/ 'I'm speaking' (lengthening not notated in script).

future positive: prefix *bέ*: *wóbɛko* 'you will go' (+ tonal changes).

immediate future: with *kɔ* 'to go': (+ lengthening of vowel as in progressive): *mẽekɔtɔ́ nsuomnám* 'I'm going to buy fish' (*tɔ* 'to buy').

past tense: lengthening or gemination of final vowel: *-y* is added for intransitives: *mẽbaay* 'I came'.

perfect: *a-* prefix + specific tonal pattern + contractions. For example, *kɔ* 'to go':

singular	1	makɔ	plural	yɛakɔ
	2	woakɔ		moakɔ
	3	wakɔ		wɔakɔ

The *past* negative is the *perfect* affirmative + low-tone nasal before stem; the *perfect* negative is the *past* affirmative + low-tone nasal before stem: e.g. *mẽŋkɔɔ* 'I haven't gone'; *mẽŋkóhũù* 'I haven't gone to see it'; *minnii* 'I haven't eaten'; *onnii* 'he hasn't eaten'; *wonnii* 'they haven't eaten'.

CAUSATIVE

ma + low-tone nasal prefix on verb: *mã nõ ŋkò* 'have him go!'

SUBJUNCTIVE

Low-tone nasal prefix + high tone on verb.

IMPERATIVE

Stem + low tones; the plural prefix is *mṍn-* + high tones: *mṍnkasa* 'would you please talk'.

CONSECUTIVE FORM

a- prefix; e.g. with *tumí* 'to be able', *mĩtumí àkɔ̀* 'I can go'.

Postpositions

Nouns are used to define spatial relationships; e.g. *ɛso* 'upper part (of sth.)', *ɔpṍŋ nõ só* 'on the table ('s top)'.

Word order

Any part of speech can be stressed by being promoted to initial position, and additionally stressed, if a noun, by the topicalizer *déɛ*. SVO is normal.

1. **M**fiase no na Ase̱m no wo̱ ho̱, na
Ase̱m no nè Nyaṅkōpo̱ṅ na e̱wo̱ ho̱, na
Ase̱m no ye̱ Onyame.
2 O̱noara na mfiase no o̱-nè Nyaṅkō-
po̱ṅ wo̱ ho̱.
3 E̱nam no so na wo̱ye̱e̱ ade nnyinā,
na wo̱aṅkwati no anye̱ biribiara a wo̱ye̱e.
4 No mu na ṅkwā wo̱, na ṅkwā no
ne nnipa hāṅṅ;
5 na haṅṅ no hyere̱ṅ wo̱ sūm mu, na
esūm no annye no.
6 ¶ Onipa bi wo̱ ho̱ a Onyaṅkōpo̱ṅ so-
maa no a ne diṅ de Yohane;
7 o̱no na o̱baa adansedi se̱ orebedi
haṅṅ no hō adanse, se̱ nnipa nnyinā mfa
no so nnye nni.
8 E̱nye̱ o̱no ne haṅṅ no, na se̱ orebedi haṅṅ no hō adanse.

ALBANIAN

INTRODUCTION

Generally regarded as the sole survivor of the Illyrian branch of Indo-European languages, Albanian (*gjuha shqipe*) is spoken today in two main dialects: Tosk (southern) and Gheg (northern). The boundary between the two forms is roughly marked by the river Shkumbini. The total number of speakers of both dialects within the Republic of Albania is about 3 million. In addition, there are some 2 million Gheg speakers in the Kosova Autonomous Region (of Yugoslavia), and a few thousand speakers of a third dialect, *arbëresh*, in southern Italy and Greece. Albanian literature, mainly in Gheg, dates from the sixteenth century (1555, Buzuku's *Meshari*). Tentative steps towards the creation of a unified national language culminated first in the adoption of the Roman alphabet (1908, Congress of Manastir) and secondly in the selection of the Elbasan (central) dialect (a form of Gheg) as the most suitable base for such a language. From 1920 to the 1950s both dialects were used for literary purposes. In 1952, however, Tosk was officially declared as the base for the new standardized literary language. In Kosova, Gheg continues to prosper as both spoken and literary language. Tosk and Gheg are mutually intelligible, and differ indeed only in certain points – most importantly in the rhotacism of Tosk: Gheg -V*n*V- = Tosk -V*r*V-; e.g. Gheg *zani* 'voice', Tosk *zëri*; and in the formation of the future tense (*see* **Verb**, below).

SCRIPT

As noted above, the Congress of Manastir (1908) provided Albanian with a standardized script based on the Roman alphabet plus *ç* and *ë*; *w* is not used. The following digraphs are used: *th* = /θ/, *dh* = /ð/, *sh* = /ʃ/, *zh* = /ʒ/, *xh* = /dʒ/, *gj* = /g'/, *nj* = /ɲ/, *ll* = /ɫ/, *rr* = /rr/.

PHONOLOGY

Consonants

stops: p, b, t, d, k, g; k', g'
affricates, ts, dz, tʃ, dʒ
fricatives: f, v, θ, ð, s, z, ʃ, ʒ, j, h
nasals: m, n, ɲ, ŋ
laterals: l, ɫ, r, rr

Vowels

Tosk has seven vowel phonemes; Gheg has twelve, including five nasal vowels. The Tosk series:

i, e, a, ə, o, u, y

/ə/ is notated as *ë*.

Stress

Stress is frequently on the penultimate syllable.

MORPHOLOGY AND SYNTAX

Noun

Albanian has two genders, masculine and feminine, with traces of an old neuter, limited now to very few words.

There are two articles, definite and indefinite. The latter is sing. *një*, pl. *ca* or *disa*; thus, *një shok* 'a comrade', *disa shokë* 'comrades'.

The definite article is affixed to the noun and is coded for gender (*cf.* **Bulgarian** and **Romanian**):

masculine affixes: *-i*, *-u*, *-ri*/*-ni*, *-a*: *mal* 'mountain', ***mali*** 'the mountain'; *zog* 'bird', *zog**u*** 'the bird'.

feminine affix: *-a*: *shtëpi* 'house', *shtëpi**a*** 'the house'; *motër* 'sister', ***motra*** 'the sister'.

PLURAL

Typical masculine plural endings are *-a*, *-e*, *-nj*, *-q(e)*, *-gj(e)*, *-ë*: e.g. *mësim* 'lesson' – *mësime*; *mal* 'mountain' – *male*; *ari* 'bear' – *arinj*; *mik* 'friend' – *miq*; *pyll* 'forest' – *pyje*; *punëtor* 'worker' – *punëtorë*.

Feminine plural: *-a*, *-e*; often no change: e.g. *lule* 'flower' – *lule*; *dhomë* 'room' – *dhoma*.

Umlaut occurs in some masculine nouns: *breg* 'coast' – *brigje*; *plak* 'old man' – *pleq*.

The plural nominative definite form ends in *-t(ë)*.

CASE

The following two paradigms show a masculine and a feminine noun declined with and without definite article, in four cases and two numbers.

Masculine: mal 'mountain'

	Singular		*Plural*	
	Indefinite	*Definite*	*Indefinite*	*Definite*
nom.	mal	mali	male	malet
gen.	mali	malit	maleve	malevet
dat.	mali	malit	maleve	malet
acc.	mal	malin	male	malevet

	Feminine: shtëpi 'house'			
	Singular		*Plural*	
	Indefinite	*Definite*	*Indefinite*	*Definite*
nom.	shtëpi	shtëpia	shtëpi	shtëpitë
gen.	shtëpie	shtëpisë	shtëpive	shtëpivet
dat.	shtëpie	shtëpisë	shtëpive	shtëpivet
acc.	shtëpi	shtëpinë	shtëpi	shtëpitë

Adjective

The attributive adjective follows the noun to which it is connected by the inflected article, e.g. masc.:

	Indefinite 'a good friend'		*Definite 'the good friend'*	
	Singular	*Plural*	*Singular*	*Plural*
nom.	mik i mirë	miq të mirë	miku i mirë	miqt e mirë
gen.–dat.	miku të mirë	miqve të mirë	mikut të mirë	miqvet të mirë
acc.	mik të mirë	miq të mirë	mikun e mirë	miqt e mirë

Certain adjectives, e.g. those derived from nouns or verbs, do not take the connecting article: *një shkollë fillore* 'an elementary school' (*fillore* ← *filloj* 'to begin').

An adjective which takes the article in attributive position keeps it in predicative position: *vendi është i bukur* 'the place is beautiful', *vendet janë të bukura* (pl.).

Pronoun

The base forms are:

	Singular		*Plural*	
	Subject	*Oblique*	*Subject*	*Oblique*
1	unë	më	na/ne	na
2	ti	të	ju	ju

Third-person forms are supplied by the demonstrative series (see below).

DEMONSTRATIVE PRONOUN/ADJECTIVE

The proximate series is based on *ky*, fem. *kjo*; the distal series is *ai*, fem. *ajo*.

The series *ai*, *ata*; *ajo*, *ato* is used for the third-person pronoun, with oblique forms *e* 'him, her', and *i* 'to him, to her'.

These forms fuse with other oblique pronouns: e.g. *më* + *e* → *ma*: *ma dha librin* 'he gave me the book'.

A noun as complement is anticipated by a pronominal copy:

Do t'**i** them edhe Abazi**t** 'I'll tell A. as well'

E njihte mirë Dini**n** 'He knew D. well'

Unë **i** fola asaj vajz**e** 'I spoke to this girl'

POSSESSIVE PRONOUNS

These follow the noun possessed; here, the singular and plural nominative forms are given for each person:

libri im	my book	librat e mi	my books	libri ynë	our book
				librat tanë	our books
libri yt	your book	librat e tu	your books	libri juaj	your (pl.) book
				librat tuaj	your (pl.) books
libri i tij	his book	librat e tij	his books	libri i tyre	their book
				librat e tyre	their books

INTERROGATIVE PRONOUN

kush 'who?', inflected for case only; *çka* 'what?'; *cili* 'which?' is inflected for gender, number, and case: *cili djal dhe cila vajzë* 'which boy and which girl?'

RELATIVE PRONOUN

që is not inflected; *i cili*, etc. is inflected; e.g.

nje ndërtesë e vogël, e cila ndryshonte fare pak nga shtëpitë e tjera
'a building which differed little from the other houses'
(*ndërtesë* (fem.) 'building'; *ndryshoj* 'to differ'; *tjeter*, (pl.) *tjerë* 'other')

Numerals

1–10: *një, dy, tre/tri* (the only numeral marked for gender), *katër, pesë, gjashtë, shtatë, tetë, nëndë, dhjetë*. 11, *njëmbëdhjetë*; 12, *dymbëdhjetë* ... 20, *njëzet*; 30, *tridhjetë*; 40, *dyzet*; i.e. *dyzet* is a vigesimal form; 60 and 80, however, revert to decimal form: *gjashtëdhjetë*, *tetëdhjetë*. 100, *(një)qind*.

Verb

The Albanian verb has two voices, active (unmarked), and medio-passive, the latter having a specific set of endings. There are six moods and eight tenses; only the indicative mood has all of these tenses, the other moods – subjunctive, conditional, optative, admirative – have present and perfect tenses, to which the subjunctive and the admirative add an imperfect and a pluperfect. The imperative mood has a present form only.

Tenses may be further sub-divided by aspect into perfective and imperfective categories. Finite forms are marked throughout for person and number.

There are two conjugations: (a) vocalic stems, e.g. *jetoj* 'I live'; and (b) consonant stems, e.g. *sjell* 'I bring'.

Tenses are primary or analytical; the latter are formed by means of the auxiliaries: *jam* 'I am', and *kam* 'I have'.

Thematic stems are affected by umlaut/ablaut, and some forms are suppletive: e.g. *shoh* 'I see'; imperfect *shihja*; aorist *pashë*.

THE AUXILIARIES

The basic forms of *jam* and *kam* are:

present: *jam, je, është*; pl. *jemi, jeni, janë*
imperfect: *isha, ishe*
aorist: *qeshë, qe* ...
subjunctive: *të jem, të jesh* ...
past participle: *qenë*

present: *kam, ke, ka*; pl. *kemi, keni, kanë*
imperfect: *kisha, kishe*
aorist: *pata, pate* ...
subjunctive: *të kem, të kesh* ...
past participle: *pasur*

MODAL VERBS

Two important modals are: *dua* 'I want' and *mund* 'I can'.

SPECIMEN CONJUGATION

Vocal stem, *kërkoj* 'I ask for, seek'.

Indicative
present: *kërko**j**, **-n**, **-n***, pl. *kërko**jmë**, **-ni**, **-jnë***
imperfect: *kërko**ja***, ***-je***, ***-nte***; pl. *kërko**nim***, ***-nit***, ***-nin***
aorist: *kërko**va***, ***-ve***, ***-i***; pl. *kërk**uam***, ***-uat***, ***-uan***
perfect: *kam, ke*, etc. *kërkuar*
future: *do të kërkoj*, *do të kërko**sh*** ... (subjunctive endings, see below).

This is the Tosk form of the future tense; the Gheg model is *kam me* + infinitive.

Subjunctive
present: *të kërkoj*, ***-sh***, ***-jë***; pl. as indicative present.
imperfect: *të* + indicative imperfect forms
Admirative
present: *kërkua**kam***, *kërkua**ke***, etc. (i.e. *kërkua* + present tense of *kam*)
Optative
present: *kërko**fsha***, ***-fsh***, ***-ftë***; pl. *kërko**fshim***, ***-fshi***, ***-fshin***

Imperative: sing. *kërko*; pl. *kërko**ni***
Past participle: *kërkuar*

Medio-passive voice: vocalic stems have the augment *-h-* in the present:
present: *kërko**hem***, ***-hesh***, ***-et***; pl. *kërko**hemi***, ***-heni***, ***-hen***
imperfect: *kërohesha*, ***-heshe*** . . .
aorist: ***u**-kërko**va***, ***u**-kërko**ve***, ***u**-kërk**ua***; pl. ***u**-kërk**uam***, ***-uat***, ***-uan***
perfect: *jam kërkuar* ... etc.

NEGATIVE

nuk and *s'* are general negating particles; *kemi* 'we have'; *s'kemi* 'we don't have'; *Goni nuk flet anglisht* 'Goni doesn't speak English.' *Mos* is used with the imperative: *mos pini duhan* 'don't smoke'.

Prepositions

(a) with nominative (usually in definite form): e.g. *nga* 'from', *tek* 'at', *gjer* 'until', etc.
(b) with accusative: e.g. *mbi* 'on', *me* 'with', në, 'in', *pa* 'without', etc.
(c) with dative (ablative): e.g. *pranë* 'near', *kundër* 'against', *mbrapa* 'after', etc.

Word formation

(a) compounding: e.g. noun + noun: *hekur* 'iron' + *udhë* 'way': *hekurudhë* 'railway'.
(b) by suffix: e.g. *-im* forming abstract nouns: *kujtimi* 'memory' (cf. *kujtoj* 'remember'); *-(t)ore* denoting locus of activity: *grunore* 'wheatfield' (cf. *grunë* 'wheat').
(c) by prefixing preposition or adverb: *në(n)* 'below' + *punës* 'working': *nëpunësi* 'employee'.
adverb + adjective: *jashtzakonshëm* (*jasht* 'outside' + *zakon* (Slav.) 'law, custom') 'unusual, extraordinary'.
privative prefix *pa-*: *pakuptueshëm* 'incomprehensible' (cf. *kuptoj*, 'I understand'; *kuptueshëm* 'comprehensible').

Prefixes frequently used to form derived verbs are: (*sh*)*për-*, *mb-*, *sh-*, *c-*: e.g. from

shkruaj 'to write', *përshkruaj* 'to describe'
jashtë 'outside', *përjashtoj* 'to exclude'
lidh 'tie', *mbledh* 'to collect'.

Word order

SVO is normal.

1 Që përpara herësë ishte Fjala, edhe Fjala
ishte me Perëndinë, edhe Fjala ishte Perëndi,
2 Këjo ishte që përpara herësë me Perëndinë.
3 Të-gjitha u bënë me anë t' asaj; edhe pa
atë nuk' ubë as ndonjë *gjë* që është bërë.
4 Nd' atë ishte jetë, edhe jeta ishte drita e
5 njerësvet. Edhe drita ndrit nd' errësirët, edhe
errësira nuk' e kupëtoj.
6 Qe *një* njeri dërguarë nga Perëndia, i-
7 cili *e kishte* emërinë Joan. Ky erdhi për dëshmim, që të apë dëshmim. Dritënë, që të be-
8 sonjënë të-gjithë me anë t' ati. Ay nuk' ishte
Drita, po *qe dërguarë* që të apë dëshmim
për Dritënë.

(Tosk dialect)

AMHARIC

INTRODUCTION

This Afro-Asiatic (Semito-Hamitic) language is South Semitic in origin but has acquired a very considerable non-Semitic element, presumably through contact with neighbouring Cushitic languages such as Oromo. The word *Amhara* is the ethnonym of the 10 to 12 million people in central and north-western Ethiopia (an area which includes the capital, Addis Abbeba) who speak *amarəñña.* As the official language of Ethiopia, Amharic is also used as a second language by about a third of the total population of Ethiopia. The main dialects are those of Gondar, Gojjam, and Shoa.

Before the late nineteenth century little was written in Amharic. Missionary activity involving the use of written Amharic was encouraged for political reasons by the Emperors Menelik II and Haile Selassie I. The first printing press for Amharic books was established in the 1880s. Through the twentieth century there has been a gradual drift from the total religious commitment of previous Ethiopian writing, towards cautious experimentation in such Western genres as the novel and the stage play, which allow social and economic issues to be raised.

SCRIPT

The Ethiopic syllabary of 26 characters, written from left to right, has been extended by seven letters denoting specifically Amharic sounds. Phonological reduction from Ethiopic to Amharic has resulted in some redundancy; thus, there are, for example, four graphs for /h/. A major omission in the script is the absence of a sign denoting gemination, which is very important, usually phonemic, in Amharic. Signs for the numerals up to 20 are derived from Greek. Words are separated from each other by the marker ':'.

PHONOLOGY

Consonants

stops: p, b, p', t, d, t', k, g, k' ʔ
affricates: tʃ, dʒ, tʃ'
fricatives: f, v, s, z, s', ʃ, ʒ, h
semi-vowels: j, w
nasals: m, n, ɲ, (ŋ)
lateral and flap: l, r;

The emphatics, i.e. glottalized consonants, are notated here as *p̣*, *ṭ*, *ḳ*, *ṣ*; /k'/ is often notated as *q*. Most consonants occur labialized. In the case of the velar series and /h/, this labialization is notated for all vowels by a specific series of graphs; in realization, however, /k°/, /g°/, /k'°/ and /h°/ precede /a/; before other vowels, the labialization tends to be lost.

Vowels

i, e, ɛ, a, ə, u, o

/ɛ/ is notated here as *ä*.

Stress

Very weak.

MORPHOLOGY AND SYNTAX

Noun

In contrast to Tigrinya and Tigre, gender is not formally marked. Nouns are treated as masculine or feminine for reasons of natural gender or by convention; thus, *färäs* 'horse', is masculine, but *baqlo* 'mule' is feminine. Inanimate objects are usually treated as masculine, but there are exceptions. Words like *ləj* 'child', can be made more specific by the addition of *wənd* 'male', or *set* 'female': *wənd ləj* 'boy'. Gender is specifically marked in the affixed definite article, the demonstratives and the second and third persons of the verb. The Semitic feminine ending *-t* reappears in certain words, e.g. *mušərrit* 'bride' (*mušərra* 'bridegroom').

The concept of gender merges in Amharic with that of dimension, giving rise to an opposition between normal size/masculine and diminutive/feminine. Thus, concord fluctuates: a noun which takes 'masculine' concord when the referent is of normal dimensions may take 'feminine' concord when departure from the norm is to be stressed; cf. *yih bet təlləq* ***nəw*** 'this house is big', but *yih bet bäṭam tənnəš* ***nəč*** 'this house is very small'.

Conversely, nouns like *ṣähay* 'sun', *çäräqa* 'moon', *kokäb* 'star', which normally take feminine/diminutive concord, acquire masculine status when unusual size is stressed; cf. *kokäb wəṭṭ****ač*** 'a star came out', but *talaq kokäb kä.sämay* ***wädäqä*** a great star fell from heaven' (Revelation, 8.10).

DEFINITE ARTICLE

-u/*-w* identifies a singular noun as masculine; the feminine affix is *-wa*/*-itu*: e.g. *bet* 'house'; ***betu*** 'the house'; *lam* 'cow', *lam****wa*** 'the cow'.

NUMBER

The plural affix is *-očč*, which takes the definite article: e.g. *bet.očč.u* 'the houses'. There are some traces of a broken plural. The numeral *and* 'one' can be used as an indefinite article.

CASE RELATIONS

The accusative is marked by *-n*: e.g. *innatwa.**n** ayyəč* 'She saw her mother'.

Genitive: the particle *yä* precedes the noun: e.g. ***yä**.Yohannəs innat* 'John's mother'; ***yä**.Ityop̣ya häzb* 'the people of Ethiopia'. The possessive marker *yä* precedes the attributive adjective: *yä ḳonjo set* 'of the beautiful woman'.

Other case relationships are expressed with the help of prefixes, circumfixes, and affixes: *see* **Postpositions**, etc., below.

Adjective

The attributive adjective precedes the noun and is formally unmarked: e.g. *təlləq bet* 'big house'. If the noun is definite, the article is affixed to the adjective: e.g. *təllə**qu** bet* 'the big house'; and similarly for the case ending in *-n*. The adjective may take the plural marker: e.g. *addis.očč bet.očč* 'new houses'.

COMPARATIVE

kä or *tä* precedes the word compared: e.g. ***kä**.Gondar Addis Ababa təlləq näw* 'Addis Abbeba is bigger than Gondar.'

Pronoun

The independent personal pronouns with copula and enclitic markers:

		Singular		*Plural*	
1		əne näññ	-ññ	əñña nän	-n
2	masc.	antä näh	-h	ənnantä naččəhu	-ččəhu
	fem.	anči näš	-š		
3	masc.	əssu näw	-w/-t	ənnässu naččäw	-ččäw
	fem.	əsswa näčč	-t		

The enclitic markers are shown in characteristic form without the linking vowels that usually precede them. They are used as the object pronouns of transitive verbs: e.g. *Bä.gäbäya ayyu.**t*** 'They saw him/her at market'; and may be anticipated by a noun or the relevant pronoun in the accusative case: e.g. *əssu.**n** ayyu.* (***t***) 'they saw him', cf. *ayyä.hu.w.at* 'I saw her'; *ayyä.ññ* 'he saw me'; *ayyä.ččəhu* 'he saw you (pl.)'.

There are respectful forms for independent second and third persons: second *ərswo*; third *əssaččäw*.

POSSESSION

This may be expressed by the affixed personal markers: sing. 1 *-e*, 2 *-əh/š*, 3 *-u/wa*; pl. 1 *-aččən*, 2 *-aččəh*, 3 *-aččäw*: e.g. *bet**e*** 'my house'; *bet**aččən*** 'our house'.

The verb 'to have' is expressed by the existential verb *allä* plus a composite ending coded for person of owner and gender and number of object(s) possessed: e.g. *all**äññ*** 'I have' (masc. sing. obj.); *all**äccəññ*** 'I have' (fem. sing. obj.); *all**uññ*** 'I have' (pl. obj. either gender).

DEMONSTRATIVE PRONOUN/ADJECTIVE

'This': masc. *yəh*, fem. *yəčč, pl. ənnäzzih*; 'that': masc. *ya*, fem. *yačč*, pl. *ənnäzziya*.

INTERROGATIVE PRONOUN

man 'who?'; *mən(dən)* 'what?'

RELATIVE PRONOUN

See Relative Clause in **Verb**, below.

Numerals

1–10: *and, hulätt, sost, aratt, ammast, səddəst, säbatt, səmmənt, zäṭäññ, assər*; 11 *asra and*; 12 *asra hulätt*; 20 *haya*; 30 *sälasa*; 40 *arba*; 100 *mäto*.

Verb

Roots are mainly two-, three-, or four-radical, the majority being triliterals. A few verbs have five radicals, and there is one monoradical – *ša* 'to want'. The citation form is, as customary in Semitic languages, the third person masculine past tense (more accurately, perfective): e.g. *mätta* 'he came', *fällägä* 'he wanted'. A typical triliteral perfective is conjugated as follows:

> singular 3 masc. *fällägä*, fem. *fällägä**čč***; 2 masc. *fälläg**h***; fem. *fällägš*; 1 *fällä**ghu***;
> plural 3 common, *fällä**gu***; 2 common, *fällä**gaččəhu***; 1 common, *fällä**gən***.

IMPERFECTIVE, OR PRESENT–FUTURE FORM

The stem is modulated by prefix and affix to provide this form, which is not predictable from the perfective form. There are two patterns, which hinge on differing treatment of the geminated second radical: that is to say, if **1**, **2**, **3** are the radicals, **1***ä***22***ä***3** may yield *yə***1***ä***23***al* or *yə***1***ä***22***ə***3***al* as present–future form: thus, *fällägä* yields *yə***F***ä***LL***ə***G***al*; but *säbbärä* yields *yə***S***ä***BR***al*.

This is, in fact, a composite form. The *-al* component is a shortened form of the existential verb *allä*, and the pronominal object is therefore infixed between the stem and the *-al* component: cf. some examples with **F***ä***LL***ä***G***ä*:

> ***əFäLLəGä.w.allähu*** 'I want him/it': ***-w-*** is the third person masculine pronominal object, and ***ə...hu*** is the present–future circumfix for first person singular.
> ***təFäLLəGə.ññ.alläh*** 'you (masc. sing.) want me'. ***-ññ-*** is the first person pronominal object, ***tə...h*** is the second person singular masculine circumfix.

The prefixes in this verbal form are the familiar Semitic series: sing. 3 *yə-/tə-*, 2 *tə-*, 1 *ə-*; pl. 3 *yə-*, 2 *tə-*, 1 *ənnə-*; and the affixes are forms of the existential verb + personal markers.

Biliterals are conjugated essentially as triliterals: e.g. *qomä* 'he stood'; ***qomku*** 'I stood'; ***yəqomal*** 'he stands'; ***əqomallähu*** 'I stand'.

Amharic has an imperative mood used only in the second person singular, and a jussive, used in the first and third person singular and plural and in second plural. The verbal noun takes the prefix *mä-*: e.g. *mäfalläg* 'wanting'; *mähed* 'going'. These forms can take the personal affixes: e.g. *kä.mähed**e** bäfit* 'before I went' (for the form *kä...bäfit*, *see* **Postpositions**, etc., below).

GERUND

The base patterns are: **1ä23**, or **1ä22ə3**: the gerund takes personal affixes similar to the possessive series: *fälləg**o**...* 'wanting ... he ...'; *fälləg**äu*** 'wanting ... we ...' e.g. *Betun šəṭ**o** yət agər məhed yəfälləgal?* 'Having sold his house, to which country does he want to go?', *fäll ə gä.š.aččäw* 'you (fem.) having wanted them'.

DERIVED STEMS

(a) *-a* prefixed to base stem changes intransitive to transitive: e.g. *moqä* 'he was warm'; ***a**moqä* 'he warmed sth. up';
(b) *-tä-* passive of transitive, e.g. *anäbbäbä* 'he read': ***tä**nabbäbä* 'it was read';
(c) *as-*: causative, e.g. *wässädä* 'he took'; ***as**wässädä* 'he had sth. taken'.

THE SHORT IMPERFECTIVE FORM

This is the present–future form minus the *-allä* component. It is used, e.g. in subordinate temporal and causal clauses, and must be introduced by such pre-posited relational conjunctions as *sə-*, *lə-*, *bə-*, * əndə-*, etc. (with juncture sandhi). Examples: *Almaz **si**mäṭṭa wädä bet əhedallähu* 'When A. comes, I'll go home'; *Yohannəs mäṣhafun **si**fälläg* 'when John was looking for the book'. And in negative: *baburu **sa.y.**mättä* 'the train not coming' = 'before the train comes'.

A conditional form is made by prefixing the relational particle *b(ə/i)* to the short imperfective: *bi.mäṭa ə.hed.allähu* 'if he comes, I'll go'.

NEGATION

For the perfective, the circumfix *al...m* is used: e.g. ***al**fälläg**äm*** 'he didn't want'; ***al**fälläg**hum*** 'I didn't want'. The circumfix for the imperfective negative is: *a*C...*m*, where C varies: cf. ***ay**fälləg**əm*** 'he doesn't want'; ***an**fälləg**əm*** 'we don't want'. With infixed pronoun object: *alfälləg**äw**əm* 'I don't want it'; *ayfällə-gaččəhum* 'he doesn't want you (pl.)'.

RELATIVE CLAUSES

These are treated as qualifiers preceding the head-word: *yä-* introduces a relative clause in the perfective; *yämmə-* in the imperfective. Cf. ***yä**mäṭṭ**aw** säw* 'the man (*säw*) who came'; ***yä**mäṭṭ**ut** säwočč* 'the men who came'; *gänzäb **yä**ṭäffabbat säw* 'the man who lost his money'; ***yämmə**norəbbat bet yəhäw* 'This is the house in which I live.' In a negative relative clause, the *-əm* component of the negating circumfix is dropped: *yämm.al.fälləggäw mäṣhaf* 'the book I don't want'.

Prepositions and postpositions

Circumfix: e.g.

bä 'in': *bä.kätäma* 'in the city';
kä 'from': *Kä.yät mäṭṭa* 'From where has he come?';

wädä 'towards, to': *kä.gära wädä ḳäññ* 'from left to right';
kä…bəhwala 'after': *Kä.hullu bəhwala mäṭṭa* 'He came after all the others';
bä…mäkakäl 'among, between': *bä.säwočč mäkakäl* 'among people';
lä…silə 'for, on behalf of': *lä.ageru silə motä* 'to die for one's country'.

Also *bä…lay* 'on', *bä…wəsṭ* 'inside'; *kä…bäfit* 'before', etc.

Word order

SOV; OSV is permissible.

በመጀመሪያው ቃል ነበረ ፤ ቃልም በእግዚአብሔር ፩
ዘንድ ነበረ ፤ ቃልም እግዚአብሔር ነበረ ። ይህ በመጀመ ፪
ሪያው በእግዚአብሔር ዘንድ ነበረ ። ሁሉ በእርሱ ሆነ ፤ ፫
ከሆነውም አንዳች ስንኳ ያለ እርሱ አልሆነም ። በእርሱ ፬
ሕይወት ነበረች ፤ ሕይወትም የሰው ብርሃን ነበረች ። ብር ፭
ሃንም በጨለማ ይበራል ፤ ጨለማም አላሸነፈውም ።

ከእግዚአብሔር የተላከ ስሙ ዮሐንስ የሚባል አንድ ፮
ሰው ነበረ ፤ ሁሉ በእርሱ በኩል እንዲያምኑ ይህ ስለ ብር ፯
ሃን ይመሰክር ዘንድ ለምስክር መጣ ። ስለ ብርሃን ሊመ ፰
ሰክር መጣ እንጂ ፤ እርሱ ብርሃን አልነበረም ።

ARABIC

INTRODUCTION

Arabic belongs to the South Central Semitic branch of the Semito-Hamitic family. Modern standard literary Arabic (*al-fuṣḥa*) is the official language of some 20 countries, ranging from Morocco on the Atlantic seaboard of Africa to the Persian Gulf states. As such, it is used in the press and other media, and is the language of diplomacy and official communication between Arab states. Basically, this literary standard is the language of the Qur'ān and the Hadith, lexically enriched, of course, largely from Arabic's own generative resources. Modernisms abound, but they are additions to a core structure which has hardly changed in a thousand years. Colloquial Arabic is spoken as mother tongue, in various dialect forms, by an estimated 150 million people. And again, as the canonical language of Islam, Arabic is understood up to a point by many millions of people, wherever the Qur'ān is taught – in Iran, Pakistan, Indonesia, East and West Africa, etc. Finally, one should mention the thousands of Arabic words that have been borrowed by Iranian, Turkic, Indian, and African languages, with little or no reciprocal borrowing by Arabic.

Arabic literature, one of the world's richest, dates from the sixth century AD, i.e. from the period immediately preceding the composition of the Qur'ān and the birth of Islam. The following periods may be broadly distinguished:

1. Pre-Islamic paganism (*al-jāhiliyya*, 'the period of ignorance').
2. The Qur'ān and the Hadith (to mid-seventh century).
3. The Umayyad period (to mid-eighth century).
4. The 'Abbāsid' period the 'golden age' of Arabic literature (to mid-thirteenth century).
5. The age of decadence (thirteenth to nineteenth centuries).
6. The nineteenth-century revival (*al-nahḍa*).
7. The twentieth century. Confrontation with European modes of thought and expression, and vast proliferation of literature in all genres.

SCRIPT

(*See* **Appendix of Scripts**.) There are two main forms: (a) Kufic, an angular script in general use up to the ninth century, and the ancestor of the present-day Moghrebi scripts of North-West Africa; (b) the flowing cursive character known as *nasxī* and its derivatives, *ta'līq* and *ruq'a*. The latter is much used in handwriting. The Arabic script is consonantal; vowels are not normally written except in pedagogic literature, and, of course, in the Qur'ān, texts of which are always fully vocalized.

PHONOLOGY

Consonants

labial: b, f, m, w
dental: t, d, n, θ, ð, s, ʃ, z, l, r
velarized emphatic: , ŧ, đ, ⱥ, ƶ
palatal: dʒ, j
velar: k, χ, ɣ
uvular: q
pharyngeal: ħ, ʕ(')
glottal: h, ʔ(')

Emphatic /ŧ/, etc. are notated here as *ṭ*, etc.

ASSIMILATION

The so-called 'sun letters': the *-l* of the article is assimilated to a following initial dental or an emphatic, e.g., *al-šamsu* → [eʃ-ʃamsu] 'the sun'; *al-nāru* → [ɛn-nɛːru] 'the fire'; *al-tājiru* → [ɛt-tɛːjiru] 'the merchant'; *al-ṭabīb* → [uŧ-ŧɔbiːb] 'the doctor'.

Vowels

long and short: i, a, u

Long vowels are notated as *ā*, etc. Initial /i, a, u/ are supported by alif in the script, and pronounced with glottal onset (hamza). /a, aː/ tend towards [ɛ, ɛː]; after the emphatic consonants, *a* → [ɔ]: e.g. *ḍaraba* → [đɔraba], 'he struck'. In proximity to *l*, /a/ → [ɛ]: *malik* → [mɛlik], *kalb* → [kɛlb].

Stress

Primary stress tends to fall on the penultimate if this is long. If the last two syllables are short; stress moves to the antepenultimate: e.g. *fallā́hun* 'a peasant'; *šáriba* 'he drank'.

MORPHOLOGY AND SYNTAX

Noun

The form of an Arabic word (*wazn*, pl. *awzān*) is related to its function. Thus, if we use C_1, C_2, and C_3 to denote the components of a triliteral root:

$C_1aC_2C_2\bar{a}C_3$ denotes the practitioner of the verbal action: e.g. *NaJJār*(*un*) 'carpenter'; *XuBBāZ*(*un*) 'baker'.

maC_1C_2*a*C_3 is a noun of place: e.g. *MaDRaS*(*un*) 'school'; *ma*ṬBaX(*un*) 'kitchen'.

C_1*a*C_2*ī*C_3(*un*) is often an adjective; may also be infinitive or broken plural (see below): e.g. *KaRīM* 'noble'; *JaMīL* 'beautiful'.

For a general note on the triliteral root, *see* **Semitic Languages**.

There are two genders, masculine and feminine, and three numbers.

ARTICLE

Indefinite status is indicated by nunation: e.g. *malik**un*** 'a king'. The definite article for all genders and numbers is prefixed *al-*: e.g. *al-maliku* 'the king'. As pointed out above, the *-l* of the article assimilates with the 'sun letters'.

GENDER

A common feminine marker is *-at*, written with tā' marbūṭa, i.e. *-h* with two dots, in the singular, but reverting to ordinary *t* in the plural: e.g. *xādimun* 'a servant': *xādim**at**un* 'a female servant'. Several common nouns are feminine, though not so marked, e.g. *al-'arḍu* 'the earth', *al-nāru* 'the fire', *al-šamsu* 'the sun'.

NUMBER

Singular, dual, and plural. The plural form may be sound or broken. The sound plural is in *-ūna*, oblique *-īna*; feminine, *-ātun*, oblique *-ātin*. Broken plural: the form of a broken plural is unpredictable, though there are certain recurrent patterns. Thus, with radicals $C_1C_2C_3$

'aC_1C_2*i*C_3*ā'u* is a plural of C_1*a*C_2*ī*C_3*un*: e.g. *ṢaDīQun* 'friend', pl. *'aṢDiQā'u*;

maC_1*ā*C_2*i*C_3*u* is a plural of *ma*C_1C_2*a*C_3*un*: e.g. *maKTaBun* 'school', pl. *maKāTiBu*.

Common broken plural forms are (omitting nunation):

C_1*u*C_2*ū*C_3: e.g. *QaLB*, pl. *QuLūB* 'heart';
C_1*i*C_2*ā*C_3: e.g. *KaLB*, pl. *KiLāB* 'dog';
C_1*u*C_2*u*C_3: e.g. *KiTāB*, pl. *KuTuB* 'book'.

Dual: masc. *-āni*, obl. *-aini*. In the feminine *-t-* is inserted: *-tani*, obl. *-taini*. Nunation drops in construct: e.g. *bābāni* 'two doors': *bābā*∅*.l-bait* 'the two doors of the house'. Formally, a broken plural is a feminine singular collective noun, and therefore takes a feminine singular adjective.

CASE

Most nouns are triptotes with three cases, nominative, genitive, accusative, with characteristic vowels *-u* (nom.), *-i* (gen.), *-a* (acc.). Diptotes have nominative in *-u* and general oblique in *-a*: e.g. triptote *al-bait**u*** 'the house'; *daxala baita.ka* 'he went into your (*-ka*) house'; *fi.l-bait**i*** 'in the house'. In the colloquial, the endings *-u*, *-a*, *-i* tend towards ∅.

THE CONSTRUCT

(Ar. *'iḍāfa*) Noun defined by noun. In Arabic, the two nouns are put in the construct relationship, whereby the first, the defining member, necessarily loses its article: thus, with *al-baitu* 'the house'; *al-rajul* 'the man': *Øbaitu.l-rajuli* [baitu.**r-r**ajul], 'the man's house'. Similarly, *al-šubbāku* 'the window': *Øšubbaku.l-baiti* 'the window of the house'. (*Cf.* **Hebrew**. In Arabic, there is no obligatory stretto of first component.)

Plural and dual in construct: *kutubu.l-mu'allimīna* 'the teachers' books'; *kitābā.r-rajuli* 'the man's two books'; *waladai.l-wazīri* 'the wazir's two sons' (acc.).

Adjective

Certain awzān (*see* **Noun**, above) are adjectives, e.g. $C_1\bar{a}C_2iC_3$, $C_1aC_2\bar{\imath}C_3$, $C_1aC_2\bar{u}C_3$: e.g. *ṣādiq* 'just, upright'; *kabīr* 'big'; *jahūl* 'very ignorant'. The attributive adjective follows the noun and takes the article, if definite: e.g. *al-baitu.l-kabiru* 'the big house'; *al-bintu.l-ḥasanatu* 'the beautiful girl'. As pointed out above, broken plural forms are construed as feminine singular for purposes of concord: e.g. *durūsun sa'batun* 'difficult lessons'. But broken plural adjectives may be used to qualify broken plural nouns denoting male humans: e.g. *rijālun ṭiwālun* 'tall men' (*ṭawīl* 'tall').

Adjectives denoting colours or bodily defects have the following pattern: masc. sing. $'aC_1C_2aC_3u$ (i.e. no nunation), fem. $C_1C_2\bar{a}C_3'u$, pl. $C_1uC_2C_3un$: e.g. *'aḥmaru* 'red', fem. *ḥamrā'u*, pl. *ḥumrun*; *'aṭrašu* 'deaf', fem. *ṭaršā'u*, pl. *ṭuršun*. The masculine form of this pattern is used for the elative (comparative); thus from *kabir* 'big', *'akbar* 'bigger'; from *jahil* 'ignorant', *'ajhal* 'more ignorant'.

Pronoun

Independent and enclitic:

		Singular		*Dual*		*Plural*	
		Independent	*Enclitic*	*Independent*	*Enclitic*	*Independent*	*Enclitic*
1		'anā	-ya, -(n)ī			naḥnu	-nā
2	masc.	'anta	-ka	'antumā	-kumā	'antum	-kum
	fem.	'anti	-ki			'antunna	-kunna
3	masc.	huwa	-hu/hi	humā	-humā	hum	-hum
	fem.	hiya	-hā			hunna	-hunna

The enclitics are bound forms attached to verbs as object pronouns, and to nouns as possessive markers. They also follow prepositions. e.g. *walad**uhu*** 'his son'; *ḍarabt**uhu*** 'I struck him'; *'alai**kum*** 'on you (pl.)'. The following sentence ilustrates all three usages:

> Ba'aθat**ni** 'umm**i** 'ilai**ka**
> 'My mother sent me to you' (*ba'aθa* 'he sent'; *'umm* 'mother'; *'ila* 'to')

DEMONSTRATIVE PRONOUN/ADJECTIVE

Masc. *hāðā*, dual, *haðāni*, pl. *hā'ulā'i*; fem. *hāðihi*, dual, *hatāni*, pl. *hā'ulā'i* 'this, these'. Masc. *ðālika*, fem. *tilka* (no plural) 'that' The demonstrative adjective precedes the noun, which is definite: e.g. *hāðā.l-kitāb* 'this book';

tilka.l-jibāl 'those mountains'.

INTERROGATIVE PRONOUN

man 'who?'; *mā* 'what?' (or, *māðā*). The introductory interrogative particle is *hal* or *'a*: e.g.

> wa hal b'imkāni.l-bašari 'an ya'rifū.l-ḥaqīqata?
> 'and is it in the power of men to know the truth?' (Gibran Khalil Gibran)

RELATIVE CLAUSES

Where the antecedent is indefinite, no link is required: e.g.

> baṭalun wahaba ḥayātahu li.bilādihi
> 'a hero who laid down his life for his country'

> bayānun ṣadara fī London
> 'a communiqué which appeared in London'

Where antecedent is definite, the linking pronoun *allaði*, fem. *allati*, is used. This has dual, plural, and oblique forms: *al-šaix..., allaði zāra London 'axīran* 'Sheikh ..., who visited London recently'.

Numerals

Professor Tritton's definition of the Arabic numerals as 'the nightmare of a bankrupt financier' is celebrated.

1: this is a pronoun agreeing in gender with its referent: masc. *'aḥadun*, fem. *'iḥdā*. The form *wāḥidun*, fem. *wāḥidatun* is an adjective.

2: *'iθnāni*, fem. *'iθnatāni* (with oblique and construct forms) is a noun in concord with referent. The dual form of the noun may also be used to indicate duality: *'usbū'aini* 'two weeks'.

3–10: the Arabic equivalents for these numerals are fully declined nouns which obey the law of inverse polarity, i.e. feminine form for masculine referent, and vice versa. e.g. *θalāθ**atu** rijālin* 'three men' (lit. 'a threesome of men'); *θalāθu marratin* 'three times'. The base forms of the numbers 3–10 are: *θalāθ-, 'arba'-, xams-, sitt-, sab'a-, θamān-, tis'a-, 'ašar-*.

11, 12: here, both components agree in gender with the referent: *'aḥada 'ašara* (masc.) 13–19: partial polarity. The ten is in concord with referent, the unit is not: e.g. *xamsa 'ašrata sanatan* 'fifteen years'. 20–99: the tens are diptotes, the units triptotes. 100 *mi'atun*; 200 *mi'atāni*, 300 *θalāθu mi'atin*.

Verb

The dictionary form is the third person masculine singular perfective: e.g. *KaTaBa* 'he wrote'. The strong verb has three radical letters; hamza, *yā*, and *wāw* are excluded. Weak verbs have hamza, *yā*, or *wāw* in initial, medial, or final position; doubly weak verbs have initial, medial, or final hamza + *yā* or *wāw*; thus, *ra'ā* 'he saw' is medial hamza + final *yā*.

Roots may have four radicals, or may be doubled verbs, i.e. geminated second radical: e.g. *ZaXRaFa* 'to adorn'; *MaRRa* 'to pass'.

Aspect rather than tense is denoted by the finite forms: perfective and imperfective. The vowel following the second radical may be *a*, *i*, or *u*, and is known as the characteristic: e.g. *KaTaBa* 'he wrote'; *ŠaRiBa* 'he drank'; *KaRuMa* 'he was noble'. The perfective is marked by suffix for person, number, and, in part, gender; the imperfective is marked by prefix and suffix for person, number, and gender (except for 1st person singular and plural): e.g.

perfective, *kataba* 'he wrote' (Arabic order of person is maintained):

		Singular	*Dual*	*Plural*
3	masc.	kataba	kataб**ā**	katab**ū**
	fem.	kataba**t**	katab**tā**	katab**nā**
2	masc.	katab**ta**	katab**tumā**	katab**tum**
	fem.	katab**ti**		katab**tunna**
1		katab**tu**		katab**nā**

imperfective indicative:

3	masc.	**ya**ktub**u**	**ya**ktub**āni**	**ya**ktub**ūna**
	fem.	**ta**ktub**u**	**ta**ktub**āni**	**ya**ktub**na**
2	masc.	**ta**ktub**u**	**ta**ktub**āni**	**ta**ktub**ūna**
	fem.	**ta**ktub**īna**		**ta**ktub**na**
1	common	**'a**ktub**u**		**na**ktub**u**

From the imperfective indicative are formed, with slight changes in final vowel, the subjunctive and the jussive.

IMPERATIVE

E.g. from *KaTaBa*: *uKTub*, pl. *uKTubū*, fem. *uktubī*, *uktubna*. The negative imperative: here the jussive is used: *lā taKTuB* 'do not write!'.

THE DERIVED STEMS

These correspond to the *binyanim* in Hebrew (*see* **Hebrew**). Servile letters are added to and/or inserted in the base form to generate extensions and modifications of the base meaning. (I is the base form; R = radical.)

Form		*Meaning*	*Example*
II:	geminate of R_2	intensive	*KaSaRa* 'he broke': *KaSSaRa* 'he smashed'
III:	vowel following R_1 lengthened	extension of meaning to involve addressee of action	*KaTaBa* 'he wrote': *Kātaba* 'he wrote to, corresponded with'
IV:	*'a* prefix	causative trans. ← intrans.	*JaLaSa* 'he sat': *'aJLasa* 'he seated'
V:	*ta-* prefixed to II	reflexive of II	*FaRRaQa* 'to separate': *taFaRRaQa* 'to be scattered'

Form		*Meaning*	*Example*
VI:	*ta-* prefixed to III	reciprocal	*ḤaRiBa* 'to be furious': *taḤāRaBa* 'to fight each other'
VII:	*n-* prefix with liaison	reflexive passive	*KaSaRa* 'he broke': *'inKaSaRa* 'it got broken'
VIII:	*-t-* inserted after R_1 + liaison	heterogeneous	*NaðaRa* 'he saw, expected': *'iNtaðaRa* 'he expected, awaited'
IX:	alif-prefix with liaison; V_1 dropped, R_3 geminated	used for colours and bodily defects	*'iḤMaRRa* 'to turn red' (cf. *ḤaMMaRa* 'to make red; *'aḤMaR* 'red': *see* **Adjective**)
X:	*sta-* prefixed with liaison	to seek, pursue, require action denoted by root	*XaLaFa* 'he remained behind': *istaXLaFa* 'he appointed a successor' (*XaLiFa* 'caliph') *akbar* 'great': *istaKBaRa* 'he regarded ... as great' *ḤaSuNa* 'to be handsome': *istaḤSaNa* 'he thought well of...'

PASSIVE

The Arabic passive is made by internal flection – *-u* after first radical – e.g. from *KaTaBa*: ***Ku**TiBa* 'it was written'; ***yu**KTabu* 'it is being written'. Similarly for the derived stems, e.g. in VIII: *'iNtaðaRa* 'he expected': ***'u**Nt**u**ðiRa* 'it was expected'. If a passive verb is used, the agent cannot be overtly specified, i.e. *ḍuriba* X 'X was struck'; but if Y, the striker, is mentioned, the sentence must be rephrased in the active voice: *ḍaraba* Y X.

NEGATIVE

Arabic has several negating particles:

lā is a general negating particle followed by a noun in the accusative or by a verb in the imperfective: e.g. *lā mahall**a** li.l-'ajab* 'there is no need to be surprised'; *lā yaktubu* 'he doesn't/didn't write'.

mā denies verbal sentences in either aspect: e.g. *mā kataba* 'he didn't write'; *mā yaktubu* 'he doesn't write'.

lam with the jussive = *mā* with perfective: *lam yaktub* = *mā kataba* 'he didn't write'.

lan + subjunctive denies the future: e.g. *lan yaktub**a*** 'he will not write'.

laisa 'is not/are not': *laisa lī 'a'dā'u* 'I have no enemies'.

PARTICIPLES
E.g. from *kataba* 'he wrote':

active: *kātib(un)* 'writing' →' writer';
passive: *maktūb(un)* 'written' (with a plural form *makātību*).

Prepositions

The noun following a preposition is in the genitive case: e.g. *fī.l-bayti* 'in the house'. The enclitic forms of the pronouns follow prepositions: e.g. *min.hum* 'of them, from them'; *fi.hā* 'in her'.

Word-formation

Originally and essentially, word-building in a 'God-given' language is reduced to the regular process of expansion of the triliteral root in accordance with the established moulds or patterns (awzān). A root capable of natural semantic expansion may have as many as 44 verbal nouns; and any root not hitherto so exploited could be used to generate new, but orthodox and therefore intelligible forms by analogy (al-qiyās). Permutation of the 28 consonants of Arabic yields over 3,000 potential bases 'theoretically existent with all their regular derivatives' (Massignon, quoted in Monteil 1960: 107). (But note phonotactic constraints on formation of roots, e.g. in neighbourhood of emphatics.) Al-qiyās was a fertile source of lexical enrichment in the Umayyad-ʿAbbāsid period.

Since the Indo-European predilection and aptitude for the formation of compound words is alien to Arabic, the problem of how best to provide the language with equivalents for modern scientific, technical, and political terms has proved a difficult one. Monteil (1960) gives an interesting account of tentative steps in this field. Many of the proposed equivalents are paraphrases rather than compounds, along the lines of, e.g., *mā fawqa.l-banafsajī* 'ultra-violet' (lit. 'what-is-beyond-violet-ness'). However, the truncated root *kahra-* (← *kahraba* 'to electrify') has been successfully used in many compound forms: e.g. *kahra-jābī* 'electro-positive'; *kahra-rākid* 'electrostatics'. Scientific and political terms with the privative prefixes *a-*, *an-*, *non-* go readily into Arabic by means of *lā-*, *γayr*, or *ʿadam*: e.g. *lā-išʿāʿī* 'non-radioactive'; *γayr mustaqīm* 'non-linear'; *ʿadam al-iʿtidaʾ* 'non-aggression'.

Word order

VSO is normal in verbal sentence, though inversions are found. SV in nominal sentence.

١ ١فِي ٱلْبَدْءِ كَانَ ٱلْكَلِمَةُ وَٱلْكَلِمَةُ كَانَ عِنْدَ ٱللهِ وَكَانَ
٢ ٱلْكَلِمَةُ ٱللهَ ✡ ٢هٰذَا كَانَ فِي ٱلْبَدْءِ عِنْدَ ٱللهِ ✡ ٣كُلُّ شَيْءٍ بِهِ
٤ كَانَ وَبِغَيْرِهِ لَمْ يَكُنْ شَيْءٌ مِمَّا كَانَ ✡ ٤فِيهِ كَانَتِ ٱلْحَيٰوةُ وَٱلْحَيٰوةُ
٥ كَانَتْ نُورَ ٱلنَّاسِ ✡ ٥وَٱلنُّورُ يُضِيءُ فِي ٱلظُّلْمَةِ وَٱلظُّلْمَةُ لَمْ
تُدْرِكْهُ
٦ ٦كَانَ إِنْسَانٌ مُرْسَلٌ مِنَ ٱللهِ ٱسْمُهُ يُوحَنَّا ✡ ٧هٰذَا جَآءَ
٨ لِلشَّهَادَةِ لِيَشْهَدَ لِلنُّورِ لِكَيْ يُؤْمِنَ ٱلْكُلُّ بِوَاسِطَتِهِ ✡ ٨لَمْ يَكُنْ هُوَ
ٱلنُّورَ بَلْ لِيَشْهَدَ لِلنُّورِ ✡ ٩

ARMENIAN, MODERN STANDARD

INTRODUCTION

This Indo-European language is spoken by about 5 million in the Armenian Republic, in Georgia and elsewhere in the CIS; and, in a slightly different form, by about a million in several Middle Eastern countries (Turkey, Lebanon) and by émigré colonies throughout the world. This second form is known as Western Armenian; Eastern Armenian is the written and spoken language used in the CIS. The two forms are mutually intelligible, indeed very close to each other. Within Eastern Armenian the sub-dialectal system is very complex: Garibian distinguishes over 50 dialects, sub-divided into seven groups, according to the method used to form the present tense.

Classical Armenian continued to be used as a written language until the nineteenth century and was the medium for the notable and very important renaissance of Armenian culture initiated by the Mekhitarist Order in Venice from the early eighteenth century onwards. In Armenia itself, the first steps towards the creation and development of a new literary language, closer to the spoken norm, were taken in the early nineteenth century by Khachatur Abovian and Ghevond Alishan. The late nineteenth century produced many outstanding writers, notably the novelists Raffi and Shirvanzade, the poets Tumanian and Isahakian, and the playwright Sundukian.

SCRIPT

(*See* **Appendix of Scripts**.) Devised by Mesrop Mashtots around the year AD 400, the Armenian alphabet has survived, almost intact, to the present day. Two letters were added in the twelfth century.

PHONOLOGY

Consonants

stops: b, p, p', dd, tt, t', g, k, k'
affricates: dz, ts, ts', dʒ, tʃ, tʃ'
fricatives: f, v, s, z, ʃ, ʒ, x, h
nasals: m, n
lateral and flap: r, rr, l, ł (→[γ]).
semi-vowel: j

The ejectives are notated here as dotted letters; like Ossete, Armenian seems to have taken these phonemes from the Caucasian languages which surround this small Indo-European enclave. There are thus five series (three of stops, two of affricates) consisting of voiced member – aspirate surd – voiceless ejective: e.g. /b – p – p'/. The contrast between the aspirate and the ejective is often phonemic: cf. *yerek* 'three'; *yereḳ* 'yesterday'. Final voiced consonants are unvoiced: e.g. *yerb* 'when' → [yer**p**]. In this article *c* = /ts/.

Vowels

front: i, e ([e] and [ɛ])
mid: a, ə
back: o, u

The vowel /ə/, represented in the script by the letter Ը, occurs unnotated in many consonant clusters: thus **գրել** 'to write', is pronounced [gərel]. It is more convenient, however, to transliterate such words without the epenthetic vowel, which is in any case fleeting and often close to a shwa: *grel*.

Stress

Stress is virtually always on the final syllable.

MORPHOLOGY AND SYNTAX

Noun

There is no grammatical gender. Armenian has two numbers. The definite article is affixed to the noun: *-ə*/*-n*: e.g. *ṭun* 'house', *ṭun***ə** 'the house'; *gini* 'wine'; *gini***n** 'the wine'. In Eastern Armenian, the indefinite article is *mi* preceding the noun; in Western it follows in the form *mə*: thus, EArm. *mi mard* = WArm. *mard mə* 'a man'. The plural marker is *-er* for monosyllables, *-ner* for polysyllables: e.g. *ṭun.***er** 'houses'; *ṭun.***er**.*ə* 'the houses'; *kayak.***ner** 'towns', *kayak.***ner**.*ə* 'the towns'.

DECLENSION

There are seven cases. Various types of declension are distinguished in the singular, differing mainly in the formation of the genitive and dative cases. There are no irregularities in the plural, as all nouns take -(*n*)*er*. Specimen declensions: *banvor* 'worker'; *gari* 'barley'; *or* 'day'.

	Singular	*Singular*	*Singular*
nom.	banvor	gari	or
gen.	banvor**i**	gar**u**	or**va**
dat.	banvor**i**	gar**u**	or**va**
acc.	banvor	gari	or
abl.	banvor**ic**	gar**uc**	or**vanic**
instr.	banvor**ov**	gar**ov**	or**ov**
loc.	—	gar**um**	or**um**

Examples of anomalous genitive formation: *hayr* 'father' – *hor*; *kuyr* 'sister' – *kroč*. All nouns in *-tyun* have a genitive in *-tyan*. Very many Armenian nouns are formed from two root words linked by *-a-*: e.g. *mayr* 'mother' + *kaγak* 'town': *mayrakaγak* 'capital city'; *hay* 'Armenian' + *-sṭan* 'place': *Hayasṭan* 'Armenia'.

Adjective

As attribute, adjective precedes noun and is invariable: e.g. *lav bareḳam* 'good friend'; *lav bareḳam.ner.i* 'of good friends'.

COMPARATIVE

With *aveli* 'more than': e.g. *spiṭaḳ* 'white': *aveli spiṭaḳ* 'whiter'. The compared nominal is in the ablative: e.g. *Yerevan.ic* (*aveli*) *meç* 'bigger than Yerevan'.

Pronoun

PERSONAL

The independent forms of the personal pronouns, with accusative case:

	Singular		*Plural*	
	Nom.	*Acc.*	*Nom.*	*Acc.*
1	yes	inj	menk	mez
2	du	kez	duk	jez
3	na	nran	nrank	nranc
	ink	iren	irenk	irenc

The full declension of *yes* 'I', for example, is: *yes – im – inj – inj – injnic – injnov – injnum*: *asek inj* 'tell me'; *inj asacin, vor...* 'they told me that ...'

POSSESSIVE ADJECTIVES

These are provided by the genitive forms of the above listed personal pronouns (*im – ko – ir*, etc.) and are paralleled by a series of personal possessive affixed markers for first, second, and third person: *-s*, *-d*, *-n*. Thus, ***im anunə*** = ***anunəs*** 'my name' (in both cases, with the definite article).

DEMONSTRATIVE PRONOUN/ADJECTIVE

Three forms closely connected with the personal endings: *ays/sa* 'this' (Lat. *apud me*), *ayd/da* (Lat. *apud te*), *ayn/na* (Lat. *apud eum*). These have plural forms: *srank*, *drank*, *nrank*; as adjectives they are invariable: e.g. *ayd ç̣ašaran.ner.um* 'in these restaurants'.

INTERROGATIVE PRONOUN

vov 'who?'; *inč* 'what?'.

RELATIVE PRONOUN

Sing. *vor*, pl. *vronk*; e.g. *duk, vor uzum ek sovorel hayeren* 'you who wish to learn Armenian'. Relative clauses may also be made with participles (*see* below): e.g. *ayn gnacoγ usanoγ* 'the student who is walking over there' (*gnal* 'to go, walk').

Numerals

1–10: *meḳ, yerḳu, yerek, čors, hing, vec, yot, ut, inn, ṭas*; 11 *ṭas.n.meḳ*; 12 *ṭas.n.yerḳu*; 20 *ksan*; 30 *yeresun*; 40 *kar̆asun*; 100 *haryur.*

Verb

The Armenian verb has active and passive voices and four moods: indicative, optative, conditional–subjunctive, and imperative. Only the indicative mood has a full set of tenses.

The infinitive ends in *-el/al*; as in Old Armenian, two bases are formed from the infinitive:

(a) the present base, formed by dropping the *-el/al*: e.g. *grel* 'to write': present base *gr-*; *ḳardal* 'to read': present base *ḳard-*; *mṭnel* 'to go': *mṭn-*.
(b) the aorist base: *-l→aç* or *-acaç*: *grel*: aorist base *graç*; *ḳardal*: *ḳardacaç*

From the present base are formed the optative, the subjunctive, the conditional, the imperfective participle in *-um*, and the future participle in *-u*. From the aorist base are formed the simple past tense and the participle in *-o*. The past participle is identical with the second base: *graç*, *ḳardacaç*.

The main auxiliary used in conjugation is *yem* = I am:
present sing. 1. em, 2. es, 3. ē; pl. 1. enk, 2. ek, 3. en ; y- anlaut if necessary.
past sing.: 1. ēi, 2, ēir, 3. ēr; pl. 1. ēink, 2. ēik, 3. ēin

Specimen conjugation: *grel* 'to write'; indicative mood (main forms):

present: grum em, es, *etc.*
past imperfect: grum ēi, ēir, *etc.*
future: grelu yem, yes, *etc.*, *or with particle* ḳə: ḳə grem (*optative*)
preterite: grel em, *etc.*
pluperfect: grel ēi, *etc.*
perfect: graç em, *etc.*
Simple aorist: sing. greci, grecir, grec; pl. grecink, grecik, grecin
Optative: sing. grem, gres, gri; pl. grenk, grek, gren

GERUNDS

The present gerund ends in *-um* (the form used in the present and imperfect tenses above) or in *-elis/alis*; the latter form is used to denote action upon which a second action is contingent: e.g. *Senyaḳ mṭnelis girkəs hanum em* 'Upon entering the room, I take my book.' The future gerund is seen as a tense formant in the future: *grelu yem*, etc. It can also be used as an infinitive of purpose; e.g. *Gnaci gradaran girk ḳardal***u** 'I went to the library to read a book'; and attributively: e.g. *ḳardalu girk* 'a book to be read'.

IMPERATIVE

Sing. *grir!* 'write!' pl. *grecek!*

HORTATIVE

Optative form preceded by *ḅiṭi*: e.g. *ḅiṭi grem* 'I am to/have to write'.

PASSIVE
The marker is *-v-*: e.g. *sirel* 'to love'; passive, *sirvel* 'to be loved'; *Vočnčacvec meķ řmbaķoçič* 'One bomber was destroyed.'

CAUSATIVE
-V*cn* -: e.g. *nsṭel* 'to sit', ***nsṭecnel*** 'to ask someone to be seated'.

NEGATIVE
The negative particle *čə* is prefixed to the auxiliary if there is one; the auxiliary then precedes the sense verb: e.g. *grum ēi* 'I was writing', ***čei*** *grum* 'I wasn't writing'; *grelu e* 'he will write': ***či*** *grelu* 'he will not write'. The negative particle for the imperative mood is *mi*.

Prepositions and postpositions

Armenian uses both.

PREPOSITIONS
With genitive case: *ařanc* 'without': e.g. *ařanc ķasķaçi* 'doubtless'; and with accusative case: *depi* 'towards': e.g. *gnum em depi hyusis* 'I am going northwards'.

POSTPOSITIONS
Usually follow the genitive case: e.g.

> *hamar* 'for': e.g. *hayreniki hamar* 'for the motherland';
> *masin* 'about': e.g. *Xosum enk girki masin* 'We're talking about the book';
> *heṭ* 'with': e.g. *nra heṭ gnaci* 'I went with him';
> *vra* 'on': e.g. *seγani vra* 'on the table'.

Word order

SVO is basic; can be altered for emphasis.

1 Սկզբումն էր Բանը. և Բանն Աստուծոյ մօտ էր. և Աստուած էր
2 Բանը։ Նա սկզբումն Աստուծոյ
3 մօտ էր։ Ամէն ինչ նորանով ե-
ղաւ, և առանց նորան ոչինչ չե-
4 ղաւ, ինչ որ եղաւ։ Նորանով էր
կեանք, և կեանքը մարդկանց լոյսն
5 էր։ Եւ լոյսը խաւարումը լոյս է տա-
լիս, և խաւարը չիմացաւ նորան։
6 Մի մարդ եղաւ Աստուածանից
ուղարկուած, անունը Յօհաննէս։
7 Սա վկայութեան համար եկաւ,
որ այն Լուսոյ համար վկայ է.
որ ամէնքը նորանով հաւատան։
8 Նա չէր Լոյսն, այլ որ Լուսոյն
համար վկայէ։

ASSAMESE

INTRODUCTION

This Eastern New Indo-Aryan language derives, like Bengali and Oriya, from the Māgadhī Prakrit. It is spoken by around 9 million people in the state of Assam, which forms linguistically an enclave between Tibeto-Burman and Mon-Khmer territories. There are two dialects, Eastern (Sibsagar) and Western (Kamarupa). The literary standard is based on the former. Assamese is one of the 14 official languages recognized in the Indian constitution.

From the thirteenth to the nineteenth centuries the Tai invaders known as the Ahoms ruled the country, their power culminating in the early eighteenth century. 'Ahom' is the normal Assamese pronunciation of the word *āsām* (Indo-Aryan sibilants reduced to /h/ in Assamese, *see* **Phonology**, below).

Literature in Assamese is recorded from the fourteenth century onwards. A distinctive and specifically Assamese genre is the historical chronicle, many of which were produced anonymously during the last two centuries of the Ahom state. There is a flourishing contemporary literature in prose media, e.g. the novel.

SCRIPT

The Bengali script, introduced in the nineteenth century, is used for writing Assamese. There is an extra letter for /w/, which has no counterpart in Bengali. Also, Assamese *r* differs from Bengali *r*.

There is an extremely poor correspondence between script and sound in this language, in that 49 graphs are available for 33 phonemes.

PHONOLOGY

Consonants

stops: p, b, t, d, k, g; with aspirates ph, bh, th, dh, kh, gh
fricatives: s, z, x, h
nasals: m, n, ŋ
laterals and flap: l, r, rh
semi-vowels: j, w

It will be noticed that, in comparison with the standard New Indo-Aryan inventory, the palatal series, *c*, *ch*, *j*, *jh*, and the retroflex, *ṭ*, *ṭh*, *ḍ*, *ḍh* are missing from the above table. In Assamese the palatals have turned into /s/, /z/, while the

IA cerebrals have merged with the dental series, and the IA sibilants are represented by /x/ and /h/.

Sandhi rules reflect both Classical Sanskrit practice (*see* **Sanskrit**) and a later series of accommodations at junctures.

Vowels

a = [ɐ], i, e, æ, a = [ɔ], o, u

These occur nasalized, and the following palatalized variants are found: [œ, y]. Diphthongs: /oi, ou/. Nasalization is marked by candrabindu ঁ.

VOWEL HARMONY

/ɔ/, /o/ followed by /i/ → [u]: e.g. *khora* 'lame man' – fem. *khuri*; /æ/ followed by /i/, /u/ → [e]: e.g. *bæta* 'son' – *beti* 'daughter'.

Stress

In Eastern dialect stress is on the penultimate syllable.

MORPHOLOGY AND SYNTAX

Noun

The basic dichotomy is between humans (masculine and feminine) and non-human (neuter). The distinction between masculine and feminine may be reflected morphologically: thus, -(*n*)*i* is a feminine marker: e.g. *burhi* 'old woman' (*burha* 'old man').

NUMBER

The plural is formed with the help of various agglutinative suffixes: *-bilak* (humans), *-bor* (animals); *-sakal* /xɔkɔl/ is an honorific suffix: e.g. *dewtasakal* 'gods'.

SPECIMEN DECLENSION

manuh 'man, human being'.

	Singular
nom./agentive	manuh**e**
acc.	manuh**ak**
gen.	manuh**ar**
instr.	manuh**ere**, manuh**ar ddara** (*ddara* is a postposition)
dat.	manuh**ak**, manuh**lai**
abl.	manuh**ar para**
loc.	manuh**at**

The same endings are added to the plural markers: e.g. *manuhbilake*, *manuhbilakak*. There is no article as such in Assamese, but a singular animate noun may acquire some degree of definiteness by the insertion of *-to-* between base and case ending: e.g. *manuhtok* 'to that man (already mentioned)'. This enclitic seems to be an importation from contiguous non-Indo-European linguistic stock. Non-Indo-European influence is also seen in the Assamese practice of adding personal markers to kinship terms in the singular: e.g. *bopai* 'my father'; *ziyer(a)* 'your daughter'; *ziyek* 'his/her daughter'.

Adjective

The adjective is not sharply distinguished from the noun, and can be declined as such. As attribute it is invariable for case, but takes fem. *-i* where necessary: e.g. *kala balad* 'black bull', *kali gai* 'black cow'.

COMPARISON

A comparative form is made by means of *koi/kari* following the locative case: e.g. *Xei gharat* ***koi*** *ei ghar daŋar* 'This house is bigger than that house.'

Pronoun

The independent personal forms are:

		Singular	Plural
	1	mai /mɔi/	ami
	2	tai /tɔi/	tahãt
hon.	2	apuni	aponasakal

In the third person the demonstratives, *i* (masc.), *ei* (fem.); *xi/xei* (masc.) *tai* (fem.) are used, with honorary forms *eõ̃* and *tẽõ̃*.

The base forms are declined, e.g. for *mai*: acc. *mok*, instr. *more/mor ddara*, abl. *mor para*, gen. *mor*, loc. *mot*: e.g. *mor bandhu* 'my friend'.

DEMONSTRATIVE PRONOUN

Not declined when used attributively: e.g. *ei manuhak* 'of this man'. The plural marker may be added to either the noun or the demonstrative, not both: e.g. *ei manuhbilake* = *eibilak manuhe* 'these people'.

INTERROGATIVE PRONOUN

kih 'who?'; *kon* 'what, which?': e.g. *kon manuh/kitap* 'which man/book?'

RELATIVE PRONOUN

yi /zi/, pl. *yibilake*. These have oblique bases: *yā-* /zaː/ for humans, *yiha-* for non-human.

Verbal participle + the particle *thaka* is also used for relative constructions: e.g. *kitap parhi thaka manuh* 'the man who is reading the book'.

Numerals

1–10: *æk*, *dui*, *tini*, *sāri*, *pãs*, *say*, *xāt*, *āth*, *na*, *dah*; 11–19 have synthetic forms; 20 *bis*; 30 *tris*; 40 *sallis*; 100 *xa*. Formation of numerals up to 100 is not predictable.

Verb

Has active and passive voices, and the following moods: indicative, imperative, subjunctive, conditional, presumptive.

Personal endings (*see* table) are the same for both numbers; where necessary *-hāk* may be added to mark plural. Gender is nowhere specified.

Personal endings:

		Present	*Past*	*Future*
1		-õ	-(i)lõ	-(i)m
2	familiar	-a	-(i)li	-(i)bi
	neutral	-ā	-(i)lā	-(i)bā
2 & 3	hon.	-e	-(i)lē	-(i)ba

The past forms are composed of the past passive participle + personal markers. The auxiliary *ach* /as/ is used with the present participle to make an analytical present tense: e.g. *mai kitap parhi achõ* /asõ/ 'I am reading a/the book'. Similarly with past indefinite: *mai kitap parhi achõilõ* /asõilõ/ 'I was reading a/the book'.

Invariable particles enter into the composition of the subjunctive, the presumptive, and the conditional. The three moods are also specifically associated with tense – the subjunctive with the past tense + *hẽten*, the presumptive with the present tense + *habalā*, the conditional with the non-finite form in *-ā* + *hẽten*: e.g. *mai gəlo hẽten* 'I'd have gone'; *xi ahise habalā* 'he must have come'.

NON-FINITE FORMS

Infinitive in -*(i)ba*: e.g. *buliba* 'to speak'.

Present participle in *-i*; past participle in *-a*. Perfective conjunctive in *-i*.

Negative: *na* /nɔ/ is prefixed to verb: e.g. *mai* ***na****karõ* 'I don't do'.

PASSIVE VOICE

The auxiliaries *ya* /za/ and *ha* /hɔ/ are used + transitive past participle. Where *ya* is used, the logical subject is in the instrumental, the logical object in the nominative: e.g. *mor ddara ei kamto kara zay* 'by me this work is done' = 'I do this work'.

Ha construction: the logical object is in the accusative, subject is in the instrumental + third person of *ha*: e.g. *Tar ddara tomak mara nahaba* 'You will not be beaten by him' (examples from Babakaev 1961).

CAUSATIVES

Add *-a*/*-wā* to the root: the second grade, in *-wa*, implies that an intermediary is involved in the action: e.g. *laru* 'to run', *laru****wa*** 'cause someone to run'; *di* 'to give', *diya* (< *di.y*(*w*)*a*) 'cause someone to give'.

Postpositions

The language has about three dozen New Indo-Aryan postpositions, plus a few drawn from Arabo-Persian.

Word order

Normally SOV.

১ আদিতে[১] বাক্য[২] আছিল, আৰু বাক্য ঈশ্বৰে সৈতে আছিল,
২ আৰু বাক্যেই আপুনি ঈশ্বৰ। তেওঁ আদিতে ঈশ্বৰে সৈতে আছিল।
৩ তেওঁৰ দ্বাৰায় সকলোৱেই হল ;[৩] আৰু যি যি হল, সেইবোৰৰ
৪ এটাও, তেওঁৰ বিনে নহল। জীৱন তেওঁতেহে ;[৪] সেই জীৱনেই
৫ মানুহৰ পোহৰ।[৫] পোহৰ আন্ধাৰত প্ৰকাশিত হৈ আছে ;
৬ কিন্তু আন্ধাৰে তাক গ্ৰহণ* নকৰিলে। ঈশ্বৰৰ পৰা পঠোৱা যোহন[৬]
৭ নামেৰে এজন মানুহ আছিল ; তেওঁৰ দ্বাৰায় সকলোৱে যেন
বিশ্বাস কৰে, এই নিমিত্তে, সেই পোহৰৰ সাক্ষ্য দিবলৈ[৭] তেওঁ
৮ সাক্ষ্যৰ অৰ্থে আহিছিল। তেওঁ আপুনি সেই পোহৰ নাছিল,
কিন্তু পোহৰৰ সাক্ষ্য দিবলৈহে আহিছিল।

BALINESE

INTRODUCTION

A member of the Malayo-Polynesian branch of Austronesian, Balinese is spoken by 3 to 4 million people in the island of Bali and some smaller adjacent islands. It has three socio-linguistic registers:

1. basa *ketah* (K): everyday Balinese for family and friendly use;
2. basa *madia* (M): basically *ketah* with an injection of more formal words for use in situations where low *ketah* would be unacceptable;
3. basa *singgih* (S): corresponds to Javanese krâmâ; a somewhat artificial construct containing many Sanskrit and Javanese words.

Many *ketah* words have no *singgih* equivalents, and have to be promoted to *singgih* status when the latter is being used. For many key concepts, however, each register has its own word; cf.

	Ketah	*Madia*	*Singgih*
'eat	naar	neda	ngadjengang
'dead'	mati	padem	séda
'live'	idup	urip	njeneng

SCRIPT

Originally Javanese. A standard romanization, based on Dutch spelling, was provided by H.J. Schwartz in Batavia in the early twentieth century.

PHONOLOGY

In the main, as in **Indonesian**. Final /k/ is not entirely glottalized. The vowel *a* in such prefixes as *pa-*, *ka-*, *ma-* is /ə/; final *a* tends to /œ/.

Stress

Tends to be on the penultimate syllable.

MORPHOLOGY AND SYNTAX

The definite article is affixed -(*n*)*é*: e.g. *batuné* 'the stone'; *guruné* 'the teacher'. Before proper nouns the article *i* is used.

NOMINAL FORMS

Simple and derived; the latter are made with such prefixes as the following:

(a) *pa-*: forms verbal noun, e.g. *rérén* 'to stop': *pa.rérén* 'the stopping'; *pa-* + ... *-an*: *pa.réré.an* 'the stopping place'.
(b) *para-/pra-*: forms collectives, e.g. *parawanita* 'women'.
(c) *ka...an*: forms abstract concepts, e.g. *ka.djegég.an* 'beauty'.

POSSESSION

Possessed – possessor: *see* **Pronoun**, below.

Adjective

Invariable; as attribute, adjective follows noun: e.g. *anaké odah ento* 'the old man' (*odah* 'old').

Pronoun

Number is not distinguished.

First person (excl.): S form is *titiang*; M form, *tiang*; K form, *itjang*.
Second person: K forms are *tjai* (masc.) and *njai* (fem.). For polite address, e.g. to strangers, *djero* can be used, at least until the caste situation has been clarified. The Malay form *tuan* is replacing the old Balinese forms. In very elevated S speech, *tjokor i ratu/tjokor i déwa* may be used, the latter to a prince.
Third person: the caste forms were *dané* for a vaiśya, *ida* for a satria or brahman, and these forms are still in use where such distinctions are called for. Omnibus forms are S *ipun* and K *ia*.

There is a general tendency to use the polite third person form when speaking of first or second person.

POSSESSION

In first and second person the personal pronoun is used: e.g. *umah tiang(é)* 'my house'. Third person: the K form is *-ne*, e.g. *limanné* 'his hand', *abian iané* 'his field' (the gemination in the first example is necessary to distinguish the form from noun + definite article, *limané* 'the hand'). S and M form: *-ipun*, e.g. *somahipun* = *rabinida* 'his wife' (*ida* is S 3rd p. pron.)

DEMONSTRATIVE PRONOUN

S *puniki* = K *ené* 'this'; S *punika* = K *ento* 'that'.

INTERROGATIVE PRONOUN

S *sira* = K *njén* 'who?'; S *punapi* = K *apa* 'what?'.

RELATIVE PRONOUN

S *sané* = K *ané*; or, *sang/kang*; e.g.

anaké ané **n**ulungin tjai 'the man who helped you'

anaké ane **t**ulungin tjai 'the man who was helped by you'

mémé bapa sang sampun nguripin titiang
'my parents who gave me life' (*nguripin* 'life')

Numerals

1–10: *sa*, *dua/kalih*, *telu/tiga*, *empat*, *lima*, *enem*, *pitu*, *akutus*, *asia*, *adasa*. These have positional variants: (a) reduplicated; (b) with *-ng*: e.g. *dua* – *dadua* – *duang*. The reduplicated form is used where the numeral is treated as a nominal; the *-ng* form where the numeral immediately precedes a noun.

Verb

Stems are neutral, and become transitive or intransitive by morphophonemic change. Nearly all intransitive verbs in Balinese have a non-nasal initial: e.g. *lunga* 'to go', *urip* 'to live'. Transitive verbs may focus either on subject or on object: if on subject, the initial is a nasal: e.g. *batuné ané mara gebeg* 'the stone was polished'; *tiang né* ***ngebeg*** *batuné* 'I polished the stone'.

Stems may be made transitive by affixation of *-ang*: e.g. *takén* 'to ask', *tak*é*n****ang*** 'to ask someone for something'. Also, transitive verbs can be intensified by addition of *-ang*: e.g. *mireng* 'to hear', *mireng****ang*** 'to pay attention to'; *ngelah* 'to own', *ngelah****ang*** 'to exercise rights of ownership'; or made causative: e.g. *uning* 'to know', *uning****ang*** 'to bring something to someone's knowledge'.

-ang also makes verbs from adjectives and nouns: *utama* 'excellent', *utama****ang*** 'to regard something as excellent'; *soré* 'afternoon', ***njoréang*** 'to do something in the afternoon'; *sugih* 'rich', ***njugihang*** 'to get richer'.

The Balinese verb appears in four forms (plus or minus affixation): (1) the simple (weak) form; (2) the strong (nasalized) form; (3) the *ka-* form; (4) the *ma-* form.

1. The simple form: the agent follows the verb, e.g.

   Buku punika tumbas tiang di pidan adji limang rupiah
   'I bought the book formerly for 5 guilders'.

2. Some examples of the nasalized form have been given above.
3. The *ka-* form focuses on verbal action; normally + *-ang/-in* affix, though this is not used for first or second person: e.g. ***katulungin*** *baan bapanné* 'helped by his father'; ***Ø****tulung****in*** *itjang/tjai* 'helped by me/you'.
4. The *ma-* form: if the base is intransitive, so is the *ma-* form; if the base is transitive, the *ma-* form is usually intransitive → passive, e.g. *padiné jén suba* ***ma****tebuk*... 'once the rice has been pounded...'; *padi ané* ***ma****tebuk* 'the pounded rice'.

Word order

Depends on verbal construction: SVO, VSO, OVS are possible.

1 Sadurung jagate puniki kaadakang antuk Ida Sang Hyang Widi Wasa,
Sang Sabda sampun wenten. Sang Sabda punika sinarengan ring Ida Sang
Hyang Widi Wasa, tur Sang Sabda punika taler maraga Widi. 2 Saking pa-
ngawit Sang Sabda punika sinarengan ring Ida Sang Hyang Widi Wasa.
3 Malantaran Sang Sabda punika Ida Sang Hyang Widi Wasa ngadakang
saluiring sane wenten. Tur tan wenten sane kaadakang sane tan malantaran Sang Sabda. 4 Sang Sabda punika maraga wit urip, tur uripe punika
dados galang manusane. 5 Galange punika macahya ring tengah petenge,
tur petenge punika tan mrasidayang ngaonang galange punika.

6 Ida Sang Hyang Widi Wasa sampun ngutus utusan Idane, sane ma-
pesengan Yohanes. 7 Dane rauh jaga midartayang pariindik galange punika ring i manusa, mangda manusane sami miragiang tur percaya. 8 Boya
ja dane Yohanes ngaraga galange punika, nanging rauh danene buat midartayang indik galange punika.

BALTIC LANGUAGES

This branch of Indo-European is of special interest in comparative linguistics because of its retention of certain very archaic features, both phonological and morphological. Baltic is genetically close to, and seems to have been always geographically contiguous with, Slavonic and Germanic. East and West forms of Baltic are distinguished. Of several East Baltic languages known to have existed, only two survive – Lithuanian and Latvian. Evidence for the extinct congeners is entirely toponymic; thus the name of the Curonians survives in Courland (Latvian: *kurzeme*). The sole attested West Baltic language – Old Prussian – survived into the seventeenth century.

The toponymic evidence shows that Baltic was formerly spoken over an area considerably exceeding its present limitations: south-eastwards across White Russia towards the Dniepr, and southwards into what is now Poland. This original habitat shrank as Baltic stock gave ground to Slavonic and Germanic. To a lesser extent, local Finno-Ugric languages have been absorbed or ousted by Baltic.

The oldest written records in Baltic are Old Prussian texts of the fourteenth century. Records in Lithuanian and Latvian date from the sixteenth century.

Both Lithuanian and Latvian are tonal, exhibit archaic Indo-European features, and share an extensive common vocabulary. In spite of this homogeneity, however, they are usually treated as belonging to different areal groupings. Thus, on areal criteria, Gyula Décsy classifies Lithuanian along with Polish, Ukrainian, Belorussian, and Kashubian: Latvian with Estonian, Vot, and Liv.

The total number of people speaking Baltic languages is probably about 5 million (including émigré populations).

See **Lithuanian, Latvian.**

BANTU LANGUAGES

INTRODUCTION

The Bantu languages form a major component of the Benue-Congo branch of the Niger-Congo family of languages; the other branches are the Kwa group, the Voltaic or Gur group, the West Atlantic group, the Mande group and the Adamawa-Eastern group. Altogether, the Benue-Congo branch comprises about 700 languages, and 500 of these are Bantu.

Geographically, the Bantu languages cover most of sub-Saharan Africa, across which they seem to have spread, eastwards and southwards, from a West African point of origin, in the early part of the first millennium AD. As in the case of the Turkic languages, dispersal was not accompanied by any marked degree of innovation on the linguistic plane; and the features which go to identify a language as 'Bantu' remained remarkably stable as the dialectal continuum expanded over great distances and through long periods of time, so that even outliers like Zulu-Xhosa, Herero, and Makua are instantly recognizable as Bantu. Indeed, it is mainly in areas close to the original Bantu homeland in West Africa that the characteristic genetic imprint is found to be somewhat modified. This may be due either to Proto-Bantu connections with contiguous languages of the isolating type (Kwa, Kordofanian, Nilo-Saharan) or to the influence of these languages on Bantu in the historical period.

At the other extreme of the Bantu continuum, the clicks in Zulu-Xhosa represent importations from neighbouring Khoisan languages. The Zulu grid of click sounds (*see* **Zulu**), for example, shows a labio-velar, a dental–velar, and a lateral–velar series, each containing four phonemes – a surd, its aspirate, its voiced allophone, and its nasal, e.g. in the dental–velar series /q, qh, gq, nq/.

The earliest descriptions of Bantu languages date from the mid-seventeenth century – e.g. Giacinto Brusciotto's Latin grammar of Kongo, published in 1659. The task of providing an internal classification of the Bantu languages based on scientific criteria, was first undertaken by W.H.J. Bleek (1862–9), who coined the name *Bantu* to designate the people and their languages. The word is a plural form meaning 'people', and functions as such in many Bantu languages; cf.

	Singular	*Plural*
Rwanda	umu.ntu 'man'	aba.ntu
Kongo	mu.ntu	ba.ntu
Zulu	umu.ntu	aba.ntu
Herero	omu.ndu	ov̇a.ndu
Swahili	m.tu	wa.tu

Lingala	mo.to	ba.to
Sotho	mō.thō	bā.thō
Shona	mu.nhu	va.nhu
Luganda	omu.ntu	aba.ntu

The Common Bantu prototype, of which these are reflexes, has been reconstructed as, sing. **mo.to*; pl. **ba.nto*.

Bleek was followed by Carl Meinhof (1901) and Sir Harry Johnston (1919). In 1948, Professor M. Guthrie published the first part of his definitive *Classification of the Bantu Languages* (complete edition, 4 vols, 1967–70). This classification lists about 700 languages (including those which Guthrie calls 'semi-Bantu') divided into 16 areal groupings, each grouping having specific phonological and morphological features.

The Bantu languages are spoken by a total of about 160 million people. Numbers for individual languages vary very considerably; between 50,000 and 100,000 is about average. Rwanda tops the list as the mother tongue of at least 10 million, followed by Swahili, Zulu-Xhosa, and Makua (in Mozambique) with 5–6 million each. The picture changes if second-language status is taken into account: Swahili, with some 50 million, then easily outstrips all its congeners.

A broad areal division, based on Guthrie's 16 zones, with the names of some of the most important representative members, is given:

1. North-West Central Africa: Duala, Fang, Buja, Lingala/Losengo;
2. West and South-West Central Africa: Kongo, Songe, Herero, Ciokwe;
3. East Central: Swahili, Sango, Bemba, Tonga, Nyanja;
4. North-East Central: Luganda, Gikuyu, Nyankole, Soga, Rundi, Rwanda, Nyamwesi;
5. South-East: Shona, Tsonga, Ronga, Makua, Yao;
6. South: Sotho, Swazi, Tswana, Zulu-Xhosa.

PHONOLOGY

Consonants

The parent Proto-Bantu language had a relatively simple inventory of stops /p, t, k/, plus /tʃ/ with their voiced, nasal, and pre-nasalized (both voiced and unvoiced) allophones: e.g.

p, b, m, ^{m}p, ^{m}b; t, d, n, ^{n}t, ^{n}d

The plural forms in the *umuntu/abantu* chart on pp. 49–50 illustrate reflexes in modern Bantu languages of the unvoiced pre-nasalized series. In Swahili, for example, the nasal has been lost, *wa.tu*; in Herero, the unvoiced has merged with the voiced series, *ova.**ndu*** (cf. a.***ndu*** in Thagicu); while in Shona the stop has been lost, *va.nhu* (cf. *wa.nu* in the Luguru language of Tanzania).

Common Bantu seems to have had no sibilants, while /s/ and several other fricatives – /ʃ, z, h, f, v/ – are widespread in the successor languages. In many of these, the fricatives and some sonants are reflexes of the parent voiced series.

Vowels

Proto-Bantu had seven vowels, /i, e, ɛ, a, ɔ, o, u/, an inventory which is characteristic today of two of Guthrie's areal groupings (North-East and North-West Central), and is also found (along with the five-vowel system) in seven others. The five-vowel system, /i, ɛ, a, ɔ, u/, is found in about 60 per cent of Bantu languages.

Tone

Proto-Bantu was probably a tone language, and tone is a general characteristic of present-day Bantu languages, where it is often phonemic. The curious phenomenon of tone reversal has been noted in Western Congo languages (high tone for Common Bantu low, and vice versa). Tone has been lost in Swahili.

Stress

Stress normally tends to the penultimate syllable.

MORPHOLOGY AND SYNTAX

Noun

It seems clear that Proto-Bantu was already in possession of the class prefix system which is now the most general and the most typical feature of Bantu morphology. Proto-Bantu had 19 classes, an inventory which has been retained in many of the daughter languages, and much reduced (usually by syncretic processes) in others; Sotho, for example, has only seven classes. Class 1, the class of human beings, is largely homogeneous over the whole field; the other classes are heterogeneous, though some of them are associated, at least in part, with certain semantic fields: e.g. trees are often in class 3, animals in class 9. In origin, the classes may well have been associated with an elaborate system of classifiers such as are found in South-East Asia. The class system has nothing to do with gender; nor is it, at least in origin, connected with an animate/inanimate dichotomy. The animate concord which is now a feature of Swahili and some other East Central languages is a recent development.

Class is marked in nouns by prefix which is then echoed by concordial coefficients in all associated parts of speech, thus producing a kind of semantic alliteration: e.g. Swahili

> **wa**geni **wa**zungu **we**ngi **wa**lifika Kenya (ili) **wa**pande mlima wa Kilimanjaro; nime**wa**ona.
> 'Many European visitors came to Kenya to climb Mount Kilimanjaro; I have seen them.'
> (*-fika* 'to arrive, come'; *-geni* 'strange'; *Mzungu* 'European'; *-ingi* 'many'; *-pande* 'to climb'; *mlima* 'mountain'; *-li* = past-tense marker; *-me-* = perfect-tense marker; *-ona* 'to see')

Classes are normally paired: a class containing singular nouns is followed by the class containing the respective plurals. Classes 1 and 2, containing singular and plural nouns denoting human beings, have been illustrated above: *umu.ntu/ aba.ntu*, etc. Similarly, class 3 comprises singular nouns with a *m-/mw-/mu-* prefix; class 4, the relevant plurals with a *mi-* prefix. The semantic field in classes 3/4 is heterogeneous, basically animate, e.g.

	Class 3	*Class 4 plurals*
Swahili	m.ti 'tree'	mi.ti
Kongo	n.ti	mi.ti
Zulu	umu.thi	imi.ti
Shona	mu.ti	mi.ti
Lingala	mw.ete	mi.ete
Luganda	omu.ti	emi.ti
Gikuyu	mu.ti	mi.ti

It will be noticed that certain prefixes – e.g. *m-* in classes 1 and 3 – are duplicated. This can only give rise to confusion in citation form; in connected utterance, oral or written, specific concordial sequence ensures semantic discrimination.

Some classes are at least partially correlated with specific semantic fields, the obvious example being class 1/2. This is on the whole atypical, however, and not consistent. *See* **Swahili** for a specific set of classes. For comparative purposes, here is the Luganda system, which is notable for the retention of classes which have been lost in other North-East Central Bantu languages:

Class	*Prefix*	*Class features and examples*
1	omu-	class of human beings: ***omu****ntu* 'man'
2	aba-	plurals of nouns in cl. 1: ***aba****ntu* 'men, people'
3	omu-	plants, trees, etc.: ***omu****ti* 'tree'
4	emi-	plurals of nouns in cl. 3: ***emi****ti* 'trees'
5	li-/eri-	with sandhi at junctures; heterogeneous field: ***ejj****inja* 'stone' (li + j- > (e)jj)
6	ama-	plurals of nouns in cl. 5: ***ama****yinja* 'stones'
7	eki-	human artefacts: ***eki****zimbe* 'building'; may have disparaging nuance: ***eki****renzi* 'overgrown youth'
8	ebi-	plurals of cl. 7 nouns: ***ebi****zimbe* 'buildings'
9	en-	heterogeneous; includes some animals: ***en****jovu* 'elephant'
10	zi-	provides plural forms for nouns belonging to various classes
11	olu-/olw-	class of long and/or thin objects: ***olu****tindo* 'bridge'
12	otu-	nouns denoting small quantities of something: ***otu****zzi* 'drops of water'
13	aka-	heterogeneous field: ***aka****mwa* 'mouth'; ***aka****ntu* 'something small'; ***aka****wungeezi* 'evening'
14	obu-/obw-	plurals of nouns in cl. 13: ***obu****mwa* 'mouths'
15	oku-	actions: ***oku****genda* 'going' (< *-genda* 'to go')
20	ogu-	augmentatives based on nouns in other classes:

		oguntu 'giant' (cf. *omuntu* 'man')
22	aga-	plurals of nouns in cl. 20: ***agantu*** 'giants'

It is worth pointing out here that Luganda has, in addition, a series of prefixes denoting high rank, which draw on class 1 for their concordial agreement, e.g. *sse-*, *nna-*, with plural forms *basse-*, *banna-*: e.g. *ssabasajja Kabaka* 'His Highness the Kabaka'.

Classes 16, 17, and 18, left blank in the above table, are the locational classes with prefixes *pa-*, *ku-*, *mu-* indicating, respectively, definite locus, indefinite locus, and locus within something: cf. Swahili *nyumba.ni* ***mwa*** *mwalimu* 'in the house of the teacher' (*-ni* is a locative suffix; *nyumba* 'house'; *mwalimu* 'teacher').

Adjective

There are very few root adjectives in Bantu. Examples are:

	'Large'		*'Bad'*
Zulu	-kulu	Zulu	-bi
Swahili	-kuu	Herero	-i
Nyanja	-kulu	Luganda	-bi
Tswana	-xolo	Kongo	-bi
		Swahili	-baya

Attributively, root adjectives follow the noun qualified, taking the proper class prefix: e.g. with root *-ema* 'good', in Swahili: *mtu mw.ema* 'a good person'; *watu wema* 'good people'; *-dogo* 'small': *wa.toto wa.dogo wa.wili* 'two small children' (*-wili* 'two') (cl. 2). Often, a relative construction is preferred, e.g. in Zulu: *umu.ntu o.na.amandhla* 'a strong man' (lit. 'a man who is strong'; relative *-a* + *u* → *o*).

Pronoun

The conjunctive pronouns, subjective and objective, are remarkably homogeneous over most of the Bantu area. Meinhof (1906) gives the Common Bantu forms for the subject verbal prefixes as:

	Singular	*Plural*
1	ni	ti/tî
2	γu	mî/mu
3	γa, γyu	βa

Reflexes of 1st person singular: e.g. Swahili *ni*; Zulu *ngi*; Luganda *n* (with variants); Kongo *n* (with variants); Duala *na*; Rundi *n*/*ndi*; Yao *ni*.

In Meinhof's table of 38 languages (1906: 88), only two – Makua and Sotho – are non-conformist, each with a *ke*/*ki* form for the first person singular.

DEMONSTRATIVE PRONOUNS

Three degrees of relative distance are normally distinguished; *see* **Swahili**.

RELATIVE PRONOUN

Many Bantu languages have no relative construction. Where such a construction exists it may take various forms:

(a) with demonstrative in the *(hu) yo* → *ye*, *(ha)o* form; with tense marker: e.g. *a.li.**ye**.soma* 'he who read'; pl. *wa.li.**o**.soma* (*-li-* is past-tense marker);
(b) subject prefix + stem + relative particle: e.g. *(mtu) a.soma.ye* '(the man) who reads';
(c) relative pronoun: e.g. in Sotho, *mōthō ea rutang* 'a person who teaches'; *bathō ba rutang* 'persons who teach';
(d) analytical construction with *amba-* (in Swahili) + relative particle: e.g. *mtu **ambaye** a.na.kuja* 'the man who is coming' (*-na-* is present-tense marker).

Indirect relative: the concordial object pronoun precedes the verb + suffixed relative form agreeing with object: e.g. *(kitu) ni.**ki**.taka.**cho*** 'the thing I want', where *kitu* is a class 7 noun, *-ki-* is the class 7 subject/object prefix, and *-cho-* is the class 7 relative pronominal form.

Verb

Most primary roots are disyllables. Derived stems are formed by suffixation, e.g. the reciprocal in *-ana*. This marker is found in many Bantu languages:

Swahili	pendana 'to love each other'
Lingala	lingana 'to love each other'
Zulu	bonana 'to see each other'
Rwanda	ku.bonana 'to see each other'
Sotho	ho.bonana 'to see each other'
Shona	onana 'to see each other'
Luganda	yombagana 'to quarrel with each other'

Similarly, with the causative ending in -V*sha* in Swahili (e.g. *weza* 'be able to', *wez**esha*** 'to enable'); this ending appears as *-ithia* in Gikuyu, as *-isa* in Zulu, as -V*sa*-V*dza*/-V*tsa* in Shona, as -V*sa* in Sotho, as *-a*/*-e* in Luganda, as *-isa* in Lingala, and as *-itha* in Herero.

Other derived stems: passive, in -(*i*)*wa*, with variants: cf.

Zulu	bon.wa 'to be seen'
Gikuyu	igu.(w)o 'be heard'
Luganda	lab.wa 'be seen'
Sotho	ho rōngŏa 'be sent' (← *rōma* 'to send': /m/ → [ŋg] before /w/)
Swahili	ku.on.wa 'be seen'

The Lingala passive is in *-ema*/*ama*: e.g. *ekosalema* 'to be done'.

Some Bantu languages have a neutral passive of state in -V*ka*(*la*), e.g. in Zulu *inkanyezi ya.bona.ka.la* 'the star was visible'; cf. *thandwa* 'to be loved', *thand.eka* 'be loving, affectionate'.

Prepositional or benefactive: e.g. -V*la*/*ra* in Zulu, *-ri*/*-er* in Shona, depending on vowel harmony; Zulu *hlala* 'to wait', *hlal.ela* 'to wait for someone'; *hamba* 'to travel'; *hambela* 'to go to visit someone'.

Antonymous: typically -V*l*/*ra*; e.g. Gikuyu, *hinga* 'to shut'; *hingura* 'to open'.

MOODS

Moods are generally marked by suffix. Most Bantu languages have seven moods: infinitive, indicative, imperative, subjunctive, perfect, continuative, relative.

The infinitive is a noun (Swahili *ku-* class, corresponding to *uku-* in Zulu, *hō-* in Sotho). The infinitive (or gerund), the indicative, and the direct imperative usually have *-a* final; the subjunctive has *-e*, the negative *-i*. Cf. Swahili.

ku.soma 'reading, to read'
ni.ta.soma 'I shall read'
soma! 'read'
ni.some (*nini*)*?* 'What shall I read?', 'What am I to read?'
si.somi 'I do not read'

Negative tense formation provides one of the criteria by which Bantu languages may be internally classified. Negation by tone pattern occurs in some, e.g. in Fang, but the use of a negative infix is much more usual and typical. For a characteristic set of negative tenses, *see* **Swahili**. Cf. Zulu:

past affirm.	*nga hamba* 'I travelled'
neg.	*a.ngi.hamba.nga* 'I didn't travel'
pres. affirm.	*ngi hamba* 'I travel'
neg.	*a.ngi.hambi* 'I don't travel'
proximate future affirm.	*ngi.za.uku.hamba* 'I shall travel shortly'
neg.	*a.ngi.zi.uku.hamba* 'I shall not travel shortly'

In Gikuyu the negative particle *-ti-* is used to negate plural verbs in principal clauses, e.g. with stem *gwāta* 'to get, take hold of'; present habitual negative plural: first person *tuti.gwat.aga*; second person *muti.gwat.aga*; third person *mati.gwat.aga*, where *-aga* is the habitual present-tense marker.

The singular forms are negated by modification of the pronominal prefix:

1	affirm	ni.ngwat.aga
	neg.	**ndi**.gwat.aga
2	affirm.	u.gwat.aga
	neg.	**ndu**.gwat.aga

The *-ti-* negative forms of certain tenses are used in an *interrogative* sense only: e.g. immediate past perfect, positive (*ni*)*nd.a.gwat.a* 'I did not get'; *-ti-* neg. *ndi.a.gwat.a?* 'Did I not get?' To negate such a tense, the negative of another past tense (the *-īte* perfect) must be used.

The negative particle may be reduplicated, e.g. Kongo *ke be.tonda ko* 'they do not love'; and may precede or follow the personal prefix, e.g. Nyanja *si.ndi.dziwa*(*i*), Shona *ha.ndi.ziwe* 'I do not know', but Duala *na.si.loma* 'I don't read'.

In general, the negative particle tends to follow the subject pronoun in the subjunctive mood, the relative version, and the participial forms: e.g. Zulu, indicative *a.ngi.hambi* 'I do not go'; subjunctive *ngi.nga.hambi* 'I may not go'. Some negative tenses in Bantu have no affirmative correlatives.

The typical Bantu verbal complex consists of prefix (subject concord marker) – tense marker – object marker – stem – modal/voice marker (with negative particle variously sited): e.g., in affirmative version, Swahili *ni.li.ki.soma* Ø 'I read (past) it' (where *ni-* is the personal subject marker for first person singular; *-li-* is the past-tense marker; *-ki-* is a class 5 object marker, referring presumably to *kitabu* 'book'; *soma* 'to read', Ø is the null marker for the indicative mood). Similarly, *ni.ta.ku.ele.za* 'I shall explain (it) to you' (*-ta-* is the future marker; *-ku-* is the second person singular object marker; *ele.za* is the causative of *elea* 'to be clear'). Cf. Gikuyu *Ni.ma.a.tu.ona?* 'Did they see us?' (*ni-* is the interrogative marker; *ma* = third person plural subject; *-a-* is the immediate past marker; *-tu-* is first person plural object marker; *ona* 'to see'). Examples from other Bantu languages:

Zulu	*u.ya.yi.thanda*	'he loves it'
	ngi.ya.ba.thanda	'I love them'
Shona	*ndi.cha.mu.ona*	'I shall see him/her (*cha* is future marker)
Sotho	*kēa mō ruta*	'I teach him'
	oa n.thata	'she loves me' (the root is ***rata*** 'to love'; *rata* → ***thata*** following /n/)
	ba m.pona	'they see me' (**n.bona* > ***m.pona***)
Lingala	*ako.li.mɔna*	'he sees it' (*-li-* is cl. 5 marker)
	bako.lo.yoka	'they hear us'

TENSE MARKERS

Considerable variation; the Swahili set is: present *-na-*; past *-li-*; future *-ta-*; perfect *-me-*; conditional *-ki-*; present indefinite *-a-*; habitual *-hu-*; narrative: *-ka-*.

Numerals

The numerals 1 to 5 inclusive are Common Bantu stock; so is the word for 10. 6, 7, 8, 9 vary very considerably from language to language; often they are missing and have to be expressed by compounds: 5 + 2, etc.

Word order

SVO is basic.

1 Yoi linaliyaaki ena limatsako, ko Yoi linaliki la
Yakomba, ko Yoi linaliki Yakomba. 2 Ende ayaaki la
Yakomba ena limatsako; 3 toma tohatotu tonunola-
maki l'ende, efan'iyema imoko iniciki inik'ende ata-
nunola. 4 Liiko li-yaaki eneyal'ende, ko liiko lo-yaaki
fololo en'ato: 5 koko fololo eololoma ena liucu, ko
liucu lit'umbak'eho. 6 Bot'omonyi am'enya, onoki
Yakomba otomaka, lina linande liyaaki Yoane. 7 E-
nde ayaki oyalama bosumoli, lacina asumola bosimo
bona fololo, lacina bato bahatu bimedya l'ende. 8 Ende
atayalaki fololo eho, ende ayaki lacina asumola bosimo
bona fololo.

Lingala

I 1 Pakutanga Shoko raivako, Shoko raiva kuna Mwari,
iro Shoko raiva Mwari. 2 Irori pakutanga raiva kuna
Mwari. 3 Zvinhu zvose zvakaitwa naye; kunze kwake
hakuna kuitwa kunyange chinhu chimwe chete chakaitwa.
4 Maari ndimo maiva noupenyu; ihwo upenyu hwaiva chiedza
chavanhu. 5 Zvino chiedza ichi chinovenekera murima, asi
rima harina kuchikunda. 6 Kwakanga kuno munhu wakanga
atumwa naMwari; zita rake wainzi Johane. 7 Iyeyu wakauya
kuzopupura, kuti apupure zvechiedza ichi kuti vose vatende
naye. 8 Iyeyu wakanga asati ari icho chiedza kwete, asi
wakauya kuti azopupura zvechiedza.

Shona

1 Tshimolohong Lentswe le ne le le teng, mme Lentswe
le ne le le ho Modimo, mme Lentswe e ne e le Modimo.
2 Le ne le le ho Modimo tshimolohong. **3** Dintho tsohle
di bile teng ka lona, mme ha ho letho le bileng teng ha
e se ka lona. **4** Bophelo bo ne bo le ka ho lona, mme bophelo e ne e le lesedi la batho; **5** lesedi le kganya lefifing,
mme lefifi ha le a ka la le hlola.

Sotho

BASQUE

INTRODUCTION

Euskara, as the Basques call their language, is an isolate, with no known congeners. Structural analogies with Caucasian languages have been pointed out, and from time to time attempts are made to connect Basque with various other languages and language families. No conclusive evidence has been adduced, however, and it seems safer to regard Basque as a relic of the prehistoric language or languages spoken in the Iberian peninsula before the arrival of Indo-European.

Basque is spoken today by over half a million people in *Euskal Herria*, the Basque country in North-Western Spain (Guipuzcoa, Vizcaya, Navarra), and by about 100,000 in the Pyrénées-Atlantiques region of France.

The language is attested in fragmentary form from c. AD 1000 onwards. The first Basque printed book appeared in 1545. Following a period of proscription, there is now a remarkable upsurge in the use of Basque in literature, in the media and in higher education. Some 5,000 books a year are now published in Basque.

SCRIPT

Roman alphabet; the orthography, which is not yet stable, has been influenced by Spanish.

PHONOLOGY

Consonants

stops: /p, b, t, d, k, g/; Saltarelli (1988) includes two palatal plosives /tj, dj/, which are notated in Basque orthography as *tt*, *dd*.

affricates: /ts, t̥s, tʃ/: notated in the orthography as *tz*, *ts*, *tx*; /ts/ is lamino-alveolar; /t̥s/ is apico-alveolar. The difference is phonemic: cf. *atzo* 'yesterday', *atso* 'old'.

fricatives: /f, z̲, s̲, ʃ/; the lamino-alveolar /z̲/ is notated as *z*, the apico-alveolar /s̲/ as *s*; /ʃ/ is notated as *x*. /z̲/ and /s̲/ have voiceless allophones before voiceless consonants or vowels.

nasals: /m, n, ɲ/;

laterals and flaps: /l, ʎ, r, rr/.

Vowels

i, e, a, o, u

diphthongs:

au, ai, ei, oi, ui

MORPHOLOGY AND SYNTAX

Basque has no grammatical gender, though a gender distinction is made in the second person singular of the synthetic conjugation: cf. *hik daukak* 'you (fam. masc.) have', *hik daukan* 'you (fam. fem.) have'.

ARTICLES

The definite article is affixed: *-a* (sing.), *-ak* (pl.), e.g. *mendi* 'mountain', ***mendia*** 'the mountain', *mendi**ak*** 'the mountains'. As indefinite article, the numeral *bat* 'one', may be used: e.g. *gizon bat* 'a man'. *Bat* may take the case endings: e.g. *mendi bat.**en** igaera* 'the ascent of a mountain'.

Noun

DECLENSION

Nine cases may be distinguished, but several additional endings occur. Basic cases of *gizon* 'man':

nominative	gizon	comitative	gizon**arekin**
ergative	gizon**ak**	inessive	gizon**an**
dative	gizon**ari**	aditive	gizon**ara**
genitive	gizon**ako** (of origin) gizon**aren** (of possession)	ablative	gizon**atik**

The plural endings may be illustrated with *etxe* /etʃe/, 'house':

nominative	etxe**ak**	comitative	etxe**ekin**
ergative	etxe**ek**	inessive	etxe**etan**
dative	etxe**ei**	aditive	etxe**etara**
genitive	etxe**en**/etxe**etako**	ablative	etxe**etatik**

The distinction between the two genitive forms is seen in a phrase such as *Bilbo**ko** arte eder**ren** museoa* 'the museum of (poss.) fine art of (origin) Bilbao' (*eder* 'beautiful, fine'; *-(r)en* = gen. ending). Cf. *Manuren semea* 'Manu's son'; *nere aitarekin* 'with my father'; *etxean* 'in the house'; *menditik* 'from the mountain'.

Adjective

As attribute, adjective follows noun, e.g. *asto txuri bat* 'a white donkey', and takes the definite article: e.g. *etxe**Ø** eder**ra*** 'the beautiful house'; *gure ahuntz polit**ak*** 'our pretty goats' (*polit* 'pretty'). Case endings are also transferred to the adjective: e.g. *ardo berria za(ha)gi berri**etan*** 'new wine in(to) old bottles' (*ardo* 'wine'; *berri* 'new'; *za(ha)gi* 'bottle').

Pronoun

The personal forms with the present tense of *izan* 'to be', are:

	Singular	*Plural*
1	ni naiz	gu gara
2	hi haiz	zu zara; zuek zarete
3	hura da	haiek dira

The resumed characteristic (*n-* in first person singular, *g-* in first person plural, *z-* in second person plural) is found throughout the verbal system (*d-* is characteristic of third person).

The ergative forms are: *nik*, *hik*, *hark*; *guk*, *zuk/zuek*, *haiek*.

The personal pronouns may take other cases: cf. *zuek Nigan, eta Ni zuengan* 'ye in me, I in you' (St John's gospel, 14.20), but see note on verbal system, below.

The possessive forms are: *nire*, *zure*, *bere*; *gure*, *zuen*, *beren*.

DEMONSTRATIVE PRONOUN

Three degrees of relative distance: *hau* 'this' – *hori* 'that' – *hura* 'that (yonder)'; these are postpositional: *gizon hori* /ɔri/ 'that man'.

INTERROGATIVE PRONOUN

nor 'who?, – with ergative, *nork*; *zer* 'what?'

RELATIVE PRONOUN

See **Verb**, below.

Numerals

1–10: *bat*, *bi*, *hiru*, *lau*, *bost*, *sei*, *zazpi*, *zortzi*, *bederatzi*, *hamar*; 11 *hamaika*; 12 *hamabi*, 13 *hamahiru*; 20 *hogei*; 30 *hogei eta hamar*; 40 *berrogei*; 60 *hirurogei*; 70 *hururogei eta hamar*; 80 *laurogei*; 100 *ahun*. That is, vigesimal system. Apart from *bat*, which follows its noun, the numerals precede the noun, which is in the singular: e.g. *bost seme* 'five sons'; *bost semeak* 'the five sons'.

Verb

As in Georgian, a relatively simple nominal system is accompanied by a very complicated verbal system. But, whereas in Georgian the complication lies in the proliferation of permutations and combinations to which the sense-verb is subjected, in Basque the sense-verb itself usually appears in simple stem or participial form, accompanied by an enormously rich network of auxiliary forms which are deictically coded for person and regimen, and which are quasi-bound in the sense that they only acquire full meaning when associated with a sense-verb stem. For example, by itself *diot* indicates action by first person singular directed in some way at third person singular, i.e. it specifies a deictic relationship. Following the stem *eman* 'to give', plus a noun, e.g. *liburu* 'book', *liburu eman* **diot**, *diot* generates the meaning '**I** give **him** a book'. If the deixis code is changed by substituting *dizut* for *diot*, the meaning becomes 'I give **you** a book'. A quantitative change can also be introduced by changing *dizut* to *dizkizut*: this indicates that '**I** gave **you** more than one object – book**s**'.

With this sort of deictic relational network at its disposal, Basque makes very sparing use of personal pronouns. Nouns continue to be marked: e.g. *Gizonari liburua eman diot* 'I give the book **to the** man.'

All Basque verbs can be conjugated thus analytically or periphrastically, but half a dozen crucially important auxiliaries and a few other verbs – e.g. *joan* 'to go', *etorri* 'to come', *eduki* 'to have', *jakin* 'to know', *esan* 'to say', *ikusi* 'to see' – retain a synthetic form of conjugation, which seems to have been formerly more widespread. As an example of a synthetic conjugation, here are the present and past tenses of *etorri* 'to come':

	Present		*Past*	
	Singular	*Plural*	*Singular*	*Plural*
1	ni nator	gu gatoz	ni nentorren	gu gentozen
2	hi hator	zu zatoz	hi hentorren	zu zentozen
3	hura dator	haiek datoz	hura zetorren	haiek zetozen

THE ANALYTICAL CONJUGATION

The most important auxiliaries are (present and past forms):

da – zen: used to conjugate intransitive verbs:
du – zuen: used to conjugate transitive verbs;
zaio – zitzaion: with indirect object; subject in possessive case;
dio – zion: polypersonal (direct and indirect objects).

Altogether, these four auxiliaries produce about a thousand forms, which are:

1. Coded for person and deixis: e.g. *diot – dizut*, as shown above.
2. Coded for number:

   (a) of subject: *du – dizut*, as shown above.
   (b) of object: *diot* indicates singular object; *dizkiot* indicates plural object.

3. Tense: from *du*, *nauzu* indicates second person/first person singular in present; *ninduzun* in past.
4. Mood: e.g. *niezaioke* indicates potential action of first person singular on third person singular, involving singular object; *niezazkioke* indicates the same deixis but involving plurality of object; *zeniezazkigukeen* indicates potential action in past by second person plural on first person plural involving a plurality of objects.

SOME NOTES ON THE MAIN AUXILIARIES

Izan 'to be'; the present tense is given above (*see* **Pronoun**); the past tense is *ni nintzen*, *hi hintzen*, *hura zen*; *gu ginen*, *zu zinen/zuek zineten*, *haiek ziren*. The general negating particle is *ez*: e.g. *ni euskalduna naiz* 'I am a Basque'; *ni ez naiz euskalduna* 'I am not ...' In the negative, *ez* plus auxiliary precede the sense-verb: e.g. *ni etorri naiz* 'I have come', *ni ez naiz etorri* 'I haven't ...'

Future: participle in *-ko* + auxiliary: e.g. *ni etorri.ko naiz* 'I'll come'.

Du – zuen: this auxiliary is used in the conjugation of transitive verbs; the nominal/pronominal subject is in the ergative with *-k*: e.g. with *ikusi* 'see': (*zu**k***) *ikusi nauzu* 'you have seen me'; (*gu**k***) *ikusi zaitugu* 'we have seen you', where *nauzu* encodes second person action on first person and *zaitugu* encodes first person plural action on second person. In *ekarri**ko** zituen* 'he was going to bring them', *zituen* encodes third person singular action on third person plural. A further example: *Maite **zintudan**, baina zu**k** ez **ninduzun** maite* 'I loved you, but you did not love me'.

Zaio – zitzaion: this auxiliary is used with stative verbs, intransitive verbs with ethic dative, and verbs whose subject is in possessive case, and is usually translated in English as transitive verb + direct object: e.g. (*niri*) *jausi zait* 'to-me it has fallen' = 'I've dropped it'; (*niri*) *jausi zaizkit* 'to-me they have fallen' = 'I've dropped them'; *gozo zaio* 'pleasant to him' = 'he likes it'; *haurrak joan zaizkio* 'the children have gone off on-him' = 'his children have left him' (where *zaizkio* indicates indirect action on third person singular by third person plural); *liburua galdu zait* 'the book has gone lost on me' = 'I've lost my book'.

Altogether, the *zaio – zitzaion* paradigm, including present, past, conditional, resultative, potential, subjunctive, and imperative forms for all persons and both numbers, has a total of about 280 forms, not all of them in everyday use.

Dio – zion: this auxiliary is used in polypersonal verbs with direct and indirect objects, of the type 'I gave it to him', *eman **nion***; cf. *eman dizkiot* 'I give him things'; *eman nizkion* 'I gave him things'; *gutun bat idatzi zion* 'he wrote him a letter'.

The *dio – zion* paradigm has a total of about 700 forms.

RELATIVE FORMS

-(e)n is added to relevant auxiliary form: *da* → *den*; *gizon**ari** eman dioda**n** ogia* 'the man to whom I gave the bread' (*ogi*); *ogia eman dida**n** gizon**a*** 'the man who gave me the bread'.

As mentioned above, in connection with *zaio – zitzaion*, the deictic grid has full conditional, subjunctive, potential, resultative, and imperative versions. Cf. *ekar **ziezagun*** 'so that he might bring us (a singular object)'; *ekar **ziezazkigun*** 'so that he might bring us (a plurality)'.

Ba- is a characteristic prefix for auxiliaries in the conditional mood: e.g. *erosi nai **ba.dituzu*** 'if you want (*nai*) to buy (*erosi*) ...'

Postpositions

These may follow plain stem or case ending: e.g. *bostak aldean* 'about 5 o'clock'; *bihar arte* 'until tomorrow'. Following genitive: *euskaldun**en** artean* 'among the Basques'; *gerla zibilar**en** ondo.**tik*** 'since the (time of) the Civil War'; *mahai(a.**ren**) azpian* 'on the table'.

Word order

Free.

Asieran Itza ba-zan,
ta Itza Yainkoagan zan,
ta Itza Yainko zan.
2 Asieran Bera Yainkoagan zan.
3 Dana Berak egiña da,
ta Bera gabe ez da egin
egindako ezer ere.
4 Beragan bizitza zan,
ta bizitza gizargia zan;
5 ta argia iluntan ageri da,
ta ilunak ez zun aŕtu.
6 Gizon bat azaldu zan
Yainkoak bidalia;
aren izena Yon.
7 Aitoŕtzat au etoŕi zan,
argiaren aitoŕtzat,
aren bidez guziek siñesteko.
8 Ez zan ori argia,
argiaz aitoŕ egitekoa baño.

BELORUSSIAN

INTRODUCTION

Belorussian is a member of the East Slavonic group of the Slavonic branch of Indo-European. Often regarded in the past as a dialect of Russian, it has now achieved official status as the language of the Belorussian Republic (capital Minsk). It derives from a complex of West Russian dialects which were spoken in the large area between the Pripet and the western Dvina, and which, from the thirteenth century onwards, coalesced towards a common norm. This process was hastened by the fact that an ecclesiastical form of West Russian was the official language of the Grand Duchy of Lithuania (thirteenth to sixteenth centuries). By the same token, Polish influence on Belorussian is due to Polish ascendancy within the Grand Duchy (Lithuanian itself was not used as a written language till the sixteenth/seventeenth centuries). Under the Russian tsars, Belorussian was proscribed. Since 1917, the language has been codified and standardized, and is now the vehicle for a considerable literature.

Belorussian means 'White Russian'. Exactly what 'white' means here is not clear. The authors (Birillo, Bulaxov, Sudnik) of the article on Belorussian in JaNSSSR, Vol. 1, 1966, interpret 'white' as meaning 'free' in contrast to the 'black' territories which were the first to succumb to the Grand Duchy in the thirteenth century.

Today, Belorussian is spoken in Belorussia and in the adjoining republics by about 9 million people. All are bilingual in Belorussian with Russian or Ukrainian.

SCRIPT

Cyrillic. The alphabet, fixed in 1933, is identical to the Russian alphabet, minus и, and plus the letters I /i/ and ў /w/. The digraphs *дж* and *dz* occur.

PHONOLOGY

Consonants

stops: p, b, t, d, k, (g)
affricates: ts, dz, tʃ, dʒ
fricatives: f, v, s, z, ʃ, ʒ, x, γ, h
nasals: m, n
lateral and flap: ł, r
semi-vowels: j, w

Followed by soft vowels, the following consonants are soft, i.e. palatalized: /p, b, f, v, m, s, z, n, l, k, g (=[h]), x, γ/. /t/ and /d/ are hard only: their soft correlatives are the affricates /ts′/ and /dz′/. These two phonemes are specifically notated in the script as ц and дз. See *ciekańnie* and *dziekańnie*, below. Note, however, that the same two letters are used to notate etymologically original /ts/, /dz/, which are hard consonants as in *tsana* 'price'.

Vowels

hard: ɪ, e, a, o, u
soft: i, ye, ya, yo, yu

/ɪ/ is notated as ы; /i/ as *i*; the remaining four soft vowels are notated as in Russian. Both the apostrophe and the soft sign ь are used in Belorussian under specific constraints to indicate palatalization. The Cyrillic soft sign ь is used to mark /l, n, z, s, ts, dz/ as soft, e.g. in word-final position: e.g. *pisac′* 'to write' (*-i-*, here, being invariably soft, does not require marking). In this entry, ɪ = hard, /ɪ/; i = soft, /i/.

Some characteristics of the Belorussian phonological system:

1. *ciekańnie*: Russ. *t′* = Bel. *c′*: e.g. t′en′ 'shadow' = *c′en′*;
2. *dziekańnie*: Russ. *d′* = Bel. *dz′*: e.g. *d′en* 'day' *dz′en′*;
3. initial *o* = /vo/, initial *u* = /vu/: e.g. *voka* 'eye', *vuxa* 'ear';
4. presence of voiced velar fricative: *gorad* 'town', /γorat/.
5. the shift of unstressed /o, ε/ to /a/ is regular in Russian, where, however, it is not notated in the orthography. In Belorussian it is notated, which complicates the inflectional system. Thus, *zólata* 'gold' – *zalatí* 'golden'.

Stress

On any syllable and movable.

MORPHOLOGY AND SYNTAX

Noun

Three genders: masculine, feminine, and neuter. Three declensions are distinguished:

1. *a*-stems: mostly feminine, e.g. *rabota* 'work', pl. *rabotɪ*;
2. *o*-stems: masculine and neuter, e.g. *stol* 'table', pl. *stalɪ*;
3. *i*-stems: feminine, *miš* 'mouse', pl. *mɪšɪ*.

A few neuter nouns can be declined either in a specific form or as (2) above: e.g. *imya* 'name' may have plural *imyonɪ* or *imi*.

Specimen declension of first declension feminine noun: *galava* 'head':

	Singular	*Plural*
nom.	galava	galovɪ
acc.	galavu	galovɪ
gen.	galavɪ	galow
dat.	galavye	galovam
instr.	galavoy	galovami
prep.	galavye	galovax

The nominal paradigms have a great many variants depending on phonetic environment: e.g. consonantal alternation in the prepositional case: *ruka* 'hand' – prep. *ruce*; *narod* 'people' – *narodze*; *malako* 'milk' – *malace*.

As in Russian, an animate/inanimate distinction is observed in the formation of the second declension masculine singular and the plural of all nouns: e.g. *brat* 'brother' – *brata* – *bratow* (gen. sing./pl.). For all nouns denoting inanimates, the accusative = the nominative.

Adjective

In general, as in Russian.

Pronoun

The first and second person series behave much as in Russian, with spelling differences: e.g. from *tɪ*, acc./gen. *cyabye*, but dative: *tabye*. The third person series is unique in Slavonic in that the palatalized onset of the oblique cases is also present in the nominative: *yon* – fem. *yana* – nt. *yano*; plural for all three genders: *yanɪ*.

DEMONSTRATIVE PRONOUN/ADJECTIVE
getɪ 'this'; *toy* 'that'.

INTERROGATIVE PRONOUN
xto 'who?'; *što* 'what?'

RELATIVE PRONOUN
As interrogative.

Numerals

Formally as in Russian, apart from spelling differences. As in Ukrainian, however, and in opposition to Russian, 2, 3, 4 are followed by nominative/accusative plural: e.g. *dva stalɪ* 'two tables'; *čatɪrɪ bratɪ* 'four brothers'.

Verb

The aspect/mood/tense system of Russian and Ukrainian is shared by Belorussian. Most Belorussian verbs are paired for aspect. The infinitive is in *-c'*, *-c* (*-cɪ* after velar).

ASPECT

Many perfective forms are made from imperative by prefixation.

Imperfective	*Perfective*
isci 'to go'	pa.isci
pisac′ 'to write'	na.pisac′
magčı 'to be able'	z.magčı

The reverse process, imperfective form from perfective, may use, e.g. *-va-*: *vıpisac′* 'to write out'; imperfective: *vıpisvac′* 'to be writing out'.

VERBS OF MOTION

As in Russian and Ukrainian, the imperfective aspect is equipped to distinguish between a generalized concept and a particular application thereof: the latter can then be made perfective: e.g. *yezdzic′* 'to travel' (in general) – *yexac′* 'to make a specific journey': perf. *pa.yexac′*.

TENSES

There are two conjugations:

(a) verbs in -(*v*)*ac′*, *-yec′*, *-nuc′*, etc.;
(b) verbs in *-ic′*, *-ıc′*, *-yec′*, etc.

Specimen present tense: conjugation (a), consonant stem: *nasıc′* 'to carry' (stress on final syllable throughout):

Singular	*Plural*
nyasu	nyasyom
nyasyeš	nyesya**cyé**
nyasye	nyasuc′

It is noteworthy that the *-e-* of the second person singular ending does not change to *-o-* under stress.

Past tense: as in Russian and Ukrainian; in masculine form, *-l* → *-w*: e.g. *Čıtaw* 'I (masc.) read'.

Future:

(a) perfective: formally, the present endings of the imperfective: e.g. *skažu* 'I shall say';
(b) imperfective: future tense of *bıt′* + imperfective infinitive: e.g. *ya budu čıtac′* 'I shall read/be reading'.

SUBJUNCTIVE MOOD

Past tense + invariable particle ьı.

IMPERATIVE

There are forms for second person singular and first and second persons plural: e.g. from *kupic′* 'to buy': *kupi*; *kupyem*, *kupicye*.

PARTICIPLES

Only the past passive participle is regularly used in spoken Belorussian: e.g. *napisanı* 'written'; *kuplyenı* 'bought'; *uzyatı* 'taken'.

Prepositions

Prepositions govern the oblique cases. Many prepositions can take more than one case, with corresponding changes in meaning. Usually, however, there is a preferred case, e.g. *dlya* 'for' with the genitive, *k/ka* 'to' with the dative, *ab* 'concerning' with the prepositional.

Word order

As in Russian.

1 На пачатку было Слова, і Слова было з Богам, і Слова было
Бог. 2 Яно было на пачатку з Богам. 3 Усе перазь Яго сталася, і безь
Яго нічога ня было стаўшыся, што
сталася. 4 У Ім было жыцьцё, і жыцьцё было сьвятлінёю людзёў. 5 І
сьвятліня сьвеце ў цямноце, і цям-
нота яе не агарнула.

6 Быў чалавек пасланы ад Бога,
імя ягонае Яан. 7 Ён прышоў дзеля
сьветчаньня, каб сьветчыць празь
Сьвятліню, каб усі ўверылі перазь
яго. 8 Ён ня быў Сьвятліня, але каб
сьветчыць празь Сьвятліню.

BENGALI (*bāṅlā*)

INTRODUCTION

This Eastern New Indo-Aryan language is the official language of Bangladesh, where it is spoken by about 110 million people, and the official regional language for another 55 million people in the Indian state of West Bengal. There are also sizable Bengali-speaking communities in Orissa, Assam, Bihar, Tripura, and Meghalaya. Along with its close congeners, Oriya and Assamese, Bengali crystallized from the Magadhi Apabhraṁśa, roughly between AD 1000 and 1200. Texts dating from this period (e.g. the esoteric Buddhist–Tantric hymns known as *Caryāpada*) show general Magadhan areal features, but are usually described as being in Old Bengali. Middle Bengali was the vehicle for a very rich literature on traditional Indian themes, which is remarkable in view of the fact that by then Bengal was Moslem; indeed, Bengal remained part of the Mughal Empire until the eighteenth century. The British take-over in the nineteenth century added a third strand to an already composite cultural scene. Bengal now became the focal point of European cultural influence in India, and literary genres, alien to the sub-continent, began to appear: e.g. the novel, first in imitation of Scott, but soon developing to culminate in the socio-political realist novel of criticism and protest. The list of outstanding names includes Sáratcandra Caṭṭopādhyāy and one figure of world stature – Rabīndranāth Ṭhākur. A key role in the formation and education of a secularized and anti-traditionalist reading public was played by critical, often pro-Marxist periodicals such as *Kallol* (1923 onwards). Mention should also be made of the rich Bengali folk-literature, the songs of the Bāuls, or wandering minstrels, and the yātrās, nocturnal celebrations of Hindu gods and goddesses.

The numerous dialects are classified by most authorities on a broad east/west basis. Some are highly divergent, e.g. the Chittagong dialect. Until the twentieth century Bengali was written in a somewhat artificial, heavily Sanskritized book-language known as *sādhu-bhāṣā*. Modern writing is almost entirely in *calit-bhāṣā*, a demotic based on the Calcutta colloquial. Even here, however, the distinction between book-language and spoken language persists; that is, even modern calit-bhāṣā is, in a sense, an artificial medium. Wherever philosophical or scientific terminology is required, of course, the limitless Sanskrit reservoir is always available. In addition, it should not be forgotten that most Bengalis are Moslems, and the language now contains several thousand Arabo-Persian words.

SCRIPT

Bengali shares with Assamese a specific derivative of the Devanagari character.

PHONOLOGY

Consonants

stops: p, b, t, d, ṭ, ḍ, k, g
aspirated: ph, (bh > β), th, dh, ṭh, ḍh, kh, gh
affricate: unaspirated: tʃ, dʒ
aspirated: tʃh, dʒh
fricatives: ʃ, s, h
nasals: m, n, ŋ
laterals and flaps: l, r, ṛ, ṛh

In Bengali, as typically in the Magadhan daughter languages, the three sibilants of Sanskrit (dental, retroflex, and palatal) have coalesced to give /ʃ/ > /s/. Consonant clusters are simplified in pronunciation: e.g. *laksya* is realized as /lɔkk^{h}o/, *anekkṣan* as /ɔnekk^{h}on/, *pakši* as /pokkhi/.

Vowels

i, e, æ, a, ɔ, o, u

All occur nasalized. Difference in length is not phonemic. The inherent vowel in the base consonantal form is /ɔ/, corresponding to Sanskrit/Hindi /a/. In the section on **Morphology and Syntax** below, *a* = /aː/, *ă* = /ɔ/.

'Vowel raising', a form of vocalic assimilation, is a characteristic feature of Bengali phonology. It can be broadly summarized as follows:

/ɔ, e, o/ → [o, i, u] if the following syllable contains /i/ or /u/
/i, u, e/ → [e, o, æ] if the following syllable contains /ɔ, a, e/ or /o/
/a/ → [e] if the preceding syllable contains /i/
/a/ → [o] if the preceding syllable contains /u/

For example, *cali* 'I go', is pronounced [coli]: /ɔ/ raised to [o] before /i/; from *šona* 'to hear': *šuni* 'I hear': /o/ → [u] before /i/; *iccha* 'wish' → *icche* : /a/ → [e], as preceding syllable contains /i/. The /ɔ/ → [o] and /e/ → [æ] shifts affect pronunciation only; the others are notated in the script.

Stress

On first syllable in citation form, on headword of phrase in speech.

MORPHOLOGY AND SYNTAX

Noun

Bengali has lost the grammatical gender system of Indo-Aryan, and has replaced it with a natural taxonomy of animate versus non-animate categories. Animates make a plural form in -(*e*)*ra*. For non-animates, there is a variety of affixes, e.g. *-guli/-a/-o*, *-šăkăl*, *-šăb*, *-šămăšto*, etc. Some vestiges remain of the typical Indo-Aryan association of certain endings with gender, e.g. the *-a/-i* opposition: *buṛa* 'old man', *buṛi* 'old woman'.

CASE

Only the genitive marker -(*e*)*r* is obligatory. There follow specimen declensions of animate *manuṣ* 'man', and non-animate *nădi* 'river':

	Singular	*Plural*	*Singular*	*Plural*
nom.	manuṣ /maːnus/	manuṣera	nădi	nădiguli
gen.	manuṣer	manuṣder (ke)	nădir	nădigulir
dat.	manuṣke	manuṣder	nădike	nădigulike
acc.	manuṣke	manuṣder	nădi	nădiguli
loc.	manuṣe	—	nădite	—

These endings are typical; for all cases except the genitive, however, there is a choice of ending. There is a tendency for the agglutinative plural suffixes *-šăb*, *-šăkăl*, etc. to be used with animates as well.

The enclitics *-ṭa/ṭi* may act as defining articles: e.g. *Năgărṭa khub băṛo* 'The town is very big.'

Adjective

As attribute the adjective is indeclinable and precedes the noun. A periphrastic comparative is made by means of *čeye* (the perfective participle of *čaoya* /tʃawa/ 'to look at') + genitive case: e.g. *Še amar čeye băṛo* 'He is older than I am.'

Pronoun

PERSONAL INDEPENDENT

In contrast to the dual base pattern found in the pronominal system of Western New Indo-Aryan, Bẹngali uses single bases to which endings are added agglutinatively: sing. 1 *ami*; 2 *tumi* (familiar), *apni* (polite); 3 *še* (familiar), *tini* (polite). The plural forms are: *amra*, *tomra*, *apnara*, *tãhara/tara*. These are declined as nouns: *ami*, *amar*, *amake*, etc.: e.g. *Tini amader kačhe prătidin ašten* 'He came to us every day' (the postposition *kačhe* 'to, at', takes genitive case).

DEMONSTRATIVE PRONOUN

Three degrees of removal are recognized: *e*, *iha*, *ini* 'this' (proximate); *o*, *uha*, *uni*, 'that' (distal); *še*, *taha*, *ta* 'that' (not visible but known).

INTERROGATIVE PRONOUN
ke 'who?'; *ki* 'what?'

RELATIVE PRONOUN
ǰe/ǰini/ǰa + correlative: e.g. *ǰe ... še*; *ǰini ... tini*

> **ǰe** lokṭa kal ekhane čhilo, **še** abar esečhe
> 'The man who was here yesterday has come again'
>
> Tumi **ǰe**khane thakbe, ami.o **še**khane thakba
> 'Where you will be, there shall I be also'

Numerals

1–10: *æk*, *dui*, *tin*, *čar*, *pãč*, *čhɔĕ*, *šat*, *aṭ*, *nɔĕ*, *dɔš*. 11–19: the forms are based on the units, ending in *-o*: e.g. *ægaro*, *baro*, *tæro*, *čoddo*, *pɔnero*. 20 *biš*; 30 *triš*; 40 *čolliš*; from 20 to 99 the forms are unpredictable, though decade + 9 is always related to the following decade: e.g. 30 *triš*; 39 *unɔčolliš*; 40 *čolliš*; 49 *unɔpɔ̃čaš*; 50 *pɔ̃nčaš*. 100 /šɔ̃to/ (the word is written as *šɔtɔ*: the second *ɔ* is raised to /o/).

Verb

Roots are mono- or disyllabic. Many derived bases are made from nouns by adding *-a*: e.g. *ghum* 'sleep': *ghumana* 'to sleep'. The rules for vowel harmony (see above) apply throughout the verbal system: e.g.

> root *čăla* 'to go': /tʃɔlo/ 'you go', /tʃ**o**li/ 'I go';
> root *dekha* 'to see'; /d**æ**kho/ 'you see', /d**e**khi/ 'I see';
> root *lekha* 'to write': /l**e**kho/ 'you write', /l**i**khi/ 'I write'.

On the basis of such alternations, Chatterji (cited in Zograph 1982) has divided Bengali verbs into seven classes.

Aspect/tense markers are added to the stem before the personal inflections: e.g. *-čh-* for imperfective/continuative, *-b-* for future, *-l-* for past.

TENSE SYSTEM
Number is not marked. The first person has one form for both singular and plural: e.g. *jaṇi* 'I know/we know'. The second person has three forms depending on status of addressee: familiar, everyday polite, and respectful; typical endings are *-i*, *-e*, *-en/-iš*, *-o*, *-en*. The third person has an ordinary form in *-e/-o* and a respectful in *en*. Thus, the form *janen*, for example, may mean 'you know' (sing./pl.), 'he/she knows' or 'they know'. The correct meaning can be fixed by the personal pronoun.

As an example of tense formation, here are the third person ordinary forms of the indicative mood of the root *kɔra* 'to do' (čalit-bhaṣa forms as pronounced):

simple present	kɔre 'does'
imperfective present	korčhe 'is doing'
perfective present	korečhe 'has done'

simple past	korlo 'did'
imperfective past	korčhilo 'was doing'
perfective past	korečhilo 'had done'
habitual past	korto 'would do'
future	korbe 'will do'
imperative mood	koruk 'let him/her (etc.) do'

NON-FINITE FORMS

There are two verbal nouns: present *-a*/*-wa*/*-na* etc., and future in -(*i*)*ba*. Participles: imperfective in -(*i*)*te*, perfective in *-iya*/*-e* and conditional in -(*i*)*le*: e.g. *Ami kičhu kărte pari na* 'I can't do anything'; *Še kătha šune apni ki bălečhilen*? 'What did you say when you heard that?'

CAUSATIVE

The marker is *-a-* between stem and ending: e.g.

jana 'to know': *janana* 'to inform' (/janano/)
dekha 'to see': *dekhana* 'to show' (/dekhano/)

PASSIVE

An impersonal construction involving nominalization is preferred: e.g. the use of the verbal noun in *-a*, etc. plus an auxiliary, /jawa/ 'to go', or /hɔwa/ 'to be'. The auxiliary does not agree with the logical subject: e.g. *amake pawa gælo* 'to-me finding it-went' = 'I was found'; *E rasta diye jawa jay na* 'this street going-along goes not' = 'One cannot go along this street.'

NEGATIVE

The particle is *na*, with allophones [ne,ni]. It is never stressed. Example: *Tar sambandhe kičhui jani ne* 'I know nothing about it.'

Postpositions

Postpositions follow either the nominative or the genitive: e.g. *ṭebiler upăr* 'on the table'; *ghărer bhităre* 'inside the house'.

The perfective participles of certain verbs, e.g. /dewa/ 'to give', /newa/ 'to take', act as postpositions: e.g. from /tʃawa/ 'to look at', /tʃeye/ has come to mean 'than' (*see* **Adjective**, above). Similarly, /theke/ from /thaka/ 'to stay', means 'from'; /diye/ from /dewa/ means 'through': *Janala diye dekhi* 'I look through the window.'

Word order

SOV is normal.

১ আদিতে বাক্য ছিলেন, এবং বাক্য ঈশ্বরের
কাছে ছিলেন, এবং বাক্য ঈশ্বর ছিলেন।
২,৩ তিনি আদিতে ঈশ্বরের কাছে ছিলেন। সকলই
তাঁহার দ্বারা হইয়াছিল, যাহা হইয়াছে, তাহার কিছুই
৪ তাঁহা ব্যতিরেকে হয় নাই। তাঁহার মধ্যে জীবন ছিল,
৫ এবং সেই জীবন মনুষ্যগণের জ্যোতি ছিল। আর সেই
জ্যোতি অন্ধকার মধ্যে দীপ্তি দিতেছে, আর অন্ধকার
তাহা গ্রহণ * করিল না।
৬ এক জন মনুষ্য উপস্থিত হইলেন, তিনি ঈশ্বর হইতে
৭ প্রেরিত হইয়াছিলেন, তাঁহার নাম যোহন। তিনি
সাক্ষ্যের জন্য আসিয়াছিলেন, যেন সেই জ্যোতির
বিষয়ে সাক্ষ্য দেন, যেন সকলে তাঁহার দ্বারা বিশ্বাস
৮ করে। তিনি সেই জ্যোতি ছিলেন না, কিন্তু আসিলেন,
৯ যেন সেই জ্যোতির বিষয়ে সাক্ষ্য দেন

BERBER

INTRODUCTION

Berber is a member of the Afro-Asiatic (Semito-Hamitic) family. For the Greeks and Romans who colonized North Africa, the local inhabitants were βάϱβαϱοι, *barbari*, who spoke a 'barbarous' tongue. The designation found its way into Arabic, and into English as Berber. An ethnonym for the mainstream of Berber tribes is *amažiγen*; the language is *tamažiγt*.

Berber seems to have been originally spoken in a strip of North African territory stretching from the Atlantic coast to the borders of Egypt. Over the last thousand years, Berber-speaking populations have spread beyond this original habitat, and today two or three hundred Berber dialects are spoken in about a dozen North African countries: Egypt, Libya, Tunisia, Algeria, Morocco, Mauretania, Mali, Burkina Faso, Niger, Chad. The total number of Berber speakers is put at c. 12 million. The principal dialects are: Shluh, Tamazight, and Riff in Morocco; Kabyle and Shawia in Algeria; Tamahaq (Tamashek) or Tuareg in several Saharan countries. Shluh is also known as *tašẹlḥait*, Shawia as *tašawit*, and Kabyle as *taqbaylit*.

SCRIPT

The oldest inscriptions in a Berber language – two diglot inscriptions found at Dugga in Tunisia – are written in Tifinag, which is still in use among the Tamahaq. This script is consonantal, written from right to left, with no way of indicating vowels. Ancient Berber inscriptions found in Libya, on the other hand, are in Roman script and are vocalized.

For administrative purposes, both Arabic and Roman scripts have been and still are used to notate Berber.

PHONOLOGY

A basic inventory includes the following phonemes:

Consonants

stops: b, d, ḍ, t, k, g
affricates: (in Kabyle and elsewhere: ts, dz, tʃ, dʒ)
fricatives: f, s, z, ẓ, ʃ, ʒ, γ
nasals: m, n
lateral and flap: l, r
semi-vowels: j, w

/ṭ, ḍ/ emphatics appear in Kabyle and other northern dialects. Several Arabic sounds – /ṣ, q, ʕ (= ain), ħ, ḫ/ – have been widely borrowed.

Consonants are long or short; long consonants are tense and held: C̄, not C.C. The contrast between C and C̄ is fundamental in Berber phonology.

Vowels

The basic contrast is between full grade /i, a, u/ and reduced or null grade /ə/ or Ø. Central Atlas Tamazight has the following inventory:

front: i, ɪ, e
central: ɛ, a, ə
back: o, ʊ, u

All with allophones.

MORPHOLOGY AND SYNTAX

Most roots have two or three radicals; mono- and quadriliterals also occur. Common Afro-Asiatic features in Berber are: *t* as feminine marker, *k* as second person marker; the prefix/suffix conjugational paradigm; broken plural.

Nouns

There are two genders in Berber, masculine and feminine. All feminine nouns have *t-* initial, and feminine nouns with a final root consonant also take *-t* following this consonant: e.g. *agmar* 'horse', *tagmart* 'mare'; *afunas* 'bull', *tafunast* 'cow'; in Tamahaq *əkahi* 'cock', *təkahit* 'hen'. The feminine *t* ... *t* circumfix is also used for certain natural phenomena: e.g. *tafukt* 'sun'; *takat* 'fire' (both of these are also feminine in Arabic).

NUMBER
(a) broken plural; (b) sound plural by affix:

(a) For example, (*a*)*drar* 'mountain', pl. *durar* or (*i*)*drarən*. In the broken plural, *-a-* is typical vocalization between R_2 and R_3 (R = radical): cf. *tamazirt* 'garden', pl. *timazar*. In Tamahaq *atri* 'star', pl. *itran*; *amagur* 'old camel', pl. *imugar*.
(b) Suffixation: the characteristic ending is *-wən* (masc.), (*w*)*in* (fem.): e.g. *amyar* 'man', p.. *imyarən*; *tamyart* 'woman', pl. *timyarin*.

DECLENSION
Nouns are free or annexed; free nouns have vocalic initial (masc.) or *t-* + vowel (fem.). In the annexed state, expressing the genitival/relational link, masculine nouns take *w-*, feminine nouns do not change (i.e. = free state).

The genitival/relational construct is also expressed by the *-n-*/*-l-* link realized as /ən/ /nə/ /əl/ /lə/: e.g. Tamahaq *amɣar* ***n*** *aɣerem* 'the sheikh of the town'; *aiis wareɣ* ***n*** *abba* 'this horse of my father'; Central Atlas Tamazight *tamazirt* ***l*** *lmɣrib* 'the country of Morocco'; *ssuq **l** l.ḥdd* 'Sunday market'; Kabyle *aḇriḏ **n** ssuq* 'the road to market'.

Adjective

No specific form; a participial construction is used: e.g. Tamahaq *yulayən* 'being good' (masc.); *tulayət* (fem.); *illa γur.i aiis yulayən* 'I have a good horse' (*illa* 'there is'; *γur.i* 'to me'). Tamazight: *lāil amẓẓian* 'small boy', pl. *luašum imẓẓian*; *tarbat tamẓẓiant* 'small girl', pl. *tirbatin timẓẓiamin*.

Pronoun

Free and affixed forms. The free forms are used only for emphasis; the set is remarkable for having feminine forms for all persons and both numbers, with the sole exception of the first person singular (in Kabyle).

The Kabyle forms for emphatic free and post-prepositional affix are:

		Singular		*Plural*	
		Free	*Affix*	*Free*	*Affix*
1	masc.	nəkk	-i	nukni	-nəγ
	fem.	–	–	nukə nti	-ntəγ
2	masc.	kəčč	-k	kunwi	-wən
	fem.	kəm	-m	kunə mti	-nkwətt
3	masc.	nətta	-s	nuṯni	-nsən
	fem.	nəttaṯ	-s	nuṯə nti	-nsətt

For example, in Tamahaq: *akal n.nəγ* 'our country'; *akal n wən* 'your (masc. pl.) country'.

There are also pronominal affix series for kinship terms and for direct and indirect object; these sets do not differ greatly from the one tabulated above. Cf. in Tamahaq:

əkfiγ **ak** 'I gave you (masc.)'
ikfa ha**sen** 'he gave them (masc.)'
ənniγ **am** 'I told you (fem.)'
inna ha**s** 'he said to him/her'

With prepositions: Tamahaq *γur.**i*** 'at my home'; *dat **əm*** 'before you (fem.)'; *gar **awən*** 'among/between you (masc. pl.)'

DEMONSTRATIVE PRONOUN

E.g. in Tamahaq and Kabyle: *wa* (masc.), pl. *wi*; *ta* (fem.), pl. *ti*.

INTERROGATIVE PRONOUN

ma 'who? what?'.

RELATIVE PRONOUN

The *wa* series can be used + resumptive pronoun, e.g. in Tamahaq: *ales **wa as** əkfiγ tiraut* 'the man who to-him I gave the letter', (i.e. . . . to whom . . .); *arabən **wi***

***asən** əkfiɣ əhari'n azrəf* 'the Arabs to whom I gave money'.

Numerals

The older (indigenous) numerical system is best preserved in Tamahaq and in the Tašelhayt of the High Atlas. Masculine and feminine forms are distinguished. The masculine forms, 1–10: *ya*(*n*), *sin*, *kṛaḍ*, *ḳḳuẓ*, *səmmus*, *sḍis*, *sa*, *tam*, *tẓa*, *mra*; the feminine forms add *-t* to these (with some variants, e.g. the feminine of *sin* is *snat*).

This indigenous series has been largely replaced by the Arabic numerals from 3 onwards.

Verb

Three bases are distinguishable: (1) C_1C_2; (2) $C_1C_2C_2$ + *a*; (3) C_1C_2 + *i/a*; i.e. base 1 is unmarked for vocalization, bases 2 and 3 are marked. It is customary to designate these bases, (1) aorist–imperative, (2) strengthened aorist, (3) preterite.

Exactly how these bases are related to tense and mood – if, indeed, the categories of tense and mood can be usefully applied to the Berber verb – is a controversial question. Different researchers have distinguished an aorist and a preterite, a past tense from a present/future, a present/past from a future; some make an aspectual distinction between perfective and imperfective. Hanoteau in his grammar of Tamahaq (1896) uses the term 'aorist' for his '*mode unique*', which can refer equally to present, past, or future: this 'aorist' can be modulated by vocalization, e.g. by *-a-* between the second and third radicals: cf. *elkemeɣ* 'I follow, have followed', *əlkemaɣ* 'I am now following'.

The general paradigm of personal markers, prefixal and suffixal, is:

		Singular	*Plural*
1		Ø R -əɣ	nə- R Ø
2		tə- R -t/-d	tə- R -əm
			tə- R -əmt
3	masc.	y/i- R Ø	Ø R -ən
	fem.	tə- R Ø	Ø R -ən(t)

DERIVED FORMS

s- causative; *t-* passive; *n-* reflexive/passive; e.g. Tamahaq forms of *əɣbər* 'to kick':

səɣbər 'to cause to beat, kick'
təɣbər 'to be beaten, kicked'
nəɣbər 'to beat, kick each other'

PARTICIPLES

y/i...n is a frequent formula: e.g. in Tamahaq *ilkəm* 'follow', participle *ilkəmən*; in Kabyle, *əkšəm* 'go in', participle *ikəšmən*.

NEGATION
In Tamahaq, *ur* is a general negator: e.g. *ur essineγ* 'I don't know'. Similarly in Tamazight, *ur d.idzi* 'he didn't come'. In Kabyle and some other dialects, /j/ acts as a negator in the past tense: e.g. *unfəγ* 'I left', *unifəγ* 'I didn't leave'.

Prefixed particles may be tense formants, e.g. *kəlad* (imperfect), *ad* (future), in Tamahaq: *kəlad irəgeh dat.i* 'he was walking in front of me'. *-d* and *-n* are directional markers: e.g. *awi* 'to take', *awid* 'to bring', *awin* 'to take away'.

Prepositions

Examples: *dat* 'before', *dəγ* 'in', *s* 'from', *γur* 'at the home of'; e.g. Tamahaq *deγ aγerem* 'in town'; *s akal ənnit* 'from his country'.

Word order

VSO.

G'LIḂD́Ā illa Aoual ; Aoual illa ŕor Rebbi, Aoual 1
illa d́'Rebbi. Ouagi illa ġ'liḃd́ā ŕor Rebbi. Irkoul 2 3
elḱaouaïdj tsououqement yīs ; oulach ain our-netsouou-
qem ara yīs, d́eg irkoul ain itsououqemen. D'eg-s ai 4
thèlla thoud́erth, thoud́erth thella tsafath g-ergazen.
Thafath thechâcha ġe-ṭlam, ṭlam our ts-iḟhim ara. 5
Illa íoun ourgaz, ism-is Yaḱyā, itsouchegâ-d s'ŕor 6
Rebbi. Yousa-d ad́-yili d́' inígi, íouakken ad́-ichehed́ ŕef 7
thafath, íouakken ad́-amnen irkoul fedéma en-*chehād̄a*-s.
Our ill'ara entsa s'iman-is tsafath, lamâna *itsouchegâ-d* 8
íouakken ad́-ichehed́ ŕef thafath.

(Kabyle dialect)

BRETON

INTRODUCTION

Breton belongs to the Brythonic branch of Celtic (i.e. P-Celtic; *see* Campbell 1991). In 1930 75 per cent of the Breton population in North-Western France, totalling about 1½ million, spoke the language; fifty years on, the percentage had dropped to just over 40 per cent. With an estimated half a million speakers, however, Breton is still outstripped only by Irish among Celtic languages. Middle Breton was used as a literary language up to the nineteenth century. The modern language is spoken in four main dialects: Léon (*leoneg*), Cornouaille (*kerneveg*), Tréguier (*tregerieg*), and the divergent dialect of Vannes (*gwenedeg*).

SCRIPT

The Roman alphabet minus q and x. The 1941 orthography known as *zedacheg* is in general use. The tilde marks nasalization. ch = /s, z/, c'h = /x, γ/, zh = /z/ (or /h/ in gwenedeg).

PHONOLOGY

Consonants

stops: p, b, t, d, k, g; labalized k°, g°
fricatives: f, v, s, z, ʃ, ʒ, x, γ, h
nasals: m, n, ɲ, ŋ
laterals: l, ʎ
rolled: r
semi-vowels: w, j

Only *l, m, n, r* are subject to gemination. Such gemination identifies the preceding vowel as short: cf. *krenan*/kreːnã/'tremble'; *krennan*/krɛnã/ 'shorten'. *ñ* is not pronounced and simply represents nasalization of the preceding vowel.

Vowels

i, e, ɛ, a, ɔ, o, œ, ø, u, y

All vowels can be long or short, and all can be nasalized, with marked variation in degree of closure. /ø/ is notated as *ö*, /y/ as *ü* in the following text.

There are several diphthongs, e.g. /ɛa, ao, ɛi, ɛ̃ɔ̃/.

Stress is movable.

Mutation

In Breton, mutation takes four main forms:

(a) Lenition: /p, t, k/ → /b, d, g/; /b, d, g/ → /v, z, x/γ/; /m/ → /v/. This mutation occurs regularly after articles (with constraints on gender, see below), certain possessive adjectives, prepositions, verbal particles, etc.: e.g. *tad* 'father': *e **dad*** 'his father'; *mamm* 'mother': *ar **vamm*** 'the mother'; *Bretoned* 'Bretons': *ar **V**retoned* 'the Bretons'. Following the definite article, lenition occurs in feminine singular and masculine plural nouns only; thus, *ar **vamm***; but *mor* 'sea', being masculine, does not mutate: *ar **mor*** 'the sea'. Example of mutation in attributive adjective: *merc'h* 'girl'; *brav* 'pretty': *ar **verc'h vrav*** 'the pretty girl'.

(b) Spirantization: /p, t, k/ → /f, z, x/. This mutation occurs after certain possessive adjectives, e.g. *ma* 'my', *he* 'her', *o* 'their': *ki* 'dog': *ma **c'hi*** 'my dog'; *penn* 'head': *ma **fenn*** 'my head'; *tad* 'father': *he **zad*** 'her father'.

Since *e* 'his' and *he* 'her' are homophones, the presence or absence of mutation in the following initial is phonemic: *e **vreur*** 'his brother'; *he **breur*** 'her brother' (*breur* 'brother').

(c) Hardening: /b, d, g/ → /p, t, k/. This mutation occurs after *ho*(*c'h*) 'your (pl.)', *az*/*ez* 'your (sing.)': e.g. *dent* 'teeth': *ho **tent*** 'your teeth'; *daouarn* 'hands': *ho taouarn* 'your hands'.

(d) Mixed: /b, d, g/ → /v, t, x/; /g°/ → /w/; /m/ → /v/. This occurs after the verbal particles *e* and *o*: e.g. *gwelout* 'to see': *o **welout*** 'seeing'.

MORPHOLOGY AND SYNTAX

Noun

The presence of an indefinite article, *un*/*ur*/*ul*, is unique in Celtic. Similarly, the definite article has three forms, *an*/*ar*/*al*, depending on following initial.

GENDER

Masculine and feminine. Gender and mutation are co-related.

NUMBER

There is a wide inventory of plural terminations, some of which induce vowel change in stem. Some common endings are:

- *-ed*: e.g. *loen* 'animal', pl. *loened*;
- *-ez*: *ti* 'house', pl. *tiez*;
- *-*(*i*)*ou*: pl. form for many inanimates: e.g. *tra* 'thing', pl. *traou* (but note exceptions such as *tadou* 'fathers', *mammou* 'mothers');
- *-i* + umlaut: e.g. *bag* 'boat', pl. *bigi*; Ø ending + umlaut: *maen* 'stone', pl. *mein*.

Stress may shift in plural: e.g. *michérour*, pl. *micheróurien* 'workers'.

Traces of a former dual appear in the prefix *daou-*/*div-*: e.g. *an daoulagad* 'the eyes'.

The ending *-enn* is added to collective plurals to make the singular: e.g. *ar gwez* '(the) trees': *gwezenn* 'a tree'; *askol* 'thistles': *askolenn* 'a thistle'.

Plural nouns take a singular verb.

POSSESSION

Possessor follows possessed object: e.g. *breur Yann* 'John's brother'. As in the Semitic construct, the noun denoting the possessed object loses the article: e.g. *gouleier an ti* 'the lights of the house'. However, other words can be interposed between N_1 and N_2, which is impossible in Semitic: e.g. *Økador vras ar bugel bihan* 'the small child's big chair' (*bras* 'big').

Adjective

As attribute, adjective follows noun, and is invariable apart from initial mutation: e.g. *an ti kozh* 'the old house'; *un den pinwidig* 'a rich man'; *ur skol vihan* 'a small school' (*bihan* 'small').

COMPARISON

The comparative is made with the ending *-oc'h* + *eget* 'than': e.g. *koant* 'pretty': *koantoc'h* 'prettier'.

Suppletive forms: *mat* 'good': *gwelloc'h* 'better'; *drouk* 'bad': *gwashoc'h* 'worse'.

Pronoun

PERSONAL

Gender is distinguished in third singular only.

		Singular		*Plural*	
		Base form	*Possessive*	*Base form*	*Possessive*
1		me	ma	ni	hon
2		te	da	c'hwi	ho
3	masc.	eñ	e	int	o
	fem.	hi	he		

Used as subject or direct object, these base forms always precede the verb, which is itself preceded by the particle *a*: e.g. *me a welit* 'you see me' (*gwelout* 'to see').

The possessive pronouns can also be used as direct object pronouns: e.g. *Da kwelout a raimp* (*warc'hoazh*) 'We'll see you (tomorrow).'

By adding personal pronominal affixes to prepositions, the ubiquitous 'conjugated prepositional' form is obtained: e.g. with *gant* /gã/ 'by, with, for, etc'.

		Singular	*Plural*
1		ganin 'by (etc.) me'	ganeomp
2		ganit 'by you'	ganeoc'h
3	masc./fem.	gantan/ganti	ganto

Similarly with *da* 'to': *din*, *dit*, *dezhan*/*dezhi*; *dimp*, *deoc'h*, *dezho*.

The prepositions *a* 'to' and *eus* 'from', share the extended bases *ac'han-* for first and second person, *anezh-* for third, and provide direct and indirect object forms: e.g. *C'hwi a gavo ac'hanon war ar blassenn* 'You'll find me in the square.'

DEMONSTRATIVE PRONOUN

Three degrees of relative distance are marked by masc. *hemañ – hennezh – henhont*; fem. *houmañ – hounnezh – hounhont.* The plural for both genders is: *ar re-mañ – ar re-se – ar re-hont.*

Enclitic forms: *an ti-mañ* 'this house'; *an ti-se – an ti-hont.*

INTERROGATIVE PRONOUN

piv 'who?'; *petra* 'what?'. Interrogative sentences are introduced by (*daoust*) *ha*(*g*): e.g. *Daoust ha brav eo am amzer?* 'Is the weather fine?' (*amzer* 'weather').

RELATIVE PRONOUN

Represented by the particle *a*: e.g. *ar paotr a welit* 'the boy whom you see'; *Setu ar paotr a zo klanv e dad* 'This is the boy whose father is ill.'

Numerals

1–10: *unan*, *daou*, *tri*, *pevar*, *pemp*, *c'hwec'h*, *seizh*, *eizh*, *nav*, *dek*; 11 *unnek*; 12 *daouzek*; 20 *ugent*; 21 *unan warn-ugent*; 30 *tregont*; 40 *daou-ugent*; 50 *hanter-kant*; 60 *tri-ugent*; 100 *kant*.

A noun following a numeral is in the singular: *deg vloaz* 'ten years'.

Verb

Breton has active and passive voices. The active voice has three moods – indicative, imperative, conditional. The indicative has past, non-past, and future tenses, and distinguishes perfective, habitual, punctual, and continuous aspects. There are three persons, singular and plural, plus an impersonal form. Tense forms may be (a) synthetic: here the verb is marked for person and number; (b) analytic: the verb is unmarked, and the personal pronoun must be present; (c) mixed, with auxiliary *bezañ* 'to be', or *ober* 'to do, make'; if *bezañ* is used, the verb is marked for person, and number. For example, the present tense of *labourat* 'to work', in three versions:

(a) Synthetic:

	Singular	*Plural*
1	bremañ e labouran 'I work now'	bremañ e labouromp
2	bremañ e labourez	bremañ e labourit
3	bremañ e labour	bremañ e labouront
	impersonal: e labourer 'one is working'	

(b) Analytic, e.g.:

1 me a labour bremañ 'I am working now'
2 te a labour bremañ

(c) Mixed, e.g.: with *bezañ* → *bez'*:

1 bez' e labouran
2 bez' e labourez
3 bez' e labour

with *ober*: base of *ober* is *gra-*, e.g:

1 labourat a ran bremañ 'I'm working now'
2 labourat a rez bremañ
3 labourat a ra bremañ

(*gra* > *ra*, following verbal particle *a*.) The three versions differ slightly in stress/focus.

Past:

(a) marked: e.g. *dec'h e labouren*, *e laboures*, *e laboure* (*-e-* is past discriminator)
(b) unmarked: e.g. *me a laboure, te a laboure,* etc.

Future:

(a) marked: sing. *e labourin*, *e labouri*, *e labouro*: pl. *e labourimp*, *e labouroc'h, e labourint (-i-/-o-* discriminators)

The (c) forms for past and future, with *ober* 'to do', are:

past, e.g.: sing. *labourat a raen*, *a raes*, *a rae*; pl. *a raemp*
future, e.g.: sing. *labourat a rin*, *a ri*, *a raio*; pl. *a raimp*

The markers *a* and *e* precede the finite verb form; *a* induces lenition, *e* the mixed mutation.

a is the syntactic linker between the subject and the verb, or between the fronted object and verb. It appears in the (b) conjugation above: *Me a labour bremañ* 'I'm working now'; *Bara a zebran bremañ* 'Bread it is I'm eating now.'

e links attributive or adverbial material, or indirect object to verb: e.g. *Er gegin e tebran* 'It's in the kitchen I'm eating now' (*kegin* 'kitchen').

The auxiliary *bezañ* (which has three sets of forms expressing state, habitual action, and spatio-temporal localization) is used to make composite tenses and the passive mood, e.g. with the past participle in *-et*.

The passive may also be expressed by the impersonal form in *-r*: e.g. *Al levr a lenner* 'The book is (being) read.'

The conditional is marked by *-f-* inserted between base and past endings: e.g. *bremañ de labourfen = bez' e labourfen = labourat a rafen bremañ* 'if I worked/ were working now'.

Imperative: the endings are: sing. 2 Ø; pl. 1 *-omp,* 2 *-it*: e.g. *komz* 'speak!' – *komzomp – komzit.*

Negative

The negative is expressed by a circumfix: *ne ... ket*. Only the marked conjugation can be negated; both *a* and *e* are then discarded: e.g. *ne labouran ket*, *ne labourez ket*, *ne labour ket*; etc.

Prepositions

Most are compatible with the personal endings (*see* **Pronoun**, above). Examples of prepositions without personal endings: *eus ar mor* 'from the sea'; *edan an douar* 'under the earth'; *goude ar bresel* 'after the war'; *e-kichen an ti-post* 'next to the post-office'. Some prepositions take an infixed personal marker: e.g. *war.lerc'h* 'after': *war-ma-lerc'h*, *war-da-lerc'h*, *war-e-lerc'h*, etc.

Word formation

By prefix, suffix, or compounding:

(a) Prefixation: e.g. *di-/dis-/diz-* is privative: e.g. *dizaon* 'fearless'; *dizampart* 'awkward'. *Peur-* gives a perfective sense: e.g. *peurskrivañ* 'to finish writing'. *enep-* 'contrary to': e.g. *enepreizh* 'injustice'; *hanter-* 'half-': e.g. *hanterzigor* 'half-open'.
(b) Suffixation: e.g. *-ded/-der* (masc./fem., no plural forms) make abstract nouns: e.g. *uhelded* 'nobility' (*uhel* 'high'). *-our* forms noun denoting agent, subject of action, or state: e.g. *klañvdiour* 'nurse'. *-erezh* forms abstract nouns: e.g. *bruderezh* 'publicity'.
(c) Compounding: various combinations, e.g. *bag-pesketa* 'fishing-boat'; *mont-dont* 'coming and going'; *pinwidig-mor* 'very rich'.

Word order

VSO is a basic formula, SVO frequent (*see* **Verb**, above).

1 Er gommansamant e oa ar Ger, hag ar Ger a oa gand Doue, hag ar Ger a oa Doue.
2 He-ma a oa er gommansamant gand Doue.
3 An holl draou a zo bet grëd drezan, hag hepzan n'eo bet grët netra hag a zo bet grët.
4 Ennan e oa ar vuez, hag ar vuez a oa goulou an dud.
5 Hag ar goulou a sclera en devalien, hag an devalien n'e deus ked e resevet.
6 Bez' e oe un den caset gand Doue, hanvet Ian.
7 He-ma a zeuaz da desteni, evit rei testeni diwarben ar goulou, evit ma credche an holl drezan.
8 Ne ket hen a oa ar goulou, mes *cased e oa* evit rei testeni diwarben ar goulou.

(Léon dialect)

BUGINESE

INTRODUCTION

A member of the Malayo-Polynesian branch of Austronesian, Buginese is spoken by about 4 million people in Southern Sulawesi (Celebes). Originally Buddhist, the Buginese were converted to Islam, along with the Macassarese, in the seventeenth century. The ethnonym is *(w)ugi'* or *to.ugi'* (*to* < *tau* 'man'); the language is *basa (w)ugi'*.

Buginese has a very rich traditional literature, still largely in manuscript form. The enormous cycle of mythological poems known as the *Surə' Galigoe* portrays and records an ethnic Sulawesi culture which is neither Islamic nor Hindu: a society of aristocratic seafarers, built on feudal lines, in which 'free men' rendered 'honourable homage' to their leaders (*see* Matthes 1874). There is also a rich prose literature, consisting of historical chronicles and *surəˀ bilang* or diaries.

SCRIPT

The Buginese–Macassarese syllabary is based on an Indian model, and retains the typically Indian method of marking vowels as super- or subscript additions to consonants. A major defect in the script is the absence of signs to denote gemination, nasalization, and glottalization. Thus ᨔᨑ can be read as *sara* 'sorrow', *saraˀ* 'rule', and *sarang* 'nest'.

Attempts have been made in the twentieth century to write Buginese in romanization.

PHONOLOGY

Consonants

stops: p, b, t, d, k, g, ˀ
affricatives: tʃ, ʤ
fricatives: Φ, s
nasals: m, n, ɲ, ŋ
lateral and trill: l, r
semi-vowels: j, w

Vowels

i, e, a, ə, o, u

/e/ and /o/ have positional variants.

Stress

Tends to penultimate syllable, but may be on antepenultimate or on final, depending on structure and composition of word or complex.

MORPHOLOGY AND SYNTAX

Article

An enclitic article is *-e* (with allomorphs), which can be added to complex: e.g. *bola.e* 'the/a house'; *bola aruŋŋ.e* 'princely house, the chief's house'; *utti u.tanəŋŋ.e* 'the bananas which I planted'. The article also serves to substantivize such units as extended verbs: e.g. *mallopi* 'to go by ship', *mallopi.e* 'a voyage'. The personal articles *i-la* (masc.) and *i-we* (fem.) are applied to Buginese proper nouns, names of boats, weapons, etc.

Noun

Buginese nouns are primary or derivatory; the latter mainly by prefixation: *pa*C-, for example, forms nouns of agency. The suffix *-aŋ* suggests something connected with or the result of the activity denoted by the base: e.g. *daŋkaŋ* 'trade', *daŋkaŋəŋ* 'goods'. Circumfix is also used: cf. from *musu*' 'war', *am.musu.r.əŋ* 'warlike actions'. This word illustrates the Buginese phonetic rule which requires the glottal stop to change to /k/, /r/, or /s/ preceding the suffix *-aŋ* or *-i*. Cf. *gau*' 'to do': *gaurən* 'to do something on someone's behalf'. There is no case system, hence word order is of crucial importance.

A possessive–relational nexus is expressed by the particle *na*: *ambo'.na səllao.na* 'the father of his friend' (where the second *na* is the second person possessive suffix).

Adjective

Most adjectives have the form *ma* + stem: e.g. *ma.lampe* 'long'; *ma.loppo* 'big'. As attribute, adjective follows noun. As predicate, the adjective forms, along with transitive and intransitive verbs, the third class of verb.

Pronoun

There are free and bound series; three persons; a plural distinction is made only with regard to first person.

	Free series	*u- series*	*-ku series*
1	ia'	u-, ku-	-(k)ku
2	idi', iko, io	ik-, ta-, mu-	-(t)ta, -(m)mu
3	ia	na-	-(n)na

An exclusive plural first person is provided by *idikkəŋ*, *ikəŋ* in the free series. The *u-* series has exclusive first person plural *ki-*, inclusive *ta-*, and the distinction appears also in the *-ku* series, but the opposition is not strictly observed.

The *u-* series forms provide the subject pronouns for transitive verbs, e.g. *u.tarima* 'I receive'; *na.tarima* 'he receives'; and the logical object in passive constructions, e.g. *u.ri.tarima* 'and they receive me' = 'I am received' (*ri* is passive marker).

The *-ku* series forms may follow nouns or verbs. Following nouns, they denote the possessive relationship: e.g. *amak.ku* 'my father'; *lopin.na* 'his boat'. Following a verb they set up a temporal or causal relationship: e.g. *ma.bela.n.na* 'when he is far away/because he is far away'; *u.tarima.mu* 'when I received you'.

A third series of bound pronouns, the *a'* series, provides object forms for transitive verbs: e.g. *ri.tarima.i* 'he undergoes reception' = 'they receive him'. *See* **Verb**, below.

DEMONSTRATIVE PRONOUN

Three-degree series: *-e/-we* 'this', *-tu* 'that', *-ro* 'that (far away)': e.g., combined with interrogative *aga* 'what?': *aga.e.tu* 'What is that?' (where *-e-* is the article). Cf. *Maloppo.i.tu bola.e* 'That house is big.'

INTERROGATIVE PRONOUN

niga 'who?'; *aga* 'what?'

RELATIVE PRONOUN

None. Relative constructions are formed with the help of bound pronouns.

Numerals

1–10: *seua/se'di, dua, təllu, əppa, lima, ənnəŋ, pitu, arua, asera, -pulo. Səppulo* is base for 11–19: e.g. *səppulo lima* 15. 20 *dua.pulo*; *-ratu* is base for hundreds.

Numeral can combine with noun: e.g. *patatauŋ* 'four years': *pata* is an alternative root for *əppa* 'four'.

Verb

Transitive and intransitive. Transitive verbs can take a passive construction, and are always correlated with an object (simple or composite). This object is copied or anticipated in the verbal form by a bound pronoun or deictic marker. Sirk (1975) gives the example: *ttiwirəŋŋ.i inanre ana'na* 'to bring food to her children'. Here, the root is *tiwi* 'to bring': the stem is made transitive–benefactive by addition of *-aŋŋ/-əŋŋ*, and then means 'to bring something to or for someone'. The object of the benefactive action, *ana'na* 'her children', is anticipated in the verbal form by the pronominal affix *-i*. The gemination of the stem initial: *tt-* is an allomorph of the active voice marker, which is *mm-* before a vowel initial.

As an example of transitive structure, Sirk (1975) gives the stem *lliaŋ* 'to sell': sell':

base form: *əlliaŋ* 'sell'
active: *mməlliaŋ* 'to (proceed to) sell'
passive: *riəlliaŋ* 'to be sold'

personalized forms: ***uəlliaŋ*** 'to be sold by me' = 'I sell'; ***muəlliaŋ*** 'to be sold by you' = 'you sell'; ***taəlliaŋ*** 'to be sold by us/you' = 'we/you sell'

Negation: by proclitic *təŋ*.

Intransitive verbs are heterogeneous in structure. Many are formed from substantives by means of prefix (*m*)*a*', and then mean 'to have to do with' (object denoted by stem): e.g. *galuŋ* 'rice-field', *ma'galuŋ* 'to work (in) the ricefield, cultivate ...'

CAUSATIVE

The prefix is *pa*C- with allomorphs: e.g. *ita* 'to see', *p*(*a*)*ita* 'to show something to someone'.

Passive: the marker is *ri-* preceding a transitive stem: cf. *ri.ləlluŋ joŋa.e* 'The deer is/was hunted.'

Both the construction of active/passive sentences, and the formation of relative clauses are illustrated in the following three sentences from Sirk (1975):

tomacca **mm**uki'.əŋŋ.**i** surə'.**e** 'the scholar who writes the letter'
surə' **ri**uki'.**e** **ri**.tommaca.**e** 'the letter written by the scholar'
surə' **na**uki'.**e** 'the letter which he writes'

Preposition

ri- is an all-purpose preposition applying to spatio-temporal frames without differentiation: this is supplied by the verb, e.g. *lləttu' ri.dusuŋŋe* 'to enter the village'; *pole ri.dusuŋŋe* 'to come out of the village'.

Word order

SVO in active construction: in passive construction V is fronted.

9. [illegible]
[illegible]
[illegible]
[illegible]
10. [illegible]
11. [illegible]
12. [illegible]
[illegible]
[illegible]
13. [illegible]
[illegible]
[illegible]
[illegible]
[illegible]
14. [illegible]
[illegible]
[illegible]
[illegible]
15. [illegible]
[illegible]
[illegible]
[illegible]

(Matt. 6: 9–15)

BULGARIAN

INTRODUCTION

The ancient Bulgars were a Turkic people speaking a language classified by Baskakov as Western Hunnic; its congener, still spoken today, is Chuvash (*see* **Turkic Languages**). The Bulgars enter history in the seventh century AD, when they moved westwards from the Crimea area, and settled to the south of the Danube, in the Balkan peninsula. Here, they gradually merged with the Slav population already established along the Black Sea coast, and even adopted the local Slavonic language. Of the original Bulgar(ian) language, only the name remains. The language now known as Bulgarian forms, together with Macedonian, the eastern branch of South Slavonic. It is the official language of the Republic of Bulgaria where it is spoken by over 8 million people. (For the 'Old Bulgarian' literary language, see Old Church Slavonic in Campbell 1991.) Through the Middle Bulgarian period (twelfth to fifteenth centuries) and again under Turkish suzerainty from the fifteenth century onwards, Bulgarian was a spoken language only, a kind of demotic accompanying the Church Slavonic literary language. By the eighteenth century it had deviated more than any other Slavonic tongue from the common Slavonic norm. The declension of the noun had disappeared, an affixed definite article had been introduced, and the infinitive had been replaced by a construction with the particle *da* plus a finite form of the verb (these are areal features, cf. Tosk Albanian, Romanian, Serbian, and, in part, Greek). In addition, Bulgarian has developed the *preizkazano naklonenie*, a set of inferential tenses which has no parallel in other European languages (but cf. **Turkic Languages**).

The first Bulgarian writer of distinction is Khristo Botev (1848–76). Two years after Botev's death, Bulgaria gained its independence, and from then until the outbreak of the Second World War, a sustained and innovative output of verse and prose appeared in Bulgarian from such writers as Ivan Vazov, Pencho Slaveykov, Peyo Yavorov, Dimcho Debelyanov, Elin Pelin, Elisaveta Bagryana, and Nikolai Vaptsarov.

There is an east/west dialect division; literary Bulgarian is based on the western dialect.

SCRIPT

Cyrillic minus *ё*, *ы*, *э*. The hard sign *ъ* is used to notate the typically Bulgarian sound /ʌ/ > /ɪ/. Here, for typographical reasons, the sound will be notated as *ă*. The Cyrillic letter *щ* is /ʃt/ in Bulgarian, not /ʃtʃ/ > /ʃʃ/ as in Russian. The soft sign *ь* denotes palatalization of the preceding consonant: *синьо* = /sin'ɔ/.

PHONOLOGY

Consonants

stops: p, b, t, d, k, g
affricates: ts, tʃ
fricatives: f, v, s, z, ʃ, ʒ, j, x
nasals: m, n, ɲ
lateral and trill: l, r

ASSIMILATION
Voiced to unvoiced and vice versa: e.g. *gradski* = /gra**t**ski/; *velikden* = /veli**g**den/. Final voiced is unvoiced: *grad* → [gra**t**]; *vrag* → [vra**k**].

Vowels

i, ɛ, a, ə, ɔ, u, ʌ(l)

The script distinguishes the palatalized vowels *yu*, *ya*. Diphthongs: /ai, oi/.

Vowel reduction is typical of Bulgarian pronunciation of unstressed syllables: e.g. /a/ → [ə]: *kníga* → [knigə]; /ɛ/ → [ɪ]: *zeléno* → /zɪlenɔ/; /o/ → [u]: *polé* → [pule].

Stress

Stress is free and can fall on any syllable. Bulgarian stress often agrees with Russian, but there are many exceptions.

MORPHOLOGY AND SYNTAX

Noun

There are three genders: masculine, feminine, and neuter. The case system has disappeared. The sole remaining inflectional distinction is that between nominative and non-nominative masculine singular, where the nominative form takes the definite article (affix): e.g. *gradăt* 'the town (nom.)'; *grada* 'the town (obl.)': *v centăra na grada* 'in the middle of the town'.
Compare:

čas**ăt** e devet i polovina 'the time is half past nine' (nom.)

V kolko čas**a** zaminavaš 'At what time are you going?' (obl.)

DEFINITE ARTICLE
Masc. hard: *-ăt*, soft: *-yat*; fem. *-ta*; neuter: *-to*; plural, all genders: *-te*/*-ta*: e.g. *gradăt* 'the town'; *borbata* 'the struggle'; *cveteto* 'the flower'; *rabotnicite* 'the workers'.

PLURAL ENDINGS
Most polysyllabic masculines take *-i* with 2nd palatalization of final consonant (*see* **Slavonic Languages**) where necessary: e.g. *rabotnik* 'workers': pl. *rabotnici*; *pedagog* 'teacher': *pedagozi*; *kožux* 'fur coat': *kožusi*.

Masculine monosyllables often take *-ove*: e.g. *plod* 'fruit', pl. *plodové*; *xlyab* 'loaf', pl. *xlyábove*; *nož* 'knife', pl. *nožóve*. Note that stress may be on stem, penultimate, or final.

The feminine plural is in *-i*; neuter: final *o* → *a*, *e* → *ya/eta*, *ne* → *niya*: e.g. *pero* 'pen': *perá*; *cvéte* 'flower': *cvetyá*; *momče* 'boy': *momčéta*.

The particle *na* is used to indicate both genitive and dative: e.g. *knigata na deteto* 'the child's book'; *davam knigata na deteto* 'I give the book to the child.'

Adjective

Adjectives are marked for gender and number. The attributive adjective precedes the noun, and the definite article, if present, is transferred to it, the distinction between masculine nominative and oblique being maintained: e.g.

golem**iyat** grad**Ø** 'the big town (*golem* 'big', *grad* 'town')

viždam golem**iya** grad**Ø** 'I see the big town'

Cf. *visok**ata** kăšta* 'the tall house'; *novo**to** pero* 'the new pen'; *golemi**te** prozorci* 'the big windows'.

PREDICATIVE
*knigata e červen**a*** 'the book is red'; *molivăt e červen* 'the pencil is red'.

COMPARATIVE
Comparative is made by prefixing *po-*: e.g. *dobăr* 'good', *pó-dobăr/-dobra/-dobro* 'better': e.g. *Našeto žilište e pó-xubavo ot tova* 'Our apartment is nicer than that one.'

Pronoun

The personal independent forms are:

sing. 1 *az*, 2 *ti*, 3 *toi*, *tya*, *to*; pl. 1 *nie*, 2 *vie*, 3 *te*

That is, the third person singular forms are marked for gender.

The pronouns have full and short oblique forms; thus, for first person, direct object full form: *mene*; short: *me*; indirect object full: *na mene*, short, *mi*. Example of full form used for emphasis:

Na tebe, ne na nego davam knigata
'I'm giving the book to you, not to him.'

Short forms: *viždam go* 'I see him'; *ne te viždam* 'I don't see you.' Both long and short forms may be used together: e.g. *na mene mi xaresva* 'I *do* like it.'

POSSESSIVE FORMS

Full forms:

		Singular			*Plural*		
1		moy	moya	moe	naš	naša	naše
2		tvoy	tvoya	tvoe	vaš	vaša	vaše
3	masc.	negov	negova	negovo	texen	tyaxna	tyaxno
	fem.	nein	neina	neino			

The short indirect object forms may also be used: e.g. *moyata kniga* = *knigata mi* 'my book'.

DEMONSTRATIVE PRONOUN

tozi 'this', *onya* 'that'. Both declined for gender and number.

INTERROGATIVE PRONOUN

koy 'who?'; *kakvo* 'what?'. Interrogative enclitic: *li*.

RELATIVE PRONOUN

koyto/koyato/koeto; pl. *koito*. If *koyto* refers to a male person, the oblique case is *kogoto*; otherwise, *koyto*: cf.

čovekăt, **kogoto** viždam 'the man whom I see'

vlakăt, **koyto** viždam 'the train which I see'

Numerals

1: *edin/edna/edno*; 2 *dva/dve*; 3–10: *tri*, *četiri*, *pet*, *šest*, *sedem*, *osem*, *devet*, *deset*. 11: *edinayset*; 12 *dvanayset*; 20 *dvayset*; 30 *triyset*; 100 *sto*.

Verb

Bulgarian verbs have perfective and imperfective aspects. The present perfective form (usually with a prefix, e.g. *uča* 'I learn', perfective ***nauča***) cannot be used independently but only in a relative capacity; cf. *trăgvam* 'I leave, start off' (imperfective); *iskam da* ***trăgna*** 'I want to leave'.

The citation form is the first person present imperfective.

There are active and passive voices; indicative, imperative/hortative, and conditional moods. In addition, Bulgarian has the unique inferential version of all eight indicative tenses (see below). Three types of conjugation are distinguished: *-e* stems, *-i* stems, and *-a/-ya* stems. Negative particle is *ne*.

THE COPULA

present: *săm*, *si*, *e*; pl. *sme*, *ste*, *sa*
past: *byax*, *be*(*še*), *be*(*še*); pl. *byaxme*, *byaxte*, *byaxa*
past participle: *bil*, *bili*

Specimen conjugation: *četá* 'I read': indicative:

> present: *četá*, *četeš*, *čete*; pl. *četem*, *četete*, *četat*
> future: present forms preceded by particle *šte*: e.g. *šte četá*
> past imperfective: *četyáx, četeše, četeše*; pl. *četyaxme, cětyaxte, četyaxa*
> past perfective: *čétox*, *čete*, *čete*; pl. *četoxme*, *četoxte*, *četoxa*
> conditional mood: with auxiliary: *bix*, *bi*, *bi čel*; pl. *bixme*, *bixte*, *bixa čeli*
> imperative: the endings are *-i*/*-ete*: *piši*, *pišete* 'write!'

THE INFERENTIAL VERSION

All indicative tenses have parallel forms in the indirect tense or reported-speech system. The indirect tense forms may be preceded by some such phrase as 'It is reported that ...' (cf. Lat. *allatum est*...) but the verb form in itself is enough to stamp the utterance as reported speech. The copula is used in all inferential tenses, except in the third person, where the participial form by itself (singular or plural) is used. Thus the inferential parallel for the present tense of *četa*, given above, is:

> sing. *četyal săm*, *četyal si*, *četyal* Ø; pl. *četeli sme*, *četeli ste*, *četeli* Ø

E.g.

> Tuk živee i semeystvoto na Ivan 'John's family too lives here';
>
> (Čuse,če)tuk živee**lo** i semeystvoto na Ivan
> '(It is said that) John's family ...'
>
> Stopanstvoto ima kăm 1,000 ovce
> 'The farm has up to 1,000 sheep' (indicative statement)
>
> Stopanstvoto ima**lo** kăm 1,000 ovce '(I'm told) the farm has ...'

As a further example, a passage from the novelist Elin Pelin in both versions:

Indicative	*Inferential*
Pisatelyat vse sedeše i vse pišeše. Toi ne znaeše počivka. Beše mnogo trudolyubiv.	Pisatelyat vse sedyal i vse pišel. Toi ne znael počivka. Bil mnogo trudolyubiv.

> 'The teacher was always sitting and writing. He never thought of taking a break. He was very much devoted to his work.'

PARTICIPLES

Use of the active past participle in *-l* has been illustrated above. The present active participle ends in *-eyki*/*ayki*: e.g. *pristigayki v grada* ... 'arriving in the town ...' The past passive participle is in *-n* or *-t*: e.g. *pisan* 'written'; *vzet* 'taken'. This participle can be used to make passive sentences: e.g. *Vestnikăt e četen ot všicki* 'The newspaper is read by all', which can also be expressed as a reflexive verb: *vestnikăt se čete ot všicki*.

Prepositions

For example, *v* 'in'; *sled* 'after'; *kăm* 'towards'; *izvăn* 'beyond': e.g. *Tazi rabota e izvăn silite mi* 'This job is beyond my powers.'

Word formation

Derivatives mainly by suffixation: e.g.

-ar: *stol* 'chair': *stolar* 'carpenter'
-nik: *rabota* 'work': *rabotnik* 'worker'
-stvo: *bogat* 'rich': *bogatstvo* 'wealth'
-ota: *čist* 'pure': *čistota* 'purity'
-ište: *igraya* 'I play': *igrište* 'playground'

Compounding is prolific: e.g. *zelenčukproizvoditel* 'market gardener' (*zelen* 'green', *-čuk*: *zelenčuk* 'vegetable'; *-tel* suffix denoting agent; *vodya* 'I lead'; *pro-*, *iz-* are prefixes denoting 'out of', 'from').

Word order

SVO is basic.

1 Въ начало бѣ Словото; и Словото
бѣше у Бога; и Словото бѣ Богъ.
2 То въ начало бѣше у Бога.
3 Всичко това чрезъ Него стана; и безъ Него не е станало нищо
отъ това, което е станало.
4 Въ Него бѣ животътъ и животътъ бѣ свѣтлина на човѣцитѣ.
5 И свѣтлината свѣти въ тъмнината; а тъмнината я не схвана.
6 Яви се човѣкъ изпратенъ отъ
Бога, на име Иоанъ.
7 Той дойде за свидетелство, да
свидетелствува за свѣтлината, за да
повѣрватъ всички чрезъ него.
8 Не бѣше той свѣтлината, но
дойде да свидетелствува за свѣтлината.

BURMESE

INTRODUCTION

This language belongs to the Burmic branch of Tibeto-Burmese family. From South-West China, where its close congener, Yi, is still spoken, Burmese was carried southwards to reach its present habitat by the ninth century AD. Here it came into contact with the Mon language and the Pali scriptures of Buddhism. The result was an amalgam: Tibeto-Burman stock with a Mon-Khmer substratum and writing system, plus a Pali–Buddhist ideological super-structure. The earliest written records in Burmese date from the eleventh century. By the twelfth century Burmese had replaced Mon as the literary language of the court.

For the study of the Pali texts, a specific genre known as *nissaya* Burmese was introduced, in which Pali words are accompanied by Burmese calques (*cf.* **Tibetan**). An interesting feature in Burmese classical verse is the so-called 'climbing rhyme', with rhymes regressing through successive four-syllable lines:

1, 2, 3, *4*, 1, 2, *3*, 4, 1, *2*, 3, *4*, 1, 2, *3*, 4 ... etc.

Burmese is the official language of the Republic of Burma, and is now spoken by about 30 million people. There are three main dialects: Central (the basis of the literary language), Arakanese, and Tavoi (Tenasserim). Over and above the dialectal division is a fundamental distinction between written and colloquial Burmese, with the latter exerting constant upward pressure on the former, as shown, for example, in the erosion of the old literary particles.

SCRIPT

Indic, derived from the Mon version of Brāhmī. There are 43 basic graphs: 11 vowels and 32 consonants. In addition, as in all Indic scripts, there are secondary forms for all vowels and for certain consonants. Eleven graphs are inherently coded for tone; for all other consonant + vowel graphs tone is indicated by subscript dot ့, by *visarga* း, or by the absence of either. Thus အာ = /a/ is *coded* for tone; အား = /à/ is *marked* for tone.

PHONOLOGY

Consonants

stops: p, ph, b, t, th, d, k, kh, g, ʔ
affricatives: ʃ, tʃh, dʒ
fricatives: θ, ð, s, sh, ʃ, z, h
nasals: m, mh, n, nh, ɲ, ŋ, ŋh
lateral and flap: l, r
semi-vowels: j, w

Sixteen of the consonants can be set out in five-term series (including aspirate sonant): surd – aspirate surd – voiced stop – sonant – aspirate sonant, e.g. for labial series: /p – ph – b – m – mh. (There is no specific graph for the aspirate sonant, which is written with the secondary form of *h*: e.g. မ = *ma*, မှ = *hma*.) Aspiration and consonant are pronounced simultaneously, and may be conventionally notated either as C*h*, or as *h*C, where C = consonant.

Most consonants can be labialized: /p°, t°, k°/, etc.; /p, b, m/ can be palatalized.

CONSONANT GRADATION

Unvoiced stop → voiced stop in intervocalic position or following a nasal: e.g. *kauŋ* + *kauŋ* → [kauŋ**g**auŋ]; *θwa* + *tɔ* → [θwà**d**ɔ́].

Vowels

i, e, ɛ, a, ɔ, o, u, ə

DIPHTHONGS

ei, ou, au, ai

Diphthongs are always followed by /ŋ/ or by /ʔ/, e.g. /eiŋ/ 'house'; /kauŋ/ '(to be) good'.

Syllables are *full*, i.e. with all components receiving their full phonetic value, or *reduced*, with vowels tending to /ə/. This characteristic is not typical of Tibeto-Burman, and may indicate Mon-Khmer influence.

The Burmese syllable must contain a vowel or diphthong, which may be preceded and/or followed by a consonant: $(C_1)V(C_2)$ where V = vowel or diphthong. There is a wide choice for C_1, but C_2 can only be /ŋ/ or /k, t, p/, realized as [ʔ]. C_1 may be followed by the semi-vowel /j/ or /w/ (i.e. palatalized or labialized).

Tones

There are three tones. The level tone is unmarked; the heavy falling tone is marked in the script by visarga and in transcription by grave accent; the 'creaky' tone is marked in the script by subscript dot, and in notation by acute accent. In addition, an abrupt (implosive or choked-off) tone occurs before the glottal stop final: this is unmarked in script. Tone marking is not consistent.

MORPHOLOGY AND SYNTAX

Noun

No grammatical gender. Where natural gender has to be specified, lexical means are employed, e.g. *má* for human females: *yá.hàŋ* 'monk' – *yá.hàŋ.má* 'nun'. *Dó* is a general plural marker: *lu* 'man', *ludó* 'people'. *Myà* is a restricted plural marker: *lumyà* 'a certain (given) number of people'. Syntactic relationships are expressed by particles following the noun. Thus, *ká* is a subject marker (literary *ði*). *Ko* is an object or directional marker, *hma* is a locative, *nέ* an instrumental marker: e.g. *eiŋ.hma* 'in the house'; *dou'.nέ* 'with a stick' (literary *hníŋ*).

POSSESSION

Literary *í* = colloquial *yέ*; Y of X is expressed as X *í/yέ* Y. This particle can be omitted; if it is, X changes tone: e.g. *θu.yέ.eiŋ* = *θú.eiŋ* 'his house'. If omitted, the objective marker *ko* induces similar tonal change.

There are several numerical coefficients, e.g. *yau'*, *ù*, for people; *kauŋ* for animals; *lòuŋ*, *chàuŋ* for objects according to shape, size, and so on. *Khú* is an all-purpose classifier which can replace any other (cf. Chinese 个 /ge/).

Pronoun

The independent personal pronouns are:

	Singular
1	cuŋ.dɔ (masc.), cuŋ.má (fem.)
2	khìŋ.bya (formal), mìŋ (general)
3	θu

Plural markers are added to make the plural series. Possessives are made by adding *í/yέ*. Again, if this is omitted, the tone of the pronoun changes: *cuŋ.dɔ.yέ* = *cuŋ.dɔ́* 'mine'.

DEMONSTRATIVE PRONOUNS

di 'this'; *ho* 'that'.

INTERROGATIVE PRONOUNS

These are based on the particle *bε* + modulators: *bε.ðu* 'who?'; *ba.go* 'what?'.

Numerals

1–10: *tí'*, *hní'*, *θòuŋ*, *lè*, *ŋà*, *chaú'*, *khú.ní'*, *ší'*, *kò*, *təs*[h]*ə*/*təse*. 20: *hní'shε*; 100: *təya*.

Verb

Verbs in Burmese may be simple, e.g. *θwà* 'to go', *sà* 'to eat'; or compound, i.e. root + root, e.g. *twé.myiŋ* 'to meet' ('meet' + 'see'). There is no inflection for person. The general predicative marker is *ði* (coll.)/*i* (lit.). This marker is further amplified by several specific markers for tense and mood: e.g. *mε* (future), *gε* (perfective), *ne* (progressive), *pyi* (inceptive). E.g.:

> təne.θə.hnai mauŋ.lu.e youŋ.hma sɔ.zɔ shiŋ.la.***gε.i*** 'One day, Maung Lu E came home from work early' (*təne.θə.hnai* 'one day, once'; *youŋ* 'place of work'; *hma* 'from' (postposition); *sɔ.zɔ* 'early'; *shiŋ.la* 'to return'; *gε* perfective particle; *i* predicative marker).

kέ/kouŋ/pi: these are used to express perfective aspect.

NEGATION
The negative marker is *mə ...phù*: e.g. *mə hmaŋ phù* 'not true'.

IMPERATIVE
Command is made more polite by addition of *pa*: e.g. *θwà.**ba*** 'please go'. An interrogative marker is *la*.

MODAL VERBS
Desiderative *chiŋ*; potential *ta'/hnain*; necessitative *yá*; conditional *yiŋ*: e.g. *twé.yiŋ* 'if ... meet(s)'; *θwa.yá.mε* '... must go'. A verbal noun is made with the *ə*-prefix (written အ = *a*, reduced to /ə/). e.g. *lou'* 'to work' – *ə.lou'* 'work' (noun); *hlá* 'to be pretty – *ə.hlá* 'beauty'.

Many verbs occur in functive–stative pairs (active–passive in Indo-European terms); the functive member has an aspirate initial which is dropped in the stative:

Functive	*Stative*
hcìŋ 'to make narrow'	ciŋ 'to be narrow'
hcwá 'to raise'	cwá 'to be lifted'
hnòu 'to waken'	nòu 'to be awake'
hlu' 'to set free'	lu' 'to be free'

As in Chinese, there are many four-syllable set phrases, which may be extended to six members. These often consist of formant + rhyming word, reduplicated: e.g. *kə.pya.kə.ya* 'hurriedly'.

RELATIVE CLAUSES
May be made with the particle *tɔ*:

> *θwà.**dɔ̀**.lu* 'the man who is going';
> *θwà.**gέ.dɔ̀**.lu* 'the man who went' (with perfective marker *kε* → *gε*);
> *θwa.mε.**dɔ̀**.lu* 'the man who will go' (with future marker *mε*).

Subjectless sentences proliferate, as as Chinese: e.g. *Pyɔ.pyɔ.ne ðe.gὲ.ði* 'Live well, die miserably.'

Compounding

Burmese has a very large stock of polysyllables built up by compounding from various parts of speech. An example shows two nouns and a verb forming a third polysyllabic noun: *nyá* 'night' + *ne* 'sun' + *sàuŋ* 'to lean' → *nyá.ne.zàuŋ* 'afternoon'.

Word order

SOV is normal.

၁ [၁]အစအဦး၌ [၂]နှုတ်ကပတ်တော် ရှိ၏။ နှုတ်ကပတ်
တော်သည် ဘုရားသခင်နှင့် အတူ[၃]ရှိ၏။ နှုတ်ကပတ်
၂ တော်သည်လည်းဘုရားသခင်[၄]ဖြစ်တော်မူ၏။-ထိုနှုတ်
ကပတ်တော်သည်အစအဦး၌ ဘုရားသခင်နှင့်အတူရှိ
၃ ၏။- ကိုယ်တော်သည် [၅]ခပ်သိမ်းသော အရာတို့ကိုဖန်
ဆင်းတော်မူ၏။ ကိုယ်တော်နှင့် ကင်းလွတ်လျက်၊ ဖန်
၄ ဆင်းသောအရာ တစုံတခုမျှ မရှိ။- ကိုယ်တော်၌ [၆]အ
သက်ရှိ၏။ထိုအသက်သည်လည်း[၇]လူတို့၏အလင်းဖြစ်
၅ ၏။-[၈]ထိုအလင်းသည်မှောင်မိုက်၌ထွန်းလင်း၍၊ မှောင်
၆ မိုက်သည် မသတ်မငြိမ်း စေနိုင်။-[၉]ယောဟန်အမည်ရှိ
သောသူတယောက်ကို ဘုရားသခင် စေလွှတ်တော်မူ
၇ ၏။-ထိုသူကိုလူအပေါင်းတို့သည်အမှီပြု၍၊ [၁၀]ယုံကြည်
ခြင်းသို့ရောက်မည်အကြောင်း၊ထိုသူသည် [၁၁]သက်သေ
ခံဖြစ်၍၊အလင်းတော်၏အကြောင်းကိုသက်သေခံခြင်း
၈ ငှါလာ၏။-ထိုသူသည်[၁၂]အလင်းတော်မဟုတ်၊အလင်း
တော်၏အကြောင်းကိုသက်သေခံခြင်းငှါသာလာ၏။-
၉ ဟုတ်မှန်[၁၃]သောအလင်းမူကား၊ဤလောကသို့ကြွလာ
လျက်၊ ခပ်သိမ်းသောလူအပေါင်းတို့အား အလင်းကို

CAMBODIAN (Khmer)

INTRODUCTION

Cambodian belongs to the Mon-Khmer sub-division of the Austro-Asiatic family. There are about 6 or 7 million speakers in Cambodia and Vietnam. The oldest inscriptions in Khmer date from the seventh century AD. From the end of the Angkor period (twelfth century) onwards, three main divisions of Cambodian literature may be distinguished: (a) Hindu influence is exemplified in the *Ream Ker*, the Cambodian version of the *Rāmāyaṇa*; in part, this is very old. (b) Buddhist influence (Cambodia became converted to Buddhism in the twelfth century). The translation of the *Tripitaka* has proved enormously influential, as, in addition to providing much of the Buddhist canon, it gave Cambodian literature a rich supply of motifs for the specifically Cambodian genre of the verse-novel. (c) the verse-novel: Cambodians seem to be particularly addicted to romantic stories of a sentimental type in which, latterly, French influence may be discerned.

SCRIPT

The Khmer script derives from a variant of Devanagari. The original Devanagari order is preserved (the retroflex and dental series have coalesced) as is the siting of the vowels; and, as in Devanagari, the consonants in their base state have a syllabic value, i.e. a back vowel inheres in each. Khmer use of this Indian material, however, introduces an essential innovation: the consonants are divided into two series or registers, in each of which one and the same vowel sign is realized differently. Thus, the system doubles the vocalic inventory (Cambodian is very rich in vowels) by giving one specific value to a vowel sign following a series 1 consonant, and quite another value to the *same* vowel sign following a series 2 consonant. Series 1 consonants are the original Devanagari voiceless stops with their aspirates (including the affricate series); series 2 consonants consist of the Devanagari voiced stops with their aspirates. For example, *kh* in series 1 represents Devanagari *kh*; *kh* in series 2 represents Devanagari *gh*. As illustration: *kh* in series 1 is ខ ; *kh* in series is ឃ ; both can be followed by the vowel sign for long *ā*: ា : but ខាត់ is pronounced [khat] ('to polish'); ឃាត់ is pronounced [khoət] ('to prevent'). For certain consonants in series 1 there is no counterpart in series 2. In such cases, the series 1 consonant can be converted to series 2 register by means of a diacritic.

PHONOLOGY

Consonants

stops: p, ph, b, t, th, d, k, kh, ʔ
affricates: ts, tʃ
fricatives: s, h
nasals: m, n, ɲ, ŋ
lateral and flap: r, l
semi-vowels: j, w

Aspiration is phonemic: cf. *thaa* 'to say'; *taa* 'old man'.

Vowels

The vocalic system is of great complexity, requiring over 30 phonemic contrasts to be notated in close transcription. There are ten basic short vowels:

front: i, e, ɛ
central: ɪ, ə, a
back: u, o, ɔ, ɑ

Ten long vowels: the above vowels doubled: /ii, ee/, etc. Ten long diphthongs:

iə, ɪə, uə, ei , əɪ, ou, ae, aə, ao, ɔə

and three short

uə, eə, oe

Cambodian is non-tonal. Stress tends to fall on the final syllable.

MORPHOLOGY AND SYNTAX

Noun

Cambodian words have no inflection of any kind, and are not readily classifiable in terms of 'parts of speech'. There are no articles: e.g. *pteəh* means 'house, a house, the house'. Number may be inferred from the context, or expressed by such modifiers as *klah* 'some', *teəng* 'all'. For example, *pii* 'two' may be added to *teəng*: *salaa.riən teəng.pii nuh* 'those two schools' (*salaa.riən* 'house of learning').

GENDER
If necessary, gender can be expressed by such lexical additions as *proh* 'male (human)', *srəy* 'female': e.g. *koun.proh* 'son'; *koun.srəy* 'daughter'.

CASE RELATIONS
Expressed syntactically with the help of various particles, or by apposition as in the genitive: e.g. *laan əwpuk* 'father's car' (*laan* 'car'; *əwpuk* 'father'), *əwpuk*

neək 'your father'; or in compound form: e.g. *tuənlee.meekong* 'the river (of the) Mekong'.

Adjective

As attribute, adjective follows noun: e.g. *salaa.riən touc* 'a small school'; *koun.srəy l'ɔɔ* 'a pretty girl'.

Pronoun

Cambodian had, and up to a point still has, a very large inventory of status-graded personal pronouns, each with correlative particles of address and response. As in the case of Lao, social change fosters the emergence of certain pronouns as neutral/polite forms of address or reference, suitable for use in most situations: e.g. for first person *khɲom*; for second person *look* (to a man), *look.srəy* (to a woman); third person *koət*. Plural forms may be made for these by adding *teəng.'ah*.

In the case of the second person, use of a title or a kinship term is preferred wherever possible. A full list of all status-graded forms is given in Jacob (1968: 158–63).

As possessives, the personal pronouns follow the noun possessed: *mday khɲom* 'my mother'.

Direct and indirect object: cf. *khɲom'aoy luy kot* 'I give money (*luy*) to him' (*kot* < *koət*).

DEMONSTRATIVE PRONOUN/ADJECTIVE

nih 'this/these'; *nuh* 'that/those': e.g. *laan nih* 'this car'; *siəwphɪw tlay pram nih* 'these five (*pram*) expensive (*tlay*) books'.

INTERROGATIVE PRONOUN

neə'-naa 'who?'; *'wəy* 'what?': e.g. *Neə'naa cang tɪw məəl kon*? 'Who wants to go to the cinema?' (*məəl* 'to see, watch').

RELATIVE PRONOUN

dael, following head-word: e.g. *Khɲom miən koun.proh məneə' dael nɪw riən nɪw laəy* 'I have a son who is still (*nɪw laəy*) at school' (*məneə'* is the classifier for person).

Numerals

1–10: *muəy*, *pii*, *bəy*, *buən*, *pram*, *prammuəy*, *prampii*, *prambəy*, *prambuən*, *dɔp*; 11: *dɔp.muəy*, 12: *dɔp.pii*; 20: *məphɪy*; 30: *saamsəp*; 40: *saesəp*; 100: *rɔɔy*.

Cambodian has about two dozen numerical classifiers.

Verb

There is no inflection of any kind. Aspect, modal categories, and tense are expressed by means of auxiliary particles which may be pre- or post-verbal. Thus, *haəy* is a post-verbal particle indicating the perfective aspect; *cɔng* is a modal auxiliary expressing wish or design.

Cambodian has no genuine passive voice; many verbals can be both active and passive, the exact meaning depending on the syntactic context.

Both prefixation and infixation are used as formative processes in Cambodian. The prefix *p-/ph-*, for example, produces causatives: e.g. *dəng* 'to know' – ***p.****dəng* 'to let know, inform'; *deik* 'to sleep' – ***ph.****deik* 'to put to sleep'. Similarly, with prefix *b*V*n-*: *riən* 'to learn' – *bɔngriən* 'to teach'.

The infix -V*m*- makes transitives: e.g. *slap* 'die' – ***səml****ap* 'to kill'; *krup* 'all' – ***kum****rup* 'to complete'; *s'aat* 'clean' – ***sam'****aat* 'to clean'.

The nasal infix makes nouns from verbs: e.g. *som* 'to ask' – ***smom*** 'a beggar'; *klaac* 'to be afraid of' – ***koml****aac* 'a timid person'.

The prefix *prɔ-* suggests reciprocity: e.g. *cam* 'to wait' – ***prɔ****cam* 'to wait for each other'.

Partial reduplication is used to express intensification or reiteration of action: e.g. *kaay* 'to dig' – ***kɔ****kaay 'to dig away at'.*

TENSE

Action is broadly classified as perfective, imperfective, or pending:

> Perfective: expressed by *baan* or *haəy*, e.g. *Maong prambuən* ***haəy*** 'It's gone 9 o'clock'.
>
> Imperfective: e.g. with *kɔmpung.tae*, corresponding to Lao *kamlang*: *Khɲom kɔmpung.tae riən phiəsaa.kmae* 'I am now learning Cambodian' (*phiəsaa* 'language', < Skt. *bhāṣā*).
>
> Pending action: e.g. with *nɪng*: *khɲom* ***nɪng*** *tɪw pteəh* 'I shall go home'.

Verbals are negated by the circumfix *mɪn ... tee*: *khɲom mɪn tɪw pteəh tee* 'I am not going home'; *khɲom sdap mɪn baan tee* 'I didn't understand' (where *mɪn* is sited between sense-verb (*sdap*) and modal (*baan*).

miən 'to have' has a negative counterpart *kmiən* + *tee*: *khɲom kmiən X tee* 'I don't have X'.

MODAL AUXILIARIES

E.g. *trəw* 'must'; *cɔng* 'want to': *khɲom trəw tɪw twəə.kaa* 'I have to go to work'. *craən-tae* denotes habitual action: e.g. *khɲom craən-tae tɪw psaa tŋay-can* 'I always go to market on Mondays': *dam yɔɔk krɔəp* 'to plant (*dam*) for grain'.

Prepositions

(a) simple, e.g. *nɪng* 'with', *pii* 'from', *ləə* 'on';
(b) verbs as prepositions: e.g. *tɪw* 'to go' = 'to(wards)'; *yɔɔk* 'to take' = 'by means of, with (in instrumental sense)'.

Word order

SVO.

១ ៙ ១កាលដើមដំបូងនោះមានព្រះបន្ទូល ហើយព្រះបន្ទូលគង់ជាមួយនិងព្រះដ៏
ជាអំម្ចាស់ស្សួរគ៌ ហើយព្រះបន្ទូលជាព្រះដ៏ជាអំម្ចាស់ស្សួរគ៌ ២កាលដើមដំបូង
ទ្រង់គង់ជាមួយនិងព្រះដ៏ជាអំម្ចាស់ស្សួរគ៌ ។ ៣របស់ទាំងអស់បានបង្កើតមកដោយពីទ្រង់
ហើយគ្មានរបស់អ្វីសោះកើតមកដែលជាមិនបានបង្កើតមកដោយពីទ្រង់នោះគ្មាន ។
៤ក្នុងព្រះបន្ទូលនោះមានជីវិត្រ ហើយជីវិត្រជាពន្លឺហ៍របស់មនុស្សលោក្យ ៥ពន្លឺហ៍
បំភ្លឺហ៍ក្នុងសេចក្ដីងងឹត តែសេចក្ដីងងឹតមិនបានទទួលពន្លឺហ៍ទេ ។
៦មានមនុស្សម្នាក់ឈ្មោះ យ៉ុន ដែលព្រះដ៏ជាអំម្ចាស់ស្សួរគ៌ចាត់ឲ្យមក ៧គាត់
បានមកសំរាប់ធ្វើជាទីបន្ទាល់ និងធ្វើជាបន្ទាល់ពីពន្លឺហ៍ ដើម្បីនិងឲ្យមនុស្សទាំងអស់
ជឿហ៍ដោយពីគាត់ ៨គាត់មិនមែនជាពន្លឺហ៍ តែគាត់លេចមកនិងធ្វើជាទីបន្ទាល់ពី
ពន្លឺហ៍ទេ

CATALAN

INTRODUCTION

Catalan belongs to the Italic family of Indo-European. As the southern member of the rich and vigorous Ibero-Gallic culture which included Provençal, Catalan shares both French and Spanish traits. At present, it is spoken by c. 6 million people (mostly bilingual) in the north-eastern coastal strip of Spain, stretching from Roussillon and Andorra (where it has official status, along with French) through Catalonia to Valencia and the Balearics. The standard literary language is based on the Barcelona dialect. In terms of literary output, Catalan is the most important minority language in Western Europe.

Writing in Catalan dates from the twelfth century. From the troubadour period – shared with Provençal – to the fifteenth century, Catalan literature held a leading place in Europe, and two writers of genius emerged: Ramón Llull, Neoplatonic visionary and philosopher, linguist, and apostle, whose *Ars Magna* offers a kind of universal conceptive calculus, in which Christian, Islamic, and Greek paradigms are convertible and expressible in terms of each other, and whose Catalan novel *Blanquerna* (c. 1284) contains the celebrated *Llibre d'amic e amat*; and Ausias March (1397–1459), the greatest poet in the Europe of his day.

From the sixteenth to the nineteenth centuries writing in Catalan virtually ceased to exist. The Catalan *renaixença* may be dated from the re-establishment of the Barcelona *Jocs Florals* in 1859, and the romantic poetry of Verdageur. A steady output of verse and prose continued until the outbreak of the Civil War, when Catalan culture was proscribed. Since the 1970s, recovery has been sustained with the help of the rich legacy of Catalan culture in exile.

The lexicon is remarkable for the large number of monosyllables of VC, CV, CVC type: e.g. *vi* 'wine', *ma* 'hand', *be* 'sheep'; *ull* 'eye; *dit* 'finger', *blat* 'wheat'.

SCRIPT

The Roman alphabet, plus certain diacritics: grave, acute, cedilla.

PHONOLOGY

Consonants

stops: p, b, t, d, k, g
affricates: tʃ, dʒ

fricatives: f, v, s, z
nasals: m, n, ɲ, ŋ
laterals and flap: l, ʎ, r
semi-vowels: w, j

[ß] is a positional variant of both /b/ and /v/. *c* has three values: /s/ before *e*, *i*; /k/ before *a*, *o*, *u*; /ɣ/ before a voiced consonant.

/tʃ/ is represented in the script by *tx* or *ig*: e.g. *puig* /putʃ/; *cotxe* /kɔtʃə/.

Vowels

i, e, ɛ, a, ə, ɔ, o, u

Reductionism is an important feature of the vowel system: unstressed /e, a/ → [ə], unstressed /o/ → [u]: e.g. *patata* [pətatə], 'potato'; *forçar* [fursa], 'force' (final *-r* drops). The acute accent is used to mark the closed /e, o/; the open values /ɛ, ɔ/ are marked by the grave. The diaeresis marks a labialized vowel after /k/ or /ɣ/: *qüestio* /k°əstio/; it also marks syllabic /i/ or /u/.

Diphthongs whose second component is /i/ or /u/ are treated as monosyllables: i.e. first component + semi-vowel /w/ or /j/.

Stress

Stress is normally on penultimate of vocalic final, or on final diphthong.

MORPHOLOGY AND SYNTAX

Noun

Nouns in Catalan are masculine or feminine. The associated articles are:

	Definite		*Indefinite*	
	Singular	*Plural*	*Singular*	*Plural*
masc.	el/l'	els	un	uns
fem.	la/l'	les	una	unes

Certain prepositions fuse with the masculine definite forms: e.g. *per* + *els* → *pels*.

The plural marker is *-s*: e.g. *un gat*, pl. *uns gats* 'cats'; *el dia*, pl. *els dies* 'days'. *-os* is used for words ending in a sibilant: e.g. *el peix* 'fish', pl. *els peixos*. Addition of the plural marker may involve some change in spelling: e.g. *taronja* 'orange', pl. *taronges*; *boca* 'mouth', pl. *boques*.

Adjective

As attribute, adjective follows noun as a rule, though many of the commonest adjectives precede, e.g. *bo/bona* 'good', *gran* 'big', and agrees with it in gender and number. A typical row is: *blanc – blanca – blancs – blanques* 'white'. A few adjectives vary in meaning according to whether they precede or follow the noun.

COMPARATIVE

The comparative is made with *més* preceding adjective followed by *que* 'than'.

Pronoun

PERSONAL

The independent personal forms are: sing. *jo*, *tu*, *el/ella*; pl. *nosaltres*, *vosaltres*, *els/elles*. A polite form of address, corresponding to the Spanish *Usted/-es*, is *Vostè/-s*.

The forms given above are also the strong object forms, with one exception: in the first person singular *mi* replaces *jo*. The strong object forms are always governed by prepositions.

The weak object forms for direct and indirect object can precede or follow the verb; e.g. in the first person singular *em* → *m'* precedes the verb; *-me* → *'m* follows, if the verb form is an infinitive, an imperative, or a gerund: e.g. *li va parlar* 'he spoke to him'; *li'l donarem* 'we shall give it (masc.) to him/her/you'; *quan em va dir* 'when he told me'; *ajuda'm* 'help me'.

Frequently, a strong form (or a noun) is copied by a weak form attached to the verb: e.g. *a vostè no l'havia vist* 'I hadn't seen you'.

Combined weak forms: the grid for all persons, and numbers yields over 200 combinations, with complex rules governing the use of full and reduced forms. The indirect precedes the direct object form: e.g. *me'l dona* 'he gives it to me'; *ha de portar-nos-els* 'he has to bring them to us'; *porta-li'ls* 'take them to him'.

POSSESSIVE ADJECTIVES

E.g., in first person, *el meu – la meva – els meus – les meves*, with weak forms: *mon – ma – mos – mes*.

DEMONSTRATIVE PRONOUN/ADJECTIVE

aquest/-a/-s/-es 'this, these'; *aquell/-a/-s/-es* 'that, those'.

INTERROGATIVE PRONOUN

qui 'who?'; *què* 'what?'; *quin/-a/-s/-es* 'what, which?'

RELATIVE PRONOUN

que (invariable) is used for both subject and object; in prepositional phrases *qui* refers to persons, *què* to things. The compound forms: *el/la qual*, pl. *els/les quals* can also be used: *sobre qui* = *sobre el/la qual* 'about whom'; *els nois, que ...* 'the boys who'.

Numerals

1–10: *un/una*, *dos/dues*; *tres*, *quatre*, *cinc*, *sis*, *set*, *vuit*, *nou*, *deu*; 11 *onze*; 12 *dotze*; 13 *tretze*; 20 *vint*; 30 *trenta*; 100 *cent*.

Verb

As in Spanish, three conjugations are distinguished: *-ar*, *-re*, *-ir*.

(a) *-ar*; this, the largest class of verbs, is fairly regular. As in Spanish, some adjustment in spelling has to be made where consonants with hard and soft values are concerned: e.g. *-c-* alternates with *-qu-*: *tanco* 'I close', *tan**ques***.
(b) *-re*: sub-divided into classes: -(C)C*re*, *-aure*, *-eure*, *-iure*, *-oure*; e.g. *prendre* 'take', *caure* 'fall', *creure* 'believe', *escriure* 'write', *moure* 'move'.
(c) *-ir*: certain verbs in this group add the increment *-eix-* between the stem and the endings: e.g. *llegir* 'read': *lleg**eix**o*.

Catalan has indicative, imperative, and subjunctive moods. The indicative mood has present, imperfect, preterite, and conditional simple tenses, plus compound tenses – perfect, pluperfect, etc. – and periphrastic tenses made with the verb *anar* 'to go'. The subjunctive mood has present, imperfect, preterite, perfect, and pluperfect forms, used, as in French and Spanish, wherever doubt, negation, possibility, apprehension, or emotion colour the utterance.

PERSONAL ENDINGS

E.g. regular verb in *-ar*, *parlar* 'to speak'.

present: sing.: *parl-o/-es/-a*; pl. *parl-em/-eu/-en*
imperfect: sing.: *parl-ava/-aves/-ava*; pl. *parl-àvem/-àveu/-aven*
preterite: sing.: *parl-í/-ares/-à*; pl. *parl-àrem/-àreu/-aren*
present subjunctive sing.: *parl-i/-is/-i*; pl. *parl-em/-eu/-in*.

The periphrastic tenses: the present tense of the verb *anar* 'to go': *vaig, vas, va*; *anem*, *aneu*, *van*. *Vaig*, etc. + infinitive expresses a preterite sense: e.g. *Vaig arribar la setmana passada* 'I arrived last week.' *Vaig*, etc. + *a* + infinitive, forms the future: e.g. *Vaig a buscar les maletes* 'I'm going to look for the cases.'

The verbs *ésser* and *estar* (corresponding in sense and usage to Spanish *ser* and *estar*) share the same past participle – *estat*. *Ésser* is used with the past participle of a sense verb to make a passive: e.g. *ha estat trobat* 'has been found'; pl. *han estat trobats*.

In compound tenses, the past participle (conjugated with *haver* 'to have') is invariable, unless a third person direct pronominal object is present. Yates gives the example:

Son boníssimes aquestes prunes; jo n'he menjad**a** una i aquest se n'ha menjad**es** dues o tres
'These plums are very good; I have eaten one, and he has eaten two or three.'

Prepositions

Several are composed of locative adverb + *de*: e.g. *dins/dintre de* 'in(side)'; *damunt de* 'above'; *sota de* 'below'.

Word order

SVO is normal.

1 En lo principi era lo Verb, y lo Verb era ab Deu, y lo Verb era Deu.

2 Ell era en lo principi ab Deu.

3 Per ell foren fetas totas las cosas, y sens ell ninguna cosa fou feta de lo que ha estat fet.

4 En ell era la vida, y la vida era la llum dels homes.

5 Y la llum resplandeix en las tenebras, y las tenebras no la comprengueren.

6 Hi hagué un home enviat de Deu ques anomenava Joan.

7 Est vingué *á servir* de testimoni pera testificar de la llum, á fi de que tots creguessen per medi d'ell.

8 No era ell la llum, sinó *enviat* pera donar testimoni de la llum.

CHINESE, CLASSICAL (Wenli)

INTRODUCTION

In a narrow sense, the term 'Classical Chinese' refers to the Chinese language and its literature from the sixth century BC to the third century AD; a period which includes the lives and works of Confucius, Mencius, Lao Tzu, Han Fei, Mo Tzu, and Chuang Tzu, to mention only the six philosopher–sages who were to have such a far-reaching effect on subsequent Chinese thought. In a broader sense, Classical Chinese begins with the *Shih Ching* ('Book of Odes'), which was compiled between the eleventh and sixth centuries BC, and which was in fact co-opted, during the central period, to form one of the 'Five Classics' (*wu jing*). The other four are:

I Jing ('Book of Changes');
Shu Jing ('Book of History');
Li Ji ('Book of Propriety');
Chun-Chiu ('Spring and Autumn Annals').

After the Burning of the Books by the Qin Emperor Shi Huang Di (213 BC), when most of this material was destroyed, the text of the Classics had to be arduously reconstructed. This took place in the early years of the Han Dynasty, whose espousal of Confucianism determined the lineaments of Chinese literature for many centuries to come. In the Confucian hegemony three factors were crucial: (1) the sacrosanctity of the classical texts; (2) the examination system based on these texts and their commentaries; (3) the supremacy of the literati who expounded the classics and set the examinations.

Outside the examination halls, a succession of poets – especially in the Tang and Sung Dynasties – some of them disreputable by Confucian standards, went on producing a lot of the world's most attractive poetry.

SCRIPT

The main source for the character inventory used in the central Classical period is the *Shuo Wen* ('explain character') dictionary of the Later Han Dynasty (published c. AD 100). Here, the characters are arranged under 540 radicals (reduced to 214 in the late Ming Dynasty). The main categories of the *Shuo Wen* classification are:

1. Simple characters, a few hundred in number, sub-divided into
   (a) pictographs: e.g.

   木 *mù* 'tree';

   山 *shān* 'mountain';

   門 *mén* 'gateway, door';

   (b) demonstratives: e.g.

   二 *èr* 'two',

   上 *shàng* 'above',

   下 *xià* 'below'.

2. Compound characters, sub-divided into (a) ideograms, (b) phonograms:
   (a) ideograms are made from two or more simple characters; e.g.

   坐 *zuò* 'to sit' is formed from

   人 *rén* 'man', reduplicated, placed over

   土 *tŭ* 'earth'.

   男 *nán* 'man', is made from

   田 *tián* 'field' + 力 *lì* 'power'.

   (b) phonograms – the most numerous class – are made from two elements: the radical fixing the character as belonging to this or that semantic group, and the phonetic which suggests the pronunciation. Example:

   聞 *wén* 'to hear':

   composed of radical

   耳 *ĕr* 'ear' + 門 *mén*.

   That is, the following information is given: the word has to do with hearing, and should rhyme with /men/.

PHONOLOGY

Reconstruction is, of course, hypothetical. The first guide to the actual pronunciation of Classical Chinese, the *Qieyun* Rhyming Dictionary, was not published until AD 601.

Consonants

Yaxontov (1965) gives the following inventory of permissible initials:

stops: p, ph, bh, t, d, th, dh, k, g, kh, gh, ʔ
affricates: ts, tʃ, dʒ
fricatives: s, ʃ, h, x
nasals: m, n, ŋ
lateral: l

The following initials were labialized: /k°, kh°, g°, gh°, n°, x°, ʔ°/. An initial consonant could be followed by *-l* and preceded by *s-* (sonants only): e.g. *bhlak* 'white' (Mod. Ch. *bai*); *smək* 'black'; *slän* 'mountain' (Mod. Ch. *shan*).

FINALS
The nasals; /p, t, k; r/.

Vowels

front: e, ɛ (+ a doubtful sound, represented here by /ɪ/)
back: ə, a, o, u

Tones

An even and a rising tone; words with /p, t, k/ ending had a specific tone, the nature of which is not clear.

MORPHOLOGY AND SYNTAX

A basic distinction is between 'full' words and 'empty' words. Pronouns count as empty words, as their exact meaning can be established only by context. The empty words – particles and pronouns – account for 25–30 per cent of all the words in a text of the central Classical period.

Given the total absence of any kind of inflection, and the polyvalent nature of Chinese words (a 'word' can be almost any part of speech in a proposition), word order is clearly of paramount importance: cf. *niǎo fēi* 'the bird flies'; *fēi niǎo* 'the flying bird'; *míng kě míng* ('name' – 'can' – 'name'; i.e. noun – modal verb – verb) in the first paragraph of the *Dao De Jing*, can be glossed as: *kě míng zhī míng* (modal verb – verb – relational particle – noun): 'the name that can be named'.

Pronoun

1st person: *yu* and *zhen* are exclusive; *wu* and *wo* are inclusive;
2nd person: *ru*, *ro*, *er*, *nai*;
3rd person: *qi*, *zhi*, *yan*; absence of a personal pronoun indicates 3rd person.

Choice of one or another pronoun seems to have depended on criteria which are no longer always clear. *Yu* and *zhen* are typically early Classical; *wu* and *wo* are associated with the later and post-Classical period.

Verb

The presence of paired verbs has been pointed out (e.g. Yaxontov 1965: 36) which are homonyms in Modern Chinese but which varied in pronunciation in the early Classical language due to the presence, in one member of the pair, of a causative or resultative formant. For example:

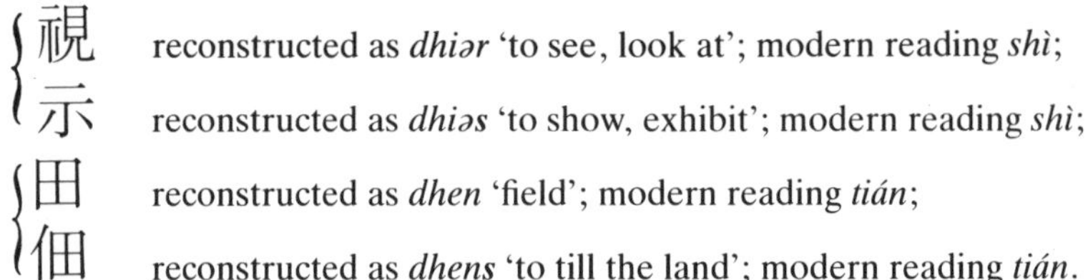

視 reconstructed as *dhiər* 'to see, look at'; modern reading *shì*;
示 reconstructed as *dhiəs* 'to show, exhibit'; modern reading *shì*;
田 reconstructed as *dhen* 'field'; modern reading *tián*;
佃 reconstructed as *dhens* 'to till the land'; modern reading *tián*.

This phenomenon has been taken as evidence for an early Chinese inflectional system which was in desuetude by the Han period.

TENSE MARKERS

Past, past anterior, future; for example, imminent future action or state may be signalled by *jiāng*: *Niǎo zhī jiāng sǐ, qí míng yě āi* 'When a bird is about to die, its song is sad' (*niǎo* 'bird', sǐ 'die', *qí* 'it(s)', *míng* 'song', *āi* 'mournful'). There are also perfective markers.

PASSIVE VOICE

May be marked by *jiàn* (modern meaning: 'to see'): e.g. *Pen-Cheng-Guo jiàn shá* 'Pen-Cheng-Guo being slain'; *Sùi sì shí ér jiàn è yān qi zhōng yě yǐ* 'If a man of forty is disliked, that is how he is going to end' (literally: 'year – four – ten – and – suffer – dislike – then – he – end – indeed – complete').

The passive may be marked by the modal auxiliary *yú*: e.g. *shā rén* 'killed men/a man'; *shā **yú** rén* 'was killed by men/a man'.

Other modal auxiliaries are: *neng* 'to be able', *gǎn* 'to dare': e.g. *Wú shuí gǎn yuàn?* 'Against whom dare I grumble?'

PARTICLES

These form the major sector of the

虛 詞 *xū.ci*,

the 'empty words', and they are of crucial importance in the Classical style. On an average, about a third of the characters in a *wenli* text are particles. They are sited throughout the discourse like signposts invested with three main functions.

1. Formally, they mark the onset, the suspension, and the conclusion of a proposition. In this role, they are not normally translatable.
2. They mark the proposition as negative, interrogative, or exclamatory; they intensify or limit its sense.

3. They have a large number of modal and prepositional (spatial and temporal) uses: concessive, causal, resultative, conditional, intentional, etc.

Some examples:

1. *fù* as initial particle:

 fù rén **zhě** jĭ yù lì **ér** lì rén
 'The man of virtue (*rén zhě*) wishing (*yu)* himself to be established (*li*), establishes others (*ren* 'other people')'

2. *ér* as limiting agent + *yĭ fū* as final exclamatory particle:

 zĭ yūe; jūn zĭ **ĕr** bù rén **zhě** you **yĭ fū**
 'The Master said: superior men (*jūn.zĭ*) who were not (*bù*) virtuous (*rén zhě*) there have been – and how!'

3. *ér* as concessive marker:

 zĭ yūe: pín **ér wú** yuàn nán
 'The Master said: to be poor (*pín*) and yet not (*wú*) grumble (*yuàn*) is hard (*nán*)'

Example of *zhī* as objective marker for referent known to audience:

 zhī **zhī** zhě bù rú haò **zhī** zhě
 'Those who know (*zhī*) it (= the Path) are not equal (*bù rú*) to those who love it'

cf. *Hŭ qiú bái shòu ér shí zhī* 'A tiger caught many animals and ate them' (*hŭ* 'tiger', *qiú* 'look for and catch', *bái* 'hundred', *shòu* 'wild animal(s)', *shí* 'eat').

The very important particle **yĭ** 以 has several meanings: e.g.

(a) by dint of, making use of: *yĭ mù zuò gōng* 'to use wood to make a bow' (*mù* 'tree, wood(en)', *zuò* 'make', *gōng* 'bow');
(b) to consider as: *yĭ guó shì wéi zhòng* 'to consider state affairs as being important' (*guó* 'country, state', *shì* 'affair(s)', *zhōng* 'important');
(c) in order to: *bŭ yĭ jué yí* 'divination (is used) in order to dispel doubt(s)' (*bŭ* 'to tell the future', 'soothsayer', *jué* 'to dispel', *yí* 'doubt(s)').

CHINESE, MODERN STANDARD

INTRODUCTION

Essentially, Modern Standard Chinese is the Northern (Beijing) form of Chinese, written in the Classical Chinese script with certain modifications (*see* **Script**, below).

During the Sung–Yuan Dynasties (twelfth to fourteenth centuries AD) *báihuà*, 'plain speech', a form of Chinese much closer to the spoken language than the *wenli* literary style, began to be used for literary purposes, e.g. in the prose passages in the Yuan drama (see, for example, the well-known *Dou E Yuan* by Guan Han-Ching). *Baihua* was also the vehicle for the prose narrative in the great Ming novels, e.g. Hong Lou Meng, the 'Dream of the Red Chamber', and Shui-hu Chuan, the 'Water Margin'.

After the fall of the Manchu Dynasty and the establishment of the Republic (1911), the movement for a national standardized language gathered momentum, accompanied by a parallel drive for the replacement of the Chinese script by some sort of phonetic alphabet. Both of these requirements were seen as indispensable first steps if universal education was ever to become a reality in China. A key part was played by the cultural revolution known as the 4 May Movement of 1919 and the implementation of the proposals for a national language first formulated by Hu Shih in the pages of the periodical *Xin Ching-nian* ('New Youth'). Finally, in 1949, *báihuà* now known as *pŭtōnghuà*, 'common language' was officially adopted as the national language of the Chinese People's Republic.

SCRIPT

For a note on the origins and nature of the Chinese written character *see* **Chinese, Classical**. Modern Standard Chinese uses the same character with the following modifications:

1. Many of the ten to twelve thousand characters in use have been 'abbreviated'; i.e. the number of strokes has been reduced, often considerably, e.g. from 16 to 5, from 19 to 9: e.g.

   爲 > 为 = (co-verb): *wèi* 'on behalf of';
   難 > 难 = *nán* 'difficult';
   禮 > 礼 = *lĭ* 'propriety, ceremony'.
2. The number of radicals has been reduced from 214 to 186. Many characters used in Classical Chinese have been discarded.

The officially adopted system of romanization is known as *pīnyīn*. The tones are indicated by diacritics: macron for level, acute for abrupt rising, inverted circumflex for low rising, grave for falling.

PHONOLOGY

Consonants

INITIALS

stops: p, b, t, d, k, g
affricates: tɕ, ts, tʂ
fricatives: f, ɕ, s, ʂ, ʐ, χ
nasals: m, n, ŋ
lateral: l
semi-vowels: j, w

Phonetically /b, d, g/ are *unvoiced* and non-aspirate; /p, t, k/ are strongly aspirated. All stops occur with labialization.
/tɕ, ts, tʂ/ are notated as *j*, *z*, *zh*, with aspirated correlatives notated as *q*, *c*, *ch*. /ɕ/ is notated as *x*, /ʂ/ as *sh*, /ʐ/ as *r*, and /χ/ as *h*.

FINALS
The vowels (see below), the nasals /n, ŋ/ following various combinations of vowels, and -/r/.

Vowels

i, ɪ, ε, ə, a, o, u, y; pinyin /i/ is [ɪ] after the retroflex sounds. /ə/ is notated as *e* or *u*: e.g. *men* /mən/, *dun* /d°ən/.

Tones

There are four tones in Modern Standard Chinese (1) high even; (2) rising, crescendo; (3) low dipping then rising; (4) falling from high level, diminuendo.

TONAL SANDHI
A tone 3 before another tone 3 changes to 2: e.g. *suó.yǐ* 'therefore', in citation form, both *suǒ* and *yǐ* are tone 3. Second components in disyllabic words are neutralized: e.g. *xièxiè̊* 'thank you'; *wǎnshång* 'evening'.

MORPHOLOGY AND SYNTAX

There is no inflection of any kind. Formally, there is nothing to distinguish any one part of speech from another. Meaning in a Chinese sentence depends on due logical order assisted by certain syntactic markers such as *ba* (indicating object), *de* (many functions; see below), *le* (past marker). Grammars of modern Chinese distinguish the following parts of speech: nouns, pronouns, numerals and measure words, transitive verbs, intransitive verbs, stative verbs, resultative verbs, auxiliary verbs and co-verbs, localizers, particles.

Nouns

May be monosyllabic: these include the oldest strata of the language: e.g. *mā* 'mother'; *mǎ* 'horse'; *chá* 'tea'; *rén* 'person'; *rì* 'sun'; *mù* 'tree'. Disyllabic: *xiān.shěng* 'first-born' = 'you' (in polite address); *dì.fǎng* 'place'; *Zhong.wen* 'Chinese language'; *péng.yǒu* 'friend'. Trisyllabic: *jiě.fàng.jūn* 'Army of Liberation'; *bàn.gōng.shì* 'office'. Polysyllabic: *bǎi.huò.shāng.diàn* 'department store' ('hundred-goods-business-place').

A pluralizing suffix *men* is available, but it is used only for pronouns and for groups; e.g. a speech may begin with the words *Tóng.zhì.**men** péng.you.**men*** 'Comrades and friends!' The suffix is not attached to singular nouns; i.e. *shū* 'book' or 'books'.

There are a couple of dozen classifiers for specific use with objects of various types and dimensions; they are bound forms, e.g. *běn*, *kuài*, *bēi*, etc.: *nèi liǎng běn shū* 'these two books'; *zhèi zhāng zhuōzi* 'this table'; *yí.kuài táng* 'a piece of candy'. *Ge* is an all-purpose classifier which can replace most of the others, unless the classifier is being used specifically without a referent: cf. *sì běn* 'four books' (the classifier identifies the referent as books).

Adjective

Adjectives in Chinese are stative verbs. If used attributively they precede the noun, often followed by *de*: e.g. *lì.shǐ duǎn* ***de*** *guó.jiā* 'a country with a short (*duǎn*) history (*lìshǐ*)'. The marker *de* is a ubiquitous and very important element in Modern Standard Chinese which has the following main functions:

1. marking attributive material, as in the above example: cf. *jīn.tián dě bào* 'today's paper';
2. to mark alienable possession: e.g. *wǒ.de shū* 'my book' (but *wǒ.**Ø** fù* 'my father');
3. hence, to form relative clauses preceding head-word: e.g. *wǒ.měn yǐ.jīng xué.guo.**de** cái.liǎo* 'the material we have already studied' (*xué* 'to study'; *guo* = perfective marker; *cái.liǎo* 'material');
4. after a stative verb if this is itself modified, e.g. by *hěn* 'very': cf. *shì hǎo péng.yǒu* 'is a good friend', but *hěn dà.**de** zhuōzi* 'a very big table'; *hěn hǎo.**de** jià.qiån* 'a very good price';
5. as loose referent: e.g. *wǒ mǎi.**de*** 'the things that I bought';
6. categorizing particle in final position: e.g. *wǒ shi zuò fēi.jī lái.**de*** 'it was by plane that I came' = 'I came by plane'.

Pronoun

PERSONAL

Sing. 1 *wǒ*, 2 *ní/nín*, 3 *tā*; plural: add *men* to sing.: *wǒ.měn*, etc. These forms function both as subject and as object: e.g. *tā gěi wǒ yi.běn shū* 'he gives me a book'.

DEMONSTRATIVE PRONOUN/ADJECTIVE, OR 'SPECIFIER'

zhèi 'this', *nà/nèi* 'that'. When these are used with nouns, classifiers are inserted between the specifier and the noun: e.g. *zhèi ge rén* 'this person'; *nèi wŭ bĕn shū* 'those five books'.

INTERROGATIVE PRONOUN
shúi 'who?'; *shen.me* /shəmmə/, 'what?'.

Numerals

1–10: *yi* (with movable tone), *èr*, *sān*, *sì*, *wŭ*, *liù*, *qī*, *bā*, *jiŭ*, *shí*; 12–19: *shí* + unit; 20 *èr.shí*; 100 *băi*; 1,000 *qiān*; 10,000 *wàn*.

Verb

Formally invariable; there are no tenses. Continuing or progressive action can be marked by *zhĕ*: e.g. *wŏ yuàn.yi̊ zhàn.zhe̊* 'I prefer to remain standing.' Impending action may be indicated by *jiù* (*yào*); the past by *gůo*: e.g. *Ní qŭ.**guo** Zhōng.guo.ma*? 'Have you ever been in China?' (*Zhong.guo* 'China'); *Wŏ méi qŭ.**guo*** 'I have never been there.'

PERFECTIVE ASPECT
le marks a change in a situation: e.g.

> Dōng.xi̊ guì.**le** 'Things (lit. 'east–west') have become expensive'
>
> Wŏ.men huì shuō Zhong.guo.huà **le** 'We can speak Chinese now' (*scil*. until now, we couldn't)
>
> Tā hē.**le** sān píng jiŭ 'He drank up three bottles of wine'
>
> Qì.chē pèng.zåi shù.shång **le** 'The car ran into a tree (*shù*)' (*qì.chē* 'car').

CO-VERBS
E.g. *zài* (locational), *yòng* (instrumental), *gĕi* (dative), *bă* ('to handle something, hold in the hands'), etc. These often have to be translated by prepositions in English: e.g. *zài fàn.guăn.r chī.fàn* 'to eat in a restaurant'; *yòng kùai.zi̊ chī.fàn* 'to eat with chopsticks'; *wŏ gĕi tā dă diàn.huà* 'I rang him'.

VERB + BOUND (LATENT) OBJECT
E.g. *kàn.shū* 'look at – book' → 'read'; *shuō.huà* 'say – word' → 'speak'; *chī.fàn* 'eat – rice' → 'eat'. These are separable: e.g. *tā kàn wan shū le* 'after he had finished reading ...'

STATIVE VERBS
E.g. *dà* 'to be big', *lĕng* 'to be cold': *Jīn.tiān zhēn lĕng* 'It's really cold today.'

COPULA
shì: often optional in positive, obligatory in negative: e.g. *wŏ* (*shì*) *Bĕijīng.rén* 'I am from Beijing'; neg. *wŏ **búshì** Bĕijīng.rén*.

DIRECTIONAL COMPLEMENTARY VERBS
lái 'to come', *qŭ* 'to go': e.g. *Tā yi̊.ji̊ng dă.diàn.huà.**lai**.le* 'He has already rung up (incoming call)'; *nèi.bĕn.shū ràng.tā măi.**qu**.le* lit. 'that-book – by-him – bought-went' = 'he bought the book and went off'.

POTENTIAL INFIX

de/*bu*: e.g. *kàn.**de**.jiàn* 'able to see'; *gǎn.**bu**.shàng* 'unable to overtake'.

NEGATION

The general marker is *bu*; the verb *yǒu* 'to have' is always negated by *méi*, never by *bu*: e.g. *Gào.sů tā méi.yǒu yòng.chů* 'It's no use telling him.'

PASSIVE

There are various markers, *bèi*, *ràng*, *jiào*, *gěi*: e.g. *tā bèi chéng.fá.le yǐ.hòu* 'after he had been punished' (*chéng.fá* 'punish'; *yǐ.hòu* 'after').

MODAL VERBS

E.g. *yīng.gāi* = *bì.děi* 'have to', *huì* 'can', *xiǎng* 'want to', etc.: e.g. *wǒ.men yīng.gāi*/*bì.děi yóng.yǔan jì.dě* ... 'we must always remember ...'

Four-character expressions

The Chinese have always been very fond of using set phrases consisting of four characters. These lapidary sayings were, and are, particularly popular as birthday and festive greetings, congratulations, etc.: e.g.

蟠桃集慶

pán.táo jí.qìng, which may be translated as 'long life and happiness galore'; *pán.táo* is a reference to the peach-tree which grew by the *yáo.chí*, the Lake of Gems, in the Kunlun palace of the Queen Mother of the West. The fruit of the tree conferred immortality.

The socio-linguistic domain of a later and more mundane age is also punctuated by this persistent rhythm. Thus, in the 1960s, the vigilant proletarian had to eschew *sān xiáng yī miè* 'three capitulations and one cut-off', observe *sì hǎo lián.duì* the 'four goods', and the *sān.bā tzuò.fēng* the 'three-eight working style', and keep his eye open for *yāo.mó gǔi.guài* 'monsters and freaks' and *niú.gǔi shé.chén* 'ox-demons and supernatural snakes', i.e. people of anti-Mao persuasion.

Word order

ba: although Chinese is essentially a SVO language, SOV is not at all uncommon. The co-verb *bǎ* provides a way of marking the object in inverted order: e.g. *wǒ **bǎ** qì.chē mǎi.**le*** 'I bought the car'.

生命之道

1 宇宙被造以前，道已經存在；道與上帝同在，與
上帝相同。2 在太初，道就與上帝同在。3 上帝
藉着他創造萬有；在整個創造中，沒有一樣不是藉着他
造的。4 道就是生命的根源，這生命把光賜給人類。
5 光照射黑暗，黑暗從來沒有勝過光。
6 有一個人，名叫約翰，是上帝所差遣的使者。7 他
來告訴人關於那光的事，目的要使大家聽見他的信息而
相信。8 他本身不是那光，而是要爲光作證。

Guóyǔ

約翰福音傳

第一章 一元始有道、道與上帝共在、道卽上帝、二是道元始與上帝共在也、三萬物以道而造、凡受造者、無
不以之而造、四生在道中、生也者人之光、五光照於暗、暗者弗識之〇六有上帝所遣者名約翰、七其至爲光
作證、使衆以之而信、八約翰非光、特爲光證耳、九眞光者臨世照萬人者也、

Wenli

CZECH

INTRODUCTION

This Western Slavonic language is the official language of the Czech Republic, spoken by around 10 million people. Czech and Slovak are mutually intelligible. Writing in Czech dates from the thirteenth to fourteenth centuries. Historically, Czech culture and literature are orientated towards Western Europe, rather than towards Moscow and the Orthodox Church. The first flowering of Czech literature was in the reign of Charles IV (fourteenth century), with Jan Hus playing a notable role in the formation of a standardized literary language. The suppression of Czech culture, associated with the Counter-Reformation, lasted until the late eighteenth century, when contact with Western sources was re-established, and a romantic renaissance ensued. This period culminated in the abortive revolution of 1848. From the late nineteenth century to the outbreak of the Second World War, Czech was the vehicle for a very rich and extensive literature in all genres, especially poetry (e.g. Vrchlický, Bezruč, Březina) and the novel (Holeček, Hašek, Čapek).

SCRIPT

Romanization plus diacritics. The orthography was rationalized, first by Jan Hus in the fourteenth century, subsequently by the Czech Brethren in their sixteenth-century translation of the Bible.

The palatalized consonants /t′, d′/ are marked by apostrophe: e.g. *ted′* 'now', *zed′* 'wall'. /t/ and /d/ are palatalized before /i/ and /je/; the latter is then written as *ě*. The palatal n /ɲ/ is notated as *ň*.

PHONOLOGY

Consonants

stops: p, b, t, d, k, g, + palatalized t′, d′
affricates: ts, tʃ
fricatives: f, v, s, z, ʃ, ʒ, j, h, x
nasals: m, n, ɲ
lateral: l
trill: r, ɼ (notated as *ř*).

/g/ occurs in foreign words only; in native words, Slavonic /g/ is represented by /h/; e.g. Russian *golub*(*ka*) = Czech *holub*. The liquids /r, l/, are syllabic: e.g. *prst* 'finger', *vlk* 'wolf'. A softened glottal stop or hamza separates vowels in final–initial contact, and in words like *naučit* 'to teach', where *-au-* is not a diphthong: *na.učit*.

Voiced consonants in final position are unvoiced: e.g. *chleb* 'bread', [xlε̄p]. Assimilation of unvoiced to voiced: e.g. *kdo* 'who?' [gdɔ]; *svatba* 'wedding' [sva**d**ba]. *Mě* is pronounced /mɲε/: e.g. *město* 'city' [mɲεstɔ].

Vowels

short: a, ε, ɪ, ɔ, u
long: aː, εː, iː, uː

Long /oː/ occurs in foreign words only. /uː/ is notated as *ů*. Diphthongs: /ou/ is native, e.g. *klobouk* 'hat'; /au, eu/ occur in loan-words.

In the thirteenth/fourteenth centuries vowel mutation after soft consonants (broadly, back/low vowels were raised to front/high) gave Czech its characteristic and very distinctive sound. Thus, *žena* 'woman', *duše* 'soul', with instrumental singular *ženou*, *duší*. Similarly, *nesu* 'I carry', but *píši* 'I write' (literary form).

Stress

Stress is invariably on the first syllable.

MORPHOLOGY AND SYNTAX

Noun

Three genders, two numbers. The original six declensions (*see* **Slavonic Languages**) are preserved in Czech:

-i/-ja feminine stems: e.g. *kost* 'bone';
-a/-ja stems: e.g. *žena* 'woman', *duše* 'soul';
-o/-jo masculine stems: e.g. *muž* 'man';
-o/-jo neuter stems: e.g. *místo* 'place', *moře* 'sea';
-ū stems: e.g. *církev* 'church' (feminine);
consonantal stems (masculine and neuter): e.g. *kámen* 'stone'.

There are seven cases including a vocative. Differentiation due to phonetic constraints is very considerable; some grammars give over 250 paradigms. There follow specimen declensions of a masculine noun – *muž* 'man' – and a feminine – *žena* 'woman':

	Singular	*Plural*	*Singular*	*Plural*
nom.	muž	muži	žena	ženy
gen.	muže	mužů	ženy	žen
dat.	muži/ovi	mužům	ženě	ženám
acc.	muže	muže	ženu	ženy

instr.	mužem	muži	ženou	ženami
loc.	muži	mužích	ženě	ženách
voc.	muži	—	ženo	—

Nominative, accusative forms for animate masculine nouns differ in singular and plural from those for inanimates.

POSSESSION

Possessor follows possessed: e.g. *mapa světa* 'a map of the world'. There are no articles.

Adjective

As attribute, adjective precedes noun, and is in full concord with it for all cases, preserving animate/inanimate distinction. Hard adjectives show gender in the nominative ending: *-ý*, *-á*, *-é*. Soft adjectives have *-í* in all three. Examples: *nový dům* (masc.) 'new house'; *stará žena* (fem.) 'old woman'; *nové divadlo* (nt.) 'new theatre'; *moderní hotel, divadlo, budova* 'modern hotel, theatre, building'.

As predicate, adjective shows concord: cf. *nový dům – dům je nový*; *nové divadlo – divadlo je nové*.

POSSESSIVE ADJECTIVES

Those based on nouns denoting males and male names: *-ův*, *-ova*, *-ovo*; females: *-in*, *-ina*, *-ino*: e.g. from *bratr*: *bratrův pokoj* 'the brother's room'; from *sestra*: *sestřin pokoj* 'the sister's room'. Compare *Karlův most* 'the Charles Bridge'; *Karlova Universita* 'the Charles University'.

COMPARATIVE

In -(*ej*)*ší*: e.g. *bohatý* 'rich' – *bohatší*; *důležitý* e.g. 'important' – *důležitější*. There are the usual suppletives: e.g. *dobrý* 'good' – *lepší*; *špatný* 'bad' – *horší*.

Pronoun

The nominative (= subject) forms are:

sing. 1 *ja*, 2 *ty*, 3 *on/ona/ono*; pl. 1 *my*, 2 *vy*, 3 *oni*

These forms are used for emphasis and contrast only. They are declined in all cases, and have weak and strong forms; e.g. for first person singular, acc./gen. *mě*, dat. *mi/mně*, instr. *mnou*.

The possessive adjectives are marked for gender in the singular, partially in plural:

sing. 1 *můj/má/mé*, 2 *tvůj/tvá/tvé*, 3 *jeho/její*; pl. 1 *náš/naše*, 2 *váš/vaše*

The third person plural form *jejich* is not marked.

DEMONSTRATIVE PRONOUN/ADJECTIVE

ten – ta – to 'this'; pl. *ti*; *tamten – tamta – tamto* 'that'. *-hle* may be added: e.g. *Líbí se mi tenhle klobouk* 'I like this hat.'

INTERROGATIVE PRONOUN
kdo 'who?'; *co* 'what?' These are declined.

RELATIVE PRONOUN
který/která/které 'which, that': e.g. *kniha, která leží na stole* 'the book which is lying on the table'. Replaced in colloquial by *co*. The literary form is *jenž* (masc.), *jež* (fem. and nt.): e.g. *cíl, jenž stojí před námi* 'the aim which lies before us'.

Numerals

1 *jeden/jedna/jedno*; 2 *dva/dvě*; 3 *tři*; 4 *čtyři*. These are declined in all cases. From 5 onwards, all oblique cases are in *-i*: 5–10 *pět*, *šest*, *sedm*, *osm*, *devět*, *deset*. 11 *jedenáct*; 12 *dvanáct*; 13 *třináct*; 20 *dvacet*; 30 *třicet*; 40 *čtyřicet*; 100 *sto*.

Verb

Taking the third person singular as criterion, we may classify Czech verbs into three groups:

(a) *-e*: e.g. *píše* 'he writes' (infinitive: *psát*);
(b) *-á*: e.g. *dělá* 'he does' (infinitive: *dělat*);
(c) *-í*: e.g. *mluví* 'he speaks' (infinitive: *mluvit*).

The *-e* groups can be further sub-divided to include *-n-* and *-uj-* stems: e.g. *tiskne* 'he presses' (infinitive: *tisknout*); *kupuje* 'he buys' (infinitive: *kupovat*).

The past or *-l* form:

-e verbs take *-l*, *-nul*, or *-oval*;
-á verbs take *-al*;
-í verbs take *-il* or *-el*.

ASPECT
As in other Slavonic languages, paired verbs. Perfective formed:

(a) by prefix: e.g. *platit* 'to pay': perf. ***za**platit*; *prosit* 'to ask': perf. ***po**prosit*; *končit* 'to finish': perf. ***s**končit*; *ptát se* 'to ask' perf. ***z**eptat se*.
(b) prefix + stem change: *odnášet* 'take away' perf. *odnést*; *přinášet* 'bring' perf. *přinést*.
(c) suppletive: *brát* 'to take': *vzít*.

Imperfectives may be formed from verbs which are inherently perfective: e.g. *padat* 'to fall': *pad**nou**t*; *dát* 'to give': *dá**va**t*.

Example of tense/aspect structure: *psát* 'to write':

	Past	*Present*	*Future*
imperfective:	psal jsem	píši (coll. píšu)	budu psát
perfective:	**na**psal jsem	**Ø**	**na**píši/u

TENSE

Specimen present tense of a *-a* verb: *dělat* 'to do': imperfective:

	Singular	*Plural*
1	dělám	děláme
2	děláš	děláte
3	dělá	dělají

Past tense or *-l* form: the auxiliary verb is not used in the third person. The *-l* form is marked for gender and number:

	Singular	*Plural*
1	čekal/-a jsem 'I waited'	čekali/-y jsme
2	čekal/-a jsi	čekali/-y jste
3	čekal/-a Ø	čekali/-y Ø

FUTURE

Future tense of auxiliary *být* = *budu* + infinitive: e.g. *budu psát* 'I shall write'. This is always imperfective. The present *form* of the perfective aspect has a future meaning: e.g. ***napíšu*** 'I shall write' (= have written).

IMPERATIVE

Both aspects have imperative mood: e.g. *Čtěte!* 'Read!' (imperfective); ***Přečtěte*** *cely text!* 'Read the whole text!' (perfective).

PASSIVE

(a) with *se*; this is associated with the change of transitive to intransitive: *Lidská práce mění krajinu* 'Human labour changes the countryside'; *Celá krajina* ***se*** *mění* 'The whole countryside is changing.'
(b) with auxiliary *být* + truncated verbal adjective: e.g. *Byl jsem vyšetřován lékařem* 'I was examined by the doctor.'

CONDITIONAL

Provided by aux. sing. *bych*, *bys*, *by*: pl. *bychom*, *byste*, *by* + *-l* form: e.g. with *rád* 'gladly': *rád bych věděl* 'I should like to know'; *rádi bychom věděli* 'we should like to know'.

PARTICIPLES

(a) present in *-cí* added to third person plural of imperfective present: e.g. *dělají*: *dělající*. The form is declined as an adjective.
(b) past active participle: *-(v)ší* replaces *-l* of perfective past; declined as adjective: e.g. *udělavší* 'having done, who has done'.
(c) past passive participle = verbal noun: *-ní/tí*: e.g. *dělání* 'doing'; *bytí* 'being'.

Negation

The general negating particle is *ne*, prefixed to verb: e.g. *nic neslyším* 'I hear nothing' (i.e. double negative).

Prepositions

Prepositions govern nouns in the accusative, genitive, dative, locative or instrumental cases. Some, e.g. *na* 'on/in/at', *pod* 'under', *před* 'in front of', take locative or instrumental for rest in a place and the accusative for motion towards, along, etc. e.g. *jsem na poště* 'I am in the post-office'; but *jdu na poštu* 'I go to the post-office'.

Word order

SVO is basic. Subject usually omitted if pronoun. Almost all permutations of word order are possible.

Na počátku bylo Slo-
vo, a to Slovo bylo u
Boha, a to Slovo byl
Bůh.
2 To bylo na počátku u
Boha.
3 Všecky věci skrze ně
učiněny jsou, a bez něho
nic není učiněno, což u-
činěno jest.
4 V něm život byl, a
život byl světlo lidí.
5 A to světlo v tem-
nostech svítí, ale tem-
nosti ho neobsáhly.
6 Byl člověk poslaný od
Boha, jemuž jméno *bylo*
Jan.
7 Ten přišel na svědec-
tví, aby svědčil o tom
světle, aby všickni uvě-
řili skrze něho.
8 Nebyl on to světlo,
ale *přišel*, aby svědčil o
tom světle.

DANISH

INTRODUCTION

Danish belongs to the Scandinavian branch of Germanic family. It is the official language of the Kingdom of Denmark, where it is spoken by over 5 million people, and joint official language of the Faeroe Islands and of Greenland. For Dano-Norwegian *see* **Norwegian**.

Writing in Danish dates from about the thirteenth century. The medieval literature is notable for its rich stock of ballads. The Bible was translated into Danish in the Reformation period. An outstanding figure of the Enlightenment was Holberg, whose influence on subsequent Danish writing was fundamental. The early nineteenth century produced one writer of world stature – Søren Kierkegaard. The modern period was inaugurated by the celebrated lectures given by Georg Brandes in the period 1870–90, the impact of which was as much socio-political as cultural (*det moderne Gennembrud* – 'the modern Renaissance'). Outstanding twentieth-century writers include Kjeld Abell, Kaj Munk and Martin Nexø.

SCRIPT

Roman alphabet, 26 letters as in English, + *æ*, *å*, *ø*.

PHONOLOGY

Consonants

stops: p, b, t, d, k, g, ʔ
fricatives: f, v, s, ʃ, h, ð, γ, j
nasals: m, n, ŋ
lateral: l
uvular trill: ʀ

All consonants are short.

The correspondence between sound and symbol in Danish is weak. *p*, *t*, *k* are aspirate /p, t, k/ only as initials. Elsewhere, *p*, *t*, *k* and *b*, *d*, *g*, tend to fuse as unaspirated /b, d, g/. Thus *lække* 'leak' and *lægge* 'lay' are both pronounced as /lεgə/; cf. in the dental series, *sist* 'last', /sisd/. /g/ is regularly elided in certain environments: cf. *nogen* 'some', /nɔ̄n/, *spørge* 'ask', /sbœrə/, *spøg* 'joke', /sbɔiʔ/, *meget* 'much', /maiəð/.

Vowels

front: i, e, ɛ, y, ø, œ
central: a
back: ɔ, o, u
neutral: ə

DIPHTHONGS
Eight glides to /u/, two to /i/.

Tone

The *stød* (glottal stop) corresponds in Danish to the acute tone in Swedish and Norwegian. The *stød* has phonemic force, as minimal pairs are thus distinguished: cf. *hund* 'dog', /hunˀ/ and *hun* 'she', /hun/.

Stress

Normally on first syllable of root word.

MORPHOLOGY AND SYNTAX

Noun

GENDER
Danish has two genders: common and neuter. The definite article is *-en* for common nouns, *-et* for neuter; *-ene* forms the plural of both genders. If, however, an attributive adjective is present, the suffixed article is dropped, and the demonstratives *den*, *det*, *de* are used instead: e.g. *hus* 'house'; *huset* 'the house'; *det store hus* 'the big house'.

NUMBER
Three possible endings: *-e*, *-(e)r*, Ø. These may be accompanied by umlaut and gemination of the final consonant: e.g. *broder* 'brother' – *brødre*; *tand* 'tooth' – *tænder*; *fod* 'foot' – *fødder*.

CASE
Only the genitive has a specific marker: *-s*. Other cases are made as in English with the help of prepositions.

Adjective

Adjective precedes noun as attribute, and takes *-t* before a neuter singular: e.g. *et godt hus* 'a good house'. For adjective with definite noun, see above.

COMPARATIVE
In *-(e)re*, with suppletive formations as in other Germanic languages: e.g. *gammal* 'old' – *ældre*; *ond* 'bad' – *værre*, etc.

Pronoun

PERSONAL

The first and second nominative forms are: *jeg*, *du*; pl. *vi*, *I*. These have objective forms: *mig*, *dig*, *os*, *der*. The third person distinguishes gender in the singular: *han*, *hun*, *den* 'he, she, it', with corresponding objective forms *ham*, *hende*, *den*. The plural is *De*, *Dem*. *De/Dem* is also the polite second person form, singular and plural.

POSSESSIVE PRONOUNS

First person *min*, *mit*, *mine*, second person *din*, *dit*, *dine*, and first person plural *vor*, *vort*, *vore*; these show concord with the object possessed. The third person forms: *hans*, *hendes*, *dens/dets* are invariable (concord, that is, with subject, not object). Similarly, the second and third person plural forms, *jeres*, *deres*, are invariable. On the analogy of *deres*, the form *vores* is replacing *vor*, *vort*, *vore*.

INTERROGATIVE PRONOUN

hvem 'who?', *hvad* 'what?'

RELATIVE PRONOUN

The interrogatives *hvem*, *hvad*, and related forms, e.g. *hvis* 'whose', are used in literary Danish, and partly in colloquial, e.g. for genitive: *Hr. Hansen, hvis broder rejser omkring i Danmark* 'Mr Hansen whose brother is travelling in Denmark'. *Som* and *der* are much used in the spoken language: *mennesker, der kan tale dansk* 'people who can speak Danish'.

Numerals

1–10: *en*, *to*, *tre*, *fire*, *fem*, *seks*, *syv*, *otte* (/-d-/), *ni*, *ti*; 11 *elleve*; 12 *tolv*; 13 *tretten*; 20 *tyve*; 30 *tredive*; 40 *fyrre*; 50 *halvtreds*; 60 *tres*; 70 *halvfjerds*; 80 *firs*; 90 *halvfems*; 100 *hundrede*.

Verb

Transitive/intransitive, weak and strong. There are active and passive voices, indicative and imperative moods, with some vestiges of a subjunctive.

NON-FINITE FORMS

Infinitive, present and past participles. The present tense for all verbs is made by adding *-r* to the infinitive in *-e*: e.g. *jeg kommer* 'I come'. There is no inflection for person or number.

The weak/strong dichotomy affects the preterite: the weak ending is *-te/-ede*, and there may be accompanying umlaut in the root: e.g. *følge* 'to follow': pres., *jeg følger*, pret. *jeg fulgte*, /fuld/.

Strong verbs have 2- or 3-stage ablaut (including past participle): e.g. *jeg drikker* 'I drink', *jeg drak* 'I drank', *jeg har drukket* 'I have drunk'; *jeg giver* 'I give'; *jeg gav* 'I gave', *jeg har givet* 'I have given'. The ablaut sequence is often close to that in English. Cf. *drikker – drak – drukket*/dregər – drag – drogəð/ 'drink'.

PASSIVE

Two forms: *at blive* 'to become' + past participle, or *-s* added to infinitive: e.g. *han blev født 1805* 'he was born in 1805'; *huset ejes af Hr. H.* 'the house is owned by Mr H'.

IMPERATIVE

= stem; polite forms can be made by means of auxiliaries.

PARTICIPLES

Present in *-ende* /ənə/; past in -(*e*)*t*. The past participle can take *-en* to agree with a common gender correlative, but the modern tendency is to avoid inflection here, and to use the -(*e*)*t* form for both genders and both numbers.

MODAL AUXILIARIES

E.g. *få*, *ville*, *måtte*, *gøre*, *skal*, etc. are used in many ways, including formation of a periphrastic future: e.g. *jeg skal komme i morgen* 'I shall come tomorrow'.

Negation

The general negating adverb is *ikke*.

Prepositions

As in English, these may be detached from the object, and take final position in the sentence: e.g. *hvad ser du på* 'what are you looking at?'

Word formation

As in German, by prefixation, suffixation, and compounding.

Word order

SVO is normal, OVS is possible, e.g. for emphasis.

I Begyndelsen var Ordet, og Ordet var
hos Gud, og Ordet var Gud.
2 Dette var i Begyndelsen hos Gud.
3 Alt er blevet til ved det, og uden det
blev intet til af det, som er.
4 I det var Liv, og Livet var Menne-
skenes Lys.
5 Og Lyset skinner i Mørket, og Mørket
fik ikke Bugt med det[1].
6 Der fremstod et Menneske, udsendt
fra Gud; hans Navn var Johannes.
7 Han kom til et Vidnesbyrd for at vidne
om Lyset, for at alle skulde komme til
Tro ved ham.
8 Selv var han ikke Lyset, men han
skulde vidne om Lyset.

DRAVIDIAN LANGUAGES

INTRODUCTION

The Dravidian stock seems to have arrived in north-west India in the fifth or fourth millennium BC. Its exact provenance is not clear. A hither/central Asian origin for the language type, if not for its present bearers, finds some support in the thesis, first advanced by Caldwell in the middle of the nineteenth century, of a lexical and morphological relationship between the Dravidian and the Uralic language families. Comparison (e.g. by Burrow 1944) of certain semantic fields seems to place a lexical relationship of some kind beyond reasonable doubt; and there are structural parallels in the tense markers, the formation of the plural, the pronominal system, and the negative conjugation. Material so far deciphered at the Mohenjo-Daro and Harappa sites also suggests a connection with Dravidian.

As regards contact between Dravidian and Indo-Aryan, it seems clear that the present polarization, with Indo-Aryan in the north and Dravidian in the south of India, is of comparatively recent date. Throughout the third and second millennia BC the two families probably coexisted in the north of India, with Dravidian gradually losing ground to Indo-Aryan. There are Dravidian words in the *Rig-Veda*, and Dravidian influence is seen in such Indo-Aryan features as the development of the retroflex series, and, later, the gradual replacement of prepositions in New Indo-Aryan by postpositions.

The process was not all one-way; the major Dravidian languages are full of Sanskrit words, and, on another front, certain features of the Dravidian outlier Brahui have been attributed to contact with its Indo-Aryan neighbour Baluchi. Andronov and Emeneau have treated parallel typological features of New Indo-Aryan and Dravidian, and their mutual interaction, as evidence of the emergence of an areal 'Indian' language type, covering New Indo-Aryan, Dravidian, and Munda.

Andronov (1965) groups the Dravidian languages as follows:

	Group	*Number of speakers* (est.)	*Location*
I	Southern		
	Tamil	55 million	Tamilnad, Sri Lanka, E and S Africa, SE Asia
	Kannada	26 million	Karnataka
	Malayalam	25 million	Kerala
	Kota	a few hundred	Kotagiri Mountains
	Toda	100,000	Nilgiri area

	Kodagu	80,000	Mercara area
II	South-eastern		
	Telugu	60 million	Andhra Pradesh, Tamilnad
III	South-western		
	Tulu	1 million	Mangalore
IV	Central		
	Kolami Naiki Parji Godaba	150,000 (Parji, 85,000)	border regions of Andhra Pradesh, Madhya Pradesh, and Maharastra
V	Gondwana group		
	Gondi	1½ million	border regions of Andhra Pradesh, Madhya Pradesh, and Maharastra
	Kui Kuvi	680,000	Orissa
VI	North-eastern		
	Kurukh	1 million	Chhota Nagpur
	Malto	100,000	Rajmahal Hills
VII	North-western		
	Brahui	400,000	Baluchistan

Andronov (1965) gives the following time-scale for separation stages:

4000 BC: separation of Proto-Brahui
3500 BC: separation of Kurukh, Malto
2500 BC: formation of Gondwana group
1500–1100 BC: separation of Central group
1100–900 BC: separation of Telugu
mid first millenniun: separation of Tulu
turn of millennium: separation of Kannada from Tamil
AD 1000–1300: separation of Malayalam from Tamil

PHONOLOGY

In initial and medial position, Dravidian phonemes are remarkably stable over the entire domain, both diachronically and synchronically. Thus, Proto-Dravidian /t-/ is everywhere reflected as /t-/, and /p-/ very largely as /p-/. The same goes for alveolar /l̠/ and /r̠/: these are characteristically Dravidian phonemes.

Typologically, the Dravidian languages are agglutinative; there is a basic dichotomy into (a) human/rational and (b) non-human/non-rational. Gender distinction appears in the southern and south-eastern languages.

Typically, there are two basic cases, direct and oblique. Further case affixes are attached to the oblique form. The first person plural distinguishes inclusive and exclusive forms. A particularly interesting feature is the Uralic type of negative conjugation.

See **Tamil, Telugu, Kannada, Malayalam**

DUTCH

INTRODUCTION

The official name of this West Germanic language is *Nederlands*. It is the official language of the Kingdom of the Netherlands, and joint official language (with French) of Belgium. There are over 14 million speakers in the Netherlands, and about 5 million in Belgium. Dutch is also the language of administration in Surinam and in the Dutch Antilles.

In the period of Germanic tribal expansion (third century AD onwards) the southern regions of what is now the Netherlands were colonized by Frankish tribes, and it was here that Old Dutch first crystallized. The transition from Middle Dutch to Modern Dutch coincided with the transfer of economic and political power to northern Holland, and the accompanying cultural polarization. It is northern (Amsterdam) usage that underlies the modern literary standard, though Brabant influence is not absent. There is a marked difference between the literary standard and the colloquials.

Writing in Old Dutch begins in the tenth century. In the subsequent history of Dutch literature three main periods may be distinguished: (a) the radiant and lyrical mysticism of fourteenth-century visionaries like Heinric van Ruysbroeck; (b) the seventeenth-century 'Golden Age'; and (c) the modern period from the mid-nineteenth century onwards: particularly rich in the social novel and in experimental verse. The novelists Multatuli, Couperus, and Schendel are outstanding. The literary monthly *De nieuwe gids* (1885 onwards) should be mentioned, as it played a seminal role in the development of Dutch culture.

SCRIPT

Roman alphabet. The standardized orthography of 1863 was revised and simplified in 1947.

PHONOLOGY

Consonants

stops: p, b, t, d, k
fricatives: f, v, s, z, x, γ, j, h
nasals: m, n, ŋ
lateral: l
uvular flap: ʀ
semi-vowel: ʋ

/tj/ tends towards retroflex [ʈ].

Vowels

front: i, e, ɛ, ɪ, œ, y
middle: ɵ, a, ə
back: ɑ, ɔ, o, u

There are eight diphthongs, which are glides to /i/ or /u/.

There is assimilation, both regressive and progressive, at junctures: e.g. *afbellen* [a**v**bɛllə(n)] 'ring off'; *opvouwen* [op**f**ɔʊə(n)] 'fold up'.

Voiced finals are unvoiced: (*ik*) *heb* → [hɛ**p**]; *hond* → [hən**t**].

/f, s/ → /v, z/ in formation of plural, and so written: *brief* 'letter' – *brieven*; *huis* 'house' – *huizen*.

Final *-n* tends to be elided: *ziekenhuis* 'hospital' → [zikəhəys].

Intrusive /ə/: e.g. *arm* /arəm/.

Stress

Normally on first syllable, disregarding weak prefixes. In compounds, stress is not always predictable.

MORPHOLOGY AND SYNTAX

Noun

Nouns are divided into those of common gender, with singular definite article in *de*, and neuters with singular definite article *het*. For both genders the plural definite article is *de*, the singular indefinite article is *een*: e.g. *de kamer* 'the room'; *het paard* 'the horse'.

The plural marker is *-en* or *-s*: e.g. *de vrouw* 'the woman', pl. *de vrouwen*; *de prijs* 'the price', pl. *de prijzen*; *de zoon* 'the son', pl. *de zoons*.
Since final *-n* is not pronounced, the opposition between singular and plural in the case of the *-en* ending is Ø/*ə*.

Adjective

The attributive adjective precedes the noun and takes *-e* for common-gender nouns: e.g. *een goede man* 'a good man'; but, *een goed boek*. The predicative adjective is not inflected.

COMPARATIVE
In *-er*, superlative in *-st*. Suppletive sets parallel to those in German and English occur: e.g. *goed – beter – best*; *veel – meer – meest*.

Pronouns

PERSONAL

For each of the six personal rows (3 singular, 3 plural) there are full and reduced subject forms, full and reduced object forms. Thus:

1st sing.	ik	'k	mij	me
3rd sing.	hij	-ie	hem	'm
	zij	ze	haar	'r

In the second person there is a choice between familiar forms: *jij*, pl. *jullie* and more formal address: *u*.

POSSESSIVE

The possessive forms are:

	Singular	*Plural*
1	mijn	ons/onze
2	jouw, je uw	**van** jullie (dat van jullie)
3	zijn haar	hun

Note: colloquial usage: *mijn broer* ***z'n*** *auto = de auto van mijn broer.*

DEMONSTRATIVE

deze, *dit* 'this', pl. *deze*; *die*, *dat* 'that', pl. *die*.

INTERROGATIVE

wie 'who?', *wat* 'what?'

RELATIVE

die with reference to common gender; *dat* with reference to neuter: e.g.

... in het decadente Haagse milieu **dat** deze schrijver kende als geen ander
'... in the decadent Hague milieu which this writer knew as no other did'

... van een levendigheid, **die** voor zijn tijd volstrekt uniek was
'... a liveliness that was quite unique for his period'

After prepositions the form is *wie* for persons, *waar* + prep. for things:

de mensen **bij wie** hij woont
'the people he lives with'

de technologische prestaties **waarop** Amerika altijd trots is geweest
'the technological achievements of which A. has always been proud'

Further to relative clauses (see above): in literary Dutch, embedding of attributive (phrase) to left of head-word is permissible: e.g. *de op de agenda staande interpellaties* 'the questions on the agenda'.

Numerals

1–10: *een, twee, drie, vier, vijf, zes, zeven, acht, negen, tien*; 20 *twintig*; 21 *een en twintig*, 30 *dertig*, 40 *veertig*; 100 *honderd*.

Verb

The citation form = infinitive, ending in -(*e*)*n*; the stem is the infinitive form minus -(*e*)*n*. A long vowel in the infinitive is written doubled in the stem: e.g. *leven* – ***leef***; *geloven* – *gel**oo**f*.

Dutch has active and passive voices, indicative and imperative moods. There are two simple tenses in the indicative: present and past.

Simple present: first person singular = stem; first plural and third plural = infinitive; second person singular and plural and third singular add *-t*: e.g. *ik kom – wij komen – hij komt*.

Formation of the simple past depends on whether the verb is weak or strong. Weak verbs add *-te/-ten, -de/-den* to the stem: e.g. *ik kookte – wij kookten*. Strong verbs make their past tense and past participle by means of single or two-stage ablaut: e.g.

> bidden 'pray' – bad – gebeden
> slapen 'sleep' – sl**ie**p – gesl**a**pen
> liggen 'lie' – l**a**g – gel**e**gen

Past participle: *ge-* + stem + *-t/d* for weak; specific form for strong has to be learnt with the verb. If the verb has a stressed prefix, *-ge-* is inserted between this prefix and the stem: e.g. *aannemen* 'accept' – *aan**ge**nomen*.

COMPOUND TENSES

These are made with specific auxiliaries: the future with *zullen*; the perfect with *zijn* or *hebben*. *Hebben* is used with transitives; intransitives involving a change of state use *zijn* (cf. *sein* with verbs of motion in German). E.g. *hij is opgestaan* 'he (has) got up'; *wij zijn naar de stad gereden* 'we drove to town'. *Zullen* and other modal auxiliaries – e.g. *laten*, *kunnen*, *moeten* – precede the infinitive they govern: e.g.

> hij is niet **kunnen** komen 'he was not able to come';
>
> hij heeft ... **laten** vallen 'he let ... drop';
>
> en ze hebben me allemaal beloofd te **zullen** komen
> 'and they all promised me they would come' (Couperus)

The modal auxiliary may even be inserted between an infinitive and its separable prefix. There are then three possibilities:

omdat ik in Amsterdam	moet overstappen 'because I have to change in A.'
	over moet stappen
	overstappen moet

PASSIVE

Both *worden* and *zijn* are used as auxiliaries in the formation of the passive voice, the latter in the perfect tense only: e.g.

> ... zal donderdag **worden** begraven '... will be buried on Thursday'
>
> het raam is gebroken 'the window is broken' (= 'the window has been broken')
>
> uit de mededeling van thans kan **worden** afgeleid, dat ...
> 'from the present announcement it can be inferred that ...'

As dummy subject, *er* may introduce a passive sentence: e.g. *er werd veel gepraat* 'a lot of talking went on' (cf. German *es wurde viel geplaudert*).

Er also = German *da* in such constructions as: *een stuk* ***er****van* = *ein Stück davon*, but, contrary to German usage, *er* can be separated from the preposition: *ik heb* ***er*** *een stuk* ***van***.

Negation

Niet follows verb negated or its object: *ik schrijf* (*de brief*) *niet* 'I don't write the letter'; but precedes modal + infinitive groupings at end of clause: *dat boek heb ik niet kunnen kopen* 'I wasn't able to buy that book'.

Prepositions

Note that the pronoun *het* cannot be used after a preposition. Instead, *er* + prep. is used (cf. *er*, above); thus, **tegen het* – *ertegen*; **in het* – *erin*.

Word derivation

Compounds are frequent, usually two or more nouns, but other parts of speech may enter into them. Example of word-building:

> antwoord 'answer'
> **ver**antwoord**elijk** 'responsible'
> verantwoordelikj**heid** 'responsibility'

Stress may shift in compound: *tóeval* 'chance', *toevállig* 'by chance'.

Word order

SVO is normal; SOV in subordinate clauses; VSO in interrogation.

1 In den beginne was het Woord en het Woord was bij God en het Woord
was God. 2 Dit was in den beginne bij God. 3 Alle dingen zijn door
het Woord geworden en zonder dit is geen ding geworden, dat geworden
is. 4 In het Woord was leven en het leven was het licht der mensen; 5 en
het licht schijnt in de duisternis en de duisternis heeft het niet gegrepen.
6 Er trad een mens op, van God gezonden, wiens naam was Johannes;
7 deze kwam als getuige om van het licht te getuigen, opdat allen door hem
geloven zouden. 8 Hij was het licht niet, maar was om te getuigen van het
licht.

ENGLISH

INTRODUCTION

The West Germanic branch of Indo-European, to which English belongs, also includes Low German, Dutch, and Frisian. English itself derives from three Low German dialects spoken by the Angles, Saxons, and Jutes, who came from Denmark, and North Germany to settle in England from the middle of the fifth century onwards. These dialects are marked by retention of the unvoiced stops /p, t, k/, which were mutated to the corresponding fricatives /f, θ, x/, in High German, and of the voiced stops /b, d, g/, which were likewise mutated to /p, t, k/. *See* **German**: Second Sound Shift. These mutations may be illustrated by such equations as:

Low German	*English*	*High German*
dör	**d**oor	**T**ür
pad	**p**ath	**Pf**ad
ski**p**	shi**p**	Schi**ff**
hei**t**	ho**t**	hei**ss**

Four main dialects took shape in *Englaland*, the 'land of the Angles':

1. West Saxon: spoken in the kingdom of Wessex and other parts of the south;
2. Kentish: the language of the Jutes in what is now Kent;
3. Mercian: spoken by the Angles in East Anglia and Humberside;
4. Northumbrian: the dialects of the Angles in north-east England and south-east Scotland.

Of these, West Saxon – King Alfred's *Englisc* – is by far the most important as the language in which most of Old English literature is written. (*See* **Literature**, below). In the eighth and ninth centuries a fresh Germanic influx came in the shape of Scandinavian settlers, whose Norse language provided English with many genetically homogeneous loan-words. From 1016 to 1042, England was, in fact, a Danish kingdom. On the linguistic plane, however, West Saxon preserved its ascendancy until the Norman invasion in 1066. The polarization of society which followed this upheaval was reflected in an equivalent polarization of language: as the language of the conquerors, Norman French assumed the dominant role, while West Saxon lost its privileged status, and joined other forms of Old English as a dialect of the English peasantry. Through the twelfth century there was little or no writing in Old English. The specific nature of Middle English, as it emerged and was consolidated between 1100 and 1500, is largely due to three factors:

1. The widely disparate rates at which the Old English inflectional system was lost in the various dialects. This dialectal divergence reached a point at which mutual intelligibility was severely impaired or even lost. The need for an accepted common norm became more and more urgent.
2. It has been calculated that about 10,000 French words were imported in the Middle English period, 75 per cent of which are still in use today. On the one hand, this represented a considerable enhancement of a language which found itself in a new political situation; on the other hand, it implied a corresponding loss of those Old English lexical resources which were no longer immediately useful.
3. The morphological core of the emergent language remained, however, that inherited from Old English.

By the late thirteenth century, the term 'English' refers to that compromise between the East Midland (< Mercian) and South-Eastern (< Kentish) dialects, which came to be known as the London dialect. In 1258, the accession of Henry III was proclaimed in 'English'. By the middle of the fourteenth century, English had replaced French as the language of the law (Statute of Pleading, 1362) and of education; and by the end of the century, Chaucer was using the London dialect to write one of the greatest poems in English. A hundred years later, the lineaments of Early Modern English are clearly discernible.

Periodization of Modern English is meaningful mainly on the phonological plane, and, within this field, primarily with regard to change affecting the vocalic system. The consonantal inventory remained largely the same from the early Middle English period onwards, and the principal morphological reductionist processes were virtually complete by the close of that period. Thus, Old English is marked by the possession of a rich and extensive system of Germanic inflection and a purely Germanic vocabulary; Middle English by extensive erosion of the morphological apparatus, and the intake of a large number of French words; Modern English by the near-total disappearance of inflection. Four periods in the development of Modern English are distinguished: (a) 1500–1620s; (b) to 1700; (c) to the end of the nineteenth century; (d) the twentieth century. In (c) and (d), due to political and economic factors, anglophone territory expands to global proportions, accompanied by a vast increase in the numbers of people using English as a second language. The extreme reductionism of Modern English accidence may be a contributory factor here.

Today, as the mother tongue of some 350 million people, English is demographically surpassed only by Modern Standard Chinese, which cannot, however, claim anything approaching the international status of English. The main components in this total are: USA 232 million speakers; United Kingdom 56 million; Canada 24 million; Australia and New Zealand 17 million.

In addition, English is the official language of several countries in Africa – Zimbabwe, Nigeria, Ghana, Uganda, Liberia – and the West Indies; and it has joint official status in India (with Hindi), South Africa (with Afrikaans) and Singapore (with Chinese, Malay, and Tamil). It is the accepted global medium in the travel industry and in international communications. Increasingly, a press conference of any importance, given anywhere in the world, will be in English, or accompanied by an immediate translation into English.

One and a half thousand years after Hengist and Horsa, the local dialect they brought with them from Denmark to Kent, shows every sign of becoming the planetary lingua franca in the twenty-first century.

Periodization of English literature

1. Old English: four manuscripts, dating from c. 1000, contain Anglo-Saxon poetry of the eighth and ninth centuries, including the heroic poem *Beowulf* and some lyrics. In prose, the outstanding items are the works of King Alfred, and the Anglo-Saxon Chronicle, which covers (with gaps) the period from Alfred's reign to the middle of the twelfth century.
2. Middle English: in the early period, the main body of work is in Anglo-Latin: e.g. Geoffrey of Monmouth's *Historia*. The transitional period includes the mediaeval romance *Sir Gawayne and the Grene Knight*, and John Langland's *Piers Plowman*. The period ends with Chaucer.
3. Renaissance: Shakespeare and the other dramatists (Marlowe, Webster); Spenser; lyric poetry.
4. The seventeenth century: Milton; Donne and the Metaphysical poets; Dryden; Bunyan.
5. The eighteenth century: Pope; Swift; the novelists, Richardson, Smollet, Sterne; Dr Johnson; *The Tatler* and *The Spectator*: Addison and Steele; William Blake; in Scotland, Robert Burns.
6. The nineteenth century: Byron and the Romantic movement; Wordsworth, Coleridge; Keats and Shelley; Tennyson, Browning, Matthew Arnold; the novelists, the Bronte Sisters, Jane Austen, George Eliot, Dickens, Hardy.
7. The twentieth century.

OLD ENGLISH

INTRODUCTION

Script

The earliest inscriptions are runic. Old English literature is written in an Irish version of the Latin alphabet, with specific forms for *f*, *g*, *r*, *s*. Later, two runic letters *þ* = /θ/, and ƿ = /w/ were added. Initially *þ* was used to indicate both /θ/ and the voiced counterpart /ð/, for which *ð* was then introduced.

PHONOLOGY

Consonants

stops: p, b, t, d, k, g
affricates: tʃ, dʒ (notated as *cg*)
fricatives: f, v, θ, ð, s, z, ʃ, x, γ, ç, h
nasal: m, n, ŋ
lateral and flap: l, r
semi-vowels: j, w

Vowels

short, ɑ, æ, ε, ə, œ, ɪ, ɔ, u, y
long: ɑː, æː, eː, œː, iː, oː, uː, yː
diphthongs: short: ea, eo; long: ēa, ēo

The long vowels never appear in the inflectional endings. They are indicated in the following text by macrons.

MORPHOLOGY AND SYNTAX

Noun

Old English had three grammatical genders: masculine, feminine, and neuter. A few nominal endings are coded for gender: e.g. *-a*, *-oþ*, *-dōm*, *-els*, *-scipe* are masculine; *-nes, -estre, -þu, -ung* are feminine.

DEFINITE ARTICLE

se 'the, that'; *þes* 'this'. *Se* has fem. form *sēo*, neuter *þæt.* All three are declined in five cases on a *þ*-initial base: e.g. masculine nom. *se*; acc. *þone*; gen. *þæs*; dat. *þǣm*; instr. *þȳ*. The common plural is: nom./acc. *þā*; gen. *þāra*; dat./instr. *þæm*.

Þes has fem. *þēos*, neuter *þis*. The masculine declension is: nom. *þes*; acc. *þisne*; gen. *þisses*; dat. *þissum*, *þȳs*. The common plural is: *þās*, *þissa*, *þissum*.

DECLENSION

Five cases, the instrumental sharing a form with the dative. There are three declensions: a strong declension, the weak or *-n* declension, and a group of minor and irregular declensions.

For example, masculine *a*-stem: *cēol* 'ship':

Singular		*Plural*	
nom.	se cēol	nom./acc.	þā cēolas
acc.	þone cēol		
gen.	þæs cēoles	gen.	þāra cēola
dat./instr.	þǣm/þȳ cēole	dat./instr.	þǣm cēolum

Feminine *o*-stem: *rōd* 'cross':

Singular		*Plural*	
nom.	sēo rōd	nom./acc.	þā rōda
acc.	þā rōde		
gen,.	þǣre rōde	gen.	þāra rōda
dat./instr.	þǣre rōde	dat./instr.	þǣm rōdum

-*n* declension: e.g. *guma* 'man': this declension has -(*a*)*n* in all four singular oblique cases, and in plural nom. and acc. The plural genitive is *gumena*, the dat./instr. *gumum*: e.g. *þǣm guman* 'to the man'; *þāra gumena* 'of the men'.

Minor declensions: e.g. *fōt* 'foot', pl. *fēt*; the mutated vowel appears in the sing. dat./instr. as well: *þæm/þȳ fēt* 'to/by the foot'. Cf. *bōc* 'book', pl. *bēc*; *tōþ* 'tooth', pl. *tēþ*; *mūs* 'mouse', pl. *mȳs*.

Adjective

All adjectives have a strong (indefinite) and a weak (definite) declension. The instrumental is formally distinguished from the dative in the indefinite singular: e.g. *cwic* 'living'; fem. *cwicu*, nt. *cwic*.

The masculine oblique cases are: acc. *cwicne*, gen. *cwices*, dat. *cwicum*, instr. *cwice*. The neuter is identical, apart from the accusative, which remains *cwic*. For all three genders, the gen. is *cwicra*, the dat. *cwicum* (no instrumental).

The weak declension is used after the definite article, the demonstratives, and the possessive pronouns: e.g. *se gōda guma* 'the good man', acc. *þone gōdan guman*, dat. *þæm gōdan guman*; pl. gen. *þāra gōdra gumena*.

Cf. Luke 15.22:

> bringað raðe þone sēlestan gegierelan
> 'bring forth the best robe' (*raðe* 'quickly'; *sēlest* suppletive superlative of *wel* 'well (good)'; *gegierele* 'robe')

Cf. John 10.11:

> Ic eom gōd hierde
> 'I am the good shepherd'
>
> gōd hierde selþ his līf for his scēapum
> 'the good shepherd giveth his life for his sheep'

COMPARATIVE
-*ra*: *earm* 'poor' – *earmra*; *bliðe* 'glad' – *bliðra*.

SUPPLETIVE FORMS
gōd 'good' – *betra*/*sēlra*; *micel* 'large' – *māra*; *yfel* 'bad' – *wiersa*; *lȳtel* 'small' – *lǣssa*.

Pronoun

The first and second persons have dual forms; the third person is marked for gender in the singular, with a common plural. Cases: nom., acc., gen. dat./instr.

	Singular	*Dual*	*Plural*
1	ic – mē – mīn – mē	wit – unc – uncer – unc	wē – ūs – ūre – ūs
2	þu – þē – þīn – þe	git – inc – incer – inc	gē – ēow – ēower – ēow
3	masc. hē – hine – his – him fem. hēo – hī – hire – hire nt. hit – hit – his – him	}	hī – hī – hira – him

Cf.

sōþ ic secge ēow 'verily I say to you'

bringað mē hider þā 'bring them hither to me' (Matthew, 14.18).

and hira gōdna dæl ofslōgon 'and slew a good number of them' (*hira*)

DEMONSTRATIVE PRONOUN
See **Definite article:** *se – seo – þæt*; *þes – þēos – þis*.

INTERROGATIVE PRONOUN
Masc. *hwā*, nt. *hwæt*; declined in five cases; *hwæðer* 'what? (which of two)'; *hwelc* 'which? (of many)'.

RELATIVE PRONOUN
þe (invariable) usually preceded by appropriate form of definite article/demonstrative *se* (Used pronominally, *se* → *sē-*.)

þæt folc, þe þær binnan wæs 'the people who were inside'

se hȳra, sē þe nis hierde and sē þe nāg þā scēap
'the hireling, that is not the shepherd, and who does not own the sheep' (*nis* 'is not'; *nag* 'does not own'; *see* **Verb**, below) (John, 15.12)

Numerals

1–10: *ān*, *twēgen*, *þrȳ*, *fēower*, *fīf*, *syx*, *seofon*, *eahta*, *nigon*, *tȳn*; 11 *endleofan*; 12 *twelf*; 13 *þrēotȳne*; 20 *twentig*; 21 *ān and twentig*, etc. 30 *þrītig*; 70 *hundseofontig*; 80 *hundeahtatig*; 90 *hundnigontig*; 100 *hundtēontig*.

Verb

As in other Germanic languages, Old English verbs are either strong (vocalic, i.e. displaying stem ablaut) or weak (consonantal). Most Old English verbs belong to the weak conjugation. There are three moods – indicative, imperative, subjunctive – and two basic tenses, present and past. The auxiliary verbs *wesan*, *bēon*, and *habban* are used to form a perfect, a pluperfect, and a future tense. The general negating particle *ne* precedes the verbal form, and may fuse with it: *ne habban* → *nabban* 'not to have'. A passive can be formed periphrastically.

STRONG VERBS

The strong verbs, which form a closed set, are divided by ablaut pattern into seven classes; examples of these (infinitive – past, third singular and plural – past particle) are:

1. rīsan – rās, rison – -risen 'rise'
2. bēodan – bēad, budon – -boden 'offer'
3. drincan – dranc, druncon – -druncen 'drink'
4. beran – bær, bǣron – -boren 'bear'
5. sprecan – spræc, sprǣcon – -sprecen 'speak'
6. faran – fōr, fōron – -faren 'go'
7. wēpan – wēop, wēopon – -wōpen 'weep'
   hātan – hēt, hēton – -hāten 'call'

All seven classes have various irregularities and sub-classes; classes 3 and 7 are particularly heterogeneous. Formation of second and third person singular present indicative from the stem often involves *i*-mutation: e.g.

cuman 'to come': cymst – cymþ
helpan 'to help': hilpst – hilpþ
grōwan 'to grow': grēwst – grēwþ

Specimen strong verb paradigm: *bīdan* 'to wait', class 1.

Indicative

present:	sing.	1 bīde, 2 bīdest, 3 bītt (<bīdþ)
	pl.	1–3: bīdaþ
past:	sing.	1 bād, 2 bide, 3 bād
	pl.	1–3: bidon

Subjunctive

present:	sing.	1–3: bīde; pl. 1–3: bīden
past:	sing.	1–3: bide; pl. biden

Imperative sing. *bīd*; pl. *bīdaþ*.
Participles: present: *bīdende*; past (*ge*)*biden*

WEAK VERBS

These were often formed from nouns and other parts of speech by means of the affix **-ja*, which induced *i-* mutation in the stem vowel of the resultant verb. According to the presence or absence of this mutation, Old English weak verbs are divided into two classes. Here, a specimen paradigm: *fremman* 'to perform' where the stem vowel represents a mutation from *-a-*:

Indicative

present:	sing.	1 fremme, 2 fremest, 3 freme
	pl.	1–3: fremma
past:	sing.	1 fremede, 2 fremedest, 3 fremede
	pl.	1–3: fremedon

Subjunctive

present:	sing.	1–3: fremme; pl. 1–3: fremmen
past:	sing.	1–3: fremede; pl. 1–3: fremeden

Imperative: sing. *freme*; pl. *fremma*
Participles: present *fremmende*; past *gefremed*

MIDDLE ENGLISH

INTRODUCTION

The twelfth century was the century of transition between late Old English and early Middle English. Almost nothing was written in English, and very little was borrowed from French. The English dialects ceased to reflect the original tribal divisions, and tended to polarize on an areal or typological basis into two groups: Northern (including Northumbrian and Mercian, from which latter the important Midland dialect was to emerge) and Southern (comprising West Saxon and Kentish). Each of these several components developed internally in terms of its own material, and at its own specific rate.

PHONOLOGY

The process of phonological change, by which Old English became Middle English, may, however, be broadly generalized. Some salient features are:

1. Weak vowels, especially in final position, were levelled to *e*; towards the end of the Middle English period strong diphthongs were also levelled:

Old English	*Middle English*	*Modern English*
nam**a**	nam**e**	name /nejm**ø**/
ber**an**	ber**en**	bear
sun**u**	sun**e**	son /sʌn/
st**eo**rra	st**e**rre	star

2. /ea/ > /æ/ > /a/: e.g. ***heard*** > ***hærd*** > ***hard***: Mod. Eng. *hard*.
3. Old English long vowels were largely maintained in Middle English. /yː/ became /iː/ in Northern dialects, and subsequently standard: e.g. Old English *fȳr* > Middle English *fīr* (Mod. Eng. *fire*/faiə/).
   Long vowels tended to be shortened before consonantal cluster: e.g. Old English *wīsdōm* > Middle English *wisdōm*.
4. The consontantal inventory remained stable, with some changes in quantity.
5. Consonantal finals of Old English nominals were replaced by vowel finals in Middle English, originating in the oblique case: e.g. Old English *cwēn*: acc. *cwēne* > Middle English *quēne* (Mod. Eng. *queen*).

MORPHOLOGY AND SYNTAX

1. Definite article gradually reduced from the Old English inflected paradigm to the single form *þe* /θe/ > /ðə/.
2. Erosion of the article is a factor in the general loss of grammatical gender.
3. Extensive erosion of the case system; by the end of the period, only the genitive *-s* remains. Even where, for a time, a modicum of inflection persisted – e.g. in the declension of Old English feminine nouns with a plural marker in *-en* – this too was finally levelled by analogy; and a generalized plural in *-(e)s* emerges. Mutating plurals are retained: *gōs – gēs* 'goose, geese'; *mūs – mȳs* 'mouse, mice', etc., though old mutating forms in the singular are levelled.
4. The adjective becomes indeclinable.
5. Prounoun: the standard Middle English system is as follows:

		Singular		*Plural*	
			Oblique		*Oblique*
1	nom.	ī, ich	mē	wē	us
2		þow	þē	yē	yow
3	masc.	hē	him		
	fem.	shē	hir(e)	þei	þeim
	nt.	(h)it	(h)it		hem

POSSESSIVE PRONOUNS
Sing.: mīn/mī – þīn, þī – his, hir(e)
pl.: our(e) – your(e) – þeir(e), her(e).

DEMONSTRATIVE PRONOUN
Early Middle English had a full declension for all three genders, with four cases in the singular, three in the plural. This was reduced in standard Middle English to a simple opposition between 'this, these'/'that, those'.

RELATIVE PRONOUN
The relative pronoun was standardized as *that*.

Verb

The standard Middle English strong-verb paradigm shows little change from that of Old English, apart from the levelling of *-a-* and *-o-* in inflections to *-e-*, the loss of *-þ* in the present indicative plural, and the shift from *-d-* to *-g-* in the present participle. Thus, the present tense of Middle English *bīnde(n)* 'to bind' is: sing. *bīnde*, *bīndest*, *bīnde*; pl. common, *bīnde(n)*. The past tense is: sing. *bǭnd*, *bounde*, *bǭnd*; pl. *bounde(n)*. Imperative: *bīnd*, *bīnd(e)*; subjunctive: pres. sing. *bīnde*; pl. *bīnde(n)*; past, sing. *bounde*; pl. *bounde(n)*; present participle: *bīndinge*; past participle: *(i)bounde(n)*.

This represents a reduction of discriminant forms from the twelve present in the Old English conjugation of *bindan*, to seven; Modern English reduces this to four.

A considerable number of Old English strong verb stems were reassessed as weak in Middle English and conjugated accordingly.

MODERN ENGLISH

The transition from Middle to Modern English:

SCRIPT

The very weak correspondence between sound and symbol, characteristic of Modern English, is due primarily to the conservation from the late Middle English period onwards of a gallicized orthography reflecting Middle English pronunciation. The orthography was consolidated by the introduction of printing (1476), and retained through a succession of phonological changes. Variant spellings were permissible into the nineteenth century.

PHONOLOGY

Vowels

The key feature in the phonological transition from late Middle to Modern English is the so-called Great Vowel Shift, which took place in the fifteenth/sixteenth centuries. Briefly, five of the long vowels were raised by one degree; the remaining two were diphthongized:

aː > æː; ɛː > eː; eː > iː; ɔː >oː; oː > uː; iː > əi > ay; uː > aw

The new long values were subsequently (through the eighteenth and nineteenth centuries) diphthongized by the introduction of a glide to reach their present values: cf.

Middle English	*Early Modern English*	*Seventeenth Century*	*Present-day*
nāme /naːmə/	/næm/	/neːm/	/neːjm/ *name*
/stɔːn/	/stoːn/	/stoːn/	/stōun/ *stone*
/ɔpən/	/oːpən/	/oːpən/	/ōupn/ *open*
/wiːn/	/wəin/	/wəin/	/wājn/ *wine*
/greːn/	/griːn/	/griːn/	/grījn/ *green*

Short vowels:

a > æ; ɪ, ɛ, u, ɔ unchanged through the sixteenth century
> ɪ, ɛ, ʌ, ɔ in the seventeenth century
> ɪ, ɛ, ɐ, ɔ in Modern English

e.g. [sune] > [sʌn] > [sɐn].

Consonants

The consonantal inventory of Modern English is:

stops, p, b, t, d, k, g
affricates: tʃ, dʒ
fricatives: f, v, θ, ð, s, z, ʃ, ʒ, h
nasals: m, n, ŋ, ɲ
lateral and flap: l, r
semi-vowels: j, w

All the stops have a measure of aspiration; /t/ and /d/ are retroflex rather than dental. All can be initial except /ŋ/; all can be medial; /h/ and /w/ cannot be final. Initial /ʒ/ occurs only in loan-words: *genre* /ʒãːr/.

Consonantal changes in transition from late Middle English/Early Modern English to present-day Standard:

1. /θ, s, f/ are voiced in weak syllables in the modern language: e.g. in gen. case: *mannes* /manəs/ > *man's* /mænz/; *with* /wɪθ/ > /wɪð/
2. /c/ voiced to /dʒ/: cf. Middle English *knǭwlę̄che* > /nɒlɪdʒ/
3. /s/ > /z/ between weak and strong vowel: *disease* /dɪzīz/
4. Middle English /h/ represented /ç/ or /xʷ/; both lost in Modern English:

   Middle English /nɪçt/ > /nɪht/ > /nɪːt/ > /nəit/ > /najt/ *night*
   /θɔuxʷt/ > /θɔːt/ *thought*

5. In Modern English /r/ tends to Ø except before a vowel; this proviso includes the so-called 'intrusive r': 'law and order' pronounced as /laːwr.ənd.ɔːdə/ Cf. here = /hiə/; her = /həː/; star = /staː/
6. /l/ was elided, from the sixteenth century onwards, between a labial vowel and a consonant: e.g. *half* > /haːf/. Cf. elision of /w/ in *towards* → /tɔːdz/.
7. /k/ dropped before /n/: *know* (sixteenth century /knou/) > /nōu/.

Stress

In Old and Middle English, the main stress was on the root syllable of inflected words. In Modern English, stress may be on almost any syllable of a word in citation form; often, variants are permissible, e.g. *cóntroversy/contróversy*. In ordinary speech, stress tends to be evenly distributed over the phrasal contour, with particles, prepositions, articles in the dips. Stress is phonemic in doublets: cf. *éxtract* (noun) – *extráct* (verb); *ábsent* (adjective) – *absént* (verb).

MORPHOLOGY AND SYNTAX

The definite article is realized as /ðə/ before consonants, as /ði/ before vowels. The now prevalent use of *a/an* as an indefinite article became generalized in the Middle English period.

Noun

Only two inflections survive – the genitive *-s* = /z/ or /s/ and the plural marker *-s*, /z/ or /s/. The apostrophe is used to separate the genitive *-s* from the singular or collective noun; the genitive of a noun with *-s* plural is marked by ': thus, singular: *boy's* pl.: boys'; collective: *men's*. A few mutated plurals survive: e.g. *mouse – mice*, *goose – geese*, etc.

Adjective

All adjectives are indeclinable.

Pronoun

Up to a point, the Middle English system survives. In the first person, both singular and plural have direct and oblique forms: *I – me*; *we – us*.

In the singular, the second person is obsolete, and the plural has been levelled to a single form: *you*.

Third person: here, the gender distinction has been preserved plus oblique forms: masc. *he – him*; fem. *she – her*; nt: *it – it*. The plural is levelled to the common form: *they – them*.

Verb

Overall, there is a general reduction from the Middle English inventory to four forms: e.g. for the verb OE *bindan*, ME *bīnde(n)*, Modern English *bind*: *bind*, *binds* (3rd person present indicative), *bound* (past tense), *binding* (present participle). Archaic forms may appear in set phrases, e.g. *his bounden duty*, where *bounden* is the old past participle (*i*)*bounden*.

Extreme reductionism has led to confusion between certain verbs, e.g. between the intransitive *lie*, whose past tense is *lay*, and the transitive verb *lay*, the former being levelled to the latter: Standard *he lay there* being accompanied in sub-standard usage by **he laid there/he was laying there*. Such a confusion is impossible in German, for example, where the verbs *liegen* and *legen* have remained distinct.

Prepositions

In Old English, prepositions governed the dative, the accusative, or the genitive. The static (dative case) versus dynamic (accusative case) opposition was found, as in Modern German.

In Modern English it is natural to close a sentence with a preposition, or even two (*the man I spoke to*; *what I have to put up with*) depending on the specific requirements of the sense-verb. The practice, which is also to be found in the Scandinavian languages, has been questioned on purist and stylistic grounds. Extreme simpicity of accidence, however, merits an equivalent degree of syntactical flexibility. Together, they help to make English, with its internationally enriched vocabulary of half a million words, readily accessible to, and usable by its global community.

1. On frymðe wæs Word, and þæt Word wæs mid Gode, and God wæs þæt Word.
2. Þæt wæs on fruman mid Gode.
3. Ealle þing wǣron geworhte ðurh hyne; and nān þing næs geworht būtan him.
4. Þæt wæs līf þe on him geworht wæs; and þæt līf wæs manna lēoht.
5. And þæt lēoht lȳht on ðȳstrum; and þȳstro þæt ne genāmon.
6. Mann wæs fram Gode āsend, þæs nama wæs Iohannes.
7. Ðēs cōm tō gewitnesse, þæt hē gewitnesse cȳðde be ðām lēohte, þæt ealle menn þurh hyne gelȳfdon.
8. Næs hē lēoht, ac þæt hē gewitnesse forð bǣre be þām lēohte.

Old English (West Saxon)

1 In the bigynnynge was the word, *that*
is, Goddis sone, and the word was at
2 God, and God was the word. This was
3 in the bigynnynge at God. Alle thingis
ben maad by hym, and with outen him
is maad noȝt, that thing that is maad.
4 Was lyf in him, and the lyf was the liȝt
5 of men; and the liȝt schyneth in derk-
6 nessis, and derknessis tooken not it. A
man was sent fro God, to whom the name
7 was Joon. This man cam in to witnessinge, that he schulde bere witnessinge of
the liȝt, that alle men schulden bileue bi
8 him. He was not the liȝt, but that he
9 schulde bere witnessing of the liȝt.

Middle English (Wyclif's translation)

N the beginning was
that Word, and that word
was with God, and that
Word was God.
2 This ſame was in the
beginning with God.
3 All things were made by it, and
without it was made nothing that was made.
4 In it was life, and that life was the
light of men.
5 And that light ſhineth in the darkneſſe
and the darkneſſe comprehended it not.
6 ¶ There was a man ſent from God,
whoſe name *was* Iohn.
7 *This* ſame came for a witneſſe, to beare
witneſſe of that light, that all men through
him might beleeue.
8 Hee was not that light, but *was ſent* to
beare witneſſe of that light.

Early Modern English (the King James Version)

1 In the beginning the Word already
was. The Word was in God's presence, and what God was, the Word was.
2 He was with God at the beginning, 3 and
through him all things came to be; without him no created thing came into being.
4 In him was life, and that life was the
light of mankind. 5 The light shines in the
darkness, and the darkness has never
mastered it.
6 There appeared a man named John.
He was sent from God, 7 and came as a
witness to testify to the light, so that
through him all might become believers.
8 He was not himself the light; he came to
bear witness to the light.

Contemporary English

ESTONIAN

INTRODUCTION

A member of the Balto-Finnic group of Finno-Ugric, Estonian is the official language of the Estonian Republic, where it is spoken by about 1 million people. There are several thousand speakers in other parts of the CIS, and some large émigré groups – for example around 70,000 in North America. The language is divided into two markedly divergent dialect groups: Northern (Tallinna keel) and Southern (Tartu keel). In their extreme forms these come close to being mutually unintelligible. The modern literary standard is based on the Northern (Tallinn) form. Centuries of German influence are reflected in the vocabulary of Estonian.

Writing in Estonian dates from the sixteenth century when religious tracts were produced in both dialects. Translation of the New Testament soon followed, and a complete Bible in 1739. A hundred years later, the appearance of Lönnroth's *Kalevala* in Finland (*see* **Finnish**) was quickly followed by the publication of a similar collection in Estonia – the *Kalevipoeg* (1857–61) edited by F.R. Kreutzwald, and by a similar upsurge of interest in the national folklore. The next important event in the history of Estonian literature was the emergence of the *Noor Eesti* group in the early twentieth century – 'Young Estonia', whose members were mainly interested in experimental verse. The period of independence in the 1920s and 1930s is the richest in Estonian literature; the main figures are the poetess Marie Under, and the novelist Anton Tammsaare, whose great novel *Tõde ja Õigus* (1926–36) offers a panoramic and detailed study of a crucial period in Estonian life, the transition from the nineteenth to the twentieth century.

SCRIPT

Roman alphabet + *ä*, *ö*, *ü*, *õ*; *c*, *f*, *q*, *w*, *x*, *y*, *z* occur only in recent loan-words. *õ* is a central vowel close to /ə/ but unrounded.

PHONOLOGY

Consonants

stops: p, t, k
fricatives: v, s, h

nasals: m, n
lateral and flap: l, r
semi-vowels: j

/p, t, k/ are unaspirated and voiceless, represented in the script by *b*, *d*, *g*; they are always short. When written as *p*, *t*, *k* they are long; when written with gemination: *pp*, *tt*, *kk* they are overlong.

PALATALIZATION

The palatalized consonants are /t′, n′, s′, l′/, not notated in script. The gradation from short to long and overlong, which affects other consonants as well as the stops, is accompanied by an increase in tenseness and a forward shift in articulation.

CONSONANT GRADATION

(*See* **Finnish.**) Consonant gradation exists in Estonian, although the phonological conditions which generate the phenomenon are no longer always present. For example, the typical Balto-Finnic genitive ending *-n* has been lost in Estonian; but *jalg* 'foot', still makes a genitive *jala*, representing former **jalan.*

Some examples of consonantal gradation:

b–v: ***leib*** (nom.) 'bread' – *leiva* (gen.)
d–j: *sõda* (nom.) 'war' – *sõja* (gen.)
g–j: *selg* (nom.) 'back' – *selja* (gen.)
b–Ø: *tuba* (nom.) 'room' – *toa* (gen.)
nd–nn: ve**nd** (nom.) 'brother' – *venna* (gen.)

Vowels

front: i, e, ɛ, œ, y
middle: ə (unrounded)
back: a, o, u

Like the consonants, the vowels, too, have three degrees of phonemic length; cf. *sada* /sada/, 'hundred'; *saada* /saːda/, 'they came'; *saada* /saːːda/, 'to receive'.

VOWEL HARMONY

Has been lost in Estonian, though there are residual traces in some southern dialects.

Stress

Stress is always on the first syllable. Any vowel of any length may appear in the first syllable; in subsequent syllables, only *a*, *e*, *i*, *u* appear.

MORPHOLOGY AND SYNTAX

Noun

No gender; no articles. There are two numbers and 14 cases. The plural nominative marker is always *-d*. The key case endings are:

Singular: nom. Ø; gen. a vowel; part. Ø, *-d/t*, or a vowel
Plural: nom. *-d*; gen. *-de/te/e*; part. *-d.*

The other cases are all constructed on the genitive base: e.g. inessive *-s*, elative *-st*, adessive *-l*, translative *-ks*.

Some examples of case usage:

genitive: *Eesti **keele** õpetaja* 'a teacher of the Estonian language';
partitive: ***Leiba** on laual* 'There is some bread on the table';
inessive: *Mina elan **linnas*** 'I live in the town';
elative: *Mina tulen **linnast*** 'I come out of the town';
essive: *Ta töötab **arstina*** 'He works as a doctor';
translative: *Sõja ajal sai ta **ohvitseriks*** 'During the war he became an officer.'

Adjective

As attribute, adjective precedes the noun and is declined in concord with it, in most, but not all, cases: e.g. *punane raamat* 'a red book'; ***punased raamatud*** 'red books'; ***punases raamatus*** 'in a red book'; ***punastes raamatutes*** 'in red books'.

COMPARATIVE
-m is added to the genitive: e.g. *Tema on minust **tugevam*** 'He is stronger than I am.'

Pronoun

Personal independent forms: long and short:

Singular: 1 *mina/ma*, 2 *sina/sa*, 3 *tema/ta*;
Plural: 1 *meie/me*, *teie/te*, 3 *nemad/nad*.

These are fully declined in 14 cases.

DEMONSTRATIVE PRONOUN
see 'this', pl. *need*; *too* 'that', pl. *tood.*

INTERROGATIVE PRONOUN
kes 'who?'; *mis* 'what?'.

RELATIVE PRONOUN
As interrogative: e.g. *raamat, mis lamab laual* 'the book which is lying on the table'.

Numerals

1–10: *üks*, *kaks*, *kolm*, *neli*, *viis*, *kuus*, *seitse*, *kaheksa*, *üheksa*, *kümme*; 11 *üksteist*; 12 *kaksteist*; 20 *kakskümmend*; 30 *kolmkümmend*; 100 *sada*. The numerals 2–10 are fully declined in all cases; from 11 onwards, the decade component in the oblique forms is invariable in genitive form; the unit component is declined: e.g. 20 *kakskümmend*; inessive ***kahe**kümnes*; illative ***kahe**kümnesse*.

Verb

Conjugational models depend on whether the stem is mutating or not. All forms of the Estonian verb can be constructed from four basic forms:

1. 1st infinitive in *-ma*;
2. 2nd infinitive in *-da/-ta/-a*;
3. 1st person present indicative;
4. passive past participle in *-tud/-dud*.

The indicative mood has four tenses: two simple and two compound. There is no future tense. As in Finnish, the auxiliary for the compound tenses is *olema* = Fin. *olla*, with present and past forms close to those in Finnish. Again as in Finnish, all positive verb forms have parallel negative forms; but whereas the negative particle is conjugated in Finnish (*en*, *et*, *ei*, etc.), Estonian has only the single form *ei*, used with all persons and both numbers. This means that the personal pronoun must be used:

SPECIMEN CONJUGATION
kirjutama 'to write':

Indicative present: sing. *kirjutan*, *kirjutad*, *kirjuta**b***; pl. *kirjutame*, *kirjutate*, *kirjutavad*;
Indicative present negative version: *ei kirjuta* (preceded by personal pronoun);
Indicative past: *kirjutasin*, *kirjutasid*, etc.;
Negative: *ei kirjutanud*;
Compound past tense: *mina olen kirjutanud*, *sina oled* ..., *mina oleme* ...;
Negative: e.g. *mina ei ole kirjutanud*.

Note reduction in Estonian to an omnibus form of the past participle, where Finnish marks number: *olen sanonut*, *olemme sanoneet*.

MOODS

Conditional: the marker is *-ksi-* + usual endings: e.g. *mina kirjutaksin*;
Imperative: 2nd p. sing. *kirjuta*, 2nd p. pl. *kirjutage*; negative: *ära kirjuta*, pl. *ärge kirjutage*;
Inferential: present, *-vat*; past, *olevat* + past participle: e.g. (*Ma kuulsin, et*) *tema õppi**vat** ülikoolis arstiteadust* '(I hear that) he's studying medicine at the university'; *Ta sõit**vat** homme Moskvasse* 'So he's going to Moscow tomorrow.'

IMPERSONAL FORMS
Present in *-takse/-dakse/-akse*; past in *-ti/-di*: e.g. *linnas ehi**takse** maja* 'a house is

being built/they're building a house in the town' (*maja* is in nominative case); *pargis jalutatakse* lit. 'it-is-gone-walking' = 'one goes walking in the park'; *räägitakse, et* ... 'it is said that ...'

PARTICIPLES

Present in *-v* (active and passive): e.g. *lugev* 'reading'; *loetav* 'being read'; *lugevad inimesed* 'people who are reading'; *loetavad raamatud* 'books that are being read'. Past in *-nud*: e.g. *Kirjutanud kirja, läks ta jalutama* 'After writing the letter he went for a walk.'

The last example also illustrates the use of the infinitive in *-ma* after verbs of motion. The infinitive in *-da* is used with such modal verbs as *oskama* 'to be able to', *tahtma* 'to want to': e.g. *Tema oskab hästi laulda* 'He can sing well.'

It is interesting to note that the partitive/accusative opposition may be used to express tense: cf.

> *ostan raamatut* 'I'm buying a/the book' (partitive case – present tense);
> *ostan raamatu*∅ 'I shall buy the book' (accusative case – future tense).

VERBAL PARTICLES

Estonian has a rich inventory of verbal particles, whose function is (a) modification of root sense, (b) aspectual, (c) directional. They are separable: e.g. *valmis tegema* 'to complete': *ta **tegi** selle töö kiiresti **valmis*** 'He did that work quickly (and finished it)'.

Some further examples:

> *alla* 'down': *alla tulistama* 'to shoot down';
> *edasi* 'onwards': *edasi töötama* 'to go on working';
> *järele* 'after': *järele jääma* 'to be left over';
> *kinni* 'shut': *kinni võtma* 'to lay hold on'.

Postpositions

Most take the genitive case. Some occur in more than one form, inflected in line with case endings. For example, from *äär* 'margin':

> *äärde* 'towards': *Läheme mere äärde* 'We go towards the sea';
> *ääres* 'at': *Istume mere ääres* 'We sit by the sea';
> *äärest* 'from': *Tuleme mere äärest* 'We come from the sea.'

Word order

SVO is normal.

1 Alguses oli Sõna, ja Sõna
oli Jumala juures, ja
Sõna oli Jumal.
2 Seesama oli alguses Ju-
mala juures.
3 Kõik on tekkinud tema
läbi, ja ilma temata ei ole
tekkinud midagi, mis on
tekkinud.
4 Temas oli elu, ja elu oli
inimeste valgus,
5 ja valgus paistab pime-
duses, ja pimedus ei ole
seda võtnud omaks.
6 Oli mees, Jumala läki-
tatud; selle nimi oli Johannes.
7 See tuli tunnistuseks,
tunnistama valgusest, et
kõik usuksid tema kaudu.
8 Tema ei olnud mitte valgus, vaid ta tuli tunnistama valgusest.

(Tallinna keel)

FINNISH

INTRODUCTION

A member of the Balto-Finnic group of Finno-Ugric, Finnish is the official language of Finland (jointly with Swedish), and joint official language of the Karelian Autonomous Republic. Finnish is spoken in Finland by around 5 million, with considerable émigré bilingual communities abroad, e.g. over half a million in North America.

The main dialectal split is into Western (South-Western, centred on Turku, and the Häme dialect, spoken by the *hämäläiset*) and Eastern (e.g. Savo dialect, spoken by the *savolaiset*). Differences between dialects are largely phonological: e.g. the /k, t, p/ stops can precede /r, l/ in Eastern forms: cf. Western *kaula* 'neck' – Eastern *kakla*; Western *eilen* 'yesterday' – Eastern *eklen*; Western *peura* 'wild reindeer' – Eastern *petra*. Also the labial final in third person singular present: Western *juo* 'he drinks' – Eastern *juop(i)*. The modern literary standard represents a successful compromise between the main dialect forms.

Finnish literature begins in 1544 with the *Rukouskirja Bibliasta* of Michael Agricola, followed in 1548 by his translation of the New Testament. Little of note followed until 1835 when Elias Lönnroth published the first version of his *Kalevala* material. The mythopoeic, ethnological, and linguistic riches revealed in *Kalevala* and its companion volume *Kanteletar* added more than one new dimension to Finnish self-awareness.

From the 1880s onwards, Finnish has been the vehicle for a rich literature in prose and verse, often fervently nationalistic but showing acute awareness of cultural crises on a European scale. Some notable names are Mika Waltari, Toivo Pekkanen, Pentti Haanpää, Paavo Haavikko, Väinö Linna, and Veijo Meri.

SCRIPT

Latin alphabet, minus *b*, *c*, *f*, *q*, *w*, *x*, *z*; plus *ä* (= /ɛ/), *ö* (= /œ/).

PHONOLOGY

Consonants

stops: p, t, d, k
fricatives: v, j, s̩, h
nasals: m, n, ŋ
lateral and flap: l, r

CONSONANT GRADATION

This is a crucially important element in Finnish phonology and morphology, affecting all declension and conjugation patterns. A 'strong' consonant, or consonant cluster initiating an open syllable, is mutated into its 'weak' correlative, when the syllable is closed by the addition of a consonant. The phenomenon (which has many complexities) can be illustrated by comparing nouns in the nominative singular (open syllable) with their genitive forms (closed by addition of the genitive marker *-n*); or by comparing infinitives (strong grade) with the first person singular (weak):

Strong	*Weak*	*Example*
pp	p	loppu – lopun 'end'
tt	t	ottaa – otan 'to take'
kk	k	kukka – kukan 'flower'
mp	mm	enempi – enemmän 'more'
t	d	katu – kadun 'street'
p	v	apu – avun 'help'
k	∅	lukea – luen 'read'

There are some important exceptions to this general rule: e.g. mutation does not take place before a long vowel (e.g. *katu* – illative *katuun*) or before the personal possessive affix (e.g. *puku* 'clothes' – *pukunsa* 'his clothes').

The process works in reverse also, i.e. strong grade is restored, for example, in the plural form of the adjective with weak grade in the singular: *rakas* 'dear' – pl. *rakkaat*.

Vowels

long and short: i, e, ɛ, a, o, œ, u, y

Length is phonemic. Long consonants and vowels are notated by gemination. There are 16 diphthongs: three rising – /ie, uo, yœ/, the rest falling, ending in /i, u/ or /y/.

Not more than one consonant can figure as syllable-initial (this goes even for foreign words: e.g. Stockholm becomes Tukholm) and words can end only in a vowel or one of the letters /l, n, r, s, t/. Final vowels tend to be aspirated.

VOWEL HARMONY

Back vowels /a, o, u/ are followed by back; front /ɛ, œ, y/ by front; /i/ and /e/ are neutral. Thus, *kymmenen* 'ten'; *omena* 'apple'; *talossa* 'in the house'; *meressä* 'in the sea'.

Formative affixes vary in orthography and pronunciation according to vowel harmony: e.g. *tuntematon* 'unknown'; *kärsimätön* 'impatient'.

MORPHOLOGY AND SYNTAX

Noun

No articles, no gender. The plural marker is *-t*, with an /-i-/ infix in the oblique cases (other than the accusative).

CASE

There are 15 cases; as illustration, the paradigm for a back-vowel noun, *talo* 'house':

	Singular	*Plural*
nominative	talo	talot
accusative	talo	talot
genitive	talon	talojen
essive	talona	taloina
translative	taloksi	taloiksi
partitive	taloa	taloja
inessive	talossa	taloissa
elative	talosta	taloista
illative	taloon	taloihin
adessive	talolla	taloilla
ablative	talolta	taloilta
allative	talolle	taloille
abessive	talotta	taloitta
comitative	—	(taloinensa)
instrumental	(talon)	taloin

Most of the cases are self-explanatory. Among the uses of the partitive are:

(a) to express indefinite quantity: e.g. *pieniä ja isoja puita* 'small and large trees';
(b) after a negative: e.g. *täällä ei ole ihmisiä* 'there's nobody here'; *en lue kirjaa* 'I don't read a/the book';
(c) after numerals: e.g. *kaksi kirjaa* 'two books';
(d) 'some': e.g. *lasi vettä* 'a glass of water'.

The adessive in *-lla*/*-lle* is used to express the verb 'to have', which is missing in Finnish: e.g. *minulla*/*meillä on*/*ei ole ystäviä* 'I/we have (no) friends'.

Adjective

As attribute, adjective precedes noun, and agrees with it in number and case: e.g. *pieni poika* 'small boy'; *pienet pojat* 'small boys'; *suuren kaupungin*/*suurten kaupunkien* (*ulkopuolella*) '(outside) the large town/s'.

COMPARATIVE

-mpi added to genitive minus *-n*: e.g. *Minä olen vanhempi kuin sinä* 'I am older than you' (*kuin* 'than').

Pronoun

Personal subject (nominative) forms: sing. 1 *minä*, 2 *sinä*, 3 *hän*; pl. 1 *me*, 2 *te*, 3 *he*. These are declined in eleven cases; e.g. the accusative forms are: *minut*, *sinut*, *hänet*; *meidät*, *teidät*, *heidät*.

POSSESSIVE AFFIXES
Sing. 1 *-ni*, 2 *-si*, 3 *-nsa/nsä*; pl. 1 *-emme*, 2 *-nne*, 3 as singular. These are added after case endings: e.g. *talossani* 'in my house'.

DEMONSTRATIVE PRONOUN/ADJECTIVES
Two-degree distinction: *tämä* 'this'; *tuo* 'that', with plural forms *nämä*, *nuo*. *Se*, pl. *ne* is neutral. All forms are declined in 12 cases.

INTERROGATIVE PRONOUN
kuka 'who?'; *mikä* 'what?'. Declined in 12 cases, the plural forms being *kutka*, *mitkä*. For all cases, the base for *kuka* is *ken-*.

RELATIVE PRONOUN
joka, pl. *jotka*, declined in 12 cases. Examples: *Tunnen kaikki, jotka asuvat tässä talossa* 'I know all those who live in this house'; *Han on mies, jonka sanaan voi luottaa* 'He is a man whose word can be relied on.'

Numerals

1–10: *yksi*, *kaksi*, *kolme*, *neljä*, *viisi*, *kuusi*, *seitsemän*, *kahdeksan*, *yhdeksän*, *kymmenen*; 11 *yksitoista*; 12 *kaksitoista*; 20 *kaksikymmentä*; 21 *kaksikymmentäyksi*; 30 *kolmekymmentä*; 100 *sata*.

Verb

The Finnish verb has active and passive voices and four moods: indicative, imperative, conditional, and potential. Tenses are simple (present, imperfect) or compound (e.g. perfect). There is no future tense. The language has an extensive apparatus of inflected participial and gerundial forms, including four infinitives. Compound tenses are made with the auxiliary *olla*, whose present tense is sing. *olen*, *olet*, *on*; pl. *olemme*, *olette*, *ovat*; the past tense is sing. *olin*, *olit*, *oli*; pl. *olimme*, *olitte*, *olivat*.

There is only one conjugation for all Finnish verbs; anomalies are phonological. The positive version is parallelled by a negative one. The negative marker is conjugated for person and number: sing. *en*, *et*, *ei*; pl. *emme*, *ette*, *eivät*: thus, *sanon* 'I say'; *en sano* 'I do not say'; *sanoo* 'he says'; *ei sano* 'he does not say', i.e. the sense-verb remains uninflected in the present. For past tense, see below.

Specimen conjugation of *sanoa* 'to say':

present tense: sing. *sanon*, *sanot*, *sanoo*; pl. *sanomme*, *sanotte*, *sanovat*; negative, *en sano*, etc.;

past imperfect: e.g. sing. *sanoin*, *sanoit*, *sanoi*; here, the negative version is made with the past participle which is marked for number: e.g. *en sanonut*, *et sanonut*, *emme sanon**eet***, *ette sanon**eet***;

perfect: e.g. *olen sanonut*, negative *en **ole** sanonut*, *emme **ole** sanon**eet***;

Conditional and potential tenses are constructed on the same principles: the former with an *-is-* infix, e.g. *sano**is**in*, *sano**is**it*; the latter with an *-e* ending, e.g. *sanonen*, *sanonet*, and the auxiliary *lienee* in the past, e.g. *lienen sanonut*.

Imperative: 2nd sing. *sano*; 2nd pl. *sano**kaa***; in the negative, the auxiliary is *älä/älkää*: *älä sano*, *älkää sano**ko***.

All parts of the Finnish verb can be constructed from three base forms – the infinitive, the first person singular present, and the third person singular past: e.g. *sanoa – sanon – sanoi*. In this example, the *-n* is stable: a mutating example is *tehdä – teen – teki* 'to do'.

PASSIVE VOICE

The passive stem is made from the active by the addition of *-ta/-tä*, *-tta/-ttä*: e.g. *sanoa* 'to say', *sano**tta*** 'to be said'. The passive voice is impersonal: *sanotaan* 'it is being said' → 'people say ...'; cf. *Yöllä nukutaan* lit. 'at-night it-is-being-slept' = 'People sleep at night'; *ei lauleta* 'there is no singing'; *Täällä eletään hauskasti* lit. 'here it-is-being-lived well' = 'Here one lives well'; *Antakaat, niin teille annetaan* 'Give and it shall be given unto you' (Luke, 6.38).

PARTICIPLES

(a) Present active in *-va/vä*; provides one way of making relative clauses: e.g. *Näen hänen tule**van*** 'I see him coming'; *Luulen hänen tulevan* 'I think he is coming'; *suomea puhuva ulkomaalainen* 'a foreigner who speaks Finnish'.

(b) Present passive: passive stem + *-va/-vä*: e.g. *Kuulen näin sanottavan* ... 'I hear it's being said ...'; *lue**ttava** kirja* 'a book that has to be read'; *minun on teh**tävä*** ... 'I have to do' (where *minun* is the genitive case of *minä*).

(c) Past active: *-nut/-nyt/-neet*; used e.g. in formation of compound tenses, see above.

(d) Past passive: formed from passive stem by changing *-a-* to *-u-*, *-ä-* to *-y-*. The partitive singular of this participle indicates anterior action in the past: e.g. ***Syötyä** lähdettiin* lit. 'there-having-been-something-of-an-eating it-was-gone' = 'After eating, I/you/he (etc.) went away.'

The following examples show how inflected impersonal forms are used to express modality, purpose, etc.: *mitä he ovat teke**mässä?*** 'What are they doing?'; *Menin Amerikkaan opiskele**maan*** 'I went to America to study'; *Minulla ei ole mitään teke**mistä*** 'I've nothing to do'; *teke**mällä*** 'by working'; *teke**mättä*** 'without working'. Motivation for the endings will be found by reference to the declension table above.

Prepositions and postpositions

Finnish has a few prepositions: e.g.

ilman 'without' with partitive, e.g. *ilman aihetta* 'without cause', *ilman rahaa* 'without money';
paitsi 'besides, except' with partitive, e.g. *Paitsi häntä en nähnyt ketään* 'Apart from him, I saw no one.'

Postpositions usually follow the genitive case:

jälkeen 'after', e.g. *juosta jonkun jälkeen* 'to run behind someone';
kanssa 'with', e.g. *lapsen kanssa* 'with the child';
aikana 'during', e.g. *kahden viikon aikana* 'during two weeks';
edessä 'in front of', e.g. *ikkunan edessä* 'in front of the window'.

Word formation

By formant affix: e.g. nouns from verbs:

-mo/*-mö* 'place where': *leipomo* 'bakery', *panimo* 'brewery';
-ja/*-jä* indicates agent: *lukea* 'to read', *lukija* 'reader';
-ri indicates agent: *juoda* 'to drink', *juomari* 'drinker'.

Nouns from nouns: e.g.

-sto/*-stö*: collective affix: *kirja* 'book', *kirjasto* 'library';
-nen is a diminutive: *kukkanen* 'little flower';
-tar/*-tär* mythopoeic female formant: *luonnotar* 'goddess of nature'; *onnetar* 'goddess of fortune'.

In a privative sense either the postposition -(*ma*)*ton* or the preposition *epä-*: *ajattelematon* 'thoughtless'; *epäluonnollinen* 'unnatural'.

-(*t*)*taa*/(*t*)*tää* makes verbs from any part of speech: *paimentaa* 'to tend, herd' (*paimen* 'flock, herd'); *ylittää* 'to exceed' (*yli* 'over, above').

Word order

SVO is normal but other sequences are possible; e.g. VS may follow adverbial material beginning sentence.

1 Alussa oli Sana, ja Sana oli Jumalan luona.
Sana oli Jumala, 2ja hän oli alussa Jumalan
luona. 3Kaikki on luotu hänen kauttaan, eikä mitään ole luotu ilman häntä. 4Hänessä oli elämä,
ja elämä oli ihmisten valo. 5Valo loistaa pimey-
dessä, mutta pimeys ei ole sitä koskaan käsittänyt.
6Jumala lähetti Johannes-nimisen miehen 7todis-
tamaan valosta, että kaikki kuulisivat häntä ja us-
koisivat. 8Hän ei ollut itse valo, hän vain todisti
valosta.

FRENCH

INTRODUCTION

French belongs to the Italic branch of Indo-European. The official language of France is spoken by over 50 million in the Republic itself, by a further 4 million Walloons in Southern Belgium, and by about 6 million in Switzerland, where it is one of the four official languages. Further afield, about 6 million French speakers live in Quebec, where they form something like 80 per cent of the population, while the francophone element in New England numbers about 1 million. For most of the 5 million inhabitants of Haiti the everyday language is Creole, but theoretically French is the official language of the island. Finally, there are sixteen francophone states running across Central Africa, in all of which French provides an official administrative and commercial medium *vis-à-vis* numerous indigenous colloquials. The total number of French speakers, including those who use it regularly as a second language, is in excess of 200 million.

Dialects

In France itself there is a broad north/south division between *langue d'oïl* (langue d'œil) and *langue d'oc*, or *occitane*; in some ways, the latter is closer to Catalan than it is to the northern dialects. Gascon in the south-west of the country is a markedly divergent occitan outlier. The sub-dialect of the Isle-de-France, known as *francien*, is the basis for the modern literary standard.

It is not too much to say that since the eleventh century French literature has provided models and set standards for the western world: an all-pervasive influence which spread in the nineteenth and twentieth centuries beyond the confines of Europe to Africa and the Far East. The history of French literature falls readily into the following six periods:

1. Eleventh to thirteenth centuries: the *chansons de geste*, including the *Chanson de Roland*; the *romans* (Arthurian cycle, *Roman de la Rose*).
2. Sixteenth century: Rabelais and Montaigne.
3. Seventeenth century: Malherbe, Descartes, Pascal, Boileau; Corneille, Molière, Racine.
4. Eighteenth century: Montesquieu; the Enlightenment and L'Encyclopédie; Voltaire, Rousseau.
5. Nineteenth century: Chateaubriand; de Vigny, Lamartine; Baudelaire, Mallarmé, George Sand, Victor Hugo, Alexandre Dumas, Gustave

Flaubert, Emile Zola.
6. Twentieth century.

SCRIPT

Latin alphabet, with three accents, circumflex, acute, and grave, and cedilla.

In the Old French period, many lexemes were, at least in writing, closer to their Latin originals than they are in Modern French, and the orthography was correspondingly more rational, with a closer correlation between sound and symbol: cf. OF *vedeir* 'see' > MF *voir*.

The period from the fourteenth to the sixteenth century brought accelerated phonetic change in which monosyllabism was a key feature, along with a consciously archaizing and sometimes misguided attempt to restore Latin orthography: e.g.

OF doit > MF doi**g**t (Latin di**g**itum)
OF pie > MF pie**d** (Latin pe**d**em)

The result is that the overall correspondence between pronunciation and notation in Modern French is weak; for example, /ɛ/ is notated in half a dozen different ways, and the proportion of mute letters is high. In this respect, French joins Portuguese in sharp contrast to Italian and Spanish.

In the nineteenth and twentieth centuries several attempts were made at achieving a limited rationalization of the orthography: e.g. the Beslais commissions in 1952 and 1965 which proposed *inter alia* a standardized plural marker in *-s* (i.e. the abolition of the *-x* marker) and the reduction of superfluous geminates. No action has been taken on these points.

PHONOLOGY

Consonants

stops: p, b, t, d, k, g
fricatives: f, v, s, z, ʃ, ʒ, ʁ
nasals: m, n, ɲ
lateral: l/ l̥
semi-vowels: j, w

Vowels

(a) oral: i, y, e, ø, œ, ɛ, a, ə, ɔ, o, u; + many diphthongs/triphthongs involving /j/, /w/ and /ɥ/;
(b) nasal: ɛ̃, ɔ̃, ã, œ̃

Some important features in the development of French phonology since the Old French period:

1. loss of affricates and of /h/;
2. strong tendency towards monosyllabism, involving 3 (below);

3. in Latin forms of $C_1V_1C_2(C_3)V_2C_4$ type, early loss of C_4 followed by loss in spoken French of V_2, thus generating a new final C_2/C_3.

By the rules of French prosody, final syllables which are mute in spoken French are given their full value in verse, e.g. if followed by a consonantal initial.

LIAISON

In word sequences whose components are closely linked by sense, e.g. article + noun, adjective + noun, verb + personal pronoun, etc., there is a follow-through between a final consonant (normally mute) and an initial vowel; in these circumstances, a voiceless fricative is voiced:

nous allons à Paris = /nu**z**al**ɔ̃z**apari/ 'we are going to Paris'
ils ont appris = /i(l)**z**ɔ̃**t**apri/ 'they have learned'

Stress

Stress tends to fall on the final syllable in citation form; in connected speech, on the focused item.

MORPHOLOGY AND SYNTAX

French has two genders – masculine and feminine – and two numbers.

Noun

Certain nominal endings are coded for gender, e.g. the following are always feminine: *-sion/-tion/-xion*; *-aison*, *-ance*; and most nouns in *-ment* are masculine. Essentially, however, gender in French is unpredictable.

A distinction between nominative (direct) and oblique case persisted throughout the Old French period, and most nouns in Modern French are derived from the oblique forms:

Latin		*Old French*		*Modern French*
noctem	>	noit	>	nuit
hominem	>	hom	>	homme
gentem	>	gent	>	gens

The plural marker is *-s*; a few nouns ending in *-eu/eau/ou* take *-x*: e.g. *le feu* 'fire' – *les feux*.

Modern French has lost all trace of declension; all syntactic relationships are expressed by means of prepositions, e.g. *de*, *à*, *pour*, etc.

Coalescence of the definite article with the preposition *de* is illustrated below. In the same way, *à* + *le* → *au*, *à* + *les* → *aux*. Unlike Italian, French does not permit coalescence of *de*/*à* with the feminine article (cf. It. *della, alla*).

Article

French has two articles. Both the definite and the indefinite article are marked for gender in the singular, and for number:

	Masculine	*Feminine*	*Plural*
definite	le	la	les (before vowel, *le/la → l'*)
indefinite	un	une	des 'some'

The preposition *de* coalesces with the definite article to produce the partitive articles: *de + le → du*; *de + les → des*; (*de + la* gives *de la*): thus, *du pain* '(some) bread'; *des livres* '(some) books'. But these forms are reduced to *de* if an adjective precedes the noun: e.g. *des miroirs* 'mirrors': ***de** grands miroirs* 'big mirrors'; *vers de nouveaux rivages* (Lamartine) 'towards new shores'.

The indefinite and partitive articles have a single negative form, *de*: e.g. *Il y a du pain* 'There is bread'; *Il n'y a pas **de** pain* 'There is no bread'.

Adjective

As attribute, the adjective usually follows its noun, but a few very common adjectives always precede: e.g. *bon* 'good', *mauvais* 'bad', *grand* 'big', *petit* 'small', etc. In either position, the adjective agrees with the noun in gender and number. Often, the siting of an adjective is a matter of style: cf.

> un emploi déréglé et passionnel du stupéfiant image (Aragon)
> 'a wild and passionate use of the stupefying image'

Feminine forms normally add *-e*: e.g. *lourd – lourde* 'heavy'. On the phonological plane, this addition very often involves activation of a mute consonant:

Masculine	*Feminine*
grand /grã/ 'big'	grande /grã**d**/
blanc /blã/ 'white'	blanche /blãš/
bon /bõ/ 'good'	bonne /bɔ**n**/

COMPARATIVE
Made with *plus* 'more': e.g. *belle* 'beautiful (fem.)' – *plus belle*. Irregular suppletive forms are: *bon* 'good' – *meilleur*; *mauvais* 'bad' – *pire*.

Pronoun

(a) Conjunctive: first and second person have nominative and oblique forms; third person has nominative + two oblique forms, direct and indirect, with gender distinguished.

		Singular	*Plural*
1		je – me	nous – nous
2		tu – te	vous – vous
3	masc.	il – le – lui	ils – les – leur
	fem.	elle – la – lui	elles – les – leur

The second person plural, *vous* is used as a polite form of address for singular.

The sequential order of the conjunctive pronouns is fixed: *me*, *te*, *nous*, *vous* (also the reflexive *se*) precede *le*, *la*, *les*, which, in turn, precede *lui*, *leur*. Following all of these come the third person oblique forms: *y* (dat.) and *en* (gen.), which are used primarily with non-human referents: e.g. *J'y vais* 'I'm going there'; *Je n'en ai jamais entendu parler* 'I've never heard of it.'

Pronominal order changes in the imperative mood: cf. *je le/les lui/leur ai donné* 'I gave it/them to him/her/them'; but *donne-le-moi* 'give it to me'. *Moi* in the last example is the first person singular disjunctive.

(b) The forms for the remaining persons are: *toi*, *lui/elle*; pl. *nous*, *vous*, *eux/elles*. These are used mainly with prepositions and for emphasis: e.g. *pour moi* 'for me'; *à toi* 'to you'; *avec eux* 'with them (masc.)'.

POSSESSIVE ADJECTIVES

The singular forms show the gender of the possessed object in all three persons: *mon – ma – mes*, etc.: *mon frère* 'my brother' – *ma sœur* 'my sister'; pl. common: *mes frères*. The plural forms, *notre*, *votre*, *leur*, are not marked for gender: e.g. *leur frère/sœur*; but show number of the possessed object: *nos*, *vos*, *leurs*.

DEMONSTRATIVE ADJECTIVE

ce/cet (masc.) – *cette* (fem.) – *ces* (pl.) 'this/that'.

DEMONSTRATIVE PRONOUN

celui-ci/celle-ci 'this one', *celui-là/celle-là* 'that one'; pl. *ceux-ci/là*; *celles-ci/là*. That is, the distal member is expressed by replacing *ci* of the proximate by *là*.

INTERROGATIVE PRONOUN

qui 'who?'; *quoi* 'what?'; *qu'est-ce qui/que*.

RELATIVE PRONOUN

qui/que; *ce qui/ce que*; with oblique forms, e.g. *dont* (gen.): *un homme qui sait le français* 'a man who knows French'; *Montrez-moi les livres que vous avez achetés* 'Show me the books you have bought'; *C'est un homme que je ne connais guère* 'He's a man I scarcely know'; *une classe dont l'utilité sociale a disparu* 'a class whose social usefulness has vanished'.

Numerals

1–10: *un/une*, *deux*, *trois*, *quatre*, *cinq*, *six*, *sept*, *huit*, *neuf*, *dix*; 11 *onze*; 12 *douze*; 13 *treize*; 14 *quatorze*; 15 *quinze*; 16 *seize*; 17–19, *dix* + unit; 20 *vingt*; 21 *vingt et un*; 22 *vingt-deux*; 30 *trente*; 40 *quarante*; 100 *cent*.

Verb

There are three main conjugations, with infinitive forms ending in *-er*, *-ir*, and *-re*. *-ir* verbs are further sub-divided into (a) verbs like *finir* 'to finish', which take the infix *-iss-* in the plural forms of the indicative and subjunctive present and imperfect, and in the imperative; and (b) those like *ouvrir* 'to open', which do not.

There are indicative, imperative, and subjunctive moods. A passive voice is formed analytically by means of the auxiliary verb *être* 'to be' plus the past participle of the sense-verb: e.g. (*ses comédies*) *n'ont pas été écrites pour la scène* '(his comedies) were not written for the stage'.

Compound tenses are made with the auxiliary *avoir* 'to have', except for verbs of motion and reflexive verbs, which use *être* 'to be': e.g. *j'ai donné* 'I have given'; *je suis allé* 'I have gone/I went'; *Il s'est couché de bonne heure* 'He went to bed early.' Both *avoir* and *être* are highly irregular.

Specimen paradigms: *donner* 'to give' and *finir* 'to finish'; forms in regular use in modern literary and spoken French:

Present indicative:

singular	1	je donne	je finis
	2	tu donnes	tu finis
	3	il/elle donne	il finit
plural	1	nous donnons	nous fin**iss**ons
	2	vous donnez	vous fin**iss**ez
	3	ils/elles donnent	ils fin**iss**ent

Imperfect: *je donn-ais*, *-ais*, *-ait*; *-ions*, *-iez*, *-aient*; *je finiss-ais*, etc.

Future: infinitive + the following endings: sing. *-ai*, *-as*, *-a*; pl. *-ons*, *-ez*, *-ont*: e.g. *je donnerai*, *il finira*.

Conditional: infinitive + imperfect endings: e.g. *je donner.ais*, *nous finir.ions*, etc.

Present subjunctive: sing. and 3rd p. pl. as present indicative (+ *-iss-* if present in indicative plural), 1st and 2nd pl. as imperfect: e.g. *que je donne*; *qu'il finisse*; *que nous donnions*; *qu'ils finissent*.

Imperative: *donne – donnons – donnez*; *finis – finissons – finissez*.

PARTICIPLES

Present: *donnant*, *finissant*; past: *donné*, *fini*. The past participle of verbs in *-re* is made with *-u*: e.g. *vendu* 'sold', *rompu* 'broken'.

These are regular verbs; there are, of course, many irregular verbs, some of which can be grouped, e.g. verbs in *-eler*, in *-yer*, in *-cer/-ger*.

A striking feature of these paradigms (and of French conjugation in general) is the homophonic nature of first, second, and third singular, usually shared by third plural as well. Thus, *donnais*, *donnais*, *donnait*, *donnaient*, are all pronounced as /dɔnɛ/; *donne*, *donnes*, *donne*, *donnent* as /dɔn/. It follows from this that the personal conjunctive pronouns have to be used to identify subject, a role in which they are often supported by use of the disjunctive series as well: e.g. *Moi, je veux vivre à la campagne* '(Me,) I want to live in the country.'

The subject pronoun cannot be omitted, even where, as in first person plural, the verb form itself provides sufficient identification: e.g. ***nous*** *avons mangé* 'we have eaten' (contrast It. *abbiamo mangiato*, and Sp. *hemos comido*).

The past historic tense (or, simple past) is found in formal literary style, though no longer in spoken or informal written style; e.g. of *donner*: sing. *je donnai, tu donnas, il donna*; pl. *nous donnâmes, vous donnâtes, ils donnèrent.*

The present subjunctive is used in subordinate clauses, following main verbs expressing emotion, doubt, opinion, prohibition, fear, etc.; also after certain subordinating conjunctions: *afin que* 'in order that', *quoique* 'although', *avant que* 'before', etc.: e.g. *Je crains qu'il* (*ne*) ***soit*** *mort* 'I'm afraid he may be dead'; *quoiqu'il* ***soit*** *pauvre* ... 'although he is poor ...'; *J'approuve qu'il le* ***fasse*** *immédiatement* 'I agree he should do it at once.' The imperfect subjunctive is virtually obsolete.

Negation

The standard negator is *ne ... pas*: e.g. *je ne sais pas* 'I do not know'. There is an increasing tendency, especially in spoken French, to drop the pre-verbal *ne*: e.g. *Je suis pas malade* (Sartre) 'I'm not ill'; *C'est pas ça qui manque* (Sartre) 'There's no shortage of it' (literally: 'That's not what's missing'). In older literary style, *pas* was often omitted: e.g. *je ne sais comment cela se fait* (Maurois) 'I don't know how one does that.'

Prepositions

Apart from their function as spatial and temporal indicators – *dans le jardin* 'in the garden', *sur la table* 'on the table' *après moi* 'after me', *à la campagne* 'in the country', etc. – certain prepositions, notably *à* and *de*, are syntactically bound to specific verbal constructions:

> *commander* ***à****/défendre* ***à*** *quelqu'un* **de** *faire quelque chose* 'order/forbid someone to do something';
>
> *enseigner* ***à*** *quelqu'un* ***à*** *faire quelque chose* 'teach someone to do something'.

Word order

SVO is basic. Simple or complex inversion occurs in certain syntactic situations.

1 Avant que Dieu crée le monde, la Parole existait déjà;
la Parole était avec Dieu, et la Parole était Dieu. 2 La
Parole était donc avec Dieu au commencement. 3 Dieu a fait
toutes choses par elle; rien de ce qui existe n'a été fait sans
elle. 4 En elle était la vie, et cette vie donnait la lumière aux
hommes. 5 La lumière brille dans l'obscurité, et l'obscurité ne
l'a pas reçue.

6 Dieu envoya son messager, un homme appelé Jean. 7 Il
vint comme témoin, pour parler de la lumière. Il vint pour
que tous croient grâce à ce qu'il disait. 8 Il n'était pas lui-
même la lumière, il était le témoin qui vient pour parler
de la lumière.

FULANI (Fulbe)

INTRODUCTION

This language (also known as Fulfulde) belongs to the West Atlantic branch of the Benue-Congo family. The total number of Fulani speakers is estimated at c. 10 million, the great majority of whom live in northern and eastern Nigeria. Others are scattered over a dozen West African states, from Chad to the seaboard.

Under the Fulani emirate of Adamawa (1806–1901) literature was mainly in Arabic. From the mid-eighteenth century onwards, a main centre of *ajami* Fulani poetry was in what is now Guinea.

PHONOLOGY

Consonants

stops: p, b, b̥, t, d, d̥, k, g, q, ˀ
affricates: tʃ, dʒ, dz
nasals: m, n
fricatives: f, s, h
lateral and flap: l, r
semi-vowels: j, w

Initial and medial /b, d, g, dʒ, j/ are frequently nasalized; notated by prefixed *m/n*. Note tendency to transfer nasalization to preceding long vowel: CV̄ + nasalization → CV̄̃.

PAIRED CONSONANTS

This a very striking feature of Fulani structure. The paired sets are:

b	w	dʒ	j
p	f	tʃ	s
d	r	g	w
		k	h

That is, stops are paired with their relative fricatives. *See* **Noun** below.

Vowels

short: a, ə, ɛ, ɪ, ɔ, u
long: a, e, i, o, u

There are seven glide diphthongs onto /j, w/.

Stress

Stress tends to long vowels.

MORPHOLOGY AND SYNTAX

Noun

No article or gender, no case system: case by position. The fundamental dichotomy in the language is human/non-human.

PLURAL

Two classes of noun are distinguished, personal and non-personal. The plural of personal nouns is formed by changing the initials as follows:

b	→ w/g	j /dʒ	→ y
ch /tʃ/	→ s	k	→ h
d	→ r	p	→ f
g	→ w/y		

These changes are reversed in the plural formation of non-personal nouns:

w	→ b/g	f	→ p
h	→ k	y	→ j/g
s	→ ch /tʃ/	r	→ d

Unvoiced *b̥*, *d̥*, *y̥*, the nasalized consonants, and the initials of loan-words do not change in either class.

Nouns in the personal class with singular in *-o*, make a plural in *-b̥e* or *'en*: e.g. ***konōwo*** 'warrior': pl. ***honōb̥e***.

Modulation of initial consonant is accompanied by a change in final vowel. Examples:

Singular	*Plural*
gorko 'male person'	***w***orbe
wordu 'dog'	***g***ordi
debbo 'female'	***reube***
reuru 'bitch'	***d***ebbi

Genitive relationship is indicated by construct: *puchu lāmid̥o* 'the king's horse'; *puchu bāba māko* 'his father's horse'.

Dative precedes accusative noun, follows accusative pronoun.

Adjective

Verbal forms supply predicative adjectival sense: an attributive form is then supplied by the neutral participle, normally in *-d̥um*, often in *-dʒum* (spelled

-jum): e.g. *wōd̥i* 'it is good', ***bōd̥d̥um*** 'good'; *woji* 'it is red' ***bodējum/bodēdʒum/*** 'red'.

The *-jum* class of noun has a personal singular form in *-jo*, with plural in *-'en* or *-b̥e*: e.g. *dan**ējo*** 'white man'; plural ***ranēb̥e***.

The *-jum* affix can be added to any word to form an adjectival derivative: e.g. *hande* 'today'; *handējum* 'today's', 'actual'.

A nasal initial in the noun is resumed in the adjective: cf. *mbōdi mbod̥ēri* 'a red snake', pl. *bod̥d̥e bod̥ēje*; *yēso wod̥ēwo* 'a red face', pl. ***gese*** *bod̥ēje*.

COMPARATIVE

Made with *b̥ura* 'to excel': e.g. *Puchu b̥uri nagge* 'A horse is better than a cow'; *Leggal b̥uri towugo dou sūdu* 'The tree is taller than the house' (*dou* 'over').

Pronoun

PERSONAL INDEPENDENT PRONOUNS

Sing. 1 *min*, 2 *an*, 3 *kanko*; pl. incl. *enen*, excl. *minin*, 2 *onon*, 3 *kamb̥e*. These are not used with verbs. Instead, the conjunctive forms are used:

	Singular			*Plural*	
	Nominative	*Accusative*		*Nominative*	*Accusative*
1	mi	yam	inc.	en	en
			excl.	min	min
2	a	ma		on	on
3	o	mo		b̥e	b̥e

POSSESSIVE FORMS

E.g. sing. 1 *am*, 2 *ma/mād̥a*, 3 *māko*. These follow the noun: e.g. *puchu māko* 'his horse'; cf. *o yi'i mo* 'he saw him'; *o dilli bē māko* 'he went with him'.

DEMONSTRATIVE PRONOUNS

o/d̥o 'this', pl. *b̥e*; *on/d̥on* 'that', pl. *b̥en*; *to/oya* 'that (further away)', pl. *b̥eya*.

INTERROGATIVE PRONOUN

moi 'who?', pl. *b̥eye*; *d̥uma* 'what?'.

RELATIVE PRONOUN

mo, pl. *b̥e*: e.g. *tigōwo* ***mo*** *a yi'i kengya* 'the merchant whom you saw yesterday'.

Numerals

1–5: *gōtel/go'o*, *d̥id̥i*, *tati*, *nai*, *jow*; 6–9 are based on 5: *jowēgo*, *jowēd̥id̥i*, *jowētati*, *jowēnai*. 10 *sappo*; 20 *nōgas*; 30 *chappand̥e tati*; 40 *chappand̥e nai*; 100 *temerre*.

Verb

The verb has three voices: active with infinitive in *-ugo*; passive with infinitive in *-ēgo*; middle with infinitive in *-āgo*.

Perfect and imperfective aspectual system rather than tense. Thus the perfect endings in the active voice are *-i*, negative *-ai*; imperfective: *-a*, *-ata*, *-an*. *No* may be added to fix action in past.

Initial of stem changes for number: e.g. *o **w**indi* 'he wrote', *b̥e **mb**indi* 'they wrote'.

SPECIMEN PARADIGM

Present: *mi d̥on **w**inda* 'I am writing', negative *mi **w**indata*; *min d̥on **mb**inda* 'we are writing', negative *min **mb**indata*.
Imperfect: *mi d̥onno **w**inda* 'I was writing', negative *mi **w**indatāno*; *min d̥onno **mb**inda* 'we were writing', negative *min **mb**indatāno*.
Future: *mi **w**índata* 'I shall write', negative *mi **w**indáta*; *min **mb**indata*.
Preterite I: *mi windi*, negative *mi windai*.
Preterite II: *mi windino*, negative *mi windaino*.
Imperative: *windu – mbinde*, negative *tā windu – tā mbinde*.

PARTICIPLES

(a) Imperfective or present: personal *bindaid̥o*, pl. ***w**indaib̥e* 'about to write'; neutral *bindaid̥un*.
(b) Perfective: personal *bindud̥o*, pl. ***w**indub̥e*; neutral *bindud̥um*.

VOICE

Passive: not much used, active forms being preferred. Pronominal forms and initial concord as for active voice.
Middle: pronominal forms and initial concord largely as for active voice.

DERIVATIVE STEMS

There are five of these;

-ina is always transitive: e.g. *o andi* 'he knew', *o andini mo* 'he informed him';
-ra, *-r*V is instrumental; *see* **Word formation**, below.
*-t*V is intensive, or expresses the contrary of stem meaning: e.g. *mab̥b̥ugo* 'to shut', *mab̥b̥itugo* 'to open';
*-d*V has various meanings: e.g. *o jangi* 'he read', *o jangidi* 'he read through and finished'.

There are several other formants of this kind, e.g. *-tira*/*-indira* expressing reciprocity: e.g. *hōfna* 'to greet, *b̥e **k**ōfnindiri* 'they greeted each other'.

Prepositions

There are a couple of dozen of these: e.g. *diga* 'from', *tana* 'without', *bāwo* 'behind' 'for': e.g. *batākewol fāgo hā alkāli* 'a letter for the judge'.

Word formation

Formation of nouns from verbs: e.g. *-ōwo* 'agent': *winda* 'to write', *bindōwo* 'writer', pl. ***w**indōb̥e*.

Noun of instrument formed from *-ra*-derived stem, with neutral endings *-d̥um*, pl. *-d̥e*; *-gal*, pl. *d̥e*; *-gol*, pl. *d̥i*: thus from *winda* 'to write': ***b**indirgol* 'pen', pl. *bindird̥i*; ***w**indirde* 'office', pl. *bindird̥e*; ***b**induki* 'writing'.

Word order

Normally SVO.

1 Har fuɗɗam Wolde wonno, Wolde ɗonno wondi be Allah,
Wolde nde Allah. 2 Har fuɗɗam o ɗonno wondi be Allah;
3 kala hunde fuh e mako lati; kala ɗum ko lati fuh ɗum lataki
bila mako. 4 Nder mako ngēndam wonno; ngēndam ɗām
ɗam annora 'yimɓe. 5 Annora kā e yaino nder nyiɓre; nyiɓre
jālaki ka.
6 Wodino gorko nulaɗo ibgo e Allah, inde muɗum Yuhanna.
7 Kaŋko o wari ngam sedamku, ha o sedna annora kā, ngam ha
moɓgal fuh nuɗɗina ngam mako. 8 Kaŋko o lataki annora
kā, amma o wari ngam o sedna annora kā.

GEORGIAN

INTRODUCTION

Georgian belongs to the South Caucasian (Kartvelian) group of languages, and is spoken by about 3½ million in the Georgian Republic. It has been a literary language since the sixth century AD. The Old Georgian period extends from the beginnings to the twelfth/thirteenth centuries; this period is rich in translation, mainly of religious works, and culminates in the work of the greatest Georgian poet, Shota Rustaveli, the author of the heroic epic *Vepkhis Tqaosani*, 'The Man in the Tiger Skin'.

It was not until the early eighteenth century that Georgia began to recover from the ravages of the Mongol conquest: King Vakhtang VI edited and completed the corpus of chronicles covering the dark period, known as *Kartlis Tskhovreba*, 'The Life of Georgia'. In the 1860s the drive for a unified literary language was led by three distinguished writers – Prince Ilia Chavchavadze, Akaki Tsereteli, and Vazha-Pshavela. Among modern writers, Niko Lortkipanidze and K. Gamsakhurdia are worthy of special mention.

SCRIPT

Old Georgian was written in the *xucuri* character, traditionally invented by Mesrop Mashtots, to whom the Armenians owe their script. In the eleventh century the ecclesiastical *xucuri* was replaced by the character known as the *mxedruli* 'civil', which is in use today. Georgian is the only Caucasian language to have developed its own script.

PHONOLOGY

Consonants

Central to the Georgian phonological system is the contrast between voiced, voiceless aspirate, and voiceless ejective phonemes (the latter notated with subscript dots in the text), found in the stops (three series) and the affricates (two series):

stops: b, p, p'; d, t, t'; g, k, k'; q
affricates: dz, ts, t's'; dʒ, tʃ, t'ʃ'
fricatives: v, s, z, ʃ, ʒ, x, γ, h
nasals: m, n
lateral and flap: l, r
semi-vowel: j

In the above inventory, /p, t, k/ are aspirates; /p', t', k'/ are ejectives (glottalized). Similarly for the affricates. Multiple clusters are frequent in Georgian; an example of a six-term cluster, given by Comrie (1981), is *mçvrtneli* 'trainer'. Such clusters have single or dual/triple release (involving shwa) depending on whether the components are homogeneous or not.

Vowels

i, ɛ, a, ɔ, u

Stress

On first syllable of disyllabics; in longer words, stress tends to fall on first and antepenultimate syllables.

MORPHOLOGY AND SYNTAX

Noun

There is no grammatical gender; if it is necessary to distinguish between sexes, defining terms may be added, e.g. for *švili* 'child': *važi.švili* 'boy–child' = 'son'; *kali.švili* 'girl–child' = 'daughter'.
There is no definite article. The numeral *ert* 'one', may be used as indefinite article.

NUMBER
The plural marker is *-eb-* following stem, preceding case markers: e.g. *çigni* 'book', pl. *çignebi*; *mta* 'mountain': *mtebši* 'in the mountains'. There is also an older literary plural in *-ni*: e.g. *dzma* 'brother', pl. *dzmani*.

DECLENSION
The following endings are added to consonant stems:

nominative	-i	instrumental	-it
ergative	-ma	adverbial	-ad
accusative/dative	-s	ablative	-dan
genitive	-is	locative	-ši

Vocalic stems drop *-i*, and take *-m* in the ergative.

Examples: *kalaki* 'town': *kalakši* 'in the town'; *samšoblo.dan* 'from the homeland'; *mațareblit* 'with the train'; *Petres çigni* 'Peter's book'. The ergative in *-m(a)* is the case of the logical subject with a transitive verb in the aorist (*see* **Verb**, below).

Adjective

The attributive adjective precedes the noun, and is, in the main, invariable. Consonant stems, however, drop *-i* in the dative (e.g. *didi* 'big', becomes *did*) and take the ergative *-ma*: cf. *patara***Ø** *bavš***ma** 'by a small child'; *did***ma** *bavš***ma** 'by a big child'; *ahal çigni* 'new book'; *ahal muzeum***ši** 'in the new museum'.

Pronoun

PERSONAL

Independent, with subject, direct and indirect pronoun markers, and possessives:

		Independent	*Subject marker*	*Direct object*	*Indirect object*	*Possessive*
sing.	1	me	v-	m	mi	čemi
	2	šen	(h) Ø-	g	gi	šeni
	3	is	-s	Ø	u	misi
plur.	1	čven	v...t	gv	gvi	čveni
	2	tkven	Ø...t	g...t	gi...t	tkveni
	3	isini	-en/-n	Ø	u	mati

Examples: *me* ***v****.çer* 'I write'; *is çer.s* 'he writes'; *čven* ***v****.çer.****t*** 'we write'; direct object with *xatav* 'to paint'; *šen* ***m****.xatav me* 'you paint me'; *isini* ***gv****.xatav.****en*** *čven* 'they are painting us'.

The subject marker of the first person ***v-*** is always dropped before the second person object marker *-g-*: i.e. *****v.g****.xatav šen* → ***g****.xatav šen* 'I paint you'. That is, the absence of a subject marker, plus the presence of a second person object marker, identifies the verb form as first person: ***g****.xedav* 'I see you'.

The independent forms, *me*, *šen*, *is*, etc., are declined, with little change in form; e.g. *me* is both nominative and ergative.

DEMONSTRATIVE PRONOUN/ADJECTIVE

As in Armenian, there are three degrees of distance, associated with the three persons: *es* (first person) 'this', *eg* (second person) 'that', *igi* (third person) 'that yonder'. These are declined and used for both numbers. The oblique base of *is* is *ama-*.

INTERROGATIVE PRONOUN

vin 'who?'; *ra* 'what?'; *romeli* 'which?': e.g. *Vin aris es ḳaci?* 'Who is this man?'; *Vis xatav.s axla es mxatvari?* 'Whom is this painter painting now?'

RELATIVE PRONOUN

-c is added to the interrogative forms: *romelic*, *vinc*, *rac*: e.g.

is çerili, romelic me gamo.v.gzavne Tbilisidan
'this letter which I sent from Tbilisi'

Ik iqo dγes **imdeni** sṭudenṭebi, **ramdenic** ik iqo gušin
'There were as many students here today as there were yesterday'

Numerals

1–10: *erti*, *ori*, *sami*, *otxi*, *xuti*, *ekvsi*, *švidi*, *rva*, *cxra*, *ati*; 11 *tert.meṭi* (*ati* → *t* + *ert* + *meṭi* 'more.'); 12 *tormeṭi*. 20–99 are constructed modulo 20: thus, 20 *oci*, 30 *oc.da.ati*, 40 *or.m.oci*; 60 *sam.m.oci.* 100 *asi.*

Verb

1. In sharp contrast to the relatively simple nominal system, the Georgian verbal system is extremely complicated and difficult to describe in brief. There are two basic contrasts: verbs are (a) static or dynamic, and (b) transitive or intransitive: the latter category includes passive and middle verbs. All static verbs are intransitive; dynamic verbs may be either transitive or intransitive. Transitive verbs require the ergative construction to be used with their aorist forms, i.e. with a direct object in the *nominative* case.

2. Georgian verbs are mono- or polypersonal. For personal indices, *see* **Pronoun**, above.

3. *Conjugation*: four types are distinguished:

I This is an active voice, and stems conjugated in it are usually transitive. Aspect is distinguished.
II Stems conjugated in this model are mostly intransitive; the second conjugation also offers one way of making passives. Aspect is distinguished.
III Denominatives are conjugated according to III. Aspect is not distinguished.
IV This is a specific conjugation for indirect verbs, whose grammatical subject is in the dative.

There is a certain amount of interchange between conjugations; e.g. verbs handled according to IV may borrow forms from II.

4. *Series and screeves*: the term 'screeve' (in Georgian *mc̣krivi*) was coined by the Georgian linguist A. Šanidze to denote a finite verbal form which may be temporal (i.e. a tense), modal, or aspectual. The screeves are arranged in three series:

(a) the present–future series, comprising the following screeves: present – future – past imperfective – conditional – first subjunctive present – first subjunctive future;
(b) the aorist series: aorist – second subjunctive (optative);
(c) the perfect series: perfect – pluperfect – third subjunctive.

5. *Version*: marked by the pre-radical vowels: (∅), *a*, *i*, *u*: ∅ is neutral; *i* denotes 'for oneself'; *u* denotes action for third party; *a* is the so-called super-essive marker: action on something. Cf.

> *çer.s* 'he writes' (neutral: no specific referential deixis);
> ***i.çer.s*** 'he writes for himself', ***mi.çer.s*** 'he writes something for me';
> ***u.çer.s*** 'he writes something for him (third party)';
> *v.**a**,çer* 'I write something on something'.

6. *Pre-verbal markers*: e.g. *a-*, *ga-*, *gada-*, *da-*, *mi-/mo-*, *čamo-*. These function as (a) aspect markers, and (b) directional markers. E.g.

> *me v.çer* 'I write': *me **da.v.**çer* 'I shall write' = 'have written' (cf. Russian perfective present form = future);
> *me **mi**.v.divar **teatrši*** 'I am going to the theatre' (*mi-* 'thither');
> *me **mo**.v.divar sadguri**dan*** 'I am coming from the station' (*mo-* 'hither').

NEGATION

The general marker is *ar*: e.g. *arapers ar vaķeteb* 'I do nothing' (double negative.

Some examples:

(a) series forms of a I conjugation verb: root *çer* 'to write':

		Singular	*Plural*
present screeve:	1	me **v**çer = I am writing	čven **v**çer**t**
	2	šen **Ø**çer	tkven **Ø**çer**t**
	3	is çers	isini çer**en**
past imperfective:	1	me **v**çer**di**	čven **v**çer**dit**
	2	šen **Ø**çer**di**	tkven çer**dit**
	3	is çer**da**	isini çerd**nen**

For the conditional, the imperfective forms are preceded by ***da-***: e.g. ***da.v.çer.di***.

(b) series forms: aorist with logical subject in ergative: e.g. ***me da.v.çer.e*** 'I wrote' (*me* is the ergative case of *me* 'I'); *sṭudenṭ.**ma da.**çer.**a*** 'the student wrote'. Optative: *sṭudenṭ.**ma** unda **da.**çer.**os*** 'the student has to write' (*unda* 'must'; *-o-* is the optative characteristic).

(c) series: perfect: verbs conjugated in this screeve are inferential: e.g. *Sṭudenṭs* ***da.u.**çer.**i.a*** *çerili* 'It would appear that the student has written the letter', where the ***-u-*** marker refers to the subject (the student) in the *dative/accusative* case, while the ***-a*** marker refers to the logical object (*çerili* 'the letter') in the nominative (cf. Turkish -miş- tenses).

POLYPERSONAL VERBS WITH SUBJECT AND OBJECT INDICES

The grid for the present screeve, for example, (either transitive or intransitive) shows 28 forms, made up as follows: four each for first and second person singular and plural; plus six each for third person singular and plural. As several of these forms would otherwise be identical, the independent forms are added: cf. *is mas **Ø**ehmareb.a* 'he helps him'; *is mat **Ø**ehmareba* 'he helps them'; *me mas **v.Ø**.ehmarabi* 'I help him'; *me tkven* (***v→Ø***) ***g***.*ehmarabit* 'I help you (pl.) (for *v→ Ø*, *see* **Pronoun**); *tkven čven **gv**.ehmarebit* 'you (pl.) help us' (*gv-* is object marker).

PASSIVE

The marker is *-i-*, *-d-*, or *-ebi-*: e.g. from *çer* 'to write': ***i.*** *çer.****eb****.a* 'is being written'. *-d-* is used with denominatives: e.g. *γame* 'night': *γam.****d****.eba* 'it becomes night' = 'night falls'.

Postpositions

These may be affixed to words in genitive, dative, or ablative case: e.g. *-tvis* 'for', affixed to genitive: *Qvela ertisa****tvis****, erti qvelasa****tvis*** 'All for one, one for all'; *-gan* 'from', affixed to genitive: *Vis****gan*** *aris es çerili?* 'From whom is this letter?'

Affixed to dative: e.g. *-ši* 'in', *-ze* 'on, at', *-tan* 'with, at ("chez")': *kalak****ši*** 'in the town'; *kreba****ze*** 'at the meeting'; *deda****stan*** 'at one's mother's'.

Independent postpositions following genitive case:

šemdeg 'after', e.g. *gaḳvetilis šemdeg* 'after the lesson';
šesaxeb 'about', e.g. *Ris šesaxeb laparaḳobs es moçape?* 'What is this pupil talking about?';
dros 'during': e.g. *omis dros* 'during the war'.

Word order

Relatively free: SVO, SOV, OSV all occur.

1. პირველითგან იყო სიტყჳ̂ა, და სიტყჳ̂ა იგი
იყო ღჳ̂თისა თანა, და ღმერთი იყო სიტყჳ̂ა იგი.
2. ესე იყო პირველითგან ღჳ̂თისა თანა.
3. ყოველივე მის მიერ შეიქმნა, და თჳნიერ
მისა არცა ერთი რა იქმნა, რაოდენი რა იქმნა.
4. მის თანა ცხოვრება იყო, და ცხოვრება იგი
იყო ნათელ კაცთა.
5. და ნათელი იგი ბნელსა შინა ჰსჩანს, და
ბნელი იგი მას ვერ ეწია.
6. იყო კაცი მოვლინებული ღჳ̂თისა მიერ, და
სახელი მისი იოანე.
7. ესე მოვიდა მოწამედ, რათა ჰსწამოს ნათლისა მისთჳს, რათა ყოველთა ჰრწმენეს მისგან.
8. არათუ იგი იყო ნათელი, არამედ რათა ჰსწამოს ნათლისა მისთჳს.

GERMAN

INTRODUCTION

A member of the West Germanic branch of Indo-European and the official language of Germany (over 76 million speakers), German is also spoken in Austria (over 7 million) and is one of the national languages of Switzerland (c. 4 million). In addition, there are large numbers of German speakers in the Soviet Union (about 1 million), in Romania (½ million), and in Alsace-Lorraine (1½ million). The world total of German speakers is around the 100,000,000 mark.

Dialects

The Second (Germanic) Sound Shift is of fundamental importance here. During the first millennium AD, part – but not all – of the continuum of emergent German speech-forms underwent a series of phonetic mutations which can be summarized as follows:

Proto-Germanic unvoiced stops became homorganic fricatives or affricates: i.e. /p, t, k/ > /f, s, x/ç/ *or* /pf, ts, kx/;
voiced stops were mutated to unvoiced: /b, d, g/ > /p, t, k/.

Where these mutations were consistently carried through, the language form known as High or Upper German resulted; its emergence can be dated to, roughly, the fifth to seventh centuries. The same mutations made a partial penetration into the central German area, but left the northern dialect area untouched. Some illustrative examples:

High German	*Low German*	*English*
i**ch**	i**k**	I (Anglo-Saxon: i**c**)
ma**ch**en	ma**k**en	ma**k**e
hei**sz**	hei**t**	ho**t**
A**pf**el	a**pp**el	a**pp**le
Schi**ff**	ski**p**	shi**p**

As the central German area gradually accepted the High German forms, the dialect situation was reduced to a basic opposition between High and Low German. The latter, also known as Plattdeutsch, has been used as a literary language, e.g. by Fritz Reuter (1810–74), and Klaus Groth (1819–99).

The historical development of High German falls into four main periods:

1. Old High German: from the conclusion of the Second Sound Shift onwards;

attested from the eighth to tenth centuries, notably in the sole surviving Old Germanic heroic ballad, the *Hildebrandslied*.

2. Middle High German: 1100–1350. The rich period of the courtly epic is dominated by Wolfram von Eschenbach, the author of *Parzival*, with its key concept of *mâze* – 'moderation, fittingness'; Gottfried von Strassburg, whose splendid version of the Tristan and Isolde story dates from c. 1210; and Hartmann von Aue, the author of *Der arme Heinrich*. The Middle High German period also produced the great Germanic epic of the *Nibelungenlied*, the source of Richard Wagner's *Ring des Nibelungen* tetralogy; and one of Europe's finest lyric poets, Walther von der Vogelweide.
3. Early New High German: 1350–1600: culminating in the Reformation and Martin Luther's translation of the Bible.
4. New High German: seventeenth century onwards.

It was Luther's translation of the Bible into the East Central German dialect (by then largely homogenized with High German) in the mid-sixteenth century that provided a firm basis for a standardized literary language. As he says in his *Sendbrief vom Dolmetschen* (1530): 'Ich hab mich des geflissen im Dolmetschen, das ich rein und klar Deutsch geben möchte', which may be freely translated: 'The task to which I have applied myself as interpreter has been to provide pure, clear German.' Luther succeeded; and his 'pure, clear German' became the language of the *Aufklärung*, and of Classical Weimar (Goethe and Schiller; Hölderlin), the language of *Bildung*, 'self-cultivation'. Through the nineteenth and early twentieth century it was the language of scholarship, of great prose (Adalbert Stifter, Theodor Fontane, Thomas Mann) and of some sublime poetry (Rainer Maria Rilke), until the days of the Third Reich, when German lost touch with both *mâze* and *Bildung*. In 1933 Karl Kraus ended his last poem with the line: *Das Wort entschlief, als jene Welt erwachte.*

SCRIPT

Until the twentieth century the Gothic script was used for German, both in print and in handwriting. Roman is now standard. Voiceless /s/ is notated as ß in word-final position, before final *-t*, and following a long vowel: e.g. *groß* 'big'; *läßt* 'lets'; *Füße* 'feet'.

PHONOLOGY

Consonants

stops: p, b, t, d, k, g, ʔ
fricatives: f, v, s, z, ʃ, ʒ, ç, x, h; [ç/x] are positional variants
nasals: m, n, ŋ
lateral and flap: l, r, ʀ
semi-vowel: j

The phonemes /ts, ps, ks, pf/ also occur, and are variously classified as affricates or as clusters.

[ç/x] as positional variants: cf. *ich* 'I' /iç/; *Buch* 'book' /bux/. The diminutive suffix *-chen* is invariably /çɛn/ whatever the preceding phoneme.

Voiced stops in word-final position are devoiced: e.g. *gab* 'gave' /gaːp/; *Tod* 'death' /toːt/.

Vowels

front: i, iː, y, yː, e, eː, œ, œː, ɛ, ɛː
central: ə, a, aː
back: u, uː, o, oː
diphthongs: ai, oi, au

MORPHOLOGY AND SYNTAX

German has three genders and two numbers. The noun has four cases.

Noun

Nominal endings are very largely coded for gender. Thus, all nouns in *-heit*, *-keit*, *-schaft*, *-ung*, and *-ion* are feminine (a very numerous class), and most nouns in *-e* are also feminine. Nouns in *-ling*, *-ich*, *-ig* are masculine; nearly all nouns in *-nis*, *-tum* are neuter (one or two exceptions), as are all nouns with the diminutive suffixes *-chen* and *-lein*. Further, most nouns with the prefix *Ge-* are neuter: e.g. *das Gebäck* 'pastry', *das Gebirge* 'range (of mountains)'.

PLURAL FORMATION

By affix: *-e*/*-en*/*-er*/*-s*; by stem mutation; by stem mutation + ending: e.g. *der Hund* 'dog' – *die Hunde*; *der Strahl* 'ray' – *die Strahlen*; *das Kind* 'child' – *die Kinder*; *das Wort* 'word' – *die Wörter*; *der Bruder* 'brother' – *die Brüder*; *die Tochter* 'daughter' – *die Töchter*.

Some nouns have two plural forms differing in sense: e.g. *das Wort* 'word': pl. *die Worte* 'words in connected utterance', *die Wörter* 'words' (as a plurality, e.g. in *Wörterbuch* 'dictionary').

Article

DEFINITE ARTICLE

der, *die*, *das* (masc., fem., neut.). These are fully declined in four cases; the accusative is distinguished only in the masculine: the following paradigm illustrates the declension of the article and the noun, as well as the weak declension of the adjective ('the good man/woman/book'):

	Masculine	*Feminine*	*Neuter*
Sing. nom.	der gute Mann	die gute Frau	das gute Buch
acc.	**den** gute**n** Mann	die gute Frau	das gute Buch
gen.	**des** gute**n** Mann**es**	**der** gute**n** Frau	**des** gute**n** Buch**es**
dat.	**dem** gute**n** Mann	**der** gute**n** Frau	**dem** gute**n** Buch
Pl. nom.	die guten Männer	die guten Frauen	die guten Bücher
acc.	die guten Männer	die guten Frauen	die guten Bücher
gen.	**der** guten Männer	**der** guten Frauen	**der** guten Bücher
dat.	**den** guten Männer**n**	**den** guten Frauen	**den** guten Bücher**n**

A few dozen nouns take -(*e*)*n* in all cases except the nominative (all masculine): e.g. *der Mensch* 'human being': *den, des, dem* Menschen; pl. *die Mensche****n***.

THE INDEFINITE ARTICLE

masculine: ein, einen, eines, einem
feminine: eine, eine, einer, einer
neuter: ein, ein, eines, einem

Adjective

As attribute, adjective precedes noun and shows concord in gender, number, and case. There are two declensions: weak, when the adjective is preceded by the definite article or other qualifier marking gender, number, and case (which is illustrated above) and strong, which is used in the absence of such a qualifier; the adjective itself then takes on the requisite markers: e.g.

	Masculine	*Feminine*	*Neuter*
nom.	gut**er** Wein	gute Frau	gut**es** Brot
acc.	gut**en** Wein	gute Frau	gut**es** Brot
gen.	gut**en** Wein**es**	gut**er** Frau	gut**en** Brot**es**
dat.	gut**em** Wein	gut**er** Frau	gut**em** Brot

The plural endings for all three genders are: *-e, -er, -en.*

There is also a mixed declension used after the indefinite article, the possessive adjectives *mein, dein*, etc., and the negating adjective/pronoun *kein*: cf. *einem guten Wein* 'to a good wine'; *einer guten Frau* 'of a good woman'.

COMPARATIVE
-er added to positive: several very common monosyllables also mutate the stem vowel: e.g. *langsam* 'slow' – *langsamer*; *lang* 'long' – *länger*; *groß* 'big' – *größer*. Suppletive: *gut* 'good' – *besser.*

Pronoun

	1	2	3
singular	ich	du	er (masc.) sie (fem.) es (neut.)
plural	wir	Ihr	sie (all 3 genders)

These are fully declined in three cases: e.g. for first person singular *ich*, acc. *mich*, dat. *mir*.

The genitive forms, e.g. *mein(er)*, *dein(er)*, etc. are very sparingly used in modern German, e.g. *es waren ihrer zehn* 'there were ten of them', though frequent in classical poetry:

Ich denke dein, wenn mir der Sonne Schimmer
vom Meere strahlt; (Goethe)
'I think of you when shimmering sunlight shines towards me from the sea'

Du and *ihr* are familiar second person singular and plural, restricted in use to certain specific socio-linguistic categories (family, school-friends, etc.). The polite form of address is *Sie* (sing. and pl.) with plural concordance; dat. *Ihnen*.

The neuter pronoun *es* is used as demonstrative and complement with the verb *sein* 'to be':

Sind **es** deine Brüder? – Ja, sie sind **es**
'is it/are these your brothers? – Yes, it is they'

DEMONSTRATIVE PRONOUN/ADJECTIVE

dieser/diese/dieses; pl. *diese* 'this, these'; *jener/jene/jenes*; pl. *jene* 'that; those': e.g. *in dieser Welt* 'in this world'; *in jenen Tagen* 'in those days' (dative endings after preposition *in*: *see* **Preposition**).

The neutral form *dies* may be used as an all-purpose demonstrative pronoun: e.g. *dies sind meine Schwestern* 'these are my sisters' (cf. Russian, *eto*).

INTERROGATIVE PRONOUN

wer 'who?', *was* 'what?'.

Wer has accusative and dative forms: *wen*, *wem*; both *wer* and *was* have a genitive: *wessen*.

RELATIVE PRONOUN

Two forms are used: (a) *der*, *die*, *das*; pl. *die*; (b) *welcher*, *welche*, *welches*; pl. *welche*. The (a) form is more usual; the masculine and neuter genitive form is *dessen*; the feminine and plural genitive form fluctuates between *deren* and *derer*: e.g. *es folgten acht Monate, während derer* ... 'eight months followed, during which ...'

The extended form, *derjenige/diejenige/dasjenige*, pl. *diejenigen*, is also available.

Numerals

1–10: *eins*, *zwei*, *drei*, *vier*, *fünf*, *sechs*, *sieben*, *acht*, *neun*, *zehn*; 11 *elf*; 12 *zwölf*; 13 *dreizehn*; 14 *vierzehn*; 20 *zwanzig*; 21 *einundzwanzig*; 22 *zweiundzwanzig*, etc. 30 *dreißig*, 40 *vierzig*; 100 *hundert*.

The numeral *eins*, when used before a noun, takes the form *ein/eine/ein*, and is declined like the indefinite article: e.g. *das kostet nur eine Mark* 'that costs only one mark'; *einer der Beamten* 'one of the officials'; *eines Morgens* ... 'one morning'.

Verb

German verbs are transitive or intransitive; formally, weak or strong. There are three moods: indicative, subjunctive, and imperative, in two voices: active or passive. The active voice has two simple tenses, present and past, and several compound tenses, made with such auxiliaries as *haben* 'to have', *sein* 'to be', *werden* 'to become'. The passive voice is entirely analytical.

The auxiliary *sein* is used to conjugate verbs denoting a change of state or place. All transitive verbs are conjugated with *haben*: cf. *ich* ***habe*** *ihm das Buch gegeben* 'I have given/gave him the book'; *ich* ***bin*** *in die Stadt gefahren* 'I drove to town' (change of place). (For position of verbal components in these examples, *see* **Word order**, below).

WEAK VERBS

The past tense is formed by adding *-te* to the stem; the past participle by prefixing *ge-* to the stem, i.e. the infinitive minus *-en*. For example, infinitive: *mach**en*** 'to make'; stem: *mach-*; past tense: *mach**te***; past participle: ***ge**macht*. Similiarly: *holen* 'to fetch' – *holte – geholt*; *sagen* 'to say' – *sagte – gesagt*.

STRONG VERBS

The past tense is made by ablaut, i.e. mutation of stem vowel. The past participle may resume either the stem vowel or the past-tense vowel, or may exhibit a further mutation: cf.

	Past	*Past participle*
l**e**sen 'read'	l**a**s	gel**e**sen
fl**ie**ßen 'flow'	fl**o**ß	gefl**o**ssen
empf**e**hlen 'recommend'	empf**a**hl	empf**o**hlen
g**e**hen 'go'	g**i**ng	geg**a**ngen

Specimen paradigms of indicative present and past tenses of weak (*holen*) and strong (*gehen*) verbs.

		Singular	*Plural*	*Singular*	*Plural*
present:	1	ich hole	wir holen	ich gehe	wir gehen
	2	du holst	Ihr holet	du gehst	Ihr gehet
	3	er holt	sie holen	er geht	sie gehen
past:	1	ich holte	wir holten	ich ging	wir gingen
	2	du holtest	Ihr holtet	du gingst	Ihr ginget
	3	er holte	sie holten	er ging	sie gingen

Certain stem vowels also mutate in the second and third persons singular of the present tense of strong verbs: e.g.

/ē > ī/: *lesen* 'read': *ich lese, du **lie**st, er **lie**st*
/a > ä/: *fangen* 'catch': *ich fange, du **fä**ngst, er **fä**ngt*
/o > ö/: *stoßen* 'push': *ich stoße, du st**ö**ßt, er st**ö**ßt*

The present subjunctive is always regular; e.g. of *tragen* 'to carry': *ich trage, du tragest, er trage*; *wir tragen, ihr traget, sie tragen*.

The past subjunctive adds *-e* to the past indicative first and third persons singular, and mutates the stem vowel if possible: e.g. *ich trüge*, *du trügest*, *er trüge*, etc.

German verbs, transitive and intransitive alike, are simple, as *tragen*, or take a separable or inseparable prefix. The following prefixes are inseparable, *be-*, *emp-*, *ent-*, *er-*, *ge-*, *ver-*, *zer-*, and, therefore, do not take prefixed *ge-* to form the past participle:

> empfehlen 'recommend': ich empfehle – ich empfahl – ich habe **emp**fohlen
> geschehen 'happen': es geschieht – es geschah – es ist **ge**schehen

The following prefixes are variable, i.e. separable or inseparable: *über-*, *durch-*, *hinter-*, *unter-*, *um-*, *voll-*, *wider*, *miß-*, *wieder-*. A verb which is used with one of these nine prefixes in an inseparable capacity has normally a secondary or derived sense. Compare with *legen* 'to lay', *setzen* 'put, place':

separable:

> wir setzten (mit der Fähre) **über**
> 'we crossed (by ferry)'
>
> sie hatte dem Kinde eine Decke über**ge**legt
> 'she had laid a blanket over the child'

inseparable:

> er **über**setzte das Buch/er hat das Buch über**∅**setzt
> 'he translated the book'
>
> ich habe es mir noch mal über**∅**legt
> 'I had second thoughts about it'

Preposition

The prepositions in German govern the genitive, the dative, or the accusative. Nine very common prepositions take either the accusative or the dative, depending on sense. For example:

with gen.	während **des** Krieges 'during the war'
with dat.	seit **dem** Krieg(e) 'since the war'
with acc.	er ging durch **den** Wald 'he went through the wood'

variable: e.g. *in*:

> er wohnt in **der** Stadt 'he lives in the town' (locus of action does not change)
>
> er ist in **die** Stadt gefahren 'he drove to town' (change of locus)
>
> das Buch liegt auf **dem** Tisch 'the book is lying on the table'
>
> er hat das Buch auf **den** Tisch hingelegt 'he laid the book on the table'

Word order

The rules governing German word order are strict, especially as regards the relative positioning of verbal components:

1. In a principal clause; basic order with a simple tense is SVO: e.g. *Ich gebe ihm das Buch* 'I give him the book.' If the tense is compound, the non-finite component goes to the end: e.g. *Ich habe ihm das Buch* ***gegeben*** 'I have given/ gave him the book.' If the sentence is introduced by anything other than the subject, e.g. by adverbial material, inversion is obligatory: e.g. *Gestern* ***habe ich*** *ihm das Buch gegeben* 'Yesterday I gave him the book.'

Use with modal verb; e.g. *müssen* 'to have to': e.g. *Er muß in die Stadt fahren* 'He has to go to town.'

If a compound tense is used, both sense-verb and modal auxiliary close the sentence in infinitive form: e.g. *Er* ***hat*** *in die Stadt* ***fahren müssen*** 'He (has) had to go to town.'

2. Relative clause: the auxiliary in a compound verb form now follows the participle: e.g. *Ich weiß, daß er in die Stadt* ***gefahren ist*** 'I know that he has gone to town'. But the auxiliary precedes the sense-verb if a modal verb is used: e.g. *Ich weiß, daß er in die Stadt* ***hat fahren müssen*** 'I know that he (has) had to go to town'; *In unserem Kreise* ***hat*** *er sich nicht mehr* ***sehen lassen können*** 'He was not able to let himself be seen again in our circle.'

In *oratio obliqua* the subjunctive is used: e.g.:

assertion:

Das billigt er nicht, aber er kann es verstehen
'He does not approve of this, but he can understand it.'

reported speech:

Er billig**e** das nicht, aber er **könne** es verstehen.

1 Im Anfang war das Wort, und das Wort
war bei Gott, und Gott war das
Wort.
2 Dasselbe war im Anfang bei Gott.
3 Alle Dinge sind durch dasselbe gemacht,
und ohne dasselbe ist nichts gemacht, was
gemacht ist.
4 In ihm war das Leben, und das Leben
war das Licht der Menschen.
5 Und das Licht scheint in der Finsternis,
und die Finsternis hat's nicht ergriffen.
6 ¶Es war ein Mensch, von Gott gesandt,
der hieß Johannes.
7 Der kam zum Zeugnis, um von dem
Licht zu zeugen, damit sie alle durch ihn
glaubten.
8 Er war nicht das Licht, sondern er sollte
zeugen von dem Licht.

GREEK, MODERN STANDARD

INTRODUCTION

Modern Greek belongs to the Hellenic branch of Indo-European. It is the official language of Greece, where it is spoken by over 10 million people, and joint official language of Cyprus; in addition, there are large Greek-speaking communities in many countries. A dialect of Greek is still spoken in few villages in Calabria.

For many centuries Greece presented the classic example of a *diglossia*. Two Greek languages were in use: (a) Demotic, the spoken language deriving from the Hellenistic koine, as modulated and developed in the Byzantine period and during the following centuries of Ottoman domination; and (b) Katharevousa, the consciously archaizing language of administration, religion, education, and literature. Katharevousa itself was written on more than one stylistic level, ranging from a semi-puristic register (advocated, for example, by Adamantios Koraïs in the early nineteenth century; a demotic base plus classical enhancement) to a high-flown literary style which was almost indistinguishable from Classical Greek. Curiously enough, the creation of an independent Greek state in 1830 proved a setback for the pro-demotic camp, as the linguistic issue became confused with political interests. Thus, from the mid-nineteenth century to the 1970s Greek continued to exist on two or even three linguistic planes, the selective use of which depended on socio-linguistic factors. Key stages in the gradual ascendancy of Demotic are:

1. The 'militant demoticism' of Psycharis (1854–1929): identification of Demotic as the expression of the modern Greek ethos: γλώσσα και πατρίδα είναι το ίδιο, 'language and fatherland are one and the same thing'.
2. 1910: Educational Society founded to promote the use of Demotic in education; countered by recognition in the 1911 Constitution of Katharevousa as the official language of the Greek State.
3. 1917: Venizelos government introduces use of Demotic in elementary schools.
4. After several setbacks – e.g. the 1952 Constitution and the Emergency Law of 1967, both of which endorsed the 1911 ruling – Demotic has now been finally and formally recognized as the spoken and written language of Greece.

SCRIPT

The 24 letters of Classical Greek, plus digraphs for certain sounds, e.g.

mp = /b/: *mpaino* = /bɛnɔ/, 'I go in';
nt = /d/: *ntunomai* = /dinɔmɛ/, 'I dress';
gx = /ŋx/: *sugxronos* = /siŋxrɔnɔs/, 'contemporary';
ts = /ts/

PHONOLOGY

Consonants

stops: p, b, t, d, k, (g) + palatalized k′
clusters: ts, dz, ks/gz, ps
fricatives: f, v, θ, ð, s, z, x, γ
laterals and flap: l, ʎ, r
nasals: m/m′, n/ŋ
semi-vowel: j

/g/ is rare.

Vowels

i, ɛ, a, ɔ, u

The former distinction between long and short vowels has been lost. All unstressed syllables are short; stressed syllables may be slightly longer or half-long. A reduction to /ə/ before or after stressed syllable is frequent. Vocalic reduction has led to considerable divergence between sound and symbol; the sound /i/, for example, is notated in no less than six different ways: η, ι,υ,ει,οι,υι.

If the digraphs *ai*, *oi* are to be pronounced as diphthongs, the *i* is marked by a diaeresis: e.g. *roloï 'watch'; kaïmaki* 'cream'.

Stress

Until recently, stress in both Demotic and Katharevousa was marked by acute, grave, and circumflex accents, a legacy from the musical pitch of Ancient Greek. In 1982, a monotonic system of accentuation was introduced by the Greek Ministry of Education; this uses the acute alone to mark stress. Use of the circumflex seems to be optional. The grave has been discarded along with the aspiration markers (*spiritus asper* and *spiritus lenis*) traditionally provided for vocalic initials.

Sandhi

Sandhi at word juncture is a fundamental feature of Greek pronunciation: e.g.

/n/ + /k/ → [ŋg]: e.g. *ston kipo* [stɔ**ŋg** ipɔ], 'in the garden'
/n/ + /b/ → [mb]: e.g. *ðen mporei* [ðɛ**mb**ɔri], 'he cannot'
/n/ + /ks/ → [ŋgz]: e.g. *ðen ksero* [ðɛ**ŋg** zɛrɔ], 'I don't know'

Crasis takes place at vocalic junctures.

MORPHOLOGY AND SYNTAX

Noun

Greek has three genders, masculine, feminine, and neuter. Some guidance as to gender may be given by the ending of a word. Thus, words ending in *-os*, *-as*, *-is* are usually masculine; words in *-i*, *-a* are typically feminine; words in *-o*, *-i*, *-ma* typically neuter.

ARTICLES
There are two articles: the indefinite article is: masc. *enas*, fem. *mia*, neut. *ena*. The definite article is: masc. *o*, pl. *oi* /i/; fem. *i*, pl. *oi* /i/; neut. *to*, pl. *ta*. This article is declined: see declension of noun, below.

DECLENSION
There are three declensions according to ending; the consonantal stems, so plentiful in Katharevousa, have been largely reduced to their accusative forms: *i elpis* 'hope' > *elpida*; *filaks* 'guard' > *filaka*.

Three typical paradigms follow: masc., *o pateras* 'father', fem., *i kardia* 'heart', neut., *to vuno* 'mountain':

Singular	nom.	o pateras	i kardia	to vuno
	gen.	tou patera	tis kardias	tou vunou
	acc.	ton patera	tin kardia	to vuno
Plural	nom.	oi pateres	oi kardies	ta vuna
	gen.	ton pateron	ton kardion	ton vunon
	acc.	tous pateres	tis kardies	ta vuna

Katharevousa formants may reappear in plural endings: e.g. *psaras* 'fisherman' – *psarades*. Notice also such forms as *to kreas* 'meat', gen. *tou kreatos*; *to γramma* 'letter', gen. *tou γrammatos*.

Adjective

As attributive, adjective precedes noun, with concord for gender, number, case: e.g.

nom.	o kalos pateras	i kali mitera	to kalo paidi
gen.	tou kalou patera	tis kalis miteras	tou kalou paidiou
	'the good father('s)'	'the good mother('s)'	'the good child('s)'

Most Greek adjectives end in *-os*, *-i/-a*, *-o*. Other endings are found, e.g. *ziliaris* 'jealous' – fem. *ziliara* – neut. *ziliariko*; pl. masc. *ziliarides*.

COMPARATIVE
In *-teros* (inflected) or with *pio* + positive: thus from *psilos* 'high': *psiloteros* = *pio psilos*.

Pronoun

PERSONAL
The personal pronouns have full, oblique, and two short forms, one of which is used as possessive marker, the other as objective pronoun. These forms are:

	Singular			*Plural*		
	Full	*Oblique*	*Short*	*Full*	*Oblique*	*Short*
1	ego	emena	mou, me	emeis	emas	mas
2	esu	esena	sou, se	eseis	esas	sas

The third person is marked for gender: masc. *autos* /aftɔs/, fem. *auti* /afti/, neut. *auto*. These are declined like the definite article, except that the feminine plural has *autes* – *auton* – *autes* /aftɛs/, etc.

POSSESSIVES
Example: *o pateras mou* /ɔ patɛraz.mu/, 'my father'.

DIRECT OBJECT
ðen ***m***. *endiaferei* 'It doesn't interest me'; *mas katalave* = 'he understood us'. Also as indirect object: *Sas aresoun ta taksiðia?* 'Do you like travelling?'; *telefonese mas* 'call us'.

DEMONSTRATIVE PRONOUN
autos, *auti*, *auto* 'this' (*see* **Personal pronoun**, above). The non-proximate series is *ekeinos*, *ekeini*, *ekeino*.

INTERROGATIVE PRONOUN
pyos – *pya* – *pyo* 'who?', with plural forms, e.g. *Pyos eina autos o anθropos?* 'Who is that man?'; *ti* 'what?'.

RELATIVE PRONOUN
Is marked for gender, e.g. *o opyos* – *o opya* – *to opyo*; and is declined like *autos*. The alternative forms *pou* and *o, ti* are indeclinable: e.g. *o neos pou irθe* 'the young man who came'; *o neos pou eiða* 'the young man whom I saw'; *o, ti θeleis* 'whatever you want'; *to spiti to opyo koitazeis* = *to spiti pou koitazeis* 'the house you are looking at'.

Numerals

1–10: *enas* '1', is fully declined (fem. *mia*) and provides the indefinite article; *duo* '2' /ðiɔ/ is indeclinable; *treis* '3' and *tessereis* '4' are declined. Thereafter indeclinable. 5–10: *pente*, *eksi*, *epta*, *okto*, *ennea*, *deka*; 11 *endeka*; 12 *dodeka*; 20 *eikosi*; 30 *trianta*; 40 *saranta*; 50 *peninta*; 100 *ekato*.

Verb

The basic division is into perfective and imperfective aspects. The perfective base is made from the imperfective base by addition of *-s*, with accompanying assimilation depending on stem final: vowel + *s* → *s*; *z* + *s* → *s*; *f* + *s* → *ps*; *g*/*γ* + *s* → *ks*. Thus:

Imperfective base	*Perfective base*
γrafo 'I write'	γra**ps**o
ðiavazo 'I read'	ðiavaso
ðialeγo 'I choose'	ðiale**ks**o

There are two conjugations: in (a) the stress falls on the root syllable preceding the ending; in (b) stress falls on the ending. For conjugation (a) the formation of the perfective aspect, as set out above, is regular; in conjugation (b) the formative element is *-is*: e.g. *milo* 'I speak' – *miliso*.

From the imperfective base the following tenses are made (verb *khano* 'I lose').

present: sing. *khano*, *khaneis*, *khanei*; pl. *khanoume*, *khanete*, *khanoun*
future: auxiliary + present forms: *tha khano*, etc. (*tha* is invariable)
past imperfect: augment in sing. 1, 2, 3, and in pl. 3: e.g. ***e****khana*, ***e****khanes*, ***e****khane*; pl. *khaname*, *khanate*, ***e****khanan*
imperfect subjunctive: particle *na* + present: *na khano* 'that I lose'
conditional: auxiliary *tha* + past imperfect forms
optative: *na* + past imperfect forms
participle: *khanontas*
imperative: sing. *khane*, pl. *khanete*; negative: *mi*(*n*) + subjunctive.

Tenses made from perfective base:

past definite: again the augment is in the singular and the third person plural: e.g. sing. ***e****khasa*, ***e****khases*, ***e****khase*; pl. *khasame*, *khasate*, ***e****khasan*
future definite: *tha* + perfective base + *imperfective* endings: e.g. *tha khasoume* 'we shall lose'
perfect subjunctive: *na khaso*
perfect: auxiliary *ekho* 'I have' + past participle: e.g. *ekho khasei* 'I have lost'

MIDDLE VOICE

The -V*mai* ending has three distinct functions:

(a) deponent: *kaθomai* 'I sit'
(b) reflexive: *ntunomai* /dinɔmɛ/, 'I dress (myself), get dressed'
(c) passive: *vlepetai* 'it is seen'

The present-tense endings, e.g. for *khanomai*, are: sing. *khan-omai*, *-esai*, *-etai*; pl. *-omaste*, *-este*, *-ontai*

The perfective stem ends in -*θ* with assimilation: *khaθika*, *khaθikes*, etc.: e.g. *sinantiθikame ksana meta ti sinaulia* 'we met again after the concert'.

PARTICIPLES

Active present *khanontas*, past *khasei*; passive present *khamenos*, past *khaθei*.

MODAL VERBS

Examples:

prepei na ton vlepo taktika 'I must see him regularly' (*prepei* 'must, should')

prepei na ton ðo simera 'I must see him today' (*ðo* is the suppletive perfective base of *vlepo* 'I see')

θelo na sou ðoso mia simvouli (*θelo* 'I want')
'I want to give you some advice' (*ðoso* is the perfective base of *ðino* 'I give')

mou aresei na ðiavazo vivlia 'I like reading books' (literally, 'to-me is-pleasing that I read books', i.e. continuous action, present indicative); but *θelo n'agoraso ena vivlio* 'I want to buy (= have bought) a book.'

Prepositions

Prepositions are simple or compound: e.g.

simple: *se* 'in(to)', which coalesces with the article: e.g. *ston*, *stin*, *sto*; *me* 'with'; *meta* 'after'; *prin* 'before'.
compound: e.g. *istera apo* 'after'; *ðipla se* 'alongside'; *pamo se* 'upon'.

Most govern the accusative, five the genitive; one -*kata*- takes either the accusative or the genitive, with change in meaning: e.g. *sto spiti* 'in the house, at home'; *stin Aθina* 'to/in Athens'; *kata ton polemo* 'during the war'; *meta ton polemo* 'after the war'; *apo tin Anglia* 'from England'; *me ta poðia* 'with the feet', i.e. 'on foot'.

Word order

SVO is basic; OV with S understood is frequent: e.g. *tin eiða* 'I saw her'.

1 Απ' όλα πριν υπήρχε ο Λόγος
κι ήταν ο Λόγος με το Θεό,
κι ήταν Θεός ο Λόγος.
2 Απ' την αρχή ήταν αυτός με το Θεό.
3 Μέσον αυτού δημιουργήθηκαν τα πάντα,
κι απ' όσα έγιναν
δεν έγινε τίποτε χωρίς αυτόν.
4 Αυτός ήταν για τα δημιουργήματα η ζωή, [α]
κι ήταν η ζωή αυτή το φως για τους ανθρώπους.
5 Το φως αυτό έλαμψε μέσα στη σκοτεινιά του κόσμου,
μα η σκοτεινιά δεν το δέχτηκε. [β]
6 Ο Θεός έστειλε έναν άνθρωπο που τον έλεγαν Ιωάννη· 7 αυτός
ήρθε ως μάρτυρας για να κηρύξει ποιος είναι το φως, ώστε με τα λόγια
του να πιστέψουν όλοι. 8 Δεν ήταν ο ίδιος το φως, ήρθε όμως για να
πει ποιος είναι το φως.

GUARANÍ

INTRODUCTION

Guaraní belongs to the Tupí-Guaraní group of the Andean-Equatorial family. It is spoken by about 2 million people in Paraguay, where it has semi-official status along with the official language, Spanish. The Paraguayan Guaranís are the descendants of Tupí tribes who migrated to the Paraguay River area in the fifteenth century. Guaraní has been a written language since its use in the Jesuit communities in Paraguay in the sixteenth and seventeenth centuries.

SCRIPT

The Roman alphabet with diacritics. A standardized orthography was agreed at the Montevideo Congress in 1950.

PHONOLOGY

Consonants

stops: ᵐb, p, ⁿd, t, k, g, ʔ
affricate: dʒ
fricatives: v, ʃ, h
lateral and flap: l, r
nasals: m, n, ɲ, ŋ
semi-vowels: j, w

Neither /b/ nor /d/ occurs apart from as the pre-nasalized phonemes. /ʃ/ is notated as *x*, /dʒ/ as *j*.

Vowels

i, e, a, o, u, y

All occur nasalized, usually marked in Guaraní script by diaeresis: *ï*, *ë*, etc. Length is not phonemic.

/y/ is a pharyngeal unrounded vowel resembling /ɯ/ or /ɪ/. Guasch (1956) compares it to the Russian ы. Its nasalized allophone is the characteristic Tupí-Guaraní sound.

Stress

Stress is, in general, unmarked on final vowel or diphthong.

MORPHOLOGY AND SYNTAX

Guaraní has no grammatical gender, nor is there a definite article. Increasing use is being made, however, of the two Spanish articles, *la* for the singular, and *lo* for the plural: e.g. *lo mitä* 'the children'. The numeral *peteï* may serve as an indefinite article for a singular noun, *umi* (a plural demonstrative) for the plural: e.g. *peteï mitäkuña paraguai* 'a Paraguayan girl'. Similarly, a demonstrative may be used as a definite article: e.g. *pe kokue jara jagua* 'the farmer's dog' (*kokue* = *chacra* 'small farm'; *jara* 'master'; *jagua* 'dog').

Noun

Initial *t-* and *h-* are movable or 'oscillating' consonants, changing to *r-* after first or second personal pronouns used as possessives, and in the inverse construct which is the Guaraní (and Tupí) genitive: cf. *tova* 'face' – *xe.rova* 'my face' (*xe* = first person pronoun); *tera* 'name' – *xe.rera* 'my name'; *oga* 'house' – *Tuparoga* 'house of God'. Many nouns which originally had a *t-* initial, are now fixed in the *r-* form.

NUMBER

The plural marker is *-kuera* (→ *nguera* by assimilation, e.g. after nasal vowel): e.g. *jagua* 'dog', pl. *jaguakuera*; *mitä* 'child', pl. *mitänguera*.

GENITIVE

By juxtaposition, the inverse of the Spanish order, with *t-/h- shift: e.g. tuva sombrero* 'father's hat'; *Ko tapo mba'e yvyra rapo.pa*? 'This root is the root of which tree?' (*yvyra* 'tree').

Pe is used to mark a direct or indirect object, and also as a locative marker: e.g. *Jagua ojuka mbarakajape* 'The dog kills the cat'; *Pe karai ome'ë avati kavajupe* 'The man (*karai*) gives maize (*avati*) to the horse'; *i.koty.pe* 'in his (*i.-*) room'; *ipopekuera* 'in his hands' (*po* 'hand').

Gui is an ablative suffix: *a.ju Paraguay.gui* 'I'm from Asuncion'.

Adjective

Adjective follows noun: *peteï kure ka'aguy hü* 'a wild black pig'; *Paraguai ñane retä porä* 'Paraguay, our lovely country' (*tetä* 'country').

Pronoun

Subject, possessive, direct and indirect object sets are distinguished (*see also* **Verb** prefixes, below):

			Subject	*Possessive*	*Direct object*	*Indirect object*
sing.	1		xe	xe	xe	xeve
	2		nde	nde	nde/ro	ndeve
	3		ha'e	i/in/ij/h(i)	ixupe	ixupe
pl.	1	incl.	ñande	ñande	ñande	ñandeve
		excl.	ore	ore	ore	oreve
	2		peë (pende)	pende	pende/po	peëme
	3		ha'e kuera	*as sing.*	ixupekuera	ixupekuera

Examples: *xe/nde kavaju* 'my/your horse ...'; *ñande ra'ykuera rera* 'the number of our sons' (*ta'y* 'son', *tera* 'number'). The base forms take postpositions: e.g. *xe.hegui* 'of me'; *xe.rehe* 'for me'; *xe.ndive* 'with me'.

DEMONSTRATIVE ADJECTIVE

Ranges through several degrees from *ko/ko'ä* 'this' (here and now), to *aipo(v)a* 'that' (unseen and unknown). Plural forms: *äva*; *umi*.

INTERROGATIVE PRONOUN

avapa 'who?'; *mba'epa* 'what?'.

Numerals

Guaraní forms are used for the first four numerals: *peteï*, *moköi*, *mbohapy*, *irundy*. Thereafter, Spanish numbers are used, though Guaraní forms exist (set out, for example, in Guasch (1956)).

Verb

There is a broad division into two classes of verb, which the Spanish writers on Guaraní call (a) *verbos areales*, and (b) *verbos xendales*.

(a) *verbos areales*: these are active/transitive, with invariable stem and personal prefixes as subject markers: these are sing. 1 *a-*, 2 *re-*, 3 *o-*; pl. 1 (incl.) *ja-/ña-*, (excl.) *ro-*, 2 *pe-*, 3 *o-*. A sub-group has 1 *ai-*, 2 *rei-*, etc.: e.g. (*xe*) ***a.****guata* 'I walk', (*nde*) ***re****guata* 'you walk'.

Tense markers are added: *va'ekue* (past), *va'erä* (future): e.g. ***re****.japo.va'ekue* 'you did'; ***re****.japo.va'erä* 'you will do'. There is also a continuative form: ***a****.japo* ***aina*** 'I am doing'; *Mba'epa* ***re****.japo* ***reina****?* 'What are you doing?'

Objective pronouns: first and second person forms precede the verb, third person forms follow: e.g. *nde* ***xe****juhu* 'you meet me'; *ha'e* ***nde****.juhu* 'he meets you'; *xe ajuhu* ***ixupekuera*** 'I meet them'; *xe ha'e ixupe peteï mba'e* 'I say (*ha'e*) something (*peteï mba'e*) to him (*ixupe*).'

(b) *verbos xendales*: these are stative forms, in which the independent pronoun precedes an adjectival or nominal stem. If the stem initial is *t-/h-*, the shift to *r-* takes place for first and second persons: e.g. with *tasy* 'sick': *xe* ***r****asy* 'I am sick'; *nde* ***r****asy* 'you are sick'; but, ***h****asy* 'he is sick'.

Both types of verb are negated by means of *nda- ... i*, as in Tupí: *nd.ai.pota.i*

'I don't want'; *nde.rei.pota.i* 'you don't want'; *nda.ore.rasy.i* 'we are not ill'.

There are, of course, numerous secondary tenses, e.g. a perfect with *kuri*: ***ajapo**/**re**japo kuri* 'I/you have done'; and a second future in *-ne*: ***a**japone* 'I shall do'.

Guaraní has two verbs meaning 'to be': (a) *aime* 'I am in/at a place'; (b) *aiko* 'I am (+ adverb)'. There is no copula; 'I am' + adjective or noun = juxtaposition: e.g. *xe tujama* 'I am old'. Nouns may be marked for tense (cf. Tupi): *-kue* (past), *-ra* (future): *mburuvixa**kue*** '(he) who was boss/chief'; *mburuvixa**ra*** '(he) who will be boss/chief'; *mburuvixa**rangue*** 'someone who was expected to become chief but did not'.

RELATIVE CLAUSE

va/gua: the referent is the subject or direct object of relative clause: e.g. *amo karai oho.**va** amongotio* 'that man who is going over there' (*oho* is third person singular of irregular verb *aha* 'go'); *amo karai a hexa.va amo* 'the man I see there'. *Ha* is used with reference to an indirect object: e.g. *amo karai a me'ë.**ha*** ... 'the man to whom I give ...'; *amo tava aju.**ha**.gui* 'that village from which I come'. Cf. *Kova.pa re.jogua va'erä?* 'Is this what you intend to buy?'; *Kova pa re.jogua va'ekue?* 'Is this what you bought?'

Imperative, conditional, potential, causal, affective moods and several modalities of motion, etc., are expressed with the help of an extensive inventory of particles.

Word order

SVO, VOS.

1 IÑYPYRŨRÂITE voí oicoma vaecue pe Ñeê, ja pe Ñeê
oi vaecue Tûpâ Ñandeyárandive, ja pe Neê jae Tûpâ
2 Ñandeyára voí. Upéva oico voí vaecue pe iñypy-
3 rúmbýpe Tûpâ Ñandeyára ndive. Upéva rupi voí
opa mbae oñemoingo ypy vaecue, ja Jese ŷ reje na
4 peteî mbaemi yepei noñemoingoi. Upe oñemoingo
ypy vaecue ipype voí, upéva voí pe Tecové, ja pe
5 Tecové jae voí umi ybypóra cuera resapéjá. Upe
Jendy ojesapé jina pytûjápe, ja pe pytûjá nda ipuacai
6 Jesé. Oi vaecue peteî cuimbae Tûpâ Ñandeyára
7 remimbou jérava Juan. Upéva ou vaecue imombeu-
jara ramo oicuaauca jaguâ pe Jesapéjarâ gui opa-
8 vave oyerovia jaguâ Jese jaerupi.

GUJARATI

INTRODUCTION

Gujarati is a Western New Indo-Ayran language and is the official language of the state of Gujarat, where it is spoken by about 25 million people. It also spreads into Maharashtra, and is spoken by Gujarati communities in every major city in India. The total number of speakers is estimated at around 30 million.

Gujarati took shape from the Gurjara Apabhraṁsa between the tenth and thirteenth centuries AD. The literature dates from the fourteenth century with mediaeval verse centring on the Rādhā–Kṛṣṇa theme.

Modern writing in Gujarati started in the late nineteenth century along with a new literary standard language, based on the Baroda dialect, as its medium. The influence of Mahatma Gandhi's writings in Gujarati can hardly be overestimated. An outstanding modern poet is Umāśankar Jośī.

Bhili and Khandesi, spoken together by around 4 million people, are usually regarded as variant forms of Gujarati, but by some authorities as languages in their own right. Apart from this questionable point, Gujarati is remarkably homogeneous over its spoken area.

SCRIPT

The specific variant of the Devanagari script used by Gujarati discards the horizontal line above the letter sequence, which is standard in Sanskrit and Hindi.

PHONOLOGY

Consonants

stops: p, b, t, d, ṭ, ḍ, k, g; all with aspirated values: ph, bh, etc.
affricates: tʃ, tʃh, dʒ, dʒh
fricatives: v/w, (f), s, ṣ, ʃ, h
laterals and flaps: l, lh, ḷ, r, rh
nasals: m, mh, n, nh, ɳ, ɳh, (ɲ), ŋ)
semi-vowels: j, w

/dʒ/ and /dʒh/ are represented as *j* and *jh*; retroflex sounds with a subscript dot.

Vowels

i, e, ɛ, ə, a, ɔ, o, u

Most occur nasalized. Each vowel is realized in four allophones, depending on position in word. These variants are not phonemic. Vowels may be accompanied by a kind of breathy 'murmur', which is perhaps associated with elision of intervocalic consonants.

Stress

Stress is barely perceptible.

MORPHOLOGY AND SYNTAX

Noun

Gujarati distinguishes masculine, feminine, and neuter genders. Gender may be identifiable from ending: thus, *-o* is typically masculine, *-ī* and *-ā* are feminine, *-ũ* is neuter. An exception is provided by the many nouns of profession, nationality, etc. which have a masculine form in *-ī*: e.g. *kaṇbī* 'peasant', *maḷī* 'gardener'. There are no articles.

NUMBER
The plural marker *-o* is added to the oblique base; this is normally identical to the nominative base, which is also the citation form. Masculine nouns in *-o*, however, make their oblique base in *-ā*: e.g. *ghoḍo* 'horse', obl. base *ghoḍā-*.

DECLENSION
There are six cases. Specimen declension of *kūtro* 'dog':
Singular

nom. kūtro
gen. kūtrāno (masc.), -nī (fem.), -nũ (neuter) (i.e. the genitive behaves as an adjective)
acc./dat. kūtrāne
instr. kūtrāe
abl. kūtrāe
abl. kūtrāthī
loc. kūtrāmā̃

The plural adds the same affixes to the pluralized stem: e.g. *kūtrā.o.-no, -nī, -nũ*, etc.

GENITIVE
Examples: *chokəra.**no** bāp* 'the boy's father'; *ghar.**nī** orḍī* 'the room of the house'; *mahātmā Gandhījī.no āšram* 'Mahatma Gandhi's ashram'.

The ablative may be used in such passive constructions as *bāp**thī** aje kām nahi thāy* 'from father today work not done' = 'Father did no work today.'

Adjective

Adjectives in *-o* show concord for gender, number, and case. Other adjectives are indeclinable, e.g. *sundar* 'beautiful'.

Pronoun

Personal base forms:

	Singular	*Plural*
1	hũ	ame (excl.), āpṇe (incl.)
2	tũ	tāme, āp
3	te/ā (demonstratives)	teo/āo

These are declined in five cases. The oblique base of *hu* is *man-*.

POSSESSIVE PRONOUN
Sing. *māro*, *tāro*; pl. *amāro*, *tamāro*; these show concord.

DEMONSTRATIVE PRONOUN
ā 'this', *te* 'that', with plural forms.

INTERROGATIVE PRONOUN
The base form *koṇ* appears as *kyo* (masc.), *kaī* (fem.), *kyũ* (neut.), with plural forms.

RELATIVE PRONOUN
Sing. *je*, pl. *jeo*, declined in all cases, e.g. gen. sing. *jenũ*, pl. *jenmũ*; with correlatives in *t-* form in principal clause: e.g.

> **je** maŋəsne mẽ pəysa apya **te** pəṭel.no bhaī che
> 'The man to whom I gave the money is the village officer's brother' (*pəṭel* 'village officer')

> **Jyāre** mumbaī jao **tyāre** māre māṭe ā be pustak lāvajo
> 'When you go to Bombay (*mumbaī*) (then) bring me those two books' (*māṭe* 'for' (postposition); *pustak* 'book')

Numerals

1–10: *ek*, *be*, *traṇ*, *cār*, *pā̃c*, *cha*, *sāt*, *āṭh*, *nav*, *das*; 11 *agiār*; 12 *bār*; 13 *ter*; 14–19 are unpredictable forms; 20 *vīs*; 30 *trīs*; 40 *cāḷīs*. The individual forms for 21 to 99 are unpredictable, though decade + 9 is always linked to the following decade: e.g. 48 is *aḍtāḷīs* (i.e. based on *cāḷīs*) but 49 is *ogaṇpacās,* based on *pacās* '50'. 100 *so*.

Verb

The infinitive ending is *-ũ*: e.g. *karvũ* 'to do'; this is the citation form.

MOODS

Indicative, imperative, subjunctive, conditional, presumptive.

Indicative mood: specimen tense formations:

Present: stem + personal inflections: e.g., for *karvũ* 'to do': sing. 1 *hũ karũ*, 2 *tũ kare*, 3 *te kare*; pl. 1 *ame karīe*, 2 *tame karo*, 3 *teo kare*. A progressive form is made from this by recapitulating the endings in the auxiliary verb *chũ*: e.g. *hũ karũ chũ, tũ kare che.*

Perfect:

(a) Intransitive verb, *āvvũ* 'to come': perfective participle, marked for gender and number, + *chũ*: *hũ āvyo/-ī/-ũ chũ* = *hũ āvelo/-lī/-lũ chũ* (*chũ* is conjugated).

(b) Transitive verb: *karvũ* 'to do': subject in oblique (instrumental) case. The participial form agrees with the object in gender and number: e.g. *mẽ karyũ che, tẽ karyũ che* = *mẽ/tẽ karelũ che* 'by-me, by-you was done'.

Past habitual: pronoun + imperfective participle, marked for gender and number: e.g. *hũ karto/-tī/-tũ* 'I was in the habit of doing'; pl. *ame kartā/-tī/-tā̃*.

Past perfective: intransitive: *hũ āvyo/-ī/-yũ* = *hũ āvelo/-lī/-lũ* 'I came'; transitive: *mẽ, tẽ . . . karyũ/karelũ.*

Future: sing. 1 *hũ karīš*, 2 *tũ karše*, 3 *te karše*; pl. *karīšũ, karšo, karše.*

The presumptive, subjunctive, and conditional moods are made by combining the perfective/imperfective participles with auxiliaries: e.g. in subjunctive: *hũ āvto/-tī/-tũ hoũ* 'I may (not) come'.

PASSIVE

In *-ā-*, e.g. from *karvũ*, *karāvũ* 'to be done'. Conjugated as in active.

CAUSATIVE

-āv/-āḍ added to stem: e.g. *karāvvũ* 'cause to do'.

NEGATION

The negative form of the copula – sing. *chũ*, *che*, *che*; pl. *chīe*, *cho*, *che* – is *nathī* /nəhiː/, which is invariable: e.g. *malik ahī̃ nathī* 'the master is not here'; *teo bīmār nathī* 'he is not ill'; *gayo nathī* 'he hasn't gone'. The particles *na* /nə/, *nahi* /nəhi/ negate personal and impersonal forms of the verb in which the copula is not used: e.g. *Kūvamā̃ kapaḍā̃ dhovā̃ nahi* 'Clothes are not to be washed in the well' (*kūvo* 'well'; *kapaḍũ* 'cloth'; *dho* 'to wash'). *Mā* is used to form a negative imperative.

Postpositions

These may follow either the base form of the noun, or one of the oblique cases. For example, with *par* 'on', *baso khursī par* 'sit on the chair', where *khursī* is in the base form.

Several postpositions follow the feminine genitive case in *-nī*: e.g. *ā bāḷak.nī taraph* 'in the direction of that boy'.

Word order

SOV is normal.

૧ સૃષ્ટિના આરંભ પહેલાં **શબ્દ**[અ]નું અસ્તિત્ત્વ હતું. તે ઈશ્વરની સાથે
૨ હતો, અને જે ઈશ્વર હતા તે જ તે હતો. • **શબ્દ** ઈશ્વરની સાથે
૩ આરંભથી જ હતો. • તેના દ્વારા જ ઈશ્વરે બધાનું સર્જન કર્યું, અને
તે સર્જનમાંની કોઈપણ વસ્તુ તેના સિવાય બનાવવામાં આવી
૪ ન હતી • **શબ્દ** જીવનનું ઉદ્‌ભવસ્થાન હતો અને એ જીવન માનવી
૫ પાસે પ્રકાશ લાવ્યું. • આ પ્રકાશ અંધકારમાં પ્રકાશે છે, અને અંધકાર
તેને કદીએ હોલવી શકતો નથી.

૬, ૭ ઈશ્વરે પોતાના સંદેશવાહક યોહાનને મોકલ્યો. • તે લોકોને એ પ્રકાશ
વિષે સાક્ષી આપવા આવ્યો; જેથી બધા માણસો આ સંદેશો સાંભળીને
૮ વિશ્વાસ કરે. • યોહાન પોતે એ પ્રકાશ ન હતો, પરંતુ પ્રકાશ વિષે તે
૯ સાક્ષી આપવા આવ્યો હતો. •

HAUSA

INTRODUCTION

This, the major language of West Africa, belongs to the Chadic branch of the Afro-Asiatic phylum. It is spoken as mother tongue by over 20 million people, and used as second language and lingua franca by at least another 10 million, and is one of the official languages of the Republic of Nigeria.

Writing in Hausa dates from the religious and literary revival associated with the Sokoto Empire established by the Fulani Usman dan Fodio in 1809. Hausa was written in Arabic script, and this *ajami* tradition lasted in general until the British occupation of Nigeria introduced the Roman script in the early twentieth century. Locally, in northern Nigeria, *ajami* writing persists. Traditional Hausa literature consists largely of verse chronicles and homiletic tracts. Prose fiction began to appear in the 1930s, drama slightly later. Poetry retains its popularity and is often broadcast.

The Kano dialect is the basis of the literary language. Very many Arabic loan-words have been integrated into Hausa; borrowing from English is also extensive.

SCRIPT

Roman alphabet with modified letters *ɓ*, *ɗ*, *ƙ* to mark the glottalized implosives; neither vowel length nor tones are marked.

PHONOLOGY

Consonants

stops: b; t, d; ʔ, k, g
glottalized/implosives: ɓ, ɗ, ƙ;
palatalized stops: k′, g′, ƙ′
labialized stops: k°, g°, ƙ°
affricates: tʃ, dʒ
fricatives: f, s, z, ʃ, f′, h
flap/roll: r, ɽ
semi-vowels: j, w

All initial vowels have glottal onset (hamza). Retroflex /ɽ/ is notated here with a subscript dot.

Vowels

short and long: i, e, a, o, u

Short /e/ = [ɛ], short /i/ = [ɪ], short /o/ = [ɔ], short /a/ = [ɐ]. Diphthongs: /ai, au/.

Tones

Two main tones, high and low, with a secondary falling tone. Tone is phonemic. Intonation is also of the greatest importance in Hausa: three cardinal intonational patterns are distinguished: declarative (stepped descending), interrogative, and vocative.

MORPHOLOGY AND SYNTAX

Noun

There are two genders, masculine and feminine, identifiable as such only in singular. Most nouns not ending in *-a*/*-aa* are masculine.

The plural takes many forms, usually involving extension and/or rearrangement (on broken plural lines; *see* **Arabic**) of singular ending, plus tonal change. In the following examples, tone is marked for illustrative purposes: *túnkìyáa* 'sheep', pl. *túmáakíi*; *sírdìi* 'saddle', pl. *síràadáa*; *gàrmáa* 'plough', pl. *gárèemáníi*; *gàríi* 'town', pl. *gárúurúwàa*. A frequent formation is the replacement of the final vowel of the singular by *ō*.C.*ī*, where C is the final consonant of the singular or its reflex: e.g. *taasaa* 'bowl', pl. *taas**ooshii***; *kaasuwaa* 'market', pl. *kaasuw**ooyii***. Many words have more than one plural form.

THE CONSTRUCT STATE

That is, linkage by *na* → *n* (masc.), *ta* → *r* (fem.), pl. *-n*. These linking elements are used in the following ways:

(a) To form the possessive relationship: e.g.

masc. *abooki.**n** ubaa* 'the friend of the father' (*abookii* 'friend');
fem. *goona.**r** ubaa* 'the field of the father';
pl. *mutaane.**n** garii* 'the people of the town'.

(b) To link preceding attributive adjective to noun: e.g.

masc. *babba.**n** gidaa* 'the big house' (*gidaa* is masculine, although ending in *-aa*);
fem. *saabuwa.**r** makarantaa* 'the new school';
pl. *saababbi.**n** littattaafai* 'the new books'.

(c) To link noun with enclitic demonstrative: e.g. *gari.**n** nan* 'this town'; *koofa.**r** nan* 'this door'.
(d) To link noun and possessive marker: e.g. *dooki.**n**.sa* 'his horse'; *goona.**r**.mu* 'our farm'.
(e) In relative-clause structure (see below).

Adjective

There is no distinction between adjectives and other nominals. Attributive nominals precede the noun they qualify, and are in gender and number concord with it. (See examples, above.)

Pronoun

PERSONAL

			Base form	*Dative*	*Possessive*
Singular	1		ni	mini	-na
	2	masc.	kai	maka	-ka
		fem.	ke	miki	-ki
	3	masc.	shi	masa	-sa
		fem.	ita	mata	-ta
Plural	1		mu	mana	-mu
	2		ku	muku	-ku
	3		su	musu	-su

The base forms have direct-object forms which are identical except for second singular, *ka*/*ki*; and third feminine, *ta*. The pronominal forms, plus linking element, underlie the verbal tense markers (see below). The possessive enclitics combine with the construct markers to provide separable possessives: *nawa*, *naka*; *tawa*, *taka*, where *-wa* is variant of *-na*: e.g. *Gida.n na.mu nee* 'This house is ours.'

DEMONSTRATIVE PRONOUN/ADJECTIVE
wannan (masc. and fem.) 'this', pl. *waɗannan* 'these'; *wancan* (masc.), *waccan* (fem.) 'that'; pl. *waɗancan* 'those'. *Nan* 'this, these' and *can* 'that, those' follow noun + construct marker: e.g. *wannan dookii* = *dooki.n nan* 'this horse'.

INTERROGATIVE PRONOUN
waa 'who?'; *mee* 'what?'. These combine with particles *nee* and *cee* to form sing. *waanee*, *waacee*, pl. *su waanee*: e.g. *Su waanee nee suka tafi goona?* 'Who (pl.) went to the field?'

RELATIVE CONSTRUCTION
Two constructions are used:

(a) with *da* (invariable): headword + *n*/*r* link + *da*: e.g. *gida.**n da** sarkii ya gina* 'the house that the chief built' (for *ya gina*, *see* **Verb**, below);
(b) *da* + *wa* → sing. masc. *wanda*. fem. *wadda*, pl. *waɗanda*; here, no linker is used: e.g. *yaaroo wanda ya zoo* 'the boy who came'.

Numerals

1–10: *ɗaya*, *biyu*, *uku*, *huɗu*, *biyar*, *shida*, *bakwai*, *takwas*, *tara*, *gooma*. 11 (*gooma*) *sha ɗaya*, 12 (*gooma*) *sha biyu*; 20 *ashirin*; 30 *talatin*. Arabic forms are used for decades. 100 *ɗarii*.

Verb

All Hausa verbs end in a vowel, and are invariable as regards tense or aspect, person, and number. The final vowel is, however, coded for transitivity and intransitivity, causativity, and certain modal nuances (see below). Specific realizations for aspect, version, person, etc. are generated via pre-verbal markers (based on the pronominal series) plus auxiliary verbal elements. One classification of Hausa verbs uses the third person plural form of these pronominal markers as indices of the various aspects and versions.

There are perfective, imperative, subjunctive, future, continuative, and habitual aspects; direct (indicative) and relative versions, affirmative, and negative; three singular and three plural + an impersonal form; the second and third singular forms are marked for gender.

DIRECT (INDICATIVE) VERSION
Perfective aspect: the pronominal series used here is illustrated with the stem *zoo* 'to come': sing. 1 *naa zoo*, 2 *kaa/kin zoo*, 3 *ya/ta zoo*; pl. 1 *mun zoo*, 2 *kun zoo*, 3 *sun zoo*. The impersonal form is *an*: e.g. *an zoo* 'one came'.

Formally, the pattern for other aspects is largely similar. Thus, e.g. for the first future, in which the auxiliary *zaa* precedes a specific set of markers:

	Singular	*Plural*
1	zan zoo	zaa mu zoo
2	zaa ka/ki zoo	zaa ku zoo
3	zai/zaa ta zoo	zaa su zoo

The direct continuative uses the auxiliary *naa* following a specific set of markers, and preceding the verbal noun: eg. *inaa zuwaa* 'I am coming'; *kanaa/kinaa zuwaa*; *yanna/tanaa zuwaa*.

The continuative paradigm plus *da* expresses 'to have': *munaa da aiki* 'We have work'. This is negated by *baa ... da*: *baa ya da aiki* 'He has no work.'

RELATIVE VERSION
The perfective and the continuative aspects have relative versions which are used in the formation of relative clauses: e.g. sing. 1 *na zoo*, 2 *ka/kika zoo*, 3 *ya/ta zoo*; pl. 1 *muka zoo*, 2 *kuka zoo*, 3 *suka zoo*. Examples: *mutaanen da suka zoo jiya* 'the people who came yesterday' (*jiya* 'yesterday'); *abin da ya cee jiya* 'what he said yesterday' (*cee* 'to say'). As the first of these examples shows, even when a nominal head-word is present, the pronominal copy is necessary.

SUBJUNCTIVE
The subjunctive marker is *su*: e.g. *su zoo* 'let them come'.

NEGATIVE
All affirmative forms, some of which are illustrated above, have negative counterparts; e.g. the negative form of the direct perfective *naa zoo* etc. is *ban zoo ba*, *ba ka zoo ba*, *ba ki zoo ba*, etc. The subjunctive negative is in *kada* + pronominal marker: e.g. *kada in zoo* 'lest I come'.

Hausa has nothing comparable to the derived stem system of Arabic, but certain terminal vowels plus accompanying tonal patterns are associated with specific meanings. Thus *ˋ-aa* verbs are always transitive, e.g. *gìrbaa* 'to harvest'; *ˋ--a* verbs are usually intransitive, e.g. *shìga* 'to enter'. Some in *ˋ--i* have centrifugal meaning, e.g. *tàfi* 'to go away'. Similarly, *-èe* verbs are transitive or intransitive, often with intensification of root meaning; *-ar* verbs are often causative, e.g. *sayar* 'to sell' (= cause to buy); many verbs in *-oo* have centripetal significance, e.g. *zoo* 'to come'; *ˋ-u* verbs are intransitive and passive, e.g. *tàaru* 'to be gathered together'.

Prepositions

Prepositions are simple, derivative, or compound. Derivative prepositions are nouns specifying location. They take the construct markers; *cikii* 'stomach': *ciki.n* 'in(side), into': *yaa shiga cikin gidaa* 'he went into the house'; *gabaa* 'breast': *gaba.n* 'in front of'.

Word formation

By affixation or compounding. Examples of affixation: *mai-* denoting presence of object or quality; *maras-* denoting its absence, e.g. *hankalii* 'mind', *mai.hankalii* 'intelligent', *maras.hankalii* 'unintelligent'; *ba-* denoting ethnic origin, profession, e.g. *ba.haushee* 'a Hausa', *ba.tuuree* 'European, English'.

Compounding: e.g. noun + noun with construct *-n*: *jirgii* 'boat' + *samaa* 'sky': *jirgin samaa* 'aircraft'; or + *kasaa* 'land': *jirgin kasaa* 'train'.

Compound + prefixed form: e.g. *tauraro.mai.wutsiya* 'star with a tail' = 'comet'.

Word order

Normally SVO.

1 [1] Tun fil azal akwai Kalma. Kalman
nan kuwa tare da Allah yake.
Kalman nan kuwa Allah ne. [2] Shi ne
tun fil azal yake tare da Allah. [3] Dukan
abubuwa sun kasance ta gare shi ne, ba
kuma abin da ya kasance na abubuwan
da suka kasance, sai ta game da shi.
[4] Shi ne tushen rai, wannan rai kuwa shi
ne hasken mutane. [5] Haske na has-
kakawa cikin duhu, duhun kuwa bai
rinjaye shi ba.
6 Akwai wani mutum da Allah ya
aiko, mai suna Yahaya. [7] Shi fa ya zo
shaida ne, domin ya shaidi hasken,
kowa yǎ ba da gaskiya ta hanyarsa.
[8] Ba shi ne hasken ba, ya zo ne domin
ya shaidi hasken.

HEBREW

INTRODUCTION

In the North-Western branch of Semitic in the first millennium BC, a distinction is made between Canaanite and Aramaic. By far the most important member of the Canaanite group is Hebrew, known from a rich literature which can be broadly periodized as follows:

1. The Bible: earliest material c. 1200 BC, latest c. 200 BC. This period includes the Babylonian exile, 587–538, and the Persian rule, 538–333.
2. The Dead Sea Scrolls and related material: these are mainly Essene writings dating from the time of the Maccabees around the turn of the millennium. Also worthy of mention is the historian Flavius Josephus (first century AD).
3. The rabbinical literature of the early centuries AD. By this time, Hebrew was no longer a spoken language, and much of the rabbinical literature, e.g. the *Talmud* and the *Targum*, is in Aramaic and based on oral tradition (cf. the hadith in Islam). Central to these writings, however, is the *Mishnah*, a first-century collection of Hebrew treatises on Jewish law.
4. The mediaeval period: the outstanding figure is Moses Maimonides (1135–1204), whose main works in Hebrew are the *Mishne Torah*, a monumental codification of Jewish law, and the *More Nevukhim*, translated by Maimonides himself from his Arabic original *Dalālat al-ḥā'irīn*, the 'Guide for the Perplexed'.

SCRIPT

The Aramaic script in which the Old Testament was written is based on a Phoenician prototype, adopted by the Israelites around 1000 BC. Like Arabic, this script runs from right to left. Originally, vowels were not marked, though three consonants, yodh, waw, and he, came to be used to notate long vowels, especially finals: yodh representing /iː, eː/, waw /oː, uː/, and he /aː/. In the seventh century AD the Massoretes – Jewish scholars working to preserve the Hebrew text of the Old Testament with maximum fidelity – introduced the system of vocalization known as the Massoretic or Tiberian. Since the consonantal structure of the text was regarded as sacred and could not be adapted in any way, vowel points were written above or below the consonants. The vocalization as now preserved represents, therefore, the pronunciation of Hebrew in the seventh century AD, and there are some grounds for believing that the original pronunciation of Hebrew was somewhat different. In addition to the long vowels mentioned above, the Massoretic system marks short /i, e, a, o, u/, plus simple shwa and three shwa augments, /ĕ, ă, ŏ/.

A key deficiency in the system is the use of ְ for both simple shwa and zero vocalization.

PHONOLOGY

Consonants

stops: p, b, t, d, ŧ, k, g, q, ʔ
affricate: ts
fricatives: f, β, θ, ð, s, z, ȿ, ʃ, χ, γ, ʕ, h, ɦ
lateral and flap: r, l
nasals: m, n
semi-vowels: j, w

The stops /b, g, d, k, p, t/ have spirant allophones: [ß, γ, ð, x, f, θ] notated in transcription as *ḇ*, *ḡ*, *ḏ*, *ḵ*, *p̱*, *ṯ*. The six stops are primarily syllable-initial, and become spirants following vowels: *bayiṯ* 'house': *ba.ḇayiṯ* /bə.ßajiθ/, 'in a house'.

The dotted letters *ṭ*, *ṣ* are the emphatics; *ḥ* represents /ɦ/.

Vowels

long and short: i, e, a, o, u + shwa /ə/ and shwa augments /əᵃ, əᵒ, əᵘ/.

Stress

Stress is generally on the final syllable, otherwise on penultimate. Stress can be marked in the script.

MORPHOLOGY AND SYNTAX

Noun

Hebrew has two genders (masculine and feminine) and three numbers; the dual is used mainly for naturally paired items, e.g. parts of the body: *einayim* 'two eyes'; *reglayim* 'two feet'.

Masculine nouns often end in a consonant and have *-im* plural marker: e.g. *ṣuṣ* 'horse', pl. *ṣuṣim*. Irregularly, some masculine nouns have the feminine plural marker *-oṯ*, e.g. *'aḇ* 'father', pl. *'aḇoṯ*; others have a modified stem: *'iš* 'man', pl. *'anāšim*.

Typical feminine singular endings are *-ah*, *eṯ/aṯ*, but many nouns with consonantal endings are feminine: e.g. *'eš* 'fire', *'erec* 'earth', *yaḏ* 'hand', *regel* 'foot', *nep̱eš* 'soul', *ḥereḇ* 'sword'. The feminine plural marker is *-oṯ*: e.g. *nep̱eš* 'soul', pl. *nep̱ešoṯ*.

The dual endings are, masc. *-ayim*, fem. *-aṯayim*.

DEFINITE ARTICLE

h- + V, where V is a vowel depending on the nature of the following initial and its vocalization: cf. *hā.'iš* 'the man'; *ha.ḥereḇ* 'the sword'; *he.hārim* 'the mountains'; *he.ḥāg* 'the festival'.

CASE

The accusative is marked by the particle *'eṯ*: e.g. *bərešiṯ bara' 'elohim '**eṯ** ha.šamayim v'eṯ ha.'arec* 'In the beginning (*rešiṯ*) God created (*bara'*) heaven and earth.'

The genitive relationship is expressed by means of the construct formula: the noun denoting the possessed object, shortened or compressed as far as possible, precedes the possessor: e.g. *qol ha.'elohim* 'the voice of God'. The feminine construct form restores the *-ṯ* ending: e.g. *torah* 'law', construct, *toraṯ-*: *toraṯ YHVH* 'the law of Jehovah'; *'iššeṯ ha.'iš ha.toḇ* 'the wife of the good man'. As in Arabic, the noun in construct cannot take the article. The masculine plural and dual ending in the construct is *-ei*: e.g. *'elohei ha.šamayim və 'elohei ha.'arec* 'the God of heaven and of earth'.

Adjective

As attribute, the adjective follows the noun, with concord in number and gender. If the noun is definite, the article is resumed with the adjective: e.g. *ha.'iš ha.ṭoḇ* 'the good man'; *ha.'iššah ha.ṭoḇah* 'the good woman'; *ha.'anašim ha.ṭoḇim* 'the good men'. As predicate, the adjective usually precedes the noun: *ṭoḇ ha.'iš* 'the man is good'. Adjectival qualification may also be expressed by construct noun plus nominal: e.g. *har ha.qodeš* 'mountain of holiness' = 'the holy mountain'.

Pronoun

Independent personal forms with enclitics (possessive):

		Singular		*Plural*	
		Independent	*Enclitic*	*Independent*	*Enclitic*
1		'ani/'anoḵi	-i	'anaḵnu	-enu
2	masc.	'attah	-ḵā	'attem	-ḵem
	fem.	'att	-eḵ	'atten	-ḵen
3	masc.	hu'	-o	hem/hemmah	-ām
	fem.	hi'	-āh	hennah	-ān

The possessive enclitics are added to the construct form: e.g. *daḇar* 'word', *dəḇar.i* 'my word', *dəḇar.enu* 'our word'; with feminine noun, e.g. *šanah* 'year', *šənaṯ.i* 'my year', *šənaṯ.enu* 'our year'. For plural of possessed object, yodh appears in the possessive suffix: *dəḇar.einu* 'our words'.

DEMONSTRATIVE PRONOUN/ADJECTIVE

Masc. *zeh*, fem. *zoṯ*, pl. *'elleh* (common) 'this, these'; masc. *hu'*, pl. *hem*; fem.

hi', pl. *hen(nah)* 'that, those'. These follow the noun and take the article: e.g. *ha.'iš ha.zeh* 'this man'; *ha.'iššah ha.zot̲* 'this woman'.

INTERROGATIVE PRONOUN

mi 'who?'; *mah* 'what?'. These are indeclinable. *Ha-* in various forms, depending on phonetic follow-up, initiates an interrogative sentence (cf. Arabic *hal*): e.g. ***ha.ṭob̲āh** ha.'ārec?* 'Is the land good?'

RELATIVE PRONOUN

'ašer, indeclinable: e.g. *vayasem šam 'et̲ ha.ad̲am 'ašer yacar* 'and he put there the man whom he had formed' (Genesis, 2.8); *ha. 'ir' ašer yaṣə' u mimmennah* 'the city from which they came'. A participial construction may also be used: e.g. *ha.'iš ha.yošeb̲* 'the man who is sitting'.

Numerals

1–19 have masculine and feminine forms; 1–10 have both construct and absolute forms. Thus, for '2':

	Absolute	*Construct*
masculine	šənayim	šənei
feminine	šətaim	šətei

Example: *va.ya'aš elohim 'et̲.šənei ha.mə'orot̲ ha.gəd̲olim* 'and God made the two great lights' (*ma'or* 'light': masc. noun with fem. pl.).

3–10: masculine forms in singular absolute; these forms modify *feminine* nouns: *šaloš, 'arba', ḥameš, šeš, šeb̲a', šəmoneh, teša', 'ešer*. The feminine form adds *-ah* to a slightly modified form of the masculine: e.g. from *šeš*, fem. *šiššah*. The feminine forms qualify *masculine* nouns: compare ***šeš** našim* 'six women', ***šiššah** 'anašim* 'six men'; ***šaloš** banot̲* 'three daughters'; ***šəlošet** banim* 'three sons'.

Verb

Hebrew verbs are strong or weak: in the former, the (triliteral) root is stable throughout the base conjugation and the derived forms. Weak verbs belong to any one of the following categories: (1) one radical is a guttural; (2) first or third radical is aleph; (3) first radical is nun; (4) first radical is yodh or waw; (5) hollow verb (second radical is yodh or waw); (6) geminated verbs.

The Hebrew verb, like the Arabic, is marked for aspect rather than tense; i.e. perfective contrasts with imperfective. Aspect coalesces with tense in the sense that the perfective aspect is very often equivalent to a past tense, the imperfective to a present or future.

The two aspects combine and complement each other in the narrative tense known as the waw-consecutive, which is a cardinal feature of Old Testament Hebrew. The first verb in such a narrative sequence is in the perfective, while following verbs, continuing the narrative, are in the imperfective – even with switch of subject. In this way, successive actions are effectively linked to initial action: the effectiveness is, of course, lost in translation, e.g. *qam ha.'iš wa.y.yomer.* 'and the man arose and **says** (= said) ...'. Conversely, a future-orientated proposition starts with an imperfective verb, and continues with perfective forms. The waw-consecutive, as the conjunction is called, is followed by gemination of the imperfective personal prefixes (*see* **Conjugation**, below) except in the first person singular, where the vowel of waw is lengthened before *'e-*. The sequence is broken by a negative (the negative particle is *lo*), and must then be re-initiated by a perfective or imperfective take-off point.

CONJUGATION

The basic *binyan* or 'structure' of the Hebrew verb is known as the Qal form. Here, as illustration, the perfective and imperfective aspects of the root *KTB* 'write':

			Perfective	*Imperfective*
singular	3	masc.	**kāṯaḇ** 'he wrote'	yi**ḵtōḇ** 'he writes/will write'
		fem.	kāṯəḇāh	tiḵtōḇ
	2	masc.	kāṯaḇtā	tiḵtōḇ
		fem.	kāṯaḇt	tiḵtəḇi
	1		kāṯaḇti	'eḵtōḇ
plural	3		kāṯəḇu	masc. yiḵtəḇu, fem. tiḵtoḇnah
	2	masc.	kəṯaḇtem	tiḵtəḇu
		fem.	kəṯaḇten	tiḵtōḇnāh
	1		kāṯaḇnu	niḵtōḇ

The other *binyanim*, the derived 'structures', are:

1. *niphal*: this is the passive of the *qal*, and is marked by the prefix *n-*: e.g. ***ni**ḵtaḇ ha.daḇar* 'the word was written'.
2. *piel*: this is the factitive of the *qal*, forming transitive verbs: it is marked by gemination of the second radical, thus corresponding to Arabic II: *qadeš* 'holy', *q**idd**aš* 'to sanctify'. It also forms verbs from nouns: e.g. *daḇar* 'word', *d**ibb**er* 'to speak'.
3. *pual*: the passive of the *piel*: e.g. *biqqēš* 'to seek', *buqqaš* 'he was sought'.
4. *hiphil*: the causative of *qal*: e.g. *šama'* 'to hear', ***hi**šmi'a* 'he caused to hear'.
5. *hophal*: the passive of the *hiphil*: e.g. *h**o**ḵtaḇ* 'it was caused to be written'.
6. *hithpael*: reflexive of *piel*; also reciprocal: e.g. ***hiṯ**ra'u* 'they looked at one another'.

The imperative has forms for second person masculine and feminine, both singular and plural. The jussive coincides largely with the imperfective (slightly truncated), is not used in the first person and has a specific negative particle: ***al** tiqtol* 'do not kill'. (It is interesting that in Exodus 20 the negative commandments are in the imperfective with the negative particle *lo*: i.e. a general exclusion, rather than contingent prohibition: *lo tircāḥ* 'thou shalt not slay'; *lo tiḡnoḇ* 'thou shalt not steal'. But cf. Exodus 20, 16: *dabər-'atāh 'immānu wa.nišmā'āh wa.'al.yiḏaber 'immānu 'elohim* 'speak thou with us and we will hear; but let not God speak with us'.)

PARTICIPLES

The active participle of the *qal* has the form *koṯeḇ* 'writing'; the passive is *kaṯuḇ* 'written'.

Prepositions

(a) Bound forms: *bə* 'in', *lə* 'to', *kə* 'like'. These replace the *h*- of the article: e.g. *b.e.harim* 'in the mountains'; *l.a.meleḵ* 'to the king'.
(b) Hyphenated forms: e.g. *'el* 'to(wards)', *'al* 'on, over, against', *taḥaṯ* 'under', *'aḥarei* 'after'. These have a specific set of personal pronominal enclitics, e.g. *'elaw* 'to him'.
(c) Free forms: e.g. *lipne* 'near'.

Word order

VSO is standard, SVO frequent.

א 1 בְּרֵאשִׁית הָיָה הַדָּבָר וְהַדָּבָר הָיָה אֵצֶל הָאֱלֹהִים וֵאלֹהִים
הָיָה הַדָּבָר. 2 הוּא הָיָה בְּרֵאשִׁית אֵצֶל הָאֱלֹהִים. 3 הַכֹּל
נִהְיָה עַל-יָדוֹ וּמִבַּלְעָדָיו לֹא נִהְיָה כָּל אֲשֶׁר נִהְיָה. 4 בּוֹ הָיוּ
חַיִּים וְהַחַיִּים הָיוּ הָאוֹר לִבְנֵי הָאָדָם. 5 הָאוֹר מֵאִיר
בַּחֹשֶׁךְ וְהַחֹשֶׁךְ לֹא הִשִּׂיגוֹ.
6 אִישׁ הָיָה שָׁלוּחַ מֵאֵת אֱלֹהִים וּשְׁמוֹ יוֹחָנָן. 7 הוּא בָּא
לְעֵדוּת, לְהָעִיד עַל הָאוֹר כְּדֵי שֶׁעַל-פִּיו יַאֲמִינוּ הַכֹּל.
8 הוּא לֹא הָיָה הָאוֹר; הוּא בָּא לְהָעִיד עַל הָאוֹר.

(John 1: 1–8)

HINDI

INTRODUCTION

A New Indo-Aryan language, Hindi has been the official language of India (along with English) since 1947. In terms of numbers it is by far the most important of the New Indo-Aryan languages. It is estimated that as many as 225 million people speak Hindi as mother tongue in the states of Bihar, Haryana, Himachal Pradesh, Uttar Pradesh, Madhya Pradesh, and Rajasthan, and several millions more speak it as a second language. In addition, there are considerable Hindi-speaking communities in many parts of the world.

In origin, Hindi stems from the same Khaṛī Bolī group of dialects which underlies its alter ego – Urdu. For a note on the historical development of these twin forms, *see* **Urdu**.

The *Rāmcaritmānas* of Tulsi Dās (late sixteenth/seventeenth century) written in the Avadhī dialect, is generally regarded as the first outstanding work in the Hindi literary tradition. In Hindi, the transition from traditional poetry to the treatment of contemporary themes in adequate language, lagged, on the whole, behind parallel developments in Bengali and Urdu. The first genuinely modern writer of any stature in Hindi was Hariścandra Bhārtendu (1850–85). With the advent of Premcand (1880–1936) Hindi prose writing, in the shape of the socio-political novel and short story, came of age. During the twentieth century his work was followed by the *āñcalik upanyās* school of novels of social criticism. Through the mid-twentieth century the *nayī kavitā* and *nayī kahānī* – the 'new poetry' and the 'new story' – movements have flourished, both preoccupied with man's predicament in a modern society.

SCRIPT

Devanagari, retaining Sanskrit conjuncts. *See* **Sanskrit**.

PHONOLOGY

Consonants

The consonantal grid is essentially as in Sanskrit. The retroflex /ḷ/ is not in Hindi; /f, z, x, γ, q/ occur in loan-words.
The opposition between the aspirate and the non-aspirate series is carefully observed, as is the opposition between the dentals and the retroflex sounds.

Vowels

short: ɪ, ə, ʊ
long: i, e, ɛ, a, ɔ, o, u

All occur nasalized. The digraph *ai* = /æ/; *au* = /ɔ/.

Stress

Stress is not phonemic.

MORPHOLOGY AND SYNTAX

Noun

Hindi has no articles. There are two genders, masculine and feminine. A typical masculine ending is *-ā*: e.g. *laṛkā* 'boy', *beṭā* 'son'. Typical feminine endings are *-ī*, *-iyā*: e.g. *laṛkī* 'girl'. Nouns with consonantal endings may be of either gender: e.g. *din* 'day' is masculine, *mez* 'table' is feminine. Sanskrit nouns retain their original gender.

CASE SYSTEM

Basically, there are two cases, direct (nominative) and oblique, plus two numbers, singular and plural. Nouns ending in the characteristic vowels *-ā*/*-ī* are declined as follows:

	Masculine		*Feminine*	
	Singular	*Plural*	*Singular*	*Plural*
direct	laṛkā	laṛke	laṛkī	laṛkiyāṁ
oblique	laṛke	laṛkoṁ	laṛkī	laṛkiyoṁ

(nasalized forms like *laṛkoṁ* can also be transcribed as *laṛkõ*).
Athematic nouns like *din*, *mez* do not change for singular oblique, but take *-eṁ* and *-oṁ* in the plural.

This system is extended by a series of postpositional markers: e.g. *ko* which marks the definite direct or indirect object: e.g. *us ādmī* ***ko*** 'to that man'; *Kisān ghoṛe* ***ko*** *ḍhūṁṛh rahā hai* 'The farmer is looking for the horse.'

The genitive relationship is expressed by means of the link *kā*, *kī*, *ke*, depending on gender and number of nouns possessed; this link follows the oblique case: e.g. *laṛ**ke kī** pustak* 'the boy's book', *laṛ**koṁ kī** pustakeṁ* 'the boys' books'.

Other case relations are expressed with the help of such postpositions as *se* 'from', *meṁ* 'in', *par* 'on', *tak* 'up to, as far as', *ne* 'by' following the oblique case: e.g. *in laṛkoṁ kī bahnoṁ ko* 'to the sisters of these boys'.

Adjective

As attribute, adjective precedes the noun; adjectives ending in *-ā* in the masculine singular behave like *kā*: all other adjectives are invariable, i.e. the feminine form in *-ī*, for example, does not change to *-e* in the oblique: e.g. *us choṭe gāṁv meṁ* 'in that small village'; but, *un choṭī mezoṁ par* 'on these small tables'.

Pronoun

PERSONAL

The basic forms with their oblique cases are: sing. 1 *maiṁ – mujh*; 2 *tū – tujh*; pl. 1 *ham – ham*; 2 *tum – tum*. The third person forms are supplied from the demonstrative series: *yah* 'this', *vah* 'that'. These have oblique forms in *is/us*.

A more formal and polite second person form is *āp*, e.g. *āp.ke beṭe* 'your son' (honorific plural) taking plural concord in verb. Used also with reference to third person.

INTERROGATIVE PRONOUN

kaun 'who?', *kyā* 'what?'

RELATIVE PRONOUN

jo, obl. *jis* (declined), with correlative *vah*: e.g. *Jo kitab us mez par hai*, ***vah*** ... 'The book that is on the table, (it) ...'; *ham.**ne** jin ādmiyoṁ.**ko** kal yahaṁ dekhā thā*, ***ve*** ... 'The men we saw here yesterday, (they) ...' (for use of agentive case with perfective verb, *ne*, *see* **Verb**, below; *ko* is the accusative particle; *ve* is plural of *vah* 'that').

Numerals

1–10: *ek, do, tīn, cār, pāṁc, chah, sāt, āṭh, nau, das*; 11 *gyārah*; 12 *bārah*; 20 *bīs*; 30 *tīs*; 40 *cālīs*; 100 *sau*.

The intermediate forms are not predictable. As in other New Indo-Aryan languages, decade + 9 anticipates the following decade; thus, 38 is *arṭīs*, continuing the *tīs* '30' decade, but 39 is *untālīs* anticipating *cālīs* '40'.

Verb

The division into finite and non-finite forms is basic:

Non-finite forms:

infinitive:	-nā	
gerundive:	-nā	
present/imperfective participle:	-tā	declined for gender and number
past/perfective participle:	-ā	declined for gender and number
conjunctive participle:	-kar(ke)	

Finite forms:

1. Synthetic: the Old Indo-Aryan flectional system is represented in Hindi by the following:

(a) The imperative: 2nd sing. = base; 2nd pl. (associated with *tum*) in *-o*. A more formally polite imperative/request is made with *-ie* (associated with *āp*): e.g. *Yah kām abhī kījie* 'Could you please do this work now.'

(b) The subjunctive: the endings are sing. 1 *-ūṁ*, 2 *-e*, 3 *-e*; pl. 1 *-eṁ*, 2 *-o*, 3 *-eṁ*: e.g. *caleṁ* 'let's go/shall we go?'; *maiṁ kyā karūṁ*? 'What am I to do?'

(c) The future (not, strictly speaking, synthetic) is made by adding the affix *-gā/-gī/-ge* to the subjunctive endings: e.g. *maiṁ dūṁgā* 'I shall give'; *ham caleṁge* 'we shall go'.

2. Compound tenses with auxiliary *hūṁ*:

(a) with imperfective participle (marked for gender and number) + *hūṁ* (inflected)

general present: *maiṁ caltā hūṁ* 'I go, am going'; *ham calte haiṁ* 'we go';
imperfect past: *maiṁ caltā thā* 'I went'; *ham calte the* 'we (masc.) went';

(b) with perfective participle (marked for gender and number) + aux.

perfective present: *maiṁ calā hūṁ* 'I have gone';
perfective past: *maiṁ calā thā* 'I had gone'

3. Perfective participle conjugated as preterite tense: e.g. *maiṁ calā* 'I went'; *ham calīṁ* 'we (fem.) went'. The perfective participle forms of five irregular verbs are very important: *karnā* 'to do' – *kiyā*; *lenā* 'to take' – *liyā*; *denā* 'to give' – *diyā*; *jānā* 'to go' – *gayā*; *honā* 'to be' – *huā*.

4. Aspectual forms with secondary auxiliaries: stem + aux.[2] + aux.[1]: e.g. a durative aspect with *rahnā* 'to remain': *maiṁ cal rahā hūṁ* 'I was going'; *ham cal rahe haiṁ* 'we (masc.) were going' (stressed as *cál.rahā.hūṁ*).

Similarly, with modal auxiliaries: e.g. *saknā* 'to be able', *cuknā* 'to complete', *milnā* 'to receive': *maiṁ hindī bol saktā hūṁ* 'I can speak Hindi'; *maiṁ khā cukā hūṁ* 'I've finished eating'.

5. Passive voice: perfective participle of sense-verb + *jānā* 'to go': e.g. *Hindī bhārat meṁ bolī jātī hai* 'Hindi is spoken in India' (*bhārat*).

6. Causative: a formal progression often produces transitive and causative verbs from an intransitive stem; the causative marker is *-vā-*: cf.

marnā 'to die', ***mārnā*** 'to kill', *marvānā* 'to have someone killed';
bannā 'to be made', *banānā* 'to make', *banvānā* 'to have something made'.

AGENTIVE CASE WITH TRANSITIVE VERBS IN PERFECTIVE FORM

The subject is in the oblique case + *ne*, the verb is in concord with the object: e.g. ***Is laṛke ne** kitāb paṛhī **thī*** 'The boy read the book' (*kitāb* is fem.). In this construction, the postposition *ne* follows the oblique form of the third personal pronoun, but the nominative (direct) form of the first and second: cf. *maiṁ.ne/tū.ne/us.ne patr likhā* 'I/you/he/she wrote the/a letter', where *likhā* agrees with *patr* (masculine). However, if a definite object marked by *ko* is present, the verbal form is that of third person singular, construed as an impersonal. An example is given in the section on the relative pronoun, above; cf. *maiṁ.**ne** un logon.**ko** pahle dekh**ā** **thā**.* 'I had seen these people before'.

Postpositions

Some of the most important have been mentioned in the foregoing sections.

Word order

SOV.

१ आदि में शब्द* था;——शब्द परमेश्वर
के साथ था और शब्द परमेश्वर था।
२ वह आदि में परमेश्वर के साथ था।
३ उसके द्वारा सब वस्तुओं की उत्पत्ति हुई,
और जो कुछ भी उत्पन्न हुआ उसमें से एक
भी वस्तु उसके बिना उत्पन्न नहीं हुई।
४ उसमें जीवन था +और यह जीवन मनुष्यों
की ज्योति था।
५ ज्योति अन्धकार में प्रकाश देती रही,
परन्तु अन्धकार उस पर कभी विजयी नहीं
हुआ।
६ परमेश्वर ने एक व्यक्ति को भेजा।
उसका नाम यूहन्ना था। ७ यूहन्ना साक्षी देने
के लिए आए कि वह ज्योति की साक्षी दें जिससे
सब लोग उनके द्वारा ज्योति पर विश्वास
करें। ८ वह स्वयं ज्योति नहीं थे, किन्तु
ज्योति के सम्बन्ध में साक्षी देने आए थे।

HUNGARIAN

INTRODUCTION

Hungarian belongs to the Finno-Ugric branch of Uralic, and is the official language of the Republic of Hungary. There is also a large Hungarian-speaking minority in Transylvania (Erdély) and the total number of speakers is between 12 and 14 million. The ethnonym is Magyar: *a magyar nyelv* 'the Hungarian language'.

From an original homeland in the Urals, where their closest congeners still live, the Magyar tribes moved westwards to reach the Carpathians and the Danube in the ninth century AD. Under the leadership of Árpád, the *honfoglalás* 'settlement' was completed by 896. The oldest monuments in Hungarian are the *Halotti Beszéd* ('Funeral Oration') of c. 1200, and the *Ó-Mária Siralom* ('Lament of Mary') dating from about a hundred years later. The fifteenth century saw a brilliant renaissance period in the reign of Matthias I Corvinus. National disaster at Mohács, where the Hungarians were defeated by the Turks, was followed by a long, slow recovery until the early nineteenth century, when the revolutionary movement produced two great poets, Petőfi Sándor and Arany János. The social and economic transformation of Hungary from the 1860s onwards brought the conditions for a tremendous upsurge in cultural creativity, both qualitative and quantitative, and Hungarian can now lay claim to one of the world's great literatures.

SCRIPT

Roman alphabet, minus *q*, *w*, *x*, *y*, + diacritics for vowel length and quality: peculiar to Hungarian is the notation of long /œ, y/ as *ő*, *ű*.

PHONOLOGY

Consonants

stops: p, b, t, d, ɟ, k, g
affricates: tʃ, dʒ
fricatives: f, v, s, z, ʃ, ʒ, j, h
nasals: m, n ɲ, ŋ
lateral and flap: l, r

All consonants can be long or short; if long, they are written doubled. At junctures, assimilation takes place: unvoiced → voiced before voiced: e.g. *nép* 'people' + *dal* 'song': *népdal* /neː**b**dal/, 'folksong'. And vice versa: voiced → unvoiced before unvoiced: e.g. *zseb* /ʒɛp/, 'pocket' + *kendő* 'kerchief': *zsebkendő* /ʒɛ**p**kendœ/, 'handkerchief'.

Vowels

For reasons of vowel harmony, the vowels are divided into:

high: i, e, œ, y
low: a, o, u

All have corresponding long values (indicated by acute accent). As regards vowel harmony, /i, iː/ are neutral and can be used with either high or low vowels; e.g. *virág* 'flower', *piros* 'red'. /e, eː/ may also occur with low vowels. In general, however, the front/back opposition is observed: cf.

a ház 'the house', *a ház**ban*** 'in the house';
a víz 'the water', *a víz**ben*** 'in the water';
*adt**am*** 'I gave', *kért**em*** 'I asked'.

Hungarian short /a/ is close to the value [ɒ]; long /a/ is [aː]. Theoretically, there is a distinction between open and closed short /e/: [ɛ] and [e]. In Budapest Hungarian the distinction is not observed. /œ/ and /y/ are notated here as *ö* and *ü*.

Liaison of final consonant to initial vowel of following word is a marked feature of Hungarian pronunciation: e.g. *nem akarok ebédelni* /ne-ma-ka-ro-ke-bé-del-ni/, 'I don't want to have lunch'.

Stress

Stress is invariably on first syllable.

MORPHOLOGY AND SYNTAX

Noun

There is no grammatical gender; the pronoun *ő*, for example, means 'he/she'. Where necessary, nouns signifying natural distinction of gender may be added: e.g. *a tanár* 'the teacher', *a tanárnő* 'the female teacher' (*nő* 'woman').

The definite article is *a*/*az*, the latter form before vowels: e.g. *az ember* 'the man'. The definite article is invariable for number: e.g. *a kép* 'the picture', pl. *a képek*. The article is assimilated to postpositions, as e.g. *a ház**ban*** 'in the house': **az.ban a házban* → ***abban** a házban* 'in that house'.

The plural marker is *-k* linked to consonantal stems by a harmonic vowel: e.g. *a ház**ak*** 'the houses'; *a könyv**ek*** 'the books'; *az ablak**ok*** 'the windows'.

CASE SYSTEM

Agglutinative affixes on stem, with harmonic vowels where necessary. With certain endings, assimilation at juncture takes place (see, e.g. comitative case in the following paradigm). In the plural, the endings are added to the *-k* marker.

Singular	nominative	a bor 'the wine'	a víz 'the water'
	accusative	a bort	a vízet
	dative	a bornak	a víznek
	illative	a borba	a vízbe
	comitative	a borral	a vízzel

The comitative ending is *-val/-vel* → *-ral/-rel* after *-r*, → *-zal/-zel* after *-z*, etc.

Variants: some stems change for certain oblique cases, e.g. *tó* 'lake', acc. *tavat*.

Adjective

As attribute, adjective precedes noun and is invariable: e.g. *piros virág* 'red flower', *piros virágok* 'red flowers'; *egy mezőgazdasági kérdés* 'an agricultural question'; (*megoldás*) *ezek**re** a mezőgazdaságiØ kérdések**re*** '(solution) to these agricultural questions'.

All adjectives can be used as nouns, and are then declined fully: e.g. *a magyar nép* 'the Hungarian people'; *a magyar**ok*** 'the Hungarians'.

COMPARATIVE

(Harmonic vowel) + *-bb*: e.g. *nehéz* 'heavy', *nehez**ebb*** 'heavier'. Some comparatives are suppletive, e.g. *sok* 'many', comparative *több*.

Pronoun

	Singular			*Plural*		
	Nominative	*Accusative*	*Enclitic*	*Nominative*	*Accusative*	*Enclitic*
1	én	engem(et)	-m	mi	minket	-unk/ünk
2	te	téged(et)	-d	ti	titeket	-tok/tek
3	ő	őt	-i/e	ők	őket	-ik

Te and *ti* are familiar. The polite second person is *Ön* or *Maga*, with third person concord. Oblique forms are made by adding the enclitic markers to the case endings; e.g. *nek**em*** 'to me', *nek**ed*** 'to you'; *benn**em*** 'in me', *benn**ünk*** 'in us'. The possessive markers are closely similar, but precede the case endings: e.g. *könyv**em*** 'my book'; *ház**unk*** 'our house'; *egy barát**om*** 'a friend of mine'; *zseb**em**ben* 'in my pocket'; *a város**aink**nak* 'of our cities'. These endings also provide the Hungarian equivalent of the verb 'to have': *könyv**em** van* 'I have a book' (lit. 'my-book is'); *könyv**em** nincs* 'I don't have a book'. Where one possessive follows another, the second has the *-nak/-nek* ending: e.g. *a tanár**om** barátjá.**nak** a könyv**e*** 'my teacher's friend's book' (where *-já-* marks possession by *tanár**om*** 'my teacher', and *-**nak*** signals the pending possessive ending *-**e***).

DEMONSTRATIVE PRONOUN/ADJECTIVE

ez 'this', pl. *ezek*; *az* 'that', pl. *azok*: e.g. *ez a könyv* 'this book'; *azok a virágok* 'those flowers'; ***ennek** az iskolá**nak** a tanulói* 'the pupils of this school'.

INTERROGATIVE PRONOUN
ki 'who?'; *mi* 'what?'.

RELATIVE PRONOUN
aki/ami/amely/amelyik: e.g. *az ember, aki beszél* 'the man who is speaking'; *az ember, **akiről** beszéltem* 'the man I spoke about'.

Numerals

1–10: *egy*, *két/kettő*, *három*, *négy*, *öt*, *hat*, *hét*, *nyolc*, *kilenc*, *tíz*; 11 *tizenegy*; 12 *tizenkettő*; 20 *húsz*; 30 *harminc*; thereafter by addition of *-van/-ven*: e.g. 40 *negyven*; 50 *ötven*; 100 *száz*.

Numerals are followed by a noun in the singular: e.g. *hat könyv* 'six books'; *tíz ember* 'ten men'.

Verb

Stems are inherently transitive or intransitive, and can be converted or extended by various modal and aspectual formants: e.g.

-tat/-tet makes causatives: *csinál-* 'to do, make', *Peter ruhát csinál**tat*** 'Peter has a suit made';
-kozik/kezik/közik makes reflexives: e.g. *véd* 'to defend', *véd**ekezik*** 'to defend oneself';
-gat/-get is frequentative: e.g. *beszél* 'to speak', *beszél**get*** 'to converse'.

The passive voice is no longer used in Hungarian; many stems are paired for transitive/active and intransitive/passive meanings: e.g. *nyít-* 'to open' (trans.) – *nyílik* 'to open (intrans.)/be opened'; *rejt-* 'to hide' (trans.) – *rejlik* 'to be hidden'.

There is a very extensive system of pre-verbal particles or prefixes, which are separable, as in German. Some of the commonest are: *be-* 'into'; *ki-* 'out of'; *le-* 'down'; *át-* 'through'; *vissza* 'back'; *meg-* is the perfective marker. Thus *megy* 'he goes', ***be**megy* 'he goes into'; *lép* 'he steps', ***ki**lép* 'he comes out'; *írja* 'he writes', ***le**írja* 'he writes down'; *fordul* 'he turns', ***vissza**fordul* 'he turns back'.

SEPARABILITY
Illustrated with verb *tenni* 'to do' + *meg-* (present third singular is *tesz*):

*hosszú utat tett **meg*** 'he's come a long way';
*mindent **meg**tenne értem* 'he'd do anything for me';
***meg** kell tennem* 'I have to do it';
*nem tesz **meg*** 'he won't do it'.

MOODS
Indicative, conditional, and a subjunctive/imperative.

Indicative: present and past tenses are made by means of personal endings added to the stem. There are two sets of these endings, one for definite, the other for indefinite complement. A subordinate clause introduced by *hogy* 'that', counts as definite. The endings are illustrated with the stem *ad-* 'give':

		Present		*Past*	
		Indefinite	*Definite*	*Indefinite*	*Definite*
singular	1	adok	ado**m**	adtam	adtam
	2	adsz	ado**d**	adtál	ad**tad**
	3	ad	ad**ja**	adott	ad**ta**
plural	1	adunk	ad**juk**	adtunk	ad**tuk**
	2	adtok	ad**játok**	adtatok	adtá**tok**
	3	adnak	ad**ják**	adtak	adtá**k**

Thus *újśagot olvasok* 'I read **a** newspaper'; *az újságot olvaso**m*** 'I read **the** paper.'

First person singular subject + second singular object are encoded in the ending *-lak*/*-lek*: e.g. *kérlek* 'I ask you'; *szeretlek* 'I love you'.

A future tense is made with the auxiliary *fog-* ('to catch') + infinitive in *-ni*: e.g. *adni fogok*/*fogom* (depending on whether complement is definite or indefinite) 'I'll give'. The present with *meg-* prefix may also have future sense: e.g. *megkérdezem a tanártól* 'I'll ask the teacher' (lit. 'from the teacher').

Conditional: the marker is *-n-* + harmonic vowel: e.g. *ad**nám*** 'I'd give' (definite object); *kér**né**k* 'they would ask'.

Imperative/subjunctive: the marker is *-j-*: note the sandhi of *j* with certain sibilants: *s* + *j* → *ss*; *sz* + *j* → *ssz*; *z* + *j* → *zz*: e.g. *olvas-* ('read') + *j* → *olvassa* 'read' (definite object). A polite request is made with *legyen szíves* 'please': e.g. *legyen szíves, olvasson* 'please read' (indefinite). *Fontos, hogy megír**jam** a levelet* 'It's important (*fontos*) that I write the letter.'

PARTICIPLES

Imperative in *-ó*/*-ő*: e.g. *a dolgozó ember* 'the working man'. The form is much used as a nominal: e.g. *a dolgozók* 'the workers'. The perfective participle is identical with third person singular past indefinite: e.g. *adott* 'he gave' → 'given'; *egy ismert író* 'a well-known writer'.

The participial form in *-va*/*-ve* denotes a state of affairs; it is often used with the auxiliary: e.g. *Az üzletek **be vannak** csuk**va*** 'The shops are closed'; *A televiziót néz**ve** elaludtam* 'While watching television I fell asleep.'

NEGATIVE

The general marker is *nem*; *ne* is used with the imperative/subjunctive: e.g. *nem megy* 'he doesn't go'; *ne menjen* 'don't go'. Negation is reduplicated: e.g. *Nem dolgoznak sehol sem*, lit. 'They're not working nowhere neither' = 'There's nobody working anywhere.'

Postpositions

For example, *mellett* 'beside', *fölött* 'above', *alatt* 'below'. They are reduplicated with demonstratives: e.g. *ez alatt a szék alatt* 'under this chair'. The postpositions take the personal markers, and show a three-way opposition for motion relative to speaker or other referent: e.g. *mellettem* 'beside me'; *mellém* 'in my direction'; *mellőlem* 'from beside me'; *fölottem* 'above me'; *fölém* '(moving) over me'; *fölülem* 'from above me'.

Word order

SOV is basic, but order is free.

1 1 Kezdetben volt az Ige, és az Ige az Istennél volt, és Isten volt az Ige. 2 Ő
kezdetben az Istennél volt. 3 Minden általa lett, és nélküle semmi sem lett,
ami létrejött. 4 Benne élet volt, és az élet volt az emberek világossága. 5 A
világosság a sötétségben világít, de a sötétség nem fogadta be. 6 Megjelent egy
ember, akit Isten küldött, akinek a neve János. 7 Ő tanúként jött, hogy bizonyságot
tegyen a világosságról, és hogy mindenki higgyen általa. 8 Nem ő volt a világosság,
de a világosságról kellett bizonyságot tennie.

ICELANDIC

INTRODUCTION

Icelandic belongs to the Germanic branch (Scandinavian sub-division) of the Indo-European family. It is the official language of Iceland, where it is spoken by about a quarter of a million people. While its Scandinavian congeners have carried reductionism to extremes, Icelandic remains close to Old Norse. This is partly due to its geographical position as an outlier. More important, however, and the major factor in its linguistic conservatism, was the presence in Iceland of the saga literature of the thirteenth and fourteenth centuries. What was kept alive was not merely a grammatical system but one of the world's great literatures. The narrative sweep, the moral power, and the sheer human interest of the sagas clearly inform the genre in which modern Icelandic writers have excelled – the epic novel, as practised by Halldor Laxness, Þ. Þórðarson, G. Hagalín, and O.J. Sigurðsson. Modern Icelandic literature has also produced many outstanding poets.

Dialectal differences are not great. The main division is between *harðmæli* in Northern Iceland, and *linmæli* in Southern Iceland (including Reykjavik). This division centres on the pronunciation of the plosives /p, t, k/ between vowels: in *harðmæli* as aspirates [p^h, t^h, k^h] and in *linmæli* as almost voiceless [b̥, d̥, g̊].

SCRIPT

Gothic until the nineteenth century. Now Roman alphabet + *æ*, *ö*, *þ*, *ð*.

PHONOLOGY

Consonants

The core of the Icelandic consonantal system is provided by the five-term series of labial, dental, and velar stops: weak non-aspirate – hard non-aspirate – weak aspirate – strong pre-aspirate – strong post-aspirate; e.g. the labial series /b̥ – p – $b̥^h$ – ^hp – p^h/. In addition, there is a palatalized velar series, in which, however, the weak aspirated member */$ɟ̊^h$/ is missing. The remaining phonemes in the consonantal inventory are:

> fricatives: f, v, þ, ð, s, ç, γ, χ, h
> nasals: voiced m, n, ŋ, ŋ′; unvoiced m̥, n̥, ŋ̊, ŋ̊′
> lateral and flap: l, l̥, r, r̥
> semi-vowel: j

The Icelandic phonological system is of extreme complexity, and the sound–symbol correspondence is correspondingly weak. The graph *k* for example represents the following nine values, depending on phonetic environment: /k, k′, kʰ, ʰk, k′ʰ, g, g′, χ, Ø/; e.g. *kalla* /kʰad̥la/, *aska* /aska/, *ekla* /εʰkla/, *kær* /k′ʰaiːr̥/, *veski* /vεsk′i/, *skammur* /sg̊amːyr/, *skyr* /sg̊′iːr/; *slikt* /sliχtʰ/, *velkt* /vεl̥tʰ/.

Long consonants are pronounced doubled.

Vowels

front: i, ɪ, ε
central: ʏ/y, œ, a
back: u, ɔ, o

Vowels tend to be diphthongized (vowel + /i/) before *-gi*/*-gj*: e.g. *boginn* /bɔiγɪn/, 'crooked, bent'.

Stress

Always on first syllable, even in loan-words: *prófessor*. Both ablaut and umlaut are very frequent in Icelandic words, the former in the strong-verb system, the latter in declension.

MORPHOLOGY AND SYNTAX

Noun

There are three genders: masculine, feminine, and neuter. The definite article is free or bound. The free article is used with a noun which is also defined by an adjective; the bound article is affixed, e.g. when a possessive pronoun follows the noun: e.g. *hinn góði maður* 'the good man'; *bókin þín* 'your book'. The free article is:

	Masculine	*Feminine*	*Neuter*
singular	hinn	hin	hið
plural	hinir	hinar	hin

These are declined in four cases: the genitive forms are: *hins*, *hinnar*, *hins*, with a common plural for all three – *hinna*.

The bound form is made by dropping the *h*(*i*)- of the free article: *hestur.inn* 'the horse', plural *hestar.nir*.

GENDER

Many endings are specific, e.g. all nouns in *-ir*, *-inn*, *-ingur* are masculine and all nouns in *-ning*, *-ung*, *-ja* are feminine. But no generally applicable rule can be given.

DECLENSION

Weak or strong; the weak declension comprises nouns ending in a vowel. Typical weak declensions: *tunga* (fem.) 'tongue'; strong: *vetur* (masc.) 'winter'; *hestur* (masc.) 'horse'

	Singular	*Plural*	*Singular*	*Plural*	*Singular*	*Plural*
nom.	tunga	tungur	vetur	vetur	hestur	hestar
acc.	tungu	tungur	vetur	vetur	hest	hesta
dat.	tungu	tungum	vetri	vetrum	hesti	hestum
gen.	tungu	tungna	vetrar	vetra	hests	hesta

Adjectives

The adjective agrees with noun in gender, number, and case. The adjective has strong and weak declensions: weak if the article or a pronoun is present. For example, the strong declension of *glaður* 'glad' is:

singular	glaður	glaðan	glöðum	glaðs
plural	glaðir	glaða	glöðum	glaðra

COMPARATIVE

The comparative is made with -(*a*)*ri*, and is always weak: e.g. *rikari* 'richer'. The usual suppletive forms are found: e.g. *góður* 'good' – *betri*; *gamall* 'old' – *eldri*; *lítill* 'small' – *minni*.

Pronoun

The base forms are:

	Singular	*Plural*	*Honorific plural*
1	ég	við	vér
2	þú	þið	þér

The third person is marked for gender:

singular	hann	hún	það
plural	þeir	þær	þau

These are declined in four cases: e.g. *ég*, *mig*, *mér*, *mín*.

The genitive forms of these personal pronouns – *mín*, *þín*, etc. – are used mainly after prepositions, and as the objective forms after certain transitive verbs: e.g. *ég vænti þín* 'I await you', *ég vænti hennar* 'I await her', *til þín* 'to you', *meðal þeirra* 'among them'. The possessive pronouns are marked for gender, number and case: e.g. *bókin mín* (fem.) 'my book', *bækurnar minar* 'my books'.

DEMONSTRATIVE PRONOUN/ADJECTIVE

Masc./fem. *þessi*, neut., *þetta* 'this'; masc. *sá*; fem. *sú*, neut., *það* 'that'. All these forms are declined in four cases, singular and plural.

INTERROGATIVE PRONOUN
hver /χɛːr/ 'who?'; *hvad* /χaːð/ 'what?'

RELATIVE PRONOUN
sem (indeclinable): e.g. *maðurinn, sem ég sá* 'the man whom I saw'; *maðurinn, sem sá mig* 'the man who saw me'.

Numerals

1–10: 1 to 4 inclusive are marked for gender: 1 *einn/ein/eitt*, 2 *tveir/tvær/tvö*. 5–10: *fimm, sex, sjö, átta, níu, tíu*; 11 *ellefu*; 12 *tólf*; 20 *tuttugu*; 21 *tuttugu og einn*; 30 *þrjátíu* (*þrír tugir*); 40 *fjörutíu* (*fjórir tugir*); 100 *hundrað*.

Verb

Verbs in Icelandic are weak or strong. There are active, passive (analytical), and middle (in *-st*) voices; indicative, imperative, and subjunctive moods.

TENSE
The present and preterite are simple, other tenses are formed by means of the auxiliary verbs: *hafa* 'have', *vera* 'be', *verða* 'become', etc. The non-finite forms are: the infinitive, and present and past participles.

WEAK VERB
Four groups are distinguished by phonological criteria; the key forms are the infinitive, the first person singular preterite, and the past participle. Examples of each class are given here; the forms shown are the infinitive, the first person singular present tense, the first person singular and plural preterite, and the past participle in its masculine form:

1. telja 'to count' – tel – taldi/töldum – talinn
2. heyra 'to hear' – heyri – heyrði/heyrðum – heyrður
3. segja 'to say' – segi – sagði/sögðum – sagður
4. elska 'to love' – elska – elskaði/elskuðum – elskaður

Most weak verbs belong to class 4. The present and preterite of *elska* are:

	Singular			*Plural*		
present	1 elska	2 elskar	3 elskar	1 elskum	2 elskið	3 elska
preterite	elskaði	elskaðir	elskaði	elskuðum	elskuðuð	elskuðu

In the subjunctive present, *i* replaces *a* of the indicative present: e.g. *elski, elskir*, etc. The past subjunctive is the same as the indicative past. The present participle is *elskandi*; past participle, *elskaður*.

STRONG VERB
Here there are seven classes, according to seven types of ablaut. The classes are set out here, showing infinitive, first person singular/plural of present, first

person singular/plural of preterite, past participle: the ablaut sequence is marked by bold typeface.

1. líta 'look' – lít/lítum – **leit**-/litum – l**i**tið
2. brj**ò**ta 'break' – brýt/brjótum – br**au**t/br**u**tum – br**o**tið
3. v**e**rða 'become' – verð/verðum – v**a**rð/**u**rðum – **o**rðið
4. bera 'bear' – ber/berum – b**a**r/b**á**rum – b**o**rið
5. g**e**fa 'give' – gef/gefum – g**a**f/g**á**fum – g**e**fið
6. f**a**ra – 'travel' – fer/förum – fór/fórum – f**a**rið
7. f**a**lla 'fall' – fell/föllum – f**é**ll/f**é**llum – f**a**llið

Conjugation of a strong verb: *gefa* = 'to give' (ablaut class 5):

	Singular			*Plural*		
present	1 gef	2 gefur	3 gefur	1 gefum	2 gefið	3 gefa
preterite	gaf	gafst	gaf	gáfum	gáfuð	gáfu

Subjunctive: present, e.g. *gefi*, *gefir*; past, e.g. *gæfi*, *gæfir*.
Participles: present, *gefandi*; past, *gefinn*.

MIDDLE VOICE

The characteristic is *-st*: e.g. *kallast* 'to be called'. The middle voice has reflexive, reciprocal, and passive sense: cf. *klæðast* 'to get dressed': *þeir heilsast* 'they greet each other'; *finnast dæmi til, að* ... 'an example can be found for ...'; *brjótast fyrir einhverju* 'to fight for something'.

PASSIVE

Auxiliary *vera* 'to be' + past participle of sense-verb, coded for gender: e.g. *bókin var gefin mér* 'the book was given to me'.

MODAL AUXILIARIES

kunna, *munu*, *skulu*, *mega*, *eiga/átt*, *vilja*, etc.: e.g.

ég kann ekki að gera það 'I can't do that';
hann sagðist mundu koma 'he said he would probably come';
ég má ekki hugsa til þess 'I can't think about this';
þu átt að læra íslenzku 'you ought to learn Icelandic'.

Negation

The general negating particle is *ekki* /ɛʰk'iː/ following the verb.

Prepositions

With accusative: *um*, *á*, *í*, *undir*, *eftir*, *fyrir*, etc.
With genitive: *til*, *án*; directionals, *sunnan* 'southwards', *norðan* 'northwards', etc.
With dative: *að*, *hjá*, *gegn*, *handa*, etc.

Examples with accusative: *á borðið* 'on the table'; *ganga á fjöll* 'to go into the mountains'; *hann fer í garðinn* 'he goes into the garden'; *það er gott fyrir sjúklinga* 'that is good for invalids'.

Examples with dative: *hann er hjá mér* 'he's with me'; *kaupa eitthvað handa einhverjum* 'to buy something for someone'.

Word order

SVO.

Í UPPHAFI var Orðið og
Orðið var hjá Guði, og
Orðið var Guð.
2. Það var í upphafi hjá
Guði.
3. Allir hlutir eru fyrir það
gjörðir, og án þess er ekkert
til orðið, sem til er.
4. Í því var líf, og lífið var
ljós mannanna;
5. Og ljósið skín í myrkrinu,
og myrkrið meðtók það ekki.
6. ¶ Maður nokkur var send-
ur af Guði, hann hèt Jóhannes.
7. Þessi kom til vitnisburðar,
til þess að vitna um ljósið, svo
allir tryðu fyrir hans vitnis-
burð.
8. Ekki var hann ljósið, held-
ur átti hann að vitna um ljósið.

IGBO

INTRODUCTION

Igbo is usually assigned to the Kwa group of Niger-Congo languages, though certain affinities with the Bantu language Efik have been pointed out. It is spoken by around 10 million people, in a variety of dialects spread over southern Nigeria, from Onitsha and Owerri to Calabar. 'Central Igbo' is a compromise standard based on the Onitsha-Owerri dialect. Writing in Igbo, as distinct from Bible translation, dates from 1932 when Pita Nwana's story *Omenuko* won a prize in a competition run by the International African Institute. From the 1970s on there has been a steady growth in the output of Igbo novels, plays, and verse. Igbo writers have also been prolific in English.

SCRIPT

Romanization dates from the inception of missionary activities in the mid-1850s. A standardized orthography was introduced in 1961. The sound–symbol correspondence is weak; e.g. the letter *s* represents /s/, s'/, /s̃/ and /s̃'/.

PHONOLOGY

Consonants

stops: /p, ph, b, bh/; these occur palatalized: /p', ph'/, etc.
/t, th, d, dh/; the palatalized dentals: /c, ch, ɟ, ɟh/;
/k, kh, g, gh/; the velars occur labialized: /k°, kh°/, etc.
fricatives: /f, v, s, z, γ, h/; these occur (except /γ/) nasalized: /f̃, ṽ/, etc. /s, z, h/ occur both palatalized and nasalized: /s̃', z̃', h̃'/; /h̃/ also labialized, /h̃°/.
lateral: l
roll: r
nasals: m, n, n', ŋ, ŋ°
semi-vowels: j, w
implosives: kp, gb

Vowels

i, ɪ, ɛ, a, ɔ, o, ɵ, u

Notated as: *i, ị, e, a, ọ, o, ụ, u*.

VOWEL HARMONY

i, e, o, u are compatible with each other; similarly, *ị, a, ọ, ụ*.

Tones

Three level tones are distinguished: high, mid, and low. The mid level tone is constrained in that it can only follow a high, i.e. no monosyllable can be mid level. Two or more non-level tones, i.e. rising/falling, are also present. Tonal contours are not fixed, and relative pitch varies considerably in the course of an utterance. Furthermore, lexical tone or citation form changes in certain environments.

Tone in Igbo is of cardinal phonemic importance.

In this description, high tone is unmarked, low tone is marked with a grave accent, mid level with a dash (').

MORPHOLOGY AND SYNTAX

Noun

Nouns fall lexically into tonal classes: e.g. for disyllables, high–high, low–high; high–low, low–low. Similarly for tri- and quadrisyllables. In various syntactic relationships, e.g. in genitive construction and in conjugational patterns, lexical tone is subject to change in specific ways: cf.

m chị̀ anụ 'I bring meat';
m̀ *chị̀ anụ* 'Do I bring meat?';
m̀ *chị̀ an****ụ́*** 'I don't bring meat'.

Meaning is thus a function of tonal pattern and word position.

There is no plural form.

Adjective

Adjectives may be formed by tonal modulation from verbs and other parts of speech: e.g. from *ịjọ́* 'to be bad', is formed *ọjọ/ọjọọ́* 'bad'; cf. *ọma* 'good'. There are few words of this type in Igbo. Any nominal can, of course, act as a modifier and follow another nominal: this collocation is equivalent to the genitive relationship: e.g. *ụlọ̀ ezè* 'house-chief' = 'chief's house'; *ụlọ̀ egh****ú*** 'goat-shed'; *àla* ***ụ́****dho* 'land of peace'; *àl****à*** *ez****è*** 'chief's domain'.

Pronoun

PERSONAL

		Separable	*Inseparable*
singular	1	mụ, m	m
	2	gị	i/ị
	3	ya	o/ọ

impersonal e/a

plural 1 anyị
2 unù
3 ñ̄a

The inseparable forms occur only as bound forms for verbal subject. There is also an emphatic form: **à***mị̂*, **à***gị̂*, **à***yâ*; *anyî*, *unû*, *ñ̄â*.

The separable forms act also as possessives: tone depends on noun modified: cf. *nn***à** *m* 'my father'; *nne* ***ḿ*** 'my mother'; *nn***à** *gị* 'your father'; *nne gị́* 'your mother'; *isi* ***ḿ*** 'my head'; *isi gị́* 'your head'.

Examples of object pronoun: *nyètu* ***ḿ*** *yá* 'give it to me'; *jù***o** *yá* 'ask him'; *dèe* *yá* 'write it'; *ži yá ùwe m* 'show him my clothes'.

DEMONSTRATIVE ADJECTIVES
à 'this', *ahụ̀* 'that'. Emphatic forms: e.g. *àmị̂*, *àgị̂*.

INTERROGATIVE PRONOUNS
These have specific tonal patterns: *ònye*/*òchu* 'who?'; *gịnị* 'what?': e.g. *ònyê bịà-rà?* 'Who came?'

Numerals

1–10: *otù*, *àbụọ́*, *àtọ*, *ànọ*, *ìse*, *ìsiì*, *àsaà*, *àsatọ́*, *tolụ́*, *ìri*. 11 *ìri nà otù*; 12 *ìri nà àbụó*; 20 *ohu*; 30 *ohu nà ìri*; 40 *ohu àbụọ́*; 50 *ohu àbụọ́ nà ìri*; 100 *ohu ìse*.

Verb

Formally simple, the Igbo verb structure is of great tonal complexity. The infinitive is marked by the high-tone prefix *i-* or *ị-*, harmonizing, that is, with the stem vowel, which is either middle or low tone: e.g. *i.sí* 'to cook', *ị.nụ́* 'to hear', *i.zù* 'to meet'.

The infinitive is negated by replacing *i-*/*-ị* with *e-*/*a-* (depending on vowel harmony) and adding the suffix *-ghị*/*-ghì*: e.g. *i.kè* 'to distribute', negative ***e****.kè.****ghì***.

A participial form is made with harmonic prefix *e-*/*a-*; this form is conjugated by one of several auxiliaries, e.g. *ị.nà* 'to do, make': *ọ nà.è.sí anụ́* 'she is cooking meat' (tone of prefix changes from *e* to *è*). Simple forms take this participial form to express protracted or habitual action: e.g. *mụ nà.a.chị anụ* 'I (usually) brought meat'.

The exact meaning – aspectual, modal, temporal – of an Igbo verb depends on tone, and on the presence or absence of certain prefixes and suffixes; the stem itself is not inflected in any way. Tonal sequence also varies depending on whether a statement is or is not initiatory.

IMPERATIVE
No prefix, certain suffixes may be used: e.g. *gwa ḿ* 'tell me!'; *gà.wa ahịa* 'set off for market!' (where *-wa* is an inceptive suffix).

ASPECT

VSO/SVO imperfective aspectual assertion: a pronominal vowel prefix is used in VSO, absent in SVO: cf. ***a.***_chị ṁ anụ_ 'I am/was carrying some meat', *m chị anụ* 'I am/was carrying some meat'.

SVO perfective: with -*r*V suffix, where V copies the stem vowel: cf. *m sì.**rì** anụ* 'I cooked some meat', *m hù.**rù** enyi* 'I saw an elephant'.

The directional suffix *te/ta* may be added: e.g. *ọ bù.tè.rè abọ* 'he brought the basket' (to a specific place), where the form *te* is demanded by vowel harmony (within the *i, e, o, u* group) and -rV copies it: ***te.re.***

SVO perfective with *e-/a-* prefix, plus open vowel suffix and *la/le* suffix: e.g. *anyị **è**.sì.**e.le** anụ́* 'we have cooked meat'. The pronominal prefix *e-/a-* is dropped if the pronominal subject preceding the verb is monosyllabic: *m sị́.e.le anụ́* but ***e.***_sị́.e.le ṁ anụ_ 'I have cooked meat'.

All affirmative forms have correlative negative forms. The prohibitive usually has the *-le/-le* suffix. In negative assertion, *e-/a-* is prefixed to the verb, and *-ghi* is added. This *e-/a-* is a verbal prefix, not to be confused with the pronominal prefix *e-/a-* discussed above: e.g. *Ewu **atá.ghi** ji ányị* 'The goat (*ewu*) didn't eat our yams (*ji*).'

Narrative form: this form takes up the thread of discourse from a preceding primary form, with no recapitulation of subject: absence of overt subject induces tonal change in both verbs and nouns.

Subordinate verb forms differing from primary forms in tone, are used to make affirmative and negative conditional and relative clauses: e.g. a relative affirmative clause with change of subject:

> *unù tìsị ùwe* 'you wear clothes'
> *ùwe unu tìsị dị mmà* 'the clothes you are wearing are good'
>
> *ewû tàrà ji* 'the goat ate yams'
> *ji ewu tàrà rìrì nne* 'the yams the goat ate were many'

Preposition

na/la 'on, in' is an all-purpose preposition: e.g. *ọ nọ nà London* 'he is in London', where *na* changes to *nà* (low tone) because of following consonant (non-nasal). Preceding a vowel, *na* is assimilated to the vowel in both tone and quality, and is written as *n'*: e.g. *na ụlọ̀ → n'ụlọ̀* 'in the house'.

Word order

See **Verb**, above.

1 NA mbu ka Okwu ahu diri, Okwu
ahu nạ Cineke di-kwa-ra, Okwu ahu
buru kwa Cineke. 2 Onye ahu na
Cineke diri na mbu. 3 Ekere ihe nile
site n'aka-Ya ; ekegh kwa otù ihe ọbula
nke ekeworo ma Ọnọgh ya. 4 Nịme
Ya ka ndu diri ; nḍ̀u ahu buru kwa Ìhè
nke madu(pl). 5 Ìhè ahu we nāmu
n'ọciciri ; ọciciri ahu ejidegh kwa ya.
6 Otù nwoke putara, onye ezitere
site n'ebe Cineke nọ, ahà-ya bu Jọn.
7 Onye ahu biara igba amà, ka ọwe gbara
Ihè ahu amà, ka madu nile we sịt̀e n'aka-
ya kwere. 8 Ya onweya abugh Ị̀hè ahu,
kama *ọbiara* ka ọwe gbara Ìhè ahu
ama.

INDO-EUROPEAN LANGUAGES

INTRODUCTION

The Indo-European family of languages comprises the following twelve branches:

1. Indic: including Vedic, Sanskrit, the Prakrits, and the New Indo-Aryan languages (NIA); the Dardic languages form a peripheral and controversial grouping within this branch.
2. Iranian: including Avestan, Old Persian, Middle Iranian (Pehlevi, etc.), the modern Iranian languages (Persian, Kurdish, Pashto, Ossetian, etc.), and the Pamir languages.
3. Anatolian: Hittite, Luvian, Palaic, Lydian, etc.; all extinct.
4. Armenian.
5. Hellenic: including Linear B Greek, Homeric and Classical Greek, New Testament Greek, and Modern Greek.
6. Albanian: formerly regarded as the sole survivor of an Illyrian branch.
7. Italic: including Latin-Faliscan, Oscan-Umbrian, Venetic, the modern Romance languages.
8. Celtic:
   (a) Continental Celtic (in Gaul, the Iberian Peninsula, and Central Europe; Galatian in Anatolia; all extinct);
   (b) Insular Celtic: (i) Goidelic: Irish, Gaelic, Manx; (ii) Brythonic: Welsh, Cornish, Breton.
9. Tocharaic (extinct).
10. Germanic:
    (a) East Germanic: Gothic (extinct);
    (b) North Germanic: Old Norse, Icelandic, the modern Scandinavian languages:
    (c) West Germanic: Old and Middle High German, Low German, Anglo-Saxon, English, modern German, Dutch, Frisian, Afrikaans; Yiddish.
11. Baltic: Lithuanian, Latvian; Old Prussian (extinct).
12. Slavonic:
    (a) South Slavonic: Old Church Slavonic, Macedonian, Bulgarian, Serbo-Croat;
    (b) East Slavonic: Russian, Ukrainian, Belorussian;
    (c) West Slavonic: Polish, Czech, Slovak, Lusatian, Slovene.

In terms of their primary expansion, that is, as located about 2,000 years ago, the Indo-European languages covered a territory stretching from Ireland to Assam, and from Norway and central Russia to the Mediterranean, the Persian Gulf, and Central India. Secondary expansion in the last four hundred years, by conquest and colonization, has placed Indo-European languages, especially English, Spanish, Portuguese, Russian, and French in every corner of the globe. The sole major language area still largely untouched by Indo-European is that occupied by its sole quantitative rival – Chinese.

As regards textual attestation, the Indo-European languages can be divided into four groups:

1. Primary stratum: centring round the second millennium BC: Hittite, Vedic, Linear B Greek.
2. Secondary stratum: first millennium BC: Greek, Sanskrit, Avestan, Old Persian, Latin, Oscan, Umbrian.
3. Tertiary stratum: first millennium AD: Gothic, Old Irish, Tocharaic, Old Church Slavonic, Armenian, early North and West Germanic.
4. Modern period: from 1000 to present: the mediaeval and modern New Indo-Aryan languages, Iranian, Romance, Germanic, Slavonic, Celtic, and Baltic languages; Modern Greek, Armenian; Albanian.

The position of Lithuanian in this tabulation is anomalous; though it is attested from no earlier than the fifteenth century AD, it belongs by virtue of its exceptionally archaic structures to the primary or, at least, the secondary stratum.

INDONESIAN

INTRODUCTION

Indonesian is a member of the Austronesian family. Two main forms of the Malayan stock are spoken and written in South-East Asia and the islands of the archipelago: (a) Bahasa Indonesia, the official language of Indonesia, spoken by around 170 million; (b) Bahasa Malaysia, the official language of Malaysia, Singapore, and the Sultanate of Brunei, spoken by around 20 million. Phonologically and morphologically, the two forms are virtually identical. Nor is there much variation in vocabulary, though local differences are frequent. The description that follows is specifically of Bahasa Indonesia.

As far back as in the ninth to twelfth centuries AD Malay was in use as the administrative language of Hindu rule in Sriwijaya (south-east Sumatra). It continued to be so used through the following centuries under the Sultans of Malacca: on the one hand, as Classical Malay, the highly organized vehicle of a rich and extensive literature, and on the other as the lingua franca for the many peoples who lived in the area. In this second form it was known as *Melayu Pasar* – 'Bazaar Malay'.

In the early years of the twentieth century it seemed likely that Dutch would emerge as the language of administration, higher education and the cultural media in the archipelago, and, in line with this, the claims of Dutch were promoted even by Indonesian intellectuals (e.g. the Budi Utomo Association). Resistance to this policy grew *pari passu* with the rise of nationalism, and in 1928, at a conference in Batavia, the ideal of a national language was first promulgated. For such a national language there could be only one base – Malay, by far the most widely used and understood of all the languages of Indonesia. Curiously, by banning the use of Dutch, the Japanese occupation fuelled this movement. On 17 August 1945, Bahasa Indonesia was officially adopted as the national language of the Republic of Indonesia.

SCRIPT

Roman alphabet. A 'perfected spelling' was recommended by the Indonesian Ministry of Education in 1972. The main change here is that *y* everywhere replaces the *j* previously used under Dutch influence: e.g. *jang* > *yang*. *j* and *c* now represent the voiced and unvoiced affricates.

Modern Bahasa Malaysia is also written in *rumi*, the *jawi* (Arabic) script being reserved for religious texts.

PHONOLOGY

Consonants

stops: p, b, t, d, k, g, ʔ
affricates: tʃ, dʒ
fricatives: f, s, ʃ, x, h;
nasals: m, n, ɲ, ŋ
lateral and flap: l, r
semi-vowels: j (notated as *y*), w

Vowels

i, ɪ, e, ə, a, ɔ, o, u

The letter *i* represents /i/ and /ɪ/; the letter *e* represents /ɛ/, /ɪ/, or /ə/; *o* represents /o/ or /ɔ/.

Stress

On the penultimate syllable, unless this contains an *e*-pepet (short *e*), no longer specifically marked in Bahasa Indonesian.

MORPHOLOGY AND SYNTAX

Roots are largely disyllabic. In the absence of prefixation, which encodes nominal and verbal properties, it is not possible to tell by inspection whether a disyllable is a noun, an adjective, a verb, or a numeral: cf. *gambar* 'picture' (noun); *hitam* 'black' (adjective/stative verb); *goreng* 'to fry' (verb); *tujuh* 'seven'.

Noun

Nouns are not marked for gender or number. Lexical means may be used to specify gender where necessary; and again, if necessary, number can be shown by reduplication (never if a numeral is present): e.g. *barang-barang itu* 'these things'; *penyakit-penyakit tropis* 'tropical diseases'; *sumber-sumber militer* 'military sources'.

DEFINITE/INDEFINITENESS

There are no articles, but the demonstratives *itu* and *ini* may be used as recapitulatory topicalizers, whose referents are known to the audience: e.g. *Undangan itu akan dipenuhi tahun ini juga* 'The invitation will be taken up this year' (the *undangan* 'invitation', having already been mentioned in the discourse; *akan* is future formant; *tahun* 'year').

All case relations are expressed by means of prepositional constructions or by apposition: e.g. *rumah makan* 'house-eat' = 'restaurant'; *pusat kebudayaan* 'cultural centre'; *buku petunjuk kota* 'guide book to the town'.

NOMINAL FORMATION BY AFFIXATION

Examples:

-an: forms resultatives, e.g. *tulis* 'to write' – *tulisan* 'something written'; *ajar* 'to teach' – *ajaran* 'doctrine'.

ke...-an: frequently used to form abstract nouns from adjectives and root nouns, e.g. *bangsa* 'people' – *ke.bangsa.an* 'nationalism'; *berani* 'brave' – *ke.berani.an* 'courage'.

pe + nasal: indicates agent or instrument, e.g. *pahat* 'to carve' – *pemahat* 'sculptor'; *dengar* 'to hear': *pen.dengar* 'listener'.

per/pen...an: abstract nouns formed by these two circumfixes may differ in respect of voice: e.g. from *kembang* 'develop': *per.kembang.an* 'development' (the passive result of a process), *pen.gembang.an* 'development' (the active process of developing something).

Adjective

As attribute, adjective follows noun, though quantifying modifiers precede: e.g. *orang baik* 'good man'; *banyak orang* 'many people'.

COMPARISON

The comparative is made with *lebih...dari(pada)*: e.g. *Malam ini lebih dingin daripada kemarin* 'Tonight is colder than yesterday.'

Pronoun

1st person: sing. *saya/aku*; pl. excl. *kami*, incl. *kita*;
2nd person: sing. *kamu/engkau/saudara/anda*; these are also plural forms;
3rd person: sing. *dia/ia*; pl. *mereka*. *Beliau* is a polite third person form.

Saudara is a generally acceptable form of polite address; *anda* is increasingly used when addressing an impersonal audience, e.g. on radio or television. *Aku*, *kamu*, and *dia* have enclitic forms: *-ku*, *-mu*, *-nya*.

Either the full form of the pronoun or its enclitic can be used as possessive: e.g. *rumah saya* = *rumah.ku* 'my house'; also as object, direct or indirect: e.g. *dia sudah menyurati saya* = *dia sudah menyurat kepada saya* = *dia sudah menyurati.ku* 'he has written (to) me'; *saya akan tinggal dengan dia/dengan.nya* 'I shall live with him'.

DEMONSTRATIVE PRONOUN/ADJECTIVE

itu 'this, these'; *ini* 'that, those'.

INTERROGATIVE PRONOUN

siapa 'who?'; *apa* 'what?'. *Apa* is used as an introductory interrogative particle: e.g. *Apa mereka belum makan?* 'Haven't they eaten yet?'

RELATIVE PRONOUN

yang: e.g. *pemilihan yang akan datang* 'the forthcoming election' ('which will come').

Numerals

1–10: *satu*, *dua*, *tiga*, *empat*, *lima*, *enam*, *tujuh*, *delapan*, *sembilan*, *sepuluh*; 11 *sebelas*; 12 *dua belas*; 13 *tiga belas*; 20 *dua puluh*; 30 *tiga puluh*; 100 *seratus*.

Classifiers

The lengthy inventory of numerical classifiers formerly used in Malay has been reduced in both languages, in Indonesian to three: *seorang* for humans; *seekor* for animals; and *sebuah* for things. Even of these, use is optional: e.g. *dia* (*seorang*) *wartawan* 'he is a journalist'.

Verb

The verb in Indonesian is not marked for person, number, or tense. Aspect and tense can be indicated by adverbial markers (see below). There is no copula. Roots are modulated by affixation. Verbs are stative, intransitive, or transitive. A transitive verb takes both a *me*(N)- prefix and a *di-* prefix; i.e. a transitive verb can be both active and passive.

VERBAL FORMANTS

Examples:

1. *ber-*: this is a formant for very many intransitives and statives, e.g. *bermain* 'to play'; *berhenti* 'to pause'; *bersumber* 'to originate in'.
2. *me*(N)-, usually with *-kan* affix: dynamic/transitive formant of wide semantic range. N here stands for a nasal, homogeneous with initial of root word: i.e. the prefix can be *me-*, *men*, *mem*, *meng*, or *meny*: Cf. *jalan* 'walk' – *men.jalan.kan* 'to drive (a car), to carry out'; *hidup* 'to live' – *meng.hidup.kan* 'to enliven, to switch on (the radio)'; *luas* 'wide' – *me.luas.kan* 'to spread'; *meng.amuk* 'to run amuck'. Initial *p, t, k, s* are dropped when *men-* is prefixed: e.g. *tangis* → *men.angis* 'to weep, cry'.
3. *mem-* acts as a subject focus marker prefixed to *per-*: cf. *kenal* 'to become friendly with' – *memper.kenal.kan* 'to introduce'; *lihat* 'to see' – *memper.lihat.kan* = *me.lihat.kan* 'to show'.
4. *di-* can be described as an object focus marker, or, in Indo-European terms, as a passive marker: e.g. *di.tunggu ke.datang.an.nya* 'his arrival is expected'; *dutabesar di.terima oleh Menteri Luar Negeri* 'the ambassador was received by the foreign minister' (*oleh* 'by'); cf. *memper.timbang.kan* 'to take into consideration', *di.timbang.kan* 'to be taken into consideration'.

NEGATIVE

The general negating particle is *tidak* preceding the word negated. A negative imperative is made with *jangan*(*lah*): e.g. *janganlah baca buku itu* 'don't read that book'.

TENSE MARKERS

Imperfective *masih*, *sedang*; perfective *sudah*. The future tense marker is *akan*.

Prepositions

Indonesian uses prepositions: e.g. *di* 'in, on, at'; *untuk* 'for'; *kepada* 'to' (a person).

Word formation

In recent years, many compounds have been formed from the initial syllables of component roots in a name, title, or designation consisting of several words: e.g. *Jatim* = *Jawa Timur* 'East Java'; *Dubes* = *duta besar* 'ambassador'; *Hankam* = *Pertahanan dan Keamanan* 'Defence and Security'.

Word order

SVO.

1 Maka pada awal pertama adalah Kalam, dan Kalam itoe bersama-sama dengan Allah, dan Kalam itoelah djoega Allah.
2 Adalah Ia pada moelanja beserta dengan Allah.
3 Segala sesoeatoe didjadikan Oléhnja, maka djikalau tidak ada Ia, tiadalah djoega barang sesoeatoe jang telah djadi.
4 Didalamnja itoe ada hidoep, dan hidoep itoelah terang manoesia.
5 Maka terang itoe bertjahaja didalam gelap, maka gelap itoe tiada sadar akan Dia.
6 Maka adalah seorang jang disoeroeh oléh Allah, namanja Jahja.
7 Ialah datang memberi kesaksian, hendak menjaksikan hal terang itoe, soepaja sekalian orang pertjaja oléh sebab Dia.
8 Maka ia sendiri boekan terang itoe, melainkan hendak menjaksikan hal terang itoe.

ITALIAN

INTRODUCTION

Belonging to the Italic branch of Indo-European, Italian is the official language of the Republic of Italy and is spoken today by over 50 million people, if the dialect form spoken in Sardinia is included. In addition, Italian is one of the three official languages of Switzerland, and is spoken in large communities in North and South America, in North Africa, and elsewhere, which probably add 5 or 6 million to give an overall total of about 60 million.

A dialectal division of Italy running roughly along the line of the Northern Appennines has long been recognized (see, for example, Dante, *De Vulgari Eloquentia*, X). To the north of this line are Piedmontese, Lombardian, Venetian, etc.; to the south lie Tuscan, Umbrian, Neapolitan, Calabrese, and Sicilian. In spite of the homogenizing influence of the standard language used by the media, most of the dialects are still very much alive, and many Italians use the language on two socio-linguistic levels – the local dialect in the family circle and among friends, Standard Italian on all more formal occasions. Certain dialectal features differ markedly from the standard norm, e.g. in the north, the palatal fricative reflex of Low Latin *pl-* as /tʃ/: e.g. /tʃatsa/ for standard *piazza*; and, in the south, the interdental fricatives of Tuscan, e.g. /θ/.

The earliest textual example of written Italian dates from the tenth century. In the ensuing 300 years, poetry was written in several dialects, until Tuscan was suddenly transmuted into one of the world's great literary languages by the genius of Dante Alighieri (1265–1321); the *Divina Commedia* was written between 1310 and 1314. Petrarca and Boccaccio complete the trio of great fourteenth-century writers. The prestige thus conferred upon Tuscan – specifically Florentine – usage ensured its adoption in the nineteenth century, when political union brought the question of a unified national language to a head. Alessandro Manzoni, who presided over the committee (1868) which took this decision, had been himself impelled to rewrite his masterpiece *I Promessi Sposi* in Florentine Tuscan (the original version, 1825–7, was in Manzoni's native Lombardian dialect; Tuscan version 1840).

SCRIPT

Latin alphabet; *j*, *k*, *w*, *x*, *y* appear in foreign words only.

PHONOLOGY

The Florentine standard inventory is given.

Consonants

stops: p, b, t, d, k, g; labialized /k/: [k°]
affricates: ts, dz, tʃ, dʒ
fricatives: f, v, s/z, ʃ
nasals: m, n, ɲ, (ŋ)
lateral and flap: l, ʎ, r
semi-vowel: j, w

/ɲ/ is notated as *gn*: e.g. *ogni* 'each' = /ɔɲi/; /k/ is notated as *c*/*ch*; /w/ is notated as *uo*: *uomo* 'man' = /wɔmo/, or *ua*: *acqua* 'water' = /akwa/. The letter *z* is unvoiced /c/ or voiced /dz/: e.g. *zucchero* /tsukεro/ 'sugar'; *zelo* /dzεlo/ 'zeal'. The distinction may be phonemic.

Vowels

i, e, ε, a, ɔ, o, u

/e,ε/ and /o,ɔ/ contrast in stressed syllables. Typically, Italian words end in vowels.

Stress

Stress is frequently on the penultimate syllable, but there are many exceptions: e.g. the third person singular past definite is always stressed on the final, as are many words marked with final grave: e.g. *virtù*, *caffè*, etc. Antepenultimate stress appears in infinitives like *vèndere* 'to sell', in the third person plural present indicative form (*màndano* 'they send'), and in many words like *mèdico* 'doctor', *àngelo* 'angel', *piròscafo* 'steamer'.

MORPHOLOGY AND SYNTAX

Italian has two genders and two numbers.

Noun

Nominal endings are, up to a point, coded for gender: e.g. most nouns in *-o* are masculine with plural in *-i*: e.g. *il bambino* 'the child' – *i bambini*; and most nouns in *-a* are feminine with plural in *-e*: e.g. *la stella* 'the star' – *le stelle*. These categories are not exclusive, however: cf. *la mano* 'the hand', pl. *le mani*; *il poeta* 'the poet', pl. *i poeti*.

Most nouns in *-e* are masculine: e.g. *il fiume* 'the river' – *i fiumi*, and all in *-zione*, *-gione*, *-udine* are feminine.

There is no declensional system; syntactic relationships are expressed by prepositions which typically coalesce with the articles, e.g.

a 'to' + *il* → *al*: similarly, *ai*, *agli*, *alla*, *alle*.
in 'in' + *il* → *nel*: similarly, *nei*, *negli*, *nella*, *nelle*.
con 'with' + *il* → *col*: similarly, *coi*, *cogli*, *colla*, *colle*.

Articles

The definite article is marked for gender and number: masc. *il* – *i*; fem. *la* – *le*. Before vocalic initial, both *il* and *la* become *l'*; *lo* is the form taken by the masculine article before such frequent initials as /ɲ/ and *s* + consonant: conditions which also change the plural *i* to *gli*: e.g. *lo squillo* 'ringing', *gli scopi* 'the aims'.

The indefinite article is masc. *un*(*o*), fem. *un*(*a*), with pl. forms: masc. *dei*/*degli*, fem. *delle*.

Adjective

The adjective agrees in gender and number with the noun, which it may precede or follow; some adjectives, e.g. of nationality, colour, always follow. A few very common adjectives have shortened forms used before masculine nouns beginning with a consonant (subject to the same constraints as those affecting the use of the definite article): e.g. *un bel dì* 'a fine day'; *un bello specchio* 'a beautiful mirror'.

COMPARATIVE

più + *di*: e.g. *Questa ragazza e più bella di quella* 'This girl is prettier than that one.'

The customary suppletive forms are found with very common adjectives: *buono* 'good' – *migliore*; *cattivo* 'bad' – *peggiore*; *poco* 'little' – *meno*; *grande* 'big' – *maggiore*.

Pronoun

The Italian pronominal system has (a) independent forms, showing a formal/informal distinction in the second and third persons. Thus, second person singular *tu* is informal, contrasting with *voi* 'you' (sing. or. pl. informal). In the third person formal *egli*/*ella* are distinguished from informal *lui*/*lei*; the plural of both is *loro*. The form chosen as the most acceptable for polite address, however, is *Lei* (sing.) pl. *Loro*, though *voi* is acceptable, especially in the south.

Secondly (b) sets of disjunctive and conjunctive pronouns, the latter subdivided into accusative and dative forms. Thus:

	Singular			*Plural*		
independent:	1 io	2 tu	3 lui, lei	1 noi	2 voi	3 loro
disjunctive:	me	te	lui, lei	noi	voi	loro
conjunctive: acc.	mi	ti	lo, la	ci	vi	li, le
dat.	mi/me	ti/te	gli/glie/le	ci/ce	vi/ve	loro

The *-e* forms are used before *lo*, *la*, *li*, *le*, and *ne* 'of it' (= Fr. *en*): e.g. *gli* + *lo* → *glielo*: *glielo diedi* 'I gave it to him'.

Conjunctive forms follow an infinitive, whose object they form: e.g. *volevo dar.glie.lo* 'I wanted to give it to him'.

Pronominal complexes, consisting of *si* → *se* or *ci* → *ce* + *la* or *ne*, follow certain verbs: e.g. *dar.se.la a gambe* 'to take to one's heels'; *metter.ce.la* 'to do one's utmost'.

POSSESSIVE ADJECTIVES

These are accompanied by the article, precede the noun, and show number and gender, except *loro* 'your/s, their/s', which is invariable: e.g. *il mio*, *la mia*, *i miei*, *le mie*, etc. but *il Loro*, *la Loro*, *i Loro*, etc.

DEMONSTRATIVE PRONOUN/ADJECTIVE

questo 'this', *quel(lo)* 'that'. These are marked for gender and number: e.g. *questo/quel ragazzo* 'this/that boy'; *quella ragazza* 'that girl'.

INTERROGATIVE PRONOUN

chi 'who?'; *che* 'what?'

RELATIVE PRONOUN

il quale, *la quale*, *i quali*, *le quali*; *che* (indeclinable): e.g. *la ragazza che vedi* 'the girl (whom) you see'; *il libro che sto leggendo* 'the book which I am reading'.

Numerals

1–10: *uno/una*, *due*, *tre*, *quattro*, *cinque*, *sei*, *sette*, *otto*, *nove*, *dieci*; 11 *undici*; 12 *dodici*; 13 *tredici*; 20 *venti*; 30 *trenta*; 40 *quaranta*; 100 *cento*.

Verb

Italian verbs may be conveniently divided into three conjugations: (a) verbs in *-are*; (b) verbs in *-ere*; and (c) verbs in *-ire*. Verbs in *-e* are further sub-divided into two classes, depending on whether the stem or the ending is stressed: e.g. *chièdere* 'to close'; *sedère* 'to sit'. Verbs in *-i* may be regular or may take a stem augment *-isc-*. An important group of *-e* verbs has irregular forms in the past definite: e.g. *prendere* 'take' – *presi*.

Verbs are transitive or intransitive, and there are indicative, imperative, and subjunctive moods. Both the indicative and the subjunctive have present and imperfect tenses; the indicative has in addition a past definite, a future, and a conditional. The non-finite forms include the infinitive, a gerund, and present and past participles. The gerund and the past participle combine with auxiliaries such as *stare* 'be', *avere* 'have', *essere* 'be' to form composite tenses: e.g. a progressive: *sto scrivendo* 'I am writing'; *stavo dicendo* 'I was saying'; and a perfect: *àbbiamo mangiato* 'we have eaten'; *sono andato* 'I went'.

The basic verbs of motion – *andare* 'go', *venire* 'come', *partire* 'depart' *entrare* 'enter', etc. – are always conjugated with *essere*. Some verbs expressing motion, e.g. *correre* 'run', may be conjugated with either *avere* or *essere*, depending on sense.

SPECIMEN PARADIGM

1st conjugation verb, *mandare* 'to send':

Indicative mood

present: mand-o, -i, -a; -iamo, -ate, -ano (stress on penultimate syllable, except in third person plural)
imperfect: mandav-o, -i, -a; -amo, -ate, -ano
past definite: mandai, mandaste, mando; mand-ammo, -aste, -arono
future: mander-o, -i, -a; -emo, -ete, -anno
conditional: mandere-i, -sti, -bbe; -mmo, -ste, -bbero

Subjunctive mood

present: mand-i, -i, -i; -iamo, -iate, -ino
imperfect: mandass-i, -i, -e; -imo, mandaste, mandassero
imperative mood: -, manda, mandi; mandiamo, mandate, mandino
gerund: mandando; past participle: mandato

PASSIVE

Can be made analytically by means of such auxiliaries as *essere*, *venire*, *andare* followed by the past participle: e.g. *Il manoscritto è andato perduto* 'The manuscript has been lost'; *Le città vengono bombardate* 'The cities are being bombed.'

Wherever possible, Italian prefers the impersonal construction with *si*: e.g. *Si parla inglese qui* 'English is spoken here.'

Negation

The general negating particle is *non* preceding the verb; negation may be duplicated or triplicated: e.g. *Non voglio niente* 'I don't want anything' (lit. 'nothing'); *Non lo vuole nessuno* 'No one wants it' (lit. 'doesn't want').

Prepositions

Simple, e.g. *di*, *a*, *con*, *per*, etc.; or compound: *davanti a* 'in the presence of, in front of'; *di lato a* 'beside'; *al di sopra di* 'above'. As in French, certain verbs take specific prepositions before a following infinitive; e.g. *dimenticare* ***di*** 'to forget', *cominciare* ***a*** 'to begin to': e.g. *mi sono dimenticato* ***di*** *avvertirti* 'I forgot to let you know'; *cominciare* ***ad*** *andare* 'to start walking'.

Word order

Depending on emphasis, SOV, VOS, VSO are all possible.

1 Al principio,
prima che Dio creasse il mondo,
c'era colui che è « la Parola ».
Egli era con Dio;
Egli era Dio.
2 Egli era al principio con Dio.
3 Per mezzo di lui Dio ha creato ogni cosa.
Senza di lui non ha creato nulla.
4 Egli era vita
e la vita era luce per gli uomini.
5 Quella luce risplende nelle tenebre
e le tenebre non l'hanno vinta.
6 Dio mandò un uomo:
si chiamava Giovanni.
7 Egli venne come testimone della luce
perché tutti gli uomini,
ascoltandolo,
credessero nella luce.
8 Non era lui, la luce:
Giovanni era un testimone della luce.

JAPANESE, MODERN STANDARD

INTRODUCTION

Today, Japanese is spoken by about 120 million, in Japan and by large Japanese communities in several parts of the world. The Ryu-Kyu language spoken in the Okinawa Prefecture is a dialect of Japanese. In Japan itself, several local dialects persist, some of which are unintelligible to outsiders, but all Japanese in Japan are taught *hyoojun-go*, the 'standard language'.

For a note on genetic affinity and the early literature, see **Japanese, Classical** in Campbell (1991).

The political, economic, and social upheaval brought about by the Meiji Restoration in 1868, could not fail to be reflected in new attitudes to literature in Japan, and the ensuing century saw a remarkable efflorescence of the novel as the relevant medium both for the naturalistic narrative and for social and psychological analysis. Themes were drawn from Sino-Japanese sources and from a great variety of western models, ranging from Zola and the Russian novelists to Kafka and Rilke, and Japanese treatment of this material is equally eclectic, covering the familiar fields of naturalism, surrealism, alienation, and existentialism, and adding a peculiarly Japanese vein of morbid lyricism. Distinguished names abound; the following cannot fail to be mentioned: Natsume Sooseki, Shimazaki Tooson, Mori Oogai, Abe Kooboo, Kawabata Yasunari, Akutagawa Ryuunosuke, Mishima Yukio.

SCRIPT

The 'standard language' is written in a combination of Chinese characters and the two Japanese syllabaries: hiragana (derived from a cursive writing of Chinese characters) and katakana (originally a kind of shorthand for mnemonic purposes).

Hiragana is used for verbal inflection and nominal particles, postpositions, etc. Katakana is used primarily for foreign words, particularly Anglo-American words which proliferate in Modern Japanese. It is also the script for telegraphese. Chinese characters figure as root words, both verbal and nominal. For example, in the complex verb form *asobanakereba.narimasen* '... have to play...' the root *aso-* 'play' is notated as the Chinese character

遊 (*yóu* 'to play')

while the remaining ten syllables (negative conditional plus negative present indicative) are in hiragana (*-n* is syllabic). Most Chinese characters used in Japanese have more than one pronunciation; a basic distinction is made between *on-yomi*, the Sino-Japanese reading (which itself may have several variants) and the *kun-yomi*, the native Japanese reading. The *on-yomi* reading of the character meaning to 'to play', given above, for example, is *yu*. Reference to this character in the dictionary (no. 4726 in Nelson's *Japanese–English Dictionary*) will show that out of about 80 compounds listed, only 25 per cent or so give

遊 its *kun-yomi* pronunciation (*aso-*); everywhere else, *yu* is used.

In 1946, an official list of 1,850 Chinese characters was adopted as the desirable inventory for everyday purposes. In 1981, this list was extended to almost 2,000. Chinese characters not included in this list are accompanied in print by their hiragana readings.

PHONOLOGY

Consonants

stops: p, b, t, d, k, g
fricatives: s, z, h
nasals: m, n, ŋ
flap: r
semi-vowels: j, w

Vowels

i, e, a, o, u

Combining the consonantal and vocalic rows, we get a grid of open syllables which provide the phonemes of Japanese. In early Old Japanese there were 112 such syllables, reduced in Heian Japanese to about 70: e.g. for the series based on *k*, *ka – ki – ku – ke – ko*. However, allophones arise in the grid: in the *s* series the fricative /ʃ/, in the *t* series the affricates /ts/ and /tʃ/, and in the *z* series the affricate /dʒ/. These are notated in the usual transcription, and here, as *sh*, *ts*, *ch*, *j*. Thus, *hajimemashite* 'how do you do' is /hadʒimemaʃte/. For the complete grid, see the Japanese script chart.

Again, for all consonants apart from /d/ and /w/ there is a three-term palatalized series; e.g. *kya, kyu*, *kyo*. In the *s* row the palatalized values are realized as /ʃa – ʃu – ʃo/; in the *t* row as /tʃa – tʃu – tʃo/, and in the *z* row as /dʒa – dʒu – dʒo/.

Final *-n* is realized as nasal [ŋ], without nasalization of the preceding vowel. That is to say, final *n* is syllabic: *Nihon* 'Japan' is pronounced /ni.ho.ŋ/.

In the transcription used here, long vowels are written doubled: e.g. *oo*. They are twice the length of single vowels; the difference is phonemic.

There are several diphthongs. When final or in contact with an unvoiced consonant: /u/ is reduced to Ø: e.g. *suki* 'likes, is fond of' → /*ski*/; *arimasu* 'is' → /*arimas*/.

Stress

Japanese has a pitch-accentuation pattern in place of tonic stress. Syllables flow evenly: a long syllable is two moras, a short syllable is one mora. Pitch is not marked; if it were, the marker would be on the last syllable of a high-pitch sequence, preceding a drop: e.g. *wakarimasen deshita* 'didn't understand': /$_{\text{wa}}$karimase$_{\text{n.}}$deshita/.

MORPHOLOGY AND SYNTAX

There is no grammatical gender; no articles. A plural marker exists but this is used mainly with pronouns. Reduplication is possible. The word *takusan* 'many', is often used: e.g. *Kuruma wa takusan arimasu ne?* 'There are lots of cars, aren't there?'; *shashin o takusan torimashita* 'took lots of photographs'.

Noun

Nouns are invariable. Syntactic relationships are expressed by means of particles. The most important of these are:

- *wa*: this is a focusing agent, which identifies or recapitulates the topic, e.g. *watashi no kaisha* ***wa*** *Oosaka ni arimasu* '(as for) my business (it) is in O'.
- *ga*: subject marker, e.g. *soto* ***wa*** *ame* ***ga*** *futte imasu* '(as for) outside, the rain is falling'; *ano hito* ***wa*** *se* ***ga*** *takai desu* '(as for) that man, stature is tall' = 'that man is tall'.
- *ni*: locative, aditive, dative, e.g. *kooen ni* 'in the park'; *imooto ni* 'to sister'; *sakura o mi* ***ni*** *ikimasu* 'go to see the cherry blossom'.
- *o*: object marker, e.g. *asa-gohan* ***o*** *tabemashita* 'ate breakfast'; *e-hagaki* ***o*** *takusan kaimashita* 'bought many postcards'.
- *no*: genitival relationship, e.g. *watashi* ***no*** *heya wa* 'my room'; *Tookyoo wa Nippon* ***no*** *shuto desu* 'Tokyo is the capital of Japan'.
- *de*: instrumental, e.g. *hikooki* ***de*** 'by plane'; *denwa* ***de*** 'by phone'.

Adjective

See **Stative verb**, below. An attributive adjective precedes the noun: e.g. *yuumei-na haiku wa* 'a famous haiku'; *takai yama wa* 'a high mountain'.

Pronoun

In general, pronouns are avoided in Japanese, especially as regards the second person. Here, the addressee's name followed by *san* should be used: e.g.

Oota.san wa nani o tabemasu ka? 'What are you having (to eat)?' (addressing Mr Oota)

Watashi, pl. *watashitachi* are acceptable first person forms; *anata* has restricted use as a second person form.

Third person: *anohito* or *anokata* 'he/she'; *kare* 'he', *kanojo* 'she'.

DEMONSTRATIVE PRONOUN

kore 'this', *sore* 'that', *are* 'that (further away)'. The demonstrative adjectives are *kono* 'this', *sono* 'that', *ano* 'that (further away)'.

INTERROGATIVE PRONOUN

dare 'who?'; *nani* 'what?'. The final particle *ka* makes a sentence interrogative: e.g. *Sono hito wa Nippon-jin desu* ***ka*** 'Is that man (is he) a Japanese?'

RELATIVE PRONOUN

See **Verb**, below.

Numerals

There are two parallel sets of numbers, native Japanese and Chinese: 1–10: Jap. *hito-*, *futa-*, *mi-*, *yon-*, *itsu-*, *mu-*, *nana-*, *ya-*, *kokono-*, *too*; Ch. *ichi*, *ni*, *san*, *shi*, *go*, *roku*, *shichi*, *hachi*, *ku/kyu*, *juu*. In enumeration, the Chinese numerals have to be combined with appropriate classifiers, e.g. *-hon* for long objects, *-satsu* for books, *-nin* for people. There are a couple of dozen of these, usually with assimilation at junctures: e.g. with *-hon*: ***ippon*** 'one' (e.g. pencil); *ni**hon*** 'two' (pencils); *san**bon*** /sa**mb**on/, 'three' (pencils). Numeral + classifier usually follow the referent: e.g. *Ki wa **roppon** arimasu* 'There are six trees (*roku* + *hon* → *roppon*).

11 *juu-ichi*; 12 *juu-ni*; 20 *ni-juu*; 30 *san-juu*; 100 *hyaku*.

Verb

There are three classes of verb: vowel stems, consonantal stems, and a small class of irregular verbs (six members). For inflectional purposes, the six bases of Classical Japanese are retained in slightly modified form:

Base	*1*	*2*	*3*	*4*	*5*	*6*
vowel class	mi	mi	miru	mire	miro	miyoo
consonant class	kaka	kaki	kaku	kake	kake	kakoo
irregular	shi/sa	shi	suru	sure	seyo/siro	shiyoo

Base 1: this is used in the formation of the negative, e.g. ***minai*** 'not to see', and the causative, e.g. ***kakaseru*** 'to cause to write'.

Base 2 provides the base for the present and past polite forms, and the desiderative: e.g. ***mimasu*** 'sees'; ***mimashita*** 'saw', ***mitai*** 'wants to see'.

Base 3: citation form, used as infinitive. Plain present tense.

Base 4: provides the conditional form in *-eba*, e.g. ***mireba*** 'would see'; *kake**ba*** 'would write'.

Base 5: imperative plain form, e.g. *kake!* 'write!'; this is permissible only in reported speech.

Base 6: prospective or hortative, e.g. *motto benkyoo* ***shiyoo*** *to omotte imasu* 'I'm thinking of doing some more studying' (*benkyoo*). This form is associated with first person only (but citation form + *deshoo* – base 6 of *da* 'to be' – is general: e.g. *Taroo wa kyoo kuru deshoo* 'Taroo will probably come today').

THE -TE/-DE (GERUND) FORM

In verbs ending in *-ru*, *-te* replaces *-ru*: *deru* – ***dete*** 'having gone out'. In *-u* verbs, root *k/g* are elided, *-de* appears after a sonant: *kaku* 'write' – *kai**te***; *shinu* 'die' – *shi**nde***; *narabu* 'line up' – *nara**nde***. There are some irregular forms: *suru* 'do' – ***shite***; *kuru* 'come' – ***kite***.

This form is much used with the auxiliary *iru/aru* to express a continuing state of affairs: e.g. *Nani o shite imasu ka* 'What is/are ... doing?' It is also used as a holding suffix in a serial utterance involving several verbs; each of these then ends in *-te/-de*, the final verb alone taking the finite ending:

Hiru-gohan o tabe**te**, oka ni nobot**te**, mati o mimashita
'Having eaten lunch, we climbed up the hill and looked at the town'

Tamago o too kat**te**, niwa e de**te**, hiru-gohan o tabemashita
'(I, we, etc.) bought a dozen eggs, went into the garden and had lunch'

The parallel with the Turkic languages is striking.

PRESENT AND PAST POLITE FORMS, POSITIVE AND NEGATIVE

present: *-masu* /mas'/, e.g. *kaki**masu*** 'writes'; neg. *kaki**masen*** 'doesn't write';

past: *-mashita* /mash'ta/, e.g. *kaki**mashita*** 'wrote'; neg. *kaki**masen deshita*** 'didn't write'.

There is a great wealth of agglutinative affixes; some of the most important are:

-eba: conditional, e.g. *ame ga fure**ba*** 'if it rains';

-tara: temporal, e.g. *hiru-gohan o tabe**tara*** 'when (I, we, etc.) eat, have eaten lunch';

-eba + *ikemasen/narimasen*: obligation, e.g. *Watashi wa Tookyoo e ikanakereba narimasen* 'I have to go to Tokyo';

-tai: desire, e.g. *Watashi moo tabetai desu* 'I want to eat too.'

PASSIVE

Infixes *-are-*, *-rare-*, e.g. *tabe**rare**ru* 'be eaten'; *kak**are**ru* 'be written'. An agent, if overtly expressed, takes the postposition *ni*: e.g. *Watashi wa kinoo ame* ***ni*** ***furareta*** 'By the rain (*ame*) I-was-rained-on yesterday.'

CAUSATIVE

The infixes are *-ase-*, *-sase-*, e.g. *tabe**sase**te imasu* 'is feeding (trans.)'. Passive and causative may be combined: e.g. *Watashi wa ka-choo-san* ***ni*** *Oosaka e ik.**ase.rare**.mashita* 'I was made to go to Osaka by my department boss.'

STATIVE VERBS

Examples: *takai* 'it is high'; *omoshiroi* 'it is interesting'. As attributes, these precede the noun. As predicates they are conjugated: past *omoshiro.katta* 'it was interesting'; negative past *omoshiro**ku**.nakatta* 'it wasn't interesting'.

RELATIVE CLAUSES

Relative clauses are placed in attributive position to the left of the head-word: e.g., using *o-tenki* 'weather', *warui* 'bad', *tokoro* 'place', *o-tenki ga warui tokoro* 'a place where the weather is bad'. Ambiguity may arise, as the deixis is not specific in Japanese: e.g. *tegami o okutta hito wa* 'the man who sent us the letter', *or* 'the man to whom the letter was sent'.

Nominalizing agents such as *toki* 'time', *koto* 'thing', are used to form other types of relative clause (verb in plain form): e.g. *asa hito ni atta toki ni wa ...* 'when you meet someone in the morning ...' (*asa* 'morning'; *au* 'to meet'); *Kare wa sensoo ga owatta* ***to iu koto*** *o shiranakatta* 'He didn't know (the thing) that the war had ended.'

HONORIFIC PREFIXES

O-, *go-* are attached to nominals and to adjectives: e.g. *Anata no* ***o-too-san*** *no* ***go****-iken wa doo desu ka?* 'What is your (hon.) father's (hon.) opinion?' A verbal form is made honorific by substituting *o-/go-* + base 2 + *narimasu*: *Yamada-san wa kore o* ***o-kaki ni*** *narimashita* 'Mr Yamada wrote this'; cf. for first person (never hon.): *watashi wa kore o kakimashita* 'I wrote this'.

Postpositions

Examples: *kara* 'from', *made* 'as far as', *de* 'in, with'.

Word order

Typically SOV.

1 初めに言(ことば)があった。言は神と共に
あった。言は神であった。

2 この言は初めに神と共にあった。

3 すべてのものは，これによってできた。できたものの
うち，一つとしてこれによらないものはなかった。

4 この言に命があった。そしてこの命は人の光で
あった。
5 光はやみの中に輝いている。そして，やみはこれ
に勝たなかった。
6 ¶ ここにひとりの人があって，神からつかわされて
いた。その名をヨハネと言った。
7 この人はあかしのためにきた。光についてあかしを
し，彼によってすべての人が信じるためである。

8 彼は光ではなく，ただ，光についてあかしをする
ためにきたのである。

JAVANESE

INTRODUCTION

Javanese belongs to the Malayo-Polynesian branch of Austronesian, and is spoken by between 50 and 60 million people in central and eastern Java. The language has been influenced, first, by Sanskrit, then, from the fifteenth century onwards by Arabic, and finally, since about 1600, by Dutch. The influence of Malay, in the shape of Bahasa Indonesia, has increased since the latter became the official language of Indonesia.

By the thirteenth/fourteenth century Old Javanese was no longer a spoken language, though it continued to be used for literature. Of particular interest in the Middle Javanese period is the *babad* literature dealing with the traditional history of Java. This period culminates in the impressive figure of Jasadipura, the eighteenth-century court poet whose work was a major factor in the emergence of the Surakarta, or Solo, dialect as the basis of modern literary Javanese.

The *wayang* – the traditional Javanese puppet theatre – draws on both Hindu and Islamic sources for its themes: e.g. on Jasadipura's reworking of the Old Javanese version of the *Mahābhārata*, Book III (*vanapurvan*).

The twentieth century has seen the growth of the social novel and other western genres; certain influential writers in this field, e.g. Senggono and Subagijo, use ngoko (*see* **Speech levels**, below). In general, however, Javanese has been more conservative than Bahasa Indonesia.

SCRIPT

The *čarakan* script was used exclusively until replaced by romanization in the twentieth century. In 1926 a standardized orthography was adopted, revised in 1972.

Speech levels

Javanese is a two-tier language. The socio-linguistic constraints which operate in many languages with regard to pronominal usage, for example, are applied in Javanese to all parts of speech, nouns, verbs, adjectives, prepositions. The two main levels are: *ngoko* or colloquial; *krâmâ* /krɔmɔ/, 'elevated'.

Ngoko is basic Javanese in the sense that it is picked up by the child at home. From school age on, however, the Javanese child has to acquire the additional and rather extensive krama lexicon for use in certain prescribed socio-linguistic situations – by young people to their elders, on formal occasions, when addressing strangers or social superiors, and so on. A compromise solution is increasingly being developed in the shape of krama madya – more formal than ngoko, less stilted than krama.

All three forms have virtually identical grammar and syntax; the differences are purely lexical. For any given referent, krama may have the same word as ngoko, an enhanced form, or a completely different word: e.g.

Ngoko	*Kråmå*	*English*
wit	wit	tree
prakara	prakawis	occasion
asu	segawon	dog
omah	griya	house
wong	tiyang	man

Use of ngoko is steadily encroaching on the krama preserve. The Javanese press uses ngoko in general. Krama itself has more than one register.

PHONOLOGY

Consonants

stops: p/b, t/d, ʈ/ɖ, k/g, ˀ
affricates: tʃ/dʒ/, t′/d′
fricatives: w, s, j, h
nasals: m, n, ɲ, ŋ
lateral and trill: l, r

Since the voiced/unvoiced values are almost indistinguishable, the stops and affricates are set out in pairs. According to Uhlenbeck, the voiced member is slightly aspirated. Initial /k/ = [q]; final /k/ = /ʔ/. No final is voiced.

Vowels

i, ɪ, e, ɛ, a, ə, ɔ, o, u

/ə/ is known as *e*-pepet; it appears in unstressed syllables, /a/ in penultimate and final syllables → [ɔ]: e.g. *nagara* /nəgɔrɔ/, 'country'.

There are no diphthongs; contiguous vowels are pronounced separately.

Stress

Stress is on the penultimate syllable unless this is *e*-pepet: e.g. *berás* 'polished rice'.

MORPHOLOGY AND SYNTAX

(N = ngoko, K = krama.)

Noun

No gender; there are no articles or plural markers; to suggest plurality N *akeh*, K *kathah* 'many' may be used. A collective can be made by reduplication: e.g. *sedulur-sedulur* (sometimes written '*sedulur 2*') 'a group of friends'.

POSSESSIVE RELATIONSHIP
See **Pronoun**, below.

Adjective

The attributive adjective follows the noun and is invariable: e.g. N *omah gedhé* = K *griya ageng* '(a/the) big house'.

COMPARATIVE
N. *luwih*, K *langkung*: e.g. N *luwih dhuwur* = K *langkung inggil* 'higher'.

Pronoun

Independent personal forms and possessive enclitics:

	Personal	*Possessive*
1	N aku, K kula	N -ku, K kula
2	N kowé, K sampéyan	N -mu, K sampéyan
3	N dhèwèké, K piyambakipun	N -e, K -ipun

There are no specifically plural forms: e.g. N *omah**ku*** = K *griya kula* 'my house(s)', 'our house(s)'; N *omahé* = K *griya**nipun*** 'his house(s)', 'their house(s)'; cf. N *sapiné wong iki* = K *lembu**nipun** tiyang punika* 'that man's cow'.

DEMONSTRATIVE PRONOUN
N *iki*, K *punika* (pronounced /menikɔ/): 'this', 'that'.

INTERROGATIVE PRONOUN
N *sapa*, K *sinten* 'who?'; N *apa*, N *punapa* /menɔpɔ/ 'what?'. The introductory interrogative particle is N *apa*, K *punapa*.

RELATIVE PRONOUN
N *kang/sing*, K *ingkang*: e.g. N *Iki wong kang arep adol omahe* = K *Punika tiyang ingkang badhé sade griyanipun* 'That is the man who wants to sell his house' (*arep* = *badhé* 'will'; *adol* = *sade* 'sell').

Numerals

For the cardinals 1 to 5 there are distinct N/K sets: N *siji*, *loro*, *telu*, *papat*, *lima* = K *setunggal*, *kalih*, *tiga*, *sekawan*, *gangsal*; 6 to 9 show common N/K forms: *enem*, *pitu*, *wolu*, *sanga*. 10 = N *sepuluh*, K *sedasa*; 11 = N/K *sewelas*; 12–15 separate N and K forms; 16–19 common forms; 20 is N *rongpuluh*, K *kalihdasa*; 30 N *telungpuluh*, K *tigangdasa*; 100 N/K *saratus*.

Verb

A few Javanese verbal stems are used in primary form, e.g. N *takon* = K *taken* 'ask'; N *ana* = K *wonten* 'be located', but the great majority of stems undergo initial nasalization before they can function as verbs. Vocalic initials take prefix *ng-*, e.g. *iris* – ***ngiris*** 'to cut'; consonantal initials take homorganic nasal, e.g. *buru* – ***mburu*** 'to hunt'; *sapu* – ***nyapu*** 'to sweep'; *rembat* – ***ngrembat*** 'to yoke'. These stems are neutral as to tense or aspect, and, since there is nothing resembling a conjugational system, adverbial markers preceding the verb may be used to indicate tense, e.g. N *tau* = K *nate* for remote past; N *wis* = K *sampun* for past; N *bakal*, *arep* = K *badhé*, *adyeng* for future. Example: K *Ratu sampun.nitih mengsah.hipun* 'The prince has overcome his enemy' (*mengsah* 'enemy').

THE -I SUFFIX

This establishes a directional relationship between a verb and its locus of action or its direct object: e.g. *lungguh* 'to sit' – *nglunggihi* 'to sit on (something)'; *-tulis* 'to write' – *nulisi kertas* 'to write on paper'.

PASSIVE

In general, the passive construction is preferred in Javanese, and there are several passive forms:

(a) The personal passive; the prefixes are N 1 *tak-*, 2 *kok-*, 3 *di-*; K 1 *kula*, 2 *sampeyan*, 3 *dipun*: e.g. N *Layang iki **tak**tulis* 'This letter is being written by me'; N *Woh iki **di**pangan wong iki* = K *Woh punika **dipun** tedha tiyang punika* 'This fruit is being eaten by this man.'
(b) Neutral passive: this is characteristic of the literary style – *-in-* infix, e.g. ***tinulis*** 'to be written'.
(c) Chance or accidental passive: formed with *ke...an* circumfix, e.g. N *maling* 'thief' – ***kemalingan*** 'to be robbed', K *pandung* 'thief' – ***kepandungan*** 'to be robbed'; N *udan* 'rain' – ***kodanan*** 'to be caught in the rain', K *jawah* 'rain' – ***kejawahan*** 'to be caught in the rain'.
(d) Two passives are coded for aspect: *ka-* perfective; *-um-* imperfective.

IMPERATIVE

In N only, as imperative forms would be incompatible with K usage. The N suffixes are *-a*, *-(n)en* for passive verbs, *-ana* for *-i* verbs.

CAUSATIVE

The suffixes are N *-aké-*, K *-aken*: e.g. N *sopir itu nglakok**aké** montore* = K *sopir punika nglampah**aken** montor**ipun*** 'the driver starts his engine'.

NEGATIVE

N *ora*/K *mboten* negate verbs: N *dudu*/K *sanès*, *dede* negate nouns: e.g. N *aku dudu wong Inggeris* = K *kula sanès tiyang Inggeris* 'I'm not English'; N *aku ora bisa basa Jawi* = K *kula mboten saged basa Jawi* 'I don't speak Javanese'.

AFFIXES

Examples:

-an, an all-purpose affix, usually with loss of initial nasalization; often indicates result of verbal action, or the instrument used: e.g. *nimbang* 'to weigh' – *timbangan* 'scales'.

ka...an makes abstract nouns, e.g. *sugih* 'rich' – *kasugihan* 'wealth'.

pa-: indicates agent, e.g. N *nulis* 'to write' – *panulis* 'writer'; K *nyerat* 'to write' – *panyerat* 'writer'.

pa...an: locus of action, e.g. N *turu* 'to sleep' – *paturon* 'bedroom'.

sa + *pa-*: extent, range, e.g. *mbedhil* 'to shoot' – *sapambedhil* 'range limit for a shot' → 'as far as ...'.

suffix *-en* forms adjectives, e.g. *uwan* 'grey hair' – *uwanen* 'grey-haired'.

Prepositions

Examples: *ing* 'in', *saking* 'from'. Composite prepositions like *ing duwur* 'up', *ing isor* 'down' are also adverbials.

Word order

Varies according to whether construction is active or passive. S normally precedes V.

1 Ing kala purwa Sang Sabda iku ana, déné Sang Sabda iku nunggil karo Gusti Allah, sarta Sang Sabda iku Gusti Allah. 2 Wiwitané Pandjenengané iku nunggil karo Gusti Allah. 3 Samubarang kabèh dumadiné déning Sang Sabda, lan samubarang kang dumadi ora ana sawidji-widjia kang ora didadèkaké déning Sang Sabda. 4 Sang Sabda kang kedunungan urip, sarta urip iku kang dadi pepaḍanging manungsa. 5 Anadéné Sang Paḍang nelahi sadjroning pepeteng, lan ora kalinḍih déning pepeteng iku. 6 Ana prija rawuh kautus déning Allah asmané Jokanan. 7 Rawuhé dadi saksi, kapatah neksèni bab Sang Paḍang, supaja dadia lantarané wong kabèh paḍa pratjaja. 8 Pandjenengané iku dudu Sang Paḍang pijambak, mung kapatah neksèni bab Sang Paḍang.

KANNADA (Kanarese)

INTRODUCTION

As regards number of speakers, Kannada comes in third place among the Dravidian languages after Telugu and Tamil; as regards age and quality of literary tradition, it runs Tamil a close second. The most important work in the early period is the *Kavirājamārga*, a rhetorical Sanskritized treatise, enlivened by glimpses of the Kannada people and their customs. Worthy of particular mention is the splendid *vacana* poetry of the Vīraśaiva saints – free verse of mystical and gnomic import in colloquial Kannada – produced in the tenth to twelfth centuries. With its extensive output of novels, drama, and verse, Modern Kannada literature is one of the most flourishing in southern India.

Kannada is the official language of the State of Karnataka. The number of speakers is estimated at about 24 million.

SCRIPT

The syllabary derives ultimately from Brahmi via the transitional script which also underlies Telugu. Order and content are as in Devanagari.

PHONOLOGY

Consonants

stops: p, b, ʈ, ɖ, t, d, k, g
affricates: tʃ, dʒ
fricatives: v, s, ʂ, l̲, ʃ, j, h
nasals: m, n, ɲ, ŋ, ɳ
lateral and flap: l, ɭ, r, r̲

/l̲/ is the retroflex fricative which tends to be pronounced as [l] in Modern Kannada. Similarly, /r̲/ tends to [r]. The stops have aspirated values, not usually found in pure Kannada words. The affricates also have aspirated values. Retroflex phonemes are notated here with a dot: e.g. /ɖ/ = *ḍ*.

Vowels

long and short: i, e, a, o, u
diphthongs: ai, au

Stress

Light stress on first syllable. All Kannada words end in vowels.

Sandhi

/j/ and /v/ are widely used in vocalic juncture: e.g. *guru* + *-u* → *guruvu* 'guru, teacher'; *ā* + *ūṭa* → *āvūṭa* 'that food'; *huli* 'tiger' + *-inda* (instr. affix) → *huliyinda* 'by the tiger'.

MORPHOLOGY AND SYNTAX

Noun

Kannada has three genders: masculine, feminine, and neuter. A typical masculine ending is *-anu*, typical feminine *-aḷu*. Plural markers are *-aru*, *-kaḷu/ gaḷu*. Thus, *sēvaka.nu* 'male servant', and *sēvaka.ḷu* 'female servant', share the plural form *sēvaka.ru*; cf. *maravu* 'tree', pl. *mara.gaḷu*; *ūru* 'village', pl. *ūru.gaḷu*. A reduplicated plural of respect is found: e.g.*dēv.aru.gaḷu* 'gods'.

DECLENSION

There are seven classes: given here is the specimen declension of *sēvaka* 'servant':

	Singular
nominative	sēvakanu
accusative	sēvakanannu
instrumental	sēvakaninda
dative	sēvakanige
genitive	sēvakana
locative	sēvakanalli
vocative	sēvakanē

Plural forms are as singular, with *-r-* replacing *-n-*: e.g. nom. *sēvakaru*, acc. *sēvakarannu*.

Adjective

As attribute, adjective is invariable, preceding noun: e.g. *doḍḍa ūru* 'a big town'.

Pronoun

The first person singular is *nān*(*u*)/*nā*, with pl. *nāvu*; similarly, the second person forms are sing. *nīnu/nī*, with pl. *nīvu*. The third person forms are marked for gender: masc. *avanu/ivanu*; fem. *avaḷu/ivaḷu*, in the singular; they share a common plural form: *avaru/ivaru*. The neuter third person form is sing. *adu/idu*, pl. *avu*(*gaḷu*)/*ivu*(*gaḷu*).

In the declension of the first person singular form, *nān*(*u*) the base for the oblique cases remains *nann-*: e.g. gen. *nanna*, acc. *nannannu*.

DEMONSTRATIVE PRONOUN
ī/*intha* 'this'; *ā*/*antha* 'that'.

INTERROGATIVE PRONOUN
Masc. *yāvanu*, fem. *yāvaḷu*; they coalesce as *yāru* 'who?'; *yāvudu* 'what?'.

RELATIVE PRONOUN
None in Kannada; *see* **Verb**, below, for formation of relative clause.

Numerals

The numerals 1–5 inclusive have each two forms reflecting gender. The neuter series is *ondu*, *eraḍu*, *mūru*, *nālku*, *aidu*; the corresponding masculine/feminine forms are *obba*, *ibbaru*, *mūvaru*, *nālvaru*, *aivaru*. From 6 onwards, there is only one form for each numeral. 6–10: *āru*, *ēḷu*, *eṇṭu*, *ombhattu*, *hattu*. 11 *hannondu*; 12 *hanneraḍu*; 13 *hadimūru*; 20 *ippattu*; 21 *ippattondu*; 30 *muvattu*; 40 *nālvattu*; 100 *nūru*.

Verb

Fundamental to the structure of the Kannada verb is the verbal noun series comprising the infinitive, the gerunds, and the participles. For the stem *māḍu* 'to do, make', the forms are:

infinitive: *māḍa*;
gerunds: present *māḍuttā*; past *māḍi*; negative *māḍade*;
participles: present *māḍuva*; past *māḍida*; negative *māḍada*.

For many Kannada verbs, the form of the verbal noun is not predictable; cf. *koḍu* 'to give' – *koṭṭu*; *koḷḷu* 'to take' – *koṇḍu*; *nagu* 'to laugh' – *nakku*.

There are three moods: indicative, imperative, suppositional.

INDICATIVE MOOD
Present tense (marker -(*u*)*tt*); past tense (marker -(*i*)*d*); future tense (marker -(*u*)*v*). Thus, from stem *māḍu* 'to do':

		Present			*Past*			*Future*	
		Sing.	*Pl.*		*Sing.*	*Pl.*		*Sing.*	*Pl.*
1	māḍ**utt**.	-ēne	-ēve	māḍ**id**	-ēnu	-evu	māḍu**v**	-enu	-evu
2		-īye	-īri		-e	-iri		-e	-iri
3	masc.	-āne	-āre		-anu	-aru		-anu	-aru
	fem.	-āḷe			-aḷu			-aḷu	
	nt.	-ade	-ave		māḍitu	-uvu		-udu	-uvu

NEGATIVE CONJUGATION
The personal affixes are added directly to the root, without infixed marker. The

negative form thus produced does duty for all three tenses: thus, the present, past, and future negative indicative of *māḍu* is:

		Singular	Plural
1		māḍenu	māḍevu
2		māḍe	māḍiri
3	masc.	māḍanu	māḍaru
	fem.	māḍaḷu	
	nt.	māḍadu	māḍavu

IMPERATIVE MOOD

Here the verb is marked for three persons, singular and plural, without distinction of gender in the third person: e.g. sing. 1 *māḍuve*, 2 *māḍu*, 3 *māḍali*; pl. *māḍōṇa* (with variants), *māḍiri*, *māḍali*.

SUPPOSITIONAL MOOD

Made by adding the personal affixes to the stem extended by the past-tense characteristic vowel *-i*: e.g. *māḍ.i.y.ēnu* 'I may/might do'.

NON-FINITE FORMS

Present–future participle: *māḍuva* 'doing, is doing, will be doing'. Past participle: *māḍida* 'was doing'. Pronominal endings may be attached to these forms to produce verbal nouns marked in third person for gender: e.g. *māḍuva.v.anu* 'he who does'; *māḍuva.va.aḷu* 'she who does'. Similarly in the negative conjugation: *māḍada* 'who is not doing'; *māḍada.va.aḷu* 'she who is not doing/did not do'.

The participial forms are used in the formation of relative clauses; the forms themselves are neutral as to voice: cf. *pāṭhavannu ōdida huḍuganu* 'the boy who read the lesson'; *huḍuganu ōdida pāṭhavu* 'the lesson read by the boy'.

Postpositions

Nouns, participles, pronouns, etc. governed by postpositions are usually in the genitive case: e.g. *oḍane* 'along with', *nanna* + *oḍane* → *nannoḍane* 'along with me'; *horatu* 'apart from', *nanna horatu* 'apart from me'.

Word order

SOV.

೧ ಆದಿಯಲ್ಲಿ ವಾಕ್ಯವಿತ್ತು ಆ ವಾಕ್ಯವು ದೇವರ ಸಂಗಡ ಕೂಡಾ
೨ ಯಿತ್ತು ಮತ್ತು ಆ ವಾಕ್ಯವೇ ದೇವರು ॥ ಅದು ಆದಿಯಲ್ಲಿ ದೇವ
೩ ರ ಸಂಗಡ ಕೂಡಾಯಿತ್ತು ॥ ಸಮಸ್ತವು ಅದರ ಕ್ರೈಯ್ಯವುಂ
ಟಾಯಿತು ಮತ್ತು ಆದದ್ದೆಲ್ಲಾ ಅದರಿಂದಲಲ್ಲದೆ ಬ್ಯೇರೆ ವಂದುಂ
೪ ಸುವುಂಟಾದದ್ದಿಲ್ಲ ॥ ಅದರಲ್ಲಿ ಜೀವವುಂಟು ಮತ್ತು ಆ ಜೀವವು
೫ ಮನುಷ್ಯರಿಗೆ ಬೆಳಕಾಗಿತ್ತು ॥ ಆ ಬೆಳಕು ಅಂಧಕಾರದಲ್ಲಿ ಪ್ರ
ಕಾಸಿಸಿತು ಆದರೆ ಆ ಅಂಧಕಾರವು ಅದರಂನ ಗ್ರಹಿಸಲಿಲ್ಲವು ॥
೬ ಯೋವಾಂನನೆಂಬ ಹೆಸರುಳ್ಳ ವಬ್ಬ ಮನುಷ್ಯನು ದೇವರ
೭ ಕ್ರೈಯ್ಯಕಳಿಹಿಸಪಟ್ಟನು ॥ ಅವನು ತನ್ನ ಕ್ರೈಯ್ಯದ ಸಮಸ್ತರು ವಿ
ಶ್ವಾಸಿಸುವ ಹಾಗೆ ಬೆಳಕಿಗೆ ಸಾಕ್ಷಿ ಕೊಡ ಸಾಕ್ಷಿಯಾಗಿ ಬಂದ
೮ ನು ॥ ಅವನು ಆ ಬೆಳಕಲ್ಲ ಆದರೆ ಆ ಬೆಳಕಿಗೆ ಸಾಕ್ಷಿ ಕೊಡುವ
೯ ದಕ್ಕಾಗಿ ಬಂದನು ॥

KASHMIRI

INTRODUCTION

By far the most important of the Dardic languages, Kashmiri is the official language of the Indian state of Jammu and Kashmir. The number of speakers is estimated at 3 million. The ethnonym is /k'aʃiːr^y/. For controversy surrounding the exact genetic status of Kashmir and the other Dardic languages, see Zograph (1982).

Alone among the Dardic languages, Kashmiri has a literary tradition dating from the thirteenth/fourteenth century. The earliest Kashmiri poetry was written by the poetess Lal Ded in the fourteenth century; later, two of the best writers in a specifically Kashmiri genre, the *lol* ('love') lyric, were also women – Haba Khotun in the sixteenth century and Arnimal in the eighteenth century.

SCRIPT

Originally, Kashmiri was written in the Sharada version of Devanagari. It is now written in the Urdu version of the Arabo-Persian script, with specific adaptations for Kashmiri phonemes.

PHONOLOGY

The Kashmiri phonological system is of considerable complexity. The following grid displays the basic phonemes, disregarding secondary articulation values. For these, see the notes following the grid.

Consonants

stops: p, ph, ṭ, ṭh, t, th, k, kh, b, ḍ, d
affricates: c, č
fricatives: s, ş, ʃ, z, ʒ, h
nasals: m, n
lateral and flap: l, r
semi-vowels: j, w

Notes
1. Stops: this is the familiar NIA series, minus the voiced aspirate member. All stops (including the aspirates) occur palatalized: /p', ph', b'/, etc., and all, except the labials, occur labialized: /t°, th°/, etc.

2. Affricates: Kashmiri has a dual series of affricates: (a) a dental series (single focus) based on /c/ pure and aspirated, each of these with palatalized and labialized correlatives: /c, c′, c°, c', c'′, c'°/ (six terms); (b) a palatal series based on /č/, pure and aspirate, with labialized correlatives (four terms). The base phoneme (dual focus) for this series is represented by Zaxar′in and Edel′man (1971) as *čǰ*.

The Kashmiri affricates appear to have a homorganic sibilant fricative onset. Examples given in Zaxar′in and Edel′man include (here simplified): *bučh* 'it stung, bit', transcribed as /b°u-ʊ-s-čh/. Similarly, for a voiced affricate: *baji* 'more, bigger', /b°əʒdʒi/.

3. Initial clusters are articulated with the help of epenthetic vowels, which harmonize with stem vowel: *drog* 'dear' /doroʊg°/.

4. /s, z, h, l, r, w/ occur palatalized; /s, z, ʃ, h, l, r/ occur labialized.

5. /m′, n′, n°/ are present.

The complete grid comprises 69 phonemes. In this entry, the retroflex phonemes are denoted by subscript dot; e.g. /ɖ/ = *ḍ*.

Vowels

short: ɪ, ə, a, o, u, œ, y
long: iː, eː, aː, oː, uː

These are basic values; all occur nasalized, and all, especially the short vowels, have many variants. Close transcription of Kashmiri is exceedingly complicated; here, a simplified approximation is used. (Long vowels are notated here as *ī*, *ē*, etc.)

The Kashmiri vocalic system has two distinctive features:

(a) Regressive assimilation, whereby the root vowel is modified by the affix (cf. *Uygur*): e.g. *pūth′* 'book'; oblique base, *poṭh′ɪ*.
(b) The so-called matra vowels – ultra-short medial and final vowels – historically present; now mute, they nevertheless induce the regressive assimilation described in (a). The matra vowels are written in index position: e.g. *host^u* 'bull elephant'.

MORPHOLOGY AND SYNTAX

Noun

Kashmiri has two genders, masculine and feminine. Gender is very unstable. A typical masculine ending is -^{u}; fem. -$^{i/ü}$: both of these matra vowels mark palatalization of the preceding consonant.

Virtually all nouns ending in the singular in a palatalized consonant are feminine.

PLURAL FORMATION

Some examples illustrating affixation and stem change: *māl* 'garland', plural *māl.ɪ*; *wat* 'way' – *wat.ɪ*; *mōl* 'father' – *məl'*; *rāt* 'night' – *rəc*; *bud* 'old woman' – *budžɪ*.

Where singular and plural do not differ, plurality is indicated by verbal concord: e.g. singular *cūr čhuh ā.mut* 'the thief came'; plural *cūr čhɪh ā.mɪt* 'the thieves came'.

DECLENSION

Four models: two masculine (-^{u} and non-^{u}) and two feminine: e.g. masculine in -^{u}:

	Singular	*Plural*
nominative	gur^u 'horse'	gur^i
oblique I	guris	guren
oblique II	guri	guryau
agentive	gur^i	

Oblique I provides the direct object; oblique II and the agentive are used as subject of transitive verb.

GENITIVE

The inflected postpositions *-h/sund*, *-un*, *-uk* are used. Some examples: *mə̄l'sund gur* 'father's horse'; *mə̄l'sɪnd' gur^i* 'father's horses'; *mə̄l'sɪnd'ɪs gur'ɪs p'aṭh* 'on father's horse'; *māl'an.hɪnd'aw gur'aw p'aṭh* 'on the horses of the fathers'.

Adjective

As attribute, the adjective precedes the noun with which it is in concord for gender, number, and case; e.g. nom. *boḍ^u mahanyuv^u* 'big man'; obl. *I baḍ'ɪs mahanvis*; pl. *baḍ^i mahaniv^i*. Cf. *baḍɪs gāmas manz* 'in the big village'; *baḍ'aw gāmaw manz* 'from big villages'.

COMPARATIVE

Example: *yɪh gur hum'ɪ gur'ɪ čhuh boḍ* 'this horse is bigger than that one', where *hum'ɪ gur'ɪ* is in obl. II.

Pronoun

	Singular		*Plural*	
	Nominative	*Oblique*	*Nominative*	*Oblique*
1	boh	me	as^i	ase
2	cə	ce	toh^i	tohe

The third person forms are supplied from the demonstrative series.

The personal pronouns have enclitic forms used with verbs: e.g. *di.m* 'give me' (where *.m* marks the first person indirect object); *wučh^u.h.as* 'they saw me'

(*.h* marks the third person agentive; *.as* is first person direct object).

Demonstrative: the series has five degrees of relative distance, ranging from *yıh* 'this (close at hand)' to *suh* (remote, invisible). All are fully declined.

INTERROGATIVE PRONOUN
k'ah 'who, what?'

RELATIVE PRONOUN
Masc. *yus*, fem. *yossa*, inanimate *yıh*; pl. *yım* (masc.), *yıma* (fem.).

Numerals

1–10: *akh, z^{a}h, trıh, cor, panc, ṣah, sath, aiṭh, nav, dah*; 11 *kāh*; 12 *bāh*; 13 *truwāh*; 20 *wuh*; 21 *akawuh*; 22 *z^{a}tōwuh*; 29 *kunatr^{a}h*; 30 *tr^{a}h*; 100 *hath*.

Verb

Non-finite forms

infinitive in *-un*: e.g. *wučhun* 'to see';
present participle in *-ān*: e.g. *wuchān* 'seeing'; this form is invariable;
past participle: four forms covering recent to remote past: e.g. *wučh^u*; to these forms, the perfective aspect marker *-mut^u-* (inflected for gender and number) can be added;
gerund in *-ıth*: *wučhıth* 'having seen, seeing'.

Synthetic forms inherited from Indo-Aryan are represented in Kashmiri by the present–future tense with the following personal endings: singular 1 *-a*, 2 *-akh*, 3 *-i*; plural 1 *-aw*, 2 *-iw*, 3 *-an*, and by the imperative mood.

All other tenses are constructed by conjugating the relevant participle with an auxiliary, *čhus/ās*, marked for person, gender, and number. The present tense of *čhus* has, for example, the following first person forms: singular, masculine *čhus*, feminine *čhes*; plural, masculine *čhıh*, feminine *čheh*: e.g. *čhus wuchān* 'I see'; *čhıh wučhān* 'we see'. The negative form is *wučhan.ay*

Future *ās-* + participle: *āsı wučhān* 'I shall see'.

The past tense of the auxiliary is based on *os-/əs-*: e.g. *ōsus wučhān* 'I was seeing'. In the past tenses, the non-finite form (apart from the present participle) agrees with the subject of an intransitive verb, with the object of a transitive. The subject of the transitive verb is then in the agentive case (*see* **Pronoun**, above) and may be recapitulated by a personal enclitic marker affixed to the participle: e.g. *me wučhu.**m*** 'I saw him' (i.e. *me* 'by me'; *wučh^u* past participle of verb 'to see'; ∅ third person implied; *-m* first person oblique enclitic).

Irregularities due to phonetic accommodation, vowel harmony, and other requirements abound in the system.

PASSIVE
The oblique case of the infinitive combines with the verb *yun* 'to come': e.g. *wučhana yun^u* 'to be seen'.

Postpositions

The case system is reinforced by an extensive inventory of postpositions, which follow the oblique cases; e.g. *k'ath* 'on', *guris k'ath* 'on the horse'; *sūtin* 'with', *Məlis sūtin āv* 'He came with his father.'

Word order

Rather free; SVO is frequent.

○ در اِبتدِا اُوس کلام تہٕ کلام اُوس خُدائس سٟیتِ تہٕ کلام باب ١
اُوس خُدا ○ یہی اُوس در اِبتدِا خُدائس سٟیتِ ○ ساری چیز سپٕنِ ٢ ٣
تٔہندِی وسیلہٕ سٟیتِ پیدٕہ تہٕ تٔہندِہ بغیر سپُن نہٕ کِنھ تہٕ پیدٕہ یہٕ پیدٕہ
سپُن ○ زِندگی آس تٔس اَندَر تہٕ سُہ زندگی آس اِنسانَن ہُند نوٗر ٤
○ تہٕ نوٗر چھُ تارِیکیہٕ اندر پرزلان تہٕ تاریکیہٕ کٔرٕ نہٕ سُہ دریافت ○ اَکھ ٥ ٦
شخصہٕ اُوس خُدایہٕ سَندِہ طرفہٕ سۆز نہٕ آمُت یَس یُوحنّا ناو
اُوس ییٚہ آو گواہیہٕ ہَندِہ خاطرِہ زِہ نوٗرس پٔٹھ دِیہ گواہی ٧
یُتھ ساری تِمَسندِہ وسیلہٕ اِعتقاد اَنَن ○ سُہ اوسنہٕ سُہ نوٗر ٨
بلکہ نوٗرس پٔٹھ اُوس گواہی دِنہٕ آمُت

KOREAN

INTRODUCTION

Korean has been variously connected with Dravidian, Austronesian, Palaeo-Asiatic, Chinese, and, most convincingly, with the Altaic languages, with which it certainly shares many grammatical features. How many of these resemblances are areal or typological, however, is a moot point, and the exact genetic affinity of Korean remains questionable. The Chinese element is very large but essentially alien. Comparison with Japanese yields a surprising wealth of morphological and syntactical similarities, but the two languages seem to have developed in parallel, rather than to be derived from a common genetic source.

Modern Korean derives from the ancient Korean Han dialect, which ousted its rival congeners thanks to the rise to political dominance of the Silla state, where it was spoken. It is spoken today by between 50 and 60 million people in North and South Korea, and in Korean colonies in China, Japan, and elsewhere. The literary norm is based on the Seoul dialect.

Until the nineteenth century Chinese was the main language of literature in Korea, and little seems to have been written in Korean. A favourite genre was the *sijo*, – a kind of ruba'i, with seven- (three + four) or eight-syllable lines. Among the most famous exponents of the *sijo* were Yun Səndo (seventeenth century), Chəng Ch'əl (sixteenth century), and Kim Sijang (eighteenth century). In the twentieth century the novel has become the main forum for the literary handling of social issues. The best-known practitioners include Yi Kwangsu and Yi Injik.

SCRIPT

In the fifteenth century the fourth Yi king of Korea, King Sejong, commissioned his scholars to produce a phonetic alphabet of 28 letters, and soon the first work in the new script, the 'Songs of Flying Dragons' was published. Chinese script continued, however, to be used for notating Korean until well into the nineteenth/twentieth century. The so-called 'mixed script' uses the indigenous alphabet plus Chinese characters; this method of writing was abandoned in North Korea after 1945, and attempts are being made to phase it out in South Korea.

PHONOLOGY

Consonants

stops: /p, t, k/, with aspirates /ph, th, kh/, and glottalized /p', t', k'/
The glottalized values are written as *pp*, *tt*, *kk*, and are sometimes described as 'implosives'. The same triad is found in the affricates: /tʃ, tʃh, tʃ'/.
fricatives: s, s', h
nasals: m, n, ŋ
lateral and flap: l, r
semi-vowels: j, w

In final position, members of the dental triad, the affricates and the sibilants are all realized as /t/; final /k, kh, k'/ → /k/; final /p, ph, p'/ → /p/. Intervocalic /p, t, k/ → [b, d, g].

Korean has an elaborate system of consonantal assimilation; e.g. stops preceding a nasal are assimilated to that nasal: e.g. *pakmulkwan* 'museum' → /panmulgwan/. In this article, /tʃ/ and its allophone /dʒ/ are notated as *c*, /tʃh/ as *ch*, /tʃ'/ as *ch'*.

Vowels

The basic inventory is:

i, e, ɛ, ɪ, ə, a, u, o

plus allophones /œ, y/. The script provides for notation of the vowels preceded by /j/ and by /w/, i.e. palatalized and labialized series. [ɔ] and [ʌ] are allophones of /ə/. Korean shows some traces of vowel harmony.

MORPHOLOGY AND SYNTAX

Noun

The nominative/subject particle, corresponding to the Japanese *ga*, is *-i* (following a consonant) or *ka* (following a vowel): e.g. *saram.i* 'the man'. Six oblique cases are formed by agglutinative affix (not inflection):

genitive	saramɪi
accusative	saramɪl
dative	sarameke
locative	(saramesə)
instrumental	saramɪro
comitative	saramkwa

In itself the noun is neutral as to number. A plurality marker is *-tɪl/-dɪl*. A focusing agent or topicalizer, corresponding to Japanese *wa*, is -(*n*)*ɪn*: e.g. *Kɪ saram.ɪn Hankuk mal.ɪl kalɪchi.lə kassɪmnita* 'As for that man, he went to teach Korean.'

Compound nouns are readily formed by apposition: e.g. *chaek.pang* 'book-store'; *chaek-sdang* 'reading table'; *chaek.kaps* 'price of books'; *Hankuk.salam* 'Korean person'.

Adjective

A participial form in *-n* provides attributive adjectives which precede the noun: e.g.

khɪ.ta 'to be big': ***khɪn*** 'big', *khɪn kənmul* 'big building';
pissa.ta 'to be expensive': ***pissan*** 'dear', *pissan chaek* 'expensive book'.

Pronoun

Until comparatively recently personal pronouns were avoided in Korean in favour of various circumlocutions, e.g. with *mom* 'body': *i mom.i* 'this body' = 'I'. In the modern language, pronouns are respect-graded: first and second person singular forms in respectful/formal language are: *cə*, *tangsin*; *na* is an acceptable form for first person singular in more informal language. For the third person the demonstrative *kɪ* is used, often plus *saram*, *puin*: e.g. *kɪ saram.ɪn* 'he', *kɪ puin.i* 'she' (cf. *ano hito wa* in Japanese). A polite form of address is *sənsaeng* = Chinese *xiānsheng*.

The pluralizing marker *-tɪl* can be added.

DEMONSTRATIVE PRONOUN/ADJECTIVE
Three degrees: *i* 'this', *chə* 'that', *kɪ* 'that yonder'.

INTERROGATIVE PRONOUN
nugu 'who?', *myəch* /myət/, 'what?'.

RELATIVE PRONOUN
None; *see* **Relative constructions** in **Verb** (below).

Numerals

The indigenous Korean numerals 1–10 are: *han(a)*, *tu(l)*, *se*, *ne*, *tasəs*, *yəsəs*, *ilkop*, *yətəl*, *ahop*, *yəl*. For the teens, these are added to *yəl*: e.g. 11 *yəl-hana*. 20 *sɪmu(l)*; 30 *səlhɪn*; 40 *mahɪn*; 100 *paek*.

A Chinese series 1–10 is also used: *il*, *i*, *sam*, *sa*, *o*, *yuk*, *chil*, *phal*, *ku*, *sip*.

Verb

With half a dozen basic agglutinative components which can be added to the stem, plus a large number of possible affixes, a Korean verb can appear in literally hundreds of forms. The basic structure can be set out as: stem – grade marker – tense/mood/aspect marker – finite indicative or interrogative marker: e.g. *kalɪchi – si – kess.imni – ta* 'will teach' (honorific register).

Neither person nor number is marked; i.e. failing a nominal subject, the personal pronoun must be used.

STEM

This can be one-, two- or three-syllable: e.g. *mək-* 'eat'; *pissa-* 'be expensive'; *kalɪchi-* 'teach'. Compounds are made with *ha-/hae-* 'to do', *po-* 'to see', and other verbs, following either a noun or a verbal form: e.g. with noun: *kongpu ha-* 'to study' (Japanese *benkyō suru*); with verbal: *mul po-* 'to inquire' (*mu.ta* 'inquire', *pota* 'to see').

GRADE

There are several socio-linguistic levels; a broad division is into plain, informal polite, formal polite, and honorific. For example, in the present tense, the informal polite style has a form close to the stem, + *yo*; the formal polite style has the infixed characteristic *-mn-*: cf.

Stem	*Informal polite*	*Formal polite*	*Respectful*
ha 'to do'	hae yo	ha**mn**ita	ha**sɪ**mnita
iss 'to be'	issə yo	iss**ɪmn**ita	iss**ɪsɪ**mnita
o- 'to come'	wa yo	o**mn**ita	o**si**mnita

Some verbs have suppletive stems for respectful/honorific usage: e.g. *mək* 'to eat': hon. *capsusita* – *capsus**ɪ**mnita* 'eat(s)'. The plain style has its own specific set of endings, used in the family and at school: senior to junior, elder to younger, and so on.

TENSE MARKERS

The informal and formal style present has been illustrated above. The past tense characteristic is *-ss-*; past anterior *-ssəss-*; future *-kess-*: e.g. in formal polite style: *ilkəssɪmnita* 'read' (past tense); *patəssəssɪmnita* 'had taken'; *kalɪchi.si.**kess.**ɪmnita* 'will teach' (hon.).

IMPERATIVE/HORTATIVE MOOD

Typical endings are *-iyo -ita*: e.g. *cusipsiyo* 'please give': *kapsita* 'let's go'. The verb stem + *ki* is a verbal noun: *Hankukmal(ɪl) paeu**ki*** '(the) learning (of) Korean'.

NEGATION

There are several interesting constructions:

1. *an* preceding finite form: e.g. *hakkyo.e kamnita* 'goes to school', *hakkyo.e an kamnita* 'doesn't go to school';
2. stem + *ci-* + *anh-*: e.g. *ka.ci anh.sɪmnita* 'doesn't/don't go';
3. stem + *ci-* + *mot hamnita*: e.g. *kaci mot hamnita* 'doesn't/don't go';
4. stem in *-l* form + *su* + *əps*: e.g. *kal su əpsɪmnita* 'can't go'; *əps.ta* 'not exist': literally, 'ability to go is not'.

INTERROGATIVE

The general characteristic is *-kka, kka yo*: e.g. *əti.e kasɪmnikka* 'Where is/are ... going?'; *Tapang.e kal kka yo* 'How about going to a tearoom?'

MODAL CONSTRUCTIONS

There are many of these: e.g.

-(*i*)*lə* 'in order to', e.g. *Hankuk mal.ɪl paeu.**lə*** 'in order to learn Korean'; *chinku.lɪl mannal**ə** wassɪmnita* 'came to meet a friend' (*chinku*);
-(*i*)*ly ko + ha-*: 'intend to', e.g. *Hankuk.e kalyəko haessɪmnita* 'intended to go to Korea';
-ko + siph-: 'want to', e.g. *yənghwa.lɪl poko siphsɪmnita* 'wanted to see a film';
-myən: 'if', e.g. *Hankuk.e ka.myən* 'if ... go(es)/went to Korea'; *maekcu.lɪl wənhasi**myən*** 'if you'd like a beer';
stem in *-l + su iss-*: 'be able to', e.g. *kal su issɪmnita* 'can go';
-(*i*)*ni kaa*: 'because', e.g. *ton.i əpsɪnikka* 'because ... has/have no money'.

RELATIVE CONSTRUCTIONS

Participial forms in *-n* (for present and past) and *-l* (future) are used attributively: e.g. *nae.ka paeu.nɪn mal* 'the language which I am learning'; *nae.ka ilk.ɪl chaek* 'the book which I'm going to read'; *hal il.i manhsɪmnita* 'the work which has to be done is much' = 'there's a lot of work to be done'. These forms can be passive: e.g. *mannal salam* 'people who are going to be met'.

Postpositions

Examples: *hakkyo aph e* 'in front of the school'; *i nyən cən.e* 'before two years' = 'two years ago'; *Səul esə Pusan kkaci* 'from Seoul to Pusan'.

Word order

SOV is normal.

처음에도가이스되도가 하나님파함긔하니도난곳 하
나님이라이도가처음에 하나님파함긔하미만물이말미
여다지며스니지은한하나토말미지안끄지오미업나니
라는에싱명이이스니이싱명이사람의빗치되여빗치어두
온되빗치오되어드오되나아지모하다라한사람이기스니
하나님이보낸바일홈은요인니라와서간증이되문빗출위
하여간증하여뭇사람이터굴말미여밋게하나터가빗치간
이요오직빗출위하여간증하엿나니라

KURDISH

INTRODUCTION

Kurdistan, where this North-West Iranian language is mainly spoken, covers large contiguous areas of Turkey, Syria, Iraq, and Iran. Kurds are also resident in north-eastern Iran (Khorasan), Baluchistan, and in the Armenian, Azerbaijani, and Turkmen Republics. Estimates as to the total number of speakers vary widely; possibly around 10 million people speak one or another form of Kurdish. The main dialects are Sorani (Iraq and Iran), and Kurmandji (Turkey, CIS, Syria).

Political and social fragmentation is reflected in the language, which has no recognized standard form, and which is or has been written in a variety of scripts – Arabic, Cyrillic, Roman, Armenian. Sorani has semi-official status in Iraqi Kurdistan, where it is the language of primary education and of the local media. Poetry has been written in Kurdish since the thirteenth century.

SCRIPT

Sorani Kurdish is written in Arabic script plus the Iranian innovations and two letters for the specifically Kurdish sounds ṟ and ḻ: inverted circumflex on Arabic *r*, *l*. The inverted circumflex is also used on a *y* or *w* bearer to denote the vowel phonemes /o/, /ə/, /ɛ/. Arabic *hā* is used to denote /ĕ/; thus, for example, the word *ferheng* 'dictionary' is written as فه‌رهه‌نگ.

In Cyrillic, /ɪ/ is represented by the Cyrillic soft sign ь; /ə/ by ә. In Sorani, the orthography is that codified by Taufiq Wahby in the 1920s, as subsequently modified by Iraqi Kurdish scholars. Treatment of certain phonemes e.g. of medial and final /iː/ and /uː/ is not always consistent.

PHONOLOGY (of Sorani)

Consonants

stops: p, b, t, d, k, g, q, ʔ
affricates: tʃ, dʒ
fricatives: f, v, s, ʃ, z, ʒ, x, γ, ħ, h, ʕ = Arabic ʿain.
nasals: m, n, ŋ
laterals and flaps: l, ḻ /ɫ/, r, ṟ /r/.
semi-vowels: j, w

/k/ and /g/ have palatalized allophones. *r* is single-flap /ɾ/; *r̲* is rolled /r/.
Kurmandji makes a distinction between the non-aspirates /p, t, k, ʃ/ and their aspirated counterparts, /ph, th/, etc.

Vowels

short: ɪ, ɛ, ʊ
long: i, e, ɛ, a, o, u

Ö is a diphthong, /əɛ/. The short vowels are unstable. Long vowels are indicated here by a macron, e.g. *ō*.

MORPHOLOGY AND SYNTAX

Noun

The definite article is -*(y)eke*: e.g. *bazar̲.eke* 'the market'; *dē.yeke* 'the village'. The indefinite article is *ēk/ē*: e.g. *pē.yēk* 'a foot'.

Gender is not distinguished grammatically; if necessary, natural gender can be marked lexically: e.g. *shēr.ī.nēr* 'lion', *shēr.ī.mē* 'lioness'. In Kurmandji, gender (masculine, feminine, common) is distinguished and marked by correlative changes in the izafe. (*See* **Persian**).

NUMBER
The usual plural marker is *-an*: e.g. *wul̲at.an* 'countries'. The definite article precedes *-an*: e.g. *žin.ek.an* 'the women'.

POSSESSION
The ezafe *-ī/-y* links two nouns in genitive relationship: e.g. *xel̲k.i.r̲ožhel̲at* 'the peoples of the Middle East'; *mela.y.mizgewt* 'the mullah of the mosque'. The ezafe is to be distinguished from the linking vowels, *e*, *ö*, *a*, *o*, *ē*, used e.g. in composite nouns: *būm.***e***.lerze* 'earthquake' (here, the linker *e* coalesces with the Arabic article: *al.arḍ* 'the earth'); *kič.***e***.čaw.r̲eš.eke* 'the black-eyed girl' (*čaw* 'eye'; *r̲eš* 'black').

(In the Kurdish spoken in Russia nouns form oblique cases: e.g. *gavan* 'shepherd', oblique, *geven*.)

Adjective

As attribute, adjective follows noun and is invariable. It is linked to its noun by the ezafe: e.g. *utel.i.baš* 'good hotel'; *šar.ek.i gewre.y taze* 'a big modern town'; *žin.ek.i kurd.i ǰiwan* 'a beautiful Kurdish woman'.

COMPARISON
A comparative is made with *-ter*: e.g. *sūr* 'red' – *sūr.ter*.

Pronoun

The personal pronouns with their enclitics are:

	Singular		*Plural*	
1	min	-(i)m	ēme	-man
2	to	-(i)t	ēwe	-tan
3	ew	-ī	ewan	-yan

The verb 'to be' is expressed by the following enclitic endings: sing. 1 *-m*, 2 *-y*, 3 *-ye*; pl. 1 *-yn*, 2 *-n*, 3 *-n*. The negative form is e.g. *nim* 'I am not', *nit*, etc.

The enclitic forms are used as possessive affixes, e.g. *čaw.an.it* 'your eyes', and as direct-object forms between prefix and root in the present tense and the subjunctive mood: e.g. *de.**m**.bīn.ē* 'he sees me'.

DEMONSTRATIVE PRONOUN

em.e (proximate), *ew.e* (non-proximate); pl. *ewane*.

DEMONSTRATIVE ADJECTIVE

em – ew; in Kurmandji a circumfix, e.g. *'əm.pyaw.ə* 'this man'.

INTERROGATIVE PRONOUN

či 'who?'; *čī* 'what?'.

RELATIVE PRONOUN

ke + definite *-e* + ezafe: e.g. *ew kitēb-**e.y ke** to de.y.bīn.ī* 'the book which you see (it)'.

Numerals

1–10: *yek, dū, sē, čuwar, pēnč, šeš, ħewt, hešt, no, de*. 11 *yazde*; 12 *duwazde*; 20 *bīst*; 30 *sī*; 40 *čil*; 100 *sed*.

Verb

As in Persian, the Kurdish verbal system is built up on the two-base pattern, the present base underlying the present–future tense, the present subjunctive, and the imperative; the past base supplies the three past tenses. The past base is obtained by dropping the *-in* ending of the infinitive; the present base is not predictable: e.g.

girtin	'to catch'	– girt	– gir
kuštin	'to kill'	– kušt	– kuž
dītin	'to see'	– dīt	– bīn

The personal endings for intransitive verbs are: sing. 1 -(*i*)*m*, 2 *-ī*/*y*(*t*), 3 *ē*(*t*); pl. 1 *īn*, 2 *-in*, 3 *-in*. Some examples of verb forms:

present tense: *de* + present stem + personal ending, e.g. *de.kew.im* 'I fall'; in negative version *na* replaces *de*: *na.kew.im*;
present subjunctive: *bi* + present stem + personal ending, e.g. *bi.kew.im* 'I may fall';
preterite: past stem + personal ending – third person marker here is **∅**, e.g. *kewt.im* 'I fell', *kewt* 'he fell'; negative: *ne.kewt(im)*;
perfect: past stem + *-uw-* + personal ending, e.g. *kewt.uw.im* 'I have fallen'; negative: *ne.m.kewt(im)*;
imperfect: *de* + past stem + personal ending, e.g. *de.kewt.im* 'I was falling'; negative: *ne.de.kewt.im*;
a pluperfect is made with the past stem of *hebun* 'to be', e.g. *kewt.i.bū.m* 'I had fallen';
an unreal conditional with the particle *-aye*, e.g. *bi.kewt.im.aye* 'if I had fallen'.

TRANSITIVE VERB

In the past tense the transitive verb is in concord with the object, and the agent is denoted by personal affix attached to that object; if no object is present, the agent marker is attached to the verb: cf. with object: *name.yek.**im** nūs.ī* 'I wrote a letter'. The agent markers are the enclitic forms of the personal pronouns (see above): cf. *nard.it.im* 'you (sing.) sent me'; *nard.im.it* 'I sent you (sing.)'; *nard.man.in* 'we sent you/them'. Examples with no object present: *xward.im* 'I ate', *xward.man* 'we ate'; neg. *ne.m.xward* 'I didn't eat', *ne.man.xward* 'we didn't eat'.

PASSIVE

The characteristic is *-r-*, with *-ē* for the present, *-a* for the past; thus, from *nūsīn* 'to write': ***nūsran*** 'to be written'; past stem: *nūs**ra***; present stem: *nūs**rē***.

The causative characteristic is *-din*: e.g. *šikan* 'to break' (intrans.) – *šikandin* 'to break' (trans.).

The past participle is made by adding *-ū/-w* to the past base. Enclitic personal markers are added to this participle to form the perfect tense: e.g. *hat.uw.im* 'I have come'.

Prepositions

Prepositions may be simple, e.g. *be* 'to', *bo* 'for'; or complex, e.g. the circumfix *le...da* 'in': ***le** kurdistan.i.emro **da*** 'in modern Kurdistan', where the circumfix encloses the ezafe phrase, which is felt as a unit. Similarly, *legel̲...da* 'with': e.g. *legel̲ dostim da* 'with my friend'.

Word order

SOV is normal.

له ابتدا کلمه بیو و آو کلمه له لای خدا بیو
هر آو کلمه خدا بیو ٢ هر آوه له ابتدا له
لای خدا بیو ٣ و بجز خواهش آوه چشتی
له موجودات وجود نات ٤ له آوه حیات
بیو و حیات نور انسان بیو ٥ و نور له تاریکی
تابان بیو و تاریکی آوه ادراك نکرد ٦ شخصی
له لای خدا هات و رسالت تا وی یحیی بیو
٧ آوه ازای شهادت هات تا و نور شهادت
بنیت تا گشت له واسطه آوه ایمان بارن ٨
آوه آو نور نبو بلکه هات تا و نور شهادت
بنیت

LAHNDĀ

INTRODUCTION

Lahndā is a member of the North-Western group of New Indo-Aryan; the name means 'western'. 'Lahndā' is an umbrella term covering an extensive group of dialects, spoken, in all, by upwards of 20 million people in western Pakistan; more precisely, in the 400 mile wide strip of territory extending from Rawalpindi to Behawalpur. The two most important dialects are Multāni and Siraiki, both of which belong to the southern group of dialects. Multāni is associated with the ancient city of Multān, an early Aryan centre of sun-god worship, and latterly an Islamic strong-point. Some portions of the Adi Granth and Sikh scriptures, are in Lahndā. At present, both Multani and Siraiki are used for literary purposes, including periodicals. Towards their eastern periphery, Lahndā forms blend gradually into the phonologically close Panjabi.

SCRIPT

As might be expected, since the great majority of its speakers are Moslems, Lahndā is written in the Arabic-Persian character plus certain additions and modifications: e.g. ٻ for /bb/, ڐ for /dd/, etc. For Multāni, the old *laṇḍa* character (related to the *šarada* script of Kashmir) may still be used.

PHONOLOGY

Consonants

The labial, dental, palatal, retroflex, and velar stops appear in five-term series with associated nasals: /p, p', b, b', bb, m; t, t', d, d', dd, n/, etc. That is, in contrast to the normal New Indo-Aryan series, the Lahndā series include the geminate sonant. /q/ with its associated fricatives /x/ and /γ/ are also present exemplifiying Arabic and Persian influence. The inventory also includes retroflex /ḷ/ and /ṛ/.

Vowels

short: i, ə, a, u
long: iː, e, ɛ, uː, o, aː

All occur nasalized. Diphthong: /au/.

Tones

There are two tones, with variations in some dialects. In the script, *h* marks the non-even (rising) tone.

MORPHOLOGY AND SYNTAX

Noun

Old synthetic forms have been more extensively preserved in Lahndā than in e.g. Panjabi.

Two genders, masculine and feminine, are grammatically distinguished. Typical masculine endings are *-a*, *-u* (long or short) and -C; typical feminine endings *-i*, *-ī*, -C. Vowel endings may be nasalized. There are many ways of marking plurality; change of vocalic final, e.g. *-a* → *-e* is common. Consonantal finals often add nasalized vowel.

There are singular and plural numbers, both having direct and oblique stems.

CASE SYSTEM

Synthetic case forms, e.g. locative in *-e*, are usually supported by agglutinative formants, e.g. *kū̃*. The synthetic form itself may show umlaut induced by loss of historically present vowel. Smirnov (1970) gives the following examples: *buškā* 'bundle of clothes': acc. ***buške kū̃***; *muṇḍur* 'stump': acc. ***muṇḍar ā̃h***.

Use of the analytical form confers definiteness on the noun, and is therefore equivalent to use of a definite article.

The genitive relationship is expressed by the relating particle *nā/nā̃/dā*.

Adjective

As attribute, adjective may precede or follow noun. Those in *-ā* agree with noun; consonant-finals are indeclinable.

Pronoun

The Multāni forms are:

Singular: 1 *mā̃* 2 *tū̃* 3 *e/o*, *īh/ūh*
Plural: 1 *assā̃* 2 *tussā̃* 3 *e/o*, *īh/ūh*
Possessive: *meḍā* 'my'; *assāḍā* 'our', etc.

With Sindhi and Kashmiri, Lahndā shares a system of pronominal enclitics, not found elsewhere in New Indo-Aryan. These are used with both nominal and verbal stems. Further, they combine with a negative particle to provide a specific negative conjugation. The enclitic pronouns can denote subject, indirect or direct object, and genitive relationship. They are marked for number, but not gender:

	Singular	*Plural*
1	-Vm, -s	-se, -hse
2	-(v)ī	-(n)/-(V)e
3	-s, -su	-n(en)

e.g. subject: *Mele gäose* 'We went to market'; object (indirect): *Hukm ḍittā hāse* 'We were given an order.'

DEMONSTRATIVE PRONOUN
The vocalic gradation series *e-*, *i-*, *u-* combines with consonants *h*/*n* to produce such forms as: *e* 'this', *in* 'these', *ūh* 'those', etc.

INTERROGATIVE PRONOUN
kaun 'who?'; *keā* 'what?'

RELATIVE PRONOUN
jo, jeṛā, jehṛā, etc.: e.g. *e zamīn jeṛī mäde kol he* ... 'This land which I possess ...' These have oblique forms.

Numerals

Close to the Panjabi numerals and equally unpredictable. A specific feature is the geminated initial in, e.g. *ḍḍū̃* 2, *ḍḍāh* 10, *bbārhā̃* 12.

Verb

The verb has personal and impersonal forms. The main impersonal forms are:

infinitive: in -V*ṇ*, etc.: e.g. *pīvuṇ* 'to drink'
imperfective participle: in -V*ndā*: e.g. *karendā* 'doing'
perfective participle: in -V*ā*: e.g. *geā* 'having gone'. This form may be active or passive
gerund in *-ī*, etc. often with supporting formant: e.g. *karī kä* '(having) done'

Personal forms. The present tense of the auxiliary verb *hovuṇ* 'to be' is: sing. *ā̃, ī, e*; pl. *ā̃, o, in*. All these forms may be preceded by *h-*. The present tense of other verbs is made by conjugating their present participle with these forms of *hovuṇ*. Change of auxiliary from *hovuṇ* to *karuṇ* 'to do', *rahuṇ* 'to remain', etc. produces other aspectual forms – repetitive, resultative, habitual, etc.

Past: an analytical form is made by conjugating the imperfective or perfective participle with the past tense of *hovuṇ*: e.g. *āhus*, *āhis*.

Future: for the future there is a standard set of sigmatic endings on the formula -V*s*V/Ṽ: e.g. *āusā̃* 'I shall come'.

ERGATIVE
The construction exists but is preferably replaced by a pronominal suffix construction, where the subject of the action appears as a pronominal suffix. It is noteworthy that an ergative construction with the gerundive (nom. form in *-nā*/*-ṇā*) can be used with reference to the future.

IMPERATIVE
Second person singular = root; plural = root + V; many dialectal variations.

SUBJUNCTIVE
Synthetic form or participle + auxiliary. The synthetic endings are close to the present forms of *hovuṇ* (see above): e.g. *šarbat piyālā pīve* 'let him/her drink a glass of sherbet'.

PASSIVE
A synthetic form is made in *-i/-ī̃*: e.g. in future: *paṛīsī* 'it will be torn up'.

NEGATIVE
nā is a general negator.

Postpositions

Postpositions express many syntactic relationships: e.g. genitive: *nā/dā* marked for gender and number: *šaks* ***nī*** *zamīn* 'the man's land' (*zamin* is feminine). The *kū̃* formant counts as a postposition: e.g. *putr ū̃ kū̃ ākhiā* 'the son said to him'; *parbhat kū̃* 'in the morning': *mä kū* 'to me'.

Locative, temporal, purposive postpositions include *appar* 'after', *bicchā* 'among', *nāḷ* 'with': *mäḍe nāḷ* 'with me'.

Word order

SOV is usual.

(۱) مُنڈھ وِچ کلام ہا اتّیں کلام خدا دے نال
ہا اتّیں کلام خُدا ہا (۲) اِیہو مُنڈھ وِچ خدا دے
نال ہا (۳) سبھے شائیں اُونکُّوں پیدا تھیاں اتّیں کہِی
شئے پَیدا نہ تھئی جو سِوا اُوندے پیدا تھئی (۴) حیاتی
اُوں وِچ ہائی اتّیں او حیاتی آدمیں دا نُور ہائی (۵)
اتّیں نُور اندھارے وِچ چمکدا ہے اتّیں اندھارے
اُوں کوں نہ سُنجاتا (۶) ہِک شخص خُدا دی طرف
کنُّوں پٹھیا گیا جَیندا ناں یُوحنّا ہا (۷) او اُگاہی ڈیونڑ
دے کیتے آیا جو نُور تے اُگاہی ڈیوے تانجو سب
(لوک) اُوندے وسیلے ایمان آنن (۸) او اوہو نُور نہ ہا
پر نُور دے اُتے اُگاہی ڈیونڑ آیا

(Multāni dialect)

LAO

INTRODUCTION

Lao belongs to the South-Western group of Tai languages, which also includes Thai, Shan, Yuan, along with many smaller languages.

After 300 years of subjugation, first to the Kingdom of Siam and then as a French colony, Laos became independent in 1954, and two years later Lao was adopted as the official language of the country. French is still widely used in government and administration, but Lao is used exclusively in the media, press, radio, and television, and is increasingly the language of education. It is the spoken and written language of about 10 million people in Laos, with extensive spread into Thailand. There are three main dialectal groupings – North, Central, and South – with a large number of local variants. The main differences between these dialects lie in the tonal structure, some dialects having only five tones (against the six of standard Lao) while others have seven. As the most developed form of Lao, and the most readily accessible to speakers of other dialects, the Vientiane dialect was the natural choice for 'standard' status, which it duly received in 1962.

SCRIPT

The Lao script, the *tua lao*, dates from about the sixteenth century. Before that, the *tham* (< Pali *dhamma*) script was used for religious texts in Lao. The *tua lao* script bears a very close resemblance to Thai, both apparently deriving from a Proto-Thai original now lost. The *tua lao* shares the etymologically motivated but now redundant duplications found in Thai.

PHONOLOGY

Consonants

The stops /p, t, k/ are non-aspirate, and are sometimes transliterated as *bp*, *dt*, *g*. They have aspirated counterparts: /ph, th, kh/. The stop series is completed by the voiced members /b/ and /d/ and the glottal stop.

affricate: dʒ
fricatives: f, v, s, h
nasals: m, n, ɲ, ŋ
lateral: l
semi-vowels: j, w

/th, k, kh, ʔ, dʒ, s, l, ŋ/ occur labialized: /th°, k°/, etc. /dʒ/ → [d']. In this article, ph, th, kh are used to notate the aspirate series, p, t, k, the non-aspirates. /dʒ/ is notated as *j*.

Vowels

The vowel system is of considerable complexity, and close transcription would involve many symbols. A simplified representation is:

high: i, ɯ, u
high-middle: iə, ɯə, uə
middle: e, ɤ, o
low-middle: ɛ, ɔ
low: a

Almost all Lao vowel phonemes have long and short values.
In this article, ɪ is used to denote the spread-lipped, i.e. unrounded central vowel.

Tones

There are six tones in standard Lao: three level (low, middle, and high), two falling (high, low) and one rising. Few Lao syllables can take all six tones. Tone can be predicted for any Lao syllable in the light of the following criteria:

1. class of letter (low, middle, or high);
2. vowel length;
3. nature of final: nasal or stop (*p*, *t*, *k*);
4. presence or absence of tone marker (*mai ek*, *mai toh*).

For more detail on this system of tone representation, *see* **Thai**. Tone in Lao is, of course, phonemic.

MORPHOLOGY AND SYNTAX

Noun

In general, very close to Thai. Basic Lao words are mostly monosyllables: e.g. *paa* ‘fish’; *nok* ‘bird’; *muu* ‘pig’. Sanskrit/Pali loan-words are plentiful: e.g. *pathet* ‘country’, *pawatsat* ‘history’. The Mon-Khmer element is represented by such words as *wat* ‘temple’, *to* ‘table’.

There is no inflection of any kind. Syntactic relationships are expressed by means of prepositions and linking particles: e.g. the genitive relationship marker *khong* (*cf.* **Thai**): *pɪm khong phai?* ‘whose book?’. In the case of inalienable relationship, simple apposition is used: *pho khooi* ‘my father’.

NUMBER

Usually ignored, but may be expressed periphastically, e.g. by *lai* ‘many’, or by classifier plus numeral. (*See* **Numerical classifiers**, below.)

Adjective

As attribute, adjective follows noun: *nam yen* 'cold water'.

COMPARISON
A comparative is made with *kwaa*: e.g. *Laaw paak phaasaa laaw keng kwa khooi* 'He speaks Lao better than I do.'

Pronoun

The personal pronoun system offers a multiple choice of status-graded forms. Certain forms are emerging as generally acceptable in normal polite communication. These are: 1st p. sing. *khooi*, pl. form *phuuakkhaw*; 2nd p. sing. *thaan*, pl. form *phuuak.thaan*; *jaw* is a more familiar form for 2nd p. sing.; 3rd p. sing. *laaw*; pl. form is *khaw.jaw*. These are both subject and object forms: e.g. *laaw maa haa khooi* 'he comes to see me'.

DEMONSTRATIVE PRONOUN
Triple series by relative distance: *nii* 'this', *nan* 'that', *phun* 'that (yonder)'. As attributive adjectives, they follow the noun: e.g. *haan nii* 'this shop'.

INTERROGATIVE PRONOUN
phai 'who?'; *nyang* 'what?'.

RELATIVE PRONOUN/ADJECTIVE
Where the antecedent is indefinite, no relative pronoun is necessary. With a definite antecedent, *thi* may be used: e.g. *khɪang thi jaw toong.gaan* 'the things that you need'.

Numerals

1–10: *nɪng*, *soong*, *saam*, *sii*, *haa*, *hok*, *jet*, *peet*, *kaw*, *sip*; 12 *sip.soong*; 20 *saaw*; 30 *saam sip*; 100 *hooi*.

NUMERICAL CLASSIFIERS
All quantified nouns are accompanied by classifiers. The formula is noun – numeral – classifier: e.g. *saang saam tua* 'elephant three bodies' = 'three elephants'; *noong.saaw saam kon* 'three sisters'; *pathet soong pathet* 'two countries' (*pathet* is both noun and classifier). An exception to the general formula is provided by *nɪng* 'one', which follows the classifier: e.g. *hɪɪan lang nɪng* 'one house'.

Verb

Many verbs are monosyllabic: e.g. *pai* 'to go', *het* 'to do', *waw* 'to speak'. Compound verbs may be:

(a) verb + verb: e.g. *huu.sɪk* 'to feel' (*huu* 'to know' + *sɪk* 'to feel');
(b) verb + noun: e.g. *aap.nam* 'to bathe' (*aap* 'to wash' + *nam* 'water'); *het.kaan* 'to work' (*het* 'to do' + *kaan* 'work');

(c) adjective + verb: *wai.khɪn* 'to hurry' (*wai* 'quick' + *khɪn* 'to move');
(d) reduplicated verb: *pai.pai.maa.maa* 'to walk here and there'.

The verb itself is invariable. Tense and aspect are generated by various particles:

perfective aspect: *dai* preceding, or *leew* following verb, e.g. *Noong dai pai het naa* '(My) brother has gone to work (in) the field'; *khooi het.kaan leew* 'I've finished working';
imperfective aspect: a typical marker is *key*, which also suggests indeterminacy, and is used in such negative sentences as *Laaw boo key pai wiang.jan* 'He has never been to Vientiane';
progressive action is indicated by the particle *kamlang*: e.g. *laaw kamlang het.kaan* 'he/she is working now'; or by *yuu*: e.g. *laaw kin.khaw yuuw* 'he is eating now';
future: particle of impending action *sii* or *ja*, e.g. *thaan sii pai haa laaw* 'you will go to see him'.

MODAL VERBS
Examples: *toong.gaan* 'to want to'; *yaak* (*dai*) 'to want to', e.g. *khooi yaak pai som wat* 'I want to visit the temple'. *Pai* 'to go' and *maa* 'to come' are used as directional particles.

NEGATIVE
The general marker is *boo*: e.g. *laaw boo het.kaan* 'he/she doesn't work'.

Prepositions

Lao is rich in spatial and temporal prepositions; e.g. *kai* 'near', *kai hɪɪan* 'near the house'; *theng* 'on', *theng to* 'on the table'; *thi* 'in(to)', *thi wat* 'in(to) the temple'; *tee...hoot* 'from ... to', *tee saam moong hoot haa moong* 'from 3 o'clock to 5 o'clock'.

Word order

SVO.

໑ ເມື່ອ ຕົ້ນເດີມ ນັ້ນ ພະທັມ ເປັນ ຢູ່ ແລ້ວ ແລະ ພະທັມ ນັ້ນ
໒ ໄດ້ ຢູ່ ນຳ ພະເຈົ້າ ແລະ ພະທັມ ນັ້ນ ກໍ ເປັນ ພະເຈົ້າ. ເມື່ອ ຕົ້ນ
໓ ເດີມ ພະອົງ ນັ້ນ ໄດ້ ຢູ່ ນຳ ພະເຈົ້າ. ສາລະພັດ ທຸກສິ່ງ ໄດ້ ເກີດ
ມີ ມາ ເພາະດ້ວຍ ພະອົງ. ແຕ່ ສິ່ງໃດໆ ທີ່ ເກີດ ມີ ມາ ແລ້ວ
໔ ນັ້ນ ບໍ່ ມີ ສິ່ງໃດ ເກີດ ມີ ມາ ໂດຍ ນອກຈາກ ພະອົງ. ຊີວິດ ກໍ ຢູ່
ໃນ ພະອົງ ແລະ ຊີວິດ ນັ້ນ ເປັນ ຄວາມສວ່າງ ຂອງ ມະນຸສໂລກ.
໕ ຄວາມສວ່າງ ນັ້ນ ກໍ ສ່ອງແສງ ຢູ່ໃນ ຄວາມມືດ ແລະ ຄວາມມືດ
ນັ້ນ ບໍ່ ໄດ້ ລົບ ຄວາມສວ່າງ ໃຫ້ ມອດ.

LAPPISH

INTRODUCTION

The Lapps (ethnonym Same/Sabme) are dispersed over a wide arc of territory extending from Dalecarlia in Sweden north-eastwards through Arctic Norway, Sweden, and Finland to the Kola Peninsula in the USSR. There are possibly 30,000 to 35,000 Lapps in around 400,000 km^2, and more than half of them live on Norwegian territory. The great majority of Lapps are bilingual in Lappish and the language of the host country, with actual use of Lappish restricted to the family and village circle. There is a broad dialectal division into Southern, Northern, and Eastern Lapp.

Virtually nothing is known about Lapp before the sixteenth century. The first printed book in Swedish Lappish appeared in 1619, in Norwegian Lappish in 1728. There is no common literary language.

In the 1950s several local Lappish organizations combined to form a Northern Council for Lappish Affairs (*Davviriikkkaid Sámiráđđi*) with representation in Oslo, Stockholm, and Helsinki. One result was the formation in 1971 of a Lapp Language Committee and in 1979 of a Lapp Writers' Union.

Genetically, Lappish is a Finno-Ugrian language, very deeply influenced by the Scandinavian languages and by Finnish: the number of Finnish loan-words is put at 2,000, that of Scandinavian borrowings at slightly more. Traces of vowel harmony are still found in Eastern dialects. It is interesting, however, that many Lapp roots, perhaps as many as 25 per cent, are neither Finno-Ugric nor attributable as borrowings to any known source: e.g. *čallet* 'write', *buktet* 'fetch', *bieggaa* 'wind'.

SCRIPT

Roman, with local additions and adaptations. In both Norwegian and Finnish Lapp, the interdentals /θ/ and /ð/ are written as ŧ and *đ*.

PHONOLOGY

Consonants

stops: p, b, t, d, k, g
affricates: ts, tʃ
fricatives: f, v, s, ʃ, θ, ð, h
nasals: m, n, ŋ
lateral and flap: l, r

/d, l, n, h/ can be palatalized in Norwegian and Finnish Lapp. Extensive palatalization of consonants is a characteristic feature of the Eastern dialects. Initial /b, d, g/ → unaspirated [p, t, k]: e.g. *baze dearvan* [paːce(t) tear[a]van], 'goodbye' (Finnish Lapp).

There is pre-aspiration of consonants /t, k/ in certain environments: e.g. (in Finnish Lapp) *guokte* [kuokhte], 'two'.

CONSONANTAL GRADATION

(*See* **Finnish**.) The Lappish system is much more elaborate than its Finnish counterpart, extending to such gradations as *rr/r*, *ll/l*, *ss/s*, *bm/m*, *k't/vt*, *k's/vs*, *ddj/j*: e.g. from **buktet** 'fetch', first person singular *buvtem*.

The weak state of long (= emphatic) geminates is identical with the strong state of short geminates; i.e.

Strong grade	*Weak grade*
kk	g
k'k	kk

The mark ' between consonants in strong geminates and other doubled letters in Norwegian Lappish indicates the presence of a shwa vowel: thus *al'bmi* /alᵊbmi/, 'sky'; in Finnish Lappish the shwa is unmarked: e.g. *olgun* /ol°kuːn/, 'outside'.

Vowels

a, æ, e, i, o, ɔ, u

/a/ may be realized as [a], [ʌ], or [ɔ]. /ɔ/ is notated as *å*.

MORPHOLOGY AND SYNTAX

Noun

The noun has two numbers and eight cases (including an abessive formed with postposition). The dual number found in the pronoun and verb is lost in the nominal declension. Specimen declensions from Norwegian Lapp:

	æd'ni 'mother'		*sabmelaš* 'Lapp'	
	Singular	*Plural*	*Singular*	*Plural*
nominative	æd'ni	ædnit	sábmelaš	sábmelažžat
genitive	ædni	edniid	sábmelažža	sábmelažžaid
accusative	ædni	edniid	sábmelažža	sábmelažžaid
illative	æd'nái	edniide	sábmelaž'žii	sábmelažžaide
inessive–elative	ædnis	edniin	sábmelažžas	sábmelažžain
comitative	edniin	edniiguin	sábmelažžain	sábmelažžaiguin
essive	æd'nin	æd'nin	sábmelaž'žan	sábmelaž'žan
abessive	ædni haga	edniid haga	—	—

Further examples of plural formation from genitive base: *æna* 'land', gen.

ædnama, pl. *ædnamat*; *rumaš* 'body', gen. *rubmaša*, pl. *rubmašat*; *suolo* 'island', gen. *sul'lu*, pl. *sul'lut*.

Adjective

The attributive form, which precedes the noun, differs from the predicative form, e.g. from Norwegian Lapp: *bar'go læ låssat* 'the work is hard', *dat læ lås'ses bar'go* 'that is hard work'; *viesso læ viel'gat* 'the house is white'; *dat læ vil'ges viesso* 'that is a white house'. Cf. in Russian Lapp: *el'l'is murr* 'high tree'; *tedd murr l'i el'l'e* 'this tree is high'.

COMPARATIVE
-t added to positive; *-mus* for superlative: e.g. *nuorra* 'young', *nuorat*, *nuoramus*; *buorre* 'good', *buoret*, *buoremus*. Adjectives of type *boaris* 'old', *viel'gat* 'white' make a comparative as follows: *boaris – boarrasæb'bo*; *viel'gat – viel'gadæb'bo*.

Pronoun

Norwegian Lapp forms: with possessive enclitic markers:

	Singular		*Dual*		*Plural*	
1	mån	-n	moai	-me	mii	-met
2	dån	-t	doai	-de	dii	-det
3	sån	-s	soai	-ska	sii	-set

These are declined in eight cases, e.g. for first person singular: *mån*, *mu*, *mu*, *munnje*, *mus*, *muina*, *munin*, *mu haga*. Nouns ending in a vowel change this vowel before certain enclitic possessives: e.g. *áč'či* 'father', *áč'čán* 'my father', *áč'čámet* 'our father'.

DEMONSTRATIVE PRONOUNS/ADJECTIVES
Three degrees of proximity: *dat* 'this' – *diet* 'that' – *duot* 'that (yonder)'. These are both singular and plural forms: cf. *dat jáv'ri* 'this lake', pl. *dat jávrit*; gen. sing. *dan jávri*, gen. pl. *daid jávriid*.

INTERROGATIVE/RELATIVE PRONOUN
There are three general words for 'who?': *gii*, pl. *gæt*, *gutte*, pl. *guđet*, *mii*, pl. *mat*; *goab'ba* means 'who/which of two?' The plural form of *goab'ba* is *goabbat*. Finally, *guttemuš*, pl. *guđemuž̌žat* means 'who/which of many?'. All of these are declined, both singular and plural, in all cases. Thus, *goabbain* 'with which of two?' (comitative case); *guđemuž̌žaiguin* 'with whom/which of many?'. Cf. *Gii ål'bmuid dat læ*? 'What man is this?' (*ål'bmuid* is plural accusative); *Mat bier'gasiid dat læt*? 'What are these things?'; *sii guđet læt dan dakkan* 'they who have done this'; *Gæsa galgan dan ad'dit*? 'To whom shall I give this?' (where *gæsa* is the allative of *gii*).

Numerals

1–10 (in Finnish spelling): *okta*, *guokte*, *golbma*, *njealljе*, *vihtta*, *guhtta*, *čieža*, *gavcci*, *ovcci*, *łogi*. 11–20: *oktanuppelohkai*, *guoktenuppelohkai*, *golbman-*, *njealljen-*, etc., with *-uppelohkai*; 20 *guoktelogi*, 30 *golbmalogi*; 100 *ĉuoði*.

The Norwegian Lapp form of *-uppelohkai* is *-ubbelåkkai*.

Verb

The verb in Lappish has four moods: indicative, conditional, potential, and imperative; and two voices: active and passive. The indicative mood has four tenses: present, imperfect, perfect, pluperfect, the latter two with the auxiliary *læt.* The present may also be used to express the future, which may also be formed analytically with the verb *gal'gat* 'shall', or *ai'got* 'want to'. Thus: *mån manan* 'I go/I shall go'; *mån aigon mannat* 'I want to go'; *mån galgan mannat* 'I shall go'.

Specimen paradigm: *ællit* 'to live', present tense:

	Singular	*Dual*	*Plural*
1	ælán	elle	ællit
2	ælát	ællibæt'ti	ælibettet
3	ællá	ælliba	ellet

Examples for *mannat* 'to go': *mån manan* 'I go'; *mån mannen* 'I went'; *mån læn mannan* 'I have gone'; *mån leddjen mannan* 'I had gone'.

IMPERATIVE

Second person singular *mana*; dual *man'ni*; plural *mannut*; + first/third person forms; *man'ni ædni lusa* 'you two, go to (your) mother' (*lusa* is postposition 'to').

CONDITIONAL

Examples: *mån manašin*, *dån manašit*.

POTENTIAL

Example: *mån manažan*.

PASSIVE

In *-uvvu(j)*; thus from *gullat* 'to hear': *man gul'luj**uvvun*** 'I am heard'; *man gul'luj**uvvujin*** 'I was being heard'.

NEGATIVE

The negative auxiliary verb + uninflected stem (in weak state):

	Singular	*Dual*	*Plural*
1	in	æn	æt
2	it	æp'pi	eppet
3	ii	æba	æi

Examples: *in låga* 'I'm not reading' (*låga* is weak stem of *låkkat* 'to read'); *æba boaðe* 'they (two) are not coming' (*boattit* 'to come').

GERUNDIVE

-min added to strong stem, e.g. *mån læn låkkamin* 'I am (engaged in) reading'.

PRESENT PARTICIPLE

The emphatic strong stem is used: e.g. *boattit* 'to come', *boat'ti* '(he) who comes'. The form can be used adjectivally: e.g. *boat'ti jakki* 'next year'.

Absence of, or failure to perform, the verbal action is indicated by the affix *-kæt'tái* attached to the weak stem; thus from *låkkat* 'to read': *Lågakæt'tai it oappa* 'Without reading you do not learn.'

Prepositions, postpositions

Lappish has one or two prepositions, many postpositions e.g. *duokkin* 'behind'; *sisa* 'inside'; *lusa* 'up to', 'as far as'. The postpositions take directional/locative markers: e.g. *Bija bårramuša bævdi **ala*** 'Put the food on the table'; *Bårramuš læ juo bævdi **al'de*** 'The food is already on the table'; *bævdi vuollai* 'under the table' (directional).

Word order

SVO.

1. Algost læi sadne, ja sadne læi Ibmel lut, ja sadne læi Ibmel.

2. Dat algost læi Ibmel lut.

3. Buokrakkan dam boft læ dakkujuvvum; ja alma dam taga i mikkege læk dakkujuvvum dast, mi jå læ dakkujuvvum.

4. Dam sist læi ællem; ja ællem læi olbmu čuovgas.

5. Ja čuovgas sævdnjadassi baitta, ja sævdnjad i dam arvedam.

6. Ibmelest vuolgatuvui olmuš, gæn namma Johannes læi.

7. Dat duođaštussan bådi, čuovgas birra duođaštet, vai buokak su boft oskuši.

8. I sån læm čuovgas, mutto (vuolgatuvvum læi) čuovgas birra duođaštet.

LATVIAN

INTRODUCTION

Latvian is a member of the Baltic branch of Indo-European. The group from which Latvian derives comprised several other languages – Latgalian, Zemgalian, Curonian – which are now extinct. Latvian is spoken by about 2½ million people, most of these in the Latvian Republic, many in other parts of the CIS, with large communities in Canada, the USA, and elsewhere.

The earliest writing in Latvian, in an orthography based on German, appeared in the sixteenth and seventeenth centuries. The first Bible translation dates from the eighteenth century. By the 1890s a standardized literary language had taken shape, which went on to flourish in the brief period of independence, 1918–40.

SCRIPT

Gothic until early twentieth century. In 1909 a switch was made to the Roman alphabet with diacritics: palatalized letters are marked by sub- or superscript dash, long vowels by the macron. /tʃ, ʃ, ʒ, dʒ/ are notated as *č*, *š*, *ž*, *dž*.

PHONOLOGY

Consonants

stops: p, b, t, d, k, g; palatalized: k′, g′
affricates: ts, tʃ, dz, dʒ
fricatives: v, s, ʃ, z, ʒ
nasals: m, n, ɲ, ŋ
lateral and flap: l, ʎ, r
semi-vowels: j, w

/f, h, x/ occur in loan-words.

ASSIMILATION

Voiced consonants are unvoiced before unvoiced and vice versa: e.g. *galds* 'table' = [gʌ**lts**]; *priecīgs* 'happy' = [priecī**ks**].

Vowels

front: i, ɪ, e, eː, ɛ, ɛː
mid: a, ā
back: uo, ɔ, u, ū

/uo/ is notated as *o*; the sound /o/ occurs in loan-words only. /ă/ = [ʌ].

DIPHTHONGS
ai, au, ei, ie + oi in loan-words.

Tones

The Central dialect, on which the literary standard is based, distinguishes three tones not notated in script: even, broken, and falling: e.g. *saule* 'sun' is even; *sir̃ds* 'heart', broken; *kàzas* 'wedding', falling.

Stress

On the first syllable with very few exceptions. This fact, coupled with a tendency to reduce the tonal system to a straight opposition between even and non-even, makes Latvian phonology very much simpler than Lithuanian, where stress is mobile and where tone is a function of the stressed syllable.

MORPHOLOGY AND SYNTAX

Noun

There are no articles. Latvian has two genders, masculine (typical endings: *-s*, *-š*, *-is*, *-us*) and feminine (typical endings: *-s*, *-a*, *-e*). Six declensions are distinguished, depending on stem ending: e.g. 1st declension: *darzs* 'garden'; 4th declension: *meita* 'girl'.

	Singular	*Plural*	*Singular*	*Plural*
nominative	dārzs	dārzi	meita	meitas
genitive	dārza	dārzu	meitas	meitu
dative	dārzam	dārziem	meitai	meitām
accusative	dārzu	dārzus	meitu	meitas
locative	dārzā	dārzos	meitā	meitās

Typical plural formations in the other declensions are: 2nd decl. *brālis* 'brother', pl. *brāļi*; 3rd decl. *tirgus* 'market', pl. *tirgi*; 5th decl. *zeme* 'earth', pl. *zemes*; 6th decl. *sirds* 'heart', pl. *sirdis*.

Some uses of cases in Latvian:

genitive: used with negative to indicate absence of something: e.g. *tur nav grāmatu* 'there isn't/aren't a book/books there' (*nav* = /nau/ 'not'), *viņa nav mājās* 'he isn't at home' (*viņa* is gen. of *viņš* 'he');
dative: used to express possession: e.g. *saimniekiem ir zirgi un rati* '(the)

farmers have horses and carts';
dative absolute: dative of logical subject + verb in relative *-ot* form: e.g. *pirmajai nedeļas dienai austot* 'as it began to dawn towards the first day of the week' (Matthew, 28.1).

Adjective

As attribute, the adjective precedes the noun and is in concord with it for gender, number, and case. The adjective can be declined in indefinite or definite form, the latter making up in some degree for the lack of definite article. The definite endings are made by the insertion of *-ai-* (nom.), *-aj-* (oblique), or by vowel lengthening; some oblique forms may be truncated for euphonic reasons: cf.

	Indefinite	*Definite*
	labs tēvs 'a good father'	lab**ai**s tēvs 'the good father'
dative	labam tēvam	labajam tēvam

COMPARATIVE
The comparative is made with *-āks*: e.g. *jauns* 'young' – *jaunāks* 'younger'; definite form: *jaunāk**ai**s* 'the younger'.

Pronoun

The nominative and genitive forms for first and second person singular and plural are: sing. 1 *es – manis*; pl. *mēs – mūsu*; 2 *tu – tevis*; pl. *jūs – jūsu*. The third person forms are marked for gender: masc. *viņš*; fem. *viņa*: pl. *viņi*, *viņas*.

DEMONSTRATIVE PRONOUNS
These also show gender: masc. *šis*, fem. *šī* 'this'; masc. *tas*, fem. *tā* 'that'; with pl. forms, *šie – šīs*; *tie – tās*.

POSSESSIVE FORMS
mūsu and *jūsu* are indeclinable. The others, *mans*, *mani*, etc., show gender and number and are declined.

INTERROGATIVE PRONOUN
kis 'who? what?'; *kurš* 'what ...?' These are declined in singular.

RELATIVE PRONOUN
As interrogative: e.g. *māja, kurā dzīvo studenti* 'the house in which the students live'; *studenti, kas dzivo ...* 'the students who live ...'.

Numerals

1–9: these have masculine and feminine forms; the masculine forms are: *viens*, *divi*, *trīs*, *četri*, *pieci*, *seši*, *septiņi*, *astoņi*, *deviņi*; fem. *viena*, *divas*, *trīs*, *četras*, *piecas*, *sešas*, *septiņas*, *astoņas*, *deviņas*; 10 *desmit*; 11 *vienpadsmit*; 12 *divpadsmit*; 20 *divdesmit*; 30 *trīsdesmit*; 100 *simt(s)*.

Verb

Verbs in Latvian are either perfective or imperfective. An imperfective verb can be made perfective by the addition of a prefix:

ņemt 'to take' (imperf.)	*iz.ņemt* 'to take out/from' (perf.)
lasīt 'to read' (imperf.)	*iz.lasīt* 'to read through and finish' (perf.)

There are three voices: active, reflexive, and passive, use of the latter is rare; and five moods: indicative, imperative, conditional, debitive, relative.

Formally, all verbs belong to three conjugational types:

(a) type *runāt* 'to speak': expansion by *-j-* throughout imperfect tense and, partially, in present: e.g. *es runāju* 'I speak', *jūs runājat* 'you speak'; *viņš runā* 'he speaks';
(b) type *dzirdēt* 'to hear': imperfect forms alone expanded by *-j-*: e.g. *es dzirdu* 'I hear'; *es dzirdēju* 'I heard';
(c) type *nākt* 'to come': monosyllabic infinitive, two syllables in present/ imperfect: e.g. *es nāku* 'I come'; *es nācu* 'I came'.

The indicative mood has three simple tenses (present, imperfect, future) and three compound (formed by copula *būt* 'to be', + active participle).

Specimen paradigm: *lasīt* 'to read'.

Present indicative: *es lasu*, *tu lasi*, *viņš lasa*; *mēs lasām*, *jūs lasāt*, *viņi lasa*
imperfect: *es lasīju*, *tu lasīji*, etc.
future: *es lasīšu*, *tu lasīsi*, *viņš lasīs*, etc.

Compound tenses: *es esmu lasījis* 'I have been and still am reading'
past: *es biju lasījis* 'I had been reading' (before something else happened)
future: *es būšu lasījis* 'I shall have read'

Negative: *ne* is prefixed to finite verb forms and takes the stress: e.g. *es nélasu*; *es négribu strādāt* 'I don't want to work'.

Debitive mood: here, Latvian has one form for all persons – the third person indicative with the prefix *jā-*. The logical subject is in the dative: e.g. *man* ***jālasa*** *grāmata* 'I have to read a/the book', where *grāmata* is in the nominative case. The accusative might be expected here, and this is indeed the case when the object is a first or second personal pronoun: e.g. *viņai* ***mani jā****redz* 'he has to see me'.

Relative: here also, there is one form for all persons, -(*š*)*ot*: e.g. *Jānis esot slims* 'it is said/they say that Janis is ill';

(*Viņš*) *šodien aizbraucot* 'He's supposed to be leaving today'

(*Viņš*) *ritu aizbrauk****šot*** 'He's supposed to be leaving tomorrow'

Reflexive mood: the infinitive has the ending *-ties*: e.g. *mazgāt* 'to wash': *mazgāties* 'to wash oneself'.

Prepositions

In the singular, prepositions follow the genitive, dative, or accusative, these reducing to the dative in the plural: cf. *aiz upes* (gen.) 'across the river'; *caur mežu* (acc.) 'through the forest'; but, *aiz upiem* 'across the rivers'; *caur mežiem* 'through the forests', where both *upiem* and *mežiem* are in the dative.

Word order

SVO.

1 Iesākumā bija Vārds, un
Vārds bija pie Dieva, un
Vārds bija Dievs.
2 Tas bija iesākumā pie
Dieva.
3 Caur viņu viss ir radies,
un bez viņa nekas nav radies,
kas ir.
4 Viņā bija dzīvība, un
dzīvība bija cilvēku gaisma.
5 Gaisma spīd tumsībā, bet
tumsība to neuzņēma.
6 Nāca cilvēks, Dieva sū-
tīts, vārdā Jānis.
7 Viņš nāca liecības dēļ,
lai liecinātu par gaismu, lai
visi nāktu pie ticības caur
viņu.
8 Viņš pats nebija gaisma,
bet nāca, lai liecinātu par
gaismu.

LITHUANIAN

INTRODUCTION

Lithuanian belongs to the Baltic branch of Indo-European. The total number of speakers, including the sizeable emigré communities in Canada, the USA, and elsewhere, is probably over 3 million. Both phonologically and morphologically the language is of extreme complexity and remarkably archaic.

There are two main dialectal divisions: *žemait* or Lower Lithuanian, and *aukštait* or Upper (High) Lithuanian. The sixteenth century saw the beginnings of Lithuanian literature in the shape of religious and devotional writings. The great landmark in the development of the literary language is the publication in 1818 of the rural epic poem *Metai* ('The Seasons') by K. Donelaitis. The modern literary language is based on the *aukštait* dialect. Writing in all genres flourished during the period of independence between the wars.

SCRIPT

Gothic until the twentieth century; thereafter Roman alphabet + *š*, *ž*, *č*, and diacritics: cedilla, superscript dot on *ė*, and macron on *ū*. *Q* and *w* are not used.

PHONOLOGY

Consonants

stops: p, b, t, d, k, g
affricates: ts, tʃ, dʒ, dz
fricatives: f, v, s, z, ʃ, ʒ, x, ɣ, j
nasals: m, n
lateral and flap: l, r

All consonantal phonemes except *j* have palatalized (soft) allophones: [p′], [b′], etc., which are used before the front series vowels, /iː, i, eː, æ, ɛ. Palatalized /l/ is [l], non-palatalized /l/ is [ɫ]. In a cluster C_1C_2 before a soft vowel, both C_1 and C_2 are palatalized, and C_2 determines the quality of C_1: e.g. *vežti* 'to lead' = [v′ɛšt′i]. Alternation of stem consonants is found throughout the inflectional system.

Vowels

front: i, iː, eː, æː, ɛ
back: a, aː, ɔ, oː, u, uː

Stress and pitch

In Lithuanian, dynamic stress is morphophonemically coupled with tone (or pitch). There are three kinds of pitch intonation, notated for reference in Lithuanian dictionaries by grave, circumflex, and acute, though not so marked in Lithuanian texts. The grave occurs with short vowels only; the other two intonations are associated with long vowels and diphthongs, the first of two moras being stressed for the acute (falling) intonation, the second for the circumflex (rising) intonation.

MORPHOLOGY AND SYNTAX

Noun

Inflectional endings in Lithuanian can be sub-divided into two classes: (a) those that attract stress, and (b) those that do not, or which deflect stress to the stem. On the basis of these complex factors, four classes of nouns and adjectives are distinguished: one class has fixed stress throughout on stem syllable; in the other three classes, stress/tone is free, shifting from stem to ending and vice versa in certain fixed patterns. An additional complication is the presence of five declensions. Together, pitch/stress class and declension type prescribe the paradigm for any given noun. Thus, *mẽdis* 'tree', for example, is a pitch/stress class 2 noun inflected according to the first declension; *akìs* 'eye', is a class 4 noun inflected according to the third declension.

There follow two specimen declensions: *výras* 'man': pitch class 1, first declension and *sesuõ* 'sister': pitch class 3, fifth declension.

	Singular	*Plural*	*Singular*	*Plural*
nominative	výras	výrai	sesuõ	sẽserys
genitive	výro	výrų	seser̃s	seserũ̜
dative	výrui	výrams	sẽseriai	seserìms
accusative	výrą	výrus	sẽserį	sẽseris
instrumental	výru	výrais	sẽseria	seserimìs
locative	výre	výruose	seseryjè	seserysè

Dual forms are found following the numeral *du/dvi* '2', and in some dialects. The genitive case is used after negated verb: e.g. *nebuvo knygų* 'there were no books'; and in a partitive sense: e.g. *Žveryne buvo meškũ̜ ir̃ kitũ̜ žveriũ̜* 'In the zoo were bears and other animals'.

Adjective

The attributive adjective precedes its noun and agrees with it in gender, number, and case. The adjective may be indefinite or definite, this latter possibility compensating for the absence of a definite article: e.g.

balta knyga '(a) white book'; *baltoji knyga* 'the (specific) white book'; *didis šuõ* '(a) big dog'; *didỹsis šuo* 'the/that big dog'.

COMPARATIVE

A comparative is made with *-esnis*, fem. *-esne*: e.g. *gẽras* [g'aras] 'good': comp. *gerèsnis/gerèsne* (fully declined).

Pronoun

The personal pronouns have singular, dual, and plural forms; they are: 1 *aš – mudu – mẽs*; 2 *tu – judu – jūs*; 3 masc. *jis – juõdu – jiẽ*; fem. *ji – jiẽdvi – jõs*. All of these are declined in six cases; the oblique base of first singular is *man-*.

POSSESSIVE PRONOUN/ADJECTIVE

This is indeclinable: sing. *mano – tavo – jõ/jõs*; pl. *mū̃su – jū̃su – jų̃*.

DEMONSTRATIVE PRONOUN/ADJECTIVE

Threefold distinction by relative distance: *šìs – šì – šiẽ/šiõs* 'this, these'; *tàs – tà – tiẽ/tõs* 'that, those'; *anàs – anà – aniẽ/anõs* 'that, those yonder'. These are declined in six cases.

INTERROGATIVE PRONOUN

Kàs 'who, what?', declined for case, not for gender/number. *Kàs* is also a relative pronoun, and there are several others which are used in both capacities: *koks, kurìs, katràs, keliñtas*, etc. Apart from *kas*, these have feminine forms: e.g. *Aš mataũ stãlą, añt kuriõ gùli knygà* 'I see a table on which lies a book'; *Mán patiñka tà knygà, kurią̃ tù mán daveĩ* 'I like the book which you gave me.'

Numerals

1–9: these agree with noun in gender, number, and case. The base (masc. nom.) forms are: *vienas, du, trỹs, keturì, penkì, šešì, septynì, aštuonì, devynì*; 10 *dẽšimt*; 11 *vienuolika*; 12 *dvylika*; 13 *trylika*; 20 *dvidešimt*; 30 *trisdešimt*; 100 *šim̃tas*.

Verb

Lithuanian verbs are perfective or imperfective. In general, perfective verbs have prefixes, but there are exceptions e.g. *gìmti* 'to be born', *mir̃ti* 'to die', are perfective; and *supràsti* 'to understand', is an example of an imperfective verb with a prefix.

Three forms are basic: (a) the infinitive minus the *-ti* ending: this is the so-called indefinite form; (b) the third person present indicative stem; (c) the third person past indicative stem. These may be identical (apart from tonal shift) as in e.g. *gyventi* 'to live': (a) *gyvén-*; (b) *gyvẽn-*; (c) *gyvẽn-*. Or they may vary, as in *eĩti* 'to go': (a) *eĩ-*; (b) *eĩn-*; (c) *ẽj-*.

There are three conjugations, the criterion being the third person present indicative ending: 1 *-a*, e.g. *dìrba* 'he works'; 2 *-i*, e.g. *mýli* 'he loves'; 3 *-o*, e.g. *móko* 'he teaches'.

The verbal system further comprises: two voices (active and passive), four moods (indicative, imperative, subjunctive, optative), and an array of tenses – 11 in the indicative – both simple and compound. There are also two infinitives, several participles, and a supine. The system will be illustrated here by the following forms: finite forms in first person singular and plural + nominative singular and plural masculine participial forms in the compound tenses. The verb is *dirbti* 'to work', which is a first conjugation verb. The auxiliary forms are from *būti* 'to be':

simple present: *dìrbu*, *dìrbame*
past frequentative: *dìrb**da**vau*, *dìrb**da**vome*
simple preterite: *dìrbau*, *dìrbome*
perfect: *esù dìrbęs*, *ẽsame dìrbę*
future: *dìrbsiu*, *dìrbsime*
future perfect: *bū́siu dìrbęs*, *bū́sime dìrbę*
pluperfect: *buvaũ dìrbęs*, *bùvome dìrbę*
progressive past: *buvaũ bedirbą̃s*, *bùvome bedirbą̃* (+ two other progressive tenses)

subjunctive:

present: *dìrbčiau*, *dìrbtume*
perfect: *bū́čiau dìrbęs*, *bū́tume dìrbę*
imperative: *dìrbk* (2nd sing.), *dìrbkite* (2nd pl.)
optative: *te-* is prefixed to third person form: *te.dirba*.

participles: e.g.

present active: *dirbą̃s*, pl. *dìrbą̃*; passive: *dìrbamas*, *dirbamì*
past active: *dìrbęs*, pl. *dìrbę*; passive: *dìrbtas*, *dirbtì*
future active: *dìrbsiąs*, pl. *dìrbsią*; passive: *dìrbsimas*, *dirbsimì*

Reflexive verbs: the marker is *-s*(*i*): this is inserted in compound verbs between prefix and stem: e.g. *aš sutinku* 'I meet'; *mẽs susitinkame* 'I meet with somone, we meet'.

Negation: *ne-* is prefixed to the affirmative form: e.g. *aš nevalgau* 'I don't eat'.

Participles are widely used to express inferential/impersonal/reported speech: e.g. *Traukinỹs* ***išeĩnąs*** *septiñtą vãlandą* 'The train is due to leave at 7'; *Mokytojas sãko, kad mokinỹs* ***ẽsąs*** *gabus* 'The teacher said that the pupil was gifted.'

PUSDALYVIS

This participial form expresses concomitant action by the subject of the principal clause: the form is in *-dam-* + *as/a* and is inflected for gender and number, not case: e.g. *Išeĩdamas profesorius pamir̃šo ãkinius* 'Going out, the professor forgot his glasses'; *Priẽš išeĩdamas paskam̃bink man* 'Before you go out give me a ring.'

PADALYVIS

This participial form expresses action by other than the subject of the principal clause. Its own subject is in the dative. The present form is in *-ant/-int*, the past in *-ius*: e.g. *aũšrai* (or *dienai*) *aũštant* 'as it is dawning' (*aušra* 'dawn'); *Sutẽmus oras atšãlo* 'As darkness fell, it grew colder' (*sutemti* 'to darken'; *atšalti* 'to turn colder').

Prepositions

Prepositions govern the genitive, the accusative, or the instrumental. Some take more than one case; *põ*, for example, is used with all three: e.g. *vaikščioti põ mišką* 'to go for a walk in the forest' (acc.); *põ žiemõs* 'after the winter' (gen.).

Word order

SVO; in the genitive relationship, possessor precedes possessed: e.g. *brólis knygà* 'the brother's book'; *Lietuvõs sóstine* 'the capital of Lithuania'; *miẽsto centrè* 'in the middle of the town'.

Pradžioje buvo Žodis, ir (tas) Žodis buvo prie Dievo, ir Dievas buvo (tas) Žodis.
2. Tasai buvo pradžioje prie Dievo.
3. Visi daiktai per tą daryti yra, ir be to nieko niera daryta, kas daryta yra.
4. Jame buvo gyvastis, ir gyvastis buvo šviesybė žmonių.
5. Ir šviesybė tamsybėje šviečia, bet tamsybė tai ne permanė.
6. Buvo žmogus, Dievo siųstas, Jonas vardu.
7 Tas atėjo liudymui, apie šviesybę liudyti, kad jie visi per jį tikėtų.
8. Jis ne buvo šviesybe, bet jeib liudytų apie šviesybę.

MACEDONIAN

INTRODUCTION

There are over a million speakers of this South Slavonic language in the Macedonian National Republic; an estimated half-million Macedonians live in Greece and Bulgaria. The literary language dates from the early nineteenth century, but it was not until after the First World War that any organized movement for Macedonian cultural expression got under way.

SCRIPT

Cyrillic with certain extra and modified letters: these are, with their phonetic values:

Ѓ = /d′/, J = /j/, Љ = /l/, Њ = /n/, Ќ = /t′/, Џ = /dʒ/, S = /dz/

PHONOLOGY

Consonants

stops: p, b, t, d, k, g; ḱ and ǵ are mid-palatal plosives, which approximate to palatalized: t′, d′
affricates: ts, dz, tʃ, dʒ
fricatives: f, v, s, z, ʃ, ʒ, j, x
nasals: m, n, ɲ, (ŋ)
laterals and flap: l, ɫ, ʎ, r

Vowels

i, ɛ, a, ɔ, u

All short – Macedonian has no long vowels. All vowels retain their full value in unstressed position (i.e. there is no reduction as in Russian). Vocalic *r* occurs: e.g. *smrt* 'death'.

Stress

On antepenult in words of three or more syllables, on first syllable of disyllable: e.g. *plánina* 'mountain': *planínata* 'the mountain', i.e. the stress shifts when a syllable is added to three-syllable word.

Both the first and second palatalizations are observed in Macedonian:

first: e.g. *rekov* 'I said' – *reče* 'he said'
second: e.g. *volk* 'wolf' – pl. *volci*

MORPHOLOGY AND SYNTAX

Three genders: masculine, feminine, and neuter. The case system has been almost entirely lost: a trace is found in nouns denoting male kin, which end in a consonant: these have an accusative form in *-a*, often followed by a dative enclitic pronoun: e.g. *brata mi* 'my brother (acc.)'. Syntactic relations in general are established with the help of prepositions, e.g. genitive with *od*, *na*, dative with *do, pri,* instrumental with *so,* locative with *v(o)*, *na, pri* (*see* **Preposition**, below).

Masculine plural forms are: *-ovci*, *-i*, *-ce*, *-ovi*, *-ni*: e.g. *grad* 'town' – *gradovi*; *prst* 'finger' – *prsti*. Feminine nouns in *-a* or a consonant make a plural in *-i*: *žena* 'woman' – *ženi.* Neuter nouns change *-o* to *-a*; *-e* to *-in'a*: e.g. *pole* 'field' – *polin'a*.

Macedonian has three postfixed definite articles:

(a) masc. *-ot*, fem. *-ta*, neut. *-to*; pl. masc./fem. *-te*, neut. *-ta*. This article is neutral, used when degree of removal need not be specified: e.g. *grad.ot* 'the town'; *žena.ta* 'the woman'.
(b) *-ov*, *-va*, *-vo*; pl. *-ve*, *-va*: used to emphasize proximate locus: 'this here'.
(c) *-on*, *-na*, *-no*: pl. *-ne*, *-na*: the distal correlative: 'that there'.

Thus: *dobriot čovek, dobriov čovek, dobrion čovek* 'the good man', depending on degree of removal, and/or topical relevance.

Adjective

Marked for gender in the singular; one common plural form; e.g. *crven* – *crvena* – *crveno*; pl. *crveni* 'red'. The attributive adjective precedes the noun and can take the article: e.g. *arna.ta kniga* 'the good book' (*aren* 'good'). For the comparative grade, *po-* is prefixed to the positive: e.g. *ubav* 'beautiful' – *po.ubav*; *golem* 'big' – *po.golem*.

The *-a-* in the masculine ending *-ar* is fleeting: *dobar čovek* 'good man', but *dobra žena* 'good woman', *dobro dete* 'good child', *dobri čoveci* 'good people'.

Pronoun

PERSONAL

The personal pronouns have indirect and direct objective forms:

	Singular				*Plural*		
	1	2	3 masc.	3. fem.	1	2	3
nominative	jas	ti	toj	taa	nie	vie	tie
indirect	mene/mi	tebe/ti	nemu/mu	nejze/i	nam/ni	vam/vi	nim/im
direct	mene/me	tebe/te	nego/go	nea/ja	nas/ne	vas/ve	niv/gi

The neuter third person pronoun *to*(*v*)*a* has the same indirect and direct forms as the masculine.

Full and shortened forms of the objective pronouns are often used together: e.g. *tebe te vide* 'he saw you (sing.)'; *toj me saka mene* 'he loves me'.

POSSESSIVE PRONOUN
moj, *moja*, *moe*; pl. *moi*; similarly, *tvoj*, *naš*, *vaš*. The third person forms are: masc. *negov -a*/*-o*/*-i*; fem. *nejzin -a*/*-o*/*-i*; pl. *nivni -a*/*-o*/*-i*. These forms are often used with the postfixed article and a linking element *-i-* where necessary: e.g. *negov.i.ot* 'his' (masc. referent).

DEMONSTRATIVE PRONOUN/ADJECTIVE
ovoj 'this'; *toj*/*onoj* 'that'; these are marked for gender, thus: *ovoj* has fem. *ovaca*, neut. *ova*; and have plural forms *ovie*, *tie*, *onie*.

INTERROGATIVE PRONOUN
koj 'who?'; *što* 'what?'. *Koj*, *koja*, *koe*, pl. *koi*, with masc. acc. *kogo*, dat. *komu*.

RELATIVE PRONOUN
koj/*što*.

Numerals

1 *eden*/*edna*/*edno*; 2 masc. *dva*, fem./neut. *dve*; 3–10 *tri*, *četiri*, *pet*, *šest*, *sedum*, *osum*, *devet*, *deset*; 11 *edinaeset* = /edinajse/; 12 *dvanaeset* = /dvanajse/; 20 *dvaeset*; 30 *trieset*; 40 *četirieset*; 100 *sto*.

Verb

As in other Slavonic languages, imperfective and perfective aspects are distinguished. Secondary imperfectives are formed from perfective verbs: e.g.

misli 'to think', perfective *raz.misli*, secondary imperfective *raz.misluva*
čeka 'to wait', perfective *do.čeka*, secondary imperfective *do.čekuva*

A different stem may be used for the perfective aspect: cf. *gleda* 'see', perfective *vidi*.

A notable feature of Macedonian is the presence of a perfect tense, constructed as in the Romance languages, by means of an auxiliary and a past participle: thus, the auxiliary *imam* 'I have', plus the neuter past participle passive: *imam raboteno* 'I have worked'.

The passive participle of an intransitive verb is used with *sum* 'I am': e.g. *jas sum dojden* 'I have come'; participle shows concord with subject.

TENSE STRUCTURE
The aorist and the imperfect are both present. *-am* has been generalized as the first person singular ending of the present tense of all verbs.

Present tense imperfective only: the endings are: *-am*, *-š*, *-Ø*; pl. *-me*, *-te*, *-*(*a*)*t*: e.g. *rabotam*, *rabotiš*, *raboti*; pl. *rabotime*, *rabotite*, *rabotat* 'I (etc.) work'.

Aorist: is formed from perfective verbs, and expresses completed action vouched for by speaker: e.g. *dojdov* 'I (start to) come, I came': *dojdov*, *dojdeš*, *dojde*; pl. *dojdovme*, *dojdovte*, *dojdoa*.

Imperfect: progressive action in the past, vouched for by speaker: the endings are the same as those of the aorist except in second and third person singular: e.g. *idev* 'I was going', *ideše*, *ideše*.

Future: A future tense is made by prefixing the particle *ќe* to the formal present of either aspect: e.g. *ќeodam* 'I shall go': *ќe pokažam* 'I shall show'. This future is negated by the formula *nema da* + present: e.g. *nema da odam* 'I shan't go'.

Imperative: *-i*, *-ete* for consonant stems; *-j*, *-jte* for vowel stems: e.g. *idi*, *idite*; *stoj*, *stojte*.

A gerund is formed from imperfective verbs; it is invariable: e.g. *odejќi* 'going'; *begajќi* 'running'.

PARTICIPLES

Past participle active: *-l*, *-la*, *-lo*; common pl. *-le*; past participle passive: *-t*, *-ta*, *-to*; common pl. *-ti*; or, *-n*, *-na*, *-no*; pl. *-ni*.

As noted above, compound tenses are made by using these participles with the auxiliaries *imam* and *sum*. In the compound form with *sum*, the auxiliary itself can be dropped in the third person singular or plural: e.g. *sum begal* 'I have been running': *begal* 'he has been running'; *begale* 'they have been running'.

Prekažanost: the inferential form corresponding to *preizkazano naklonenie* in Bulgarian (*see* **Bulgarian**) is used in the second and third persons in Macedonian: e.g. *toj rabotel* (= compound past minus auxiliary) *cel den* '(they tell me) he worked all day'.

A pluperfect is made with the imperfect form of *sum* + the active past participle of either aspect: *bev/beše* (etc.) *storil* 'I/you (etc.) had done'.

Conditional: invariable particle *bi* + past participle active: *toj bi došol* 'he would come'.

Prepositions

All Macedonian prepositions govern the nominative base form, even if an oblique form is available.

1. Во почетокот беше Словото, и Словото беше во Бога,
и Бог беше Словото.
2. Тоа во почетокот беше во Бога.
3. Сé постана преку Него и без Него ништо не стана, што
постана.
4. Во Него имаше живот и животот им беше светлина на
луѓето.
5. И светлината во темнината свети, и мракот не ја опфати.
6. Имаше еден човек по име Јован, пратен од Бога;
7. тој дојде за сведочанство, да сведочи за Светлината, та
сите да поверуваат преку него.
8. Тој не беше светлина, туку да сведочи за Светлината.

MALAYALAM

INTRODUCTION

This South Dravidian language is spoken by about 24 million people in Kerala, and is one of the officially recognized state languages of India. Lexically, Malayalam is close to Tamil from which it seems to have diverged in comparatively very recent times, perhaps during the thirteenth century AD. The earliest literary monument in Malayalam is a *Rāmacarita* in a recension dating from the fourteenth century, though the work itself may be older.

There are two main points of difference between Tamil and Malayalam: the personal endings of the verb, present in Tamil, have been lost in Malayalam; and, second, the extent of borrowing from Sanskrit is considerably greater in Malayalam. From the nineteenth century onwards, there has been a gradual tendency for the colloquial language to replace the heavily Sanskritized literary style.

The outstanding figure in the history of Malayalam literature is that of Tuñcatt' Eẓuttacchan (sixteenth century), to whom we also owe the modern Malayalam script.

SCRIPT

The syllabary is in order and content an exact copy of the Devanagari grid. There are numerous ligatures, including graphs for geminated consonants.

PHONOLOGY

Consonants

stops: p, t, ṭ, k; with aspirated and voiced/voiced aspirate values: e.g. /p, ph, b, bh/
affricates: tʃ, dʒ; with aspirated values
fricatives: j, v, s, ṣ, ʃ, h
nasals: m, n, ɲ, ŋ, ɳ
laterals and flaps: l, ḷ, r, ṟ, ṛ

/ṟ/ tends towards dental [t]. Retroflex phonemes are notated here with a subscript dot, e.g. *ṛ*.

Vowels

short and long: i, e, a, o, u
diphthongs: ai, au

Sandhi based on homogeneous assimilation is very extensive; glides /j/ and /w/ are used at vocalic junctures. The distinction between single and geminated consonants is phonemic.

Stress

Slight; on first syllable.

MORPHOLOGY AND SYNTAX

Noun

Three genders – masculine, feminine, and neuter – are distinguished, and certain endings are gender-specific, e.g. masc. *-an*, *-kāran*; fem. *-i*, *-tti*, *-kāri*. Sanskrit words retain their original gender; cf. *kumāran* 'son'; *kumāri* 'daughter'; *mīnkāran* 'fisherman'; *mīnkāri* 'fisher-woman'. Lexical gender: e.g. *āṇpakṣi* 'male bird'; *peṇpakṣi* 'female bird'.

NUMBER
The plural is formed in three ways:

(a) with *-kaḷ*: e.g. *vīṭu* 'house', pl. *vīṭukaḷ*. Juncture with *-kaḷ* is subject to sandhi: *maram* 'tree', pl. *maraṁkal*;
(b) masculine nouns in *-an* change this ending to *-ar*: e.g. *manuṣyan* 'man' – *manuṣyar*;
(c) honorific plural in *-mār*: e.g. *amma* 'mother' – *ammamār*.

CASE SYSTEM
There are seven cases. As specimen, declension of *manuṣyan* (masc.) 'man':

nominative	manuṣyan	instrumental	manuṣyanāl
accusative	manuṣyane	genitive	manuṣyante
comitative	manuṣyanōṭu	locative	manuṣyanil
dative	manuṣyannu		

Plural is *manuṣyanmār*, to which the same endings as set out above are added.
The base for the oblique cases often varies from the nominative. For example, *maram* 'tree', adds the oblique endings to the base *maratt*, extended by *-in-*: e.g. *maratt.in.ōṭu*. Similarly, *malayāḷattil* 'in Malayalam'.

Adjective

Malayalam has very few true adjectives. As attribute, the adjective precedes the noun: *nalla* 'good', *periya* 'big'. *nalla veḷḷam* 'good water'.

Adjectives may be nominalized: e.g. *nallavaḷ* 'a good woman' (cf. third person feminine pronoun).

Pronoun

The basic personal forms are:

		Singular		Plural
1		ñān	incl.	nām/nammaḷ, excl. ñaṅṅaḷ
2		nī		niṅṅaḷ
3	masc.	avan/addēham		avar(kaḷ)
	fem.	avaḷ		
	nt.	atu		ava, atukaḷ

These are declined in all cases. The oblique base of *ñān* is *en-*: thus, *enne, ennōṭu, enikku, ennāl, ende, ennil.* Possessive pronouns: e.g. *ente* 'mine' *avante* 'his', *avaḷute* 'hers'.

DEMONSTRATIVE PRONOUN
The three genders are distinguished in the singular: *ivan – ivaḷ – itu* 'this'; *avan – avaḷ – atu* 'that'. In the plural, *ivan* and *ivaḷ* combine to give plural *ivar*, in opposition to neuter plural *iva*. Similarly, *avar* (masc./fem. pl.) – *ava* (neuter).

INTERROGATIVE PRONOUN
ēvan, ēvaḷ (sing. masc., fem.) 'who?', pl. *ār/ēvar*; *ētu* (neuter) 'what?', pl. *ēva.*

RELATIVE PRONOUN
See **Participle**, below.

Numerals

1–10: *oru/onnu* (this is not a gender distinction), *raṇṭu, mūnnu, nālu, añju, āṟu, ēṟu, eṭṭu, onpatu, pattu*; 11 *patinonnu*; 12 *pantraṇṭu*; 13 *patimūnnu*; 20 *irupatu*; 30 *muppatu*; 40 *nālpatu*; 100 *nūṟu.*

The noun following a numeral is in the singular if it is neuter, plural if masculine/feminine: e.g. *mūnnu kutira* 'three horses'; but *raṇṭu peṇkaḷ* 'two sisters'.

Verb

Thanks to the elimination of person and number (except in the imperative), the verbal system in Malayalam is considerably simpler than that of the other Dravidian languages. All verbal forms are built on the basis of the root, which takes such endings as -(*k*)*kuka*, -*yuka* to express the infinitive. Verbs in -*kkuka* are strong; verbs with any other infinitive ending are weak.

There are four moods: indicative, imperative, conditional, and necessitative.

Indicative mood: tense formation:

Present: -(*k*)*kunnu* is added to the root, e.g. *ñān vāyikkunnu* 'I read'; *niṅṅaḷ vāyikkunnu* 'you (pl.) read'.

Present progressive: *-uṇṭu* or *-kontirikkunnu* is added to present form, e.g. *ñān naṭakkunnuṇṭu* 'I am walking'; *avar samsariccu.koṇṭirikkunnu* 'they keep on talking'.

Past: formation here is much more heterogeneous and irregular: the marker is *-tu* or *-i*, with extensive stem modulation and sandhi: e.g.

	Past tense
čeyyuka 'to do'	čeytu
snēhi.kkuka 'to love'	snēhičču
varuka 'to come'	vannu
paṟayuka 'to speak, say'	paṟaññu
vīṟuka 'to fall'	vīṇu

Future: two forms are possible: (a) *-um* added to present minus *-unnu*, e.g. *avan čeyyum* 'he will do/make'; (b) in *-u/ū*, usually with link consonant, e.g. *varū* 'will come'; *koṭuppu* 'will give'.

Imperative mood: the second person singular is provided by the root: e.g. *pō* 'go!'. For the second person plural *-in* is added: e.g. *pōvin*! This mood has first and third person forms in *-ṭṭe*, and a polite form in *-ālum*: e.g. *tannālum* 'please give'.

Conditional mood: the marker is *-āl* or *-eṅkil*: e.g. *čeyt.āl* 'if ... does/do/did'.

Necessitative mood: has three tense forms: cf. *paṟayēṇḍunnu* 'has to say'; *paṟayēṇḍi* 'had to say'; *paṟayēṇḍum* 'will have to say'.

NEGATIVE CONJUGATION

The characteristic marker is *-ā-*: e.g. *paṟa.y.**ā**.yka* 'not to speak'. Present, past, and future negative tenses can be formed either by *-ā-* + tense ending, or by affixation of the particle *-illa*: e.g. *paṟa.y.**ā**.yunnu* = *paṟa.y.unn.illa* 'don't/ doesn't speak': *paṟay.ā.ññu* = *paṟaññ.illa* 'didn't speak'; *paṟay.ā.yum* = *paṟaka.yilla* 'will not speak'.

FORMATION OF RELATIVE CLAUSES

The participial form is neutral as to voice: cf. *pustakam vāyičča strī* 'the woman who read(s) the book'; *strī vāyičča pustakam* 'the book read by the woman'.

Malayalam has about 20 auxiliaries, which express perfect/imperfective aspect, and modality (benefactive, inceptive, terminative, etc.). Thus, *vekkuka* (past tense *večču*) 'to put' for perfective, *kolluka* (past tense *koṇṭu*) 'to take' for imperfective: e.g. *čeytu.večč.irunnu* '... (he etc.) made (and completed)'.

Postpositions

Examples: following nouns in genitive case: *nāṭuvē/naṭuvil* 'between, among'; *vīṭukaḷute naṭuvil* 'between/among the houses'; *mukaḷ* 'on': *marattin mukaḷ* 'on the tree'; *kīṟē* 'under, beneath'; *vrikshattin kīṟē* 'beneath the tree'. In these two examples, *maram*, genitive, *marattin(te)* is the native Dravidian word for 'tree';

vriksha is a Sanskrit loan-word. *čurrum* 'round': *sūryante churrum* 'round the sun'; *mutal … ōḷam* 'from … to'; *janičča divasam mutal maraṇattōḷam* 'from day of birth to death'.

With locative case: e.g. *ūṭē* 'through': *nagarattilūṭē* 'through the town'.

Word order

SOV.

ആദിയിൽ വചനം ഉണ്ടായിരുന്നു ആ വചനം ദൈവ
ത്തൊടു കൂട ആയിരുന്നു ആ വചനം ദൈവവും ആയിരുന്നു *
ആയത ആദിയിൽ ദൈവത്തൊടു കൂട ആയിരുന്നു * സക ൨
ലവും അവനാൽ ഉണ്ടാക്കപ്പെട്ടു ഉണ്ടാക്കപ്പെട്ടതൊന്നും അവ ൩
നെ കൂടാതെ ഉണ്ടാക്കപ്പെട്ടതുമില്ല * അവനിൽ ജീവൻ ഉണ്ടാ ൪
യിരുന്നു ആ ജീവൻ മനുഷ്യരുടെ വെളിച്ചം ആയിരുന്നു * വി ൫
ശെഷിച്ചും ആ വെളിച്ചം ഇരുളിൽ പ്രകാശിക്കുന്നു എങ്കിലും ഇ
രുൾ അതിനെ പരിഗ്രഹിച്ചില്ല *
ഒരു മനുഷ്യൻ ദൈവത്തിൽനിന്ന അയക്കപ്പെട്ടിരുന്നു അ ൬
വന്റെ നാമം യൊഹന്നാൻ എന്നായിരുന്നു * ആയവൻ ൭
താൻ മൂലം എല്ലാവരും വിശ്വസിക്കെണ്ടുന്നതിന ആ വെളിച്ച
ത്തെ കുറിച്ച സാക്ഷിപ്പെടുത്തുവാനായിട്ട സാക്ഷിയായി വ
ന്നു * അവൻ ആ വെളിച്ചം ആയിരുന്നില്ല ആ വെളിച്ചത്തെ ൮
കുറിച്ച സാക്ഷിപ്പെടുത്തുവാനായിട്ട (അയക്കപ്പെട്ടവൻ) അ
ത്രെ *

MAORI

INTRODUCTION

Maori belongs to the East Polynesian branch of the Austronesian family, of which it is the most southerly member. When Cook discovered New Zealand in the eighteenth century the Maori population numbered about 300,000, and had been in the islands for over 500 years. At present, Maori is spoken by around 100,000, which makes it in terms of numbers the leading Polynesian language. English has had a considerable effect on the vocabulary of Maori, and some effect on the syntax. Dialect forms vary mainly in phonological detail and in the lexicon. The first Maori grammar appeared in 1815 (Kendall).

SCRIPT

In the 1820s a phonetic script for Maori was devised in Cambridge. Bible translation soon followed.

PHONOLOGY

With ten consonants and five vowels Maori has the richest phonological inventory of any East Polynesian language.

Consonants

The stops are /p, t, k/ with their associated nasals /m, n, ŋ/; /f/ and /w/ are present, and an alveolar /r/ close to /l/. The glottal /h/ tends to [ʔ] in one dialect. /f/ is written as *wh*: e.g. *whare* = /farɛ/.

Vowels

long or short: i, e = [ɛ], a, o = [ɔ], u

Long vowels are notated either by doubling or by macron.

Stress

Stress is on the first long vowel or diphthong; if neither is present, then on the first syllable.

MORPHOLOGY AND SYNTAX

For a general note on Polynesian structure *see* **Polynesian Languages**. The parts of speech in Maori may be broadly divided into two categories: bases and particles. Nominal bases are compatible with preposited nominal particles; verbal bases are compatible with pre- and postposited process particles. Internal flection is limited to certain plural formations occurring in a very few nouns, e.g. *tangata* 'person', pl. ***tāgata***; *wahine* 'woman', pl. ***wāhine***. Plurality is normally established by the article, by pronominal concord, or by the presence of a numeral: e.g. *te kōtiro* 'the girl', ***ngā*** *kōtiro* 'the girls'.

Nominal particles

1. Indefinite article: *he*, e.g. *he kōtiro* '(a) girl/girls'.

2. Definite article: *te*, pl. *ngā*, e.g. *te rākau* 'the tree', *ngā rākau* 'the trees'.

3. Article with proper nouns: *ko/a*. *Ko* is used if a name is the first word in the sentence: e.g. *Ko Tiare te māhito* 'Charles is the teacher'; *Kei Ākarana a Tiare* 'Charles is in Auckland'.

4. Demonstratives: *tēnei* 'this', proximate to first person, pl. *ēnei*; *tēnā* 'that', proximate to second person, pl. *ēna*; *tērā* 'that', removed from both, pl. *ērā*. Examples: *ēnā māhita* 'those teachers (near you)'; *tēnei whare roa* 'this long house'. Demonstrative pronoun follows predicate: e.g. *he whare tēnei* 'this is a house'. The sentence is introduced by *ko* if the noun is definite: e.g. *Ko te māmā tēnā* 'That is the mother.'

5. Object, target marker: *i*, e.g. *E mātakitaki ana ngā tamariki* ***i*** *te hōiho* 'The children are watching the horse' (for *e...ana*, *see* **Process particles**, below).

6. Possessive markers: *o* and *a* series. *See* **Polynesian Languages** for general note on alienable/inalienable possession in Polynesian. The Maori taxonomy is not entirely clear. The *a* series includes kin (spouse, child), animals (unless used in transport), articles of food, various disposable items, etc. The *o* series includes immovable property, relatives not in the *a* category, articles of clothing, etc. Cf. *te wahine* ***a*** *Hohepa* 'Joseph's wife'; *te matua* ***o*** *Hohepa* 'Joseph's father'. Similarly, *na/no* are used for 'belonging to', with reference to these two categories: e.g. *he potae* ***no*** *te mahita* 'a hat belonging to the teacher'.

7. Agentive markers: *e/ki*, e.g. *I matakitia te kēmu* ***e*** *ngā tamariki* 'The game was watched by the children' (for passive verb form, see below; *tamariki* is irregular plural formation from *tamaiti* 'child').

8. Locative markers: *kei/kei* + noun → preposition, e.g.

(a) *kei Ākarana a Tiare* 'Charles is in Auckland';
(b) *kei runga i* 'on top of, on'; *kei raro i* 'under'; *kei roto i* 'in', etc.: e.g. *Kei runga i te tēpu te pukapuka* 'The book is on the table'; *Kei tawhiti te maunga* 'the mountain is far away.'

The pronominal system

PERSONAL PRONOUNS

	Singular	*Dual*	*Plural*
1	ahau/au	tāua (2nd + 1st p.)	tātou (2nd + 1st p.)
		māua (3rd + 1st p.)	mātou (3rd + 1st p.)
2	koe	kōrua	koutou
3	ia	rāua	rātou

POSSESSIVE PRONOUNS
These are closely related to the above listed pronominal forms. In the first person plural, both dual and plural subject have inclusive and exclusive forms, the former in *t-*, the latter in *m-*. All possessive forms are marked with *tā* or *tō*, plural *ā*/*ō*, with reference to the possessive markers described in 6 above. Thus *tā tāua* denotes singular *a*-category object belonging to us two; *ō rātou* denotes a plurality of *o*-category objects belonging to them (several); *ō tāua tamariki* 'our children' (dual inclusive); *ā māua tamiriki* 'our children' (dual exclusive).

Process/verbal particles

These generate tenses:

1. Simple past: *i*, e.g. *i haere a Hohepa* 'Joseph went'.
2. Present continuous: *kei te* + verb, e.g. *kei te mahi rātou* 'they are working'.
3. Continuous action, neutral as to tense: *e* + verb + *ana*, e.g. ***e** tākaro **ana** ngā tamariki* 'the children are/were/will be playing'; ***e** mahi **ana** ngā tāngata* 'the men are/were/will be working'.
4. Past continuous: *i te* + verb, e.g. ***i te** mahi a Hohepa* 'Joseph was working'.
5. Perfective: *kua*, e.g. ***kua** tae mai te rangatira* 'the chief has arrived'.
6. Onset of action in narrative: *ka*, e.g. *ka haere te pahi* 'the bus left'.
7. Agent-focus in future: *ma* + agent + *e* + verb, e.g. ***Ma** Hohepa **e** hanga te whare* 'It's Joseph who will build the house'.
8. Agent-focus in past: *na* + agent + *i* + verb, e.g. *Na rātou **i** waiata ngā waiata Māori* 'It was you (pl.) who sang the Maori songs.' *Ma*/*na* may indicate future/past even where no verb is present: e.g. *na rātou ngā waiata Māori.*
9. Imperative: *e* + verb/*me* + verb.
10. *kāhore*/*ekore* negates verb: e.g. *kei te mahi a Hohepa* 'Joseph is working'; *kāhore a Hohepa i te mahi* 'Joseph is not working' (*kei* is not compatible with *kāhore*).
11. Supplementary particles: e.g. *tonu*, stresses continuation of action; *pea* marks potentiality, feasibility; *rawa* intensifier; *nē*, *nēra* interrogative.

PASSIVE
A variety of endings turn active verbs into passives, e.g *-a*, *-ai*, *-tia*: *I matakit**ia** te kēmu* 'The game was watched.' The passive endings are also used to make a polite imperative: e.g. *Whakamāori**tia*** 'Please translate into Maori'. Here, *whaka-* is the causative prefix.

A verbal noun is made in *-anga*: e.g. *kōrero* 'to speak' – *kōrerotanga* 'speaking'.

RELATIVE CLAUSES

There are several constructions, e.g. *Ko ia te tangata i haere mai inapō* 'He is the man who came yesterday'; *Ko as te tangata i kite* ***ai*** *au inapō* 'He is the man I saw yesterday' (*haere mai* 'to come'; *kite* 'to see'; ***ai*** used if subject changes).

Agent-focus in relative clause: cf. *te tangata* ***nāna nei i*** *hanga te whare* 'the man who built the house'; *te tangata* ***māna e*** *hanga te whare* 'the man who will build the house'.

Numerals

1–10: (*ko*)*tahi*, *rua*, *toru*, *whā*, *rima*, *ono*, *whitu*, *waru*, *iwa*, *tekau*. 11 *tekau mā tahi*; 12 *tekau mā rua*; 20 *rua tekau*; 100 *kotahi rau*.

Word order

VSO is basic and normal (V is a verbal complex).

I TE timatanga te Kupu, i te Atua
ano te Kupu, ko te Kupu ano te
Atua.
2 I te Atua ano tenei *Kupu* i te
timatanga.
3 Nana nga mea katoa i hanga; a
kahore tetahi *mea* kihai hanga e ia *o*
nga mea i hanga.
4 I a ia te oranga; a ko te oranga
te maramatanga mo nga tangata.
5 E witi ana te maramatanga i roto
i te pouritanga; a kihai tangohia e te
pouritanga.
6 ¶ He tangata ano i tonoa mai i
te Atua, ko Hoani tona ingoa.
7 I haere mai ia hei kai korero, kia
korero ai ia ki te Maramatanga, kia
wakapono ai *nga tangata* katoa i a ia.
8 Ehara ia i taua Maramatanga,
na, *i tonoa mai ia* kia korero ki taua
Maramatanga.

MAPUDUNGU

INTRODUCTION

Mapudungu, also known as Mapuche or Araucanian, is classified by some authorities as a Penutian language, as an outlier, that is, of a North American Indian stock. Others allocate it to the Andean-Equatorial family. When the Spaniards arrived in Chile they found three groups of Araucanians, one of which – the Pikumche (*piku* 'north', *che* 'people') – was speedily conquered. By the eighteenth century the southern group too had lost its specific identity. The central group, however, the Mapuche (*mapu* 'land', *che* 'people') has maintained its identity as a socially compact and self-aware indigenous grouping, and, as such, takes second place only to the Quechua-Aymara and the Guaraní. They number about 250,000 in Chile, with a further 100,000 in Argentina. The Mapuche call their language Mapudungu (*mapu* 'land', *dəŋun* 'to speak').

SCRIPT

If written, Mapudungu is notated in the Roman alphabet. Félix (1916) uses the additional letters, *ə*, *ü*, *ŋ*, *ñ*, plus *tr* for the emphatic ejective /ʈʂ̰/.

PHONOLOGY

Consonants

stops: p, t, d, k; q (*see* **Vowels**, below)
affricates: tʃ, ʈʂ̰
fricatives: f, s, ʒ
nasals: m, n, ɲ, ŋ
lateral and flap: l, ʎ, r
semi-vowels: j, w

Félix distinguishes allophones of /t, n, l/, which he notates as *ṭ·*, *n·*, *l·*. In this article, these allophones are not marked. *d* tends to [ð]; *sh* = [ʒ].

Vowels

i, e, a, o, u, ə

Félix uses *ü* to denote a very guttural [ɪ] sound, uttered with the lips in position for [e]. In some descriptions of the language, the sound is compared to the

Guarani *y*. In certain positions, e.g. as initial followed by *i*, *ü* acquires a consonantal value between [g] and [q]; e.g. *üi* 'man': [qɪ].

/ə/ in Mapudungu has several values, depending on consonantal environment; e.g. preceding /f/ → /œ/.

Stress

On the penultimate syllable for vocalic finals; on final for consonantal. There are exceptions; e.g. first person plural forms ending in the semi-vowel /j/ are stressed on the final syllable.

MORPHOLOGY AND SYNTAX

Noun

Mapudungu has no grammatical gender. Natural gender is indicated by lexical means: e.g. *wentru che* 'man-person'; *domo che* 'woman-person'. *Wentru* and *domo* are also used to differentiate grade: e.g. *wentru kal* 'coarse wool'; *domo kal* 'fine wool'.

An animate/inanimate opposition is reflected in the use of *pu* as a plural marker for nouns denoting animate; some authorities give *yuka* as an equivalent marker for inanimate nouns: *Chi* may be used as a definite article: e.g. *chi wentru* 'the man'; *pu wentru* '(the) men'.

The numeral *kiñe* 'one', functions as indefinite article: e.g. *kiñe wesha ad niei ñi kawellu* 'my horse has a nasty habit' (*wesha* 'bad'; *ad* 'custom'; *niei* 'has'; *ñi* 'my').

A collective plural for animates is made with *wen*: e.g. *fotəmwen* 'father and son', where *fotəm* denotes 'son' (with reference to father). Similarly *pəñeñwen* 'mother and child' (male or female).

A partitive plural is made with *ke*: e.g. *alü ke che* 'many people' (*alü* 'many'). *Ke* is placed between the attributive adjective and the noun: *küme ke kawellu* 'good horses'.

Infixed *-ume-* and *-ye-* also act as pluralizing formants: e.g. *pofreŋe.**ume**.lu* 'those who are poor' (*-lu* is the participial form used to form relative clauses); *aku.**ye**.i fentren che* 'many people arrived' (*akun* 'to arrive'; *fentren* 'many').

Compounding is frequent in Mapudungu: e.g. *küdau* 'work' – *küdau.fe* 'worker' – *küdau.we* 'place of work'; *piku.m.che* 'people of the north' – *piku.kürəf* 'north wind'.

Syntactic relations are expressed by particles: *ñi* (gen.), *meu* (loc., abl., etc.). *ñi* is used following nouns denoting persons: *chau ñi ruka* 'father's house (*ruka*)'. Otherwise, the genitival relationship is expressed by simple juxtaposition: *lelfün kulliñ* 'the animals (*kulliñ*) of the pampas (*lelfün*)'; integral part tends to precede whole: *reu lafken* 'the waves (*reu*) of the sea'. Prepositions help to clarify the situation. These are often derived from nouns, e.g. *furi* 'shoulders' come to mean 'behind': *furi ruka meu* 'behind the house' (*ruka*); *fei ni furi meu* 'behind him' (*fei* 'he, him'); *pərəmfiñ ñi pəchü fotəm kawellu meu* 'I accustomed my little son to the horse' (use of *fotəm* shows that the father is speaking; *pəchü* 'small'; *pərəmn* 'to accustom, train').

-tu is the formant for an instrumental sense: e.g. *namu.tu* 'by foot'; *kawellu.tu* 'by horse'.

Adjective

The adjective is invariable, and, as attribute, precedes the noun: e.g. with the noun *lafken* 'stretch of water': *fücha lafken* 'the sea'; *pəchü lafken* 'a lake'. Cf. *nieiñ wesha antü* 'we're having (*nieiñ*) a bad (*wesha*) day' (not getting much).

The adjective can take the plural marker: *pu fücha* 'the old (people).' A comparative is made with *doy*(*el*): e.g. *iñche doyel mai wesha loŋko ŋen* 'my headache is really (*mai*) getting worse' (*loŋko* 'headache'; *ŋen* 'I am').

Pronoun

The personal forms are:

	Singular	*Dual*	*Plural*
1	iñche	iñchiu	iñchiñ
2	eimi	eymu	eymn
3	fei	feyeŋu	feyeŋn

Truncated forms of these serve as possessives. *Ñi* functions both as 1st person singular possessive and as a general marker: *ñi chau* 'my father', *ñi chau eŋu* 'their (dual) father', *mi chau* 'your father', *ñi ruka* (*y*)*eŋn* 'their (plural) house' and as oblique forms: *elueyeu eŋn pətrem* 'he gave them tobacco' (*pətrem*).

DEMONSTRATIVE ADJECTIVE/PRONOUN

təfa, *təfei* (masculine/feminine; singular/plural): e.g. *təfa.chi pu mapuche* 'these Mapuche'; *təfei.chi küdau meu* 'in this work'; *iñche fei kim.la.n* 'I don't know this' (*kimn* 'to know'; *-la-* negative marker).

INTERROGATIVE PRONOUN

inei 'who?'; *chem* 'what?'.

Mapudungu has interrogative verbs, e.g. *chemn* 'What to do?'; *chum.a.imi* 'What will you do?; *chum.ke.imi* 'What are you doing?'

RELATIVE PRONOUN

None; the participle in *-lu* is used, if necessary with the adjectival formant *chi*: thus, from *akun* 'arrive': *aku.lu* '(he) who arrives/has arrived'; *aku.fu.lu* 'who was arriving'; *aku.a.lu* 'who will arrive'; *aku.a.fu.lu* 'who would arrive'. This form is negated by *no*/*nu*: *aku.no.lu*, *aku.no.fu.lu*, etc. In the passive, *-lu* is added to the passive marker *-ŋe-*: *küpal.ŋe.lu* 'who was carried'.

Numerals

1–10: *kiñe, epu, küla, meli, kechu, kayu, relqe/reqle, pura, ailla, mari*; 20 *epu mari*; 30 *küla mari*; 100 *pataka*. *Meli semana* 'four weeks'; *küla rupa* 'three times'.

Verb

The infinitive ending is *-n*, which can be added to other parts of speech to form verbs: e.g. *küme* 'good' – *kümn* 'to be good'.

Many Mapudungu verbs are semantically dense information-packs, the root meaning being extended by modal, circumstantial, affective overtones, all of which would be expressed adverbially in Indo-European languages: for example, cf.

> *piñmalkan* (root *pin* 'to say'): 'to denigrate someone who is, along with others, present, without confronting him/her directly';
> *inakonkəlen* (root *konkəlen* 'be inside something'): 'to be in a region, house or family where one was not born; i.e. is a stranger'.

Verbs are transitive (primary or derived) neutral or impersonal. They are fully conjugated in three persons and three numbers. The personal endings are reduced reflexes of the personal pronouns. There are active and passive voices and four moods: indicative, imperative, optative, subjunctive. In the indicative, the following tenses are distinguished: base form (present/past) has null marker; imperfect has *-fu-*, future *-a-*. The personal endings are: sing. 1. *-n*, 2. *-imi*, 3. *-i*; dual 1. *-iyu*, 2. *-imu*, 3. *-inu*; pl. 1. *-iñ*, 2. *-imn*, 3. *-iŋn*.

The ambivalent base form is interpreted primarily as a past tense in the case of dynamic verbs, i.e. verbs of movement; otherwise as a present; thus *akun* (base form) 'I arrived'; *nien* 'I have'.

POLYPERSONAL VERBS

As Félix (1916) emphasizes in his *Diccionario*, it is misleading to illustrate the Mapudungu verb by setting out such forms as *elun* 'I give', *eluymi* 'thou givest', *eluy* 'he/she gives' (from *elun* 'to give'). These are deficient in that one must give something to someone: i.e. the transitive verb form must be polypersonal:

> *elufiñ* 'I gave it to him'; negative: *elu.la.fi.ñ*: future: *elu.a.fi.ñ*, negative *elu.la.i.a.fi.ñ*
> *elu.la.qeneu* 'he didn't give it to me' (*-la-* is the negative infix);
> *elueyeu* 'he gave it to them';
> *elune.a.imi* 'they'll give it to you'.

Such forms, coded for both subject and direct and/or indirect object, can be further generated from simple transitive roots by the addition of such formants as (*e*)*l*, *lel*, (*n*)*ma* to the root: e.g. from *küpaln* 'to bring, draw something', are formed *küpal.el.n*/*küpa.ma.n* 'to bring, draw something to someone'; *küpa.lel.fi.ñ manshana* 'I brought him/her apples'.

Further examples of polypersonal verbs in Mapudungu:

> *ŋillan* 'to buy': *ŋillaleneu* 'he bought it for me', *ñi chau ŋillaleneu təfachi kawellu* 'my father bought me this horse';

akuln 'to bring, carry': *akul.**el**.eneu ñi chumpiru* 'he brought me my hat';
puwəln 'cause to arrive somewhere else': *iñche fei puwəl.**el.a**.qeyu mi ruka meu* 'I'll get it to your house for you';
anümn 'to plant': *anüm.**el.ye.a**.qeyu mi manshana* 'I'll plant your apple trees for you'.

DERIVED STEMS

The following formants (among many others) are used to generate aspectual and modal meanings:

(*ma*)*ke*, customary/habitual action: e.g. *weñei* 'he steals' – *weñe.ke.i* 'he's always stealing';
ŋilla, causative: e.g. *ŋilla.faln* 'to have made, order to be made';
küpa, desiderative: e.g. *küpa.amu.la.i* 'he doesn't want to go';
məñal, inceptive with future tense, completive with past tense: e.g. *məñal.pra.kawelln, akui witran* 'I had just mounted the horse when a stranger arrived';
pepi, potential: e.g. *pepi.amu.la.ian* 'I shan't be able to go', *təfachi ruka pepi.məlen ŋelai* 'one may not be in this house';
(*ə*)*rke*, continuative: e.g. *fei weñeñ.ma.rke.eneu ñi kawellu* 'so then he goes and steals my horse';
rupa(*n*), terminative, perfective: e.g. *rupan.küdau.fu.iñ* 'we had finished working';
(*ə*)*rpu* marks intermediate stage in action: e.g. *nütram.ərpu.i* = *pi.rpu.i* 'he said' (while something else was going on), *la.rpu.i Temuco* 'he died in Temuco' (on journey from Valdivia to Santiago), *aŋkan.tu fele.rpu.i* 'as time went on, he became blind';
pu, perfective infix: e.g. *trann* 'to fall' – *tran.pu.i* 'he fell', *küdau.pu.an* 'I'll go and do a day's work (and finish it)', *məle.pu.an hospital meu* 'I'll go to hospital (and be cured there)';
tu marks return to original state or condition: cf. *küpai* 'he came' (of a stranger), *küpa.**tu**.i* 'he came' (return of a native), *amu.**tu**.i* 'he went away' (from where he did not belong).

PASSIVE

ŋen is added to transitive stems: e.g. *ñi elu.ŋen* 'I am given'.

VERBAL PREFIXES

Examples:

fente-, terminative, 'as far as': e.g. *fente.dəŋun* 'to fall silent, having been talking', *fente.kənun* 'to stop doing something';
wəño- indicates reversal, return: e.g. *wəño.kintun mapu* 'to return to see the land' (i.e. escape death), *wəñonmatuimi mi kure?* 'Has your wife returned to your side?'

NEGATION

The general negating infix is *-la-*: e.g. with root *femn* 'to do something specific' – *fem.**la**.n* 'I did no such thing'; *koilatun* 'to tell lies' – *koilatu.**la**.n* 'I'm not lying'.

-la- may be reinforced by *newe*; e.g. with root *adtun* 'to find something pleasing': *iñche newe adtu.ke.la.fiñ chi dəŋu* 'I do not find this matter (*dəŋu*) at all pleasing' (for the ending *-fiñ*, indicating first person → third person deixis, *see* **Polypersonal Verbs**, above).

-keno-/-ki-, negates the imperative: e.g. *küpa.keno.pe* 'he is not to come'.

Prepositions

Examples:

> *aŋka* (basic meaning, 'stomach') 'in the middle of': *aŋka n.amun nien ñi kutran* lit. 'in the middle of the leg I have my pain', i.e. 'my leg hurts in the middle';
>
> *inau/inafel* + *meu* 'close to': *iñche ñi inau meu* 'close to me';
> *minche* 'below': *minche ruka meu* 'below the house';
> *wente* 'upon': *wente mesa* 'on the table'.

Many verbs carry specific spatial information, rendering pre- or postpositions superfluous; cf. *takunaqkəlen* 'to be below and covered by something': *piuke takunaqkəlei ponon meu* 'The heart is below the lungs (*ponon*) and covered by them'. *Meu* is an all-purpose locative postposition, exemplified several times in this article.

Word order

As described above, if V is a transitive verbal complex, it is coded for S and O. Where nominals are present, order is rather free: SOV, OVS, and SVO are all possible.

1. Llitun meu deu felefui ta Dungun, ka feichi Dungun Ngünechen engu felefui, ka feichi Dungun, Ngünechen nga tfei.
2. Fei tfa rüf llitun meu Ngünechen engu felefui.
3. Kom küfchi dungu, fei ta ñi deumel ta tfei, ka ngenofule fei chem no rume ñi deumyel, ngelayafui.
4. Fei meu mlefui ta mongen, ka tfeichi mongen, ta che ñi pelom ta tfei.
5. Ka ta pelom, pu dumiñ meu llemllemi ka ta pu dumiñ yerpulaeyeu.
6. Mlefui mai kiñe wentru Ngünechen ñi werküel, fei mai Juan pingefui.
7. Fei mai küpai pifalngealu, ka ñi wülpayafiem pi falchi dungu ñi felen kai feichi pelom, ñi feyentuam kom che fei meu.
8. Fei ta pelom no fel, re ta ñi pifalpatiem ñi felen tfeichi pelom.

MARATHI

INTRODUCTION

As one of the official state languages of India, Marathi is spoken by about 50 million people in Mahar̄ashtra, with some degree of spread into adjacent territories. There are also outlier groups of Marathi speakers in Dravidian country. There are three main dialects: dēsī, the base for the modern standard literary language; kōṅkaṇi /kokni/ the dialect spoken in Goa; and Eastern Marathi, which shades gradually into Oriya and Eastern Hindi.

The Mahārāṣṭrī Prakrit from which Marathi derives differed markedly from the Śauraseni and Māgadhī Prakrits underlying most of the other New Indo-Aryan languages, and this difference continues today to mark Marathi off from its congeners. Dravidian influences seem also to have played a part in the formation of Marathi, particularly in the structure of the verbal system.

Writing in Marathi dates from the thirteenth century, when Jñāneśvar wrote his commentary on the *Bhagavadgītā*. Jñāneśvar is also the first of the poet–saints, the long line of Marathi poets who wrote hymns in honour of the god Viṭhobā of Panḍharpūr. The most celebrated of the poet–saints are Nāmdev (fourteenth century) and Tukārām (seventeenth century). Under Western influence, the novel and the short story figure very prominently in modern Marathi writing. Hari Nārāyaṇ Āpṭe (1864–1919) was the first Marathi novelist to deal candidly with social issues in his fiction.

SCRIPT

The Bal Bodh ('understood by children') version of the Devanagari script is used for Marathi. Vocalic /r̥/ and /l̥/, short and long, are missing.

PHONOLOGY

Consonants

stops: p, b, t, d, ʈ, ɖ, k, g
affricates: ts, dz, tʃ, dʒ
fricatives: v/f, s, ʂ, ʃ, h
nasals: m, mh, n, nh, ɳ
lateral and flap: l, lh, ɭ, r, rh
semi-vowel: j

All of the stops and affricates have aspirated correlatives, except /ts/: /ph, bh/, etc. Retroflex sounds are notated in the following text with dots, e.g. /ɖ/ = ḍ.

Vowels

short: i, a, u (where a = [ʌ] or [ə])
long: iː, eː, aiː = [əi], auː = [əʊ], aː, oː, uː

In the script, length is marked (here by a macron) but is not phonemic; nasalization is neither marked nor phonemic, and seems to have acquired an optional or spontaneous character except in the first person endings of the indicative mood.

The pronunciation of consonantal clusters is assisted by an epenthetic vowel; e.g. *garᵃmī* 'hot'; *jaṅgᵃlāt* 'in the jungle'.

VOWEL REDUCTION
/a/ tends to be full in a first syllable, reduced in final and in a syllable preceding a full vowel.

MORPHOLOGY AND SYNTAX

Noun

With Gujarati, Marathi shares a three-gender system of masculine, feminine, and neuter. Words in *-ā* are typically masculine, in *-ī* feminine. Neuter endings were typically nasalized, but this feature has been lost in modern Marathi.

NUMBER
Broadly speaking, most plural direct forms are identical with their singular direct forms, or simply add thereto a long vowel: e.g.

	Singular direct	*Plural direct*
masculine	hāt 'hand'	hāt
	bājū 'side'	bājū
feminine	bhiṅt 'wall'	bhiṅtī
	šāḷā 'school'	šāḷā
neuter	ghar 'house'	gharẽ
	ḍokē 'head'	ḍokī̃

CASE
Direct and oblique forms: the oblique form is incomplete without one or another of the agglutinative case affixes, or a postposition. Thus, the genitive case is provided by the oblique base plus the affix *cā/cī/cẽ* (i.e. marked for gender).

The dative/aditive marker is *lā*, which is also the objective marker for an animate object: e.g. *Tyānẽ āpᵃlyā mitrālā pāhilẽ* 'He saw his friend.' The instrumental/agentive marker (illustrated in the last example) is *-nẽ*.

These case affixes have plural forms: e.g. for the genitive, *-ce, -cyā, cī̃*; agentive pl. *-nī̃*.

An ablative case is made with -(*h*)*ūn*/*tūn*: e.g. *gharūn* 'out of the house'; *khiḍ*[a]*kītūn pāh*[a]*ṇē* 'to look out of the window'.

Comitative: the affix is *śī*: e.g. *dus*[a]*ryā desāṅśī sah*[a]*kāry*[a] 'collaboration with other countries'.

Adjective

Variable or invariable; the former are marked for gender and number, and take -*yā* in the oblique for all three genders and both numbers: e.g. *cāng*[a]*lā mul*[a]*gā* 'good son': *cang*[a]***lyā*** *mulālā* 'to the good son'.

Pronoun

PERSONAL INDEPENDENT

	Singular	*Plural*
1	mī	āmhī
2	tū̃	tumhī

These are declined in all cases; e.g. for the first person singular: aditive/dative, *malā*; agentive, *mī*/*myā̃*; comitative, *mājhāśī*; ablative, *mājhāhūn*.

The third person forms are supplied by the demonstrative series: *to* (masc.), *tī* (fem.), *tē̃* (neut.), with plural forms: *te, tya, tī̃.*

POSSESSIVE ADJECTIVES
mājhā 'my', *ām*[a]*cā* 'our', etc.

INTERROGATIVE PRONOUN
koṇ 'who?'; *kāy* 'what?'

RELATIVE PRONOUN
jo.

Verb

In broad outline, the Marathi verbal system is similar to those of its New Indo-Aryan congeners. At many points, however, it is much more complicated, and this complication is due to several factors:

1. the retention of certain archaic Indo-Aryan features, e.g. the endings of the subjunctive and the imperative moods;
2. the concomitant growth of secondary forms, both synthetic and analytic;
3. the wide expansion of participial constructions of a Dravidian rather than a New Indo-Aryan type: e.g. material which would figure as a verbal dependent clause in other languages becomes a nominal member of the principal clause in Marathi;
4. the presence of an ergative construction with specific conditions for object–predicate agreement;
5. an elaborate system of personal endings with many archaic variants.

NON-FINITE FORMS

infinitive: in *-ũ*: e.g. *karũ* 'to do'
supine: *-āyā/-āv^{a}yā*: takes certain case endings, e.g. with aditive, *bheṭāy^{a}lā yēṇẽ* 'to come to see someone'.
participles: imperfective with characteristic *-t-*, long and short forms: e.g. *karīt(ā)* 'doing'; shortened form: *karat*; perfective with characteristic *-(i)l/-(i)lel* + gender and personal marking: i.e. *kelā* 'having done' (irregular formation from *karũ̄* 'to do'); future participles: in *-ṇār* (invariable).
gerunds: imperfective: *-(i)tā/-(i)tānnā*; perfective: *-ūn*.

Examples: supine: *lihāy^{a}cā kāgad* 'writing paper'; *pyāy^{a}cē pāṇī* 'drinking water'; imperfective participle: *tī hasat mhaṇālī* 'laughing, she said'; perfective participle: *tyannī lihililī nāṭ^{a}kē* 'plays written by him'; gerund: *Tī māṇ^{a}sē jivant as^{a}tā mṛtā-samān* 'These people, though alive, are as good as dead.'

CONJUGATION

Synthetic forms:

(a) primary: simple past indicative, simple future, imperative;
(b) secondary: simple present formed from imperfective participle, simple past formed from perfective participle. Analytic forms: provided by participles plus auxiliary verb.

There are two conjugations:

(a) intransitive verbs: characteristic is *-a/e-*;
(b) transitive verbs: characteristic is *-i/ī-*.

NEGATION

na precedes certain verbal forms (future, optative, infinitive, etc.); *nā* follows inflected forms. *Nāhī* is the negative copula.

PERSONAL ENDINGS

		Past	*Future*	*Imperative*	*Simple present*		
					Masc.	*Fem.*	*Neut.*
Singular	1	-ẽ/-ī	-en/-in	-ũ	-to	-te	-te
	2	-es/-is	-(i)šil	ø	-tos	-tes	-tes
	3	-e/-i	-el/-il	-o	-to	-te	-te
Plural	1	-ũ	-ũ	-ũ		-to	
	2	-ā	-al	-a		-ta	
	3	-at/-it	-(i)til	-ot		-tat	

In the paradigm, all vowels are long; all first person forms are nasalized in both singular and plural; and past and simple present forms for the second person plural are also nasalized. The nasalization here is a stable feature inherited from southern Apabhraṁśa.

COMPOUND FORMS

The perfective participle is marked for person; the imperfective participle appears in the shortened form (e.g. *karat*) and is invariable.

Some examples of tenses in the indicative mood:

general present: e.g. *Vāgh ǰaṅg*^{a}*lāt rāh*^{a}*tāt* 'Tigers live in the jungle'
present continuous: e.g. *Āǰ phār gar*^{a}*mī hot āhe* 'Today is (being) very hot.'
In the colloquial the participle and the auxiliary tend to fuse: e.g. *kar*^{a}*to ahe* → *kar*^{a}*toy*^{h} = is doing
past habitual: e.g. *Te dar*^{a}*roǰ kāmālā ǰāt asat* 'They went every day to work'
future (presumptive): e.g. *To vidyārthī hoṇār* 'He's going to be a student'.
Passive: the locative case of the gerund of the sense-verb may be used + *yẽṇẽ* 'to come': *Tyālā ispit*^{a}*lā̃t neṇyā̃t ālẽ* 'He was taken to hospital.'

ERGATIVE

If the perfective participle or a related form appears in the predicate, this predicate agrees with the object which is in the direct state, while the logical subject is in the agentive: e.g. *mī̃ don bāy*^{a}*kā pāhily**ā*** 'I saw two women' (lit. 'by-me were seen ...').

A neutral construction is also possible in certain conditions, e.g. if no direct object is expressed: e.g. *putrā**nẽ** mhaṭ*^{a}***lẽ*** 'the son said'.

Double concord is also possible but only if the agent is second person singular pronoun: the predicate then agrees with the object in gender and number, but with the subject in person: cf. ***tū*** hẽ kām kelẽ*s* 'you did this work'; but *mī hẽ kām kelẽ*∅ 'I did this work'.

Postpositions

There is some duplication between case affixes and postpositions: e.g. *muṁbaīt* (locative case) = *muṁbaī madhye* 'in Bombay'.

Word order

SOV is basic in nominal construction.

पर्व ॥ १ ॥ प्रारंभीं शब्द होता आणि तो शब्द ईश्वराज
२ वळ होता आणि तो शब्द ईश्वर होता ॥ तोच प्रारंभीं ईश्वराज
३ वळ होता ॥ त्याने सर्व उत्पन्न केलीं आणि जें जालें तें त्याज
४ वांचून कांहीं उत्पन्न जालें नाहीं ॥ त्यामध्यें जीवन होतें आ
५ णि तें जीवन माणसांचा प्रकाश होता ॥ आणि तो प्रकाश अं
धारांत प्रकाशला आणि अंधाराने त्यास धरिलें नाहीं ॥
६ ईश्वरापासून पाठविला [असा] येक माणुस होता त्याचें नाव
७ योहान्न ॥ तोच आपणाकडून अवघ्यानीं विश्वास करावा ह्मणोन
८ त्या प्रकाशाविषईं साक्ष द्यावयास साक्षकरितां आला ॥ आप
ण तोच प्रकाश नव्हता परंतु त्या प्रकाशाविषईं साक्षी देण्यास
९ [आला] ॥

MONGOLIAN, MODERN

INTRODUCTION

Khalkha Mongolian is the official language of the Mongolian People's Republic, where it is spoken by about 2½ million people. Another 2 million speak it in the Inner Mongolian Autonomous Region of the CPR, with up to half a million in other areas of Northern China.

SCRIPT

For the Old Mongolian script, *see* **Appendix of Scripts**. In 1941 the Cyrillic alphabet was taken over en bloc for literary Khalkha, though not all of the Cyrillic letters are, in fact, required for the adequate representation of Mongolian phonemes. Two new letters had to be added: ө and ү. In comparison with the classical script, Cyrillic gives a closer, though still far from perfect, notation for Khalkha speech.

PHONOLOGY

Consonants

stops: p, b, t, d, g
affricates: ts, dz, tʃ, dʒ
fricatives: v, s, z, ʃ, x
nasals: m, n, ŋ
lateral and flap: l, ɫ, r
semi-vowels: j, w

An important distinction is made between vocalized consonants (the seven consonants /m, n, g, l, b, v, r/) and the non-vocalized (the remaining nine consonants). In what follows here, a *7* means one of the seven vocalized; a *9* means one of the others. The basic rule is that a *7* must be preceded or followed by a vowel; a *9* can follow a *7* without intervening vowel. Thus, if two consonants are in final position, the first must be a *7*, the second is *9*: e.g. *bold* 'steel'; *uls* 'country'.

In medial position, three consonants may be contiguous only if the middle one is a *9*: e.g. *boloxgüi* 'not allowed' = /bolxgwe/

Vowels

front: i, e
central: ə, ủ, ỏ
back: a, o, u

All occur both short and long, and all have several allophones. Thus the letter *i* for example, represents [i, ɪ, e]; *o* represents [ɔ, å, ɐ]. The symbol ʏ, represented here by *ủ*, is close to /ʉ/ when short, to /y/ when long; the symbol ɵ, represented here by *ỏ*, = /ə/ or /œ/: e.g, *ỏmỏn* 'south' /œmənə/, /œmᵊnə/.

Vowel length is phonemic: cf. *xol* 'far', *xool* 'food'. Long vowels are written doubled. Short vowels are given their full value only in first syllables; thereafter they tend to be reduced to /ə/. Final short vowels are notated in the script only after *g* and *n*. Thus *bagš* 'teacher' is actually /bagʃɪ/, which explains why the dative case is *bagšɪd*.

VOWEL HARMONY

The basic division is between front and back vowels; /i/ is neutral: e.g. *margaašaas* 'from tomorrow'; *ỏnỏỏdrỏỏs* 'from today'; *xoyordugaar* 'second'; *negdủgeer* 'first'. Certain final particles, e.g. the negative *gủi* /gwe/, are not affected by vowel harmony.

Stress

On first syllable if the word has no long vowel; otherwise on first long vowel.

MORPHOLOGY AND SYNTAX

Mongolian has no grammatical gender and no articles.

Noun

Case inflection is by affix marked for vowel harmony. As illustration, declension of *mal* 'cattle, livestock':

nominative	mal	ablative	malaas
accusative	maliig	instrumental	malaar
genitive	maliin	comitative	maltai
dative	mald		

n-stems: in these, the so-called 'fleeting' *n* is dropped in the nominative, but surfaces in certain oblique cases: e.g. *mori* 'horse': dat. *morind*; abl. *morinoos*.

The comitative affix *-tai* is used to indicate possession: e.g. *bi xoyor mori.tọi bain* 'I have two horses'.

NUMBER

Collective markers are affixed, e.g. *-nar*, *-uud*, *-čuud*: e.g. *nom* 'book', pl. *nomuud*; *zaluu* 'youth', pl. *zaluučuud*.

Double decension is frequent, with affixes strung together: e.g. *nȯxȯr* 'friend', gen. case *nȯxriin* + dative ending *-d* → *nȯxriind* 'at my friend's house'.

Adjective

As attribute, adjective precedes noun and is invariable: e.g. *ulaan nom* 'red book'; *ulaan nomuudtoi* 'having red books'.

COMPARATIVE

Made with the ablative case: e.g. *Ȯnȯȯdȯr ȯčigdrȯȯs dulaan* 'Today (it) is warmer than yesterday'.

Pronoun

The personal subject forms, with bases for oblique cases:

	Singular			*Plural*		
1	bi	obl. base	nad-	bid	obl. bases	bid-/man-
		except gen.	min-			
2	či		či-/ča-	ta		tan-

The third person forms are supplied by the demonstrative pronouns *ter* and *ene*, with plurals *ted*, *ed*; oblique bases: *tüü-*, *üün-*, *ted-*, *ed-*. The pronouns are declined in all cases. The plural form *ta* is used as the polite form of address for the singular.

INTERROGATIVE PRONOUN

xen 'who?'; *yu* 'what?'.

RELATIVE PRONOUN

None; for formation of relative sentences, *see* **Verb**.

Numerals

1–10; these are all *n*-stems except *xoyor* 2: *neg*(*en*), *xoyor*, *gurav*, *dürüv*, *tav*(*an*) *zurgaan*, *doloon*, *naim*(*an*), *ies*(*ȯn*), *arav*/*arvan*; 11 *arvan neg*; 12 *arvan xoyor*; 20 *xori*(*n*); 30 *guč*(*in*); 40 *dȯč*(*in*); 100 *zuu*(*n*).

Verb

The fundamental distinction is between perfective and imperfective aspects; each aspect has a tense system in which past is opposed to non-past. This yields four base forms, with each of which a specific affix is associated:

perfective past	*-v*	imperfective past	*-džee*
perfective non-past	*-laa*	imperfective non-past	*-na*

These forms are not marked for person and cannot be negated. For negation purposes, the verbal nouns are used plus the negative marker *-güi* /gwe/. Thus, the past system is negated by adding *güi* to the verbal noun in *-san*: e.g. *ter irev* 'he came': *ter irsen**güi*** 'he didn't come'. The non-past system uses the verbal noun in *-x* + *güi*: e.g. *bi meden* 'I know', *bi mede**xgüi*** 'I don't know'. The verbal noun in *-dag* is used to denote customary or repeated action: e.g. *ter Ulaanbaatart suudag* 'he lives (is resident in) Ulaan Baatar Xot'.

IMPERATIVE

The bare stem serves as a peremptory imperative: e.g. *yav* 'go!'. The ending *-aarai* is used for a polite request: e.g. *saiŋ yawaarai* lit. 'go well!' = 'goodbye'. The imperative is negated by *bitgii*: *bitgii yav* 'don't go'; the existential verb (copula) by *biš*: *bagš end biš* 'The teacher is not here.'

CONVERBS

These forms, which are always used in conjuction with finite verbs, play a crucially important part in Mongolian syntax by linking one action to another in various aspectual, temporal, sequential, and modal ways: e.g.

Converb in *-dž/č* (imperfective), used as holding device in sequence of verbs, closed by finite verb: *Bi doloon cagt boso**dž** öglöönii xool ide**dž**, nom unši**v*** 'I got up at seven, ate breakfast and read a book' (lit. 'rising ... eating ... I read ...'); *Nar garč, dulaan bolo**n*** 'When the sun rises, it gets/will get warm'; *nar garč, dulaan bolov* 'When the sun rose, it got warm.'

Converb in *-aad* (perfective) relates conclusion of one action to ensuing action(s): e.g. *Bid xuvcas ömsö**öd**, öglöönii xool id**eed**, nomın sand or**ood**, nom unšina* 'Having got dressed, eaten breakfast and gone to the library, we shall read books' (*xuvcas* 'clothes', *nomın san* 'library', *unšix* 'to read').

-saar refers to passage of time since an action, or result of that action: e.g. *Deed surguuld ors**oor** xeden džil bolov?* 'Since going to the university, how many years is it?' (*deed* 'big' *surguul* 'school', *džil* 'year').

CONDITIONAL/CONCESSIVE

-bal, e.g. *cas or**wol*** 'if it snows'; *dulaan bol**bol*** 'if it turns warm'.

TERMINATIVE

-tal, e.g. *ir**tel*** 'until ... come(s)'; *gar**tal*** 'until ... go(es)'.

RELATIVE CLAUSES

Verbal nouns are treated as attributive adjectives, e.g. *unšix nom* 'a book which is to be read'; *nom unši**dž** bai**gaa** xüüxed* 'the child who is reading the book'; *bidnii xii**sen** adžil* 'the work which we did'.

Postpositions

Postpositions follow nominative, genitive, ablative, or comitative cases: e.g.

with nominative: *dotor* 'in', e.g. *tasalgaan dotor* 'in the room';
with genitive: *tuxay* 'about', e.g. *šine baišingin tuxay* 'about the new building';
with ablative: *xoiš* 'after', e.g. *xuvisgalaas xoiš* 'after the revolution'.

Word order

SOV is basic.

31. Тэндэ Тӯни Эхэ
ахá дӯнэт ирэ̄т, газá бáйжи, Тӯни иргэхэé илэгэбэ.

32. Тэндэ улагхи Тӯни
хажӯда гхӯжи байсарá;
зарминин Тӯндӯ: мэнэ
Шини Эхэ ахадӯнэр, газá
бáйжи. Шамáй бэдэрнэ,
гэжи Тӯндӯ айлада.

33. Алатхада, Тэрэ зар-
лик болó: Мини Эхэ эгхэ-
гэбэл, Мини дӯнэр хэ̄т би?

34. Тигэт Тӯни хажӯда
гхӯкшиди ширтэн, ижи:
мэнэ Мини Эхэ, Мини
ахадӯнэр эдэ бáйна;

35. тэрэ юндаб гэхэдэ,
Бурхани дýрайги бӯтэ̄к-
ши, тэрэ Мини дӯ, ухин
дӯ, Эхэм мӯн, гэжи зар-
лик болó.

(Mark 3: 31–5)

NAMA

INTRODUCTION

The most important of the Hottentot languages (Khoisan family), Nama is spoken by about 40,000 in Namibia and by a further 50,000 Bergdama (who are non-Khoisan) in the same area. Nama is also spoken by a small group of Bushmen. Nama is the only Hottentot language with any form of writing (in Roman script).

PHONOLOGY

Consonants

p	m			
t	n	ts	s	r
k	k^h			
h	x			

CLICKS

These were defined by Beach (1938) in terms of 'influx' and 'efflux':

Four types of influx:

	Abrupt	*Affricate*
gingival	≠	/
post-alveolar	!	//

Five types of efflux:

		Glottal stop	*Glottal friction*
smooth velar	γ	ʔ	h
delayed velar	x		

Plus nasalization, notated as *n*.

Combining these, we get the following grid of click sounds:

≠(γ)	≠x	≠ʔ	≠h	≠n
/(γ)	/x	/ʔ	/h	/n
!(γ)	!x	!ʔ	!h	!n
//(γ)	//x	//ʔ	//h	//n

Vowels

i, e, a, o, u

/a/ is reduced to [ə] before certain vowels

Tone

There are three tones, high, middle and low; high is indicated by an acute accent, low by a grave.

MORPHOLOGY AND SYNTAX

Noun

Three genders: masculine, feminine, and common. Three numbers.

	Singular	*Dual*	*Plural*
masculine	-p, -i	-khà	-ku
feminine	-s	-rà	-tì
common	-'ì	-rà	-ìǹ -ǹ

Examples: */írip* 'male jackal'; */írís* 'female jackal'; */írí'ì* 'some jackal or other'. The female form may be suppletive: e.g. *tàtáp* 'fathe'; *màmás* 'mother'. Hagman (1977) points out an interesting transfer of gender marker to indicate departure from norm: *'oms* 'house'; *'omi* 'unusually large house'.

ASSOCIATIVE/GENITIVE RELATIONSHIP

The particle is *tì* following possessor, e.g. *'áop tì 'oms* 'the man's house'; *seetáfrikàp tí póótàp* 'the South African border'.

Adjective

Simple or derived. As attribute, adjective precedes noun, with *-xà* ending. Thus, from root *//am̃i* 'water', *//am̃xà !xáis* 'watery place'. The privative ending is *'o*: e.g. *//ám'o !xáis* 'waterless place'. Nama uses apposition also to express attribution: e.g. */ṓãp ≠xaríp* 'the boy, the small one' = 'the small boy'.

Pronoun

As specimen, the masculine forms in three numbers of first, second, and third persons:

	1st person		*2nd person*	*3rd person*
	Exclusive	*Inclusive*		
singular	tiíta	—	saáts	//'ĩĩp
dual	siíkxm̀	saákxm̀	saákxò	//'ĩĩkxà
plural	siíke	saáke	saáko	//'ĩĩku

Similarly for feminine: e.g. *tiíta – saás – //'ĩĩs*; and common dual/plural: e.g. *siím̀*

– saárò – //'ĩĩrà.

The common plural second person *saátù* yields the polite form of address.

POSSESSIVE PRONOUNS

tíí 'my', *sáá* 'your': e.g. *tíí 'oms* 'my house'.

DEMONSTRATIVE PRONOUN

nee 'this?'; *//nãã* 'that'.

INTERROGATIVE PRONOUN

tarí'ì 'who?'; *taré'ì* 'what?'.

Numerals

Decimal system: 1–10 are root words: */ úí, / ám, !noná, hàká, kóro, !naní, hũũ, //xáísá, kxòese, tìsí*; 100 *kái tìsí* 'big ten'.

'aa is used as an itemizer: e.g. *hàká tìsí !noná 'aa* '43 bits'.

Verb

Aspect and tense are distinguished by marker:

	Imperfective aspect	*Perfective aspect*	*Tense*
recent past	kòrò	kò hãà 'ií	kò
distant past	kèrè	kè hãà 'ií	kè
present	ra/ta	Ø hãà Ø	Ø
future	nĩĩ ra	nĩĩ hãà	nĩĩ
indefinite	kàrà	kà hãà Ø	kà

The personal pronouns can be used as verbal objects, but there is in addition a series of verbal suffixes marked for gender and person/number:

1st person: masc. *-te*, *-kxm̀*, *-ke*; fem. *-te*, *-'m̀*, *-se*; common *-'m̀*, *-ta*;
2nd person: masc. *-tsi*...
3rd person: masc. *-pi*...

Cf. *//'ĩĩku ke //'ĩĩpà kè mũũ* = *//'ĩĩku ke kè mũũ**pi*** 'they saw him', where the first version uses the full pronominal form, the second the pronominal suffix.

PASSIVE

The marker is *-hè*: cf.

'áop ke tarásà pérépà kè màa
'The man gave the woman bread'

tarás ke 'áop xaa pérépà kè màa**hè**
'The woman was given bread by the man' (*xaa* is postposition 'by'; *màa* 'give').

There are also reflexive (*-sn*) and reciprocal (*-ku*) suffixes.

STATIVE VERB
Tense marker + predicate + copula (*'ií* or Ø): e.g. *'áop ke kè !á͞i'ii* 'the man was good'.

NEGATIVE
tama + *kè*, *kò*, *kà*, Ø + *hà͞a* + *'ií* (for past tenses): e.g. *ná͞as ke !á͞i tama hà͞a* 'that is not good'.

MODAL VERBS
(Aux.) e.g. *//xáa* 'be able'; *//'óá* 'be unable'; *≠áó* 'to want to'; *//'i͞ip ke nee /ó͞ásà ra ≠áó* 'He wants this girl'.

Postpositions

Simple or compound: e.g. *'áí* 'on, at'; *!na͞a* 'in(to)'; */xáa* 'with'; *≠'oákunis /xáa* 'by plane'.

Word order

Structure of active verbal sentence: S + tense marker + (imperfective aspect marker) + active verb + (perfective aspect marker). The aspect markers are, of course, mutually exclusive.

Word order in general is flexible; items may be promoted or postponed for reasons of emphasis.

1 Koeroep nas ke koemssa ha ore koemss ke Tsoeikwap dewa hai, siihii koemss ke Tsoeikwaza.

2 Nees ke koeroep na Tsoeikwap dewa hai.

3 Howagoen ayip ka ke diihii, ooike ayip oossií goeigaree diitama, diihiikeenga.

4 Ayipnap ke oeiiba ha, oeiip ke kooin dii naapba.

5 Naapke kayp nara naa, oop ke kaypba nauoeg a bii tama ha.

6 Nabap ke kwii kooiba Tsoeikwapga ke tzii hii, tallip ons Johannip tamira kayhip.

7 Neep ke ha, naapgap nii hoeaaka, howan nii ayipga koemka.

8 Apip ke naatamaba, gaweep ke tziihii, naap gap nii mii ka.

NAVAJO

INTRODUCTION

Navajo, also spelled Navaho, belongs to the Apachean sub-group of the Athabaskan branch of the Na-Dené family. The Navajo call themselves *t'áá diné* 'the people', and the language is *diné bizaad* (*saad* 'words': ***bi.****zaad* 'his words'). Navajo is spoken by about 130,000 Indians in New Mexico, Arizona, Colorado, and South-East Utah. Almost alone among North American Indian languages it is on the increase, being widely used in the conduct of affairs in the Navajo Reservation, and in its local media, radio, journalism, and some literature.

SCRIPT

Roman alphabet plus ' for glottal stop in pre- or intervocalic position; consonants marked with ' are ejectives: *t'* = /t'/. Barred *ł* is used for /ł/; the cedilla is used to mark nasalization. High tone is marked by an acute accent.

PHONOLOGY

Consonants

Authorities differ as to the exact composition of the Navajo consonantal inventory. The following phonemes are generally accepted:

stops: p, t, k; th, kh; t', k', ʔ
/p, t, k/ are non-aspirated, unvoiced and are notated as b, d, g; the aspirates /th, kh/ are notated as t, k; the glottal stop is the most frequent sound in Navajo.
affricates: ts, ts', dz, tʃ, tʃ', dʒ
fricatives: s, z, ʃ, ʒ, γ, ç, h, x, γ°, x°; j, w
nasals: m, n
laterals: l, ł, tł, tł', dl
palatalization: the consonants k, g, t, x, h, are always palatalized before /e/ ké 'shoe' = /kh'é/ The same consonants are labialized before /o/: tó 'water' = /th°ó/.

Vowels

The basic series is:

i, e, a, o

Young and Morgan (1976) give three vowel lengths: short, long, over-long (before /d, '/). Length is phonemic: e.g. *bita'* 'between them' – *bitaa'* 'his father'. All vowels occur nasalized. Long vowels are written as digraphs.

Tone

High or low, plus two glides, rising and falling. The high tone is marked by the acute accent, the low tone is unmarked. In digraph vowels, an acute on the first component indicates falling glide; acute on the second marks rising tone.

MORPHOLOGY AND SYNTAX

There is no grammatical gender: e.g. *bi* 'he, she, it'.

Noun

There is a fairly small inventory of basic monosyllables, e.g. *sǫ'* 'star', *kǫ́'* 'fire', *dził* 'mountain'. Nouns involving inalienable possession, e.g. the parts of the body, family relationships, are cited with the impersonal possessive prefix *'a/'á*: e.g. *'akee'* 'foot' (necessarily belonging to someone), *'ála'* 'hand'. Certain verb forms may be used as derived nouns: *neest'ą́* 'it has matured' = 'fruit'; *'ólta'* 'reading is completed' = 'school'.

COMPOUNDS

Example: noun + noun: *tózis* 'waterbottle' (*tó* + *zis*); postposition + verb: *bee'eldǫǫh* 'gun' (*bee* 'with it'; *'eldǫǫh* 'makes an explosion').

NUMBER

Navajo has singular, dual, and different categories of plural, including a distributive plural, conceived as a grouping of individual items rather than a mere plurality. These refinements emerge in the verb; the noun itself is rarely marked for plurality, e.g. *dził* 'mountain(s)'. Kinship nouns take a specific ending in *-ke*, e.g. in Mark, 3.34: *kǫ́ǫ́ shimą́á dóó shi.tsilí**ké*** 'behold, my mother and my brethren'; *shiye'* 'my son' – *shiye'**ké*** 'my sons'.

POSSESSION

Phrases like 'the man's horse' are rendered as 'the man – his horse': *hastiin **bi**.łį́į́'*, where *bi-* is the third person possessive marker.

Adjective

Qualifying material is usually supplied by the third person forms of impersonal verbs – 'to be thick/sharp/green', etc. The relative formant *-ígíí* can be used: e.g. in Luke 5.36–9, 'new wine' is rendered as 'wine that is new': *wain ániid.**ígíí***.

There are also a few adjectival suffixes: e.g. *-tsoh* 'big', *-chil(í)* 'small': *dinétsoh* 'big man'; *łį́į́chilí* 'small horse'.

Pronoun

The independent subject pronouns are:

	Singular	*Dual*	*Distributive plural*
1	shí	nihí	danihí
2	ní	nihí	danihí
3	bí	bí	daabí
3a	hó	hó	daahó

3a is the impersonal form. These forms are prefixed to nouns as possessives: normally low tone, but certain nouns require a preceding possessive prefix to be high tone, e.g.

low tone series: *shi.tsii*' '(it is) my head', *ni.tsii*', etc.;
high tone series: *shí.la*' '(it is) my hand', *ní.la*', etc.

shi.*yáázh* ***bi.****chidí* 'my son's car'.

The pronominal forms are also used predicatively: e.g. *'eii łįį'* ***bí*** 'That horse is his'; lengthened, + glottal closure, the same form indicates acquisition: e.g. *'eii łįį'* ***bíí'*** *silįį'* 'That horse became his'.

DEMONSTRATIVE PRONOUN/ADJECTIVE
díí 'this, these'; *'eii* 'that, those'; *'éí* 'that' (remote).

INTERROGATIVE PRONOUN
háa 'where?'; *háishą'* 'who?'; *ha'át'íishą'* 'what?'. Cf. Matthew, 12.48: *Háishą'* ***shi.****má nilį, áádóó háishą'* ***shi.****tsilíké danilį* 'Who is my mother and who are my brethren?' (*nilį/danilį* 'is/are').

Numerals

1–10: *łáá'ii, naaki, táá', dįį', 'ashdla', hastą́ą́, tsosts'id, tseebíí, náhást'éí, neezná.* 11–19: the format is, unit – *ts* – *'áadah*: e.g. 11 *ła'ts'áadah,* 12 *naakits'áadah.* 20 *naadiin*; 21 *naadįįła'*; 22 *naadiinaaki*; 30 *tádiin*; 40 *dízdiin*; 100 *neeznádiin*.

Verb

Semantically and formally, Navajo verbs can be divided into two categories:

(a) Static verbs, including adjectivals; these have perfective or continuative form alone, and are thus conjugated.

(b) Dynamic or active verbs: these generally focus on certain physical properties of their objects, e.g. *shosh* 'to place slender, stiff objects side by side, e.g. planks across a stream', *mas* 'to roll a round object'. Here, dictionary definitions often appear to be no more than a catalogue of basic activities, but many of these roots yield impressive mytho-poeic metaphors in modern Navajo;

e.g. *'ááł* 'to handle a round, bulky object', is used of the sun-bearer, who 'carries the sun' across the sky.

Some active stems are coded for number; thus, the stem *tééł* 'to lie down' (with reference to a singular referent) – *tish* 'to lie down', (with reference to two persons) – *jah* (plural).

In both (a) and (b) the root is a monosyllable CV or CVC. The initial C is subject to consonantal sandhi at juncture with preceding prefixes and classifiers. The root itself is a variable which appears in several differentiations, each of which has specific aspectual and/or modal meaning. For active roots, these are future, imperfective, continuative, perfective, reiterative, optative, progressive, neutral, habitual. Not all of these are in use for every root. Those actually in use are listed, for any given root, in a Navajo–English dictionary. Thus, the entry for the root meaning 'to say (it)' appears in the Young–Morgan dictionary (in 1976: 165) as follows:

niił, niih (ní), niid, 'niih, ne'

these being the future, imperfective (continuative), perfective, reiterative, and optative bases. For each of these, the requisite personal prefixes are then listed. Six forms are normally sufficient to provide all twelve forms of the personal pronoun grid (*see* **Pronoun**, above): for *niił*: *dideesh, didíí, didoo, jididoo, didii, didooh*: the paradigm for the future base:

	Singular	*Dual*	*Plural (three or more)*
1	dideesh.niił	didii'.niił	dadidii'.niił
2	didíí.niił	didooh.niił	dadidooh.niił
3	didoo.niił	didoo.niił	dadidoo.niił
3a	jididoo.niił	jididoo.niił	dazhdidoo.niił

It will be seen that the six forms given in the dictionary cover the singular and the dual first and second persons. Thereafter, the same forms recur, with *da-* prefix in the plural, and syncope in 3a.

It should not be imagined that the pronominal prefixes given here are valid for other verbs: there are hundreds of variants: for example, the pronominal series for the future base of the root *t'ąs – t'ąs – t'ą́ą́z – t'ąs – t'ąąs* 'to cut in spiral fashion', is: *náhidínées – náhidíníił – néidínóol – náhizhdínóol – náhidíníil – náhidínóoł*.

The tense system is based on the available stems, e.g. the present tense is formed from the imperfective or the continuative stem + a specific pronominal series: e.g. from *jił* 'to carry something along on one's back': sing. *yishjił – yiłjił – yoołjił*; dual: *yiiljił – ghołjił*. A past tense is formed from the perfective aspect, again with its specific pronominal series: e.g. from *ghał* 'to eat it': *yishghal – yinílghal – yoolghal*.

Certain periphrastic forms are available for future and past: e.g. *yishą́* 'I'm eating it' – *yishą́ą́* ***dooleeł*** 'I'll be eating it' – *yishą́ą́* ***ńt'*éé*** 'I was eating it'.

NEGATION

By circumfix, *doo...da*: e.g. *dayoosdlą́ą́d* 'they believed'; ***doo*** *dayoosdlą́ą́d* ***da*** 'they did not believe'.

OBJECT PRONOUN

In the verbal complex, the object pronoun immediately precedes the pronominal prefix + base unit; the *-l-* classifier (see below) may intervene: e.g. ***shi.****didoo.niił* 'he will say it to me'; ***bi.****didíí.niił* 'you (sing.) will say it to him'.

CLASSIFIERS

These precede the stem: *-ł-* causative, *-l-* passive: cf. *hółbį'* 'you are building a hogan', *halbį'* 'a hogan is being built'; *ńdiíłtłoh* 'you will make it wet', *ńdiíltłoh* 'you will get wet'.

These examples are from Young and Morgan (1976).

PREFIXES

Navajo has a large inventory of verbal prefixes which confer specific modal and directional meanings on verb complexes: e.g.

'ahá: conveys idea of bisection, e.g. *'ahádeeshgish* 'I'll cut it in two' (root *gish*);
ch'í: making a linear exit, e.g. *ch''ídeeshááł* 'I'll go out' (e.g. from a house) (root *gaal*);
hada: downward motion, e.g. *hada.díí.tłish* 'you'll fall down' (root *tłish*).

Order of items in verbal complex: prefix – pronominal subject – object – classifier – stem.

RELATIVE CLAUSE

The relative formants *ígíí* and *ii* are widely used. *shił nizaad.ígíí* 'the one (place) that I think is far' (*shi.ł* 'according to me'; *nizaad* 'far').

Postpositions

Young and Morgan list about 50 of these; they are usually cited with the 3rd person pronoun *bi-*, e.g. *bi.k'ee* 'on account of him'; *bi.náká* 'through it'; *bi.ł* 'with him'; *bi.deijígo* 'above it': *góne'* in. *'atiin bi.deijígo tsin 'íí'á* 'Above the trail stands a tree.'
sodizin bá hooghan góne' ná'át'oh doo bee haz'ą́ą da 'smoking is not permitted inside the church' (where *sodizin bá hooghan* 'house of prayer', 'church'; *góne'* 'in'; *ná'át'oh* 'smoking'; *bee haz'ą́ą* 'permitted'; *doo...da* is negating circumfix.)

Word order

Free as regards S,V,O in nominal sentence; order of components in verbal complex is of course fixed.

Saad jílíinii

1 Hodeeyáadi Saad hojíló̜, 'éí Saad Diyin God bił
hojíló̜, 'índa 'éí Saad Diyin God jílį́. 2 T'áá 'éí hodeeyáadi
Diyin God bił hojíló̜; 3 t'áá'ałtsoní hanahjį' dahazlį́į́',
'índa dahólónígíí t'áałá'í ndi t'áá hádingo t'áadoo ła' da-
hazlį́į' da. 4 'Iiná hwii' hóló̜, 'áko 'éí 'iiná nihokáá' dine'é
bee bá 'adińdíín. 5 'Éí 'adińdíín chahałheełjį' 'adiníłdíín,
'áko chahałheeł doo bidéé łníi da.

John 'adińdíín yaa ch'íhoní'ą́

6 Diné léi' John wolyéego, Diyin God bits'ą́ą́dóó yíl'a'.
7 T'áá hó hwee 'ééhózin doo biniyé jiníyá, 'adińdíín nilíi-
nii baa ch'íhozhdoo'áałgo, diné t'áá'ałtso hanahjį' da'iidoo-
dląął biniyé. 8 Hó 'éí doo 'adińdíín jílį́į da, ndi 'adińdíín
t'óó baa ch'íhozhdoo'ááł biniyé jiníyá.

NEPALI

INTRODUCTION

In the *Linguistic Survey of India*, Grierson (1903–28) classified Nepali as belonging to Eastern Pahari (see Zograph 1982). The linguistic continuum in north-west India is one of great complexity; dialects overlap and merge into one another, with few hard and fast boundaries. Nepali itself seems to be a composite language consisting of (a) an Indo-Aryan substratum of Śauraseni type, which was the language of the Khasa tribes in the Himalayan foothills some two thousand years ago, an ancestry which survives in the local name of the language – Khas Kurā (*kurā* 'speech'); (b) the related New Indo-Aryan language brought to Central Nepal by the Rajput invaders in the mid-eighteenth century, a development associated with the rise of the Gurkhas; (c) the new literary standard fostered by press and radio, which makes heavy demands on the Sanskrit reservoir; and finally, (d) one should mention the pervasive influence, especially in the more outlying colloquials, of the Tibeto-Burman languages – e.g. Newari – which have always surrounded the Pahari languages.

Nepali is now the official language of the Kingdom of Nepal where it is spoken by about 8 million people. It is also spoken by substantial minorities in Sikkim, Bhutan, parts of Assam, and in Darjeeling. The first tentative steps towards a literary language were taken in the eighteenth/nineteenth centuries along traditional Indian lines (a version of the *Rāmāyaṇa* by Bhānubhakta Ācāryā). The modern literary language is based on the Kathmandu norm.

SCRIPT

Devanagari.

PHONOLOGY

Consonants

stops: p, b, t, d, ʈ, ɖ, k, g; all with aspirates: ph, th, etc.
affricates: tʃ, dʒ with aspirates
fricatives: v, s, ʂ, ʃ, j, h
nasals: m, n, ɳ, ɲ, ŋ
lateral and flap: l, r, ɽ, ɽh

Vowels

ə, i, e, a, o, u

All occur long and short, except /oː/ which is long only. All occur nasalized: nasalization is marked either by *candrabindu* or by *anusvār (see* **Sanskrit**). There are two diphthongs: /əy/, /əw/, also nasalized. Nasalization and stress are phonemic; length is not.

MORPHOLOGY AND SYNTAX

Noun

There are no articles. Gender plays little part in Nepali structure, though the markers of its historical presence could hardly be entirely absent from a New Indo-Aryan language. Very generally, in nouns denoting human beings, *-o*, *-ā* are masculine endings, *-ī* is feminine: e.g. *chorā* 'son', *chorī* 'daughter'. The basic opposition in Nepali is human/non-human, and this is reflected in the use of the acc./dat. marker *-lāī* (see below).

Plural: the all-purpose suffix is *-harū*, added to the singular form.

DECLENSION

Genitive: the affix is *-ko*/*kī* for masculine/feminine; *-kā* for plural: e.g. *chorāko kitab* 'the boy's book'; *Nepālkā šaharharū* 'the cities of Nepal'.

Acc./dat. *-lāī* marks the oblique case, with reference to human beings: e.g. *bābu chora**lāī** lin.cha* 'the father takes the son'; *timī**lāī*** 'to you'; *bābu pustak**Ø** lin.cha* 'the father takes the book'.

The instrumental/agentive marker is *-le*. The locative *-mā*: e.g. *Annapūrṇā paščim Nepālmā cha* 'Annapurna is in Western Nepal'; *may.le* 'by me'.

Adjective

As attribute, adjective precedes noun. Many are invariable; those in *-o* change this to *-ī* for feminine and *-ā* for plural. In the colloquial, the *-o* form suffices for both numbers: e.g. *rāmrā vidyārthī.harū* 'good students'; *rāmrī chorī* 'good girl'.

Pronoun

Socio-linguistically complex in that there are three possible forms for second and third persons, depending on social status of person spoken to or of:

first person: the sole form is *ma*, pl. *hāmī*(*harū*);
second person: low grade *tã*; middle grade *timī*; high grade sing. *tapāī̃*, pl. *tapāī̃harū*;
third person: low grade *u*/*yo*; middle grade *yinī*/*unī*, pl. *yinīharū*/*unīharū*; high grade *yahā̃*/*vahā̃*, pl. *yahā̃harū*. Example in high grade: *Tapāī̃.ko jāt ke ho* 'Sir, what is your caste?'

The gender distinction made in the verb, where the second and third persons have masculine and feminine forms, is not reflected in the pronominal system.

POSSESSIVE PRONOUN

The forms are *mero/-ī/-ā* 'my'; *hamro*, etc. 'our'; *tapāĩko*, etc. 'your'.

DEMONSTRATIVE PRONOUN/ADJECTIVE

Sing. *yo*, pl. *yī* 'this, these'; *tyo*, *tī* 'that, those'.

INTERROGATIVE PRONOUN

ko 'who?'; *ke* 'what?'

RELATIVE PRONOUN

The *jo* (oblique *jas*)/*je* formula exists (*see* **Hindi**) but relative clauses are more idiomatically expressed by means of the participle in *-ne*, or the first perfect participle in *-eko*: e.g.

Kāṭhmāṛəw̃ ǰā**ne** bas 'the bus which is going to Kathmandu'

bholi āu**ne** vidyārthī 'the student who is coming tomorrow'

hijo ā**eko** mānche 'the man who came yesterday'

Numerals

1–10: standard New Indo-Aryan forms; beyond 10 the numerals are unpredictable as regards individual form, though the overall pattern agrees with that in other NIA languages, with decade + 9 linked to the following decade; e.g. 30 *tīs*; 38 *aṭhtīs*; 39 *unancālīs*; 40 *cālīs*, 100 *ek say*.

Verb

In certain features – personal and impersonal forms, finite and non-finite, simple tenses (stem + personal ending), compound tenses (participle + conjugated auxiliary) – the Nepali verb conforms to the standard New Indo-Aryan model. It has, however, three unique features: (a) specific negative forms for many tenses; (b) a future in *-lā*; (c) a semi-ergative construction with transitive verbs: the participial predicate agrees with the *subject*, which is, however, in the oblique (agentive) case.

The infinitive is in *-nu*: e.g. *garnu* 'to do', with secondary forms in *-na* (the verbal noun) and *-nā* (used with postpositions). From this, the primary base is found by dropping *-nu*. The following participles are formed on this base or on a secondary associated base:

1st perfect:	*-eko*
2nd perfect:	*-e*
imperfect:	*-da/do/dā/dəy*
conjunctive:	*-era*, *-ī*, *-īkana*
infinitival:	*-ne*

The two auxiliaries *cha* (locative, existential) and *ho* (copula) are fully conjugated. There are imperative, indicative, and optative moods.

INDICATIVE MOOD

Specimen tense formation of *garnu* 'to do', primary base *gar-*:

simple indefinite: primary base + *cha*: e.g. *ma garchu* 'I do', *unī garcha* 'he does', *garche* 'she does'
present continuous: imperfect participle + *cha*: e.g. *ma gardəy chu* 'I am doing'
simple past: stem + endings: *-ẽ*, *-is*, *-yo*; pl. *-yə̃w*, *-yəw*, *-e*: e.g. ***məyle** garẽ* 'I did'
two perfect tenses: 1st/2nd perfect participle + *cha*: subject in agentive: e.g. ***məyle** gareko chu/garechu* 'I have done'
future: base + endings: *-ũla, -lās, -lā*; pl. *ə̃wlā, əwlā, -lān*; e.g. *ma garũlā* 'I shall do'

IMPERATIVE MOOD

The honorific imperative is made by adding *-hos* or *-holā* to the infinitive: e.g. *garnu.hos* 'do!'; *Basnuhos/Basnuholā* 'Please take a seat' (*basnu* 'to sit'). This form is negated by prefixing *na-*: e.g. *na.garnu.hos* 'don't do!'.

OPTATIVE MOOD

The endings of the optative or injunctive mood are shown here, attached to *gar-*:

	Singular	*Plural*
1	garũ̄	garə̃w
2	gares	gare
3	garos	garūn

Example: *bholi pānī na.paros* 'Let it not rain tomorrow!' (*parnu* 'to fall').

PASSIVE

-i is added to the base: e.g. *garinu* 'to be done'; *sunincha* 'it is heard'; *dekhincha* 'it is seen'.

CAUSATIVE

-āu/-ā is added to base– e.g. *gar**ā**unu* 'to cause to do'.

NEGATIVE CONJUGATION

As mentioned above, all Nepali verbs have parallel negative conjugations. Thus the simple indefinite negative of *garnu* is:

	Singular	*Plural*
1	gardina	gardəynə̃w
2	gardəynas	gardəynəw
3	gardəyna	gardəynan

The second and third person forms are masculine. The negative endings are added directly to consonantal stems such as *gar-*. Vocalic stems are nasalized before the endings are attached: e.g. from *jā-* 'to go': *ma jā̃dina* 'I do not go'. The negative of *che* is *chəyna*; of *ho*, *hoina*.

Some grammars give as many as 24 tense/aspect paradigms in the indicative mood, about half of these being doublets; e.g. *gareko cha* 'he did/has done', with doublets *gare cha* and *gareko ho*.

Postpositions

Examples: *-mā* 'in', *-bāṭa* 'with, from', *-sita* 'at'. *Sita* is used to express the verb 'to have'; *sãga* is also used: e.g. *Ma.sãga pəysa chəyna* 'I have no money on me'; *gar.nā.ko lāgi* 'so as to do'

Word order

SOV.

१ थाल्नि माँ बचन् थियेा अनि बचन् भगुवान् सङ्
२ थियेा अनि बचन् भगुवानै थियेा। उ थाल्नि माँ
३ भगुवान् सङ थियेा। सबै थाेक् का सिर्जना उइ
देखि भयेा अनि ज्ये सिर्जायेकेा छ क्येइ थाेक् पनि
४ उ बिना सिर्जायेकेा छैन। उस् माँ जीउँनि थियेा
अनि त्यो जीउँनि मान्छे हरु का उज्यालेा थियेा।
५ अनि त्यो उज्यालेा अँध्यारेा माँ चम्कन्दै छ तर
अँध्यारेा ले त्येस्लाइ माँन्येन॥
६ एक् जना मान्छे भगुवान् का पट्टि बाटेा पठाईयेा
७ त्येस्को नाँउ योहन् थियेा। त्येस्को बाटेा ले सबै
जना ले पत्त्याउन् भन्ने खातिर् ले त्यो उज्यालेा का
बिषय् माँ साँचि दिँनु लाइ उ साँचि का लागि आयेा।
८ उ आफै ता त्यो उज्यालेा थियेन तर त्यो उज्यालेा
९ का बिषय् माँ साँचि दिँनु लाइ आयेा।

NIVKH

INTRODUCTION

Presumably an isolated Palaeo-Siberian language, Nivkh (also known as Gilyak) is of doubtful affinity. Some connection with American Indian languages and with the Tungus family has been pointed out. It is spoken by around 3,000 to 4,000 people on the lower Amur and on the island of Sakhalin.

SCRIPT

In the 1930s a Roman-based script was introduced, with a switch to Cyrillic in 1953: the following additional letters were used: *g, q, γ,* ꞔ (the last of these represents the voiced fricative /ʁ/). At present, Nivkh does not appear to be written.

PHONOLOGY

Consonants

stops: p, b, t, d, k, g, q, ɢ
affricate: tʃ'
fricatives: f, v, s, z, x, γ, χ, h, ʁ
nasals: m, n, ɲ, ŋ
lateral and trill: l, r, ř = ɾ
semi-vowel: j

Palatalized t′,d′ occur, and aspirated p', t', k', q'.

CONSONANTAL ALTERNATION

This characteristic feature of Nivkh affects word-initial and suffix-initial consonants, the mutation being triggered by the final of the preceding word or syllable. Typical mutation series are: /p – v – b; t – r – d; t′ – z – d′; k – γ – g/. There are about 20 such series; inspection of them shows, for example, that no Nivkh word has a citation form with voiced plosive initial: cf. *tɪf* 'house' (citation form): /t/ → /r/ after /k/, e.g. *ɪtɪk rɪf* 'father's house'; /t/ → /d/ after vowel, e.g. *oγlagu* ***dɪf*** 'children's home'.

Vowels

i, ɛ, a, ɪ, o, u

The long vowels /iː, aː, oː, uː/ also occur, mostly as a result of the elision of the velar and uvular spirants /γ/ and /ʁ/: e.g. [oːla] 'boy' < /oγla/. Vowel length is phonemic: cf. *t'ūr* 'fire', *t'ur* 'peas'. In this article, /ɛ/ is notated as *ẹ*.

MORPHOLOGY AND SYNTAX

Noun

The noun is marked for number, case, and possession.
The plural marker is *-ku* + allophones *-xu*, *-gu*, etc. depending on the nature of the final consonant: e.g. *ɪtɪk* 'father', pl. *ɪtɪk.xu*; *oγla* 'boy', pl. *oγla.gu*. Reduplication is also used to form plurals.

CASE SYSTEM
Absolute/nominative + seven oblique, e.g. from *ɪtɪk* 'father': *ɪtɪk.ax* (dat./acc.), *ɪtɪk.rox* (dat./adit.), *ɪtɪk.uin* (loc,), *ɪtɪk.γir* (instr.).

POSSESSION
The markers are sing. 1 *n'i*, 2 *či*, 3 *p'i*; e.g. *n'rɪf* 'my house', *črɪf* 'your house'; *p'rɪf* 'his/her house; one's own house'. Third singular prefixes: *i-*, *e-*, *vi-*, etc. may also be used.

Adjective

Non-existent in Nivkh; all qualification is expressed verbally.

Pronouns

PERSONAL INDEPENDENT
Sing. 1 *n'i*, 2 *či*, 3 *yif*; dual 1 *mẹgi*; pl. 1 *n'ɪŋ* (excl.), *mer* (incl.), 2 *čɪŋ*, 3 *yivŋ*. There are several variants for these, especially for the third person plural. The pronouns are declined in all cases: e.g. in first person singular: *n'ax* 'to me/me' (acc.); *n'ux* 'from me'; *n'iγir* 'by me', etc. Pronominal direct and indirect objects are expressed by personal pronominal prefixes: e.g. *yif n'rod'* 'he (*yif*) helped me (*n'*)'; *n'i yi.z.n.ɪ.d'* 'I'll call him' (where *-nɪ-* is the future marker).

DEMONSTRATIVE PRONOUN/ADJECTIVE
tɪd' 'this' (prox.); *(a)hɪd'* (distal); *kud'* 'that' (absent, but formerly mentioned).

INTERROGATIVE/RELATIVE PRONOUNS
aŋ/aγ 'who(m), whose', *sid'* 'what'; *řad'* 'who, which of several, whose': cf. *Tɪd' řad' rɪvŋa* 'Whose house is this?'; *Aŋ nɪd'nɪ.dox q'aud'*, *hɪd' yin'.dox q'aud'* 'He who does not work, does not eat' (for negative construction with *-dox q'aud'*, see below).

Numerals

Nivkh has specific sets of numerals for the enumeration of various categories of objects – boats, people, animals, fishing-nets, small round objects, long thin objects, etc. Panfilov (1962) lists 26 such sets. For example, 'three' with reference to people is *t'aqr*; to animals, *t'or*; to boats, *t'ẹm*; to sweep-nets, *t'for*; etc. It is noteworthy that the palatalized *t'* remains stable as initial in all variants, and the same stability applies in other numbers. Thus, *n'* is the initial for the 26 variants of *n'im* 1, and *m* is the initial for all variants of *mim* 2.

Verb

The Nivkh verb has voice, aspect, mood, and tense in affirmative, negative, interrogative, and affective versions. Quantitative aspects of the action may also be expressed.

VOICE

Active, hortative, reflexive, reciprocal. There is no passive voice as such: thus, *xa n'ivx* 'the man who is shooting' *or* 'the man being shot at'.

The base or active voice comprises intransitive verbs, two sets of transitive verbs (the first set with the object in absolute case, the second with the object in dative/aditive case), and the reflexive verbs with a *p'*- prefix: e.g. *ɪtɪk vid'* 'father goes'; *Muinɪ n'ivx **p'**alγazid'* 'The sick man resigned himself to his fate.'

ASPECT

Perfective, reiterative, habitual, durative; e.g. the perfective aspect is marked by *-γɪt*, often plus reduplication of base: *Utkuoʁla mu xorixori.γɪt.t'* 'The boy stopped rowing the boat.' Reiterative, intensifying, and habitual aspectual forms also show reduplication, the latter plus *-xɪ*: e.g. *ɪtɪk vivi.xɪ.d'* 'father likes to walk'. Aspect markers may be compounded.

Intensification of action or quality may also be expressed by phonetic change: initial surd → related voiced stop: e.g. *tuzla-* 'cold' – ***duzla-*** 'very cold'.

A general indicative mood marker is *-d'/t'* (cf. the demonstrative endings), to which the pluralizing affix *-ku/xu/gu* etc. may be added. Tense: past/present marker is null; future has *-nɪ*. The verb is marked for person only in the imperative mood which shows 1, 2, 3 sing., 1, 2, 3 plural, and 1 dual.

Other moods include an inferential or presumptive, made with the endings *-uvr/ɪvr* etc. + *iaγalo*: e.g,. *Čai q'avd'**avr** iaγalo?* 'The tea is (presumably) hot?'; also a conditional and a concessive.

Nivkh has a wide range of participial and gerundial forms which retain tense, aspect, and voice identity, are not declined, and make a plural form by reduplication. For example, a temporal clause formant in *-(f)kẹ*: *Či mat'kak**ẹ*** *čɪtɪk mud'* 'When you were small, your father died'; and a form in *-pa/-ba* meaning 'as soon as': *yif tɪftox p'rɪ**ba*** 'as soon as he comes home'.

NEGATION
E.g. by affix *-tox*/*-dox* + *q'aud'* as auxiliary: *yif p'rɪ***dox** *q'au.γit.lẹ* 'he didn't come', *lɪx kɪ***dox** *q'au.ŋan* 'when it doesn't rain'; and as attribute: *pil.***dox** *q'au dɪf* 'a not-so-big house'. Used by itself *q'aud'* means 'is/are not': e.g. *Naf toluin čo q'aud'* 'Now there's no fish in the sea' (*čo* 'fish').

Postposition

Nivkh uses postpositions.

Word order

SOV is normal. There is no ergative construction in Nivkh.

NORWEGIAN

INTRODUCTION

Norwegian is a member of the Scandinavian branch of the Germanic family of the Indo-European languages. It is spoken by about 4 million people.

From the fourteenth to the early nineteenth century Norway was part of Denmark, and Danish was the written, and, at least as far as the educated and urbanized classes were concerned, the spoken language of the country. With the end of Danish hegemony in the nineteenth century, nationalistic demands began to make themselves heard for 'pure' or 'rural' Norwegian, harking back via the many dialects to the Old Norse of the Middle Ages, in preference to the alien, though genetically very closely connected, Danish. Groups of intellectuals explored the potentialities of various dialects in search of a basis for a *landsmål* or popular speech, to replace the Danish norm of the *riksmål* or state language. Here, a crucial part was played by Ivar Aasen, whose grammar, based on the very conservative West coastal dialects, appeared in 1864, to be followed by a dictionary in 1873. Of course, a Doric, however pure linguistically, was bound to have an uphill struggle against the social prestige and the economic use-value of the Dano-Norwegian *riksmål*, and it took the rest of the century for a somewhat artificial construct like *landsmål* to emerge as a serious contender. The Nynorsk, 'New Norwegian', that took shape from Aasen's pioneer work, received official sanction in 1884; and by 1892 individual schools were empowered to choose it as language of instruction, in preference to Standard Norwegian. In 1907, an orthographical reform changed the Dano-Norwegian intervocalic voiced plosives *b*, *d*, *g* to their unvoiced counterparts *p*, *t*, *k*, thus falling into line with actual Norwegian pronunciation. A further reform in 1917 brought more sectors of *riksmål* – or *bokmål* as it was by then known – into line with *landsmål* usage. In 1938–9 an attempt was made to create a new unified norm – *samnorsk*. This never got off the ground.

Today, both Standard Norwegian and Nynorsk are joint official languages of Norway. Theoretically, they have equal status, and are used at all levels and in all walks of life. In practice, however, Standard Norwegian remains very much in the ascendant. Only about 16 or 17 per cent of Norwegians – resident mainly in the coastal fringe and in the central mountains – actually speak Nynorsk as mother tongue, and this percentage is reflected in Nynorsk's share of the media. The urban population remains solidly committed to Standard Norwegian, the leading language of administration, business, and the media.

In all linguistic matters, the Norsk Språkråd acts in an advisory capacity for the Norwegian government.

Since formally *bokmål* differs little from Danish (*see* **Danish**), Nynorsk forms are mainly considered here.

SCRIPT

The Roman alphabet + *æ*, *ø*, *å*.

PHONOLOGY

Consonants

stops: p, b, t, d, k, g
fricatives: f, v, ç, s, ʃ, j, h
nasals: m, n, ŋ
lateral and flap: l, r

Retroflex /ʈ, ɖ, ɳ, ɭ/ occur in *bokmål* and in eastern dialects. Geminated consonants are long.

Vowels

Notated as *i*, *y*, *e*, *ø*, *æ*, *a*, *å*, *u*, *ʉ*; all occur long or short *i* represents /i/ and /ɪ/; *e* represents /e/ and /ɛ/; *ø* = /œ/; *å* = /ɔ/. Unstressed *e* tends to become /ə/.
Diphthongs: /ei, œ, ai, aʉ, ɔy/. That is, Nynorsk retains Old Norse diphthongs.

Tones

Two tones or pitch contours are distinguished: one is a rising tone (single tone) used in all monosyllables; the other is a falling–rising tone (double tone) used in polysyllables.

Stress

Nearly always on first syllable.

MORPHOLOGY AND SYNTAX

Noun

Uniquely among the Scandinavian languages, Nynorsk retains a distinct feminine gender with a specific indefinite article: masc. *ein*, fem. *ei*, neut. *eit*. Masculine and feminine definite articles coalesce into *den*; neuter, *det*.

DECLENSION
Typical series for three genders: indefinite, definite with affixed article, plural indefinite, plural definite with affixed article:

masc.	ein fiskar	fiskar**en**	fiskar**ar**	fiskar**ane**	'fisherman'
fem.	ei jente	jent**a**	jent**er**	jent**ene**	'girl'
nt.	eit hus	hus**et**	hus**Ø**	hus**a**	'house' (*huset* = /husɛ/)

Umlaut of the stem vowel takes place in certain types of masculine and feminine nouns: masc. *son* 'son' – *søner*; *bonde* 'farmer' – *bønder*; fem. *hand* 'hand' – *hender*; *bok* 'book' – *bøker*

The old *-i* declension of feminine nouns is retained in certain dialects: e.g. *ei sky* 'a cloud': *sky**i*** – *sky**er*** – *sky**ene***.

Adjective

Typically, the Nynorsk adjective is marked for masculine/feminine (common form), neuter and plural in strong form: e.g. *hard* – *hard**t*** – *hard**e*** 'hard'; *ny* – *ny**tt*** – *ny**e*** 'new'; and by *-e* for all three genders and both numbers in the weak form: e.g. *den*, *det*, *dei*, *harde* ...

COMPARISON

The comparative is made with *-are*: e.g. *farleg* 'dangerous' – *farleg**are***. As in other Germanic languages certain adjectives have suppletive comparative forms: e.g. *god* – *betre* – best; *liten* 'small' – *mindre*.

Pronouns

		Singular			*Plural*		
		Subject	*Object*	*Possessive*	*Subject*	*Object*	*Possessive*
1		eg	meg	min	vi/me	oss	vår
2		du	deg	din	de/De	**dykk/Dykk**	**Dykkar**
3	masc.	han	han/honom	hans			
	fem.	ho	henne	hennar	dei	dei	deira
	nt.	det	det	(dess)			

Min, *din*, *vår* are inflected for gender and number: e.g. *min*, fem. *mi*, neut. *mitt*, pl. *mine*.

There is a tendency in Nynorsk to insert possessive pronouns such as *hans* and *hennar* between the nouns in a genitive relationship: e.g. *far **hans** Per* 'Per's father'; *bror **hennar** Lise* 'Lise's brother'.

DEMONSTRATIVE PRONOUNS

denne	– dette	– desse	'this, these'
den	– det	– dei	'that, those'

The latter is used as definite article for an adjective + noun complex: ***den** gamle **mannen*** 'the old man'; ***det** nye **huset*** 'the new house' (i.e. duplication of marker).

INTERROGATIVE PRONOUNS

kven 'who?', *kva* 'what?'

RELATIVE PRONOUN

som, *då*. These are invariable; *som* can be omitted if it is not the subject of a relative clause.

Numerals

1–10: *ein/ei/eitt*; *to*, *tre*, *fire*, *fem*, *seks*, *sju*, *åtte*, *ni*, *ti*; 11 *elleve*; 12 *tolv*; 13 *tretten*; 20 *tjue*; 30 *tretti*; 40 *førti*; 100 *hundre*.

Verb

Strong/weak, transitive/intransitive. Extreme reductionism: all verbs have one form for all persons in the present, and, similarly, one past form.

Compound tenses are made with the auxiliaries *å vera* 'to be', *å ha* 'to have'. The present and past forms of these are: *vera*: *er*, *var*; *ha*: *ha*, *hadde*.

There are four formal classes of weak verb: e.g.

1. Single ending *-a*(*r*): *å fiska* 'to fish': pres. *fiskar* /fiska/; past *fiska*; pp. *fiska*.
2. Four endings: *å kjenna* 'to know': pres. *kjenner*; past *kjende*; pp. *kjent*.
3. Four endings, sometimes with umlaut: *å spørja* 'to ask': *spør* – *spurde* – *spurt*.
4. Four endings: *å bu* 'to dwell': *bur* – *budde* – *butt*.

STRONG VERBS

Two- or three-stage ablaut is found in virtually all strong verbs in Nynorsk. The past has no dental ending; the present has no ending, apart from stems ending in a stressed vowel, which take *-r*: e.g. *få* 'get', pres. *får*. Main ablaut patterns (infinitive – past tense – past participle):

> e – a – o: vera 'to be' – var – vore
> e – a – e: lesa 'to read' – las – lese
> i – ei – i: gli 'to glide' – glei – glide
> e – a – u: brenna 'to burn' – brann – brunne
> y – au – o: krypa – 'to creep' – kraup – krope

PAST PARTICIPLES

These behave as adjectives ending in *-en* (masc./fem.), *-e* (neut.), *-ne* (pl.): e.g. *komen* – *kome* – *komne* 'arrived'.

> mannen er komen frå ... 'the man has come from ...'
> barnet er kome 'the child has come'
> dei er komne 'they have come'

FUTURE

Expressed by auxiliaries such as *skal* and *vil* + infinitive. These auxiliaries are often omitted with verbs of motion.

PASSIVE

The *-st* passive is characteristic of Dano-Norwegian rather than of Nynorsk. Usually, the auxiliaries *verta*, *bli*, or *vera* + past participle combine to give a passive sense: e.g. *huset vert bygt* 'the house is being built' (or, *huset blei bygt*).

Negation

The general particle of negation is *ikkje*.

Prepositions

For example, *bak(om)* 'behind', *gjennom* 'through', *kring* 'around', *med* 'with', *på* 'on', *åt* 'for'.

Word order

SVO.

1 I opphavet var Ordet, og Ordet var hjå Gud, og
Ordet var Gud. 2 Han var i opphavet hjå Gud.
3 Alt vart til ved han, og utan han vart ikkje noko
til av alt det som er til. 4 I han var liv, og livet var
ljoset åt menneska. 5 Og ljoset skin i mørkret; men
mørkret tok ikkje imot det.
6 Det stod fram ein mann, send av Gud; Johannes
var namnet hans. 7 Han kom for å vitna; han skulle
vitna om ljoset, så alle skulle koma til tru ved han.
8 Det var ikkje han som var ljoset; men han skulle
vitna om ljoset.

(Nynorsk)

PANJABI

INTRODUCTION

Panjabi is the most important of the North-Western group of New Indo-Aryan languages. It is the official language of the Indian state of Panjab, and the major language in the Panjabi province of Pakistan. Estimates of the total number of Panjabi speakers vary from 40 to 70 million. It may be taken that the higher figure includes the estimated 20 million speakers of the closely related and contiguous language Lahndā (*see* **Lahndā**). No statistics appear to be available for the number of Panjabi speakers in Pakistan.

On the religious and cultural plane, the language has a very special significance for the Sikhs, whose holy book, the Adi Granth, is the oldest text in the Gurmukhi script (1604). The word *Gurmukhi* means 'from the mouth of the guru'. There is a considerable body of mediaeval literature, but, in general, Panjabi had to wait until the late nineteenth century before it stood much chance of competing with Urdu as a medium for literature. Today, the language is the natural medium in the state of Panjab for education, the media, and a large and flourishing literature.

The colloquial language falls into three fairly well-defined groupings:

(a) Central: the Mājhī (Amritsar/Lahore) dialect which provides the basis for the literary language;
(b) the Ḍōgrī group in northern Panjab;
(c) the more markedly divergent western dialects which gradually merge into Lahndā.

SCRIPT

The Gurmukhi script is derived from Brahmi, and is set out in the same arrangement as the Devanagari. The vowel inherent in the base form of the consonant is short *a*. Other vowel signs are added as in Devanagari.

Tone

Three tones are distinguished; the even tone is unmarked, the other two are indicated in the script as follows: the letter *h*, or a voiced aspirate, signals a low tone on the following vowel; the *h* is mute, the aspirate is devoiced, e.g. script form *ghoṛā* 'horse', realized as /kòṛaː/. The same signals following a vowel mark it as high, e.g. script form *cah* 'tea', realized as /cá/.

PHONOLOGY

Consonants

stops: p, b, t, d, ʈ, ɖ, k, g; with aspirated surds ph, th, ʈh, kh
affricates: tʃ, tʃh, dʒ
fricatives: f/v, s, ʃ, z, x, h
nasals: m, n, ɳ, ɲ, ŋ
lateral and flap: l, ɭ, r, ɽ
semi-vowels: j, w

The voiced aspirates *bh*, *dh*, etc. do not figure in the phonological inventory though they occur in the script, e.g. as tone markers (see above). /dʒ/ is represented here as *ǰ*.

Vowels

short: ɪ, ə, u
long: i, e, ɛ, a, ɔ, o, u

In this article, /ɪ/ is represented by *i*, /ə/ by *a*, and /ŭ/ by *w*. All vowels have nasalized allophones.

Stress

Stress is a function of the qualitative/quantitative distribution of vowels.

MORPHOLOGY AND SYNTAX

Noun

Two grammatical genders, masculine and feminine. Typical masculine endings are *-ā*, *-ā̃*: *kamrā* 'room'. Most nouns in *-ī* are feminine: e.g. *roṭī* 'bread'. The gender of inanimates is not always stable.

NUMBER
Masculine nouns ending in a consonant remain unchanged; those in *-ā* change this to *-e*: e.g. *ghoṛā – ghoṛe*. Typically, feminine nouns in *-ī* add *-ā̃*: e.g. *billī* 'cat' – *billīā̃*.

DECLENSION
Analytic. Postpositions are added to the oblique base of the noun, which is, e.g., *-e*/*-ẽ* for masculines in *-ā*/*-ā̃*. Feminine nouns and all masculines with consonantal final remain unchanged for oblique case.

Plural oblique forms: *-iā̃* for masculines in *-ā*/*-ā̃*; *-ā̃* for most other masculine and feminine nouns alike. Examples of these forms: *mwṇḍā* (masc.) 'boy': *mwṇḍe nū̃* 'to the boy, the boy (acc.)', *mwṇḍiā̃ nū̃* 'to the boys, the boys (acc.)'; *kwrsī* 'chair': *kwrsiā̃ ute* 'on the chairs'.

Genitive: the affix is *dā* following the oblique case; the affix *dā* is in concord for gender, number, and case with the possessed object: e.g. *mwṇḍe* ***dā*** *ghoṛā* 'the boy's horse'; *mwṇḍe* ***de*** *ghoṛe* 'the boy's horses'; *mwṇḍe* ***diã*** *ghoṛiã* ***nũ*** 'to the boy's horses'.

Other case markers are: *ne*, agentive; *to*, ablative; (*u*)*te*, locative.

Adjective

The adjective precedes the noun qualified. Adjectives ending in *-ā* are declined like nouns in *-ā*: e.g. *navā* 'new': *nave ghar dā* 'of a new house'; fem. in *-i*. Adjectives ending in a consonant, e.g. *lāl* 'red', are indeclinable.

COMPARISON

A comparative is made by adding *-erā* to the base: e.g. *vaḍḍā* 'big' – *vaḍḍerā*. If the adjective ends in *-ṛā*, the retroflex *ṛ* is transferred to the affix: *-eṛā*.

Pronoun

PERSONAL

The direct personal forms are:

	Singular	*Plural*
1	/mɛ̃/	asiŋ
2	tū̃; āp	twsiŋ

The oblique forms are *mɛ̃*, *tɛ̃*, *asā̃*, *twsā̃*.

The third person forms are supplied from the demonstrative series.

POSSESSIVE PRONOUNS

merā 'my', *terā* 'thy', *sāḍā* 'our', *twāḍā* 'your': declined as adjective.

DEMONSTRATIVE PRONOUN

There are several sets, with two degrees, proximate and less proximate: the opposition *e*/*o* is basic.

INTERROGATIVE PRONOUN

/kɔŋ/ 'who?'; *kī* 'what?'

RELATIVE PRONOUN

jo + correlative *wh*, etc. in principal clause: e.g. *Mɛ̃ ǰo/ǰeṛā nāval kharīdiā wh chetī gwmm ho giā* 'The novel which I bought soon went lost.'

Numerals

1–10: *ikk*, *do*, *tinn*, *cār*, *panǰ*, *che*, *satt*, *aṭṭh*, *nɔ̃*, *das*; from 11 to 99 the forms are unpredictable. As in several other New Indo-Aryan languages, decade + 9 is based on following decade: e.g. 30 is *tīh*, 38 is *aṭṭhtī*, but 39 is *wntālī*, anticipating *cālī* '40'. Similarly, 49 is *wnanǰā*; 50 *panǰāh*; 100 /sɔ/.

Verb

The infinitive ending is *-ṇā/-nā*: e.g. *ǰāṇā* 'to go', *laṛnā* 'to fight'.

SIMPLE (SYNTHETIC) NOUNS
These are limited in Panjabi to the imperative: e.g. *kar/karo* 'do' (familiar); with more formal requests expressed by the endings *-ī/-īo*: e.g. *twsiŋ bɛ̄ṭhīo* 'please sit'; the subjunctive: *mẽ karā̃, tū̃ karẽ*, etc.; and the simple future: *-gā, gi*, pl. *ge, gīā̃* added to the subjunctive: e.g. *mẽ karā̃.gā.*

COMPOUND TENSES
These are made by combining the imperfective participle in *-dā*, and the perfective participle in *-iā* of the sense-verb, marked for gender and number, with the copula *hoṇā*: e.g.

> with the imperfective participle: present indicative: *mɛ̄ bɛ̄ṭhdā/dī hā̃* 'I (masc./fem.) am sitting'; pl. *asiŋ bɛ̄ṭhde/dīā̃ hā̃* 'we (masc./fem.) are sitting';
> with the perfective participle: perfect: *mɛ̄ bɛ̄ṭhdā/ī hā̃* 'I (have) sat'.

In all tenses formed with the perfective participle, the logical subject of a transitive verb is in the oblique form followed by the postposition *ne*. The participle shows gender and number concord with the object, the verb is in third person: e.g. *Tobi ne kapṛe toe* 'The washerman washed the clothes.'

There are suppositive, subjunctive, and conditional moods, all made from the participles plus auxiliaries.

PASSIVE VOICE
A specific participle in *-īdā* can be used; or an analytical form, the perfective participle of a transitive verb + *ǰāṇā* 'to go': e.g. *Pāṇī mwṇḍe tõ pītā ǰāndā hɛ* 'Water is drunk by the boy' (*pāṇī* is masc.). A two-fold gradation in ending turns intransitives into transitives, and thence into causatives: e.g. *dekhṇā* 'to see', *dikhāuṇā* 'to show', *dikhvāuṇā* 'to cause to be shown'.

Various verbs are used as auxiliaries to generate aspectual and modal nuances – inceptive, reiterative, intensive, terminative, etc.: e.g. *bannh rakhiṇā* 'to bind strongly'; *dass uṭṭhṇā* 'to start speaking'.

Postpositions

Dā, nū, and *ne* have already been mentioned. There are many more.

Word order

SOV is normal; indirect object precedes direct.

ਪਿਰਥਮੇ ਬਚਨ ਸਾ; ਅਰ ਬਚਨ ਪਰਮੇਸੁਰ ਦੇ ਸੰਗ ਸਾ; ਅਰ ੧ ਕਾਂਡ
ਬਚਨ ਪਰਮੇਸੁਰ ਸਾ। ਇਹੋ ਪਿਰਥਮੇ ਪਰਮੇਸੁਰ ਦੇ ਸੰਗ ਸਾ। ੨
ਸਭ ਕੁਛ ਉਸ ਤੇ ਰਚਿਆ ਗਿਆ; ਅਤੇ ਰਚਨਾ ਵਿੱਚੋਂ ਇੱਕ ੩
ਵਸਤੁ ਉਸ ਤੇ ਬਿਨਾ ਨਹੀਂ ਰਚੀ ਗਈ। ਉਸ ਵਿੱਚ ਜੀਉਣ ਸਾ; ੪
ਅਰ ਉਹ ਜੀਉਣ ਮਨੁੱਖਾਂ ਦਾ ਚਾਨਣ ਸਾ। ਅਤੇ ਉਹ ਚਾਨਣ ੫
ਅਨ੍ਹੇਰੇ ਵਿਖੇ ਚਮਕਿਆ; ਪਰ ਅਨ੍ਹੇਰੇ ਨੈ ਤਿਸ ਨੂੰ ਕਬੂਲ ਨਾ
ਕੀਤਾ। ਪਰਮੇਸੁਰ ਦੀ ਵਲੋਂ ਜੂਹੰਨਾ ਨਾਮੇ ਇੱਕ ਮਨੁੱਖ ੬
ਭੇਜਿਆ ਹੋਇਆ ਸਾ। ਉਹ ਸਾਖੀ ਨੂੰ ਆਇਆ, ਜੋ ਚਾਨਣ ੭
ਉੱਪੁਰ ਸਾਖੀ ਦੇਵੇ; ਤਾਂ ਸਭ ਲੋਕ ਉਸ ਦੇ ਵਸੀਲੇ ਤੇ ਪਤੀਜਣ।
ਸੋ ਆਪੇ ਉਹ ਚਾਨਣ ਨਹੀਂ ਸਾ; ਪਰ ਉਸ ਚਾਨਣ ਦੀ ਉਗਾਹੀ ੮
ਦੇਣ ਆਇਆ ਸਾ।

PASHTO

INTRODUCTION

Pashto belongs to the Eastern Iranian branch of the Indo-European family of languages. Since 1936 it has been the official language of Afghanistan (along with Dari/Farsi Kabuli) and is now spoken in Afghanistan and north-west Pakistan (Pashtunistan) by around 15 million people. The main dialect split is between Eastern (Mašriqi, Pešawari) Pashto and Western (Kandahari).

Writing in Pashto began in the sixteenth century. The seventeenth century produced the national poet of Afghanistan, Khushḥāl Khān Khaṭak; also many mystical *dīwāns* of Sufi inspiration. Typical of the rich Afghan folk literature is the *landey*, a short pithy verse form which has been compared to the Japanese haiku. The twentieth century has seen a rapid growth in political and social journalism and other contemporary genres, with concomitant innovation in language.

Pashto is rich in Arabo-Persian loan-words.

SCRIPT

The Arabic script, plus the Persian innovations, is further extended by specific letters for the following Pashto sounds: /ʈ, ɖ, ɳ, ts, dz, ʒ̣, ɽ, ʃ̣, e, əj/.

PHONOLOGY

Consonants

stops: p, b, t, d, ʈ, ɖ, k, g, q, ʕ, ʔ
affricates: ts, dz, tʃ, dʒ
fricatives: f, s, z, ʃ, ʒ, (ʃ̣, ʒ̣), x, γ, h
nasals: m, n, ɳ
lateral and flap: l, r, ɽ
semi-vowels: j, w

The retroflex fricatives /ʃ̣, ʒ̣/ are characteristic of Western Pashto. Retroflex sounds are represented here with dots.

Vowels

i, e, a, aː, ə, o, u

Vocalic length is not phonemic; /ə/ is always stressed.

Stress

Stress is on any syllable, movable and phonemic.

MORPHOLOGY AND SYNTAX

Noun

Pashto has two genders – masculine and feminine – and two numbers – singular and plural. Typical masculine endings are *-aj*, *-ə*, *-u*; nearly all nouns ending in a consonant are masculine. Feminine endings are *-a*, *-ā*, *-i*, *-o*, *-əj*. Examples: masc. *saṛaj* 'man', *plār* 'father'; fem. *koṭa* 'room', *ārzo* 'wish'.

NUMBER

Consonantal endings take the plural marker *-una* (*-ān* for animates); nouns in *-aj* change this to *-i*; feminine nouns in *-a* take *-e*/*-i*: e.g. *kor* 'house' – *koruna*; *saṛaj* 'man' – *saṛi*; *koṭa* 'room' – *koṭe*; *mdzəka* 'country' – *mdzəki*.

Phonetic assimilation of various kinds occurs at junctures; suppletive forms and the Arabic broken plural are also found.

CASE

There is a simple opposition between the direct (nominative) and oblique forms. In practice, the oblique form of masculine nouns in *-ə*, *-i*, *-u*, or with consonantal ending, is identical with the direct form; the singular oblique of all other masculine and all feminine nouns equals the plural direct; and all plural obliques are in *-o*: e.g. for the masculine noun *špun* 'shepherd': pl. direct = sing. oblique *špānə*, pl. oblique *špano*; and for *lmundz* 'prayer': pl. direct = sing. obl. *lmāndzə*; pl. obl. *lmandzo*. Each of these examples shows umlaut of the stem in the formation of the plural and the oblique case; this is very frequent in the Pashto nominal system.

POSSESSION

The marker is *də* preceding the possessor in the oblique case: e.g. *də koṭ**e** war* 'the door (*war*) of the room'; *də halək plār* 'the father of the boy'.

Adjective

As attribute, adjective precedes the noun. Where phonetically possible, the adjective takes gender and number concord, with stem umlaut. At most, an adjective can have four forms (masc. sing./pl.; fem. sing./pl): e.g. *soṛ – saṛə́ – saṛá – saṛé* 'cold'; *loj kor* 'big house'; *loj**a** koṭa* 'big room'; *loj**i** koṭe* 'the big rooms'.

COMPARATIVE

Made with *tər*, which functions as a preposition governing the compared object, not as the normal Iranian adjectival affix: e.g. *Ahmad* ***tər*** *Madmud məšr dəj* 'A. is older than M.' (cf. Persian: *A. az M. mosenn**tar** ast*).

Pronoun

The direct personal forms have oblique and enclitic forms:

		Singular			*Plural*	
		Direct	*Oblique*	*Enclitic*	*Direct/oblique*	*Enclitic*
1		zə	mā	-mi	mu.ž	-mu
2		tə	tā	-di	tāsi	-mu
3	masc.	daj	də	-e/je	duj	-e/je
	fem.	dā	de			

In addition to their function as direct objective pronouns, the oblique forms appear in the ergative construction (see below); they also take postpositions. The enclitics are used as possessive markers, and as direct objects in the present and future tenses; they may also replace the oblique forms in the ergative construction: e.g. *hewād* ***mi*** 'my homeland'; *zə* ***di*** *winəm* 'I see you'. The oblique pronominal forms preceded by *z*, *s* or *da/ə* function as possessive pronouns: sing. 1 *z.mā*, 2 *s.tā*, 3 *da.də* (masc.), *də de* (fem.); pl. 1 *z.mu.ž*, 2 *s.tāsi*, 3 *də duj*: *zma wror* 'my brother'; *də duj žəba* 'their language'.

DEMONSTRATIVE PRONOUN/ADJECTIVE
Three degrees of removal: *dā* 'this' – *daγa* 'that' – *haγa* 'that (yonder)'; these have oblique forms.

INTERROGATIVE PRONOUN
cok /tsok/ 'who?'; *ča* 'what?'.

RELATIVE PRONOUN
čə: e.g. *saṛaj* ***čə*** *num* ***je*** *Mahmud dəj* 'the man whose name is M.', i.e. with resumptive enclitic: ... *num je* 'his name'.

Numerals

1–10: *jau*, *dwa*, *dre*, *calor*, *pindzə*, *špaẓ*, *owə*, *atə*, *nəh*, *las*; 11 *jawolas*; 12 *dwolas*; 13 *djārlas*; 20 *šəl*; 30 *derš*; 40 *calweṣt*; 100 *səl*.

Verb

All forms are derived from two bases, the present and the past. The past base of most verbs is identical to the infinitive base; the present base is not predictable, and suppletive forms are frequent. Compare:

Infinitive/past base	*Present base*
wistəl 'to take out'	bās-
tləl 'to go'	dz-
lidəl 'to see'	win-

TENSE STRUCTURE
The present tense is made from the present base, the past from the past base. The present indicative endings are, for *wājəl* 'to say':

	Singular	*Plural*
1	wājəm	wāju
2	wāje	wājəj
3	wāji	wāji

PAST TENSE

(a) Intransitive verbs: the personal endings (as in present tense, except for third person) are added to the infinitive, i.e. the past base: in the third person, gender is distinguished: e.g. *rasedəl* 'to arrive':

		Singular	*Plural*
1		rasedələm	rasedəlu
2		rasedəle	resedələj
3	masc.	rasedə	rasedəl
	fem.	rasedəla	rasedəle

(b) Transitive verbs: here the ergative construction is used; the agent is in the oblique case, the object in the nominative/direct; the verb agrees in gender and number with the object: e.g. *saṛi ṣ̌ədza lidəla* 'by-the-man the-woman seen' = 'the man saw the woman'.

The ergative construction is also used with certain intransitive verbs denoting human reactions and affective states: e.g. ***mā*** *žaṛəl* 'by-me wept' = 'I wept'.

ERGATIVE CONSTRUCTION WITH A PRONOMINAL OBJECT

Example: *zə* ***je*** *lidələm* 'I by-him my-(being)-seen' = 'he saw me'; future: particle *bə* + present, e.g. *zə bə tā winəm* 'I shall see you'.

ASPECT

The perfective aspect of a simple imperfective verb can be made by prefixing *wu-*: e.g. *wu-rasedəm* 'I arrived' – *zə ṣ̌ār ta wu.rasedəm* 'I reached the town'; but many verbs have suppletive perfective forms: e.g. imperfective *kawəl* 'to do, make' – perfective *kṛəl*; imperfective *kedəl* 'to become' – perfective *šwəl*.

PASSIVE VOICE

The auxiliary is *kedəl/šwəl*: e.g. *lidəl kedəl* 'to be seen'.

CAUSATIVE

The characteristic is *-wəl* affixed to the present stem: e.g. *lwastəl* 'to read' – *lwalawəl* 'to have someone read'.

There are also imperative and optative moods, and a conditional form.

PARTICIPLES

(a) Present: the infinitive ending *-əl* is replaced by the characteristic *-unk-* + singular/plural masculine/feminine endings: thus from *tləl* 'to go', *tl.unk.aj* 'going' (masc. sing.); *tl.unk.i* (plural referent of either gender).
(b) Past: *-aj* is affixed to the infinitive: e.g. *tləlaj* 'having gone'. This form is used to make a perfect tense with the auxiliary *jəm*; the participle is inflected for feminine singular and for common plural: e.g. *rasedəlaj jəm* 'I have

arrived'; *rasedəli di* 'they (masc./fem.) have arrived'.

NEGATION

The general negating particle is *na/nə*, which attracts the stress: *muž paštanə́ nə́ ju* 'We are not Pathans'; the imperative is negated by *ma.*

Modal auxiliaries are used much as in Persian.

Prepositions and postpositions

Both are found in Pashto (e.g. *be* 'without', *tər* 'on', which are prepositions; *ta* 'to(wards)', postposition following the oblique case) but the usual form is the circumfix: e.g. *pə... ki* 'in', *pə ṣ̌ār ki* 'in the town'; *tər...lāndi* 'under', *tər mez lāndi* 'under the table'; *lə...na* 'from, out of', *lə ṣ̌ār na* 'out of the town'.

Word order

SOV.

١ په ابتدا کښ کلمه وه او هغه کلمه اَلله څخه وه او هغه کلمه اَلله وَه ١
٢ دغه په ابتدا کښ اَلله څخه وَه ٣ ټول څيزونه په دي سره وشول او بې ٢ ٣
له هغې هيڅ شي له هغو نه چه شوي دي و نه شه ٤ په هغې کښ ژوندون ٤
وه او هغه ژوندون نُور دَ انسان وُه ٥ او نُور په تياري کښ ځليده او تياري ٥
هغه و نه پيژاند ٦ يَو سړي له جانب دَ اَلله نه واستولي شه چه نُوم ئې يُوحَنّا ٦
وَه ٧ هغه دَ شاهدئ دَپارَ راغي تا چه په نُور شاهدي ولي تا چه ټول دَده ٧
په واسطي ايمان راوړي ٨ دي هغه نُور نه وُه بلکه راغي چه په نُور شاهدي ٨
ولي

PERSIAN

INTRODUCTION

Persian belongs to the South-West Iranian branch of the Indo-European family. The name 'Persia(n)' derives from Parsa, the province from which the Sasanid Dynasty originated. The language is also known as Farsi, which is an Arabicized form of Parsa (Arabic has no /p/ sound). Persian is spoken by about 30 million people in Iran, and, in slightly variant form, by 5 million in Afghanistan (known here as Dari), and by about 3 million in the Tadzhik Republic. There are a number of important dialects within Iran itself (e.g. Luri, Bakhtyari, Mazandarani).

The development and use of Middle Persian (Pehlevi – see Campbell 1991) was interrupted in 642 when the Arabs conquered Iran. When Persian reappears in the tenth century it is not based on any one identifiable Middle Persian dialect, it is rich in Arabic loan-words and it is written in the Arabic script. It should be pointed out, however, that Persian was Arabicized only as regards the appropriation of Arabic lexical items, including the broken plural and the derived stems (*see* **Arabic**). Thus, while the root *ʿZL*, for example, is not conjugated in Persian, its passive participle appears in compound verbs plus auxiliary: e.g. *maʿzul shodan* 'to be dismissed', *maʿzul kardan* 'to dismiss'. There are thousands of such Arabo-Persian complexes in the language, but Persian structure itself was hardly modified to accommodate this new and inexhaustible influx.

A thirteenth-century writer like Saʿdī uses both languages, e.g. in the *Golistan*, but separately, a *hikāyat* (tale) in Persian being often followed by a *bayt* (couplet) in Arabic. Writing three centuries earlier, Ferdousi could consciously eschew Arabic words in his nationalistic epic, the *Shāhnāme*.

The great classical period of Persian literature runs from the tenth to the fourteenth centuries. Apart from Ferdousi, the national poet, the list of great names includes Rūdakī (ninth/tenth centuries), Nāṣere Khosrou (eleventh century), Neẓāmī and Omar Khayyām (eleventh/twelfth century) Aṭṭār, Jalāloddin Rūmī, Saʿdī (thirteenth century), Ḥāfeẓ (fourteenth century).

SCRIPT

Arabic with the addition of four letters for sounds which do not occur in standard Arabic: /tʃ, ʒ, g, p/. Retention of certain Arabic letters without their original phonemic values (e.g. Arabic /ḍ/ > Persian /z/) has led to considerable duplication in notation: there are four letters for /z/, three for /s/. The Arabic emphatics are found only in Arabic loan-words.

PHONOLOGY

Consonants

stops: p, b, t, d, k, g, ɢ, ʔ
affricates: tʃ, dʒ
fricatives: f, v, s, z, ʃ, ʒ, x, ɣ, h
nasals: m, n
lateral and flap: l, r
semi-vowel: j

The hamza onset /ʕ/ occurs medially in such verb forms as the second person plural imperative, e.g. *begu'īd* 'say'.

Vowels

The long vowels *i, a, u* = /iː, ɔː, uː/ are notated in the Arabo-Persian script; the short vowels, not notated, are /æ, ɛ, ɔ/; there are two diphthongs /ɛi/ and /ɔu/.

In this article /ɔː/ is notated as *ā*; *a* without a macron is /æ/.

Stress

Stress falls on final syllables, excluding enclitics, in nouns, pronouns, adjectives, verbal infinitives, and verbal forms without prefixes. Stress shifts to prefix *mi-* in imperfective tenses, and thence to preceding negative marker, if this is present: cf: *xarídam* 'I bought' – *mí.xaridam* 'I was buying' – *ná.mi.xaridam* 'I was not buying'.

MORPHOLOGY AND SYNTAX

Noun

Persian has no grammatical gender and no articles. The unmarked noun denotes a class of objects rather than a single element of that class: *man ketāb xōš dāram* 'I like books'. The noun is made specific by the addition of unstressed *-i*: *ketāb.i* 'a book'.

For specific plurality there are two markers, *-ān* and *-hā*. In classical usage, a distinction was (and is) made between *-ān* for humans, and *-hā* for inanimates and animals. The modern tendency is for *-hā* to be used indiscriminately. Both *-ān* and *-hā* are stressed.

The Arabic broken plural coexists in Persian with *-ān/-hā*. Thus, *ketāb* 'book' may be pluralized as *ketābhā*, or as *kutub* (Arabic broken plural). In a few cases, the Arabic plural alone is used: e.g. *xabar* 'news' – *axbār*; *hadd* 'frontier' – *hodūd*.

The marker *-rā* serves to identify a noun as the object of a transitive verb: e.g. *bačče.rā dīd* 'he saw the child'. *-rā* may follow *-i*: *pādešāh.i.rā šonidam, ke...* 'I heard of a king, who ...' (Sa'dī, *Golestan*, 1.).

POSSESSION

The formula X's Y is expressed in Persian as Y-*e* X; the unstressed *-e* link is known as the *ezāfe*: e.g. *doxtar.**e** ān mard* 'that man's daughter'; *tamām.**e** tājer.hā.**ye** doulatmand.**e** šahr* 'all the rich merchants of the city' (where the attributive adjective, *doulatmand* 'rich', is also connected to its preceding noun by the ezāfe). In this example, if the word *tājer.hā* 'merchants' is to be the object, *-rā* must be affixed, not to *tājer.hā* but to *šahr*: i.e. the whole ezāfe phrase is felt to be a unit, which must, as a unit, be rounded off by the objective marker.

Adjective

As attribute, adjective follows noun, to which it is linked by the ezāfe, and is invariable: e.g. *manzal.e bozorg* 'the big house'; *melal.e mottahad* 'the United Nations'; *dāneš.ju.**ye** irānī* 'the Iranian student'; *kuh.hā.ye boland* 'high mountains'.

COMPARATIVE

In *-tar*: e.g. *Īn ketāb az ān ketāb bozorg.tar ast* 'This book is bigger than that book.'

Pronoun

Independent personal forms with enclitics:

	Singular		*Plural*	
	Independent	*Enclitic*	*Independent*	*Enclitic*
1	man	-am	mā	-emān
2	to	-at	šomā	-etān
3	u	-aš	išān	-ešān

The objective pronouns are the same as the independent forms above, with the exception that *man* becomes *mā*: e.g. *mārā dīd* 'he saw me'. The enclitics may also be used as object pronouns: e.g. *be.u goftam* = *goftam.**aš*** 'I said to him'.

The enclitics are used as possessive markers: e.g. *ketāb.**am*** 'my book' (this may also be expressed as *ketāb.**e** man*, i.e. independent form with izāfe link). The plural pronoun *šomā* provides the polite form of address for second singular; similarly, *išān* is used as the polite form of reference to a singular third person (with plural concord).

DEMONSTRATIVE PRONOUN/ADJECTIVE

in 'this, these'; *ān* 'that, those'. They take the plural marker *-hā*: e.g. *ānhā kord.and* 'these (people) are Kurds'.

INTERROGATIVE PRONOUN

ki 'who?'; *če* 'what?': e.g. (*porsidand*) *ke haqiqat.**e** tasawwaf čist* (← *če ast*) '(asked) what is the true meaning of Sufism' (Golestan, 2.24). The particle *āyā* initiates a sentence requiring a yes/no answer.

RELATIVE PRONOUN
The linking particle *ke* follows the head-word: e.g. *mardi.ke diruz raft* 'the man who went off yesterday'; *manzel.i.ke ānjā manzel mi.konam* 'the house in which I live'.

Numerals

1–10: *yak, do, se, čahār, panǰ, šeš, haft, hašt, noh, dah*. 10–19: unit + *dah*, the units varying slightly: e.g. *yazdah, davāzdah, sizdah*; 20 *bīst*; 30 *sī*; 40 *čehel*; 100 *sad*.

Verb

The two basic oppositions are: (a) between present and past stems; (b) between perfective and imperfective aspects.

The infinitive ending is *-tan*/*-dan*/*-idan*: the *-an* is dropped to give the short infinitive, which is also the past stem, e.g. from *xaridan* 'to buy', *xarid* = past stem = third person singular past, 'he/she bought'.

Theoretically, the present stem is obtained by dropping the whole of the infinitive ending: in the case of *xaridan*, *-idan* is dropped, leaving *xar-*. There are, however, very many irregular formations: e.g. from *āmadan* 'come', *ā-*; from *raftan* 'go', *raw-*; from *kardan* 'do, make', *kon-*.

The personal enclitic markers used in conjugation are: sing. 1 *-am*, 2 *-i*, 3 *-ast*/*-ad*; pl: 1 *-im*, 2 *-id*, 3 *-and* (humans), *-ast*/*-ad*.

The auxiliary used in the formation of composite tenses is *budan* 'to be', whose present stem is *bāš-*. All Persian verbs are constructed and conjugated on this model; the only irregularity lies in the formation of the present stem.

ASPECT
Briefly, imperfective forms are marked by a prefix: *mi-*, *be-*; perfective forms have no prefix. Thus from *xaridan* 'buy':

> Imperfective aspect, present or past stem: *mí.xarim* 'we are buying'; *bé.xarim* 'that we may buy' (subjunctive); *mí.xa**rid**.im* 'we were buying'.
> Perfective aspect, past stem: *xaríd.im* 'we bought'; *xaridé.im* 'we have bought'; *xāhim xaríd* 'we shall have bought/we shall buy'.

All of these forms are negated by prefixing *na-*, except in the case of the subjunctive, where the *be-* is dropped before *na-* is prefixed: thus *na.mi.xarim* 'we are not buying'; *na.**Ø**.xarad* 'he is not to buy'.

A passive voice can be made with the auxiliary *šodan* 'to become': e.g. *koštan* 'to kill' – *košte šodan* 'to be killed', where *košte* is the past participle. The passive form cannot be used in Persian if the agent is specified.

IMPERATIVE
Prefix *be-* + present stem: *be.xar* 'buy!', pl. *be.xarid*. Necessitative and potential forms are made with the subjunctive; the former uses the third person singular of *bāyestan* 'to have to': *bāyad be.xarim* 'we have to buy'; *bāyad be.ravim* 'we must

go'. The potential forms are made with *tavānestan* 'to be able': *mi.tavānam be.ravam* 'I can go'.

Several other Persian verbs are used as auxiliaries with Persian or Arabic nominals or verbals, especially *kardan* 'to do, make' (present stem, *kon-*); cf. with *šodan* 'to become': *vāred šod* 'he entered'; *xārej šodand* 'they went out', where *vāred* and *xārej* are Arabic active participles.

Prepositions

Some, e.g. *az* 'from', *tā* 'until, as far as', *bar* 'on', *ba* 'with', do not need the ezāfe: e.g. *az šahr* 'from the town'; *tā emruz* 'till today'. Others, such as *bedun* 'without', *pošt* 'behind', *ru-* 'on', require the ezāfe: e.g. *ru.ye miz* 'on the table', *bālā.ye kuh* 'up on the mountain'

Word order

SOV.

بود درا بتدا کلمه و انکلمه نزدخدابود وان کلمه خدابود * وهمان درابتدا نزد
خدابود* وهرچیز بوساطت اوموجودشد و بغیراز وهیچ چیزازچیز های که موجودشده
است وجود نیافت * دراوحیات بودوان حیات روشنائی انسان بود * وان روشنائی
درتاریکی میدرخشید وتاریکی درنمییافتش * شخصی بودکه ازجانب خدافرستاده
شده که اسمش یحیی بود * واوبرای شهادت امدتا انکه شهادت بران نوردهدتا
انکه همه بوساطت اوایمان اورند * واوخودروشنائی نبود بلکه امده بود که بران
روشنائی شهادت بدهد *

POLISH

INTRODUCTION

Polish is usually regarded as the sole survivor of the Lechitic sub-group of West Slavonic languages, though some authorities treat the dialect form known as Kashubian as a separate language. The written record in Polish begins in the fourteenth century – apart from the famous sentence found in a thirteenth century Latin document: 'daj ać ja pobruczę a ty poczywa' (in modernized spelling), presumably uttered by a considerate miller to his spouse: 'I'll grind for a bit, you take a break.' The first great Polish writer is Jan Kochanowski in the sixteenth century, the author of *Treny*, a beautiful threnodic sequence on the death of his little daughter. The Romantic period produced at least four outstanding figures, all of whom spent most of their productive years in emigration: Adam Mickiewicz, the national poet of Poland, whose *Pan Tadeusz* (1843) is a splendid apotheosis, both of Polish aspirations and of the Polish past; Juliusz Słowacki, Zygmunt Krasiński, and Cyprian Norwid. In the early years of the twentieth century two novelists produced masterpieces: Stefan Żeromski's *Popioły* ('Ashes'), a saga of the Napoleonic era in Poland, rich in rapturous and lyrical descriptions of the Polish countryside, and Władysław Reymont's *Chłopi* ('The Peasants'), an encyclopaedic survey of Polish peasant life in the nineteenth century. This novel received the Nobel Prize in 1924; a previous Nobel laureate was Henryk Sienkiewicz (for *Quo Vadis?*) in 1905. An impressive school of post-Second World War poets includes such individual voices as Tadeusz Różewicz and Zbigniew Herbert. In 1980 the Nobel Prize for Literature went again to a Polish writer – Czesław Miłosz.

Today, Polish is spoken by some 40 million people in the Republic of Poland, of which it is the official language. In addition there are about 6 million Poles in the USA, and several hundred thousand elsewhere.

SCRIPT

The Roman alphabet, plus marked letters for specific Polish sounds: *ą*, *ć*, *ę*, *ł*, *ń*, *ó*, *ś*, *ź*, *ż*.

PHONOLOGY

Consonants

stops: p, b, t, d, k, g
affricates: tɕ, dʑ, ts, dz, tʃ, dʒ
fricatives: f, v, ɕ, ʑ, s, z, ʃ, ʒ
nasals: m, n, ɲ
laterals and flap: l, ł (→ w), r
semi-vowels: j, w

/tɕ/ (notated as *ć*) and /dʑ/ (notated as *dź*) are pre-palatal, in opposition to alveolar /tʃ/ and /dʒ/.

Vowels

oral: i, ɛ, a, ɔ, u
nasal: ɛ̃, ɔ̃

Vowels are not reduced in unstressed position, in contrast to Russian, for example. Final voiced consonants are unvoiced, e.g. *mąž* 'husband' → [mɔ̃ʃ]. There is also an elaborate system of assimilation, both preparatory and regressive, at junctures: e.g. with prepositions: *w Polsce* 'in Poland' → [**f**]*Polsce*; *pod tytułem* 'under the title' → *po*[**t**].*tytułem*]; *odporność* 'resistance' → *o*[**t**]*porność*.

Stress

Invariably on penultimate syllable, except in foreign words like *fábryka*, *polítyka*; the conditional particle *-by* does not affect stress: e.g. *zróbił* 'he did'; *zróbiłby* 'he would do'.

MORPHOLOGY AND SYNTAX

Noun

Polish has three genders, two numbers, and seven cases, if we include the vocative. There are no articles. Certain noun endings are coded for gender, e.g. most nouns in *-a* are feminine, as are all nouns in *-ość*; nouns ending in hard consonants are masculine; all in *-e* and *-o* are neuter.

DECLENSION

There are four main types:

1. *a*-stems (mostly feminine): e.g. *kobieta* 'woman', *noga* 'leg, foot';
2. *o*-stems (masculine): e.g. *pan* 'gentleman, Mr > you' (polite 2nd person);
3. *o*-stems (neuter): e.g. *miasto* 'place, town';
4. *i*-stems (feminine): e.g. *noc* 'night'.

An animate/inanimate opposition appears in *masculine o*-stems, where the accusative case of a noun denoting an *animate being* takes the form of the genitive, an opposition reflected in adjectival and pronominal concord: e.g. (*Pamiętam*) *mojego starego ojca* '(I remember) my old father' (*mój* 'my (masc.)', *stary* 'old', *ojciec* 'father'). In the plural genitive, this animate/inanimate opposition is replaced by a more restrictive one, which sets up an opposition between men on the one hand, and everything else on the other: cf. the following three masculine nouns: *chłop* 'peasant', *rolnik* 'farmer', *pies* 'dog': for the first two, the plural accusative = plural genitive: *chłopów*, *rolników*; but, *pies* has plural genitive *psów*, acc. *psy* = nominative.

Specimen declensions: *noga* 'leg, foot'; *pan* 'gentleman'; *noc* 'night'

	Singular	*Plural*	*Singular*	*Plural*	*Singular*	*Plural*
nom.	noga	nogi	pan	panowie	noc	noce
gen.	nogi	nog	pana	panów	nocy	nocy
dat.	no**dz**e	nogom	panu	panom	nocy	nocom
acc.	nogę	nogi	pana	panów	noc	noce
instr.	nogą	nogami	panem	panami	nocą	nocami
loc.	no**dz**e	nogach	panu	panach	nocy	nocach

Note consonant alternation in the declension of *noga*: *g/dz*. This is frequent in Polish inflection; cf. *ręka* ('hand') pl. *ręce*; *brat* 'brother', pl. *bracia*.

Adjective

As attribute, adjective normally precedes noun, and is in concord for gender, number, case. For example, the hard stem *pełny* 'full': masculine and feminine singular, plural for male persons:

	Masculine	*Feminine*	*Plural (men)*
nom.	pełny	pełna	pełni
gen.	pełnego	pełnej	pełnych
dat.	pełnemu	pełnej	pełnym
acc.	pełnego/pełny	pełną	pełnych
instr.	pełnym	pełną	pełnymi
loc.	pełnym	pełnej	pełnych

Examples:

każdego polskiego miasta 'of each Polish town'

Mamy piękną pogodę 'We're having fine weather'

naszym kochanym córkom 'to our dear daughters'

COMPARATIVE

(*ej*)*szy* added to base form: e.g. *stary* 'old' – *starszy*; *trudny* 'difficult' – *trudniejszy*. The comparative is, of course, declined as a normal adjective. The comparative may also be formed with the adverb *bardziej* 'more': e.g. *bardziej głęboki* 'deeper'.

Pronoun

PERSONAL

The independent personal pronouns are:

		Singular		*Plural*
1		ja		my
2		ty		wy
3	masc.	on	male persons:	oni
	fem.	ona		
	nt.	ono	others:	one

These are fully declined; e.g. the other cases of first person singular are: gen. *mnie*; dat. *mnie*, *mi*; acc. *mnie*, *mię*; instr. *mną*; loc. *mnie*. The polite second person form of address is *Pan*/*Pani*: e.g. *Proszę Pana, gdzie Pan teraz pracuje?* 'Excuse me (for asking), where are you working at present?'

POSSESSIVE

The first and second person possessive adjectives – *mój*, *moja*, *moje*; *twój*, *twoja*, *twoje* – with plural forms – *nasz*, *nasza*, *nasze*; *wasz*, *wasza*, *wasze* – agree with their referents in gender, number, and case. The third person forms, *jego*, *jej*, *jego*; pl. *ich* (all three genders), are invariable. The polite second person forms, *pana*, *pani*, with pl. *państwa*, are also invariable.

DEMONSTRATIVE ADJECTIVE

ten, *ta*, *to* 'this'; two plural forms: *ci* for male persons, *te* for everything else. *Tamten*, *tamta*, *tamto* 'that'. All forms are fully declined.

INTERROGATIVE PRONOUN

kto 'who?'; *co* 'what?' Fully declined. *Czy* is an introductory interrogative marker, requiring a yes/no answer: e.g. *Czy samolot często się opóźnia?* 'Is the plane often late?'

RELATIVE PRONOUN

który, *która*, *które* 'who'; *kto*, *co* 'which': e.g.

chłopiec, który przyszedł pierwszy 'the boy who came first'

chłopcy, których uczyłem 'the boys (whom) I taught'

ten, kto to zrobił 'the one who did it'

Numerals

The Polish numerical system is of considerable complication. 1 *jeden*: this is a regular adjective, fully declined; 2 *dwaj*, gen. *dwóch* for male persons only; fem. *dwie*, other masculine and neuter, *dwa*; 3 *trzej*, *trzech* (male persons only); otherwise, *trzy*; similarly for 4 *cztery*. From 5 onwards, numbers have two forms only; a nom./acc. uniflected form for all referents except male persons; and an inflected form in *-iu* which provides all cases for male human referents, and the oblique cases for other nouns. Thus: *pięć biletów*, *pięć kobiet* 'five tickets', 'five women'; but, *pięciu mężczyzn* 'five men'. From 5 upwards, the noun is in the genitive plural, the verb in the singular (third person neuter): e.g. *pięciu panów* 'five men', *pięc kobiet* 'five women', *Pięc psów mieszka w tym domu* 'Five dogs live in this house.'

Verb

The Polish verb has imperfective, perfective, iterative, and semelfactive aspects; a periphrastic passive voice; three moods – indicative, imperative, and conditional; present, past, and future tenses; non-finite forms.

ASPECT

Formation of perfective from imperfective aspect is, typically, by addition of prefix, which often changes not only the aspect but also the meaning of the verb: cf. from *pisać* 'to write': perfective ***napisać*** 'to have written'; with change in nuance: ***dopisać*** 'to add to something in writing'; ***podpisać*** 'to sign'; ***zapisać*** 'to make a note of'.

Some perfective forms are suppletive: e.g. *brać* 'take' – *wziąć*; *mówić* 'speak' – *powiedzieć*.

Secondary imperfective forms are generated from the perfective aspect by lengthening of the stem: e.g. *dopisać*: *dopisy**wa**ć*; or by ablaut: *odnieść* 'take' – *odnosić*.

The *-ywa-* infix is also typical of the iterative aspect: e.g. *pisy**wa**ć*:

> W młodości pisywał wiele listów
> 'When he was young, he was in the habit of writing many letters.'

Semelfactive: a characteristic ending of the semelfactive infinitive is *-nąć*: e.g.

> Nagły, daleki, jadowity głos drgnął w lasach (Żeromski, *Popioły*)
> 'A sudden sound, far-off and baneful, stirred in the forest.'

Compare:

> Ogary poszły w las. Echo ich grania **słabło** coraz bardziej aż wreszcie **utonęło** w milczeniu leśnym.
> 'The hounds had moved off into the woods. The echo of their belling grew fainter and fainter until at last it was submerged in the silence of the forest.'

In this sentence (also from *Popioły*) *słabnąć* is an imperfective verb describing a process – 'to weaken' – which is brought to an end by the perfective verb *utonąć* 'to sink'.

TENSE STRUCTURE

Indicative: the past tense distinguishes gender in the singular, and, in the plural, the male human preserve, characteristic of the nominal declension. Specimen paradigm: *czytać* 'to read':

Present: sing. 1 *czytam*, 2 *czytasz*, 3 *czyta*; pl. 1 *czytamy*, 2 *czytacie*, 3 *czytają*.

Past: sing. 1 *czytał.em/am*, 2 *czytał.eś/aś*, 3 *czytał/czytała/czytało*; pl. 1 *czytaliśmy/czytałyśmy*, 2 *czytaliście/czytałyście*, 3 *czytali/czytały*.

Future: sing. 1, 2, 3: *będę/będziesz/będzie czytał/a/o*; pl. *będziemy/będziecie/będą czytali* (male humans only), *czytały* (others). Thus: *będziemy czytali* 'we shall read/be reading' (men speaking); *będą czytały* 'they (not men) will be reading.'

The future forms given here are *imperfective* only. The perfective future is made by adding the present imperfective endings to the perfective stem:

Jutro **na**pisze do niej list
'He'll write (= have written) a letter to her tomorrow.'

Compare:

∅Pisze ten list od dwóch godzin
'He's been writing that letter for two hours.'

CONDITIONAL

The endings sing. *bym*, *byś*, *by*; pl. *byśmy*, *byście*, *by* are added to the third person singular and plural past tense of the sense-verb: the male human restriction is observed. Thus: *pisali.by* 'they (men) would write'; *pisały byśmy* 'we (not men) would write'.

IMPERATIVE

Often formed from third person singular present tense (imperfective) by dropping last letter: e.g. *pisze* 'he writes': *pisz!* 'write!', pl. *pisz.cie!*; or by dropping last letter of third person plural (verbs in *-ać*): e.g. *czytają → czytaj!*

PARTICIPLES

Present in *-ąc*: e.g. *niosąc* 'carrying'; *widząc* 'seeing'. These are declined as adjectives: e.g. *kochająca córka* 'a loving daughter'. When used adverbially, the participle is indeclinable:

Wchodząc do kościoła Mariackiego, Zosia podziwiała słynny ołtarz
'Entering the Maria Church, Zosia admired the famous altar.'

The past participle (perfective verbs) has the ending *-wszy/-łszy*: e.g. *wróciwszy na swe miejsce* 'having returned to his place'; *wyszedłszy* 'having gone out'.

PASSIVE VOICE

Formed analytically with the auxiliary *być* 'to be' (imperfective) or *zostać* 'to remain' (perfective), plus passive past participle in *-ny/-na/-ne*, *-ty/-ta/-te*: e.g. *wszystko było zamknięte* 'everything was closed'; *...został zastrzelony* '... was shot dead'.

Negative

The general marker is *nie*; double and triple negatives are frequent.

Prepositions

Most Polish prepositions govern the genitive case, including the partitive genitive; the accusative, locative, and instrumental cases are also used. Some prepositions take more than one case, depending on sense: e.g.

Samolot poleci nad miasto 'The plane will fly away over the town' (acc.)

Lecimy nad miastem 'We are flying above the town' (instr.)

Word order

SVO is general.

1 Na początku było
Słowo, a Słowo było u Boga,
a Bogiem było Słowo.
2 To było na początku u
Boga.
3 Wszystkie rzeczy przez
nie się stały, a bez niego nic
się nie stało, co się stało.
4 W niém był żywot, a
żywot był światłością lu-
dzi.
5 A światłość w ciemności
świeci, ale ciemność jéj nie
ogarnęła.
6 Był człowiek posłany
od Boga, któremu imię było
Jan.
7 Ten przyszedł na świa-
dectwo, aby świadczył o świa-
tłości, aby przezeń wszyscy
uwierzyli.
8 Nie był ci on światłością,
ale, aby świadczył o świa-
tłości.

POLYNESIAN LANGUAGES

Geographically, the Polynesian languages fall into the following three clearly defined groups:

(a) Western Polynesian: Tongan, Niue, Samoan, East Uvean, East Futunan, the Ellice Islands language, and Tokelau.
(b) Eastern Polynesian: Maori, Rarotongan, Tahitian, Tuamotuan, Marquesan, Hawaiian, Mangarevan, Rapanui.
(c) The outliers. The following languages are spoken in the neighbourhood of the Solomon Islands: Sikaianan, Luangiuan, Rennellese; in the neighbourhood of the New Hebrides: Pileni, Mae, West Futunan, Aniwan, Mele-Fila, Tikopian; Nukuoro and Kapingamarangi are northern outliers; West Uvean is spoken in the Loyalty Islands. There are several smaller languages.

Genetically, however, neither the exact provenance of the Polynesian languages nor their internal relationships are so clear. Until the 1930s, Polynesian, Indonesian, and Melanesian-Micronesian were regarded as the three branches of the so-called 'Austronesian' family, a viewpoint which has not been entirely discarded. In 1934–8 Otto Dempwolff argued on phonological grounds that Polynesian, Melanesian, and Micronesian should be regarded as forming a single unit, to which the name 'Oceanic' was given. A third hypothesis (Kähler, 1962) identifies Polynesian as an outlying sub-division of the Indonesian branch.

As regards internal relationships within the group, various classifications have been proposed: e.g. that of Pawley (1936), who distinguishes (a) Tongic, consisting of Tongan and Niue; (b) Samoic, comprising Samoan, Ellice Islands, Tokelau, East Futunan, and the outliers: (c) East Polynesian. In this classification, the New Hebridean languages form a specific group among the outliers.

The linguistic question is throughout beset by the problem of when and from where the various island groups were first settled. Tonga seems to have been the scene of the earliest colonization (before 1000 BC), by settlers coming from Indonesia and New Guinea, followed by Samoa (more than 2,000 years ago) and Niue. From the central springboards of Tonga and Samoa, penetration of eastern Polynesia proceeded over the subsequent 1,000 years (Hawaii in the eighth century AD, New Zealand about 1200). Many island groups have probably been subjected to several successive waves of colonization.

SCRIPT

Only one form of indigenous writing is known to have been used in Polynesia – the Easter Island script (rongorongo), which has not yet been deciphered. Roman-based alphabets have been introduced for several Polynesian languages, usually in association with a translation of the Bible, in whole or in part.

PHONOLOGY

Consonants

The Proto-Polynesian consonantal system has been reconstructed as:

p, f, w, m; t, n, s, l, r; k, ŋ; h, ʔ

In contemporary Polynesian, Proto-Pol. /p, t, k, m, n, ŋ/, are retained unchanged in virtually all cases; /f, s, r/l/ are retained in approximately half; /w, h, ʔ/, are retained in about 15 per cent of daughter languages. Where these are not retained, /w/ > /v/, /h/ > Ø, /ʔ/ > Ø. The former contrast between /r/ and /l/ has been lost, so that these letters represent notation for one and the same sound. Vocalic systems have been retained almost unchanged. Extreme reductionism is found in Hawaiian where Proto-Pol. /t/ > /k/, /ŋ/ > /n/, and /r, h, ʔ/ are all reduced to Ø. This gives a total of eight consonants. Tongan has the richest consonantal inventory. Certain consonantal clusters are found in some of the outliers, e.g. /mb, nd/ in Mae and in Pileni. These may be the result of Melanesian influence.

The extreme poverty of the consonantal structure means that very few monosyllabic forms are possible (in the case of Hawaiian, only 45). However, it is precisely these monosyllabic forms that provide the nominal and verbal particles which abound in Polynesian languages, and which are crucially important for their syntax. The great majority of Polynesian roots are bivocalic, of (C)V(C)V type.

Vowels

i, e, a, o, u

MORPHOLOGY AND SYNTAX

In parallel with the high degree of phonological isomorphism, there is also considerable structural similarity between the various Polynesian languages. Some generally valid points are here set out, with examples where helpful.

1. Authorities on Polynesian languages do not always agree as to what exactly constitutes a Polynesian 'word', since boundaries between 'words' tend to be fluid. However, three classes of items which go towards generating 'words' can

be distinguished: (a) the (open) class of auto-semantic roots; (b) the affixes which can be prefixed or suffixed to items in (a); (c) particles. Classes (b) and (c) are closed. Example in Tongan: *ko e nofo'anga'a Tolu* 'Tolu's dwelling-place' (where *nofo* 'to sit' is a root; *'anga*, location marker, is an affix; *Tolu* is a proper name; *ko* is introductory particle; *e* is defining particle; *'a* is attributive particle).

2. Reduplication (partial or total) occurs widely and is a highly productive way of expressing reiteration, plurality, intensification or diminution, semantic extension, etc.: e.g. reiteration: Samoan, *eva* 'talk' – *evaeva* 'talk a lot, spend (the evening) talking; intensification: Tahitian *roa* 'long' – *roroa* 'very long' (partial redup.); plurality: Tongan *lahi* 'big' – *lalahi* (pl. form of adjectival base); semantic extension: Tahitian *arui* 'night' – *aruiarui* 'twilight', Tongan *moho* 'cooked' – *momoho* 'ripe'.

3. Internal inflection. Rare: occurs as plurality marker: e.g. Tongan *fefine* 'woman' – pl. *fafine*; *tangi* 'weep' – *tengihia* 'weep for, lament'.

4. Nominal and verbal particles gravitate to left-hand side of nucleus; adverbial particles gravitate to right.

5. Preposited particles: examples from a West Polynesian (Tongan), and East Polynesian (Marquesan), and from an outlier language (Nukuoro):

Nominal particles:

(a) prepositions

	Tongan	*Marquesan*	*Nukuoro*
focus marker	ko	'o	go
agentive marker	'e	e	e
alienable possession	'a	a	a
inalienable possession	'o	o	o
relative marker	'i	i	i

(b) determinatives

definite article (sing.)	he/'e	te	de
personal article	a	a	a

Verbal particles:

aspect/mood/tense markers			
(a) inceptive	ka	'aa	ga
(b) perfective	kuo	ua/uu	gu
tense			
(a) past	na'a, na'e, ne	i	ne
(b) non-past	e/'e, te	e	e

6. Pronouns: singular, dual, plural short forms, with exclusive/inclusive contrast in first person:

			Tongan	*Samoan*
singular	1	excl.	u/ou/ku	ou/'ou
		incl.	te	ta
	2		ke	'ee
	3		ne	'ee
dual	1	excl.	ma	maa
		incl.	ta	taa
	2		mo	('ou)lua
	3		na	laa
plural	1	excl.	mau	maatou
		incl.	tau	taatou
	2		mou	('ou)tou
	3		nau	laatou

7. Plurality markers are sited between determinative and nucleus: e.g. Tahitian *e **mau** fare* 'houses'; *te **mau** fare* 'the houses'.

8. Demonstratives. Triple-term series by degree of distancing in space or in topicalization: e.g. Tahitian *teie – tena – tera*; Maori *teenei – teena – teera*; Tongan *ni – na – ia*.

9. The numerals are largely isomorphic over the whole field. 1–10 in Tongan: *taha, ua, tolu, fā, nima, ono, fitu, valu, hiva, hongofulu*; Samoan: *tasi, lua, tolu, fa, lima, ono, fitu, valu, iva, sefulu*.

10. Alienable/inalienable possession. Practically all Polynesian languages make a distinction between alienable and inalienable possession: a distinction which has to do not so much with the nature of the objects thus apportioned as with the relationship between them and the natural or contingent owner. Typically, the alienable series is marked by *-a-* , the inalienable series by *-o-*. The taxonomy into *-a-* and *-o-* categories may vary from one socio-linguistic milieu to another, but essentially the key point remains that the *-a-* series is subject-related, the *-o-* series object-related. With regard to the situation in Maori, Biggs (1969: 43), *Let's Learn Maori*, Wellington; quoted in Krupa (1982), writes: 'Possession of anything towards which the possessor is dominant, active or superior, is expressed by *a*; possession of things in respect of which the possessor is subordinate, passive or inferior, is expressed by *o*.' And Buse (1960: 123), 'Rarotongan personal pronouns: forms and distribution', BSOAS, 1960, quoted in Krupa (1982: 115), offers the following interesting information on the Rarotongan series:

> as a rule, a person stands in an A-relationship to his or her descendants, employees, spouse, lover (all acquired relationships), animals (not the horses), food, crops, instruments, tools, machinery, movable property (not means of transport). He stands in an O-relationship to his ancestors, employers (relationships which he is not responsible for, or in which he does not play the controlling part), parts of the body, clothing, buildings, conveyances, abstractions.

For examples of the *-a-* and *-o-* categories in practice, *see* **Samoan, Maori.**

11. Negation. Negative markers are usually accompanied by positional and structural readjustment of the positive order. In some languages the negative markers are coded for tense (e.g. in Tahitian). There are specific markers for prohibition.

12. Sentence structure. Both nominative–accusative and ergative constructions are found; some Polynesian languages have both. As in certain American Indian languages, an ostensible 'object' may be absorbed as a constituent of the verbal complex: 'he shoots (a) bird(s)' → 'he is-a-bird-shooter'. That is, an intransitive sentence results. See Krupa (1982: 122–33) for a full discussion of this interesting point.

13. Word formation. (a) root + affix (prefix or suffix); (b) reduplication; (c) compounding. Examples from Tahitian:

(a) *Fa'a* + root, e.g. *aogā* 'useful' – ***fa'a****aogā* 'to utilize'; ***fa'a****samoa* 'in Samoan'. Root + *a*, e.g. *nofo* 'to sit' – *nofo***a** 'chair'.
(b) *Fulu* 'feather': e.g. *fulufulu* 'hair'.
(c) *Tusi* 'to write' + *tala* 'story': *tusitala* 'story-teller, writer'.

Word order

VSO is usual. SVO is found in certain outliers.

PORTUGUESE

INTRODUCTION

Portuguese belongs to the Italic branch of the Indo-European family. It is the official language of Portugal, where it is spoken by about 9 million people, and of Brazil, where the number of speakers is estimated at about 125 million. In addition, it is the language of administration in Angola, Mozambique, Guinea-Bissau, Cape Verde, and San Tomé e Príncipe. Other islands of Portuguese speech are Goa, East Timor, and Macao.

Roman occupation of the western seaboard of the Iberian peninsula lasted from 200 BC to the fourth century AD. Subsequently, Visigoths and Moors came and went, but the Vulgar Latin spoken in Roman Gallaecia and Lusitania had become firmly established, and, by the time the Moors were expelled (the reconquest was complete by 1267) it was spreading to the rest of what is now Portugal. The phonological complexities of Modern Portuguese were already inherent in the Vulgar Latin of Gallaecia, which retained the vocalic structure of Latin while at the same time discarding some of the key consonants which supported it. The Portuguese literary language (from the thirteenth century onwards) is based on the south-central dialect of Lisbon/Coimbra. The literature is extensive and rich in all genres; in the modern period, particularly strong in lyric poetry, the essay and the novel.

In the fifteenth/sixteenth centuries Portuguese was the first Indo-European language to spread to sub-Saharan Africa, and the first to rejoin its congeners in India.

SCRIPT

The Latin alphabet minus *k*, *w*, *y*; diacritics are used: acute, grave, circumflex, cedilla, and tilde, the latter to indicate nasalization in the absence of a nasal consonant. The correspondence between symbol and sound is weak: five vowel symbols do duty for 17 sounds, while 18 consonants have some 30 values. For example, the letter *s* is realized, depending on phonetic environment, as /s/, /z/, /ʃ/ or /ʒ/: cf. *todas as mesmas senhoras* 'all the same ladies', realized as: /tod**ɛz.**aʒ.meʒməʃ**.s**ɪɲorəʃ/

EUROPEAN PORTUGUESE

PHONOLOGY

Consonants

stops: p, b, t, d, k, g
fricatives: f, v, s, z, ʃ, ʒ
nasals: m, n, ɲ
laterals and flaps: l, ɫ, ʎ, r, ʀ
semi-vowels: j, w

The affricate /tʃ/ appears in northern Portuguese. /b, d, g/ have allophones [ß, ð, γ]

Vowels

i, e, ε, a, ɐ, ə, ɔ, o, u

Basic series, expanded by diphthongs. All vowels occur nasalized (by tilde, or by presence of a nasal consonant). Assimilation and sandhi, both consonantal and vocalic, play a key role in Portuguese pronunciation, in conjunction with tonic stress, which is accompanied by marked reduction of unstressed vowels. The stress pattern is phrasal rather than local: Cf. *Esta manhã vou escrever umas cartas* 'This morning I'm going to write letters', realized as: /εʃtə mãɲ**ã** vɔʃ.krəv**er**.uməʃ.k**ar**təʃ/; *que se divirta bem* 'have a good time', /kəsədəv**ir**təbẽi/ – stress marked by bold print.

MORPHOLOGY AND SYNTAX

Noun

Nouns are masculine or feminine, singular or plural. Some nominal endings are gender-related, e.g. *-a*, *-ção*, *-são* are feminine, *-o* is masculine. Gender is not predictable from consonantal endings: thus, *amor* is masculine, but *cor* is feminine.

ARTICLES
Definite: *o* (masc.), *a* (fem.), pl. *os*, *as*; indefinite: *um*, *uma*; *uns*, *umas*.

PLURAL
The marker is -(V)*s* with a wide range of phonological adjustment at junctures, e.g. *a liçao* 'the lesson', pl. *as lições*; *a viagem* 'the journey', pl. *as viagens*; *o hotel* 'the hotel', pl. *os hoteis*.

CASE
Relations are expressed analytically with the help of prepositions, many of which coalesce with the article: *em* 'in' + *o* → *no*, *de* + *a* → *da*, etc.

Adjective

A basic opposition is Ø for masculine, *-a* for feminine, but many adjectives have identical forms for both genders. The attributive adjective may either precede or follow the noun; there is a preferred order for many adjectives. ANA is frequent: e.g. *um velho costume militar* 'an old military custom'.

Pronoun

(a) Strong: subject forms and emphatics:

sing.	1 eu	2 tu	3 masc. ele, fem. ela
pl.	1 nos	2 (*vos*, archaic; *see* **Polite address**, below)	3 masc. eles, fem. elas

The emphatic forms used with prepositions are identical except for first person singular which has *mim*: e.g. *para mim* /mĩ/ 'for me', and the second person singular which has *ti*.

(b) Weak: direct and indirect object: the direct object forms are:

sing.	1 me	2 te	3 masc. o, fem. a
pl.	1 nos	2	3 masc. os, fem. as

In the indirect object series, *me*, *te*, and *nos* are unchanged; *o* and *a* have the same indirect form, *lhe* /ʎe/; *os* and *as* have the form *lhes*.

POLITE ADDRESS
There are two forms: (a) *você(s)*; (b) *o senhor*, *a senhora*. Both of these forms require third person concord (cf. Sp. *usted*).

POSSESSIVE ADJECTIVE
Forms show gender throughout: e.g. *meu/minha*, *teu/tua*.

PRONOMINAL ORDER
In positive sentences, weak oblique pronouns are usually hyphenated to right-hand side of verb, indirect preceding direct: e.g. *ele dá-no-los* 'he gives them to us'; *ele dá-mo* 'he gives it to me' (*me* + *o* → *mo*). In negative, relative, optative, clauses, etc. the weak object precedes the verb: e.g. *quando a vi...* 'when I saw her ...'; *se me permite...* 'if you will allow me'.

A striking feature of Portuguese structure is that the oblique pronoun can be infixed between verb stem and personal ending, in the future and conditional tenses: e.g. *dar.**lhe**.iamos* 'we would give you/him'.

DEMONSTRATIVE PRONOUN/ADJECTIVE
Three degrees of removal: *este* 'this' – *esse* 'that' – *aquele* 'that (yonder)'. These are declined.

INTERROGATIVE PRONOUN
quem 'who?', (*o*) *que* 'what?'

RELATIVE PRONOUN
qual is declined for gender and number: *o qual*, *a qual*; pl. *os quais*, *as quais*. *Que* is invariable, with either singular or plural antecedent.

Numerals

1–10: *um/uma*, *dois/duas*, *três*, *quatro*, *cinco*, *seis*, *sete*, *oito*, *nove*, *dez*; 11 *onze*; 12 *doze*; 13 *treze*; 14 *catorze*; 16 ***dezasseis***; 20 *vinte*; 100 *cem*. The *dois/duas* distinction of gender reappears in the hundreds for 200 onwards: e.g. *duzentos/duzentas*.

Verb

Three conjugations, characterized by infinitive ending: *-ar*, *-er*, *-ir*. There are active and passive voices; indicative, imperative, and subjunctive moods. The indicative active has six simple tenses (stem + personal ending) and four compound (auxiliary *ter* 'to have' + past participle). Typical personal endings are (here, for present of *-ar* verb): sing. *-o*, *-as*, *-a*; pl. *-amos*, (*-ais*), *-am*. Similar endings are added to the remaining tenses, whose first person forms are (*comprar* 'to buy'): imperfect *comprava*; preterite *comprei*; future *comprarei*; conditional *compraria*; pluperfect *comprara*; past participle: *comprado*: e.g. *tenho comprado* 'I have bought', *tem comprado* 'he has bought'.

The inflected infinitive: i.e. the infinitive plus the endings: sing. 1 Ø, 2 *-es*, 3 Ø; pl. 1 *-mos*, 2 *-des*, 3 *-em*. This peculiarly Portuguese construction is used to avoid subordinate clauses of various kinds: e.g. *ao chegar eu* 'when I arrive(d), will arrive'; *depois de* (*eles*) *chegarem* 'after they have/had arrived, will arrive'; *Acho melhor não fazeres questão* 'I think it will be as well if you don't make an issue of this'; *ouvi-os dizerem que...* 'I heard it being said that ...'.

Passive voice: is made with *ser* 'to be' + past participle.

THE VERB 'TO BE'
ser/estar: *ser* denotes essential, permanent properties; *estar* denotes a temporary and contingent state of affairs: *Lisboa é em Portugal* 'Lisbon is in Portugal'; *estamos em Lisboa* 'we are in Lisbon'. *Estar* is also used with the present participle to express continuous action: e.g. *está olhando para...* 'he/she is looking at ...'.

Negation

Não precedes the verb negated, often reinforced by second negative following verb: *não tenho nada* 'I have nothing'.

Prepositions

The basic series – *a* 'to', *ante* 'before', *após* 'after', *em* 'in', *para* 'for', etc. – is greatly extended by the use of nominals/adverbials + *de*: e.g. *abaixo de* 'below';

através de 'through'; *em lugar de* 'instead of'; *por detrás de* 'behind'.

Word order

SVO is normal.

BRAZILIAN PORTUGUESE

INTRODUCTION

About 120 million people speak Brazilian Portuguese (*brasileiro*) in a variety of dialects. The Paulista dialect (of São Paulo and district) and the Carioca dialect of Rio de Janeiro vary, for example, in the pronunciation of the sibilants /s, z/; Paulista /s/ = Carioca /ʃ/, Paulista /z/ = Carioco /ʒ/: e.g. *as ruas* 'the streets' – Paulista /ɐz.ʀuəs/, Carioca /ɐʃ.ʀuəʃ/.

PHONOLOGY

Portuguese was transplanted to the New World in the early sixteenth century. By the late seventeenth century phonological divergencies between the two languages, European and Brazilian Portuguese, had developed. Some of the more important are (EP = European Portuguese; BP = Brazilian):

1. EP /ʀ/ becomes a fricative in BP: /h, x, ʁ/: e.g. *dormir* 'to sleep' is /duhmih/ in BP.
2. /t, d/ in EP become the corresponding affricates in BP, if followed by /i/: e.g. *bom dia* /bõ.dʒiə/ 'good day'; *sétimo* = /sɛtʃimu/ 'seventh'; *depressa* /dʒiprɛsə/ 'hurry'.
3. Clusters tend to be simplified in BP: e.g. *facto* → /fatu/; *secção* → /sesɐ̃ũ/.

MORPHOLOGY AND SYNTAX

Largely as in EP, but *haver* 'to have' has been completely replaced by *ter*, even in the impersonal usage: *Ha água gelada* → *Tem água gelada* 'There is iced water.' The weak pronominal object, which tends to follow the verb in EP, precedes it in BP: e.g. *Eu a vejo quase todos os dias* 'I see her almost every day.'

SECOND PERSON FORM OF ADDRESS
você(s) or *o senhor/a senhora*.

LEXICON
BP vocabulary differs from EP in two respects. Firstly, for many everyday objects and verbs BP often uses an alternative Indo-European root: e.g. EP *o comboio* 'the train' is *o trem* in BP; EP *o tabaco* 'tobacco' is BP *o fumo*; EP *pôr* 'to put' is BP *botar*.

Secondly, however, BP has borrowed a large number of words from various

African and South American Indian languages, especially from Tupian, with which Brazilian has been in close contact for centuries. Some outstanding Brazilian writers have drawn heavily on this exotic reservoir, which is particularly rich in terms for native fauna and flora, and, as a result, passages in their writings may be incomprehensible to an EP speaker, and indeed not always immediately clear to a BP speaker. For example, in his collection of short stories *Sagarana* (where *rana* is a Tupí affix meaning 'similar to, quasi', and *saga* is the Norse word), not only does Guimarães Rosa exploit the vocabulary peculiar to the *sertanejo* (the inhabitant of the *sertão*, the outback) but Portuguese morphology and syntax are drastically modulated to harmonize with this exotic element.

1 No Principio era a Palavra, e a Palavra estava junto de Deos, e a Palavra era Deos.
2 Esta estava no principio junto de Deos.
3 Por esta forão feitas todas as cousas, e sem ella se não fez cousa nenhuma do que fui feito.
4 Nella estava a vida, e a vida era a luz dos homens.
5 E a luz resplandece nas trevas; e as trevas não a comprehendêrão.
6 Houve um homem enviado de Deos, cujo nome *era* João.
7 Este veio por testemunho, para que testificasse da Luz, para que todos por elle cressem.
8 Elle não era a Luz: mas para que testificasse da Luz.

(European Portuguese)

QUECHUA

INTRODUCTION

Quechua belongs to the Quechuamaran branch of the Andean Equatorial grouping. The original habitat of the Quechua people seems to have been in the Apurímac–Ayacucho area of what is now Peru. Here arose the Inca Empire, which was known up to the Spanish Conquest as *Tahuaninsuyu* 'the four regions' (*tahua* 'four', *suyu* 'region'). Quechua, the predominant language of the empire, was spoken in two versions: the ruling caste spoke Inca Simi, which was presumably a high-caste register of the Kråmå type (*see* **Javanese**), although some authorities believe it to have been a secret language; the ordinary people spoke Runa Simi, or 'popular language'. From the mid-sixteenth century onwards, the tribal name Kechwa/Quechua came to be used to designate Runa Simi.

For several reasons, with proselytizing high among them, the Spanish establishment encouraged the spread of Quechua. The language was taught at the University of Lima (founded in 1551), and in 1560 Domingo de Santo Tomás produced the first Quechua grammar. At the same time, however, the active promotion of Quechua over a huge area extending from Ecuador to Argentine, led inevitably to its dilution and degeneration. It is now spoken in various dialect forms throughout Peru and Bolivia and in much of Ecuador, by something like 8 million people. During the 1970s, Quechua enjoyed a brief period of semi-official status in Peru, from which it was demoted in 1979.

There are two main dialect forms: Cuzco Quechua, the Bolivian standard, and Ayacucho Quechua, the Peruvian standard. The main difference between them is a phonological one – the presence in Cuzco Quechua of a three-way opposition in the stops and affricates: surd – glottalized (ejective) surd – aspirate surd, e.g. /p – p' – ph/. There are also minor grammatical differences, e.g. the 1st person plural (inclusive) pronoun is ***ñoqanchik*** in Ayacucho, ***ñoqanchis*** in Cuzco. The two dialects are mutually comprehensible. The description which follows here is essentially of Ayacucho Quechua.

The most important literary work in Quechua is the drama *Ollanta*, which is in the Cuzco dialect, and is probably post-Conquest in date.

SCRIPT

Runa Simi was unwritten. The first official Quechua alphabet was drafted in 1939 and adopted in 1946. It contains 21 letters of the Roman alphabet.

PHONOLOGY

Consonants

stops: p, t, q, k
affricate: tʃ
fricatives: s, γ, χ, h
nasals: m, n, ɲ
laterals and flaps: l, ʎ, r, rr
semi-vowels: j, w

/b, d, g, f/ occur in Spanish loan-words. /k/ and /q/ tend to be realized as fricatives /χ/ and /γ/.

Vowels

The basic phonemic vowel series is /i, u, a/. /i/ → [e, ε], and /u/ > [o, ɔ], in contact with uvular /q/.

Stress

Stress, if unmarked, is invariably on the penultimate syllable. A final syllable may be stressed and is then so marked: *arí* 'yes'. As suffixes are added cumulatively to the base, stress moves progressively to the right: e.g. *wási* 'house', *wasikúna* 'houses', *wasikunápaq* 'for the houses'.

MORPHOLOGY AND SYNTAX

There is no grammatical gender. Natural gender can be denoted by coded words, e.g. *warmi* for female, *qari* for male. Thus *wawa* 'child' – *warmi wawa* 'little girl'.

ARTICLES
No definite article. The suffix *-qa* acts as a topic marker. The numeral *huk* 'one' may be used as an indefinite article. The plural marker is *-kuna* suffixed to noun and followed by the case ending.

Noun

All Quechua nouns are declined according to one and the same paradigm: e.g. *wasi* 'house':

	Singular	*Plural*
nom.	wasi	wasi**kuna**
gen.	wasi**pa**	wasi**kunapa**
dat.	wasi**paq**	wasi**kunapaq**
	wasi**man**	wasi**kunaman**
acc.	wasi**ta**	wasi**kunata**
abl.	wasi**manta**	wasi**kunamanta**
iness.	wasi**pi**	wasi**kunapi**

In addition to *-kuna*, there is a plural form in *-s*, borrowed from Spanish, and used after vowel finals: e.g. *wawas* 'children', *warmis* 'women'.

POSSESSION
The possessed object takes the relevant personal possessive marker: e.g. *wasipa **punkun*** 'the door of the house'; ***Incap** **ususin*** 'the Inca's daughter'; *warminpa **sutin*** '**his** wife's name' (*-n* is the third person possessive marker (see below)).

INESSIVE
Used for both place and time: e.g. *wasipi* 'in the house'; *ñaupa ñaupa pachapi* 'long, long ago' (*pacha* 'time'). *-pi* is also used adverbially: e.g. *baratulla**pi** rantiy* 'to buy cheaply'.

Adjective

The adjective precedes the noun and is invariable: e.g. *hatun wasi* 'big house' – *hatun wasikunapi* 'in the big houses'; *Pay sumaq llaqtaykiman rin* 'He goes to your beautiful village' (*pay* 'he'; *sumaq* 'beautiful'; *llaqta* 'village'; *-yki* is poss. ending 2nd p.; *-man* is dat. ending; *riy* 'to go').

COMPARATIVE
-manta + *aswan* 'than': e.g. *Qaqa**manta aswan** kapkam kay tantaqa* 'This bread is harder than rock' (*qaqa* 'rock', *tanta* 'bread').

Pronoun

The independent personal pronouns are:

	Singular	*Plural*
1	ñoqa	incl. ñoqanchik, excl. ñoqayku
2	qam (Cuzco: qan)	qamkuna
3	pay	paykuna

These are declined as nouns: e.g. *ñoqanchikpaq* 'for us'.

POSSESSIVE MARKERS
Sing. 1 *-i/-y*, 2 *-iki/-yki*, 3 *-n*; pl. 1 *-nchik* (incl.),*-yku* (excl.), 2 *-ykichik*, 3 *-nku*: e.g. *wasi**n*** 'his/her house'; *wasi**ikichik*** 'your (pl.) house'. For agent–patient markers, *see* **Verb**, below.

DEMONSTRATIVE PRONOUN/ADJECTIVE
Three degrees of removal: *kay* 'this' – *chay* 'that' – *wak* 'that (yonder)'.

INTERROGATIVE PRONOUN
pitaq 'who?'; *imataq* 'what?': e.g. *Pitaq yachachi**sunkichik** runasimi**ta?*** 'Who is teaching you (pl.) *runa simi*? the verbal ending *-sunkichik* encodes action by 3rd person on 1st. *-chu* is an enclitic interrogative particle: e.g. *Pirwanu**chu** kanki?* 'Are you (sing.) a Peruvian?'

RELATIVE PRONOUN
mayqin, ima, pi(chus) are used in Cuzco Quechua (there is no relative pronoun

in Ayacucho Quechua): e.g. *chay warmi mayqin.manta.chus rimani* 'that woman of whom I am speaking'.

Participial construction: e.g. *yaku haypaq runakuna* 'the people who have received water (*yaku*)'; *ñoqa.pa risqay llaqtam* 'the village I am going to' (*llaqtam* 'village'; *riy* 'to go'); *llamka**sqa**y chakra* 'the field which I tilled' (*llamkay* 'to till, work').

Numerals

1–10: *huk*, *iskay*, *kimsa*, *tawa*, *pichqa*, *soqta*, *qanchis*, *pusaq*, *isqon*, *chunka*. 11 *chunka hukniyoq*; 12 *chunka iskayniyoq*; 13 *chunka kimsayoq*; 20 *iskay chunka*; 30 *kimsa chunka*; 100 *pachak*; 200 *iskay pachak*.

Verb

The Quechua verb is fully conjugated for three persons in both numbers, singular and plural; in the first person plural a distinction is made between inclusive and exclusive. There are no irregular verbs; all verbs are conjugated according to one and the same paradigm. The three basic tenses are present, past, and future.

The infinitive ends in *-y*: e.g. *riy* 'to go'; *karunchay* 'to go away'; *llamtay* 'to work'.

Present tense: e.g. of *karunchay*:

	Singular	*Plural*
1	karuncha.ni	incl. karuncha.nchik; excl. -.yku
2	karuncha.nki	karuncha.nkichik
3	karuncha.n	karuncha.nku

Past tense: the same endings are added to the stem plus the past marker *-rqa-*, e.g. *karuncha.**rqa**.ni*, *karuncha.**rqa**.nki*. These endings are close to those of the possessive pronouns (*see* **Pronoun**, above).

Future tense: there are specific endings for first and third persons; second person is as above.

	Singular	*Plural*
1	karuncha.saq	incl. karuncha.sunchik; excl. -saqku
2	karuncha.nki	karuncha.nkichik
3	karuncha.nqa	karuncha.nqaku

A progressive tense is made by infixing *-chka-*: e.g. *Imatataq ruwa.**chka**.nkichik?* 'What are you (pl.) doing?': *hamu.chka.ni* 'I'm coming'.

CONDITIONAL

The affix is *-man-*: e.g. *apa.nchik.man* 'we would take'.

PAST NECESSITATIVE

Stem + *na* + personal ending + *mi* + *kara*: e.g. *ri.na.y.mi kara* 'I had to go'; cf.

ri.na.y.si kasqa 'it is said that I had to go'/'apparently I had to go' (for the *si*... *sqa* component, see **Bound Affixes**, below).

GERUNDS

The affixes are *-spa-*, *-stin-*, and *-pti-*, e.g. from *takiy* 'to sing': *Taki**stin** llamka.chka.nku* 'While singing, they go on working'; *Taki.**pti.n** kusiku.**ni*** 'I am happy when (*pti*) he (*-n*) sings'; *tapu.wa.**spa*** '(he) having asked/asked me'.

The *-wa-* in this last example is the 1st person object marker *wan*, the *-n* being elided before *-spa*; some further examples of the agent–patient pronominal infix/affix system: *uyari.**wa**.rqa.**nki*** 'you (sing.) listened (*rqa* for past tense) to me'; *uyari.**wa**.rqa.**nkichik*** 'you (pl.) listened to me'; *tapu.**y.ki*** 'I ask you (sing.)'; *tapu.**y.kichik*** 'I ask you (pl.)'; *yanapa.**su.nki*** 'he will help you (sing.)'; *yanapa.**su.nkichik*** 'he will help you (pl.)'.

Ignoring plural endings, the basic formulae, then, for the present tense are: *-yki* 'I – you'; *-wanki* 'you – me'; *-wan* 'he – me'; *-sunki* 'he – you': e.g. *qam.ta Inca muna.sunki* 'the Inca loves you' (*Ollanta* 154). There is a parallel set for the future tense, e.g. *-say.ki* 'I – you', *wan.qa* 'he – me'.

IMPERATIVE

-y (sing.), *-ychik* (pl.); negated by *ama...chu*, e.g. *ama lloqsi.ychik.chu* 'don't go out' (*lloqsiy* 'to go out').

BOUND AFFIXES

Quechua has a very extensive inventory of bound affixes which may be used with either nominals or verbals, and which confer all sorts of nuances – delimiting, concessive, dubitative, reassuring, etc. – on the thematic core. For example, *-si* added to the subject, with *-sqa* added to the verb, generates an inferential form: e.g. *pay.**si** llamta.**sqa*** 'it is said that he worked; he seems to have worked'.

NEGATION

The circumfix *manam...chu* is used: e.g. *manam yachan.nki.chu* 'you (sing.) don't know'; *manam payta tari.nku.chu* 'they don't find him'; *pay.**pa** mana tayta.**n** kan.chu* 'he has no father' (lit. 'of him – not – his father – is not').

Postpositions

The case endings are supported by various postpositions. Many of these can also be added directly to the stem: e.g.

- *-nta* 'by means of', e.g. *chaka**nta** mayu.ta chimpa.ni* 'I cross the river by the bridge';
- *-rayku* 'for the benefit of', e.g. *Mama.y.rayku tukuy tuta llamka.ni* 'I work all night for the sake of my mother' (*tuta* 'night');
- *-mantapacha* 'since, from', e.g. *wasimantapacha* 'from the house', *qayna watamantapacha* 'since last year'.

Word order

SVO, SOV.

1 Qallariynimpim Simi karqa, Simitaqmi Dioswan karqa, Simitaqmi Dios karqa. 2 Paymi qallariy-
nimpi Dioswan karqa. 3 Tukuy imakunam paywan
rikurirqa, ima rikuriqpas mana paywanqa manam
rikurirqachu. 4 Kawsaymi paypi karqa, kawsay-
taqmi karqa runakunapa kanchaynin. 5 Kanchaymi
akchirin tutayaypi, tutayayñataqmi mana hapirqa-
chu.

6 Diosmanta kachamusqa runam karqa, Juan
sutiyuq. 7 Paymi hamurqa testificakuypaq, kanchaymanta testificanampaq, chay hinapi paywan llapa-
llan iñinankupaq. 8 Payqa manam kanchaychu karqa, aswan kanchaymanta testificaqpaqmi.

(Ayacucho dialect)

ROMANIAN

INTRODUCTION

Romanian belongs to the Italic branch of the Indo-European family. It is spoken by around 20 million people in Romania, while 2½ million speak the morphologically identical, phonologically slightly divergent form known as Moldavian in the Moldavian Republic. Other forms of Romanian, spoken by small numbers of people, are: Aromanian in Greece and Albania; Megleno-Romanian in the southern border areas, and Istro-Romanian in Istria.

The language described here is, genetically, Daco-Romanian: i.e. it derives from the Low Latin superimposed on a Dacian substratum in the Roman colony of Dacia between the second century BC and the third century AD. It is not clear how this original nucleus disintegrated into divergent and, geographically, widely separated forms. As regards Daco-Romanian itself, the main dialectal division is between Muntenian in the south, and Moldavian in the north and north-east. The modern literary language is based on Muntenian usage.

There is a rich body of oral traditional literature in Romanian, culminating in one of the world's great poems, the *Mioriţa* ballad. From the sixteenth century onwards, historians and theologians began to use Romanian in place of the Old Church Slavonic hitherto used for administrative and religious purposes in the Moldavian and Wallachian principalities. Modern writing in Romanian can be dated from the Romantic period in the early nineteenth century. The period from the late nineteenth century to the Second World War produced an extensive literature of very high quality, particularly strong in poetry and the novel: worthy of special mention are the novelists Liviu Rebreanu, Camil Petrescu, George Călinescu, and Marin Preda, and the poets Lucian Blaga, Tudor Arghezi, and Ion Barbu.

SCRIPT

The Cyrillic script continued to be used until well into the nineteenth century, and is indeed still used for Moldavian in the Republic. In Romania, the language is written in the Roman alphabet, extended by the following letters for specifically Romanian sounds: *ă, â, î, ş, ţ*. *â* and *î* are both pronounced as /ɪ/ (*see* **Phonology**): *â* was the form in use until 1953, when it was everywhere replaced by *î*. In 1965, *â* was restored in all words belonging to the semantic–etymological field based on the word *român* 'Romanian': thus, *România, româneşte.*

PHONOLOGY

Consonants

stops: p, b, t, d, k, g
affricates: ts, tʃ, dʒ
fricatives: f, v, s, z, ʃ, ʒ, h
nasals: m, n
lateral and flap: l, r
semi-vowels: j, w

/ʃ/ is notated as *ş*, /ts/ as *ţ*, /ʒ/ as j, /dʒ/ as *ge*/*gi*.

Exceptionally for a Romance language, Romanian tolerates initial clusters such as *mr-* (*mreajă* 'net trap'), *hl-* (*hleios* 'marshy'), *ml-* (*mlaştină* 'marsh').

Vowels

i, e = [e] or [ɛ], ɪ, ă = [ə], a, o = [o] or [ɔ], u

/ɪ/, notated as *î*, *â*, is central, closed, unrounded, and tense, produced in the velar region; represented in Moldavian as ы. Final *-i* often indicates palatalization of final consonant: e.g. *munţi* /munts'/ 'mountains'. There are several diphthongs.

MORPHOLOGY AND SYNTAX

Noun

Nouns in Romanian are masculine, feminine, or ambivalent; the latter behave as masculines in the singular, as feminines in the plural. Most words in this category, conveniently classed as neuter, denote inanimate objects. Consonantal endings are masculine or neuter; typical feminine endings are *-a*, *-e*, but some nouns in *-e* are masculine, e.g. *peşte* 'fish', *cîine* 'dog'.

NUMBER
In general, masculine nouns take *-i*, feminine *-e*/*-i*, neuter, *-uri*. The masculine and feminine endings frequently induce phonetic change in the noun, e.g. regressive assimilation, accommodation of final consonant: e.g. *strada* 'street', pl. *străzi* 'student', pl. *studenţi*; *masa* 'table', pl. *mese*; *carte* 'book', pl. *cărţi*.

ARTICLES
(a) Indefinite: *un* (masc.), *o* (fem.), inflected for case and number:

masculine

un student bun 'a good student'
unui student bun 'of/to a good student'
unor studenţi buni 'of/to good students'

feminine

o maşină bună 'a good car'
unei maşin**e** bun**e** 'of/to a good car'
unor maşine bune 'of/to good cars'

Similarly, *un*, *unui*, *unor* for neuter nouns.

(b) Definite: uniquely for a Romance language, the definite article is affixed to the noun: masc. *-ul/-l*; fem. *-a*; neuter *-ul/-l*. The masculine form *-le* also occurs. Where an adjective is present, the suffixed article is often attached to the adjective: cf. *bun**ul** student* = *student**ul** bun* 'the good student'. Plural *bun**ii** studenţi*; oblique case sing. *bun**ului** student* 'of/to the good student'; pl. *bun**ilor** studenţi*. Similarly in the feminine: *bun**ei** maşin**e*** 'of the good car', pl. *bun**elor** maşine*; and neuter: *bun**ului** hotel* 'of/to the good hotel', pl. *bun**elor** hotel**uri***.

(c) The possessive article: masc./nt.: *al*, pl. *ai*; fem. *a*, pl. *ale*. These are used:

(i) in concord with the independent possessive adjectives:

masc.: cîinele este **al meu** 'the dog is mine'
fem.: cartea este **a mea** 'the book is mine'
pl.: cărţile sînt **ale mele** 'the books are mine'

(ii) as resumptive linking agent in genitive construction, e.g. where an adjective intervenes:

politica României 'Romania's policy'

but:

politica externă **a** României 'Romania's foreign policy'
o clasă socială 'a social class'

but:

un studiu amănunţit **al** unei întregi clase sociale
'a detailed study of an entire social class'

existenţa lumii materiale şi **a** sufletului
'the existence of the material world and of the soul'

It follows from the above that there are two sets of endings for Romanian nouns and adjectives, depending on whether they are definite or indefinite. The difference between the two sets is not great.

Adjective

As explained above, the adjective may follow the noun, but often precedes and then takes the article. The adjective is always in concord with the noun, and may have as many as four forms, due to inflection. Cf. *crud* 'raw, cruel': fem. sing. *crudă*; masc. pl. *cruzi*; fem. pl. *crude*.

Pronoun

The personal pronouns have each one subjective and four objective forms. Thus, for the first person singular:

sbj.: eu
direct obj. stressed: (*pe*) *mine*; unstressed: *mă*
indirect obj. stressed: *mie*; unstressed: *îmi*

Similarly for second and third persons. The third person masculine forms are: *el* – (*pe*) *el* – *îl* – *lui* – *îi/i*.

In the second person, *dumneata* is preferred for singular, *dumneavoastra* for singular/plural in polite address. The latter always takes the second person *plural* form of the verb.

The preposition *pe* precedes the stressed objective form, which is then accompanied by the unstressed form preceding the verb: e.g.

L-am văzut **pe** Ion lînga pod 'I saw John near the bridge'
Pe mine mă cunoaște multă lume 'Many people know me'
Cine **te**-a învațat **pe tine** să/că...? 'Who taught you to ...?'

In general, *pe* is used, like *a* in Spanish with nouns denoting animate beings, but cf.:

însușirile **pe care** trebuie să **le** posede un scriitor
'the qualities which a writer must possess'

DEMONSTRATIVE PRONOUN/ADJECTIVE
acest(*a*) 'this'; *acel*(*a*) 'that'; the forms with *-a* follow the noun, which is then definite: e.g. *acel student* = *student**ul** acela* 'that student'. All forms are fully declined for gender, number, and case.

INTERROGATIVE PRONOUN
cine 'who?'; *ce* 'what?'

RELATIVE PRONOUN
care 'who, which'; fully declined.

al doilea din cei opt copii **ai** unei familii **al cărei** destin si **ale cărei** migrații sînt ...
'the second of the eight sons of a family, whose fate and whose peregrinations are ...'

In ***al cărei***, *al* refers to *destin* (masc.), *cărei* to *familia* (fem. in oblique); in ***ale cărei***, *ale* refers to *migrații* (fem.), *cărei*, again, to *familia* (in oblique). Dative forms are recapitulated by the unstressed indirect pronoun: *omul* ***căruia i-am*** *vorbit* 'the man to whom I spoke (to him)'.

Numerals

1–10: *un* 'one' is used as indefinite article (see above); as a numeral, it has the feminine form *una*. *doi* 'two' (masc.) has a feminine form *două*: e.g. *doi prieteni* 'two friends'; *două sticle* 'two bottles'.

The remaining numbers are invariable: 3–10: *trei, patru, cinci, șase, șapte, opt, nouă, zece*; 11 *unsprezece*, 12 *doi/două.spre.zece*; 20 *douăzeci*; 30 *treizeci*; 40 *patruzeci*; 100 *o sută*; 200 *două sute*.

Verb

It is customary to distinguish four conjugations, representing the Latin conjugations in *-ā, -ē, -e, -ī*: e.g. *a cîntá* 'to sing'; *a vedeá* 'to see'; *a fáce* 'to make, do'; *a auzí* 'to hear'.

There are indicative, imperative, subjunctive, and conditional moods. The indicative mood has simple (present, imperfect, preterite) and compound (perfect, two periphrastic future) tenses. The auxiliaries are *a avea* 'to have' and *a fi* 'to be'; *voi* 'to want' appears in the compound future.

The present tense of *avea* is: sing. *am – ai – are/a*; pl. *avem – aveți – au*. Specimen paradigm of *a cînta* 'to sing' indicative present in full, thereafter first person singular.

> Present: sing. 1 *cînt*, 2 *cînți*, 3 *cîntă*; pl. 1 *cîntăm*, 2 *cîntați*, 3 *cîntă*
> Imperfect: *cîntam*
> Preterite: *cîntai*
> Perfect: *am cîntat*
> Future: *voi cînta*; *am să cînt*. The form *am să cînt* consists of auxiliary + *să* + subjunctive: the subjunctive is identical to the present except in the third person singular where *cînt**e*** replaces *cîntă*.
> Conditional: auxiliary (*aș – ai – ar*, etc.) + infinitive: *aș cînta* 'I'd sing'.

The stems of many first conjugation verbs are expanded in the present tense by the element *-ez-*: thus, *a lucra* 'to work', has: *lucr**ez**, lucr**ezi**, lucr**ează***; Similarly, fourth conjugation stems are expanded by *-esc*: e.g. *a lipsi* 'to be missing': *lips**esc**, lips**ești**, lips**ește***.

Passive: with auxiliary *a fi*: e.g. *casa a fost vîndut**ă*** 'the house was sold'; *casa ar fi fost vîndută* 'the house would have been sold'.

Imperative: the polite form = second person plural indicative present: *întrebați-**l** și **pe el*** 'ask him too'.

The uninflected past participle is used, following the preposition *de*, in a gerundive or passive infinitive sense:

> Erau aici multe de văzut
> 'There were many things to be seen here'
>
> De auzit am auzit dar n'am înțeles
> 'I heard what there was to be heard but I didn't understand'
>
> un studiu temeinic **al** căilor de urmat în vederea ...
> 'a thorough study of the ways to follow with a view to ...'

Negation

The negative marker throughout the verbal system is *nu*.

Prepositions

Primary prepositions – *sub* 'under', *în*, 'in', *după* 'after', *peste* 'on', etc. – govern the direct case, undefined (i.e. without the article) unless the noun is itself qualified by an adjective or numeral: e.g. *după război* 'after the war'; *după **primul** război mondial* 'after the First World War'; *în traducere* 'in translation'; *într'o traducere reușită* 'in a successful translation'.

Secondary prepositions beginning with primary prepositions like *de-*, *în-* etc. take the oblique case: e.g. *de.asupra clădirii* 'above the building'; *reacția îm.potriva convențiilor* 'the reaction against the conventions'.

Word order

SVO; OSV is possible.

In început erá Cuvântul, și Cuvântul erà la
Dumnezeu, și Dumnezeu erà Cuvântul. 2 Acesta erà în început la Dumnezeu. 3 Printr'însul
tot fu făcut, și fără dânsul nu fu făcù nici măcar
ceva ce este făcut. 4 Vieața erà intr'însul, și
vieața erà lumina oamenilor. 5 Și lumina în
întunerec se arată, și întunerecul nu o prinse.
6 Fost-a un om trimis, dela Dumnezeu, al cărui
nume *erà* Ioan; 7 Acesta venì spre mărturie,
ca să mărturisească pentru lumină, ca toți să
crează printr'însul. 8 Nu erà acela lumina, ci
venì ca să mărturisească pentru lumină.

ROMANY

INTRODUCTION

Until well into the eighteenth century the gypsies were something of an enigma, both as regards their origins and their language. The very fact that they were popularly supposed to have come from Egypt (the word *gypsy* is a corruption of *Egyptian*) was enough to invest the language with mystery. It is now clear that the gypsies (the ethonym is *roma*) emigrated from India in a succession of waves towards the end of the first millennium AD. One of these waves proceeded via Iran into Anatolia, South Russia, and the Balkans, to reach Western Europe by the fifteenth century, Britain by the sixteenth. A following wave seems to have taken a more southerly route via Iran, Syria, and the Mediterranean into North Africa and the Iberian Peninsula. By the twentieth century, groups of gypsies leading a more-or-less nomadic form of life were present in all European countries and in many other parts of the world, and the Romany language, originally a specific form of New Indo-Aryan, had been substantially differentiated into two or three dozen dialects – a process in which contact with the languages of the host peoples played a crucial role.

Three main factors have gone towards shaping the Romany language as it appeared in its nineteenth-century heyday:

1. progressive simplification of the Middle Indian phonological system;
2. erosion of synthetic forms and their replacement by analytical means;
3. assimilation of lexical items and phonological and morphological features belonging to the languages of the host countries.

The first two points are also characteristic of the new Indo-Aryan languages in the sub-continent. So is the third, up to a point, but to nothing like the same extent as in the case of Romany.

Vencel′ and Čerenkov (1976) divide European Romany into eight main groupings:

1. ruska roma, lotfitka roma; in north Russia, Latvia, Estonia, central Poland;
2. sinti: Germany, France, Poland, Slovakia, Austria, north Italy;
3. servika roma, ungrike roma: Slovakia and Hungary;
4. erlides, ursari, drindari: Bulgaria, Macedonia, Serbia, Romania, Crimea;
5. lingurari, zletari, kekavyari (grouped together as čacě rom): the Vlach areas of Romania and Moldavia;
   kelderari: originating in the Hungaro-Romanian border country, now scattered world-wide from the CIS to Argentine;

lovari: belt extending from Russia across Europe to England, with spread to USA;
gurbeti: Bosnia and Herzegovina;

6. servi, plaščunuya: Ukraine;
7. fintike roma: Finland;
8. volšenenge kale: Wales.

Until the early twentieth century, gipsies were normally bilingual in Romany and the language of the host country. The latter has now succeeded in reducing Romany everywhere to the level of a domestic patois.

SCRIPT

Both Roman and Cyrillic have been used for the few publications, mainly of a religious nature, which have appeared in Romany. Gypsy folklore, tales and poems, have been collected and published in Eastern Europe and in Britain (by the Gypsy Lore Society).

PHONOLOGY

Consonants

stops: p, b, p', t, d, t', k, g, k'
affricates: ts, dz, tʃ, dʒ
fricatives: f, v, s, z, ʃ, ʒ, x, γ, h
nasals: m, n, ɳ, ŋ
laterals and flaps: l, ɫ, r, ɹ, ɽ
semi-vowels: j, w

The retroflex pair /ɽ/ɽ'/ is found only in drindari; /ɹ/ is limited to lingurari. /p', d', k'/ are aspirates. Most consonants, including the aspirates, have corresponding palatalized values, /p′, b′, p″/, etc.

The voiced affricates are largely absent in group 5, but are widespread through groups 1–4, 6–8 inclusive.

Vowels

front: i, e/ɛ
central: ɪ, ə, ɔ, a
back: o, u
diphthongs: ai, ei, oi, ui

Nasalized /ã, ũ/ occur, e.g. in Romanian Romany. All vowels tend to /ə/ in unstressed position.

Stress

Varies from one dialect to another under influence of stress patterns in host language. Thus, it is transferred towards initial in Hungarian Romany, towards a long vowel in Latvian Romany. In pure Romany (New Indo-Aryan) words, the main stress is on the final syllable. In the oblique cases, this stress moves to the penultimate: e.g. in Russian Romany: *romá* 'gypsies', *roméstɪr* (ablative).

Treatment of Middle Indian sounds:

1. Aspirated voiced stops are devoiced: Skt *bhūmi* > /p'uv/'earth'; *bhrāta* > /p'ral/ 'brother'.
2. Intervocalic /-t/ > /l,r/: Skt *bhrāta* > /p'ral/ 'brother'; *gata* > /gelo/ 'gone'; *gītā* > /gili/ 'song'.
3. Retroflex series disappears: Skt *vāṭa* > /bar/ 'enclosure'; *varṣa* > /bɛrʃ/ 'year'.
4. /s, s/ /s, ʃ/: Skt *kāṣṭha* > /kaʃt/ 'wood'.
5. /tr-/ is retained: Skt *triṇī* > /trin/ 'three'.

VOCALIC CHANGE

Some examples:

Sanskrit		*Romany*
agni	>	/yag/ 'fire'
caura	>	/cor/ 'thief'
mṛta	>	/mulo/ 'dead'
daśa	>	/deʃ/ 'ten'
śṛṇoti	>	/ʃunel/ 'hears'
hṛdayam	>	/yilo/ 'heart'

MORPHOLOGY AND SYNTAX

Article

The definite articles *o* (masc.) and *e* (fem.), singular and plural, are borrowed from Greek: the oblique form is *e* (with variants). Thus, *o rom* 'the gypsy', *e romeske* 'to the gypsy'.

Noun

The basic dichotomy is animate/inanimate; animates are masculine or feminine. There are two numbers. Formally, the animate/inanimate opposition, and the masculine/feminine opposition are differentiated only in the oblique base (i.e. inanimates have base form = accusative = nominative).

Plural: *-a*, *-e*: e.g. *rom* 'gypsy', pl. *roma*; *chavo* 'boy', pl. *chave*.

There are six cases; five of these have endings added agglutinatively to the base oblique form = accusative.

	Singular	*Oblique*	*Plural*	*Oblique*
masculine	rom	rom**es**	roma	rom**en**
feminine	romn'i	romn'**a**	romn'**a**	romn'**en**

Thus, in Russian Romany:

	Singular	*Plural*
nominative	rom	roma
accusative	rom**es**	rom**en**
dative	rom**eske**	rom**enge**
locative	rom**este**	rom**ende**
ablative	rom**estɪr**	rom**endɪr**
com./intrumental	rom**essa**	rom**enca**

Genitive case: formed with *-ker-* + final vowel marked for gender:

romés.**ker.o** chavo 'the gypsy's son'
romes.**ker.i** chai 'the gypsy's daughter'
romes.**ker.e** chave 'the gypsy's children'
romeŋ.**ger.o** chavo 'the gypsies' son'
romeŋ.**ger.e** chave 'the gypsies' sons'

Adjective

Attributively, adjective precedes noun and agrees with it in gender and number. Case is restricted to two: nominative or oblique (group 6 (*see* **Introduction**) may decline adjective in all six cases): e.g. *baro rom* 'big gypsy', fem. *bari romn'i*; pl. *bare roma*; obl. *bare*(*s*) *romende*.

COMPARATIVE
A comparative is made in -(V)*d*V*r*, e.g. *bari**dir*** 'bigger'.

Pronoun

Gender is distinguished in third person singular: sing. 1 *me*, 2 *tu*, 3 masc. *ov*, fem. *oi*; pl. 1 *ame*, 2 *tume*, 3 *on*. These are declined in six cases: base for first singular is *man*; for third masc. *łes*, fem. *ła*; pl. *łen*.

POSSESSIVE

sing. 1 miró, mirí, miré (→ mo, mi, me)
2 tiró, tirí, tiré (→ to, ti, te)
3 masc. łéskoro, etc., fem. łesk'eri, etc.
pl. 1 amaró, etc.; 2 tumaró, etc.: 3 łeŋgoro

DEMONSTRATIVE
adava 'this', *odova* 'that'. These vary widely in dialects. The Welsh forms are *kadava*, *kodova*.

INTERROGATIVE
ko(*n*) 'who?'; *so* 'what?'

RELATIVE
For Russian Romany Vencel' (1964) gives *savi*, pl. *save*.

Numerals

1–10: *ek'*, *dui*, *trin*, *štār*, *pamž*, *šov*, *efta*, *oxto*, *en'a*, *deš*; 11 *deš.u.yek*; 12 *deš.u.dui*; 20 *biš*; 30 *tranda*; 40 *štar.var.deš*; 50 *pamž'.var.deš*; 100 *šeł*.

Verb

Marked for person and number; gender is marked in participial form only. There are two moods, indicative and imperative; in some dialects a conditional–optative mood may be expressed analytically.

Four tenses are usually distinguished: present – future – past imperfective – past perfective. In certain dialects, the present has a future sense.

A reflexive form can be made from all transitive verbs.

Aspect is not a feature of the Romany verb, but certain prefixes associated with aspect in other languages have been borrowed, e.g. *za-* from Russian, *pše-* from Polish, and *fer-* from German. There are three conjugations.

Specimen paradigm: first conjugation verb, *čin-* 'write'; Russian Romany forms:

present: *čin.ava*, *-esa*, *-eła*; pl. *-asa*, *-ena*, *-ena*
past perf.: *čin-d'om*, *-d'an*, *-d'a*; pl. *-d'am*, *-dle*, *-dle*
past imperf.: *čin-avas*, *-esas*, *-ełas*; pl. *-asas*, *-enas*, *-enas*
future: in Russian Romany formed from present tense of *le-* 'to take' + *tə* + truncated present: sing. *łava tə činav*, *łesa tə čines*, *łeła tə činel*; pl. *łasa tə činas*, *łena tə činen*, *łena tə činen*.
imperative: second singular = root; second plural adds *-n*.

Present tense of auxiliary *ov-* 'to be': sing. *som*, *san*, *si*; pl. *sam*, *san*, *si*.

NEGATION

In general, indicative tenses are negated by *na* preceding verb; imperative by *ma*. In German Romany, a negative marker *či* or *gar* follows verb (influence of *nicht*?): Rmy *činava či/gar* = Gm. *ich schreibe nicht*.

PARTICIPLE

This is formed from third person plural base of past perfective: marked for gender and number: e.g. *bikindło*, *-i*, *-e* 'sold' (masc., fem., pl. common); *kerdo*, *-i*, *-e* 'done'; *džindło*, *-i*, *-e* 'known'. The participle can be active or passive, and is neutral as to tense.

Prepositions

The nominal declension set out above refers mainly to nouns denoting animate beings. Other nouns are rarely declined in this way, and here prepositions are brought in to express syntactic relationships. In some dialects, a distinction is made between a dynamic situation (motion towards or into something) and a static (rest in a place). Thus, in servika/ungrike roma, *andro veš* 'into the forest'; *andro vešeste* 'in the forest'.

Word order

SVO is normal.

31. Atunči avile leski dey tay vi leske phral. Ašile avri
tay tradine ekh vorba te avel avri lende. 32. Vi but žene
bešenas kote tay phende, "Ašun, tyiri dey tay tyire phral si
avri. Mangen tu te žas lende." 33. Tay dya anglal o Isus,
"Kon si muŕi dey tay muŕe phral?" 34. Tay dikhlya pe
kodolende kay bešenas truyal leste tay phendya, "Katka
bešen muŕi dey tay muŕe phral. Kongodi kerel e voya le
Devleski, vo si muro phral tay muŕi phey tay vi muŕi dey."

Kelderari
(Mark 3: 31–5)

RUSSIAN

INTRODUCTION

This East Slavonic language is the official language of the CIS, where it is spoken by about 160 million people as mother tongue, and, as second language, by the national minorities totalling around 60–70 million.

The dialectal split of East Slavonic into Russian, Ukrainian, and Belorussian dates from the end of the first millennium AD. The earliest writing in the Kievan and Mongol periods (eleventh to fourteenth centuries) was in Old Church Slavonic, i.e. a literary medium based on South Slavonic: an influence which was fortuitously promoted by an influx of South Slavonic clerics after the fall of Constantinople in 1453. Thus fortified, the written language, which had previously permitted some intermingling with East Slavonic forms, remained aloof from the more and more divergent East Slavonic spoken language until the eighteenth century, when, as part of the modernization programme of Peter the Great, agreement on a standardized written and spoken norm was recognized as a most urgent necessity. What emerged was to some extent a compromise between written South Slavonic and spoken East Slavonic – a compromise which can still be traced in the modern Russian language, e.g. in the presence of doublets representing East and South Slavonic versions of Proto-Slavonic roots, e.g. ESlav. *golová* 'head', SSlav. *glavá* 'chapter'.

A main dialectal division in the Russian speech area is that between northern and southern pronunciation, and features of both have found their way into the standardized language. Thus, what is known as *akan'e*, the reduction of unstressed /o/ to [ə, a], is originally a southern trait, but is now a phonological component of standard Russian, one which is not, however, reflected in the orthography. *See* **Phonology**, below. On the other hand, the northern pronunciation of /g/ as [g] is now standard, versus the southern pronunciation [ɣ].

Modern Russian literature begins with the scholar, poet, and linguist Lomonosov in the eighteenth century; his Russian Grammar was published in 1755. A first high point was reached in the early nineteenth century with two outstanding poets: Alexander Pushkin and Mikhail Lermontov. Over the ensuing half-century, Turgenev, Gogol', Dostoevski, Tolstoy, and Goncharov wrote some of the world's best novels, and Anton Chekhov some of its best plays. A third efflorescence came in the very early years after the Revolution, with the experimental poetry of Blok, Mayakovsky, Khlebnikov, Mandel'stam, and others. From the 1930s until the advent of *perestrojka,* writing in Russia has suffered from dual political pressure: on the one hand, internal in the shape of government decrees delimiting the writer's field (e.g. the Zhdanovščina), and, secondly, external, in that apparently non-conformist works have tended to be hailed for political reasons as masterpieces. From hundreds of names, those of Pasternak, Paustovsky, and Bulgakov rate special mention.

SCRIPT

Cyrillic. The 'civil alphabet' (*grazhdánskaja ázbuka*) was introduced in the place of the Church Slavonic script as part of Peter the Great's language reform in the middle of the eighteenth century. In 1917/18 certain redundant letters were discarded, and this is the form now in use.

PHONOLOGY

Consonants

stops: p, b, t, d, k, g
affricates: ts, tʃ
fricatives: f, v, s, z, ʃ, ʒ, x
nasals: m, n
lateral and flap: l, r
semi-vowel: j

With certain exceptions (noted below) all Russian consonants occur in pairs: one non-palatalized, one palatalized: thus, for example, the stops can be set out in two rows as /p, b, t, d, k, g/ and /p′, b′, t′, d′, k′, g′/ (though velar palatalization is rare). The exceptions are provided by the affricate /ts/ which is hard only, while /tʃ/ is always soft. The fricatives /ʃ, ʒ/ are always hard, the other fricatives are ambivalent, as are /m, n, l, r/. Finally, the Cyrillic letter щ, pronounced as /ʃː/ has no hard counterpart. In the Cyrillic script, the soft sign ь is used to signal that an ambivalent consonant is palatalized: e.g. *den′* 'day'.

It should be noted that *g* in masculine and neuter adjectival and pronominal genitive forms is pronounced as /v/: e.g. *jego* /yəvo/, 'his'.

Vowels

Symmetrically divided into hard and soft series; specifically notated in the Cyrillic script.

hard: ɨ, ɛ, a, o, u
soft: i, e, ja, jo, ju

As will be seen, the difference between /a/ja, o/jo, u/ju/ is one of palatalization only. In the other two cases, there is an additional difference in quality: /ɨ/i, ɛ/e/.

An extremely important feature of Russian phonology is the extensive reductionism which affects all unstressed vowels except /u/. Unstressed /o/, in particular, tends to become [a]; this phenomenon is known as *akan'e*. Where two or more unstressed vowels (not /u/) precede the tonic stress, the reductionist or neutralization process is graduated through more than one stage of the secondary vowel inventory. Again, this is particularly evident in the case of /o/; cf. *xorošo* /xərʌʃɔ/, 'well, good'; *golova* /gəlʌva/ 'head'. In this article, consonants preceding a soft vowel are understood to be soft (apart from exceptions noted above): e.g. *délo* /d'ela/, plural *delá* /d'əla/ 'affair(s)'; ы is notated as y. In broad transcription both Cyrillic е and э are usually notated as Roman *e*. In this article, э is notated as *ẹ* to distinguish it from the soft counterpart; that is to say, wherever *e* appears, it is soft, and the preceding consonant is palatalized. Initial *e* is /je/.

Stress

Free, occurring on any syllable of a word. Stress is mobile within the inflectional system: cf. *oknó* 'window', pl. *ókna*; *délo* 'affair', pl. *delá*; *pisát'* 'to write': *ja pišú* 'I write', *my píšem* 'we write'.

MORPHOLOGY AND SYNTAX

Noun

Russian has no definite or indefinite article. There are three genders, two numbers and six cases plus a rarely used vocative. Some endings are coded for gender: *-a* (fem.) (though nouns in *-a* denoting male persons – e.g. *mužčina* 'man', *deduška* 'grandfather' – are masculine), *-o* (nt.), consonant (masc.).

Examples of declension: *a*-stem, *stena* 'wall'; masc. *o*-stem, *stol* 'table'; *i*-stem, *dver'* 'door'.

	Singular	*Plural*	*Singular*	*Plural*	*Singular*	*Plural*
nom.	stena	steny	stol	stoly	dver'	dveri
acc.	stenu	steny	stol	stoly	dver'	dveri
gen.	steny	sten	stola	stolov	dveri	dverjej
dat.	stene	stenam	stolu	stolam	dveri	dverjam
instr.	stenoj	stenami	stolom	stolami	dver'ju	dverjami
prep.	stene	stenax	stole	stolax	dveri	dverjax

Animate/non-animate opposition: for masculine singular nouns referring to living creatures, and for all plural animate nouns, the accusative = genitive. Compare

My posetili zavod 'We visited the factory' (acc. = nom.)

My vstretili molod**ogo** inžener**a** 'We met the young engineer' (acc. = gen.)

The genitive case is always used with the negated verb 'to be in a place' → 'to exist': e.g. *Otveta net/ne bylo* 'There is/was no reply.' This turn of phrase is also used to express the notion of 'having/not having': e.g. *U menja mašin**a*** 'I have a car': *U menja mašiny net* 'I haven't got a car.' The object – especially if abstract –

is usually in the genitive after negated verbs: e.g. *Oni ne obratili nikak**ogo** vnimanij**a** na ego slova* 'They paid no attention at all to his words.'

Adjective

Adjectives have long attributive forms, preceding the noun, and short predicative forms; the long forms may also be used predicatively, very frequently in the instrumental case after the verb 'to be': e.g. *Mongol'skie voiny byli lovk**imi** i bespoščadn**ymi*** 'The Mongol warriors were cunning and ruthless.'

Specimen declension of attributive adjective: masculine hard, *staryj* 'old':

	Masculine	*Neuter*	*Feminine*	*Plural*
nominative	staryj	staroe	staraja	starye
accusative	staryj/-ogo	staroe	staruju	starye
genitive	starogo	starogo	staroj	staryx
dative	staromu	staromu	staroj	starym
instrumental	starym	starym	staroj	starymi
prepositional	starom	starom	staroj	staryx

COMPARATIVE

The formant is *-ee/-ei/-e*: e.g. *sil'nyj* 'strong' – *sil'n**ee***. Before the comparative ending *-e*, consonant alternation takes place: e.g. *dorogoj* 'dear' – *doro**že***; *krepkij* 'strong' – *krep**če***; *suxoj* 'dry' – *su**še***. A periphrastic form with *bolee* 'more than', can also be used: e.g. *Ẹta kniga interesnee, čem ta = Ẹta kniga bolee interesna, čem ta* 'This book is more interesting than that one.'

Pronoun

PERSONAL PRONOUNS

sing. 1 *ja*, 2 *ty*, 3 *on/ona/ono*; pl. 1 *my*, 2 *vy*, 3 *oni*

These are declined in six cases; e.g. for first person singular *ja*:

gen. *menja*; dat. *mnje*; acc. *menja*; instr. *mnoj*; prep. (*obo*) *mnje*

Throughout this pronominal declension, the accusative is identical with the genitive. The possessive adjectives are: *moi*, *tvoi*, *naš*, *vaš*, for first and second persons singular and plural. These are declined in six cases. The possessive pronoun of the third person is *ego* (masc., nt.), *ejo* (fem.), *ix* (pl.); these forms are indeclinable: *ja videl ego/ejo/ix brata* 'I saw his/her/their brother'.

DEMONSTRATIVE PRONOUN

ẹtot/ẹta/ẹto, pl. *ẹti* 'this/these'; *tot/ta/to*, pl. *te* 'that/those'. Again, these are fully declined in six cases. However, only the neuter form *ẹto* can function by itself as a subject (i.e. without a noun): cf.

Ẹti knigi – učebniki 'These books are textbooks'

Ẹto – učebniki 'These (which we have here) are textbooks'

INTERROGATIVE PRONOUN

kto 'who?'; *čto* 'what?' Both are fully declined.

RELATIVE PRONOUN

Masc. *kotoryj*, fem. *kotoraja*, nt. *kotoroe*: always agrees with referent in number and gender; case agreement depends on function of relative pronoun in sentence.

Ja xoču uspet′ na poezd, kotoryj otxodit v 10 časov
'I want to catch the train which leaves at 10'

Dajte mnje knigi, kotorye ležat na stole
'Give me the books which are lying on the table'

Zavtra k nam pridët tovarišč, kotor**ogo** my davno ne videli
'Tomorrow a friend of ours is coming to see us, whom we haven't seen for a long time'

Ja uže pročital knigu, kotor**uju** on mnje dal
'I have already read the book which he gave me'

Numerals

1 *odin*, *odna*, *odno*; pl. *odni* can be used to mean 'some'. 2 *dva* (masc. and nt.), *dve* (fem.). 3–10: *tri*, *četyre*, *p'at'*, *šest'*, *sem'*, *vosem'*, *dev'at'*, *des'at'*; 11 *odinnadcat'*; 12 *dvenadcat'*; 20 *dvadcat'*; 30 *tridcat'*; 40 *sorok*; 50 *pjat'desjat*; 60 *šest'desjat*; 70 *sem'desjat*; 80 *vosem'desjat*; 90 *devjanosto*. (Note final *t'* in units and teens, final *t* in decades.) 100 *sto*.

Nouns in the nominative following 2, 3, 4, or any numeral whose last digit is 2, 3 or 4, take the genitive singular: *četyre doma* 'four houses'; *dvesti šest'desjat četyre nedeli* '264 weeks'. Numerals upwards of 4, i.e. from 5 inclusive take the genitive plural: e.g. *šest' knig* 'six books', *pjat'sot čelovek* 'five people'.

The cardinal numbers are declined: e.g. 3 *tri*: nom., acc. *tri*, gen., prep. *trjox*, dat. *trjom*, inst. *tremja*. Cf. *tri sestry* 'three sisters'; *v 'Trjox sestrax'* 'in "The Three Sisters"' (Chekhov's play): *On sčital 'Trjox sestjor' komedijej* 'He regarded "The Three Sisters" as a comedy'.

From 5 to 30 inclusive, declension is modelled on that of *dver'*. In compound numerals ending in *-desjat*, both components are declined; e.g. from *pjat'desjat* 50 gen., dat., prep. *pjatidesjati*; inst. *pjatjudesjatju*. Cf. the following two sentences from Solzhenitsyn (*V Krugle Pervom*):

(a) uspešno upravljal vnešnim xodom **dvuxsot** vos′m**i**desjat**i** od**noj** žizn**i** i služb**oj** pjat**i**desjat**i** nadziratel**ej**
literal translation: 'successfully managed the outward behaviour of 281 lives and the duties of 50 warders'

(b) s desjat**i** večera snova zasvetjatsja tysjač**i** i tysjač**i** okon sorok**a** pjat**i** obščesojuzn**yx** i dvadcat**i** respublikansk**ix** ministerstv
literal translation: 'at 10 in the evening/ anew will-light-up / the thousands

and thousands of windows / of the 45 All-Union (ministries) and of the 20 ministries of the Republics'.

The two adjectives in the second passage – *obščesojuznyx* and *respublikanskix* – are governed by the numerals 45 and 20 and are therefore in the genitive plural. The same case, however, the genitive plural, is also used where an adjective qualifies a masculine or neuter noun and follows 2, 3, or 4 (or a compound numeral whose last digit is one of these) which, as pointed out above, require the noun governed to be in the genitive **singular**: cf. *dva* ***bol'šix*** *doma* 'two big houses'; *tri* ***važnyx*** *izvestija* 'three important items of news'. This rule may also apply to feminine nouns, although here the nominative is perhaps more usual: *dve* ***bol'šie/bol'šix*** *knigi* 'two big books'.

Certain adjectives always precede the numeral plus noun phrase, and are then in the plural nominative: *pervye dva goda* 'the first two years'.

There are further constraints governing, for example, the treatment of adjectives used as nouns.

Collective numerals: e.g. *dvoe* 'twosome', *troe* 'threesome'. Apart from these, collectives are made with the suffix *-ero*: *četvero* 'foursome', *pjatero, desjatero*, etc. A following noun is in the genitive plural: *četvero oxotnikov/studentov/rabočix* 'a foursome of hunters/students/workers'. The form denotes male persons. Similarly, where no noun is expressed, the referent is usually understood to be male: *Ix bylo četvero* 'There were four of them', though the presence of females in the collective is not excluded. Cf. *Semero odnogo ne ždut* 'Seven don't wait for one'. The cardinal numeral may replace the collective: *On prožil tam četvero sutok* = *On prŏzil tam četyrjox sutok* 'He stayed there four days' (*sutki* '24 hours'). The form may be used with a preposition: *On svernul listik tezisov* ***včetvero*** *potom* ***vvos'mero*** 'He folded his page of points in four and then in eight' (Solzhenitsyn).

Approximation can be expressed by inversion: *rublej sto* 'about a hundred roubles'.

Verb

The Russian verb has two aspects (perfective, imperfective), two moods (indicative, imperative), two synthetic tense forms (past and present), and two conjugations. Imperfective verbs make an analytic future tense with the help of an auxiliary – the synthetic future of the verb *byt'* 'to be' (which is defective in the present): sing. *budu, budes', budet*; pl. *budem, budete, budut*. The sense verb is in the imperfective infinitive: *ja budu načinat'* 'I shall begin'; *my budem pisat'* 'we shall write'. The perfective future is expressed by what is formally the present tense of the perfective: *ja napišu* 'I shall have written'.

Where the perfective aspect is generated from the imperfective by prefixation, the endings of the perfective future are the same as those of the imperfective present: *ja čitaju* 'I read' (imperf. pres.), *ja pročitaju* 'I shall have read' (perf. fut.). Where the perfective aspect is formed by other means, the endings differ: cf. *davat'* (imperf.)/ *dat'* (perf.): *ja daju* (imperf. pres.) *ja dam* (perf. fut.).

Similarly, a conditional/subjunctive is made from the past tense of both imperfective and perfective verbs plus the particle *by*: *esli by u menja bylo mnogo deneg* 'if I had a lot of money' (Gorky); *ja uexal by na Kavkaz* 'I'd go to the Caucasus'.

ASPECT

In general, the imperfective form denotes incomplete action, action in progress (present, past, or future) without specific cut-off point, or repetitive action. The perfective aspect denotes completed action, past or future: e.g.

My stojali (imperfective) pod derevom, poka ne končilsja dožd'
'We stood under the tree (process) until the rain stopped (cut-off point)'

Formation of perfective aspect:

(a) By prefixation: as in Polish, the prefix has a dual role: over and above perfective aspect, it may also modify the root meaning, usually within the same semantic field. Prefixes also serve to form inceptive and semelfactive verbs.

(i) simple perfectivity is illustrated by such pairs as *čitat'* 'to be reading' – ***pro**čitat'* 'to read through and finish'.

Včera učenik **sidel i čital** ves' den'
'Yesterday, the pupil sat and read all day'

Učenik **pro**čital knigu i pošol gul' jat'
'The pupil finished the book and went for a walk'

(ii) change of meaning: e.g. *pit'* 'to drink' – ***vy**pit'* 'to drink up' – ***za**pit'* 'to take to drink'.

dat' (perfective) 'to give'	**vy**dat' propusk 'to issue a pass'
	zadat' vopros 'to put a question'
	otdat' knigu 'to return a book'
	podat' primer 'to set an example'

(iii) inception of action: e.g. *plakat'* 'to weep ' – **za**plakat' 'to start crying'; *dut'* 'to blow' – **po**dut' 'to start blowing'.

Ženščina **za**plakala 'The woman began to cry'

Podul silnyj veter 'A strong wind got up'

(b) Aspect is also generated by modulation of the verbal ending: e.g. imperfective forms are made from perfective by infixing -(*i*)/(*y*)*va*-: e.g. *vstat'* (perf.) 'to rise' – *vsta**va**t'* (imperf.)

Segodnja ja **vstal** očen' rano 'Today I got up very early'

Letom ja často **vstaval** s vosxodom solnca
'In summer I often got up at sunrise'

(c) By alternation of *a*/*i*: e.g.

Imperfective	*Perfective*
rešat' 'to solve'	reš**it**'

končat′ 'to finish'	konč**i**t′
pokupat′ 'to buy'	kup**i**t′

(d) By *-nu-* infix: e.g. *nagibat′* 'to bend' – *nag**nu**t′*.

(e) Some perfective forms are suppletive: e.g. *brat′* 'to take' – perf. *vz′jat′*.

PASSIVE VOICE

This is analytical: *byt′* 'to be', + passive participle in *-n*: e.g. *On byl soslan v Sibir′* 'He was banished to Siberia.'

TENSE STRUCTURE

Compared with that of Serbo-Croat, for example, the Russian tense system is simple, and depends for its amplification on the aspectual system. The two simple tenses may be described as past and non-past, the latter subsuming present and future. Only imperfective verbs can have a present tense in the exact meaning of the word; the formal equivalent made from a perfective verb has a future perfect meaning: cf. *on čitaet* 'he is reading'; *on **pro**čitaet ẹtu knigu* 'he will (have) read this book through'.

The past form is made by dropping the *-t′/-ti* of the infinitive, and adding the following endings: *-l* (masc.), *-la* (fem.), *-lo* (nt.), *-li* (pl. common): e.g. *on čital* 'he was reading'; *ona čitala* 'she was reading'; *oni čitali* 'they were reading'. And in the perfective *on pročital ẹtu knigu* 'he read the book'; *ona pročitala*, etc.

Paradigms in illustration of these two tenses: conjugation I: *rabotat′* 'to work'

		Non-past
singular	1	ja rabotaju
	2	ty rabotaeš
	3	on etc. rabotaet
plural	1	my rabotaem
	2	vy rabotaete
		oni rabotajut
		Past
singular		ja, ty, on rabotal
		ja, ty, ona rabotala
		ono rabotalo
plural		my, vy, oni rabotali

Only regular forms have been shown here. There are many irregularities, involving consonantal alternation. Verbs in *-č′* make their past tense, for example, as follows: *moč′* 'to be able': past: masc. *mog*, fem. *mogla*, nt. *moglo*; pl. *mogli*.

DETERMINATE AND INDETERMINATE VERBS

Russian has 14 verbs of motion, each of which has two specific imperfective forms: one denotes vectorial motion (i.e. non-random), usually undertaken on purpose; the other, the indeterminate paired member, simply expresses the category of motion in a given modality ('walk', 'run', 'swim', 'fly', etc.) without a specification as to vector or intention: e.g. *xodit'* 'to go on foot' (indeterminate imperfective); *idti/itti* 'to go on foot' (determinate imperfective: directed motion) with perfective *prijti*, made from determinate imperfective: cf. *ja **xožu** medlenno* 'I am a slow walker'; *Ja **prišol** k vam pogovorit' o važnom dele* 'I've come to you to discuss something very important.'

Similar sets of paired verbs are:

Indeterminate	*Determinate*
jezdit′ 'to go, not on foot'	jexat′
letat′ 'to fly'	letet′
plavat′ 'to swim'	plyt′

NON-FINITE FORMS

Russian has present and past participial forms, both active and passive: the present active participle has the formant *-ušč/-jušč, -ašč/-jašč*: *čita.**jušč**.ij* 'reading' → 'who is reading'; *govor.**jašč**.ij* 'speaking' → 'who is speaking'. The past active participle: the formant is *-vš/-š*: e.g. *čita.**vš**.ij* 'having read, who had read'.

These participles are declined as adjectives: e.g.

dl′ja lic, **govorjaščix** na russkom jazyki 'for people who speak Russian'

My besedovali s pisatelem, **napisavšim** povest′ o ...
'We were talking with a writer, who has written a story about ...'

Passive participles: the formants are, for the present -V*m*; for the past *-nn/-t*; e.g. *čita.**em**.yj* 'being read'; *pro.čita.**nn**.yj* 'having been read, which was read'. The formation of the passive participle of verbs ending in *-it′* involves extensive consonantal alternation: cf. *vozvratit′* 'to give back' – *vozvra**ščj**onnyj*; *kupit′* 'to buy' – *kupl′jennyj.* Compare:

Čitatel′ vozvratil knigu 'The reader returned the book'

čitatel′, vozvrati**vš**ij knigu 'the reader who returned the book'

kniga, vozvra**ščj**onnaya čitatelem
'the book which has been returned by the reader'

IMPERFECTIVE AND PERFECTIVE VERBAL ADVERBS

Examples: *čita**ja*** 'while reading'; perfective: *pro.čita**v*** 'having read':

On sidel v sadu, čita**ja** knigu
'He was sitting in the garden, reading a book'

Zakonči**v** rabotu, on otdyxaet/otdyxal/budet otdyxat′
'Having finished work, he rests/rested/will rest'

Prepositions

The Russian prepositions are specifically associated with certain cases, e.g. *k* 'towards' with the dative, *ot* 'from', *bez* 'without', *dlja* 'for' with the genitive, etc., for example, *v* meaning 'in' or 'into'. As in German, the distinction here is between rest in a place and motion towards or into a place: *v teatre* (prep.) 'in the theatre'; *v teatr* (acc.) 'into the theatre'. Similarly, the preposition *na* is used with the accusative to denote direction of action: *upal na pol* 'fell to the floor', or certain periods of time: *na leto* 'for the summer', and with the prepositional case to denote location at or on a surface: *na stole* 'on the table', often with occasion stressed rather than locus: *na koncerte* 'at the concert', *na vojne, na fronte* 'in the war, at the front'.

An opposition between exact and inexact quantity is expressed by *v* with the same two cases: *zajom v pjat' funtov* 'a £5 loan' (exact quantity); *prosčjot v pjati funtax* (prep.) 'an error of £5'. Verbs may be followed by a variety of prepositions depending on nuance: *Mat' dumala o syne* 'The mother was thinking about her son'; *dumat' nad kakim-nibud' voprosom* 'to think a question over'.

Word order

Free; SVO, SOV are common; O(S)V occurs, e.g.

den′gi	rabočim	platili	neregul′jarno
'money	to-the-workers	they-paid	not-regularly'

1 Въ началѣ было Слово, и Слово
было у Бога, и Богъ было Слово.
2 Оно было въ началѣ у Бога. Все
3 Имъ получило бытіе, и безъ Него не получило бытія ничто,
4 что ни получило бытіе. Въ Немъ была
5 жизнь, и жизнь была свѣтъ человѣковъ. И
свѣтъ во тьмѣ свѣтитъ; но тьма не объ-
6 яла его. Былъ человѣкъ, посланный отъ
7 Бога, именемъ Іоаннъ. Сей пришелъ для
свидѣтельства, чтобы засвидѣтельствовать о свѣтѣ, дабы всѣ увѣровали чрезъ
8 него. Не *самъ* онъ былъ свѣтъ, но *былъ по-*
сланъ, чтобы засвидѣтельствовать о свѣтѣ.

SAMOAN

INTRODUCTION

Samoan belongs to the Malayo-Polynesian branch of the Austronesian family and is spoken by about 200,000 people in Samoa, New Zealand, and other parts of the Pacific area. Since 1962 Samoan has been the official language (along with English) of Western Samoa, and is used for education and journalism; there are several newspapers and periodicals. Literacy in Samoan dates from the 1830s, when work began on the translation of the Bible. The rich corpus of Samoan folk literature was preserved and transmitted orally.

SCRIPT

As English. The letter *g* = /ŋ/.

PHONOLOGY

Consonants

Three stops, /p, t, k/; three nasals, /m, n, ŋ/; fricatives, /v, f, s/; the lateral /l/ alternates with /r/. /h/ is found mainly in foreign words. The glottal stop /ˀ/ is also present, but is not stronger than a hamza pause.

Vowels

short: ɪ, ɛ, ə, ɔ, u
long: i, e, a, ɔː, u

Represented by *i*, *e*, *a*, *o*, *u*. There are four diphthongs beginning with /a/ + glide to /e, i, u, o/; also /ei, ou/.

Stress

Usually on penultimate; on any final diphthong.

MORPHOLOGY AND SYNTAX

For note on general structure of Polynesian, *see* **Polynesian Languages**.

Noun

A few nouns have specific forms – e.g. *tamaloa* 'young man', pl. *tamaloloa* – but, in general, number is marked by specific articles. Thus, *le/lee* marks a noun as definite and singular, *se* as indefinite and singular. The corresponding plural markers are Ø and *ni*: e.g. *'o le fale* 'the house', *'o se fale* 'a house'; *'o fale* 'the houses', *'o ni fale* 'some houses'. In these examples *'o* is a focusing particle which introduces the (nominal) subject of discourse. It figures normally in initial position; i.e. in VSO order (typical of Polynesian) it is dropped.

POSSESSION

Possessed object precedes possessor: e.g. *'o le ulu* ***o*** *le tama* 'the boy's head'. Here, *o* is the possessive marker indicating inalienable possession, or possession which is independent of the possessor's wish or intention. In contrast, the *a* marker is used with contingent or voluntary possession: e.g. *'o le solofanua* ***a*** *le tama* 'the boy's horse'. *See* **Polynesian Languages** for a general note on the *a/o* possessives.

Adjective

As attributive, the adjective follows the noun, and agrees with it in number. Many adjectives have specific plural forms, either by partial reduplication or by elision of one syllable: e.g. *lapo'ā* 'big', pl. *lapopo'a*; *manaia* 'beautiful', pl. *mananaia*; *puta* 'thick, fat', pl. *puputa*; *pa'epa'e* 'white', pl. *pa'pa'e*.

COMPARISON

A comparative can be made with the formula *'ua sili ona* ...: e.g. *'ua sili ona maualuga lenei mauga i lenei* 'This mountain is higher than that' (*maualuga* 'high'; *lenei* 'this/that'; *mauga* 'mountain').

Pronoun

The personal forms are:

	Singular	*Dual*		*Plural*	
		Inclusive	*Exclusive*	*Inclusive*	*Exclusive*
1	a'u/o'u/'ita	ta'ua/ta	ma'ua/ma	tatou	matou
2	'oe/e	oulua/lua		outou/tou	
3	ia/na	laua/la		latou	

These are both subject and object forms. Choice of long or short form may be positional: e.g. short form of first and second person pronouns is preferred immediately preceding a verb: e.g. *sa* ***e*** *nofo i se nofoa* 'you (sing.) sat in a chair'.

POSSESSIVE PRONOUNS

Formally associated with the pronominal series set out above. They take initial *l* for a singular possessed object, and drop this *l* for the plural; they are also marked in accordance with the *a/o* series. Thus: *lo'u* 'my (*o*-series object)', *la'u* 'my (*a*-series object)'; *'la'u ta'avale* 'my car', *'o a'u ta'avale* 'my cars'.

DEMONSTRATIVE PRONOUN/ADJECTIVE
lenei 'this', pl. *nei* 'these'. There are three forms for 'that': *lea – lenā – lelā*, with plural forms *ia – nā – lā*.

INTERROGATIVE PRONOUN
ai 'who?'; *'o le.a* 'what?', pl. *'o a*.

RELATIVE PRONOUN
'o le, pl. *o'e*; preceded by preposition: (*i*) *ai*, following the verb: e.g. *'o le teine sa o'u va'ai* ***i ai*** 'the girl whom I saw (her)'.

Numerals

1–10: *tasi, lua, tolu, fa, lima, ono, fitu, valu, iva, sefulu*; 11 *sefulu ma le tasi*; 12 *sefulu ma le lua*; 20 *lua sefulu*; 30 *tolu**ga**fulu*; 100 *selau*.

The numeral may precede or follow the noun it quantifies. If it follows, *e* is used as linking particle: e.g. *'o maile* ***e*** *tolu* 'three dogs'. *'o fafine e to'a lima* 'five women', where *to'a* is the classifier for human beings.

Verb

Three classes may be distinguished: (a) transitive verbs, (b) stative verbs, and (c) adjectival or qualitative verbs. Transitive verbs take a direct object, with or without the preposition *i*. Many verbs have a plural form, made by reduplication of the first or second syllable or of the whole word: e.g. *lafo* 'to throw', pl. *la**la**fo*; *alofa* 'to love', pl. *alo**lo**fa*; *tu* 'to stand', pl. *tutu*. Some plural forms are suppletive, e.g. *alu* 'to go,' pl. *o*.

A reciprocal form is made with the help of the prefix *fe* + suffix (*a*)*i*: e.g. ***fe**alofa.n.**i*** 'to love one another'; *sa **fe**misa'**i** i māua* 'we two were quarrelling'.

The suffixes *-ina*, *-a*, with allomorphs, added to the stem, produce a form traditionally described as 'passive voice': e.g. *amata* 'to begin' – *amata**ina*** 'to be begun'; *alofa* 'to love' – *alofa**gia*** 'to be loved'; *inu* 'to drink' – *inu**mia*** 'to be drunk'. Since these suffixes are used, however, in contexts where a passive sense is impossible, they are now regarded rather as aspectual markers of completed action, and are so listed, e.g. in Arakin's grammar of Samoan (1973).

In itself, the verbal stem is neutral as to tense. Tense, or better, aspect, can be expressed by modulation of the stem by the prepositive verbal particles. The most important of these are:

e: imperfective, denoting present or future habitual action;
te: imperfective, denoting present or future indefinite action;
o lo'o: imperfective, denoting continuous action;
o le ā: imperfective, denoting future action;
'ua: perfective, denoting completed action in past, whose effect persists into present; also used with impersonal verbs;
sa/na: perfective, denoting completed action in the past

Examples: *'ua alu le va'a i Apia* 'the boat has gone to Apia' (*le va'a* 'the boat'); *o lo'o moe le tama* 'the boy is sleeping' (*moe* 'to sleep'); *o le ā'o'u alu i le tifaga* 'I shall go to the cinema'; *o le ā sau 'o le to'alua o le taule'ale'a i le nu'u* 'The wife ('*o le to'alua*) of the young man (*o le taule'ale'a*) will come (*o le ā sau*) into the village (*i le nu'u*)'.

The prepositive particle *se'i* denotes the optative: *ina* + stem + *ia*, the imperative.

CAUSATIVE

The prefix is *fa'a*, e.g. *pa'ū* 'to fall' : *fa'apa'ū* 'to drop'; *aogā* 'useful' – *fa'aaogā* 'to make use of'.

NEGATIVE

The general marker is *lē*, preceding verb, e.g. *'ua lē sau 'o ia* 'he hasn't come' (*sau* 'to come').

DIRECTIONAL MARKERS

Example: *atu* denoting movement away from focus; *mai* towards focus. *A'e* can be used for upward, and *ifo* for downward motion in the same way.

Prepositions

Examples: *i* 'in, on', etc.: e.g. *i Apia* 'in Apia, to Apia'; *'o le tusi i le laulau* 'The book is on the table.' *I* also means 'about': e.g. *'o le tala i Samoa i Sisifo* 'the story about Western Samoa'. *E* marks the agent, animate or inanimate: e.g. *e le tamaaloa* 'by the man'; *e le afā* 'by the storm'.

Composite prepositions include *e aunoa ma* 'without', *seia o'o i* 'until'.

Word formation

Derivatives are made by affix or by compounding:

(a) Prefix + stem: e.g. the many *fa'a* words (see Causative, above).
(b) Stem + suffix: e.g. verb + suffix, *galue* 'to work' – *galuega* 'work'; noun + adjective, *matagofie* (*mata* 'eye' + *gofie* 'light') 'light on the eye' = 'pretty'.
(c) Compounding: noun + noun, e.g. *fuamoa* 'fruit–hen' = 'hen's egg', *potu.moe* 'room–sleep' = 'bedroom'; verb + noun: *tusi.tala* 'write–story' = 'writer'.

Word order

VSO is normal.

Sa i le amataga le Lo- 1
kou, sa i le Atua le
Lokou, o le Atua foi le
Lokou. Oia foi sa i le 2
Atua i le amataga. Na 3
ia faia mea uma lava; e
leai foi se mea e tasi sa
fai e lei faia e ia. O ia 4
te ia le ola; o le ola foi
lea, o le malamalamao ta-
gata. Ua pupula mai foi 5
le malamlama i le pouli-
uli, a e lei tali atu i ai, e
le pouliuli.
Ua feauina mai, mai 6
le Atua, le tasi tagata, o
Ioane lona igoa. Ua sau 7
ia o le molimau, na te
faailoa mai i le malama-
lama, ina ia faalogo *i ai*
o tagata uma lava, ia te
ia. E le o le malama- 8
lama ia, a ua sau ia e faailoa mai i lea lava mala-
malama.

SANSKRIT

INTRODUCTION

Sanskrit belongs to the Indo-Aryan branch of Indo-European. The name is an anglicization of *saṃskṛta* 'polished, purified' (in contrast to *prākṛta* 'natural, unadorned', and hence by extension, 'vulgar, vernacular').

Indo-Aryan speakers seem to have entered India from the north-west during the second millennium BC. The Aryan kindreds are spoken of as 'immigrants' in the *Rig-Veda*, which was composed c. 1200 BC, and in this sense Ananda Coomaraswamy compared the *Rig-Veda* to the Old Norse *Landnámabók*. Vedic, the oldest stratum of Indo-Aryan, differs in several respects from the Classical Sanskrit described in this article. A note on these differences is appended.

The term Classical Sanskrit, the literary medium of the Hindu establishment and the Brahmin upper classes, covers the language and its literature from the fourth century BC (when the language was precisely and comprehensively codified by the unique linguistic genius of Pāṇini) to the twelfth/thirteenth centuries AD. Throughout this long period, spoken forms of Middle Indo-Aryan – already evident in the Aśokan inscriptions of the third century BC, and the Pali texts – went on diverging from *saṃskṛta*, which continued, however, to be written by scholars as a living language, and to function as a lexical reservoir for the emergent New Indo-Aryan languages. Sanskrit is still used to some extent as a suitable medium for scholarly writing, and, amazingly, a few thousand people in India still claim it as 'mother tongue'.

Periodization of Sanskrit literature:

1. 1200–200 BC. Composition of the Vedic corpus comprising (a) the liturgical canon: *Ṛgveda* (*Rig-Veda*), *Yajurveda*, *Sāmaveda*, *Atharvaveda*; (b) the exegetical texts: *brāhmaṇas*, *āraṇyakas*, *upaniṣads*, all dating from the second half of the first millennium BC.

   Both (a) and (b) are held to be *śruti*, i.e. 'heard' in the beginning by divinely inspired *ṛṣis* (in contrast to other authoritative but not divinely inspired texts which are *smṛti* 'remembered').
2. The two great epics, the *Mahābhārata* and the *Rāmāyaṇa*, composed and added to, from some years BC to about the eighth century AD.
3. The drama: AD 400–1000; the great figure here is Kālidāsā (fifth century AD) author of such plays as *Śakuntalā* and *Vikramorvasīya*.
4. The *purāṇas*, composed from BC to about the fifteenth century AD; repositories of Hindu lore concerning the 'five essential themes' – the

creation of the universe, its destruction and regeneration, the genealogies of the gods, the solar and lunar kings, the progenitors of the human race.

5. The *tantras*: similar in substance to the *purāṇas*, but concerned mainly with *śakti*, the female principle inherent in the god Śiva.

SCRIPT

Devanagari, developed from *brāhmī*.

PHONOLOGY

Classification of the sounds of the language in terms of positional series is very important in Sanskrit philology, and is retained here: each series has five terms: voiceless non-aspirate, voiceless aspirate, voiced non-aspirate, voiced aspirate, homorganic nasal: the consonants, as set out in the Devanagari script, are accompanied by the short vowel *-a* = /ə/:

Consonants

velar:	ka	kha	ga	kha	ṅa
palatal:	ca	cha	ja	jha	ña
retroflex:	ṭa	ṭha	ḍa	ḍha	ṇa
dental:	ta	tha	da	dha	na
labial:	pa	pha	ba	bha	ma

In addition, Sanskrit has the sibilants *ś* (palatal), *ṣ* (retroflex), and *s* (dental); the voiced pharyngeal *h*, the dental liquid *l*, alveolar or retroflex *r*, and the semi-vowels *y* = /j/ and *v*. Voiceless *ḥ* in final position is known as *visarga*.

FINAL CONSONANTS

A Sanskrit word cannot have more than one final consonant, which must be one of the following: /k, ṭ, t, p, ṅ, n, m, r, ḥ/ (visarga is marked in the script as two dots :).

Any other etymologically legitimate final must therefore be converted to one of the permissible finals:

palatals and *h* → *k*, *ṭ*: e.g. *vāc* 'speech' → *vāk*; *samrāj* 'supreme ruler' → *samrāṭ*;
retroflex → *ṭ*: e.g. *prāvṛṣ* 'rainy season → *prāvṛṭ*;
dentals → *t*: e.g. *suhṛd* 'friend' → *suhṛt*;
labials → *p*: e.g. *kakubh* 'summit' → *kakup*;
s, *r* → *ḥ*: e.g. *kavis* 'poet' → *kaviḥ*.

SANDHI

May be external, i.e. between words in a sentence, or internal, between stem and affix. In both cases, the purpose is to avoid hiatus and to promote the smooth and homorganic assimilation of sounds. The system in Sanskrit is very elaborate; a few examples must suffice:

dental + palatal; vowel + vowel: e.g. *yat ca ucyate* → *yaccocyate* 'as it is said'; *tat jāyate* → *tajjāyate* 'that is born'; *tān jayati* → *tāñjayati* 'he conquers them'
dental + dental nasal: e.g. *jagat nāthaḥ* → *jagannāthaḥ* 'lord of the world'
retroflex + *h*: e.g. *dviṭ hasati* → *dviddhasati* 'the enemy laughs'

Vowels

i, iː, e, a, aː, o, u, uː
ai, au
syllabic ṛ /r̩/ and ḷ /l̩/ (ṝ is rare)

A vowel is nasalized by *anusvāra*, represented by superscript dot in Devanagari, and transliterated as *ṃ*; e.g. *taṃ* = /tã/.

MORPHOLOGY AND SYNTAX

Sanskrit has three genders, three numbers (including a dual), and eight cases.

Noun

Stems may be uniform or flexible.

1. uniform stems: e.g.

a-stems: masc. *grāma* 'village', *deśa* 'country'; nt. *vanam* 'forest';
i/ī-, *u/ū*-stems: fem. *nadī* 'river', *mati* 'thought, mind', *vadhū* 'woman, bride', *dhenu* 'cow'; masc. *muni* 'sage', *guru* 'teacher';
ṛ-stems: masc. *pitṛ* 'father', and fem. *mātṛ* 'mother';
consonant stems: dental: *suhṛd* (masc.) 'friend'; palatal: *vāc* (fem.) 'speech'; retroflex: *dviṣ* (masc.) 'enemy'.

Specimen paradigms: masc. *a*-stem: *grāma* 'village'; fem. *i*-stem: *nadī* 'river'; consonantal stem: *vāc* (fem.) 'speech':

	Singular	*Dual*	*Plural*
nominative/vocative	grāmah	grāmau	grāmāḥ
accusative	grāmam	grāmau	grāmān
instrumental	grāmena	grāmābhyām	grāmaiḥ
dative	grāmāya	grāmābhyām	grāmebhyaḥ
ablative	grāmāt	grāmābhyām	grāmebhyaḥ
genitive	grāmasya	grāmāyoḥ	grāmānām
locative	grāme	grāmāyoḥ	grāmeṣu
vocative	grāma	grāmau	grāmah

	Singular	*Dual*	*Plural*
nominative/vocative	nadī	nadyau	nadyaḥ
accusative	nadīm	nadyau	nadīḥ
instrumental	nadyā	nadībhyām	nadībhiḥ
dative	nadyai	nadībhyām	nadībhyaḥ
ablative	nadyāḥ	nadībhyām	nadībhyaḥ
genitive	nadyāḥ	nadyoḥ	nadīnām
locative	nadyām	nadyoḥ	nadīṣu

	Singular	*Dual*	*Plural*
nominative/vocative	vāk	vācau	vācaḥ
accusative	vācam	vācau	vācaḥ
instrumental	vāca	vāgbhyām	vāgbhiḥ
dative	vāce	vāgbhyām	vāgbhyaḥ
ablative	vācaḥ	vāgbhyām	vāgbhyaḥ
genitive	vācaḥ	vācoḥ	vācām
locative	vāci	vācoḥ	vākṣu

2. Flexible stems: for example, the reduplicated perfect active participle in *-vas* has three stems, e.g. *cakr̥vas* '(he) having done': middle stem, *cakr̥vat*; strong stem, *cakr̥vāṃs*; weak stem, *cakruṣ*. The strong stem appears in the singular nominative, vocative, accusative, the dual nominative, vocative, accusative, and the plural nominative, vocative. Elsewhere, the middle or weak stem appears, the middle, for example, being used with the dual and plural instrumental and dative: *cakr̥vadbhyām/-bhiḥ*.

There are, of course, many variants, and the declension system is further complicated by internal sandhi.

Examples of case usage:

Nominative: *sa pandit**o**.bravīt* 'that pandit said'; *kalo gacchati* 'time passes'; *vyāghro māṇuṣam khadati* 'the tiger eats man'.

Accusative: *Dharma**ṃ** śrotum ihāgataḥ* '(I) have come hither to hear the law'; *brāhmaṇ**am**.āyānt**am**.avalokya* 'seeing the Brahmin coming'; *patavam dadāti* 'it gives skill'.

Instrumental: *vyāghre**ṇa** vyāpāditaḥ khāditaśca* '(was) seen by the tiger and eaten'; ***kena**.cit sr̥gal**ena** avalokitaḥ* 'was seen by a certain jackal'; *daiv**ena** deyam* '(to be) given by Fate'; *Balo mukhaṃ hast**ābhyām** gūhati* 'The boy hides his face with his hands'; *prakr̥t**yā*** 'by nature'.

Dative: *Viprāya gāṃ dadāti* 'He gives a cow to the Brahmin'; *yuddh**āya** gacchati* 'he goes to war'; *Kūpaṃ putre**bhyaḥ** khanati* 'He digs a well for his sons.'

Genitive: + noun replaces verb 'to have' in Sanskrit, e.g. *arīṇāṃ rathā bhavanti* 'the enemies have chariots'. Genitive absolute: used in contemptuous or slighting sense: e.g. *pasyat**o** mūrkh**asya*** 'while a fool was looking on'.

Locative: *grīṣme* 'in summer'; *rājakuleṣu* 'in royal families'. Locative absolute: *tasmin nirgate* 'when he had gone out'; *astam gate savitari* 'when the sun had set'.

Ablative: *munir.vanāt gacchati* 'the sage goes from the forest'; *ahāryatvāt* 'because of (its) being unlikely to be stolen'.

Vocative: *Mitra – kuśalaṃ te* 'Friend – hail to thee!'; *Bho bho, paṇḍitāḥ śruyatām* 'Ho, pandits give ear!'

Adjective

Declined in concord with nominal and on same lines. Many adjectives are formed with the suffixes *-mat, -vat* (masc. forms) meaning 'possessed of', 'possessing': e.g. *jñāna.vat* 'possessing knowledge'; *rūpa.vat* 'having form' → 'shapely, handsome'.

Adjective + noun can often be rendered in Sanskrit by a compound: e.g. *su.janaḥ* 'a good man'; *dur.janaḥ* 'a bad man'.

Pronoun

PERSONAL

The base forms of the personal pronouns are:

sing.: 1 *aham*, 2 *tvam*, 3 *saḥ/sā/tat* (i.e. the third person distinguishes gender)
dual: 1 *āvām*, 2 *yuvām*, 3 *tau/te/te*
pl.: 1 *vayam*, 2 *yūyam*, 3 *te/tāḥ/tāni*

These are declined in seven cases. The oblique forms of first singular are based on *ma-*: *mām*, *mayā*, *mama*, etc. Similarly, for *vayam*: *asmān*, *asmābhiḥ*, etc.

DEMONSTRATIVE PRONOUN

ayam 'this', *asau* 'that': fully declined.

INTERROGATIVE PRONOUN

kaḥ (masc.), *kā* (fem.), *kim* (neuter) 'who?'

RELATIVE PRONOUN

yaḥ/yā/yat may be used, but Sanskrit often prefers to make a relative clause into an adjectival compound. Both forms are shown in this sentence from the *Hitopadeśa*:

asti kaścid evaṃbhūto vidvān **yo** mama putrāṇāṃ nityam.unmārgagāminām- anadhigata.śāstrāṇām.idānīṃ nītiśāstropadeśena punar.-janma karāyituṃ samarthaḥ

Here, ***yo*** refers to *vidvān* 'learned man': 'is there any such learned man, **who** ... can (*samarthaḥ*) bring about (*karāyitum*) the rebirth (*punar.janma*) of my sons (*mama putrāṇām*) **who**-are-continually (*nityam*)-going-in-evil-ways (*un.mārga.gāminām*) and-who-have-not-as-yet-studied-the-śāstras. (*nītiśāstra-upadeśa* 'instruction in social and political ethics': *-ena* is the instrumental case ending: 'by instruction in ...'; sandhi: *-a* + *u-* → *-o-*)

The interrogative *kaḥ* forms may also be used: e.g. *parivartini saṃsāre mṛtaḥ* ***ko*** *vā na jāyate* 'who (when) dead (*mṛtaḥ*) in the round (*parivartin*) of existence (*saṃsāra*) is not born again ...'

Numerals

1–10: *eka*, *dvi*, *tri*, *catur*, *pañca*, *ṣaṣ*, *sapta*, *aṣṭa*, *nava*, *daśa*; 11 *ekādaśa*; 12 *dvādaśa*; 20 *viṃśati*; 30 *triṃśat*; 40 *catvāriṃśat*; 100 *śataṃ*.

Eka is declined as a pronoun, *dvi* as an adjectival dual; 3 onwards as nominals.

Verb

VOICE

An active voice is opposed to a medio-passive. The active voice is known as the *parasmaipada* ('word for another'); the middle voice is the *ātmanepada* ('word for oneself'); the passive is identical to the ātmanepada, except in the present and imperfect tenses. There are indicative, imperative, and optative moods.

TENSE

The indicative mood has five main tenses, which can be formally divided into two groups: group 1 contains the present and the imperfect, in which the personal endings are added to the *base*, often with a linking agent; in group 2 the personal endings are added to the *root* (or root + sibilant); this group comprises the perfect, and aorist, and the future.

The base to which the personal endings are added in group 1 is formed in ten different ways; in other words, there are, in this respect, ten classes of verb. The formation of these classes involves the important phenomenon of vowel gradation: briefly, normal grade vowels *a*/*ā*, *i*/*ī*, *u*/*ū*, *ṛ*, *ḷ*, are said to have a strengthened grade (known as *guṇa*) and a doubly strengthened grade (known as *vṛddhi*). The guṇa grade of *u*/*ū*, for example, is *o*, the vṛddhi is *au*; similarly, *i*/*ī* – *e* – *ai*; *ṛ* – *ar* – *ār*. For example, in class I: *budh* 'know' – ***bo****dh*, ***bo****dhati*: guṇa grade in present tense; in class III *bhṛ* 'carry': pres. (*bi*)*bh****ar****ti* (guṇa), perf. *babh****ā****ra* (vṛddhi)

In illustration of the personal endings, here are the parasmaipada and ātmanepada forms of the present tense of the first conjugation, class I verb *bhū* 'to be':

	Parasmaipada			*Ātmanepada*		
	Singular	*Dual*	*Plural*	*Singular*	*Dual*	*Plural*
1	bhavāmi	bhavāvaḥ	bhavāmaḥ	bhave	bhavāvahe	bhavāmahe
2	bhavasi	bhavathaḥ	bhavatha	bhavase	bhavethe	bhavadhve
3	bhavati	bhavataḥ	bhavanti	bhavate	bhavete	bhavante

Imperfect: with stressed augment: for example the singular parasmaipada forms are: 1 ***á****bhavam*, 2 ***á****bhavaḥ*, 3 ***á****bhavat*; plural: *abhavāma*, *abhavata*, *abhavan*.

Optative: characteristic *-e-*: sing. 1 *bhaveyam*, 2 *bhaveḥ*, 3 *bhavet*; pl. *bhavema*, *bhaveta*, *bhaveyuḥ*.
Aorist: sigmatic or non-sigmatic, both with augment: there are seven forms: e.g. from *diś-* 'to point'; *a.dik.ṣ.at* = third person sigmatic aorist
Perfect: by reduplication: e.g. *kṛ* 'to do', perfect, *cakāra*. Verbs which cannot be reduplicated make a periphrastic perfect, consisting of feminine noun in the accusative case + perfect of *kṛ* or of *as (babhūva)*: *bibharāṃ babhūva* 'he has been a-carrying'.
Future: *-sya-/-iṣya* added to stem: e.g. *dāsyati* 'he will give'.

Ātmanepada forms may be construed as active or passive, depending on the context; often, parasmaipada and ātmanepada forms can be neatly opposed: e.g. in *Bhagavadgītā*, II. 19: *nā'yaṃ hanti na hanyate* 'that one neither slays nor is slain'.

Compounds

A characteristic feature of Sanskrit is the formation of compound words, sometimes of enormous length and intricacy, especially in the work of such late authors as Bāṇa (seventh century AD) and Subandhu (eighth century) where the facility is carried to excessive lengths. There are many types of compound; three are fundamental:

1. The *dvandva*: two members of equal status, or equally in focus, normally with dual ending: e.g. *mṛgakāk**au*** 'a deer and a crow'.
2. The *tatpuruṣa*: the first member qualifies the second; often adjective + noun (then known as *karmadhāraya*): e.g. *nīla* 'blue' + *utpala* 'lotus' → *nīl**o**tpalam* 'a blue lotus'; *dus* 'bad', + noun: *du**r**janaḥ* 'a wicked man'.
3. The *bahuvrīhi*: adjectival compound replacing relative clause. Theoretically, there is no limit to the number of component elements. A final noun loses its nominal character and takes adjectival status. Examples: *prāptajalo grāmaḥ*: this can be analysed as *sa grāmaḥ yaṃ jalaṃ prāptam*, i.e. 'the village which has been reached by water supplies'; *bahuvīraḥ deśaḥ* 'a country with many heroes'; *śāntomanāḥ muniḥ* 'the sage whose mind is at rest' (see also the example given in Relative pronoun, above).

Postpositions

Postpositions are virtually absent, as the elaborate case system meets most requirements. The following may be mentioned:

anu 'after', *prati* 'towards'; these follow the accusative case;
antar 'within' (with locative);
puras 'before' (with genitive);
ā 'from, up to': precedes ablative, and can also mean 'until'; cf. the following compound (from *Kathāsaritsāgara*, Chapter xvii: 'Story of Ahalyā'): *ā vanāntara.saṃcāri.rāghava.ālokana.āditi* 'until you come (*āditi*) to a

sighting (*ālokana*) of Rāghava (descendant of Rāghu, i.e. Rāma) wandering (*saṃcāri.n*) within the wood (*van.āntara*) = 'until you see Rāghava wandering in the woods'. A compound which illustrates the use of *ā* and the manner in which a prepositional relationship, which is felt to be a detached unit in English, is integrated with the rest of the concept in Sanskrit.

PREPOSITIONAL ADVERBS

These forms, which developed from the case system, are widely used in Sanskrit to express an extensive range of temporal and spatial relationships: e.g.

with accusative: *ubhayataḥ* 'on both sides of';
with instrumental: *samam* 'together with';
with ablative: *param* 'beyond, after';
with genitive: *agre* 'before, in the presence of'.

Word order

The concept is hardly applicable to Sanskrit, partly because of the preference for compounds.

आदौ वाद आसीत्, स च वाद ईश्वराभिमुख आसीत्, स १ १
च वाद ईश्वर आसीत्। स आदावीश्वराभिमुख आसीत्। तेन २
सर्व्वमुद्भूतं, यद्यदुद्भूतं तन्मध्ये च तं विना न किमप्युद्भूतं। तस्मिन् ३
जीवनमासीत्, तज्जीवनञ्च मनुष्याणां ज्योतिरासीत्। तज्ज्योति- ४
श्चान्धकारे राजतेऽन्धकारस्तु तन्न जग्राह। ५
अथेश्वरसकाशात् प्रहितो नर एकः समुद्बभूव, तस्य नाम योहन ६
इति। स साक्ष्यार्थमाजगाम, ज्योतिरधि तेन तथा साक्ष्यं दात- ७
व्यमासीत्, यथा सर्व्वे तेन विश्वासिनो भवेयुः। स ज्योति र्नासीत्, ८
अपि तु ज्योतिषि साक्ष्यदाने नियुक्तः।

SEMITIC LANGUAGES

INTRODUCTION

This group of related languages, formerly known as the Semito-Hamitic family, is now classified as part of the Afro-Asiatic family, whose other members, apart from Semitic, are:

(a) Egyptian; attested from the third millennium BC (Old Egyptian) to its latest stage, Coptic, still in use, up to a point, in the Coptic Church;
(b) Berbero-Lybian (*see* **Berber**);
(c) the Cushitic/Omotic languages in north-east Africa, whose best-known members are: Afar (Danākil), Oromo (Galla), Somali, Walamo (*see* **Somali**);
(d) the Chadic languages: over a hundred languages in north-west Africa, including Hausa, Angas, Margi, Somrai (*see* **Hausa**).

Culturally, by far the most important of the Afro-Asiatic member groups is the Semitic, conventionally divided into:

1. North-East Semitic: Akkadian, Babylonian, Assyrian. Records begin c. 2350 BC and continue to c. 500 BC.
2. North-West Semitic: Ugaritic, Hebrew, Phoenician, Aramaic, Syriac, Samaritan, Mandaean; records from mid-second millennium BC. Represented today by Ivrit, Modern Assyrian (Syriac), Maltese.
3. South Semitic: Arabic, South Arabic (Sabaean-Himyaritic), Ethiopic and the modern Semitic languages of Ethiopia.

Semitic phonology, morphology, and lexicon provided the mould for the formulation, and, in part, the promulgation of the world's two great monotheisms, Judaeo-Christianity and Islam: twin Semitic mappings of the human condition and its metaphysical superstructure, which have achieved global significance, and which have influenced other languages and cultures to a degree hardly matched, if at all, by any other language system. Judaism and Islam agree, moreover, in conferring an extra-linguistic dimension upon their holy books by designating these as *ipsissima verba*, 'the Word of God'. In the Qur'ān it is explicitly reiterated that the Mosaic Law and the Christian Gospel are chronologically earlier but still valid revelations from the one God, which are now subsumed and sealed by the Qur'ānic text; and it is in this sense that the Jews and the Christians are accepted in the Qur'ān as *ahl al-kitāb*, 'the people of the Book'; *al-kitāb*, 'the Book', being the divine exemplar of Islamic theology, the uncreated Word of God (see Qur'ān XXVI, IV, V, XVII).

Semitic promulgation of Semitic monotheism was, however, reserved for Arabic alone. The scriptures of Judaism and Christianity were obliged to seek their wider audiences via translation into non-Semitic media – Greek (the Septuagint and the New Testament), Latin and, in due course, the European successor languages. For the Arabs, on the contrary, the Qur'ān inspired, informed and sustained the great wave of territorial, religious and cultural conquest, and the creation of a multilingual Islamic community. As W. Montgomery Watt puts it:

> In the century after Muḥammad's death many thousands accepted Islam in this way (*scil.* by becoming 'protected persons') and Muḥammad's little state became a vast empire. This could not have come about but for the Qur'ānic conception of the holy war, which in turn is linked with the distinctive conception of the Islamic community and polity. Thus the later Islamic state, even at the economic level, is in certain respects an embodiment of the Qur'ānic vision. (1968: 109)

Client and conquered communities alike acquired the Arabic script, along with at least a ritual participation in, at best a mastery of the Arabic language. Some of the linguistic results are to be seen in the wealth of Arabic words assimilated into a string of non-Semitic languages, ranging from Spanish and Portuguese to Swahili and Javanese, many of which still use the Arabic script. And, at the eastern extremity of the domain of Arabic expansion, it is intriguing to find, in the Buginese and Macassarese translations of the New Testament, the gospels each introduced by an Islamic exordium in Arabic: 'In the name of Allah, the Compassionate, the Merciful, and to Him we pray, to God most high.'

Today, the total number of people speaking Semitic languages is approaching 200 million, with Arabic in its various forms accounting for more than 160 million.

SCRIPTS

The earliest script used for a Semitic language – Akkadian – was the cuneiform borrowed from Sumerian. A consonantal cuneiform alphabet was used for Ugaritic in the second millennium BC. The consonantal Phoenician alphabet, dating from the late second millennium BC was also used for Hebrew, Moabite, and Samaritan. There was also a consonantal Aramaic script, from which was derived the square Hebrew character and the Classical Arabic script. Finally, the South Arabic scripts, from which is derived the Ethiopic syllabary used for Ethiopic, Amharic, Tigre, and Tigrinya.

VOWEL NOTATION

In part, present in Akkadian cuneiform (*a*, *i*, *u*, *e*). Specific notation of vowels in North-West and South Semitic appears much later: Masoretic in Hebrew, Estrangelo and Nestorian in Syriac, the Arabic short-vowel signs, were all introduced in the late first millennium AD. The Ethiopic syllabary, which notates seven vocalic values by modulation of consonantal base forms, dates from the fourth century AD.

Throughout the first millennium BC the consonants *y* and *w* were used in North-West Semitic to notate /iː/ and /uː/, while *h* was used to notate final *e*, *i*, *o*.

PHONOLOGY

Consonants

As reconstructed, the Proto-Semitic consonantal inventory is as follows:

stops: p, b, t, d, ŧ, đ, k, g, q, ʔ
affricate: ts
fricatives: θ, ð, s, ʃ, ɕ, ꞩ, z, γ, χ, ħ, ʕ, h
nasals: m, n
lateral and flap: l, r

Nearly all of the Proto-Semitic consonants are retained virtually intact in all daughter languages where these sounds are present. One important exception is that Proto-Semitic /p/ became /f/ in South Semitic: cf. North Semitic ***pqd*** 'to seek' > Arabic ***fqd***.

ASSIMILATION
Occurs in all Semitic languages. Two examples are: the sun letters in Arabic (*see* **Arabic**) and the stop → fricative process in Hebrew (*see* **Hebrew**).

Vowels

Proto-Semitic had three basic vowels:

long and short: i, a, u

Stress

The exact position and the nature of stress in Proto-Semitic are unknown.

MORPHOLOGY AND SYNTAX

The key genetic characteristic in the Semitic languages is the presence of the consonantal root: usually of three consonants, though bi- and quadriliterals are common: e.g. from Arabic: *HRB*, *QNʿ*, *SLM*, *SQṬ*.

There are phonotactic constraints on the identity of the three radicals: e.g. identical consonants cannot figure in first and second position, nor can consonants which, though not identical, belong to the same phonetic series.

It seems likely that both bi- and triradicals were present in Proto-Semitic, since biradical nominals – *yad* 'hand', *dam* 'blood', etc. – are found in the oldest Semitic strata.

Each root represents an undifferentiated semantic nucleus. Specific, i.e.

meaningful, differentiations within that semantic field are generated by set vocalic patterns, servile consonants, prefixes, suffixes. e.g. in Arabic: root *KTB*: *KaTaBa* 'he wrote'; *KaTaBtumā* 'you two wrote'; ***ya****KTuB* 'let him write'; *KiTāB* 'book'; *KuTuB* 'books'; ***ma****KTaB* 'bureau', 'office'; *KāTiB* 'clerk'; ***ma****KTūB* 'written'; ***ista****KTaBa* 'he wished to write'.

All Semitic languages have noun, pronoun, verb, adverb, adjective, preposition, conjunction.

Noun

Two genders, masculine and feminine, are found throughout the family. A typical feminine marker is -(*a*)*t* – -*ā* in Hebrew and Syriac. All members have examples of masculine nouns with feminine endings, and feminine nouns which have no feminine ending: e.g. Arabic: *khalifat*[u] 'caliph'; *nafs* (fem.) 'soul'.

NUMBER

The dual is present, along with singular and plural. The dual is rare in Ethiopic. A characteristic trait is the formation of secondary plural from primary plural form: cf. Arabic: *balad* 'country, place'; pl. *bilād*; secondary pl. *buldān*. Plural forms may be external (sound) or broken (internally inflected). In North-West Semitic -*im* (masc.), -*ot* (fem.) are typical plural endings (Hebrew). The broken or internal plural is regularly found in South Semitic only; for examples *see* **Arabic**.

DEFINITENESS/INDEFINITENESS

In Hebrew and Arabic, definiteness is expressed by the definite article; in Syriac by the emphatic state in -*ā*. A suffixed article developed in Amharic. Both mimation and nunation are present in Akkadian, but are not associated with definiteness or indefiniteness. Neither is present in Hebrew, Syriac, Aramaic, Ethiopic. In Arabic, nunation marks indefiniteness.

DECLENSION

Three basic cases, nominative, genitive, accusative, marked in Akkadian and in Arabic in singular paradigm by -*u*, -*i*, -*a*. For diptotes this is reduced to -*u*, -*a*. North-West Semitic has lost inflection by ending.

POSSESSION

The typical pattern is the construct: possessed + article + possessor: e.g. in Arabic, *ibnu'l.malik*[i] 'the king's son'. In North-West Semitic and in the Ethiopic successor languages' expression of possession by means of genitive particle replaces the construct: Syriac: *də*; Hebrew–Ivrit: *šel*; Amharic *ya*... (preceding possessor).

Adjective

Adjective follows noun and agrees with it in Akkadian, Hebrew, Syriac, and Arabic. Feminine form in -*t*. Usage fluctuates in Ethiopic.

Pronoun

The pronominal system is virtually isomorphic for the entire field. The only markedly divergent forms occur in Akkadian in the oblique cases. There are independent forms and suffixed forms, these serving as possessive markers and as pronominal objects. As example of isomorphism, cf. first person singular: Akkadian *anāku*; Ugaritic *'ank*; Hebrew *'ānōkī*; Syriac *'enā*; Arabic *'anā*; Ethiopic *'ana*.

DEMONSTRATIVE PRONOUN
Two-term series, distinguishing 'near' from 'far'.

INTERROGATIVE PRONOUN
Isomorphic for whole family: typical forms: *man* 'who?'; *min/ma* 'what?'.

Numerals

Decimal system. A curious and possibly unique feature is the reversal of gender which takes place when the numbers 3 onwards (i.e. excluding 1 and 2) are used with nouns: the feminine form of the numeral is used with masculine nouns, the masculine form with feminine nouns. For examples *see* **Hebrew**, **Arabic**. The system is eroded in Ethiopic.

Verb

From the bare root (bi-, tri-, or quadriliteral) further stems (versions) are generated by such devices as gemination of second radical, vowel lengthening, introduction of servile consonants, or combinations of these. These versions express modifications of the root sense: intensification, causativity, reciprocity, reiteration, etc. Not all possible versions are represented in all the Semitic languages, and the tendency over their recorded history is to reduce the inventory. Stem II (gemination of second radical), for example, is found in all members; stem III, however, seems to be in South Semitic only (lengthened first vowel). For derived stem paradigms, *see* **Hebrew**, **Arabic**.

A possible connection between the second vowel (in triliteral) and the dichotomy: action/state (contingent or permanent) is clearest in South Semitic; cf. Arabic: ***kataba*** 'he wrote' (action); ***salima*** 'he was well' (contingent state); ***ḥasuna*** 'he was good-looking' (permanent state).

The vocalic theme: *u – i – a* denotes passivity: e.g. from root *QTL* 'to kill', ***qutila*** 'he was killed'.

CONJUGATION
The Semitic verb is aspectual rather than tense-related. The imperfective aspect is implicit in conjugation by personal prefix + suffix (coded for number); conjugation by personal suffix alone (again showing number) expresses the perfective aspect. Examples from Arabic: ***yaktubāni*** 'they two (masc. dual) are writing' (imperfective); *katabat* 'she wrote' (perfective).

MOODS

It is not entirely clear to what extent modal versions of the verbal system were present in Proto-Semitic.

In North-West and South Semitic, vocalic patterns generating the subjunctive and the jussive, the waw-consecutive in Hebrew, etc. are applied to the imperfective form. Thus, in Arabic, change of *-u* to *-a* + apocope of final *-ni*/*-na* gives subjunctive, apocope of final vowel gives jussive: e.g. ***yaktubu*** 'he writes'; ***yaktuba*** 'he may write'; ***yaktubØ*** 'let him write'. In Ethiopic the subjunctive is an imperfective form only. In Akkadian, however, modal patterns were applied to the perfective aspect also.

All Semitic languages have an imperative mood with prefix–suffix formation: e.g. Arabic: ***uktub***, pl. ***uktubū*** 'write!'.

There is no consistency in the formation of the infinitive. All members of the group have active and passive participial forms.

Weak verbs are also found throughout the group. These involve *w*, *j* in any radical position, and verbs with the glottal stop. Verbs may be doubly weak, e.g. hollow verbs with initial hamza. In doubled verbs, the second and third radicals are identical: e.g. *SRR* 'to please', *MRR* 'to pass'.

NEGATIVE

By negative particle: *lo*, *lā*, *lan*, *ul*(*a*), etc. In Ethiopic, by prefix *i*-. There are specific forms for the negative of the copula: e.g. Hebrew *ayin*, Arabic *laisa*.

Prepositions

The *b*- series, meaning 'in/by', etc., *l*- series, meaning 'to', *k*- series, meaning 'like', etc., and *mn*- series, meaning 'from', are all isomorphic throughout the family. In Ethiopic daughter languages, a tendency has developed to introduce postpositions, sometimes with preposition as well; e.g. Amharic ... *lay* 'on'; *ba*...*wəsṭ* 'in'.

Word order

Nominal sentences SVO; verbal sentences VSO. SOV is found in Akkadian; SVO appears in Assyro-Babylonian.

SERBO-CROAT

INTRODUCTION

This South Slavonic language is spoken by about 18 million people, and has been present in the Balkans since the sixth/seventh centuries. Since the Middle Ages the area has been divided on two planes – socio-linguistically between Orthodox (Serbia) and Catholic (Croatia), with a Moslem component in the south; and dialectally between Štokavian (east, centre, and south-west), Kajkavian (north) and Čakavian (west). These names are derived from the words for the interrogative pronoun 'what?', which are respectively *što, kaj,* and *ča.* In the early nineteenth century Vuk Stefanović Karadžić chose Štokavian as the basis for the reformed Serbian literary standard, at the same time as Ljudevit Gaj was engaged on a similar project for Croat. In 1850 a Literary Accord was signed in Vienna, recognizing Štokavian as the basis for the new unified language, Serbo-Croat. Not that this accord put an end to dialectal variation; on the contrary, new Štokavian itself falls into three mutually intelligible dialect forms: Ekavian (in Serbia), Ijekavian (western Serbia and Croatia) and Ikavian (Dalmatia and parts of Bosnia). The latter is no longer used as a literary language, but the other two, centring respectively on Belgrade and Zagreb, are about equally distributed and used interchangeably. They differ on some morphological points (see below) and, most noticeably, in the pronunciation of the mid front vowel *e*: e.g. Belgrade *sneg* 'snow' = Zagreb *snijeg*; *reka* 'river' = *rijeka*; *lep* 'beautiful' = *lijep.*

Writing in both forms of Serbo-Croat dates from the eleventh/twelfth centuries. Pride of place must go to the Serbian folk epic – the *srpske narodne pjesme*. There are two main cycles, one centring on the disastrous Battle of Kosovo, the other on the heroic figure of Marko Kraljević. Recited by wandering minstrels to the accompaniment of the gusla, through the centuries of Ottoman domination, the *narodne pjesme* came to the attention of Western writers in the late eighteenth century and were enthusiastically received by protagonists of the Romantic movement, such as Herder and Goethe. Much of the corpus was recorded in 1933–4, an enterprise sponsored by Yale and Columbia and edited by Béla Bartók.

From the mid-nineteenth century onwards through the twentieth century a large, high-level output in all literary genres has been sustained in both languages. Among them, the names of the Nobel laureate Ivo Andrić in Serbian, and of Miroslav Krleža in Croat deserve to be singled out.

SCRIPT

In the Orthodox area, Cyrillic has been used since the twelfth century. The use of the Roman alphabet in the Catholic area (Croatia) dates from the fourteenth century. The 1818 dictionary of Vuk Stefanović Karadžić presented an adapted Cyrillic with additional letters, represented as digraphs in the revised Croat orthography: ћ /ć/; џ /dʒ/; ђ /đ/; љ /lj/; њ /nj/. The orthography for both forms was further standardized in the Pravopis of 1960.

PHONOLOGY

Consonants

stops: p, b, t, d, k, g
affricates: ts, tʃ, ć, dʒ, đ
fricatives: f, v, s, z, ʃ, ʒ, x
nasals: m, n, ɲ
laterals and flap: l, l′ (ʎ), r
semi-vowel: j

/tʃ/dʒ/ are palato-alveolar, /ć/đ/ are palatal.

Vowels

i, e, a, o, u + syllabic r

The pure vowels are long or short.

TONE

The combination of vowel length + rising/falling intonation yields four tones: long rising: ′; long falling: ˆ; short rising: `; short falling: ̏. The tones are not marked in written Serbo-Croat. Tone may shift and change within a word; e.g. *lèkar* 'doctor', acc. *lekára*. Tone is phonemic: cf. *grâd* 'city' – *grȁd* 'hail'. Consonant alternation and vowel gradation: e.g. *pisati* 'to write' – *pišem* 'I write'; *plakati* 'to weep' – *plačem* 'I weep'; *smrt* 'death' – *umreti* 'to die' – *umoreti* 'to kill'.

Stress

Stress is intimately bound up with tone; thus, monosyllables have only falling tone (short or long); in polysyllables, a falling tone can only be on the first syllable, a rising tone cannot be on the final.

MORPHOLOGY AND SYNTAX

Noun

Serbo-Croat has three genders, two numbers, seven cases, including a vocative. Four main types of declension are distinguished: *a*-stems (mostly feminine), *i*-stems (masculine and feminine), masculine and neuter *o*-stems, consonantal stems. For example, the paradigms for *kuća* 'house' (*a*-stem), *selo* 'village' (neuter *o*-stem):

	Singular	*Plural*	*Singular*	*Plural*
nom.	kuća	kuće	selo	sela
voc.	kućo	kuće	selo	sela
gen.	kuće	kućā	sela	selā
acc.	kuću	kuće	selo	sela
dat.	kući	kućama	selu	selima
loc.	kući	kućama	selu	selima
instr.	kućom	kućama	selom	selima

Formally, the most interesting point in the declension system is the plural genitive in *-ā*. Dative and locative have virtually fused. In masculine singular animate nouns, acc. and gen. forms are identical, e.g. *retko vidam tvog brata* 'I seldom see your brother'.

Adjective

The indefinite adjective has survived in Serbo-Croat: e.g. *star čovek* '(an) old man', *stari čovek* 'the old man'; but is used mainly predicatively: e.g. *Dan je lep* 'It's a nice day.'

The attributive adjective precedes the noun and is fully declined in concord: e.g. *ovaj mladi čovek* 'this young man'; *ta mlada devojka* 'this young girl'; *naše lepo selo* 'our beautiful village'.

The animate distinction is preserved for masculine singular: e.g. *ovog mladog čoveka* (acc. and gen. forms are identical) '(of) that young man'.

COMPARATIVE

-(j)ji/a/e, with palatalization in monosyllables as phonologically necessary: cf. *slab* 'weak' – *slabiji*; *jak* 'strong' – *jači*; *brz* 'fast' – *brži*; *sladak* 'sweet' – *slađi*.

Pronoun

sing. 1 *ja*, 2 *ti*, 3 *on/ona/ono*; pl. 1 *mi*, 2 *vi*, 3 *oni/one/ona*

These are declined in seven cases (with obvious omissions, e.g. no vocative in first person). The oblique cases of first singular are: *mene* (acc./gen.) *meni*, *meni*, *mnom*. Those of the third person singular and plural have *nj-* initial; e.g. for *on*: acc./gen. *njega*, dat. *njemu*, loc. *njemu*, instr. *njime*.

THE POSSESSIVE PRONOUNS

moj/moja/moje, *tvoj/tvoja/tvoje*, *naš*, *vaš*: 3rd sing. masc. *njegov*, fem. *njen*, pl. *njihov*, are fully declined in seven cases.

ENCLITIC PRONOUNS

These have genitive/accusative and dative forms. They can never take first place in a sentence, and the dative form always precedes the genitive/accusative: cf.

On će mi ga dati = daće mi ga 'he will give it to me'

On je rekao da će mi ga dati 'He said that he would give it to me'

Da li mu je rekao da nas je njegov drug video
'Did he tell him that his friend saw us?'

For the enclitic forms of the verb shown here (*će* and *je*), *see* **Verb**, below.

DEMONSTRATIVE PRONOUN
ovaj, *ova*, *ovo* 'this (near me)'; pl. *ovi*; *taj*, *ta*, *to* 'this (near you)'; *onaj*, *ona*, *ono* 'that'; pl. *oni*. All are fully declined.

INTERROGATIVE PRONOUN
ko 'who?'; *šta/što* 'what?' – declined, without vocative.

RELATIVE PRONOUN
koji, *koja*, *koje*: e.g. *čovek koji je bio sa mnom* 'the man who was with me'. *Što* may also be used: e.g. *Što snaga ne može, pamet učini* 'What force cannot do, brains can.'

Numerals

jedan/jedna/jedno and *dva/dve/dva* (1 and 2); nouns following *dva/dve/dva* take *-a* for masculine (an old dual ending) and *-e* for feminine nouns: e.g. *dva dana* 'two days'; *dve godine* 'two years'.

The same endings follow *tri* 3 and *četiri* 4.

5–10: *pet*, *šest*, *sedam*, *osam*, *devet*, *deset*; 11 *jedanaest*; 12 *dvanaest*; 20 *dvadeset*; 30 *trideset*, 40 *četrdeset*; 100 *sto*.

From 5 on, the cardinals are followed by nouns in the plural genitive: e.g. *petnaest danā* 'fifteen days'.

Verb

The Serbo-Croat verb is notable for the presence of tense forms which cut across the essentially aspectual structure, e.g. an imperfect (formed from imperfective verbs) and an aorist (from perfectives), with both of these forms tending to lose ground to a composite perfect tense formed from verbs of either aspect. Remarkably, Serbo-Croat perfective verbs also form what is morphologically a present tense: cf. *dajemo* 'we are giving' (imperfective), *dok ne damo* 'until we give' (from perfective verb *dati*).

Verbs are divided into six classes by the joint criteria of infinitival ending and present tense. Thus, the very numerous class of *-iti* verbs has a present tense in *-im*: e.g. *govoriti* 'speak' – *govorim*; *držati* 'hold' – *držim*. Verbs in *-ati*: present in *-am*: e.g. *gledati* 'look at' – *gledam*; in *-ovati*, with present in *-ujem*: e.g. *putovati* 'travel' – *putujem*.

ASPECT
The root may be perfective or imperfective: e.g. *kup-* 'buy' is perfective, *pis-* 'write' is imperfective. Perfectives are made from imperfectives (a) by prefix,

e.g. *pisati* – ***na**pisati* 'write'; *piti* 'drink' – ***po**piti* 'drink up'; (b) by change in stem: e.g. *skakati* (imperfective) – *skočiti* (perfective) 'to jump'. As in other Slavonic languages, prefixation often generates not only perfectivity but also a semantic change in the word.

Secondary imperfective verbs can be formed from perfectives by expansion of the stem: e.g.

perfective	snábdeti 'to supply'	imperfective	snabdévati
	zaúzeti 'occupy'		zaúzimati

TENSE FORMATION

Present: e.g, of *ráditi* 'to work' (all Serbo-Croat verbs take *-m* in the first person singular present tense):

sing. 1 radim, 2 radiš, 3 radi; pl. 1 radimo, 2 radite, 3 rade

Imperfect: e.g. of *kupovati* 'to buy':

sing. 1 kupovah, 2 kupovaše, 3 kupovaše; pl. 1 kupovasmo, 2 kupovaste, 3 kupovahu

Aorist: naučiti (perf.) 'to learn':

sing. 1 naučih, 2 nauči, 3 nauči; pl. 1 naučismo, 2 naučiste, 3 naučise

Perfect: e.g. of *čekati* (imperf.) 'to wait':
The active participle of *čekati* is: sing. *čekao* (masc.), *čekala* (fem.), *čekalo* (neuter); pl. *čekali*, *čekale*, *čekala*. These forms are conjugated with the present tense of *biti*:

sing. 1 sam, 2 si, 3 je; pl. 1 smo, 2 ste, 3 su.

Thus: *čekao sam* 'I (masc.) have waited, have been waiting'; *čekale su* 'they (fem.) have waited, have been waiting'.

These enclitic forms may precede the subject; e.g. *svi **su** pokušaji propali, da* 'all efforts (*pokušaj* 'effort') to... failed' (*propasti* 'to fail'); *Taj **je** komad oštra satira gradskog života* 'The play is a biting satire on city life.'

Future: the short forms (enclitic) of the verb *hteti* 'to want' are used with the infinitive of the sense-verb:

sing. 1 ću, 2 ćeš, 3 cé; pl. 1 ćemo, 2 ćete, 3 će.

The auxiliary may precede or follow the infinitive: e.g. *ja ću imati* = *imaću posetiću vas kad dođem u Beograd* 'I'll visit you when I come to Belgrade'; ***neću** vas posetiti kad...* 'I shan't visit you...'.

Active participle: as illustrated in the perfect tense above, the participle is made by dropping *-ti* of the infinitive and adding *-o*/*-la*/*-lo*; *-li*/*-le*/*-la*. The passive participle in *-n*/*-na*/*-no*, *-jen*/*-jena*/*-jeno* is declined as an adjective: e.g. *kupovan*, *kupovana*, *kupovano* 'bought'.

The use of the infinitive after modal verbs, frequent in English and many other languages – 'I want/have/ought **to go**' – is avoided in Serbo-Croat, which, like Bulgarian, prefers a construction with *da* and a finite verb: *moram da idem* 'I have to go'; *neću da pitam* 'I don't want to ask'.

Negative particle: *ne*.

Prepositions

Govern genitive, accusative, dative, locative/prepositional, or instrumental cases. Some prepositions, e.g. *u*, *za*, take either the accusative, the genitive, or the instrumental: cf.

> *za* with instrumental: *sedeti za stolom* 'to be seated at table'
>
> *za* with accusative: *sesti za stol* 'to sit down/seat oneself at table'
>
> *za* with genitive: *za turskog vremena* 'during the Turkish era'

Of particular interest is the series of paired prepositions: *nad/iznad* 'on, above', *pos/ispod* 'under', *pred/ispred* 'in front of', *za/iza* 'behind', *među/između* 'among, between'. The simple forms take the accusative or instrumental depending on whether motion towards something is involved, or rest in a place: e.g.

> ići pred pozorište 'to go to the front of the theatre' (acc.)
>
> čekati pred pozorištem 'to wait in front of the theatre' (instr.)

The *iz-/is-* forms take the genitive, and may suggest comparison; cf.

> nad gradom 'above the town' (instr.)
>
> **iz**nad prosečnog 'above average' (gen. case, with nuance of comparison; *prosečon* 'average')

Word order

Rather free; SVO/VSO are both frequent. The question of word order is complicated by the pronominal and verbal enclitics, which often require SOV.

У почетку бјеше ријеч, и ријеч бјеше у Бога, и Бог бјеше ријеч.
2. Она бјеше у почетку у Бога.
3. Све је кроз њу постало, и без ње ништа није постало што је постало.
4. У њој бјеше живот, и живот бјеше видјело људима.
5. И видјело се свијетли у тами, и тама га не обузе.
6. Посла Бог човјека по имену Јована.
7. Овај дође за свједочанство да свједочи за видјело да сви вјерују кроза њ.
8. Он не бјеше видјело, него да свједочи за видјело.

SINDHI

INTRODUCTION

Sindhi belongs to the North-Western group of the New Indo-Aryan languages (NIA), and is spoken by between 6 and 10 million people in Pakistan and Baluchistan. After partition, over 1 million Sindhi speakers moved to India and settled in large cities such as Delhi, Bombay, and Poona. There are several dialects. The literary language is based on the central Vicoli dialect, which does not differ greatly from the Northern or Siraiki dialect. Though basically a New Indo-Aryan language, Sindhi shows very marked Islamic influence, with both Arabic and Iranian traits.

Writing in Sindhi began in the seventeenth century and even the earliest work shows the cross-culture eclecticism which is so striking in Sindhi literature of the eighteenth and nineteenth centuries. A classical high point is reached in the great *risālō* of Shāh 'Abdu'l-laṭīf Bhitā'ī (1689–1752).

SCRIPT

In 1852, the Arabic script used to write Sindhi was augmented by signs for the following specific Sindhi phonemes:

the retroflex series: ʈ, ʈh, ɖ, ɖh, ɽ, ɳ
the aspirates: ph, bh, th, dh, ch, gh;
the nasals: ɲ, ŋ
the implosives: ɓ, ɗ̣, ʄ, d̠ʒ(subscript dot indicates retroflex; /d̠ʒ/ is implosive /dʒ/); Zograph (1982) notates these as *b̄/b*', *d̄/ḍ*', *j̄/j̄*', *ḡ/g*'.

As in Urdu and Iranian generally, there is some redundancy in the script. Thus, /s/ has three graphs, /z/ has five.

PHONOLOGY

Consonants

stops: p, b, t, d, ʈ, ɖ, k, g, q; with corresponding aspirates /ph, bh/, etc., except /q/
implosive or recursive stops: ɓ, ɗ, ʄ
affricates: tʃ, dʒ; with aspirates: /tʃ', dʒ'/ and implosive /d̠ʒ/
fricatives: f, v, s, z, ʃ, x, γ, h
nasals: m, n, ɳ, with corresponding aspirates: mh, nh, ɳh; ɲ, ŋ
laterals and flap/trill: l, lh, r, ɽ, ɽh
semi-vowel: j

In this entry retroflex sounds are indicated by a dot, implosives by subscript macrons.

Vowels

i, e, a, o, u

Short or long, apart from /o/ which is always long. The short vowels /i, a, u/ are realized as [ɪ, ə, ʊ]. /ɔ/ is represented by the diphthong [au]. All vowels occur nasalized.

A striking feature of Sindhi is the presence of short final vowels, which tend to be weakly articulated, but which have a phonemic function.

MORPHOLOGY AND SYNTAX

Noun

GRAMMATICAL GENDER

Masculine and feminine nouns share all five vocalic endings, but *-o* and *-u* are typically masculine, *-ī* and *-e* are typically feminine: e.g. *naru* 'man'; *nāre* 'woman'.

NUMBER

Typically, masc. *-o* → *-ā*: e.g. *ghoṛo* 'horse' – *ghoṛā*; feminine in -(*i*)*iū*/-*ū̃*: e.g. *nāre* 'woman' – *nāreū̃*.

DECLENSION

Direct and oblique forms are distinguished. The direct form is also the form used for the direct object; the oblique form provides the indirect object: e.g. from nouns in *-o*, oblique case *-e*, from fem. in *-ī*, oblique *-ia*. *See* **Postposition**, below.

Sindhi has an instrumental in *-ā̃* (with variants): e.g. *kamā̃* 'by work', *hathā̃* 'by hand'. Masculine singular nouns in *-u* have a locative case in *-e*: e.g. *hathe* 'in the hand'.

Adjective

As attribute, adjective precedes noun. Many adjectives are indeclinable, but those with vocalic endings are usually inflected for gender, case, and number. Partial inflection (e.g. gender and case, not number) is also found.

COMPARISON

A comparative is made with the oblique case + *khā̃*/*khō̃*/*khū̃*: e.g. *Hī chokaro hūa chokarē khā̃ caṇo āhē* 'This boy is better than that boy.' Sindhi also uses the Iranian comparative in *-tar*, and the Arabic elative of *'aF'aL* type.

Pronoun

PERSONAL

With gender distinction in third person singular: sing. 1 *mā̃*, 2 *tū̃*, 3 masc. *hū*/*hīu*; fem. *hūa*/*hīa*; pl. 1 *asī̃*, 2 *tavhī̃*, 3 *hū̃*. These have oblique forms, sing. *mū̃*, *to*, *huna, hina*, pl. *asā̃, tavhā̃, hunane*; and enclitics, sing. *-me, -i/-e, -se*; pl. *-ū̃/sū̃, -va, -ne.* The enclitics can be used as possessives, and with postpositions: e.g. ***ḏaḏume*** 'my grandfather'; ***khē.me*** 'to me'; ***sā̃se*** 'with him' instead of *mū̃ khe, huna sā̃.*

DEMONSTRATIVE PRONOUN

hī 'this'; *hū* 'that'. These are masculine direct forms; the feminine are *hīa, hūa.* Plural: masc. *hī*, fem. *hū.*

INTERROGATIVE PRONOUN

kēru 'who?', oblique, *kāhē*; *keharo* 'what?'

RELATIVE PRONOUN

Masc. *jo*, fem. *jā*, with oblique and plural forms, has a correlative in *so*: e.g. *Jo ḍauṛando so thakibo* 'Who runs quickly soon gets tired.'

Numerals

1–10: *hiku, ḇa, ṭī, cār, panja, cha, sata, aṭha, nav, ḏaha.* 11–99: unpredictable; as is usual in NIA languages, decade + 9 is linked to the following decade: 20 *vēha*; 28 *aṭhāvēha*; 29 *unṭēha*; 30 *ṭēha*; 100 *sau*.

Verb

Infinitive is in *-aṇu* (intrans.): e.g. *halaṇu* 'to go'; *-iṇu* (trans.): e.g. *khāiṇu* 'to eat'.

Participles: imperfective in *-ando/-īndo*: e.g. *halando* 'going'. Perfective is in *-yo*: e.g. *paṛhio* 'having read'; this participle is active if the verb is transitive, passive if intransitive. A passive imperfective participle is made with *-ibo*: e.g. *paṛhibo* 'being read'.

Gerundial forms: e.g. in *-ē/-ī, khāē* 'having eaten'; in *-iṇo/-aṇo, vaṭhiṇo* 'requiring to be taken'.

Personal forms: Sindhi has imperative, indicative, subjunctive, and conditional moods. Tense forms are simple or compound.

Simple: e.g. the subjunctive, which consists of stem + personal ending: sing. 1 *halā̃*, 2 *halē̃*, 3 *halē*; pl. *halū̃*, *halo*, *halane*: these forms are preceded by the personal pronouns.

Compound tenses: the format is personal pronoun + participle (imperf./perf.) + personal endings, *or*, + auxiliary: *huaṇu/tho/āh*: e.g. *mā̃ halando hose* 'I was going'; *asī halandiū̃ huyū̃sī* 'we were going' (first person plural, feminine).

About a dozen compound tenses are made in this way to express various shades of complete/incomplete, habitual, frequentative, action. There are two compound present tenses, which are virtually doublets: cf. *mā̃ khāiā̃ piā̃ tho* 'I eat and drink' (regularly or all the time); i.e. the subjunctive of the sense-verb plus the auxiliary *tho*, marked for gender and number. The second compound present is made with the imperfective participle and the auxiliary *āh-*: *Kamlā ine madrāsīa khē piyār kandī āhē* 'Kamla is in love with this Madrasi.'

There are three futures: e.g. first future made from the imperfective participle with personal endings: *mā̃ halanduse* 'I shall go.'

The first future of the verb *huaṇu* 'to be' is used with the imperfective or perfective participle; the participle is marked for gender and number, the auxiliary for gender, number and person: e.g. *mā̃ halyo hūnduse* 'I (masc. sing.) shall go'.

The negative participle is *na*.

Passive voice: the active base takes *-j/-ij* infix: e.g. *māriṇu* 'to beat', *mārǰaṇu* 'to be beaten'.

Postpositions

One of the most important is *jo/jī*, plural forms *jā/jū̃*, which provides the genitival link between a noun in the oblique case and a following noun: e.g. *chokarē jo nālo* 'the boy's name'; *hāriune jī zamīn* 'the peasants' earth'.

Khē marks direct and indirect object: e.g. *māṇhūa khē ḏisaṇu* 'to see the man'; *mū̃ khē ḏiaṇu* 'to give to me'; *huna khē kamu karaṇo āhē* 'to him, work is to be done' = 'he has to work'.

Khā̃ 'from', *sā̃* 'with', etc.

Word order

SOV.

مُنڍ ۾ ڪلامُ هو ۽ ڪلامُ خُداءَ ساڻُ هو ۽ ڪلامُ پاڻ خُداءُ هو (٢) سو
اُهو مُنڍئِي ۾ خُداءَ ساڻُ هو (٣) ۽ سڀئِي شيُون تنهِ ڪان پَيدا ٿِيَ ۽
پَيدائِش ۾ تنهِ ڌاران ڪا هِڪڙِي شئُ بِ نہ پَيدا ٿِي (٤) تنهِ ۾ جِياپو هو
سو جِياپو ماڻهُنِ جو سوجهِرو هو (٥) ۽ اُهو سوجهِرو اُوندَهِ ۾ پِئِي چِمڪيو
پر اُوندَهِ تنهِ کي نہ مَڃيو ∴
(٦) تہ هِڪڙو ڄڻو خُداءَ موڪليو تنهِ جو نالو يوحنُ هو (٧) اُهو شاهِدُ
ٿِي سوجهِري جِي ساکَ پرڻ آيو سو اِنهِي لاءِ تہ سڀئِي تنهِ ڪري وِيساهُ
آڻِينِ (٨) تہ اُهو پاڻ سوجهِرو نہ هو پر تنهِ سوجهِري جِي ساکَ پرڻ آيو ∴

SINHALESE (Sinhala)

INTRODUCTION

This Indo-Aryan outlier has developed over the last 2,000 years in isolation from its New Indo-Aryan congeners, and, not suprisingly, exhibits a number of unusual, not to say unique, features, due in part to Dravidian influence. The earliest records of literary Sinhalese date from the thirteenth/fourteenth centuries AD. This literary language has continued to be used into the twentieth century, and differs markedly from the colloquial Sinhalese which is described in this article. Much of classical Sinhalese literature is derivative, an ornate recycling of Indian motifs, e.g. the *sandeśa* ('message-poem') model and jātaka themes.

Sinhalese is now the official language of Sri Lanka, where it is spoken by about 12 million people. Its only close relative is the Mahl dialect spoken in the Maldive Islands.

SCRIPT

The Sinhalese script, introduced in the tenth/eleventh centuries derives from Grantha, a South Indian version of the Brahmi script, and is both influenced by and close to Dravidian scripts such as Telugu and Kannada.

PHONOLOGY

Consonants

stops: p, b, t, d, ʈ, ɖ, k, g
affricates: tʃ, dʒ
fricatives: v/w, s, ʂ, ʃ, h
nasals: m, n, ɳ, ɲ, ŋ
laterals and flap: l, ɭ, r
semi-vowels: j, w (allophone of v)

The aspirates /ph, bh/, etc. are retained in the script for the due notation of Sanskrit loan-words. Similarly, /ʂ/ and /ŋ/ occur only in Sanskrit loan-words. In the spoken language, /l/ and /ɭ/ have coalesced.

An interesting feature of Sinhalese phonology is provided by the semi-nasals, which occur in association with voiced consonants: e.g. *am̆ba* 'mangoes'. In the verbal system, a semi-nasal occurring in citation form may acquire full nasal status in the past tense: cf. *ban̆dinavā* 'to tie' – past, *bändā*.

Vowels

i, e, ɛ, a/ʌ/ə/, o, u

These six short vowels have correlatives. /a/ as initial and in closed syllables is [a]; elsewhere it is [ʌ], [ə]; e.g. *kapanavā* [kapənəva:] 'to cut'.

The realization of Sinhalese words in connected speech is marked by elision, crasis, and assimilation, aimed at avoiding hiatus and promoting euphony.

MORPHOLOGY AND SYNTAX

Noun

GENDER

The basic contrast is between animate and inanimates; animates are further subdivided into masculine and feminine. Characteristic masculine endings are: *-ā*, *-vā/-yā* added to the root. There is no specific feminine ending, but *-ī* is common, and there are several feminine affixes: e.g. *-dena*, *-ikāva*, *-dēviya*. Neuter, i.e. inanimate, nouns usually end in *-ya*, *-va*, *-a*.

NUMBER

Many masculine and some feminine nouns in *-ā* change this ending to *-ō* in the plural: e.g. *piyā* 'father', pl. *piyō*. Again, final *-ā* may change to *-u*, with gemination of final consonant: e.g. *putā* 'son', pl. *puttu*.

Neuter nouns often add *-val*: e.g. *pāra* 'way', pl. *pāraval*. Apocope is also frequent: e.g. *pota* 'book', pl. *pot*.

An indefinite form, corresponding in sense to the indefinite article in English, is made by suffixing *-(e/a)k*: e.g. *minihā* 'man' – *minihe**k*** 'a man'; *puṭuva* 'chair' – *puṭuva**k*** 'a chair'.

DECLENSION

Various cases are listed in grammars; the basic cases, used also in the spoken language, are as follows: *minihā* 'man': acc. *minihā*(*vā*); dat. *minihāṭa*; gen. *minihāgē*; abl. *minihāgen*; instr. *minihāvisin*. The plural of *minihā* is *minissu*, acc. *minissun*, to which form the genitive, dative, etc. affixes are attached.

Neuter: e.g. *puṭuva* 'chair': dat. *puṭuvaṭa*; gen. and loc. *puṭuvē*; abl. *puṭuven*. The plural of *puṭuva* is *puṭu* (nom. and acc.); the dative is *puṭuvalaṭa*, gen. and loc. *puṭuvala*, abl. *puṭuvalin*.

Adjective

The adjective precedes the noun and is indeclinable: e.g. *loku minihā* 'big man'.

Pronoun

INDEPENDENT PERSONAL FORMS

First person: *mama* or *man*; pl. *api*. These are declined: e.g. *maṭa* 'to me'. second person: for polite address, pronouns are avoided, and titles or kinship terms (i.e. third person forms) are preferred; e.g. *mahattayā* 'Sir', is a suitable form of address for all males; the feminine counterpart is *nōnā* (*mahattayā*). third person: *eyā* is acceptable for 'he'; equivalent plural form *ē gollo*: e.g. *ē gollanṭa* 'to them'.

DEMONSTRATIVE PRONOUN
oya 'this'; *ara* 'that'; *ē* is a general demonstrative.

INTERROGATIVE PRONOUN
kavda 'who?'; *mokāda* 'who?'; *monavā* 'what?'. *-da* is an interrogative particle affixed to verb or to any other focused element in the sentence: e.g. *Eyā enne heṭa.**da**?* 'Is it tomorrow that he is coming?' (*enne* is relative present participle of *enavā* 'he is coming').

RELATIVE PRONOUN
See **Verb**, below.

Numerals

1–10: *eka*, *deka*, *tuna*, *hatara*, *paha*, *haya*, *hata*, *aṭa*, *namaya*, *dahaya*; 11 *ekolaha*; 12 *dolaha*; 13 *dahatuna*; 14 *dahahatara*; 20 *vissa*; 30 *tiha*, 40 *hataliha*; 100 *siyaya*.

Verb

The citation form is in *-navā*: e.g. *karanavā* 'to do, make'. In colloquial Sinhalese, this form serves as a present–future form for all three persons, singular and plural: e.g. *mama/eyā karanavā* 'I/he shall/will do'. Similarly, colloquial Sinhalese has a general preterite form in *-ā* for all persons and both numbers. Two conjugations are distinguished, according to the way in which this past tense is formed:

1. Verbs with present form in *-**a**.navā* change this to *-uvā* with stem ablaut: e.g. *ō* → *ē*, *o* → *e*, *ū* → *ī*, *a* → *ä*: e.g. *labanavā* – *läbuvā* 'received'; *hōdanavā* – *hēduvā* 'washed'.
2. Verbs with present form in *-**i**.navā* change this to *-iyā*, again with stem ablaut: e.g. *arinavā* – *äriyā* 'sent'. There are several irregular formations, e.g. *denavā* 'gives' – *dunnā*; *yanavā* 'goes' – *giyā*; *bonavā* 'drinks' – *bivvā* or *bunnā*.

An indefinite future with a potential nuance is made with the endings *-yi*/*-vi*: e.g. *Eyā mē väḍa kara.yi* 'He will/may do this job.' In written Sinhalese, the following personal markers are added to stems to form a present tense: sing. 1 *-mi*, 2 *-hi*, 3 *-yi*; pl. 1 *-mu*, 2 *-hu*, 3 *-ti*: e.g. *mama kara.mi* 'I do'. The same affixes, with some variations, are added to the colloquial preterite to form a perfective tense: e.g. *karanavā* 'to do', coll. pret. *kaḷā*, lit. pret. *mama kaḷe mi*.

PARTICIPLES

present: the *-vā* ending of the present is dropped: e.g. *kanavā* → *kana* 'eating';

past: made in various ways, e.g. from past tense with shortening of final vowel: e.g. *bässā* 'sat down' – *bässa* 'having sat down'; *giyā* 'went' – *giya* 'having gone'.

The participles are neutral as to voice: cf. *minihā kana bat* 'the rice the man is eating'; *bat kana minihā* 'the man who is eating rice'.

GERUND
The perfective gerund has the ending -(*al*)*ā*: e.g. *balanavā* 'looks at' – gerund, *balā*/*balalā*. The subject of the sentence is in the dative: e.g. *eyā**ṭa** väḍa hamāra karalā* 'when he has finished the work' (*väda* 'work'; *hamāra karanavā* 'to finish').

IMPERATIVE
Several endings, e.g. *-nna*, e.g. *karanna* 'do'. The imperative is negated by means of the particle *epā* following the infinitive in the dative case: e.g. *Mē karan**ṭa** epā!* 'Don't do this!'

CAUSATIVE
The characteristic is *-va-*, with agent in dative: e.g.

> Lamayā väḍakārayā**ṭa** kiyāla aṁba kaḍa**va**navā
> 'The boy is getting the servant to pick mangoes' (*lamayā* 'boy', *kaḍavanavā* 'picks', *aṁba* 'mango', *kiyāla* 'having said')

CONDITIONAL
The *-ā* of the past tense → *ot*(*in*): *keruvot* 'if ... were to do', 'if ... do/does'.

MODAL VERBS
Example: *puluvan* 'can', with dative subject: *ma**ṭa** mēka karanna puluvan* 'I can do this'; but the desiderative modal verb with *kämati* has the subject in the nominative.

COMPOUND VERBS
Sinhalese has a large inventory of compound verbs (noun + verb, verb + verb) giving reciprocal, benefactive, durative, etc., nuances to the sense: e.g. *sellam.karanavā* 'to play'; *gahā.gannavā* 'to fight' (reciprocal of *gahanavā* 'to strike').

NEGATIVE
The general marker is *nä*: e.g. *Gaha loku nä* 'The tree is not big.' *Nemeyi* 'is not' is used to negate the gerundial forms: e.g. *balalā nemeyi* 'not having looked at it'.

Postpositions

These can take case endings: cf. *gaňgin megoḍa* 'this side of the river'; *gaňgin egoḍa.**ṭa*** 'to the other side of the river'.

Word order

SOV.

1. පටන්ගැන්මෙහිදී වාක්‍යයානෝ සිටිසේ
ක; වාක්‍යයානෝ දෙවියන්වහන්සේ සමග සිටිසේක;
2. ඒ වාක්‍යයානෝ දෙවියන්වහන්සේව සිටිසේක. එම
තැනන්වහන්සේ පටන්ගැන්මෙහි දෙවියන්වහන්සේ
3. සමග සිටිසේක. ඒ තැනන්වහන්සේ කරණකොට
ගෙණ සියල්ල මවනලද්දේය. මවනලද කිසිවක් උන්ව
4. හන්සේ නැතුව නොමවනලද්දේය. උන්වහන්සේ
තුළ ජීවනය තිබුණේය; ඒ ජීවනය මනුෂ්‍යයන්ගේ
5. ආලෝකය වූයේය. ආලෝකය අඳුරෙහි බබලන්නේ
ය. අඳුර ඒක පිළිගත්තේ නැත.
6. දෙවියන්වහන්සේ විසින් එවනලද යොහන් නම්
7. මනුෂ්‍යයෙක් සිටියේය. ඔහු තමන් කරණකොටගෙ
ණ සියල්ලන් විසින් අදහන පිණිස, ඒ ආලෝකයට සා
8. ක්ෂිදෙන්ට සාක්ෂිකාරයෙක්ව ආයේය. ඔහු ඒ ආලෝ
කය නූවූයේය; නුමුත් ඒ ආලෝකයට සාක්ෂිදෙන පිණි

SLAVONIC LANGUAGES

INTRODUCTION

Within the Indo-European family, the Slavonic languages form a compact and, morphologically homogeneous group with a large common stock of basic vocabulary. Phonologically, the individual languages show more variation; the nasal vowels of Common Slavonic have been retained only in Polish, and tone is found only in Serbo-Croat and Slovene. The degree of homogeneity suggests that dialectal variation from a common Slavonic stock is fairly recent. This common parent language seems to have persisted into the early years of the first millennium AD; by about 600 the individual Slavonic languages were beginning to take shape. When the Old Church Slavonic literary language appears in the ninth century some of its characteristic features are identifiably South Slavonic. In the main, however, this literary language is still close to Common Slavonic. The original diffusion of Common Slavonic into Eastern, Western, and Southern dialects remains the basis for contemporary classification of the Slavonic languages: Eastern Slavonic comprises Russian, Ukrainian, and Belorussian; Western Slavonic, Polish, Czech, Slovak, Lusatian (also known as Sorbian or Wendish, with two literary and spoken norms, Upper and Lower); South Slavonic comprises Serbo-Croat, Slovene, Bulgarian, and Macedonian. Extinct Slavonic languages include Polabian (Lechic group of West Slavonic).

SCRIPT

Old Church Slavonic was written in two scripts, Glagolitic and Cyrillic, both expressly designed for its adequate notation. Glagolitic is no longer used. Slavonic languages are now written either in Cyrillic or Roman, depending on religious and cultural affinity. Russian, Ukrainian, Belorussian, Serbian, Bulgarian, and Macedonian, traditionally associated with the Eastern Orthodox Church, use Cyrillic; the others, under Catholic influence, use Roman.

PHONOLOGY

Three inter-connected phenomena are fundamental in the process whereby Common Slavonic became differentiated from the Indo-European matrix. These are: (a) the loss of final IE consonants; (b) the monophthongization of IE diphthongs, and the reduction of phonemic length in vowels to a neutral grade; (c) successive stages of palatalization.

(a) loss of final consonant: cf. Greek *hupnos* – Slav. *sunŭ*; Latin *axis* – Slav. *osĭ*; Latin *taurus* – Slav. *turŭ*.
(b) monophthongization: cf. Lithuanian *eĩti* – Slav. *iti* 'to go'; Latin *cruor*, Greek *kreas* – Slav. *kruvĭ* 'blood, flesh'.
(c) By the first palatalization (which antedated the process detailed in (b)), the Indo-European phonemes /k, g, x/, if followed by IE front vowels, were mutated to /tʃ, ʒ, ʃ/. The second palatalization followed the monophthongization process; and monophthong reflexes thus produced caused preceding /k, g, x/ to become /ts, ʒ, s/ʃ/. Cf. as an example of the first palatalization IE **g°īuos*, Lith. *gývas* – Slav. *živŭ* 'alive'; of the second, Lith. *kaina* – Slav. *tsena* 'price'. A third palatalization produced the same mutations of /k, g, x/ *following* front vowels: e.g. Germanic *kuningaz* – Slav. *kŭnĕžĭ*, Russian *knjaz'* 'prince'.

Vocalic system of Common Slavonic:

i, ɪ, e, a, o, u; nasalized: ę, ǫ;

Common Slavonic had the sequence C_1Vl/rC_2, where V is /e/ or /o/. The sequence is conveniently exemplified by **tort*, whose reflexes in the successor languages are then *torot* (the 'full vowel' – *polnoglasie* – form found in Russian), *trot*/*trat*. /e/ and /l/ can be inserted in the formula to produce analogous forms: **tolt – tolot – tlot*/*tlat*, etc.: e.g.

Common Slav. **gard-* 'town'. The reflexes are:

East Slav.: Russian: *gorod*, Ukrainian: *horod*
West Slav. (a) Polish: *gród*; Lusatian: *hród*/*grod;* (b) Czech/Slovak: *hrad*
South Slav.: Old Ch. Slav.: *gradŭ*; Serbo-Croat: *grâd*; Slovene: *grâd*; Bulgarian: *grad*

Common Slav. *bergŭ* 'bank, steep slope'

East Slav.: Russian: *bereg*; Ukrainian: *bereh*
West Slav. (a) Polish: *brzeg* /bʒɛk/; Lusatian: *brjoh*/*brjog*; Polabian: *brig*; (b) Czech: *břeh*; Slovak: *breh*
South Slav.: Old Ch. Slav. *brĕgŭ*; Serbo-Croat: *brêg*/*brîg*/*brijeg*; Slovene: *brêg*; Bulgarian: *brĕg*.

The *jers*, ъ and ь; these are the Common Slavonic reflexes of IE /*u, *i/: e.g. IE *supn-*, Skt *sup-*, GK. *hupnos*, Slav. /sŭnŭ/ 'sleep'. Reflexes in modern Slavonic languages:

Common Slav. *sŭnŭ: Russian: son*; Polish and Czech: *sen*; Lusatian: *són*/*soń*; Serbo-Croat: *sȁn*; Slovene: *sán*/*sèn*; Bulgarian: *sŭn*.
Cf. Common Slav. *dĭnĭ* 'day': Russian: *djen'*; Polish: *dzień*; Lusatian: *dźeń*/*źeń*; Czech: *den*; Serbo-Croat: *dân*; Slovene: *dân*/*dên*; Bulgarian: *den*.

Reflexes of the nasalized vowels: e.g. from Common Slav. *rǫka* 'hand, arm': Old Ch. Slav.: *rąka*; Russian: *rukà*; Polish: *ręka*; Czech: *ruka*; Lusatian: *ruka*;

Serbo-Croat: *ruka*; Slovene: *róka*; Bulgarian: *rŭkà*.

Stress was mobile in Common Slavonic, falling on any syllable. The situation in the modern languages is as follows:

(a) Russian, Ukrainian, Belorussian: stress is mobile;
(b) Slovene, Bulgarian: stress mobile, with certain restrictions;
(c) Serbo-Croat: mobile; in Common Slavonic cognates, the Serbo-Croat stress frequently falls on the syllable *preceding* the stress in the (a) and (b) languages: cf. Russian: *govorít'* 'to speak'; Slovene: *govoríti*; Serbo-Croat: *govóriti*; Russian: *ženà* 'woman'; Bulgarian: *ženà*, Serbo-Croat: *žéna*.
(d) Polish, Czech, Slovak, Lusatian: stress fixed; in Polish on the penultimate, in the others on the initial syllable.

In the closely associated Baltic languages, stress is free in Lithuanian but nearly always word-initial in Latvian.

MORPHOLOGY AND SYNTAX

Nominal system

Typically, the Slavonic languages have seven cases, including a vocative. A striking innovation in the declension system, *vis-à-vis* Indo-European practice in general, is the opposition 'masculine animate versus other' set up in the singular paradigm originally, but extended to the plural in Russian: cf. *ja vižu dom* 'I see a/the house' (*dom* 'house': acc. case = nom.); *ja vižu brata* 'I see the brother' (*brat* 'brother': gen. *brata*). That is to say, if the referent is a masculine animate, the objective case is assessed as a genitive, and so expressed.

The same assessment of the objective case as a genitive may take place if the verb is negated: e.g. *ja vižu dom* 'I see the house': *ja **ne** vižu doma* 'I don't see the house', though here there are specific restrictions.

The two Slavonic languages which have acquired a postpositional definite article – Bulgarian and Macedonian – have also discarded the case system.

A dual number is conserved in Slovene and in Lusatian.

Adjective

Originally Slavonic had weak indefinite and strong definite forms, the latter being made by the affixation of pronominal gender markers to the weak form: e.g. from *dobŭr* 'good': masc. *dobry.ji*, fem. *dobra.ja*, neuter *dobro.je* (in Old Church Slavonic).

Verb

As exemplified in Old Church Slavonic, the verbal system of Indo-European is reduced to one voice (active), two moods (indicative and imperative), and three formally distinguished tenses: aorist, present, past. The aorist was to vanish in Eastern and Western Slavonic, though it is preserved in South.

The comparative poverty of this inventory is successfully offset by the elaborate aspectual system, which is one of relatively recent date. The basic dichotomy in the aspectual system is that between perfective (completed) and imperfective action; beyond this, the system is capable of endless refinements and very subtle nuances.

The perfective future is expressed by the present-tense form of perfective verbs; an imperfective future is made with the help of an auxiliary verb.

An inferential mode has been developed in Bulgarian and Macedonian.

See articles on individual languages.

SLOVAK

INTRODUCTION

This West Slavonic language was joint official language (with Czech) of the Republic of Czechoslovakia. It is spoken by about 5 million in The Republic of Slovakia and adjacent areas. In addition, there are sizeable Slovak communities in the USA and in Canada. Slovak is very close to Czech, the two languages being mutually intelligible.

A literary norm for Slovak was successfully codified in the mid-nineteenth century by L′udovit Štúr, who based his dictionary (1846) on the central dialect. Hardly had this advance been achieved, however, when the 1867 *Ausgleich* gave the Hungarians a free hand to pursue their policy of magyarization throughout their domains. Slovak cultural interests were severely restricted, and in 1875 the Matica Slovenská, a cultural institution roughly equivalent to a Slovak Academy, was forced to close – not to reopen till independence came in 1918. In the early part of this period, the journal *Slovenské Pohl′ady*, edited by S.H. Vajanský, played an important part in keeping Slovak cultural aspirations alive. Panoramic surveys and steadfast reaffirmations of Slovak beliefs and customs were provided by the poet Pavol Országh (Hviezdoslav) and the novelist Martin Kukučin, whose masterpiece *Dom v stráni* appeared in 1903. It was left to the poet Ivan Krasko to open European horizons to Slovak writers; and between the wars Slovak writing in general reflected the European cultural scene. Latterly, dissident writers like Ladislav Mňačko have attracted much attention.

SCRIPT

The Roman alphabet + diacritics: acute accent on long vowels; *č*, *ň*, *š*, *ž*; *l′*, *t′*, *d′*; *ô* = /wɔ/.

PHONOLOGY

Consonants

stops: p, b, t, d, k, g; /t/ and /d/ occur palatalized: t′, d′
affricates: ts, dz, tʃ, dʒ
fricatives: f, v, s, z, ʃ, ʒ, x, ɦ
nasals: m, n, ɲ
laterals and flap: l, ʎ, r
semi-vowels: j, w

Final *v* = [u̯] or [w].

Vowels

i, iː, ɛ, ɛː, a, aː, e, eː, ɔ, ɔː, u, uː

/i, iː/ are notated as *i, í, y, ý*. Syllabic /l̩/ and /r̩/ when long are notated as *ĺ, ŕ*. Vowel length is phonemic.

THE RHYTHMIC RULE

In Slovak, two long syllables cannot be contiguous; e.g. *ženám* 'to the women' is permissible, but in *piesňam* 'to the songs' the *-ám* ending must be shortened to *-am*, as the diphthong *-ie-* of the first syllable is long. There are, however, several important exceptions to this rule.

Stress

As in Czech, stress is invariably on the first syllable.

MORPHOLOGY AND SYNTAX

Noun

Slovak has three genders, two numbers. In its basic patterns – nominal and adjectival declension, the pronominal system, the aspectual structure of the verb – the language is close to Czech. Both languages observe the animate/inanimate opposition, though Slovak goes further and agrees with Polish in treating male humans as a special category in the plural. In declension, Slovak has lost the vocative case which is retained in Czech. The Czech phenomenon known as *přehláska* – the fronting of /a, aː/, /ɔ, ɔː/ to /e, ie/ and of /u, uː/ to /i, iː/ – is unknown in Slovak: cf. Czech *duše* 'soul', acc. *duši*; Slovak *duša*, *dušu*. In the neuter soft declension, e.g. of *srdce* 'heart', where Czech has the forms pl. dat. *srdcím*, instr. *srdci*, loc. *srdcích*, Slovak has *srdciam*, *srdcami*, *srdciách*.

Specimen declension of masculine hard stem (animate) with adjective:

	Singular	*Plural*
nom.	dobrý chlap 'good chap'	dobri chlapi
gen.	dobrého chlapa	dobrých chlapov/xlapou̯/
acc.	dobrého chlapa	dobrých chlapov
dat.	dobrému chlapovi	dobrým chlapom
instr.	dobrým chlapom	dobrými chlapmi
loc.	dobrom chlapovi	dobrých chlapoch

Pronoun

The human male category is again singled out for special marking: 3rd p. pl. *oni* with reference to men, *ony* for other categories.

The first person singular pronoun *ja* has the following oblique forms: acc./gen. *mňa*, *ma*; dat. *mne*, *mi*; prep. (*o*) *mne*; instr. *mnou*.

POSSESSIVE ADJECTIVES
Example: *môj*, *môjho*, *môjmu*, where *-o-* is the labialized /^{w}o/.

Numerals

Basically as in Czech, but Slovak has a specific open set for use with animates: these forms have genitive/accusative cases: e.g. 2–5: *dvaja*, *traja*, *štyria*, *piati*, with gen./acc. forms *dvoch*, *troch*, *štyroch*, *piatich*: e.g. *Boli sme piati* 'There were five of us.'

Verb

All infinitives in Slovak end in *-t'*. Five classes of verb are distinguished:

1. *a*-conjugation: e.g. *volat'* 'to call' – present tense 1st p. *volám*, 3rd pl. *volajú*;
2. *i*-conjugation: e.g. *robit'* 'to work' – *robím* – *robia*;
3. *e*-conjugation: e.g. *niest* 'to carry' – *nesiem* – *nesú*;
4. *ne*-conjugation: e.g. *kradnút'* 'to steal' – *kradnem* – *kradnú*;
5. *uje*-conjugation: e.g. *pracovat'* 'to work' – *pracujem* – *pracujú*.

Perfective aspect: formed from imperfective either by prefix, as in *robit'* – *urobit'*; by the ending *-nút'*, e.g. *siahat'* 'to touch, disturb' – *siahnút'*; by vowel change: e.g. *chytat'* 'to take' – *chytit'*; or by suppletion: e.g. *brat'* 'to take' – *vziat'*, *klást'* 'to put' – *položit'*.

The only simple tense in Slovak is the present, the personal endings are:

sing. 1 *-m*, 2 *-š*, 3 Ø; pl. 1 *-me*, 2 *-te*, 3 *-ú*/*-jú*/*-ia*

In contrast to Czech, Slovak has only one ending for the 1st person singular: *-m*.

Specimen paradigm: robit′ 'to work' (imperfective):

Indicative present:

	Singular	*Plural*
1	robím	robíme
2	robíš	robíte
3	robí	robía

The past tense is made by conjugating the auxiliary verb *byt'* 'to be' with the inflected past participle:

	Singular	*Plural*
1	robil, -a, -o som	robili sme
2	robil, -a, -o si	robili ste
3	robil, -a, -o Ø	robili Ø

Future: the future tense of *byt'* + infinitive of imperfective verb: e.g. *budem*, *budeš*, *bude robit'*. The perfective future is made by adding the present-tense endings (as above) to the perfective stem: e.g. ***urobím***, ***urobíš***, ***urobí***.

Non-finite forms: from *robit'*: active participle *robiaci*; gerund *robiac*; passive participle *robený*.

Preposition

Most Slovak prepositions take the genitive case, e.g. *do* 'to, for', *bez* 'without', *namiesto* 'instead of', *spod* 'from under', etc.: e.g. *íst' do práce* 'to go to work'; *lístky do divadla* 'tickets for the theatre'. *Cez* 'through', and *pre* 'because of', take the accusative: e.g. *dívat' sa cez oblok* 'to look out of the window'; *priniesol som to pre teba* 'I've brought this for you'.

Some occur in pairs, e.g. *medzi* with accusative or instrumental, *spomedzi* with the genitive: e.g. *dedina medzi horami* 'a village among the mountains'; *vyjst' spomedzi stromov* 'to come out from among the trees'; *l'udia spod Tatier* 'folk from the Tatra foothills'. Optionally, prepositions may be tripled: e.g. *s.po.pred, s.po.pod.*

Na 'on', *po* 'up to, after, along', etc., *o* 'about', *v/vo* 'in', take the accusative or the locative: e.g. *prišiel v poslednú chvíl'u* 'he came at the last moment'; *v minulom roku* 'last year'. *Za* 'at the time of', 'during', 'at', etc. takes three cases: genitive, accusative, instrumental: e.g. *hovorit' za niekoho* 'to speak about, talk of someone'; *sadnút' si za stôl* 'to sit down at table'; *sediet' za stolom* 'to sit/be seated at table'.

Word order

SVO is basic, with considerable freedom, depending on emphasis, style, and nuance.

Na počiatku bolo Slovo, a to Slovo bolo u Boha,
a to Slovo bol Bôh. 2 To *Slovo* bolo na počiatku
u Boha. 3 Všetko je skrzeň učinené, a bez neho
nenie nič učinené, čo je učinené. 4 V ňom bol
život, a ten život bol svetlom ľudí, 5 a to svetlo
svieti vo tme, a tma ho nezadržala. 6 Bol *istý* od
Boha poslaný človek, ktorému *bolo* meno Ján.
7 Ten prišiel na svedoctvo, aby svedčil o tom
svetle, aby všetci uverili skrze neho. 8 Nebol on
tým svetlom, ale *nato prišiel*, aby svedčil o tom
svetle.

SLOVENE

INTRODUCTION

Slovene belongs to the South Slavonic group of the Slavonic branch of Indo-European. It is spoken by between 2½ and 3 million people in the Republic of Slovenia. The earliest specimens of written Slovene date from the eleventh century. In fact the so-called *Brižinski spomeniki*, the 'Freising Monuments', provide the oldest known text in a Slavonic language in Latin script. Slovene literature proper begins in the sixteenth century, when Primož Trubar translated the Bible into Slovene. The greatest Slovene poet is generally taken to be Franc Prešeren (1800–49). The most distinguished modern writers are the novelist and playwright Ivan Cankar and the poet Oton Zupančič.

SCRIPT

Roman alphabet with diacritics: *č, š, ž*.

PHONOLOGY

Consonants

stops: p, b, t, d, k, g
affricates: ts, tʃ
fricatives: f, v, s, z, ʃ, ʒ, h (x)
nasals: m, n, ɲ
laterals and flap: l, ʎ, r
semi-vowels: j, w

A key point in Slovene phonology is the labialization of /v/ and /l/ in post-vocalic or syllable-final position to /w/: e.g. *bil* = [biw] or [bii̯]; *polno* [powno], [pou̯no]. The voiced stops are devoiced in final position: *ubog* = [ubok] ('poor').

Vowels

Notated as *i, e, a, o, u*, where *e* = /e/ and /ɛ/, *o* = /o/ and /ɔ/. Stress-bearing vowels may be long or short, unstressed vowels are always short. The neutral vowel /ə/ is notated as *e*: e.g. *poguben* 'ruinous', /pogubən/.

Tone

Dialectically, rising and falling tones affect long vowels. The modern tendency in the standard literary language is to neutralize this distinction.

Stress

Stress occurs on any syllable of a word. In general, it tallies with stress in Serbo-Croat, but there are many discrepancies: cf; SC *dèset* = Sl. *desȅt* 'ten'; SC *júnak* = Sl. *junȁk* 'hero'; SC *mȇso* = Sl. *mesȍ* 'meat'.

MORPHOLOGY AND SYNTAX

Slovene has three genders: masculine, feminine, and neuter; and three numbers, the dual being retained in the noun, pronoun, adjective, and verb.

Noun

-u/-u stems have disappeared in Slovene; *-i* and *-a* stems are mainly feminine; *-o* stems are masculine; neuter stems are in *-o* or *-e*. Each gender has a specific plural characteristic: masc. *-i*, fem. *-e*, nt. *-a*. For example:

masculine: sing. *klobuk* 'hat'; dual *klobuka*; pl. *klobuki*;
feminine: sing. *žena* 'woman'; dual *ženi*; pl. *žene*;
neuter: sing. *mesto* 'place'; dual *mesti*; pl. *mesta*.

Example of masculine noun in six cases, three numbers:

	Singular	*Dual*	*Plural*
nom.	klobuk	klobuk.**a**	klobuk.**i**
gen.	klobuk**a**	klobuk.**ov**	klobuk.**ov**
dat.	klobuk**u**	klobuk.**oma**	klobuk.**om**
acc.	klobukØ	klobuk.**a**	klobuk.**e**
loc.	klobuk**u**	klobuk.**ih**	klobuk.**ih**
instr.	klobuk**om**	klobuk.**oma**	klobuk.**i**

The direct object of nouns denoting animate beings takes the genitive form: e.g. *vidim mlad**ega** gospod**a*** 'I see the young man' (for the declension of the adjective see below). The accusative of feminine nouns in *-a* is in *-o*: e.g. *hiša* 'house': *Moj brat kupi to hišo* 'My brother is buying that house'; and the feminine plural genitive is the stem minus *-a*: e.g. *teh hišØ* 'of these houses'.

Some irregularities occur in all three genders; e.g. fem. *hči* 'daughter', pl. *hčere*; neuter, *uho* 'ear', pl. *ušesa*.

Adjective

The adjective is in concord for gender, number, and case throughout as attribute, and has a determinate form (cf. **Baltic Languages**): e.g. *lep vrt* 'nice garden'; *lepi vrt* '**the** nice garden'. Examples: *priden deček* 'diligent boy': gen./ acc. *pridnega dečka*; *s pridnim dečkom* 'with, by a diligent boy'.

DUAL

Example in feminine: *lepi ženi* 'two beautiful women'; *z lepima ženama* 'with the two beautiful women'.

DERIVED ADJECTIVES

Examples: *brato**v** klobuk* 'the brother's hat'; *sestri**n** klobuk* 'the sister's hat'; *brato**vo** obuvalo* 'the brother's footwear'.

COMPARATIVE

The formant is -(*ej*)*š*-: e.g. *lep* 'beautiful' – *lepši*; *hud* 'bad' – *hujši*; *sladek* 'sweet' – *slajši*. Slovene has a few suppletive formations for common adjectives: e.g. *dober* 'good' – *bolje*/*boljši*.

Pronoun

The independent personal forms are:

	Singular	*Dual*	*Plural*
1	jaz	midva	mi
2	ti	vidva	vi

The third person forms are marked for gender:

	Masculine	*Feminine*	*Neuter*
singular	on	ona	ono
dual	onadva	onedve	onedve
plural	oni	one	ona

All these forms are declined in six cases.

The possessive pronominal adjectives are: 1st p. sing. *moj*, pl. *naš*; 2nd p. sing. *tvoj*, pl. *vaš*; 3rd p. sing. masc. *njegov*; fem. *njen*; pl. common: *njihov*. For example: *mati in njen sin* 'the mother and her son'; *oče in njegov sin* 'the father and his son'.

The pronominal object is placed between the auxiliary and main verb in the past compound tense: e.g. *jaz sem **ga** videl* 'I have seen him/I saw him'; *mi smo **ga** videli* 'we have seen him'. But, in future, *jaz mu bom dal* 'I shall give to him'.

DEMONSTRATIVE PRONOUN/ADJECTIVE

Marked for gender: *ta* – *ta* – *to*, i.e. the masculine and feminine forms are identical: e.g. *ta deček je majhen* 'this boy is small'; *ta deklica je majhna* 'this girl is small'. The plural forms are *tisti* – *tista* – *tisto*. All forms are declined.

INTERROGATIVE PRONOUN

kdo 'who?'; *kaj* 'what?'.

RELATIVE PRONOUN

kateri – *katera* – *katero*; with dual and plural forms, declined in all cases: e.g. *slon, od katerega dobivamo slonovo kost* 'the elephant from which we get ivory'.

Ki may also be used: e.g. *deček, ki dela* 'the boy who is working'; *deček,* ***ki mu*** *dam knjigo* 'the boy to whom I give a book'. *Kdor* is used to mean 'the one who ...': e.g. *kdor kupuje in prodaja* ... 'he who buys and sells ...'

Numerals

1 and 2 show gender: 1 *ed/en* (masc.), *ena* (fem.), *eno* (nt.); 2 *dva* (masc.), *dve* (fem./nt.). 3–10: *tri, štiri, pet, šest, sedem, osem, devet, deset*; 11 *enajst*; 12 *dvanajst*; 13 *trinajst*; 20 *dvajset*; 30 *trideset*; 40 *štirideset*; 100 *sto*.

Verb

The infinitive ends in *-ti* (with few exceptions). Grammars of Slovene divide verbs into six categories according to the characteristic linking the stem to the *-ti* ending:

			1st person singular present
1	-ni-:	dvig**ni**ti	dvig**nem** 'I raise, lift (perf.)'
2	-e-:	žel**e**ti	žel**im** 'I wish'
3	-i-:	govor**i**ti	govor**im** 'I speak'
4	-a-:	del**a**ti	del**am** 'I do'
5	-ova/-eva:	kup**ova**ti	kup**ujem** 'I buy'
6	-Ø-:	nesti	nes**em** 'I carry, take (perf.)'

Consonant alternation occurs as in other Slavonic languages:

pisati 'to write': *pišem* 'I write'
hoteti 'to want': *hočem* 'I want'
lagati 'to tell a lie': *lažem* 'I lie'

For conjugation purposes, the six categories reduce to three types with characteristic vowels: *-a-*, *-e-*, *-i-*.

Specimen paradigm of regular *-a-* type: *delati* 'to do':

Present indicative:

	Singular	*Dual*	*Plural*
1	jaz delam	midva delava	mi delamo
2	ti delaš	vidva delata	vi delate
3	on dela	onadva delata	oni delajo

Past, future, and conditional are all formed by means of the participial form: sing. *delal*, dual *delala*, pl. *delali*, conjugated by the auxiliary verb *biti* 'to be': thus:

jaz sem delal 'I did', *midva sva delala* 'we two did';
jaz bom delal 'I shall do', *mi bomo delali* 'we (pl.) shall do';
on bi delal 'he would have done', *onadva bi delala* 'they two would have done'.

Irregular verbs may have suppletive forms, phonological irregularities, and synthetic tense-forms, e.g. *iti* 'to go':

present tense: sing. *grem*, *greš*, *gre*; pl. *gremo*, *greste*, *gredo*;
past: *jaz sem šel, ti si šel*
future: *jaz pojdem, ti pojdeš*

ASPECT

As in other Slavonic languages, imperfective (including duratives) and perfective (including inceptives). Some examples of perfective/imperfective formations:

Perfective	*Imperfective*	*Perfective*	*Imperfective*
pasti 'fall'	padati	spoznati 'get to know'	poznati 'know'
skočiti 'jump'	skakati	kupiti 'buy'	kupovati 'buy often'
ukrasti 'steal'	krasti		

PASSIVE

Infrequent in Slovene, the active voice being preferred. The past participle in *-t*, *-en*, *-n*, is used; phonetic accommodation at junctures: e.g. *kupiti* 'buy' – *kupljen*; *nositi* 'carry, bear' – *nošen.*

NEGATION

The general marker is *ne*: e.g. *ne delam* 'I don't do'. *Ne sem* → *nisem* 'I'm not', *ne imam* → *nimam* 'I don't have'.

After a negated transitive verb, the genitive case replaces the accusative: e.g. *jaz nimam knjige/klobuka* 'I haven't got a book/hat'; cf. *Mojega očeta ni doma* 'My father is not at home' (*oče* 'father', gen. *očeta*).

Infinitive: use of the infinitive is avoided, especially where subject switch is involved: cf. *Prijatelj me prosi*, (*da*) *naj grem domov* 'My friend is asking me to go home' (*naj* is an optative particle).

Prepositions

Prepositions may govern genitive, dative, accusative, locative, or instrumental case. Several take two cases, depending on whether rest in a place or motion towards a place is involved. Thus, *jaz grem v šolo* 'I go to school' (acc.); *učenec je v šoli* 'the pupil is in school' (loc.); *v teh hišah* 'in these houses' (loc.).

Word order

SVO in principal clause, with inversions in subordinate clauses.

V začetku je bila beseda, in
beseda je bila pri Bogu, in Bog
je bila beseda.
2. Ta je bila v začetku pri
Bogu.
3. Vse je po njej postalo, in
brez nje ni nič postalo, kar je
postalo.
4. V njej je bilo življenje, in
življenje je bilo luč ljudém,
5. In luč v temi sveti, in tema je ni zapopadla.
6. Bil je človek poslan od Boga, kteremu je bilo ime Janez.
7. Ta pride na pričevanje, da
priča za luč, da bi vsi verovali
po njem.
8. On ni bil luč, nego da priča za luč.

SOMALI

INTRODUCTION

The Somali language (*afka Soomaaliga*) belongs to the Cushitic branch of the Afro-Asiatic family. Since 1973 it has been the official language of the Republic of Somalia, where it is the mother tongue of about 2½ million people; a further 1½ million speak the language in Kenya and Ethiopia. Until the twentieth century the rich corpus of Somali traditional poetry was preserved and transmitted almost exclusively by word of mouth. The declamation of poetry seems to be peculiarly well suited to the emotional needs of a nomadic society composed of contentious clans; and just as in early Arabic verse, the panegyric, the dirge and the lampoon figure prominently in Somali verse. Given the mass appeal and the tenacity of the oral tradition, it is not surprising that radio has proved a major factor in the contemporary development of Somali culture.

SCRIPT

Closely associated with the oral tradition and a distrust of innovation went a reluctance to commit Somali utterance to any form of imported script. Attempts made in the early twentieth century to introduce an adapted form of the Arabic script were not very successful. As in the case of Oromo, the Amharic syllabary was also tried; and two indigenous alphabetic scripts were invented in the 1920s and 1930s. In 1972 a standardized national orthography, based on the Roman alphabet, was introduced by the Somali Language Committee, and a year later Somali became the vehicle for education in Somalia. The immediate result was a spectacular increase in literacy. Since then, there has been a rapid upsurge in the output of Somali periodicals and books in all genres.

The standardized script has all the Roman letters except *p*, *v*, *z*. The letter *c* is used to denote the pharyngeal fricative ʿain (as in Arabic); ' denotes hamza. The following digraphs are used: *dh* = /d'/, *kh* = /χ/, *sh* = /ʃ/.

PHONOLOGY

Consonants

stops: b, t, d, k, g, q, ʔ; /d'/ is a post-alveolar ejective
affricate: dʒ
fricatives: w, f, s, ʃ, j, χ, ʕ, h, ħ
nasals: m, n
lateral and flap: l, r

[p] and [ß] occur as allophones of /b/; [γ] of /g/; [tʃ] of /dʒ/.

Vowels

In broad transcription:

long and short: i, e, ɛ, a, ɔ, o, u

Long vowels are written doubled: *Soomaaliya* 'Somalia'. Length is phonemic. In close transcription, /ɵ/ and /ʉ/ are distinguished.

Tone

The question of tone in Somali is controversial; intonation is associated with tonic stress, and is phonemic: *árday* 'student' – *ardáy* 'students'.

MORPHOLOGY AND SYNTAX

Noun

Somali has two grammatical genders, masculine and feminine. The enclitic definite article is marked for gender: initial *k-* (masc.), *t-* (fem.), plus vowel series *-a*/*-ii*/*-u*. The initials assimilate with certain stem finals, thus producing masc. *g-*/*Ø-*/*h-* and fem. *d-*/*ḍ-*/*s-*: e.g. *nin.ka* 'the man'; *naag.ta* 'the woman'; *buug.ga* 'the book'; *aabba.ha* 'the father'; *gabadh.dha* 'the girl'. The *-a* forms are neutral, i.e. without special deixis. There is a tendency for the *-u* forms to be used as subject markers, provided the subject is not qualified: cf. *macallin.ka* 'the teacher' (citation form); *macallin.**ku** wuxuu oronayaa* 'the teacher is speaking' (*oro* 'to say'; for *wuxuu* *see* **Verb**, below). The *-ii* forms play a specific part in the formation of relative clauses: *see* Relative pronoun, below.

Focus markers are syntactically obligatory in indicative sentences. Thus, in answer to the question *Yaa yimid?* 'Who has come?' two answers are possible: *Axmed **baa** yimid*, or *Axmed **waa** yimid*. In the former, Axmed is in focus as the person who came; in the latter, the verbal fact of 'coming' is stressed. Cf.

Axmed **baa** Jaamacadda buugag geeyay
'**Axmed** took books to the University.'

Axmed Jaamacadda buugag **waa** geeyay
'Axmed **took books** to the University.'

The two sentences differ only in the selection of focused component.

PLURAL FORMATION

There are several types:

(a) by partial or selective reduplication; this is the commonest form of plural formation for masculine monosyllables: e.g. *nin* 'man', pl. *niman*; *dab* 'fire', pl. *dabab*;
(b) by affixing -(*y*)*o*: e.g. *gabadh* 'girl', *gabdho*;
(c) masculines in *-e*/*-i* take *-yaal*: e.g. *shaqaale* 'worker', pl. *shaqaalayaal*;

(d) Arabic loan-words may take the Arabic broken plural, or the Somali *-o*: e.g. *miskin* 'poor man', pl. Ar. *masaakiin*, or Som. *miskiinno*.

It is interesting that many nouns taking the *k*- determinative series in the singular, have the *t*- series in the plural, i.e. show inverse polarity in gender (cf. use of numerals in Semitic generally). Thus: *buug.**ga*** 'the book', pl. *buugag.**ta*** 'the books'; *macallin.**ka*** 'the teacher', pl. *macallimiin.**ta*** 'the teachers'; *qaran.**ka*** 'the nation', *Qaramma**da** Midoobey* 'The United Nations'.

POSSESSION

The noun denoting the possessor may precede or follow possessed object: e.g. *guri.ga naag.ta* 'the house of the woman'; *buugga Maryam* = *Maryam buuggeeda* 'Mary's book' (where *-geeda* (← *-keeda*) is the feminine possessive definite ending); *nolo.sha dad.ka Soomaalidu* 'the life of the Somali people' (*nolol* 'life').

Adjective

As attribute, adjective follows noun: e.g. *buugga cusub* 'the new book'; *meel fog* 'a far-off place'. The use of attributive adjectives is not typical of Somali, which prefers to rearrange the sentence in terms of stative verbs: e.g. *weyn.aa* 'was big'. An attributive adjective qualifying a plural referent is itself in plural form: e.g. *wiil weyn* 'a large youth', pl. *wiilal waaweyn*; *buug cusub* 'a new book', pl. *buugag cucusub*: *cashar fudud* 'an easy lesson', pl. *casharro fudfudud.*

COMPARATIVE

ka + positive: e.g. *ka weyn* 'bigger'; *ka yar* 'smaller'.

Pronoun

The personal pronouns with their enclitic, object and possessive forms are as follows:

			Subject		*Object*		*Possessive*
			Full (emphatic)	*Enclitic*	*Simple*	*Prepositional*	
Sing.	1		anigu/a	aan	i	ii	kayga
	2		adigu/a	aad	ku	kuu	kaaga
	3	masc.	isagu/a	uu	ø	u	kiisa
		fem.	iyadu/a	ay			keeda
Pl.	1	incl.	innagu/a	aynu	(i)na	(i)noo	keenna
		excl.	annagu/a	aanu			kayaga
	2		idinku/a	aad	idin	idiin	kiinna
	3		iyagu/a	ay	ø	u	kooda

Examples: *guri.gayga* 'my house'; *guri.ga waa kayga* 'the house is mine'.

For feminine possessed objects the possessive series has the *t*- prefix: e.g. *tayga*, *taaga*. For plural objects the possessive forms have infixed *-w-*: e.g. *kuwayga*, *kuwaaga*.

Use of objective forms: e.g. ***u** keen macallinka buugga* 'bring the book to the teacher'; *buugaggii baa Axmed **kuu** keenay* 'Axmed brought the books to you';

*buugaggii b**aan** **kuu** keenay* 'I took the books to you'.

DEMONSTRATIVE PRONOUN/ADJECTIVE

The basic forms are: proximate *kan/tan* 'this', pl. *kuwan*; distal *kaas/taas* 'that', pl. *kuwaas*. There is assimilation at junctures: e.g. *buuggaas* 'that book'; *naag.taas* 'that woman'.

INTERROGATIVE PRONOUN

Formed from definite article + invariable interrogative marker *ma*: e.g. ***Maxaad*** *dhigaysaa?* 'What are you writing?'; ***Muxuu*** *dhigayaa?* 'What is he writing?'; ***Kumaad*** *araktay?* 'Whom did you see?'

RELATIVE CONSTRUCTIONS

There is no relative pronoun as such. The focusing particle, obligatory in principal clauses, is absent in the relative. *-kii/-tii* is affixed to the head-word in a relative clause involving action in the past, *-ka/-ta* similarly used for action in the present. El-Solami-Mewis (1987) gives the following examples:

> Nin**ka** gurigan dhisaya **waa** weyn yahay
> 'The man who is building this house is big'
>
> Nin**kii** gurigan dhisey **wuu** weyn yahay
> 'The man who built this house is big' (*guri* 'house'; *dhiso* 'to build'; *weyn* 'big').

Numerals

1–10: *kow, laba, saddex, afar, shan, lix, toddoba, siddeed, sagaal, toban*; 11 *kow iyo toban*; 12 *laba iyo toban*; 20 *labaatan*; 30 *soddon*; 40 *afartan*; 50 *konton*; 100 *boqol*.

The numeral precedes the substantive, which is in the singular if masculine; if feminine, the ending *-ood* (not a normal plural marker) is added; cf. *saddex cashar* = 'three lessons', *afartan qof* 'forty people'; but *saddex walaal**ood*** = 'three sisters'.

Verb

The verb has affirmative and negative conjugations; three moods (indicative, imperative, subjunctive); and two basic tenses (present, past) with a compound future. The tenses are further sub-divided into simple and progressive forms. The verbal stem is identical to the imperative singular: e.g. *qaad* 'take'; *akhri* 'read'; the plural is in *-a*: e.g. *qaada* 'take!' (pl.) *akhriya* 'read!'.

Verbal endings encode gender (third person singular) number, tense, mood, and modality.

There are four conjugational types:

1. consonantal: e.g. *keen* 'to bring', verbal noun, *keenid*;
2. in *-i/-ii/-ee*: e.g. *iibi* 'to buy', verbal noun, *iibin*;
3. derivative medio-reflexive: e.g. *joogsan* 'to stop', verbal noun, *joogsasho*;
4. stative–attributive: e.g. *weynaan* 'to be big', verbal noun, *weynaansho*.

TENSES

General present, e.g. of *keen*:

		Singular	*Plural*
1		keenaa	keennaa
2		keentaa	keentaan
3	masc.	keenaa	keenaan
	fem.	keentaa	

Present continuous: sing. *keenayaa*, *keenaysaa*, *keenayaa/keenaysaa*; pl. *keenaynaa*, *keenaysaan*, *keenayaan*. Simple past: sing. *keeney*, *keentey*, *keeney/keentey*; pl. *keenney*, *keenteen*, *keeneen*.

In affirmative sentences the subject – verb – object complex is always accompanied by an inflected particle, e.g. *waxaa*: *anigu* ***waxaan*** *dhigay**aa** warqad* 'I am writing a letter'; *adigu* ***waxaad*** *dhigay**saa** warqad* 'you are writing a letter'; *isagu* ***wuxuu*** *dhigay**aa** warqad* 'he is writing a letter'.

Future: this tense is formed from three elements: the infinitive of the sense-verb, the inflected particle *waa*, and the inflected present of *doonid* 'to want': e.g. ***waan*** *keen doon**aa*** 'I shall bring'; ***waad*** *keen doon**taa*** 'you will bring'; ***wuu*** *keen doon**aa*** 'he will bring'.

The characteristic of the subjunctive is *-o*: eg. *waa**n** keeno*, *waa**d** keento*, ***wuu*** *keeno*.

A compound form, consisting of the particle *leh* plus inflected forms of the verb *ahay* 'to be', is used along with *waxaa* to express the verb 'to have': e.g. *anigu waxaa**n** leeyahay guri* 'I have a house'; *adigu waxaa**d** lee**d**ahay guri* 'you have a house'; *isagu* ***wuxuu*** *leeyahay guri* 'he has a house'.

An impersonal passive is formed with the impersonal pronoun *la*: e.g. *guri.ga waa* ***la*** *dhisi* 'one builds the house' = 'the house is being built.'

USE OF SUBJUNCTIVE IN SUBORDINATE CLAUSES

Example: *Dawladda waxay ka codsatay guddiga inuu qor**o** buugagii dugsiyada hoose* 'The government requested the committee to write books for the elementary schools' (*dawlad.da* 'government'; *guddi.ga* 'committee'; *qor* 'write'; *dugsi.**ga** hoose* 'elementary school').

NEGATION

The general negating particle is *ma*; the imperative is negated by *ha*: e.g. *ha keenin* 'do not bring'. In the indicative tenses, *-o/-to* replace *-aa/-taa*, i.e. take subjunctive characteristics: e.g. *ma aan keen**o*** 'I do not bring'; *Muqdisho ma* ***aan tago*** 'I am not going to Mogadiscio'. The past form, *ma keenin* is invariable for all persons: e.g. *ma aan keenin* 'I did not bring'.

Prepositions

The prepositions combine with pronominal forms and with each other. Thus, *lagu* may be either the impersonal passive particle *la* plus the second person pronominal marker *-ku*, or, *la* + the preposition *ku* 'in, by means of': cf. *Maryam baa shaah* ***noo*** *keentay* 'Mary brought tea for us' (where *noo* is first person plural object marker *na* + directional marker *u*); *lacag.tii buu naga qaaday* 'he took the money from us' (where *naga* = *na* (as in previous example) + preposition *ka* 'from'). Syntactically, the directional markers *ku, ka, la, u* always qualify the verb (which they precede), not the noun; i.e. the word order is: marker – verb – noun. Cf. *gurigayga wuxuu* ***ku*** *yaala Muqdisho*: literally, 'my-house it **in** is-situated Mogadiscio'; i.e. 'My house is situated in Mogadiscio.'

The prepositions *gud* 'on', *hoos* 'under', *ag* 'beside', etc. are treated as nominals and take the possessive markers: e.g. *gud.kiisa* 'on' (with masc.), *hoos.tooda* 'under' (with pl.), *hoos.teeda* 'under' (with fem.), *ag.tiisa* 'near him', *ag.teeda* 'near her'; *dariishad.da ag.teeda* 'beside the window'; *sariir.ta gud.keeda* 'on the bed'.

Word order

SVO is basic, but not obligatory; order is free, the inflected particles serving to articulate the logical structure of a sentence.

1 Horti waẖa jirey Hadal, Hadalkana
waẖu lajirey Ilahey, Hadalkana waẖu aha
Ilahey. 2 Kan waẖu lajirey Ilahey horti.
3 Kuli waẖa lugusubiyey kan. Waẖ walba
olasubiyeyna masubsamen asaga laan tisa.
4 Guda hisana waẖa kujirtey nolol, nolo-
shana wahay eheyd nurki dadka. 5 Nur-
kana waẖu kaiftima mugdiga daẖdisa mugdiga mauawodin. 6 Waẖa sobaẖey nin
ousodirey Ilahey, magai̲sana wa Yohana.
7 Kan waẖu uimadey marag inu umaragkao̲
nurka kuli hahelane iney kuaminan dara-
disa. 8 Asaga maeheyn nurka, ilowse waẖu uimadey inu kamaragkao̲ nurka.

SPANISH

INTRODUCTION

Spanish belongs to the Italic branch of the Indo-European family of languages. It is the official language of the Kingdom of Spain, where it is spoken by about 50 million, and of a long chain of Latin American countries, running from Mexico to Argentina, giving a total of a little under 300 million speakers. This figure includes the Spanish-speaking population of Puerto Rico, certain areas in the USA, and a few enclaves in North Africa.

The Roman presence in the Iberian Peninsula – then inhabited largely by Celtic tribes – dates from the late third century BC. Through the first century BC to the seventh century AD, Hispania formed part, first of the Roman Empire and, after the third century AD, of the Visigothic Kingdom. Some traces of this Germanic influence remain in the Latinate vocabulary bequeathed by the Romans. A far larger alien component is provided by the Arabic brought in by the Moorish invaders from the seventh century onwards. There are still some 4,000 Arabic words in modern Spanish. By the eleventh century the main dialectal watershed between Castilian in the north and Andalusian in the south had taken shape, and the language of the twelfth-century epic *El Cantar de mio Cid* is already clearly Castilian. Through the succeeding three centuries Castilian consolidated and extended its status as the 'Spanish' language; a pre-eminence due in part to the fact that the Reconquista – the gradual expulsion of the Moors from Andalusia, leading finally to the unification of the country in the fifteenth century – was launched from, and successfully prosecuted by Castile.

The main dialectal division in the modern language is still that between north (Castilian) and south (Andalusian); other dialects, such as Aragonese, are moribund. Catalan is a language in its own right, and Galician is a Portuguese outlier. A key phonetic difference between Castilian and Andalusian is the phenomenon known as *seseo*: in Andalusia, *c* before *e/i*, and *z*, are pronounced as /s/ instead of the Castilian interdental fricative /θ/. *Seseo* is also characteristic of much of the Spanish spoken in Latin America, a plausible hypothesis here being that the language brought by the conquistadores to the New World in the sixteenth century and onwards was in fact *s*-Spanish; i.e. the /θ/ pronunciation was not lost in Latin American Spanish, it was never there.

A second key characteristic of Latin American Spanish is the pronunciation of *ll* – Castilian /ʎ/ as /j/ or /ʒ/. Practice here varies from one country to another; e.g.

calle 'street' is pronounced as /kaʎe/ in Peru, as in Castilian, becomes /kaje/ in Venezuela, and /kaʒe/ in Argentine and Uruguay.

The earliest recognizable Spanish is found in some tenth-century glosses to Latin texts. The subsequent history of Spanish literature can be periodized as follows:

1. Twelfth to fifteenth centuries: epic and romance; *El Cantar de mio Cid*, the story of Spain's national hero, Rodrigo Díaz, known as el Cid (from Arabic *sayyid* 'lord, master'). Also in this period fall the important encyclopedic works produced in the reign of Alfonso the Wise (thirteenth century) such as the enormous *General Estoria*, the *Siete Partidas* and the *Estoria de España*.
2. The *siglo de oro*, the Golden Age (sixteenth to early seventeenth centuries): ushered in (1499) by the humorous and realistic masterpiece *La Celestina*. This period includes three of Spain's greatest writers: Garcilaso de la Vega, Miguel de Cervantes, and Lope de Vega; the original picaresque novel, *Lazarillo de Tormes*; the early and fascinating accounts of life in the New World, e.g. the *Historia verdadera de la conquista de la Nueva España*, by Bernal Diaz del Castillo; and the works of the great Spanish mystics, Fray Luís de León, Santa Teresa de Avila, and San Juan de la Cruz.
3. The seventeenth century: Gongora and the movement for re-Latinization: *conceptismo* and *culteranismo*; one great writer – Calderón de la Barca.
4. The late nineteenth century; the revival of the novel: Benito Pérez Galdós.
5. Early twentieth century the 'generation of 1898': Azorín, Angel Ganivet, Antonio Machado, Pio Baroja, and Miguel de Unamuno: politico-social, religious, and cultural reassessment of the modern world in general and of Spain in particular.
6. The period of the Civil War: Federico Garcia Lorca, Camilo Jose Cela.

The late nineteenth and the twentieth centuries have seen a remarkable proliferation of distinguished writers in Latin America. Outstanding among so many are: Argentine: Jorge Luis Borges; Chile: Pablo Neruda; Mexico: Octavio Paz; Colombia: Gabriel Garcia Marquez; Nicaragua: Ruben Dario; Peru: Cesar Vallejo, Mario Vargas LLosa.

SCRIPT

Latin alphabet plus tilde (to mark palatal /ɲ/) and acute accent. Certain letters, e.g. *b*, *c*, *g*, have positional variant sounds; e.g. *c* = /k/ before a back consonant, /θ/ before a front; *b* = /b/ as initial, /ß/ between vowels; *g* = /x/ before *e*, *i*, otherwise = /g/. There are four digraphs: *ch* = /tʃ/, *ll* = /ʎ/, *qu* = /k/, *rr* = /r/.

Spanish introduces questions and exclamations with inverted markers: *¿a que hora termina Vd. el trabajo?* 'When do you finish work?'; *¡Que lástima!* 'What a pity!'

PHONOLOGY

Consonants

stops: p, b, t, d, k, g
affricate: tʃ
fricatives: f, θ, s, x
nasals: m, n, ɲ
laterals and flaps: l, ʎ, ɾ, rr
semi-vowels: j, w

/d/ has allophone [ð]. /s/ has [z] allophone, e.g. in *mismo* 'same', /mi**z**mo/. /n/ has homorganic allophones before certain consonants: e.g. *enviar* 'send' = [ɛ**mb**jar]; *incapaz* 'unable' = [i**ŋ**kapaθ]. *h* is silent: e.g. *hombre* 'man' = [ɔmbre]. /l/ and /r/ alternate in uneducated speech in Latin American: e.g. *calma*/*carma*.

Vowels

i, e, a, o, u
Diphthongs: ai, au, ei, eu, oi

Stress

Normally tends to the penultimate syllable, except in consonantal endings where final stress is frequent: e.g. *el algodón* 'cotton'; *el almacén* 'store'; but *el azúcar* 'sugar', *el árbol* 'the tree'. Final stressed vowels, e.g. in preterite, are marked by acute: *compré* 'I bought'. Antepenultimate stress also occurs: *lámpara* 'lamp', *póliza* 'policy, certificate'.

MORPHOLOGY AND SYNTAX

Two genders, masculine and feminine; two numbers.

Articles

	Masculine	*Feminine*	*Plural*
definite:	el	la	los/las
indefinite:	un	una	unos/unas 'some'

For example, *Los unos dicen que sí y los otros que no* 'Some say yes, the others no.'

In contra-distinction to usage in French and Italian, the Spanish definite article can be used pronominally: e.g. *mi libro y* ***el*** *de Pedro* 'my book and Pedro's'.

The plural marker is -(*e*)*s*.

Adjective

As attribute usually follows, but some common adjectives precede noun and may be truncated: *buen(o)* 'good', *mal(o)* 'bad': e.g. *Hace buen/mal tiempo hoy* 'It's good/bad weather today.'

Position of adjective may affect meaning, cf. *un hombre grande* 'a big man', *un gran hombre* 'a great man'.

COMPARATIVE

This is made with *más* + *que*: e.g. *Este libro es más barato que ése* 'This book is cheaper than that one.' Spanish has retained the Latinate suppletives: *bueno* 'good' – *mejor*; *malo* 'bad' – *peor*; *pequeño* 'small' – *menor*; though *más pequeno* and *más grande* are used with reference to size.

Pronoun

PERSONAL

All the basic personal pronouns except first and second singular are marked for gender:

		Singular	*Plural*
1		yo	nosotros/nosotras
2		tu	vosotros/vosotras
3	masc.	él	ellos/ellas
	fem.	ella	

A polite second person form of address is provided by *Usted*, abbreviated in writing to *Vd.*, with plural *Ustedes* (*Vds.*), with third person verbal concord.

There are three sets of object pronouns in Spanish. The direct object set is:

	Singular	*Plural*
1	me	nos
2	te	os
3	le/la/lo	los/las

These precede the verb, unless this is in imperative or infinitive form: *le/les esperamos a Vd./Vds.* 'we are expecting you]masc. sing./fem.pl.)'. The *a* in this example is the so-called 'personal *a*', which must precede an object noun denoting a person; cf. *Tendré oportunidad de conocerle a Vd. personalmente* 'I shall have a chance to get to know you personally.'

The direct object pronouns are the same as the direct, with the exception that the gender-marked forms for the third person are reduced to *le/les*: *le parece bien a ella* 'it seems OK to her'; *¿En qué puedo servirles?* 'What I can do for you (pl.)?' *Le/les* → *se* before an object pronoun with an *l-* initial: e.g. *se lo digo a Vd.* 'I say it to you' = 'I tell you'.

PREPOSITIONAL FORMS

These are identical to the subject forms, except in the first and second person singular which have *mí* and *ti*: *para mí* 'for me'; *un regalo para ti/para Vd.* 'a present for you'.

PREPOSITIONAL ADJECTIVES

The singular forms, *mi*, *tu*, *su*, have two-way marking for number: e.g. *mi libro* 'my book'; *mis libros* 'my books'. The first and second person plural forms are marked in addition for gender of possessed object: e.g. *nuestros libros* 'our books'; *nuestra casa* 'our house'.

DEMONSTRATIVE ADJECTIVE AND PRONOUN

Three-degree gradation:

este, esta, estos, estas 'this, these' (associated with 1st p.)
ese, esa, esos, esas 'that, those' (associated with 2nd p.)
aquel, aquella, -os, -as 'that, those yonder' (associated with 3rd p.)

The pronominal forms are identical, but take an acute accent: e.g. *esa tienda y ésta* 'that shop and this one'.

INTERROGATIVE PRONOUN

quién 'who?', *qué* 'what?'

RELATIVE PRONOUN

que is both subject and object and is invariable: e.g. *los puntos que se han tratado hoy* 'the points which have been dealt with today'. For greater precision, *el cual/la cual, los/las cuales* may be used.

Numerals

1–10: *uno* (→ *un/una* before nouns), *dos*, *tres*, *cuatro*, *cinco*, *seis*, *siete*, *ocho*, *nueve*, *diez*; 11 *once*; 12 *doce*; 13 *trece*; 14 *catorce*; 15 *quince*; 16–19: *diez y seis*, etc.; 20 *veinte*; 30 *treinta*; 40 *cuarenta*; 100 *ciento* (→ *cien* before a noun).

Verb

Three conjugations are distinguished, in *-ar* (the great majority), *-er*, *-ir*. The verb has three moods: indicative, imperative, subjunctive.

Specimen regular paradigm: *tomar* 'to take':

		Present indicative	*Present subjunctive*	*Preterite*	*Imperfect*	*Future*
sing.	1	tomo	tome	tomé	tomaba	tomaré
	2	tomas	tomes	tomaste	tomabas	tomarás
	3	toma	tome	tomó	tomaba	tomará
pl.	1	tomamos	tomemos	tomamos	tomábamos	tomarémos
	3	toman	tomen	tomaron	tomaban	tomarán

Note: the second person plural is not shown in these paradigms, as it is of very limited use.

The conditional adds the endings: *-ía*, *-ías*, *-ía*; *-íamos*, *-ían* to the infinitive. The imperfect subjunctive has alternative endings: either *tomara*, *tomaras*, *tomara*; *tomáramos*, *tomaran*, or *tom-ase*, *-ases*, *-ase*, *-ásemos*, *-asen*.

The *-er* and *-ir* conjugations have virtually the same endings, with a few exceptions, e.g. in the imperfect, where *comer* 'to eat' has *comía*, *comías*, *comía*; *comíamos*, *comían*. The *-er* verbs can distinguish between the first plural forms in the present and the preterite: e.g. *comemos* 'we eat', *comimos* 'we ate'. Tenses based on the infinitive differ, as might be expected, in vowel pattern. Both tenses of the subjunctive are much used in Spanish.

Departures from the regular pattern are found, e.g. in root-changing verbs: *mover* 'move' – present *muevo*, *sentir* 'feel, hear' – *siento*, *dormir* 'sleep' – *duermo*, but many apparent irregularities are due to orthographical requirements: e.g. the alternation of *z*/*c* = /θ/, *g*/*gu*, *c*/*qu* = /k/.

There are, however, many genuinely irregular verbs: e.g.

	Present	*Past participle*
decir 'say'	digo	dicho
hacer 'do'	hago	hecho
ir 'go'	voy	ido
saber 'know'	se	sabido
conocer 'know'	conozco	conocido

Continuous tenses are made with the auxiliaries *estar* 'to be', *ir* 'to go' plus present participle: e.g. *estoy hablando*/*estamos hablando* 'I/we am/are speaking'; *está escribiendo la carta* 'he is writing the letter'.

The distinction between the two verbs *ser* and *estar*, both meaning 'to be', is very important; broadly, *ser* is the copula, used of any permanent identity; *estar* denotes a contingent state of affairs: cf. *El señor López* ***es*** *español* 'Mr L. is Spanish'; *El Señor López* ***está*** *malo* 'Mr L. is ill'.

The perfect tense is made by conjugating the auxiliary verb *haber* 'to have' with the past participle of the sense-verb: e.g. *he hablado* 'I have spoken'; *han hablado* 'they have spoken'.

In contra-distinction to French and Italian, verbs expressing motion are conjugated in Spanish with the auxiliary *haber*: e.g. *he venido* 'I have come'; *he ido* 'I have gone'.

Negation

The negating particle is *no* preceding the verb, with resumption of negation in pronominal or other associated material: e.g. *no viene nadie* 'no one is coming'; *no tengo nada* 'I have nothing'; *no hace nunca frio* 'it's never cold'.

Prepositions

Worthy of particular mention is the combination of the preposition *con* 'with', with the pronominal forms *mí*, *ti*, and *si*: *conmigo* 'with me'; *contigo* 'with you'; *consigo* 'with oneself'.

Word order

Both SVO and VSO are regular.

1 En el principio era la Palabra; y la Palabra estaba con Dios: y
la Palabra era Dios.
2 Esta en el principio estaba con Dios.
3 Todas las cosas fueron hechas por ella; y sin ella, nada se hizo en
lo que ha sido hecho.
4 En ella estaba *la* vida; y la vida era la Luz de los hombres.
5 Y la Luz resplandece en las tinieblas; mas las tinieblas no la com-
prendieron.
6 Hubo *un* hombre enviado de Dios, llamado Juan.
7 Este vino como testigo, para dar testimonio acerca de la Luz, á
fin de que todos creyesen por él.
8 No era él la Luz, sino *enviado* para dar testimonio de la Luz.

SUNDANESE

INTRODUCTION

Sundanese belongs to the Malayo-Polynesian branch of the Austronesian family, and is spoken by between 15 and 20 million people in west Java. The modern literary standard is based on the Bandung dialect.

The earliest folk literature in Sundanese dates from the fourteenth century. Since the middle of the nineteenth century the language has been the vehicle for a flourishing modern literature in all genres. It is also used in primary education and in the local media.

SCRIPT

Until the seventeenth century Sundanese was written in the Javanese script, known in this context as *cacarakan*. Conversion to Islam in the twelfth/thirteenth century brought the use of the Arabic script. Since mid-nineteenth century romanization.

PHONOLOGY

Consonants

stops: p, b, t, d, k, g
affricates: tʃ, dʒ
fricatives: s, h
nasals: m, n, ɲ, ŋ
lateral and flap: l, r
semi-vowels: w, j

Final *k* as /k/, not /ʔ/ as in Indonesian. Similarly, final *d*, *g* = /d/, /g/. The affricates are notated as *tj* and *dj*.

Vowels

i, ɛ, a, ə, œ/ʌ, o, u

/ɛ/ is notated as *e*, /ə/ as *ĕ*.

Stress

Stress is normally on the penultimate syllable, unless this has *ĕ*, when stress moves to final.

MORPHOLOGY AND SYNTAX

The more or less elaborate coding of respect levels, characteristic of Javanese, Madurese, etc., is also found in Sundanese, where four levels are distinguished: high *basa lĕmĕs*; neutral *basa sĕdĕng*; everyday *basa kasar*; low *basa tjohag*. Equivalents are not evenly distributed in the four levels. Thus, the verb 'to sleep' is expressible in all four: b. lĕmĕs *kulem*; b. sĕdĕng *sarè*; b. kasar *saré*; b. tjohag *molor*. However, *artos*, the b. lĕmĕs word for 'money' has a b. kasar equivalent, *duit*, but no equivalents in b. sĕdĕng or b. tjohag. Similarly, 'house' is *rorompok* in b. lĕmĕs, *bumi* in b. sĕdĕng, and *imah* in b. kasar, but has no b. tjohag equivalent. *See* **Pronoun**, below.

Many roots are formally neutral and can be syntactically exploited as nominals or verbals, e.g. *djalan* 'way' (nominal), 'to go' (verbal). This ambivalence extends to loan-words: e.g. *sakola* 'school; to go to school'.

Noun

Root, e.g. *imah* 'house', *djalma* 'man'; derivative: e.g. with prefixes *pa-*, *pi-*, *ka-*, circumfix *pa...an*, etc. All prefixes have variants, depending on initial of stem; e.g. *pa-* appears as *pa-*, *pam-*, *pang*, *pan-*, *panj-*. Thus are formed nouns of agency: e.g. *dagang* 'to trade' – *padagang* 'trader'. Also nouns denoting verbal action: e.g. *bantu* 'to help' – *pangbantu* 'help(ing)'.

The circumfix *pa...an* forms nouns denoting locus of action, or activity engaged in: *mandi* 'to bathe' – *pamandian* 'bath-house'; *madat* 'opium' – *pamadatan* 'opium-smoker'.

Partial reduplication and compounding are prolific sources of nouns: e.g. *sato* 'animal' – *sasatoan* 'cattle'; *ngomong* 'speak' – *mĕsin-ngomong* 'gramophone'.

The plural number can be indicated by complete reduplication, e.g. *djalma* 'man '– *djalmadjalma* 'people'; by partial reduplication + *-an*, e.g. *kembang* 'flower' – *kĕkĕmbangan* 'flowers'; or by infixed *-ar/al-*, e.g. *budak* 'child' – *barudak* 'children'.

Adjective

See **Verb**, below.

Pronoun

All four speech levels have complete sets of personal pronouns in three persons and two numbers. The b. kasar set for normal everyday usage is:

	1	*2*	*3*
singular	kuring, sim kuring	maneh, silaing	manehna
plural	kuring kabeh	maraneh, maneh kabeh	maranehna

In second and third persons, note the use of pluralizing infix *-ar-* mentioned above. Sundanese does not possess the personal pronominal enclitics for first and second persons found in Javanese and Bahasa Indonesia. The third person does, however, have *-na*: e.g. *imahna* 'his house'.

DEMONSTRATIVE PRONOUN
ieu 'this' – *eta* 'that' – *itu* 'that yonder'; *ieu* and *eta* may precede the noun, *itu* always follows.

INTERROGATIVE/RELATIVE PRONOUN
saha 'who?'; *naon* 'what?'.

Numerals

1–10: *hidji, dua, tilu, opat, lima, gěněp, tudjuh, dalapan, salapan, sapuluh*; 20 *dua puluh*; 100 *ratus*.

Verb

As stative verbs, adjectives are included under this heading. All predicative forms can be marked for plurality by means of the *-ar/al-* infix: e.g. *geulis* 'be beautiful', pl. *galeulis*; *alus* 'be good', pl. *aralus*.

The verb is neutral as to aspect, mood, or tense, and is not marked for person except for third, which may take *-eun*. Various particles are used to articulate the course of action as narrated in the flow of speech: thus, *geus* and *parantos* suggest that ongoing action has reached a result, i.e. is 'perfective', while *(a)tjan* suggests that this point has not yet been reached. In other words, *geus* or *parantos* will normally refer to the past; but the aspectual distinction can apply to any time frame. The future can be more pointedly specified by the use of *bakal* or *baris*. The auxiliary *pating* indicates co-operative action; concomitant action is suggested by *keur* or *nudja*: e.g. imperfective: ***keur** matja naon?* 'What are you reading?'; perfective: ***geus** dahar?* 'Have you eaten already?'; future: *Sabulan deui kuring **bakal** papanggih djeung manehna* 'I shall meet him in a month'.

VERB FORMATION
By prefix, suffix, infix, or circumfix:

By prefix: (the index indicates the number of possible variants)

nga^4- forms transitives, e.g. *nga.duruk* 'to burn something'; *nga.djawab* 'to answer';
pi-/mi- make transitives from verbal roots, nouns or adjectives; e.g. *garwa* 'wife' – *migarwa* 'to take a wife';
ba-/si- make reflexive verbs from intransitive roots, e.g. *ba.robah* '(be) change(d)';
di- is a passive formant, e.g. *di.batja* 'to be read' – *eta buku dibatja ku kuring* 'this book is read by me' (*ku* is prepositional subject marker).

By suffix: e.g. *-an/-keun/-eun*. The latter denotes chance passivity, e.g. *hudjan.eun* 'to be caught and soaked in a downpour'. *-an* and *-keun* are transitive markers: e.g. *meupeuskeun gělas* 'to smash the glass'.

By circumfix: e.g. *nga*[4]-...*an/keun*; *pang...keun*: e.g. from *diuk* 'sit' – *nga.diuk.an* 'to occupy'; *lagu* 'song' – *nga.lagu.keun* 'to sing a song'.

NEGATIVE

The general negating particle is *teu*, preceding the verb.

MODAL AUXILIARY VERBS

Example: *hajang* 'to want to', *embung* 'not to want to'; *bisa* 'to be able to': e.g. *kuring teu bisa ... njuratan* 'I can't write'.

Prepositions

Examples: *di* 'in', e.g. *di pasar* 'in the bazaar'; *ti* 'from'; *ku* marks the subject or the instrumental, e.g. ... *dibatja ku kuring* 'read by me' = 'I read'; *ku kapaludara* 'by plane'; *ka* marks object, e.g. *kuring ngabantu ka indung* 'I help mother'.

Word order

Free: SVO, VSO, OVS. Qualifier follows qualified.

دِنَ اُوتْنَ كْبْس اَيَا فَقَنْدِكَ تَيْهْ اَرِي فَقَنْدِكَ تَيْبَا اَيْنَا د اَللّٰه

2. سَرْتَ فَقَنْدِكَ تَيْبَا بَا اَللّٰه ٭   اَرِي اَيْتَ تَيْبَا دِنَ اُوتْنَ

3. كْبْس اَيَا د اَللّٰه ٭   سِنِسْكَرَ بَا كُوْ اَيْتَ دِجَدِكَنْنَنَا اَرِي سَجَبْنَا كُوْ اَيْتَ مَهْ هَنْتَ اَيَا فِسَنْ اَنُوْ دِجَدِكَنْ دِنَ

4. سَكَبِيهْنَ نُوْ كْبْس دِجَدِكَنْ ٭   دِنَ جَرُوْ اَيْتَ فَقْتْيَنَا هُرُوْف

5. تَيْهْ اَرِي اَيْتَ هُرُوْف تَيْبَا بَا جَهَيَا مَنُوْس ٭   دَمِي جَهَيَا تَيْبَا غَكْبِيرَ دِ نُوْ فُوَايِكْ اَرِي كُوْ فُوَايِكْ تَيْبَا هَنْتَ دِتَرِمَا ٭

6. اَيَا هِج جَلمَ نُوْ دِفُورْغ كُوْ اَللّٰه جَنْفَنْنَنَا يَوْهَنَيِسْ ٭

7. فَقْسُومْفَقْنَ فِمْرَتِيْلَكَنْنَ // بَدَيْ مَرْتِيْلَكَنْ فُرْكَرَ جَهَيَا تَيْبَا

SWAHILI

INTRODUCTION

Swahili belongs to the North-East Coastal Bantu group of the Benue-Congo family. The name is derived from the Arabic *sawāḥil*, the broken plural of *sāḥil* 'coast'. Estimates of the numbers speaking Swahili vary from 50 to 70 million and upwards; the great majority of these are bilingual, with Swahili used as a second language alongside other Bantu mother tongues (Chinyanja, Shona, Luba, etc.) and as a lingua franca for speakers of non-Bantu languages. Swahili is the national language of Tanzania and of Kenya, and is a main language in parts of Zaire and the Congo. There are many dialect forms spread over an enormous area stretching from the Somali border to Mozambique, and from the Comoro Islands to the Congo. The first steps towards the creation of a standardized Swahili were taken in 1930, when the Inter-Territorial Language Committee was formed. African participation in this body began in 1946, with representatives from Kenya, Tanganyika, Uganda, and Zanzibar. The work of standardizing the language is now in the hands of the Institute of Swahili Research in Dar es Salaam.

Swahili has had a Moslem background since the period of the Zenj Empire (tenth to fifteenth centuries). The growth of Swahili as an international trade language dates from about the thirteenth century. Contact with Arabic and other languages is richly reflected in the lexicon. The classical verse literature, dating from the mid-seventeenth century and reaching a high point in the eighteenth/nineteenth centuries, was centred on the coastal strip of Kenya. During the twentieth century the centre of gravity in Swahili creative writing has moved to Tanzania, as English has gained the upper hand in Kenya.

SCRIPT

Until the late nineteenth century (and occasionally thereafter) Swahili was written in the Arabic script. The romanization now in use has all the letters of the English alphabet except *c*, *q*, and *x*.

PHONOLOGY

Consonants

stops: p, b, t, d, k, g
affricates: tʃ, dʒ → [d′]
fricatives: f, v, s, z, ʃ, h
nasals: m, n, ɲ, ŋ
lateral and flap: l, r
semi-vowels: j, w

/θ, ð, x, γ/ occur in words of Arabic origin.

Some grammars make a distinction between aspirate and non-aspirate /p, t, k/, and quote such pairs as /paa/ 'roof', /p^{h}aa/ 'gazelle'.

Vowels

a, ε, i, ɔ, u

All are short.

Stress is invariably on the penultimate. Exceptionally for a Bantu language, Swahili has no tones. A degree of vowel harmony characterizes suffixation: cf. *timia* 'to be complete', *kimbia* 'to run'; *tokea* 'to appear', *pokea* 'to receive'.

MORPHOLOGY AND SYNTAX

Noun classes

(*See* **Bantu Languages**.) Swahili has fewer classes than some of its congeners, owing to the fusion in Swahili of certain classes having phonetically similar prefixes. Traditionally, fourteen classes were distinguished, by allocating two classes, singular and plural, to each semantic field. This system can be simplified by putting both singular and plural in one class: e.g. the m-/wa- class,

Class 1 – people: *mtu* 'person', pl. *watu*; *mtoto* 'child', pl. *watoto*.
Class 2: singular marker *m-*, pl. *mi*; heterogeneous, includes plants, trees, various natural phenomena, e.g. *mti* 'tree', pl. *miti*; *mlima* 'mountain', pl. *milima*.
Class 3: heterogeneous, singular marker *ki-*, pl. *vi-*, e.g. *kitu* 'thing', pl. *vitu*; *kisu* 'knife', pl. *visu*.
Class 4: heterogeneous, singular marker Ø, *ji-*, pl. *ma-*, e.g. *jicho* 'eye', pl. *macho*; *Øduka* 'shop', pl. *maduka*. Most nouns in this class have no concord in the singular.
Class 5: heterogeneous, known as the *n-* class, this is the largest noun class in Swahili, as it contains all loan-words. Singular and plural are identical: e.g. *nyumba* 'house(s)'; *nyoka* 'snake(s)'; *dakika* 'minute' (Arabic).
Class 6: heterogeneous, but many abstract nouns in *u-* sing., with no plural,

e.g. *usafi* 'cleanliness'; *uzuri* 'beauty'; *Udachi* 'Germany'.
Class 7: the locative class contains only one noun: *mahali* 'place', with a rather complicated system of concord involving the locus markers *p-*, *k-*, *m-*. *See* Location, below.

The class system outlined above, while characteristic of the Swahili noun, is cut across by a simple animate/non-animate opposition, in the sense that nouns denoting animates, especially rational animates, take class 1 concord in adjective and verb, whatever their own formal grammatical class. Thus, *ndugu* 'younger brother' is a class 5 noun, but 'a good brother' is *ndugu **m**zuri*, i.e. the attributive adjective *-zuri* 'good' takes class 1 concord, *m-*. *Samaki* 'fish' (Arabic) is also class 5; but 'small fishes' is *samaki **wa**dogo*.

POSSESSION
The stem *-a* is marked for concord with the class to which the possessed object belongs. The order then is possessed object – class marker + *a* – possessor: e.g. *kitabu **cha** mtoto* 'the child's book'; *watu **wa** Tanzania* 'the people of Tanzania'; *nyumba ya mtu* 'the man's house'. An attributive adjective comes between the possessed object and the particle: e.g. *nyumba **n**dogo ya mtu* 'the man's small house'.

LOCATION
The markers *p-*, *k-*, *m-* take class concord: *p-* gives a definite fix, *k-* an indefinite, *m-* refers specifically to location within something. Thus, 'there' can be translated in more than one way, e.g. ***upo pale*** 'it is there' (definite fix, e.g. *meza**ni*** 'on the table'); ***wako kule*** 'they are thereabouts'; ***imo** nyumbani* 'it is in the house' (different class concords are used in these examples).

The postposition expressing the locative case is *-ni*.

Adjective

The attributive adjective follows the noun qualified and has class concord: e.g. ***mtu mwema*** 'good man' (cl. 1); ***kisu kikali*** 'a sharp knife' (cl. 3); ***watoto Wazungu wengi*** 'many European children'. Comparatively few adjectives are of Bantu origin; many are borrowed from Arabic, and these are all indeclinable: e.g. *chumba **Ø**safi* 'clean room'.

Compound adjectives are formed with the *-a* linking particle marked for concord: e.g. ***chakula cha** kizungu* 'European food'.

COMPARATIVE
Periphrastic with *kupita/kuliko*: e.g. *Mlima wa Kilimanjaro ni **m**refu kuliko mlima wa Kenya* 'Mount Kilimanjaro is higher than Mount Kenya' (*-refu* 'tall').

Pronoun

The subject prefixes for the *m-/wa-* class are: sing. 1 *ni-*, 2 *u-*, 3 *a-*; pl. 1 *tu-*, 2 *m-*, 3 *wa-*. The object infixes for the same class are: sing. 1 *ni-*, 2 *ku-*, 3 *m-*; pl. 1 *tu-*, 2 *wa-*, 3 *wa-*. For all other classes, the object infix equals the subject prefix; e.g.

for the *ki-/vi-* class, 'it' is *ki-/-ki-*; 'they' is *vi-*; 'them' is *-vi-*. In such sentences as 'he gave it to me', 'it' need not be expressed: e.g.

a.li.ni.pa *a-* = subject prefix, *m-* class, 3rd p. 'he';
li = past-tense marker (*see* **Verb**, below);
ni = indirect object, *m-* class, 1st p. 'to me';
pa = root verb, 'to give'.

Cf. *ni.li.**ki**.nunua* 'I bought it', where the presence of ***ki*** indicates that I bought something specific belonging to the *ki-* class. Cf. *ni.li.**m**.wona* 'I saw him'; *a.li.**ni**.ona* 'he saw me' (*-ona* 'to see'; *w* is a euphonic glide).

THE INDEPENDENT EMPHATIC PRONOUNS
mimi – wewe – yeye; pl. *sisi – ninyi – wao*; these can never replace the subject prefixes, but have to be used e.g. in the habitual aspect which does not take subject prefixes.

POSSESSIVE PRONOMINAL MARKERS
Sing. 1 *-angu*, 2 *-ako*, 3 *-ake*; pl. 1 *-etu*, 2 *-enu*, 3 *-ao*. These are modulated by the appropriate class markers: eg. ***vitabu vile vyangu*** 'these books are mine'; ***nyumba yetu*** 'our house'; ***Ørafiki wema wangu*** 'my good friends'.

DEMONSTRATIVE PRONOUN
The proximate series is based on the particle *ha-* + class marker; the distal series by combining the class markers with *-le*. Assimilation and some anomalies occur in both series: e.g. ***kijiji hiki*** 'this village', ***vijiji hivi*** 'these villages'; ***chumba kile*** 'that room', ***vyumba vile*** 'those rooms'.

INTERROGATIVE PRONOUN
nani 'who?'; *nini* 'what?'.

RELATIVE PRONOUN
See **Verb**, Relative clause, below.

Numerals

The numerals are adjectives, and the units 1, 2, 3, 4, 5, 8 take class concord; 6, 7, 9, being Arabic, do not. 1 *-moja*; 2 *-wili*; 3 *-tatu*; 4 *-nne*; 5 *-tano*; 8 *-nane*. 6 *sita*; 7 *saba*; 9 *tisa*; 10 *kumi*. 11 *kumi na -moja*; 12 *kumi na -wili*; 20 *ishirini*; 30 *thelathini*, etc. (*see* **Arabic**); 100 *mia* (Arabic). Examples: ***visu vitatu*** 'three knives'; ***visu Øsabu*** 'seven knives'; ***watoto wanne*** 'four children'; ***watoto** kumi na **mmoja*** 'eleven children'.

Verb

The infinitive form for Bantu stems is *ku* – stem – *a*: e.g. *ku.fany.a* 'to do'. For Arabic stems: *ku* – stem – *e/i/u*: e.g. *ku.fikr.i* 'to think'.

INDICATIVE FORMS
The general formula is subject marker – tense sign – stem. The present

characteristic is *-na-*; the past, *-li-*; the future, *-ta-*: e.g. *ni.**na**.soma* 'I am reading'; *ni.**li**.soma* 'I read (past)'; *ni**ta**soma* 'I shall read'. Other characteristics are: perfect *-me-*; subjunctive Ø; conditional *-ki-*. Examples: *i.**me**.fika* 'it has arrived'; *tu.**Ø**.ngoje* 'let us wait'; *ni.**ki**.kaa* 'if I wait'.

PASSIVE

The passive of transitive verbs is made by inserting *-w-* between stem and final: e.g. *ku.soma* 'to read' – *ku.som.**w**.a* 'to be read'; *ku.jua* 'to know' – *ku.ju.**liwa*** 'to be known'. The second example shows the expanded passive marker *-uliwa-* (four variants) added to stems ending in *-ua/-oa*.

CAUSATIVE

-sha is added to stem: e.g. *kutelemka* 'to go down' – *kutelem**sha*** 'to lower'.

HABITUAL MOOD

The characteristic is *-hu-*; subject markers are not used. Thus, e.g. ***hu**soma* means '... is/are habitually reading'; and person must be specified by other means, e.g. the use of the emphatic personal pronouns.

THE PREPOSITIONAL FORM

Example: *a.na.wa.som.ea* 'he/she is reading to them': here, the ending *-ea* marks the prepositional form which is used when the verb is benefactive, i.e. the action is performed to or on behalf of someone else: *wa* is the infixed pronominal object: '(to) them', referring e.g. to *watoto* 'the children'. Formally, *i/e* is inserted before the final vowel. As in the passive, *-l-* may figure as a euphonic glide component: e.g. *-pata* 'to get' – *patia* 'to get for someone'; *-chukua* 'to carry' – *-chuku**li**a* 'to carry to/for someone'

NEGATION

For most tenses, negative subject markers are used which are prefixed directly to the stem in the present tense, i.e. dropping *-na-*: class 1, sing. 1 *si-*, 2 *hu-*, 3 *ha-*; pl. 1 *hatu-*, 2 *ham-*, 3 *hawa-*; the stem final changes to *-i*: e.g. ***ha**somi* 'he doesn't read'; ***hatu**jui* 'we don't know'.

The *-li-* past is negated by *-ku-* with negative prefix: e.g. ***ha.ku.**soma* 'he did not read'. Future: ***si**.ta.kwenda* 'I shall not go'; ***ha**.ta.soma* 'he will not read'.

RELATIVE INFIX

An alternative form of the demonstrative pronoun in *-o* provides the base *-yo* for the relative infix, which is marked for concord (*yo* → *ye* in class 1): e.g. *ni.li.**ye**.soma* 'I, who read (past)'; *mtoto. a.li.**ye**.soma kitabu* 'the child who was reading a book'.

A second way of making a relative clause is to use the base *amba-* + relative marker, as above: e.g. *mtu ambaye a.na.soma* 'the person who is reading'; *watu ambao wa.na.soma* 'the people who are reading'. Thus, *ni.na.ye.soma* = *mimi ambaye ni.na.soma* 'I who am reading' (*amba-* cannot be sentence-initial).

IMPERATIVE

The stem alone provides an abrupt command. A polite request is made with the formula *u* – stem – *e*: e.g. ***ufany.e*** 'would you be so kind as to ...' (sing.); pl. *m.fany.e*.

Prepositions

Several nouns take the possessive *ya*: e.g. *juu ya* 'on', ***ndani ya*** **'inside'**. Others take *na*: e.g. *mbali na* 'far from'; *karibu na* 'close to': e.g. *ni.na.kaa karibu na mji* 'I live close to the town'.

Word order

SVO is basic. In the verbal complex, the object infix precedes the stem, and may anticipate an overtly expressed object, thus conferring definite status on the latter: e.g. *ni.li.**ki**.nunua kitabu* 'I bought **it** the book' (i.e. a specific book).

1 Hapo mwanzo kulikuwako Neno, naye Neno aliku-
2 wako kwa Mungu, naye Neno alikuwa Mungu. Huyo
3 mwanzo alikuwako kwa Mungu. Vyote vilifanyika
kwa huyo; wala pasipo yeye hakikufanyika cho chote
4 kilichofanyika. Ndani yake ndimo ulimokuwa uzima,
5 nao ule uzima ulikuwa nuru ya watu. Nayo nuru
yang'aa gizani, wala giza halikuiweza.
6 Palitokea mtu, ametumwa kutoka kwa Mungu,
7 jina lake Yohana. Huyo alikuja kwa ushuhuda, ili
aishuhudie ile nuru, na wote wapate kuamini kwa
8 yeye. Huyo hakuwa ile nuru, bali alikuja ili aishu-
hudie ile nuru.

SWEDISH

INTRODUCTION

Swedish belongs to the East Scandinavian branch of Common Scandinavian (part of the Germanic branch of Indo-European). The Old Swedish period runs from the thirteenth to the early sixteenth century.

The emergence of the modern Swedish language and literature can be dated with some precision: in the 1520s King Gustav Vasa dissolved the union with Denmark, and, more importantly, Catholicism was replaced by the Lutheran Church. The first translation of the Bible into Swedish appeared in 1547. From the late-nineteenth-century realists and Strindberg onwards, Swedish literature has produced a large crop of distinguished writers, working mainly in the field of experimental poetry and in the critical analysis of society and the arts.

The literary language is based on the central (Stockholm) dialect. Some of the outlying dialects are highly divergent, e.g. that of Dalecarlia.

SCRIPT

The Roman alphabet + *å*, *ä*, *ö*.

PHONOLOGY

Consonants

stops: p, b, t, d, ʈ, ɖ, k, g
fricatives: f, v, ç, s, ʂ, ʃ, h
nasals: m, n, ɳ, ŋ
laterals and flap: l, ɭ, r
semi-vowel: j

/p, t, k/ are aspirated; the retroflex series /ʈ, ɖ, ɳ, ʂ, ɭ/ plus the retroflex clusters such as /ʈʂ, ɖʂ, ɳʂ/, are generally signalled in the script by *r* + C: e.g. *mord* 'murder', /muːɖ/ (in close transcription [mʊːɖ]; *korn* 'grain', /kuːɳ/ ([kʊːɳ]). Word-final /r/ has the same effect on a following initial /s/: e.g. *för sent* 'too late', /fəʂeːnt/. There is a tendency for /ʃ/ to become /ʂ/: e.g. *skinn* 'skin', /ʃin/ > [ʂin].

Vowels

Some 20 vowel sounds, differing in quantity and quality, are represented by nine letters: *i*, *e*, *a*, *o*, *u*, *y*, *å*, *ä*, *ö*; basically, they can be classified as:

(a) front unrounded: short ɪ, e, ɛ
long i, e, ɛ
(b) central: short ʏ, a, œ/ɵ, ʉ, ə
long ʏ, a, ø, ʉ
(c) back rounded: short u, ɔ
long u, o

In close transcription, the following central rounded phonemes are distinguished:

/œ/, e.g. *først* /fœʂʈ/, 'first';
/ɵ/, e.g. *just* /jɵst/, 'just, exactly';
/ø/, e.g. *överens* /øːvərɛns/, 'agreed';
/ʉ/, e.g. *ju* /jʉ/, 'indeed'.

In the central rounded area, close transcription of Swedish will distiguish between /ɵ/ as in *upp* 'up' and /ə/ as in *törst* 'thirst' (with retroflex /ʂ/).

Tone

Two tones are distinguished: the single or falling tone, which affects monosyllables (ignoring affixed endings, e.g. the definite article) and the double tone, the second component of which has a slightly higher onset pitch than the first. Both components have a downward glide. This second tone affects most polysyllables. Tone may be phonemic; the example usually quoted is *anden*; pronounced with single tone, this means 'the duck'; with double tone, 'the spirit'.

In speech, elision of final consonants is typical: e.g. *var vänlig och kom* 'do (be friendly and) come!', is realized as [va.vɛnli.o kom].

Stress

Normally, the main stress is on the first syllable, with secondary stress on the first syllable of a second component in a compound. Final unstressed vowels tend to be reduced to /ə/.

MORPHOLOGY AND SYNTAX

Noun

There are two genders: common and neuter. The indefinite article precedes: *en* for common, *ett* for neuter: e.g. *en blomma* 'a flower', *en bil* 'a car'; *ett barn* 'a child', *ett äpple* 'an apple'.

The definite article is suffixed: -(*e*)*n* for common nouns, -(*e*)*t* for neuter: e.g. *blomman* 'the flower', ***bilen*** 'the car'; *barnet* 'the child', *äpplet* 'the apple'.

Plural markers are: *-ar*, *-or*, *-er*, *-n*, *-Ø*: this gives five declensions: *häst* 'horse'

– *hästar*; *flicka* 'girl' – *flickor*; *tand* 'tooth' – *tänder*; *äpple* 'apple' – *äpplen*; *barn* 'child' – *barn***Ø**.

Umlaut may affect the stem as in *tand/tänder*; cf. *son – söner*, *bror – bröder*. To these plural markers, the plural definite article is affixed: *-na* for common, *-en* for neuter nouns: e.g. *flickor.na* 'the girls'; *barnen* 'the children'.

The demonstrative pronoun *den/det/de* is also used as a definite article, especially where an adjective intervenes: thus, *en stor bil* 'a big car', becomes in the definite form ***den** stora **bilen*** 'the big car', similarly, ***den** unga **flickan*** 'the young girl'; pl. ***de** stora **bilarna*** 'the big cars'; and in neuter: ***det** långa **brevet*** 'the long letter', ***det** vita **huset*** 'the white house'. That is, definiteness is doubly marked.

In modern Swedish the plural definite marker *de*, tends to be replaced by *dom*.

CASE SYSTEM

Of the old case system only the possessive *-s* remains. This can be added to the affixed article: e.g. from *flicka* 'girl': *en flickas* 'a girl's'; *flick**ans***, *flick**ors***, *flickor**nas***.

Adjective

Adjective precedes noun as attributive and is marked for neuter and for plural: e.g. *grön* 'green': *ett grön**t** hus*, *de grön**a** husen*.

COMPARATIVE

The comparative is in *-are* (indeclinable), often with umlaut in the stem: e.g. *stor* 'big' – *större*; *låg* 'low' – *lägre*.

Pronoun

PERSONAL

The third-person singular forms distinguish masculine/feminine. The subject forms with their objective correlatives are:

		Singular		*Plural*	
		Subject	*Object*	*Subject*	*Object*
1		jag	mig	vi	oss
2		du; ni	dig; er	Ni	Er
3	masc.	han	honom	de	dem
	fem.	hon	henne		
	nt.	det	det		

The *ni/er* forms tend to be avoided as somewhat old-fashioned, with a corresponding increase in the use of *du*. Periphrastic forms of address for second person are much in use.

DEMONSTRATIVE PRONOUN/ADJECTIVE

den/det/de have already been mentioned. Another form is *denna/detta/dessa*.

INTERROGATIVE PRONOUN
vem 'who?', *vad* 'what?'

RELATIVE PRONOUN
som; invariable: e.g. *mannen, som jag talade med* 'the man I was talking to'; *tabletter, som man löser upp i vatten* 'tablets which one dissolves in water'.

Numerals

1–10: *en/ett, två, tre, fyra, fem, sex, sju, åtta, nio, tio*; 11 *elva*; 12 *tolv*; 13 *tretton*; 14 *fjorton*; 15 *femton*; 20 *tjugo*; 30 *trettio*; 40 *fyrtio*; 100 *hundra*.

Verb

Transitive/intransitive, with active and passive voices. There are two moods: indicative and imperative. The indicative has two simple tenses, a present and past. The supine is used with the auxiliary *att ha* to form a perfect tense. The past participle is used only as an adjective: e.g. *en av Sveriges mest* ***lästa*** *författare* 'one of Sweden's most (widely) read authors'.

INDICATIVE MOOD
The present tense is made by adding *-r* to the infinitive for all persons: e.g. *att gå* 'to go', *jag går* 'I go'; *skriva* 'write', *jag skriver* (/a/ > /e/).

PAST TENSE
Here, there are three weak conjugations and one strong:

Weak

(a) past tense ending *-ade*, supine in *-at*: e.g. *jag kallade, jag har kallat*.
(b) past tense ending *-de*, supine in *-t*: e.g. *jag glömde, jag har glömt*.
(c) past tense ending *-dde*, supine in *-tt*: e.g. *jag trodde, jag har trott*.

The roots in these examples are, *kalla* 'to call', *glömma* 'forget', *tro* 'believe'.

Strong verbs: these show one- or two-stage ablaut: e.g.

	Present	*Past*	*Perfect*
skriva 'write'	skriver	skrev	har skrivet
ligga 'lie'	ligger	låg	har legat

Formerly, singular and plural forms of the past tense of strong verbs were distinguished, and these plural forms may still be found in the literary language: e.g. *skrevo* 'we/you/they wrote'; *lågo* 'we (etc.) lay'.

In the perfect tense, the auxiliary *har/hade* is often dropped: cf. *I södra Småland . . . stod en rödmålad kvarn med de största vingar, som någon* ***sett*** *i hela bygden* 'In southern Småland ... stood a red-painted mill, with the biggest sails anyone (had) ever seen in all the countryside' (V. von Heidenstam: *Fem Berättelser*).

MODAL AUXILIARIES

Examples: *må/måtte*, *kan/kunde*, *skall/skulle*, *vill/ville*, etc.

jag måste skriva hem i dag 'I must write home today.'
jag ville skriva hem i dag 'I wanted to write home today.'
jag kan inte skriva hem i dag 'I can't write home today.'

PASSIVE VOICE

Either the *-s* form or the form with *att bli* + supine: e.g. *brevet har skrivits* = *brevet har blivit skrivet* 'the letter has been written'. The *-s* form is much used in general statements, public announcements, notices and recipes: e.g. *affären stänges kl. 5* 'the shop closes at 5'.

Deponent verbs have the passive *-s* form with active meaning: *jag hoppas, att du*... 'I hope that you will ...'; *Minns du, var han bor*? 'Do you remember where he lives?'

Negation

Inte follows a finite verb, but is inserted between auxiliary and non-finite form, except in relative clauses, where it precedes auxiliary:

han sade, att han ***inte*** *kunde göra det* 'he said that he couldn't do that';
han har inte sett 'he hasn't seen';
jag kan inte skriva 'I can't write'.

Prepositions

As in English, a preposition can be placed at the end of a phrase: e.g. *Vilka program brukar de titta* ***på*** 'Which programme are they accustomed to look **at**?'

Word order

SVO is normal; VSO in principal clause if subordinate material or a relative clause begins the sentence: *Just när han ska stänga dörren, kommer någon springande* 'Just as he is about to close the door, someone comes running up'.

I begynnelsen var Ordet, och Ordet var hos Gud, och 1*
Ordet var Gud. Han var i begynnelsen hos Gud. Allting 2
har blivit till genom honom, och utan honom har ingen-
ting blivit till av allt det som finns till. I honom var liv, 4*
och livet var människornas ljus. Och ljuset lyser i mörkret, 5*
och mörkret har icke fått makt med det.
En man uppträdde, sänd av Gud; hans namn var Jo- 6*
hannes. Han kom som ett vittne, för att vittna om ljuset, 7*
för att alla skulle komma till tro genom honom. 8

TAGALOG

INTRODUCTION

A member of the Indonesian branch of Austronesian, and native to central and southern Luzon, Tagalog has spread far beyond its original confines, and is now the official language of the Philippines, taught in all schools and spoken, either as mother tongue or as second language by up to 40 or 50 million people (approaching 75 per cent of the total population).

A common stock of Malayo-Polynesian root words provides the central lexical core of Tagalog, but the language has been subjected to several cultural influences and these are reflected in the Sanskrit, Dravidian, Arabic, and Chinese loan-words it contains. Since the sixteenth century a large number of Spanish loan-words have been more or less completely assimilated, and there is a more recent and substantial Anglo-American component. Some native literature seems to have existed before the Spanish conquest, but this was destroyed without trace by the Catholic authorities. The first Tagalog book, a Spanish–Tagalog religious digloss, was published in 1593; a Tagalog Bible appeared in 1704. A notable contribution to the enrichment and propagation of Tagalog was made in the middle of the nineteenth century by Baltazar, known as Balagtas, who instituted the poetry contests known as *balagtasan* (the derived verb is *makipagbalagtasan*, 'to take part in a poetry contest'). The National Language Institute for the promotion of Tagalog was founded in 1936.

SCRIPT

From the late sixteenth century onwards, use of the Roman alphabet accompanied the spread of Catholicism. The letters *c*, *f*, *j*, *q*, *v*, *x*, *z* are not used. The digraph *ng* is used to denote /ŋ/.

PHONOLOGY

Consonants

stops: p, b, t, d, k, g, ʔ
fricatives: s, h
nasals: m, n, ŋ
lateral and flap: l, r
semi-vowels: w, j

[d] and [r] are allophones of the same sound, and alternate with each other.

Vowels

i, e, a, o, u

Unstressed /i/ → [ɪ]; unstressed /o/ → [u]. There are half-a-dozen diphthongs closing on /y/w/.

Stress

There are five types of accentuation, known by Tagalog names; stress is phonemic:

1. mabilis: acute on last syllable, e.g. *anák* 'child', *bulaklák* 'flower';
2. malumay: stress on penultimate, not marked, e.g. *lalaki* 'man';
3. malumi: weak stress on penultimate + grave on last syllable, which has glottal stop, e.g. *batà* 'child';
4. maragsa: strong stress on final + glottal stop marked by circumflex, e.g. *masamâ* 'bad';
5. mariin: two stressed syllables, e.g. *pàgawáan* 'factory'.

MORPHOLOGY AND SYNTAX

Noun

No grammatical gender. Syntactic relationships between words are expressed by a series of articles/markers which identify the status of the noun (proper or common, focused or non-focused), its number (singular or plural), and governance (direct/indirect object, genitive or passive relationship). These articles are:

	Proper				*Common*			
	Subject	*Genitive*	*Indirect*	*Passive*	*Subject*	*Genitive*	*Indirect*	*Passive*
sing.	si	ni	kay	ni	ang	ng	sa	ng
pl.	sina	nina	kina	nina	+ mga			

ng is pronounced /naŋ/, *mga* as /maŋah/. Examples: ***si*** *Pedro ay lalaki* 'Pedro is a man'; ***ang mga*** *sapatos ay malilínis* 'the shoes are clean'; ***ang*** *bahay* ***ng*** *lalaki ay bago* 'the man's house is new' (*ay* /ɛ/ is the copula).

Adjective

As attribute, adjective may precede or follow noun; the euphonic ligature /ŋ/ connects A with N, N with A: cf. *matandâ* 'old', *babae* 'woman': *matanda**ng** babae* = *baba**ing*** *matandâ* 'old woman'; *ang baháy* ***na*** *malakí* = *ang malakí**ng** baháy* 'the big house'. The plural of adjectives may be marked by partial reduplication: e.g. *matandâ* 'old', pl. *matatandâ*.

Pronoun

Pronouns have subject series, *ng* series (genitive, instrumental), and *sa* series used as indirect objects. The subject series is: sing. 1 *akó*, 2 *ikáw*, 3 *siyá*; pl. 1 incl. *táyo*, excl. *kamí*, 2 *kayó*, 3 *silá*; The possessive/oblique forms are pre- or postpositive; e.g. for singular 1, 2, 3, the prepositive forms are: *akin*, *iyo*, *kaniya*; postpositive: *ko*, *mo*, *niya*; thus, *ito ay aklat* ***ko*** = *ito ay aki**ng** aklat* 'this is my book'. Cf. *binasa* ***ko*** *ang aklat* 'read – by me – the book', i.e. 'I read the book'.

For *binasa*, *see* **Verb**, below.

DEMONSTRATIVE PRONOUN

Three degrees of removal, in the *ang* series: *ito* 'this', *iyan* 'that', *iyon* 'that' (further away); with *ng* and *sa* forms.

INTERROGATIVE PRONOUN

sino 'who?'; *ano* 'what?'.

RELATIVE PRONOUN

See **Verb**, below.

Numerals

1–10: *isá*, *dalawá*, *tatló*, *ápat*, *limá*, *ánim*, *pitó*, *waló*, *siyám*, *sampû*; 11 *labí**ng** isá*; 12 *labí**n**dalawá*; 13 *labí**n**tatló*; 20 *dalawampû*; 30 *tatlumpû*; 100 (*i*)*sandaán*.

Verb

Formally, a Tagalog verb consists of a root (which may be reduplicated) and an affix or affixes (prefix, suffix, infix). Verbs are classified in terms of (a) aspect, and (b) their focus determinant affixes, such as *mag-*, *um-*, *i-*, etc. The affixes convey information on how the verb form is to be construed *vis-à-vis* the other items in the sentence; one might describe them as signposts marking the structure of the sentence with particular reference to the agent–patient–beneficiary relationship; depending on choice of affix, one of these three main participants in an action is said to be 'focused'. Furthermore, locational or instrumental factors in the action may be focused.

Aspect: four aspects are distinguished: neutral – perfective – imperfective – intentional (future); e.g. for root with *ma*(*g*)- prefix: *tulog* 'sleep' the four forms are: *ma.tulog* – *na.tulog* – *na.tu.tulog* – *ma.tu.tulog*. Cf. *aral* 'study': *mag.aral* – *nag.aral* – *nag.a.aral* – *mag.a.aral*; for root with *-um-* infix, see *sulat* 'write', below.

Combining the four aspects with the four focus patterns, we get a 16-term grid, which may be illustrated with the base *sulat* 'write':

	1	*2*	*3*	*4*
I	sumulat	sulatin	sulatan	isulat
II	sumulat	sinulat	sinulatan	isinulat
III	sumusulat	sinusulat	sinusulatan	isinusulat
IV	susulat	susulatin	susulatan	isusulat

Accompanying pronouns are selected, to show the appropriate deixis, from the *ang*, *ng*, *sa* series (*see* **Pronoun** above).

Tagalog has a preference for what in other languages would be called passive constructions, and for predicate-initial sentences. Thus the sentence 'the man is eating' can be rendered in the same order as *ang lalaki ay kumákain*, but more idiomatically as *kumákain ang lalaki*, where the copula *ay* is dropped. No distinctions for gender, person, or number are made (though certain prefixes can act as pluralizers). Some authorities describe the perfective/imperfective aspects as 'past' and 'present'.

The pilot role of the key affixes will become clearer from some comparative examples:

1. Agent is in focus: the affixes are e.g. *mag-*, *-um-*. *-um-* is an infix except in verbs with initial vowel. The structure is *-um-* verb + agent in *ang/si* form + adverb etc.: e.g. from root *dating* 'to come' (Indonesian, *datang*): *dumating si Pedro kahápon* 'Pedro came yesterday'; imperfective *d**umara**ting*; perfective *d**um**ating*; future *d**ara**ting*. Cf. John XVI, 32:

   Marito, ang oras ay d**umara**ting, oo d**um**ating na

   'Behold, the hour cometh (imperf.) yea, is now come (perf.)'

2. Patient is in focus: the affixes are: *-in*, *-an*, *i-*, *ma-*. The structure is *-in* verb + agent in *ni/ng* case + patient in *ang* case: *binasa **ni** Pedro **ang** aklat* 'Pedro read the book'. Main forms: infinitive *basa**in***; imperfect *b**in**abasa*; perfect *b**in**asa*; future *babasa**in***.

3. Location or direction of action is in focus: the affixes are *-in*, (*h*)*an*, *pag...an*. The structure is *-an/-in* verb + agent in *ni/ng* case + target in *ang*: e.g. ***nilapitan ni** Pedro **ang** bundok* 'Pedro drew near to the mountain.'

4. Beneficiary or instrument of action is in focus: the affixes are *i-*, *ipag-*, depending on whether active form of the verb has *-um-* or *mag-* (see 1 above). *I-* is correlated with *-um-*, *ipag-* with *mag-*. The structure is *i-/ipag-* verb + agent in *ni/ng* case + beneficiary in *si/ang* case + object in *ang* case: e.g. ***i**binibili **ko si** Pedro **ng** aklat* 'I buy a book for Pedro.'

These examples may serve to illustrate the basic structure of the Tagalog verbal system. The following four Tagalog sentences can all be translated by the same English sentence; but the four different 'focusings' require four different verb forms in Tagalog, with related changes in the markers:

1. Bumibili ***si** Pedro* **ng** aklat sa lunsod para kay Fidel.
2. Binibili **ni** Pedro ***ang** aklat* sa lunsod para kay Fidel.
3. Binibilhan **ni** Pedro **ng** aklat ***ang** lunsod* para kay Fidel.
4. Ibinibili **ni** Pedro **ng** aklat **sa** lunsod ***si** Fidel.*

In each sentence the focused component is italicized. The general English translation is 'Pedro is buying a book in town for Fidel.'

There are, of course, many other affix patterns which generate other verbal senses: cf. *matúlog* 'to sleep'; *mátulog* 'to drop off unintentionally'; *makatulog* 'to be able to sleep'; perfective *nakatúlog*.

NEGATION

The general negating particle is *hindî*: e.g. *hindî magandá si Linda* or *si Linda ay hindî magandá* 'L. is not pretty'; *hindî siya magandá* 'she is not pretty'. The prohibiting particle is *huwág*: e.g. *huwág mong insulat* 'don't write' (*mo**ng*** 'by you').

RELATIVE CLAUSES

Introduced by the ligature *na/ng*: e.g. *si Pedro ang lalaki**ng** bumabasa/bumasa/babasa* 'P is the man who is reading/was reading/is going to read'.

Prepositions

sa is virtually an all-purpose preposition in Tagalog, either by itself or as extended by modifiers: e.g. *sa mesa* 'on the table', *sa lunsod* 'in town', *sa Maynilà* 'in, to, from Manilla'. *Sa gitna* 'between', *sa loob* 'inside', *sa labas* 'outside'.

Word order

There is a broad division into predicate-initial and non-predicate-initial sentences. Examples of both will be found in the foregoing.

1 Nang una'y siya'y Verbo
na, at ang Verbo ay sumasa
Dios, at ang Verbo ay Dios.
2 Ito sa pagpapasimulâ ay
sumasa Dios.
3 Ang lahat nang manḡa
bagay ay guinauâ niya; at
alin man sa lahát nḡ manḡa
guinauà ay hindi guinauà
cung hindì siya'y cainalam.
4 Sa caniya naroroon ang
buhay, at ang buhay ay si-
yang ilao nang manḡa táuo
5 At lumiliuanag ang ilao
sa manḡa cadiliman; data
pua't hindì napag-unauà ang
ilao nang cadiliman.
6 Nagcaroon nang isáng
táuo na sinugò nang Dios,
at pinanḡanḡalanang Juan.
7 Ito'y naparitong sacsí
upáng patotohanan ang ilao,
at nang dahil sa caniya'y
sumampalataya ang lahát.
8 Hindì siya ang ilao; cung
dì upang magpatotoo sa ilao.

TAMIL

INTRODUCTION

This South Dravidian language is spoken by about 50 million people in Tamilnadu, where it has had official language status since 1956. There are also up to 3 million speakers in Sri Lanka, and at least another million scattered through South-East Asia, Indonesia, Polynesia (Fiji), South Africa, and Guyana. Tamil has a long history, with an epigraphical record dating from more than 2,000 years ago. Ancient Tamil literature dates from about the same period, the main monuments being (a) the *Tolkāppiyam*, a grammar of the language and also a socio-linguistic document of great interest and importance; (b) the *Tirukkuṛal*, the 'Tamil Veda', a kind of handbook of secular wisdom by the fifth-century poet Tiruvaḷḷuvar; and (c) two vast collections of short poems, the *Pattupāṭṭu* ('Ten Songs') and the *Eṭṭuttokai* ('The Eight Anthologies'), which provide a psychologically detailed mapping of human life in terms of its key twin facets: love and war. Many of the war poems are quasi-historical and take up themes concerning wise governance, in the manner of the Sanskrit classics; the love poems are set in five existential 'landscapes', each with its specific tensions and solutions. With such a classical past, Tamil is not surprisingly one of the leading literary languages in the sub-continent today.

The word 'Tamil' covers a highly complex set of socio-linguistic levels and relationships. In the first place, there is a basic distinction between literary Tamil and spoken Tamil. The literary language can be further sub-divided into (a) Classical Tamil and (b) modern standard literary Tamil of press, radio, and literature. Spoken Tamil itself exists in half a dozen main dialects (the Sri Lankan form is the most archaic) with an East-Central form emerging as a spoken standard. Finally, on the socio-linguistic plane there is an opposition between a Brahmin high register with its own specific lexicon, and various lower-caste registers. There are signs that spoken Standard Tamil is becoming increasingly acceptable within the framework of the modern literary standard.

SCRIPT

The Tamil syllabary derives via Granth forms from the Brahmi script. The grid consists of 18 consonants × 12 vowels (including two diphthongs). Five Grantha letters are used for Sanskrit words, and there is a sign for the *visarga*. As in Devanagari, short *a* is inherent in the base form of the consonant.

PHONOLOGY

Consonants

The core of the Tamil consonantal inventory consists of the following eighteen phonemes:

stops: p, ʈ, t̠, k
affricate: tʃ
fricatives: j, v, ʐ
nasals: m, n, n̠, ɳ, ɲ, ŋ
lateral and flap: l, ɭ, r, ɽ

The phonemic distinction between dental /t/, alveolar /t̠/ and retroflex /ʈ/ is explicit in the script. The five *n* sounds are each specifically graphed.

Positionally determined allophones, however, share one and the same graph with the core consonant on which they are based: cf.

Core phoneme	*Allophone sharing graph*
k	g, x
tʃ	ʤ, s, ç
ʈ	ɖ, ɽ
t	d, ð
t̠	d̠, ɹ̠
p	b, ß

Thus, /tʃ, ʤ, s, ç/ are all notated as ச. The /tʃ/ value is found in medial position, in association with /ʈ/ or /t̠/; /ʤ/ is found medially following /ɲ/; /s/ is initial or intervocalic; /ç/ – which often approaches /ʃ/ – is found in loan-words.

Similarly, /t̠, d̠, ɹ̠/ are all notated as ற. Colloquial pronunciation of /t̠/ as /t̠r̠/, that is, as a fusion of two allophones, has spread to the literary language: e.g. *ku*t̠t̠*am* 'fault, blame' is pronounced as /kut̠t̠r̠am/ or /kuttram/.

In this article, the alveolar phonemes are marked by subscript macron; the retroflex phonemes by subscript dot: *t̠*/*ṭ*.

Vowels

Short and long values are distinguished in the script:

short: ɪ, ɛ, ʌ, ɔ, u
long: i, e, a, o, u

There are two diphthongs, both notated in the script: /ai/ and /au/.
Vowels are nasalized before a final nasal consonant, which is then not released: e.g. *pustakam* /puttaxā/ 'book'; *vantom* /vəŋdō/, 'we came'.

Sandhi is of crucial importance in Tamil pronunciation, and may or may not be notated in the script. The insertion of a homogeneous linking element at junctures is particularly frequent.

Stress

Stress is weak and may fall on any syllable.

MORPHOLOGY AND SYNTAX

Noun

There is no definite article. The numeral *oru* '1', may be used as an indefinite article. Use of the accusative case of a neuter noun identifies it as definite.

GENDER
Tamil divides nominals into two classes: rational/human as opposed to non-human (neuter). Within the rational class, a distinction is made between masculine and feminine.

NUMBER
Singular and plural. A typical plural marker added to singular, is *-kaḷ*; the stem-final may be modified: e.g. *āḷ* 'person' – *āṭkaḷ* 'persons'; *nāy* 'dog' – *nāykaḷ*; *pasu* 'cow' – *pasukkaḷ*. Further plural markers occurring in the literary language are: *-r*, *-ār*, *-mār*, *-ir*. A typical plural marker in the spoken language is *-nga*: e.g. *āḷu* 'man', pl. *āḷunga*.

The formant *-tt*(*u*)- marks the oblique base of neuter nouns in *-am*: e.g. *paṭam* 'picture', oblique case *paṭatt-*, acc. *paṭattai*.

There are eight cases. All are predictable, given the singular oblique base and the plural nominative. As specimen declension, *pāl* 'milk':

nominative	pāl
accusative	pālei
instrumental	pālāl
comitative	pālōṛu
dative	pālukku
locative	pālil
genitive	pālin/pāl.uṭaya

Similarly, for *maram* 'tree': e.g. *maram*, *marattei*, *marattāl*. In the plural, the same endings are added to the plural marker *-kaḷ*, etc.

GENITIVE RELATION
Possessor precedes possessed: e.g. *Rāvin̲ makan̲in̲ makan̲* 'Rao's son's son'.

Adjective

A few forms deriving from Old Tamil neuter plural nominal forms are used attributively in Modern Tamil, preceding the noun and invariable: e.g, Old Tamil *periya* 'large objects' – Mod. Tamil 'large'; Old Tamil *nalla* 'good objects' – Mod. Tamil 'good': *periya paiyan̲* 'big boy'; *nalla sankati* /sangaðɪ/, 'good news'.

Pronoun

PERSONAL

		Singular	Plural
1		nāṉ	nām (incl.), nāṅkaḷ (excl.)
2		nī	nīr, nīṅkaḷ
3	masc.	avaṉ	avarkaḷ
	fem.	avaḷ	
	neut.	atu	

Pronouns in Tamil are nominals and are so declined. Thus for first person singular *nāṉ*: e.g. acc. *eṉṉai*, dat. *eṉakku*, gen. *eṉ/eṉṉiṉ*.

DEMONSTRATIVE PRONOUN
Three degrees of relative distance: *inta* 'this' – *anta* 'that' – *unta* 'that (yonder)'. These are invariable: e.g. *inta maram* 'this tree': *inta nāṛu.xaḷ* 'these countries' (*nāṛu* /na:ḍɪ/ 'country').

INTERROGATIVE PRONOUN
Unlike the demonstrative series, the interrogative series is marked for number, gender, and case. Thus, *evaṉ* 'who?' = 'what man?'; *evaḷ* 'who?' = 'what woman?'; *evar*(*kaḷ*) 'who?' = 'which people?'; *etu* 'what?'. Addition of final *-ā* turns an affirmative statement into a question: e.g. *maturaikku.p.pōvīrkaḷ* 'you will go to Madura' – *maturaikku.p.pōvīrkaḷā?* 'Will you go to Madura?'

RELATIVE PRONOUN
None. For relative constructions, *see* **Verb**, Participles, below.

Numerals

oṉṟu, *iraṇṭu*, *mūṉṟu*, *nāṉku/nālu*, *aintu*, *āṟu*, *ēḻu*, *eṭṭu*, *oṉpatu*, *pattu*; 11–19: *patiṉ/paṉṉ* + units, e.g. 15 *patiṉaintu*. 20 *irupatu*; 30 *muppatu*; 40 *nāṟpatu*; 100 *nūṟu*; 200 *irunūṟu*.

Verb

There are personal and impersonal forms. Personal forms are conjugated in three moods (indicative, imperative, and optative); the indicative mood has present, past, and future tenses. The affirmative paradigm has a negative counterpart, which has the same three moods but no tenses. Both affirmative and negative paradigms have an extensive array of participial forms and verbal nouns.

The citation form of a Tamil verb is in dental consonant + *al*: e.g. *seytal* /seyðal/. Most roots are mono- or disyllabic. Inflected forms are made from two bases: (a) root = first base; (b) root + -(*k*)*k* formant.

TENSE MARKERS

present: *ir/-ind/-itp* etc. added to second base;
past: *-t/-tt/-nt* added to first base;
future: *-p/-pp/-v* added to either base.

Specimen conjugation (affirmative) of *seytal* 'to do, make':

present: *sey.k.ir.ēn*, *-āy*, *-ān/-āḷ/-atu*; *sey.k.ir.ōm*, *īrkal*, *-ārkaḷ*, *sey.ki.nrana*;
past: *sey.t.ēn*, *-āy*, *-ān/-āḷ/-atu*; *sey.t.ōm*, *-īrkaḷ*, *-ārkaḷ*, *-(an)a*;
future: *sey.v.ēn*, *-āy*, *-ān/-āḷ/seyyum*; *sey.v.ōm*, *-īrkaḷ*, *-ārkaḷ*, *-(an)a*.

Similarly, from root *iru-* 'to be': first person singular present, *iru.kk.ir.ēn*; past *iru.nt.ēn*; future *iru.pp.ēn*. These are, of course, written forms, pronounced e.g. /irıgire:n/.

IMPERATIVE

Second person singular (impolite) = root: *sey!* 'do!'. Plural forms are used for polite request: *seyuṅkaḷ* 'please do'.

OPTATIVE

The markers are *-ka* or *-aṭṭum* on either base: e.g. *seyyaṭṭum* 'may he do'.

NON-FINITE FORMS

Participle in *-a* (present or past) *-um/-untu* (future): e.g. *seykira*, *seyta*, *seyyum*. The gerund has a dental marker (*t*, *tt*, *nt*) + back vowel; i.e. the form is that associated with past tense, but the tense of the gerund is that of the main finite verb.

A cardinal rule of Tamil syntax is that only one finite verb can figure in a sentence; any other verbs occurring in the sentence must be in gerundial form.

The participles can be both active and passive depending on context: e.g. *pāṭam paṭitta paiyan* 'the boy who read the lesson'; *paiyan paṭitta pāṭam* 'the lesson read by the boy'.

The infinitive is in *-a*. This is used, e.g., with the word *vēṇṭum* to express obligation: *poka.vēṇṭum* 'must go'; *koṭukka.veṇṭumā?* 'must give?' (interrogative *-ā*).

THE NEGATIVE PARADIGM

There are synthetic and analytic forms. The (older) synthetic form adds personal endings directly to stem. Thus from *sey-*: *sey.y.ēn*, *-āy*, *-ān/-āḷ/-ātu*; *sey.y.ōm*, *-īr*, *-ār/-ā*. These forms are neutral as to tense.

The analytic forms: here, the positive singular neuter participle is combined with *illai* 'not', to form a negative series which is neutral as to person, number, and gender, but which has the tense markers: e.g. *nān/nī*, *avan* etc. *seykiratillai/seytatillai* 'I/you don't do/didn't do'. There are other analytic negative forms.

RELATIVE CONSTRUCTIONS

As there is no relative pronoun, relative sentences are transferred to the left-hand of the head-word; the verb form is the past, present, or future third person neuter, minus *-tu*: e.g. *pāṭam sollukira paiyan* 'the boy who is saying his lesson';

anta.p.paiyaṉ paṭitta pāṭam 'the lesson which that boy studied'; *nāṉ eẓutum kaṭitam* 'the letter which I shall write'.

Third-person pronouns may be added to participial forms as follows: *paṭitta.avaṉ* 'he who has read'; *paṭikkir.avaṉ* 'he who is reading'; *paṭikkir.avaḷ* 'she who is reading'; *paṭipp.avarkaḷ* 'they who will have read'.

Postpositions

Postpositions proliferate in many variant forms. They are used with both nominal and verbal stems; nouns are in nominative, accusative, genitive, dative, locative case: e.g.

nominative: *itu* ***mutal*** *atu* ***varai*** *patiyuṅkaḷ* 'read from here to there';
genitive: *kīẓ* 'under' – *atan.kīẓ* 'under it'; *māṭu* 'towards' – *eṉ vittu.matē.vāruṅkaḷ* 'come to my house';
accusative: *paṟṟi* 'about, concerning' – *atai.p.paṟṟi ninaivu* 'recollections of this';
dative: *appuṟam* 'after' – *sāpāttukkappuṟam* 'after eating'.

Tamil makes much use of onomatopoetic words and echo-words.

Word formation

(a) compounds: e.g. *paṇputtokai* compounds (= Skt *karmadhāraya*), where one component defines the other: e.g. *kalluppu* 'rock salt' (*kal* 'stone'; *uppu* 'salt'); *marappeṭṭi* 'wooden box' (*maram* 'wood'; *peṭṭi* 'box'); *maruttuccālai* 'chemist's shop' (*maruntu* 'medicine'; *-cālai* = suffix denoting place, institution).
(b) Many suffixes are used to make nouns from other nouns, and nouns from verbs.
(c) Lengthening of root vowel is also used: e.g. *pōr* 'war' (*poru-* 'to make war').

Word order

SOV is normal.

1 ஆதியிலே வார்த்தை இருந்தது,
அந்த வார்த்தை தேவனிடத்திலிருந்
தது, அந்த வார்த்தை தேவனாயிருந்
2 தது.–அவர் ஆதியிலே தேவனோடிருந்
3 தார்.—சகலமும் அவர் மூலமாய் உண்
டாயிற்று; உண்டானதொன்றும் அவ
ராலேயல்லாமல் உண்டாகவில்லை.—
4 அவருக்குள் ஜீவன் இருந்தது, அந்த
ஜீவன் மனுஷருக்கு ஒளியாயிருந்
5 தது.–அந்த ஒளி இருளிலே பிரகாசிக்
கிறது; இருளானது அதைப் பற்றிக்
கொள்ளவில்லை.

6 தேவனால் அனுப்பப்பட்ட ஒரு
மனுஷன் இருந்தான், அவன் பேர்
7 யோவான்.—அவன் தன்னால் எல்லா
ரும் விசுவாசிக்கும்படி அந்த ஒளியை
க்குறித்துச் சாட்சிகொடுக்க சாட்சி
8 யாக வந்தான்.—அவன் அந்த ஒளி
யல்ல, அந்த ஒளியைக்குறித்துச் சாட்
சிகொடுக்க வந்தவனாயிருந்தான்.

TELUGU

INTRODUCTION

This South-East Dravidian language is the language of the Andhra people. Since 1966 it has been the official language of the state of Andhra Pradesh, which was formed from the Telugu-speaking districts of the former Presidency of Madras along with the nine Telangana regions of the Nizam's Dominions. In terms of numbers, Telugu is certainly the largest Dravidian language, being now spoken by about 55 million people, 8–10 per cent of whom live in neighbouring territories, such as Karnataka and Tamilnadu. There are four main dialects, in all of which there is a marked distinction between colloquial forms and the literary language. The latter is itself divided between the older and heavily Sanskritized literary model, and the emergent Modern Standard Telugu.

Literature in the classical literary language goes back to the eleventh century AD; its first great monument is the *Mahābhārata* translation by Nannaya (thirteenth/fourteenth century). This early literature is in a language which is more than half Sanskrit. A major part in the revival of Telugu literature after several centuries of stagnation was played by K. Wirēśaliṅgam, the first Telugu writer to develop a modern prose style. While New Indo-Aryan words still abound in Telugu, the purely Sanskrit element is being reduced, and the modern literary standard tends to converge with educated use of the Central colloquial.

SCRIPT

The Telugu syllabary is derived from a variant of the Asokan Inscription character. The Devanagari order is maintained, and there are many composite ligatures. Strangely, there is no graph for the past-tense characteristic /æː/ (transcribed below, in the section on verbs, as *E*).

PHONOLOGY

Consonants

stops, p, b, t, d, ṭ, ḍ, k, g
affricates: ts, dz, tʃ, dʒ
fricatives: v/w, s, ś, ʃ, h
nasals: m, n, ṇ, ɲ, ŋ
laterals and flap: l, ḷ, r

All of the stops have aspirated forms, found only in Sanskrit loan-words. The latter pair of affricates have aspirated forms. /ś/ occurs in Sanskrit loans, as do the latter two nasals.

The retroflex /ɽ/ found in Tamil, is missing. [ts] and [tʃ] are positional variants of one graph, pronounced [ts] before a front vowel, [tʃ] before a back. Similarly, the graph *v* represents /ß/ before a front vowel, /w/ before a back. In the spoken standard, *t/d* are realized as [θ/ð].

Vowels

short: ɪ, e, a, o, u
long: i, e, æ, a, o, u

VOWEL HARMONY
This category is not typical of Dravidian; in Telugu it reduces to a choice between /u/ and /i/ in certain affixes, e.g. the dative case ending *ku/ki*, *nu/ni*: cf. *bidda.ku* 'to the boy'; *tammuni.ki* 'to the younger brother'.

SANDHI
Notably by insertion of glide sounds (/j, v/) at short vocalic junctures, or by fusion/elision.

MORPHOLOGY AND SYNTAX

Noun

There is no definite article. The numeral *oka* '1' may be used as an indefinite article.

GENDER
In the singular, the opposition is between masculine and non-masculine, the latter category including all nouns denoting females; in the plural, the dichotomy changes to rational versus non-rational, with females promoted to rational status. Grammatical gender is not formally marked, but is made explicit e.g. by concord of noun with verb in third person which is gender-coded, or by the use of a similarly coded demonstrative pronoun.

A typical masculine ending is *-ḍu*, with a feminine correlative in *-rālu*: e.g. *snēhituḍu* '(male) friend' – *snēhiturālu*.

NUMBER
-lu is added to the singular: e.g. *bidda* 'boy' – *biddalu*. There are many variants, cf. *illu* 'house' – *iṇḍḷu* 'houses'.

DECLENSION
There are four cases: a specimen declension follows, for *tammu-* 'younger brother':

	Singular	*Plural*
nominative	tammu.ḍu	tammu.lu
genitive	tammu.ni/ḍi	tammu.la
dative	tammu.niki	tammu.laku
accusative	tammu.ni	tammu.lanu

For most Telugu nouns, the oblique base = genitive base = nominative (minus -*ḍu*). Many nouns, however, have widely varying oblique bases; cf. *īllu* 'house', obl. base, *īnṭi*; *yēru* 'river' – *yēṭi*; *pannu* 'tooth' – *panṭi*.

Adjective

The few genuine adjectives are indeclinable and precede the noun. They are Dravidian root words, e.g. *manci* 'good', *cheḍḍa* 'bad', *tella* 'white': *manci pustakam* 'good book'; *pedda ceṭṭu* 'big tree'.

Pronoun

The personal pronouns are:

	Singular		*Plural*	
	Direct	*Oblique base*	*Direct*	*Oblique base*
1	nēnu	nā	mēmu/manamu	mā/mana
2	nīvu	nī	mīru	mī

In the plural first person, *mēmu* is exclusive, *manamu* inclusive, with oblique forms as shown. The third person forms exhibit gender and are graduated for social status. They are, in addition, marked for relative proximity, the *i-* series referring to persons close at hand, the *a-* series to those further away. Thus:

	Familiar	*Respectful*	*Honorific*
masculine	vīḍu/vāḍu	itanu/atanu	vīru/vāru
feminine	idi/adi	īme/āme	vīru/vāru

Plural forms for both genders: *vīṇḍlu/vāṇḍlu*, *vīḷḷu/vāḷḷu*, *vīru/vāru*.

DEMONSTRATIVE PRONOUN/ADJECTIVE
The bases are in *i-* for proximate, *a-* for distal: *idi* 'this', *adi* 'that'.

INTERROGATIVE PRONOUN
The base is *ē-*: *ēvaḍu* 'who?' (masc.); *ēvi* 'what?'.

RELATIVE PRONOUN
None; for relative constructions *see* **Verb**, below.

Numerals

1–10: *okaṭi*, *renḍu*, *mūḍu*, *nālugu*, *aidu*, *āru*, *ēḍu*, *enimidi*, *tommidi*, *padi*. 11 *paḍakonḍu*; 12 *pannenḍu*; 13 *paḍamūḍu*; 20 *iruvai*; 30 *muppai*; 40 *nalabhai*; 100 *nūru*, or *vanda*.

Verb

As in other Dravidian languages, there are positive and negative conjugations. Verbal bases are usually disyllabic, and the (C)VCCV formula (i.e. with gemination of the intervocalic consonant) is very common. There are indicative and imperative moods, and a basic series of present, past, and future tenses with analytical secondary forms. The tense system distinguishes number and person (with exceptions, e.g. in negative past). Gender is marked in the third person. The non-finite forms underlie the finite.

Thus, from the root *cheppu-* 'to speak', are derived the infinitive *cheppa*, the verbal noun *cheppa.ḍamu*, the verbal participles, present *chepputu*, past *cheppi* (with elision of the *-a*) and the conditional verbal participle in *-te*. In connected speech or written narrative, all verbs are in such participial forms apart from the finite verb which winds up the sentence.

The participles provide formants for relative clauses, present e.g. *cheppa.tu-na*, past, *cheppina*, indefinite *cheppē*: e.g. *chepputunna* '(he, etc.) who is speaking'; *cheppina* '(he, etc.) who was speaking'. Such forms are neutral as to voice: cf. *ataḍu campina puli* 'the tiger (*puli*) killed by him', *atanni campina puli* 'the tiger that killed him', where the same past participial form does duty for both active and passive sense: cf. *nēnu tāgina niḷḷu* 'the water I drank'; *mīr rāsin(a) uttaram* 'the letter I wrote'.

PERSONAL FORMS

The personal endings are: sing. 1 *-nu*, pl. *-mu*; 2 *-vu*, pl. *-ru*. In the third person singular masculine *-ḍu* is contrasted with *-di* (feminine and neuter); the plural form *-ru* covers masculine and feminine, i.e. the rational category reappears, contrasting with *-vi* for the irrational category. These endings are added to stem + present marker *-utu-* + *unnā* to form the present tense: e.g. *chepp.ut.unnā.nu/vu/ḍu*.

Past tense: here, the modern standard literary and colloquial characteristic is /æ:/, which has no specific graph in the script; here transcribed as *E*: e.g. *cheppE.nu/vu/ḍu*. The third person singular feminine varies: e.g. *chepp.in.di*. Analytical forms with the auxiliary *uṇḍu* denote continuous present/past tenses.

Future: unlike Tamil, Telugu does not have a specific future characteristic. The present form in *-ut* is used, without *-unnā*: e.g. *chepp.utā.nu/vu/ḍu* 'I etc. shall speak'.

NEGATIVE CONJUGATION

Present: the personal markers are affixed to the infinitive, e.g. *cheppa.nu/vu/ḍu* 'I, etc. do not speak'; or, analytically, e.g. *cheppa.ḍamu lēnu/lēvu/lēḍu* 'I am not one who speaks'.

Past: infinitive + *lēdu* for all persons and both numbers: e.g. *nēnu cheppa.lēdu*, *nīvu cheppa.lēdu*; i.e. the personal pronouns must be used here, as the verb form is invariable.

PASSIVE

Grammars give a passive form made with the auxiliary *paḍu* 'to feel, suffer, fall', etc., but this does not seem to be much used. More idiomatic is the use of the past participle plus the auxiliary *un* 'to be'.

IMPERATIVE MOOD

The second person positive markers are, sing. *-u*, pl. *-aṇḍi*. The prohibitive is made by pre-fixing the negative marker *-k-* to these endings: e.g. *pāḍaṇḍi* '(please) sing'; *weḻ**lak**aṇḍi* '(please) don't go'.

CAUSATIVE

The marker is *-inc-*, e.g. *tāgu* 'to drink' – *tāg**incu*** 'to give to drink'. This marker is also used to make transitive verbs from nouns: e.g. *prēma* 'love' (Sanskrit) – *prēmincu* 'to love'.

Various affixes are used to generate potential, necessitative, etc. modal forms: e.g. with *-gala-*: *cheppa.galanu* 'I am able to speak'.

Postpositions

Postpositions are very numerous in Telugu; all follow the oblique stem. They are either simple, e.g. *tō* 'with', *valla* 'by means of', or compound, e.g. *lōnunci* 'from, out of'; *taravāta* 'after', *venaka* 'behind': e.g. *Mā inṭi venaka tōṭa unnadi* 'Behind our house is a garden.'

Word order

SOV; indirect object precedes direct: e.g. *nēnu ataniki ā sommu istānu* 'I'll give him the money.'

1 ఆదియందు వాక్యముండెను వాక్యము దేవుని
2 యొద్దనుండెను వాక్యము దేవుడైయుండెను। ఆయన
ఆదియందు దేవునియొద్ద నుండెను సమస్తమును ఆ
3 వాక్యము మూలముగా కలిగెను। కలిగియున్న దేది
యు ఆయనవలననే తప్ప మరి యెవరివలన కలుగ
4 లేదు। ఆయనలో జీవముండెను ఆ జీవము మనుష్యు
5 లకు వెలుగైయుండెను। వెలుగు చీకటిలో ప్రకాశిం
చుచున్నది గాని చీకటి దాని గ్రహింపలేదు.
6 దేవుని యొద్దనుండి పంపబడిన యొక మనుష్యుడు
7 వచ్చెను అతని పేరు యోహాను। అతని మూలముగా
అందరు విశ్వసించునటుల అతడా వెలుగునుగూర్చి
8 సాక్ష్యము చెప్పుటకు సాక్షిగా వచ్చెను। అతడా
వెలుగై యుండలేదు గాని యా వెలుగునుగూర్చి

THAI

INTRODUCTION

Thai is the official language of Thailand and is spoken by about 40 million people. It is the most important member of the Tai family which also includes Lao, Shan, and Yuan. From the twelfth to the twentieth centuries the country was known as Siam, the language as Siamese. In 1939 the country was officially designated *mɪang thai*, the Thai Kingdom.

There are four main dialects, differing mainly in tonal and phonological respects. The literary language is based on the central dialect, which includes the Bangkok standard. Thai contains many Sanskrit and Pali words, imported mainly in the Ayutthaya period (fourteenth to eighteenth centuries).

The oldest work in Thai literature is the Buddhist cosmography known as the *Traiphūm* (Sanskrit *tribhuvana*), which dates from the fourteenth century. Both the Thai version of the *Rāmāyaṇa*, the *Rāmakrien*, and the national epic, the *Khun Chāng Khun Phāēn*, are ancient in substance, but both are known only in nineteenth-century recensions. A very important sector of Thai literature consists of the historical chronicles known as the *Phongsāwadān* and the *Prachum Phongsāwadān*, edited and analysed by the great Thai polymath Prince Rajanubhab Damrong. Mention should also be made of the *nirāt* literature, devoted to man as migrant and wanderer, a favourite genre of Thai poets in the seventeenth to nineteenth centuries. During the twentieth century the social novel has come to the fore.

SCRIPT

The Thai script, dating from the late thirteenth century, seems to have been borrowed in part from the Khmer version of a South Indian script. It has no ligatures. The short vowel ɔ is inherent in the base form of the consonant. Degree of redundancy is high, with five graphs for /kh/, six for /th/, three for /s/, etymologically explicable but no longer phonetically necessary. Consonants are sub-divided into low, middle, and high class.

The division into classes is partially phonological, in that the unaspirated consonants are grouped as middle, the aspirated consonants as high or low class. Thus /k/ has a middle-class graph, /kh/ a high-class. The spirant surds appear in both high and low classes: of four letters denoting /s/ three, sited as in Devanagari between the semi-vowels and *h*, are high class; the fourth, placed in Thai in the palatal series, is low. The Thai letters corresponding in locus to the retroflex series in Devanagari, are very rarely used.

PHONOLOGY

Consonants

stops: b, p, ph, d, t, th, c, (g), k, kh, (ʔ)
affricates: tʃ
fricatives: f, s, h
nasals: m, n, ŋ
lateral and flap: l, r
semi-vowels: j, w

/c/ (or /tç/) is a voiceless, unaspirated fortis stop, sometimes described as close to /t'/ and often transcribed as its allophone /dʒ/: e.g. the future marker จะ = /dʒə/. /tʃ/ is the aspirated correlative.

Permissible consonantal finals are the nasals and /p, t, k, r, l/. As finals, /p, t, k/ are pronounced as unreleased [t]; /r/ and /l/ as [n].

Vowels

front: i, e, ɛ
back rounded: u, o, ɔ
back unrounded: ɪ, ə, a

All vowels occur long or short; length is phonemic.

Thai has fourteen diphthongs and three triphthongs; distinctions here are very subtle.

Tone

There are five tones, three level and two oblique: middle – low – falling – high (acute) – rising. Some authorities sub-divide the high tone into (a) plain high, and (b) constricted high.

Tone in a Thai word is determined by certain factors, and is therefore predictable. The following factors are relevant: e.g. for a typical Thai morpheme C_1VC_2:

1. class of C_1 consonant: low, middle, or high;
2. presence or absence of tone marker: there are two tone markers, *mai-ek*, *mai-to*;
3. vowel length;
4. nature of C_2 consonant: nasal (/m, n, ŋ/) or /p/t/k/; /r/l/;

Thus, for a C_1VC_2 morpheme, where C_1 is a low-class consonant, the following possibilities arise:

1. no tone marker, C_2 is not /k, t, p/: tone is even (middle);
2. V is short, C_2 is /k/, /t/, or /p/; mai-to may be present: tone is acute (high);
3. C_1 is preceded by a high-class /h/, and mai-ek is present: tone is low;
4. C_1 is preceded by high-class /h/: tone is rising;

5. C_1 is preceded by high-class /h/, and mai-to is present: tone is falling;
6. V is long, with C_2 = /k/, /p/ or /t/: tone is falling.

Analogous rules apply for middle- and high-class initials, which prescribe low tone in words with *k*, *p* or *t* final, whether V is long or short, and for CV and $C_1C_2VC_3$ morphemes. In the latter case, if C_1 and C_2 cannot be pronounced together, i.e. there is a shwa between them, the word is treated as disyllabic and subject to specific tone rules.

MORPHOLOGY AND SYNTAX

Noun

The FSI *Thai Reference Grammar* (Noss 1964) points out that this, the largest class of Thai words, is also the most open, as lexical innovations are usually generated in the form of nominals. Thai nouns are monosyllabic: e.g. *nam* 'water'; *vua* 'buffalo; *ma* 'horse'; or polysyllabic:

(a) by prefixation, e.g. *khua:m-* 'condition of being ...' used to make abstracta: e.g. *khua:mrak* 'love'; *khua:mru* 'knowledge'; *khua:mdi:* 'goodness';
(b) by compounding: e.g. *nam.ta* 'water-eye' = 'tears'; *khon.khrua* 'person-kitchen' = 'cook'; *cha:ŋ.ma:j* 'artisan-wood' = 'carpenter'.

There is no declension of any kind. Genitive relationships are expressed either by apposition, or by use of the particle *khɔ:ŋ*: e.g. *ŋa:n khɔ:ŋ khaw* 'his work'; *khɔ:ŋ khraj* 'whose?'.

PLURAL

Distinguished, if at all, by numeral or a particle such as *la:j* 'many': e.g. *ci:n la:j khon* 'many Chinese'.

CLASSIFIERS

Example: *khon* (for people), *tua* (animals), *lem* (books), *ton* (plants). The order is: noun – classifier – numeral: e.g. *ma: sɔ:ŋ tua* 'two dogs'; *phu:jiŋ sa:m khon* 'three women'.

Adjective

As attribute, adjective follows noun: e.g. *ba:n jaj* 'big house'. The classifier may serve to identify a non-overtly expressed referent: e.g. *tua jaj* 'the big one' (scil. animal).

COMPARATIVE

Made with *kwa:*: e.g. *di: kwa:* 'better'.

Pronoun

The pronominal system is socio-linguistically complex. Some generally acceptable forms are shown here:

first person singular: *phom* (masc.), *dichan* (fem.) (these are formal); pl. *raw*;
second person singular: *khun/than* (these are formal); *thə:* informal;
third person: *khaw*.

For the plural second and third persons the singular forms may be used. Kinship terms and titles are often preferable.

DEMONSTRATIVE PRONOUN/ADJECTIVE

ni: 'this', pl. *law.ni:*; *nan* 'that', pl. *law.nan*. These follow the noun: e.g. *nai ro:ŋ.rɪan nan* 'in that school'; *caag rɪan ni:* 'from this house'.

INTERROGATIVE PRONOUN

khraj 'who?'; *'araj* 'what?'. Interrogative particles: *maj, rɪ*: both with rising tone: *Sabaj di: rɪ:?* 'Are you well?'

RELATIVE PRONOUN

thi may be used: e.g. *Pha:sa: thi khon thai phu:t khy: pha:sa: thai* 'The language which Thai people speak is the Thai language' (*khy*: is the copula).

Numerals

1–10: *nɪŋ, sɔ:ŋ, sa:m, si:, ha:, hog, jed, pɛ:d, kaw, sib*; 11 *sib.et*; 12 *sib sɔ:ŋ*; 20 *ji: sib*; 30 *sa:m sib*; 100 *rɔ:j*.

Verb

Thai verbs are monosyllabic, e.g. *tham* 'do', *paj* 'go', *ru:* 'know'; or polysyllabic, e.g. with prefix *pra-*, which acts as a transitivizing formant, *gan* 'to ward off' – *pra.gan* 'to insure', *lun* 'to wake up' – *pra.lun* 'to waken someone'; or compounds, e.g. verb + noun *tham.ŋan* 'to work', noun + verb *kham.tham* 'to question', *kham.tɔ:b* 'to answer'. In certain compounds the second component has lost its primary meaning, and, when a real object is overtly expressed, this umbral object is discarded: e.g. *kin.khaw* 'eat rice' – *khaw kin.khaw* 'he eats' (in general); but, *khaw kin ponlamaj* 'he eats fruit'.

RESULTATIVES

Example: *lɛ:hen* 'to see and recognize' (*lɛ:* 'to look at'; *hen* 'to see'); *nɔ:n.lap* 'to go to sleep' (*nɔ:n* 'to lie down'; *lap* 'to fall asleep'). The negative *maj* is inserted between the components of such a compound: e.g. *phom nɔ:n.maj.lap* 'I can't get off to sleep'.

ASPECT AND TENSE

the simple present is expressed by the verb alone: e.g. *khaw hen* 'he sees'; *Raw paj Hua.hɪn boj.boj* 'We often go to Hua Hin.'
past tense: the marker is *daj*, e.g. *khaw daj paj* 'he went';
future: the marker is *ca'*, e.g. *Wan ni: raw ca' pai du lakhɔ:n* 'Today we'll go to the theatre';
progressive: *kamlaŋ ... ju*, e.g. *chan kamlaŋ kin ju* 'I am eating';

perfective: *lɛ:w*; also a conjunction meaning 'and then', e.g. *Khaw kin.khaw lɛ:w pai tham.ŋan* 'Having eaten, he goes off to work.'

MODAL VERBS
Examples: *khuan* 'should, ought to'; *tɔŋ* 'must'; *ja:g* 'want to'; e.g. *Khaw khuan ca' paj thamŋan* 'He will have to go and work.'

NEGATION
The general negative marker is *mai*: e.g. *chan paj maj daj* 'I cannot go' (*daj* 'to be able'). The negative command is made with *ya:* 'do not'.

Prepositions

Examples: *naj* 'in' – *naj na:* 'in the field'; *thi* 'in, at' – *thi ba:n* 'at home'; *ta:m* 'along' – *ta:m khlɔ:ŋ ni* 'along this canal'.

Polite adjuncts: *khrap* is added by men to both statements and questions, *kha* by women: e.g. *Wan ni: wan 'araj khrap?* 'What day is it today?' (man speaking).

Word order

SVO.

๏ ในที่เดิมนั้นพระลอโฆเปนอยู่ แลเปนอยู่ด้วยกันกับ
พระเจ้า พระลอโฆก็เปนพระเจ้า ท่านก็อยู่กับพระเจ้าในที่
เดิม ท่านได้สร้างไว้ซึ่งสารพัดทั้งปวง ที่เปนอยู่นั้นมิได้
เปนนอกจากท่านสักสิ่งใดสิ่งหนึ่งเลยหามิได้ ในท่านชี
วิตรมีอยู่ ชีวิตรนั้นเปนที่ส่องสว่างแก่มะนุษย์ทั้งหลาย
สว่างนั้นก็ส่องแสงในที่มืด แต่ว่าซึ่งมืดนั้นมิได้รับเข้า ฯ
๏ แล้วก็ยังมีคนหนึ่ง รับใช้แต่พระเจ้ามา ชื่อว่าโยฮัน ฯ
นั้นมาเปนพญาณมากล่าวด้วยความสว่างนั้น จะให้คนทั้ง
ปวงเชื่อเพราะท่าน โยฮันจะได้เปนความสว่างนั้นหามิได้
ท่านมาเปนพญาณว่าด้วยความสว่างนั้น

TIBETAN

INTRODUCTION

Tibetan belongs to the Bodish branch of the Sino-Tibetan family of languages. The ethnonym is *bod.pa* (whence Bodish) pronounced as /pœpa/. Tibetan is spoken by about 4 million people: 1½ million in Tibet, where it has joint official status with Chinese, 1 million in Nepal and India, the remainder in south-west China.

The literary language dates from the seventh century AD, when Buddhism began to penetrate into Tibet. The enormous task of translating the Sanskrit/Pali canon into Tibetan began in the eighth century and was not completed until the fourteenth. The Tibetan canon comprises two main divisions: the *Kanjur* (in Tibetan, *bKa'.'gyur* 'word-change', the Buddha's own words in translation) and the *Tanjur* (*bsTan.'gyur* 'treatise-change', i.e. the translation of the commentaries). The Tanjur alone is in 225 volumes. Part of the translators' task was to provide a lexicon of calques on Sanskrit technical terms, in consistent and one-to-one correspondence with their originals. A measure of the accuracy with which this was accomplished is given by the fact that it is often possible to reconstruct with some certainty Sanskrit originals, which have been lost, from their Tibetan calques.

The old literary language was used for a large output of philosophical, philological, and historical works till the nineteenth/twentieth century. Worthy of particular mention is the great mystic and poet Milarepa (Mi.la.ras.pa; eleventh century). Since the late nineteenth century a new literary language, approximating more to the spoken language, has emerged.

SCRIPT

In the seventh century King Srong.brTSan.sGam.po commissioned a group of scholars to study Indian writing systems with a view to finding a script for Tibetan. Brahmi was chosen as a suitable model. In the Tibetan version, the phonological series are ordered as in Devanagari, but the voiced aspirate member is missing, e.g. in the velar series, *ka – kha – ga – nga* (minus *gha*). As in Devanagari, the short vowel *a* is inherent in the base consonant. The other vowels are marked by superscript and subscript signs.

PHONOLOGY

Consonants

stops: b, p, t, d, ʈ, ɖ, k, g; palatalized: k′, g′
affricates: ts, dz, tʃ, dʒ
fricatives: s, z, ʃ, ʒ, h
nasals: m, mh, n, ɲ, ɲh, ŋ, ŋh
laterals and flaps: l, lh, r, rh
semi-vowels: j, w

Vowels

Short /a/ inheres in the base consonant; the other four basic vowels are (in Tibetan order) /i, u, e, o/. Depending on phonetic environment these are realized as: [i, e, ė, ɛ, ɔ, o, u, y/ʉ, œ/ə, ȯ]. [ė] and [ȯ] are tense, closed.

In the remainder of this article, the standard transcription of Tibetan is used. For reasons of space, only selected words are shown in phonetic transcription. Tone is not marked.

Tibetan spellings which have already occurred above, require some explanation. The basic point is that prefixed letters may precede the word-initial consonant: these prefixed letters are themselves silent, but may affect the sound of the word-initial: e.g. in *bsTan.'gyur*, *T* is the initial of the first component, which is pronounced /tėn/. In the classical literary language, the verb *sTon* /tœœn/ has a past root which is spelled *bsTan*, the form found in this compound, which is pronounced as a whole /ten.kuu/.

This retention of the traditional and etymological orthography means that the correspondence between sound and symbol is very weak. For example, *kra*, *khra*, *gra*, *phra*, *bra*, *sGra*, *bsGra* are all ways of writing the phoneme /ʈa/.

In Tibetan dictionaries, words are entered under word-initial consonant, i.e. ignoring the prefixed letters. Taking C = consonant, V = vowel sequence *i*, *u*, *e*, *o*, P = prefixed letter, the dictionary entry sequence is CV, C*y*V, C*r*V, PCV, PC*y*/*r*V, PPCV. Final consonants are ordered in sequence.

Tone

There are four tonal phonemes: mid (neutral), high, low, falling. These are not marked in the script, but can be deduced from the initial consonant or consonant cluster + vowel. High and low tones inhere in consonants: in a four-term series (velar, palatal, dental, etc.) the first two have high, the second two low tone: e.g. *kā – khā – ga̱ – nga̱*; *cā – chā – ja̱ – nya̱*.

The inherent tone of an initial can be changed by a prefixed, superscript, or subscript consonant: e.g. *d* prefixed to a low-tone initial raises it to high; thus *ma* is a low-tone consonant, but ***dMar*** /maa/, 'red', is high tone.

Final consonants introduce a further complication by affecting the tone, quality and length of the base vowel; e.g. *na* is low tone, but addition of *-d*, e.g. in *nad* /nɛɛ̀/ produces falling tone.

Tibetan is very rich in two-, three- and four-term compounds. In these, assimilation and vowel attraction cross junctures in a kind of vowel harmony which is, however, not consistent: e.g. /re/ + /tuun/ gives /rintuun/, 'wish, desire'.

MORPHOLOGY AND SYNTAX

Noun

The lexical repertory of Tibetan consists of a large number of monosyllabic morphemes which are either independent or dependent (bound). Many independent morphemes serve as words in their own right, e.g. *ri* 'mountain', *mi* 'human being', *rta* 'horse', *'bri* /ʈi/ 'to write'. Bound morphemes comprise morphological and syntactic formants.

GENDER

There is no grammatical gender; certain particles may mark natural gender, e.g. *po*/*mo*: *grogs* /ʈhɔɔ/ 'friend' – *grogs.po* 'male friend', *grogs.mo* 'female friend'; *rgyal.po* /kɛɛ.po/ 'king'; *rgyal.mo* 'queen'.

ARTICLE

The demonstrative *'di*/*de* may be used as a definite article: the numeral *gCig* (with variants depending on final letter of noun) as indefinite: e.g. *mi 'di* 'the man'; *mi chen-po 'di* 'the big man'; *sTag.gCig* 'a tiger'.

NUMBER

The plural markers are *tsho* or *rNams*; the noun itself is invariable: e.g. *dMag.mi* /məə.mi/ 'soldier' – *dMag.mi.tsho* 'soldiers'.

SYNTACTIC RELATIONS

Four linking particles are of crucial importance, and each of these appears in four different allophones, depending on the final letter of the previous word. They are the genitive/relating particle, which is *kyi* after *d, b, s*; *gi* after *g, ng*; *gyi* after *n, m, r, l*; and *'i* after vowels: cf. *bod.**kyi** skad* /phöö.qi qɛɛ/ 'the Tibetan language'; *gser.**gyi** me.tog* 'golden flower'.

The agentive particle is, similarly, *kyis, gis, gyis, s*.

The other two key particles are the gerundial particle *de*/*te*, and the conjunctive particle *cing*/*šing*/*zhing*.

Locational and other markers follow the genitive particle: e.g. *LHa.sa.i byang.phyogs.la* 'in the northern part of Lhasa'.

AGENTIVE

In Tibetan, the agentive case marks the subject of all tenses of an active verb, i.e. for a transitive verb with an object the marker (C)*s*: *bzo.pa mang.pos sha nyo.gi.yod*/*nyos.pa.red*/*nyo.gi.red* 'Many (*mang.po*) workers (*bzo.pa*) are buying (*nyo*) meat (*sha*)/bought meat/will buy meat.' (For structure of verb, see below.) Also *khyed.rang.**gis** las.ka byas.pa.red* 'by-you the work was done' = 'you did the work'; *sTag.**gis** gYag bSad.pa.red* 'The tiger (*sTag*) killed yaks.'

Adjective

As attribute, adjective follows noun, precedes plural marker, and is invariable.

COMPARATIVE
Can be made by isolating the first syllable: e.g. *yag.po* 'good'; *yag.* 'better'.

Pronoun

PERSONAL

		Singular		Plural	
		Standard	*Honorific*	*Standard*	*Honorific*
1		nga	—	nga.tsho	—
2		khyod	khyed.rang	khyod.tsho	khyed.rang.tsho
3	masc.	kho	khong	kho.rang.tsho	khong.rang.tsho
	fem.	mo	khong	mo.rang.tsho	khong.rang.tsho

Possessive forms: e.g. *nga.**i**, khyed.rang.**gi***.

DEMONSTRATIVE PRONOUN/ADJECTIVE
'di 'this', *de* 'that': e.g. *mi 'di.tsho* 'these men'.

INTERROGATIVE PRONOUN
su 'who?'; *ga.re* 'what?': e.g. *'di su.**i** deb red?* 'Whose is this book?'

Numerals

1–10: *gCig, gNyis, gSum, bZHi, lNGa, drug, bDun, brGyad, dGu, bCu*. These are pronounced: /tsig, nyii, sum, ši, nga, thuu, tyyn, kɛɛ, qu, tsu/. 11*bCu.gCig*; 12 *bCu.gNyis*; 21–99: unit + ten + specific formant for each decade: e.g. 45 *bZhi.bCu.zhe.lNGa*. 100 *brGya* /ka/.

Verb

Tibetan classifies verbs as follows:

(a) Active verbs, mainly transitive verbs with an object; the subject is in the agentive case; e.g. *khyed.rang.**gis** las.ka byas.pa.red* 'you did the work'.
(b) Verbs of perception and of movement; the subject is in the nominative: e.g. *nga mthong.gi.'dug* 'I see'; *nga. Bod.la phyin.pa.yin* 'I went to Tibet'.

Copula and existential verb: the copula has *yin* for first person and *red* for second/third: e.g. *kho dmag.mi red* 'he is a soldier'; *nga bzo.pa yin* 'I am a worker'. The existential verb has *yod.* for first person, *'dug* or *yod* for second/third: e.g. *Bod.la zhing.pa mang.po yod.pa.red* 'There are many farmers in Tibet.'

In Classical Tibetan, classes (a) and (b) have four temporal/modal stems characterized by vowel and/or consonantal change: e.g. for *gCod.pa* 'to cut':

Present stem	*Past stem*	*Future stem*	*Imperative*
gCod	bCad	gCad	CHod

In Modern Tibetan, the tendency is for the past and present stems to oust the other two.

TENSE STRUCTURE

The general formula is: stem + particle + auxiliary: e.g. *nga 'gro.gi.**yod*** 'I go'; *khyed.rang 'gro,gi.'**dug*** 'you go'; *nga.tshos gYag.mang.po nyo.gi.yod* 'we are buying many yaks' (*nyo* = 'to buy'); *ngas khang.pa.gCig nyo.gi.yin* 'I'll buy a house'; *khong.tsho lHa khang.la 'dug* 'they are in the temple'.

The formula -.*la* + existential verb is also used to express 'to have something': e.g. *Nga.**la** khang.pa gCig **yod*** 'I have a house'; *Phrug.gu/ṭhuqu/tsho.**la** smyug.gu/ñuqu/mang.po **yod*** 'The children have lots of pens.'

NEGATION OF TENSE

The negative particle *ma/mi* is introduced into the auxiliary slot: e.g. *nga 'gro.gi.yod* 'I go' – *nga 'gro,gi.**med*** 'I don't go' (*ma* + *yod* → *med*); *kho za.gi.'dug* 'he eats' – *kho za.gi.**mi**.'dug* 'he doesn't eat'; *'di gYag red* 'this is a yak' – *'di gYag* (*yin.pa*) ***ma**.red* 'this isn't a yak'.

The past tense of verbs of perception and involuntary action is made with the auxiliary *byung* /tshung/ or *song* (the former for first, the latter for second/third person), and is negated by placing negative particle *ma* between stem and auxiliary: e.g. *nga khyed.rang.gi grogs.po* /ṭhɔɔ/ *mthong.**ma**.byung* 'I haven't seen your friend'.

RELATIVE CLAUSES

Normally precede their antecedent to which they are linked by the genitive particle

(cf. Chinese 的 *de*):

e.g. *Khos bris.pai phyag.bris* /tshəəṭii/ *ga.par.'dug?* 'Where is the letter he wrote?'; *khyed.rang.**gis** nyos.pai shing.tog* 'the fruit you bought'; *nga.tshos lHa.sa.la bTang.pai yi.ge* 'the letter(s) we sent to Lhasa'. Note that the stem in itself is neither active nor passive, but combines both: e.g. *bTang.pai dNGul* 'the money which was sent (given)'; *dNGul bTang.pai mi* 'the man who sent the money'. Note also the formant *mkhan* 'the one who performs the verbal action': e.g. *'dir las.ka byed.**mkhan**.(tsho)* 'the person(s) who is/are working here'.

Honorifics

Like several other oriental languages, Tibetan is a two-tier language. Everyday words are paralleled by honorific forms for use in communication with or in reference to more or less exalted personages, and also in polite conversation with equals or strangers: e.g. *'gro.ba* 'to go' – hon. *phebs.pa*; *za.ba* 'to eat' – hon. *bZhes.pa*; *mig* 'eye' – hon. *sPyan* /tsɛɛn/.

An honorific term often serves as a kind of radical for a series of further terms in the same semantic field. For example, the honorific for the 'mind' (the everyday word is *sems*) is *thugs* /thuù/. On this word as basis, compounds are constructed as, for example: *thugs.smon* /thuqmyyn/, 'prayer'; *thugs.mos*

/thuqmœœ/, 'aspirations'; *thugs.bSam* /thuusəm/, 'thinking'.

Lexicon

As mentioned above, Tibetan Buddhist literature contains a large number of specialist religious and philosophical terms which are calques on Sanskrit terms. As an example, we may take the Tibetan term *shes.rab.kyi.pha.rol.tu.phyin.pa* which renders the Skt word *prajñāpāramitā* 'reaching the further shore of knowledge' = 'attainment of complete insight' (*shes.rab* '(great) knowledge'; *pha.rol* 'the other side'; *phyin.pa* 'attain'; *kyi* is the genitive particle; *tu* is a terminative particle).

Compounds

Very many Tibetan words are compounds of various kinds:

(a) synonymic (a.b, where a = b), e.g. *sgra* 'sound' + *skad* 'sound': *sgra.skad* 'sound', /ta.qεε/;
(b) a.b, where a modifies b, e.g. *gNam.gru* /nəm.ʈu/, 'sky boat' = 'aircraft';
(c) a.b, where a is opposite or complement of b, e.g. *che.chung* 'big–small' = 'size'; *po.mo* 'male–female' = 'sex';
(d) a.b, where b modifies a, e.g. *blo.mTHun* 'mind – being in harmony' = 'comrade'.

Word order

SOV is basic, where S is often in the agentive case. There are several examples above.

༄༅། །ཡོ་ཧ་ནན་གྱིས་ཡི་གེར་བཀོད་པའི་འཕྲིན་བཟང་ཞེས་བྱ་བ་བཞུགས་སོ།།

།དཀོན་མཆོག་གི་ཐོག་མ་མེད་པའི་བཀའ་ཡེ་ཤུ་མ་ཤི་ཀའི་ངང་ནས་མི་རུ་སྒྱུར་བ་དང་། ཡོ་ཧ་ནན་ཁྲུས་
གསོལ་མཁན་གྱིས་དེ་ལ་དཔང་བྱས་པ་དང་། དེའི་རྗེས་གྱིས་ཉེ་གནས་སྔ་མ་རྣམས་ཁོང་གི་དྲུང་དུ་འོངས་
པའི་ལེའུ་སྟེ་དང་པོའོ། 1།ཐོག་མར་བཀའ་ཡོད་ལགས་པ་དང་། བཀའ་དེ་ནི་དཀོན་མཆོག་གི་སྤྱན་
སྔར་བཞུགས་པ་དང་། བཀའ་དེ་ནི་དཀོན་མཆོག་ལགས་པ་ཡིན། 2།དེ་ནི་ཐོག་མར་དཀོན་མཆོག་གི་
སྤྱན་སྔར་བཞུགས་སོ། 3།བཀའ་དེས་ནི་ཇི་ཡོད་པ་ཐམས་ཅད་མཛད་པ་ཡིན་ཏེ། དེ་མེད་པར་ཅི་ཡང་མ་
བྱུང་བ་ཡིན། 4།དེའི་ནང་ན་གསོན་པ་ཉིད་འདུག་སྟེ། གསོན་པ་ཉིད་དེ་ནི་མི་རྣམས་ཀྱི་འོད་པོ་དེ་ཡིན།།
5།འོད་པོ་དེ་ནི་མུན་པའི་ནང་དུ་སྣང་བར་མཛད་ཀྱང་། མུན་པས་དེ་འཛིན་པར་མ་ཐུབ་སོ། །
6མི་དཀོན་མཆོག་གིས་མངགས་པ་ཞིག་བྱུང་སྟེ། དེའི་མིང་ཡོ་ཧ་ནན་ཞེས་བཏགས་སོ། 7།མི་དེ་དཔང་
པོར་བྱུར་ཏེ། འོད་ལ་དཔང་བྱེད་པའི་རྗེས་གྱིས་མི་ཐམས་ཅད་དད་པར་འགྱུར་བའི་ཕྱིར་དུ་བྱུང་ངོ། །

TURKIC LANGUAGES

The Turkic branch of the Altaic family comprises about 30 languages spoken over a vast area extending from Istanbul and the Balkans to the frontier areas of the People's Republic of China, and to Yakutia in the far north-east of Siberia. The total number of speakers lies between 80 and 90 million, with Osmanli Turkish accounting for about half of this figure; in second place come Kazakh and Uzbek, each with around 12 million, followed by Tatar and Azerbaijani with 5 million, and Chuvash, Kirgiz, and Turkmen with about 1½ million each.

Apart from Chuvash, whose specific peculiarities point to its early separation from mainstream Turkic, and Yakut, which has been considerably affected by its Tungusic neighbours, the family, as a whole, is remarkably homogeneous, lexically, phonologically, and morphologically. Thus, some degree of mutual intelligibility is possible over the whole field, which can, indeed, be seen as a dialectal continuum, with few, if any, sharp boundaries between contiguous representatives.

It is this very homogeneity of the Turkic languages which complicates any attempt at internal classification. Several classifications are available, based on phonological, morphological, and historical criteria. The following classification is that given by the Turkologist N.A. Baskakov (in *Jazyki Narodov SSSR* 1966): the names of dead languages are in parentheses:

A. Western Hunnic
1. Bulgarian (Old Bulgarian), Chuvash.
2. Oguz
   - (a) Oguz-Turkmen: (Oguz), Turkmen, Trukhmen;
   - (b) Oguz-Bulgarian: (Uz, Pecheneg), Gagauz;
   - (c) Oguz-Seljuk: (Seljuk, Old Turkish) Azerbaijani, Osmanli Turkish, some dialects of Crimean Tatar.
3. Kipchak
   - (a) Kipchak-Oguz: (Kipchak, Polovets), Kumik, Karaim, Karachaev-Balkar;
   - (b) Kipchak-Bulgarian: (Golden Horde Western language), Tatar, Bashkir;
   - (c) Kipchak-Nogay: Nogay, Kazakh, Karakalpak.
4. Karluk
   - (a) Karluk-Uygur: (Karakhanid and post-Karakhanid Turkish);
   - (b) Karluk-Khoresmian: (Chagatay, Golden Horde Eastern language, Old Uzbek), Uzbek, Uygur.

B. Eastern Hunnic
1. Uygur group:

   (a) Uygur-Tukuy (Old Uygur, Old Oguz, Old Kirgiz), Tuvin;
   (b) Yakut;
   (c) Khakass, Shor, Chulim Tatar, Altay (northern dialects);

2. Kirgiz-Kipchak group: Kirgiz, Altay.

Synoptic table of the Turkic consonantal inventory (based on Baskakov (1966)):

stops: p, b, t, d, k, g, q, ɢ: + hamza /ʕ/ and palatalized t′, d′, k′, g′
affricates: ts, dz, tʃ, dʒ; palatalized ts′ dz′ tʃ′ dʒ′
fricatives: f, v, θ, ð, s, z, ʃ, ʒ, x, γ, h, ɦ; palatalized: s′, z′ x′, ʃ′ ʒ′
nasals: m, n, ɲ, ŋ
laterals and flaps: l, ɫ, r, ʀ
semi-vowel: j

About 60 per cent of these phonemes will be found in the inventory of the average Turkic language.

COMMON FEATURES

1. Agglutinative structure, root + affixes; the roots are remarkably stable over the whole field and over long periods of time.
2. Vowel harmony is characteristic of the whole group, and even tends to persist in the *spoken* form of languages, in which it has been discarded as a component in the literary standard, e.g. Uzbek. Basically, Turkic vowel harmony reduces to the rule that front vowels in a linguistic unit – e.g. stem plus endings – are followed by front vowels, back vowels by back. Specific treatment of the category of rounded versus unrounded vowels varies from one language to another within the family. In many members, roundedness tends to be neutralized through a vowel sequence initiated by a rounded vowel: e.g. in Turkish ***öneri*** 'suggestion'; ***görüşme*** 'interview'.

   In Kirgiz, on the other hand, a four-fold pattern involving front rounded, front unrounded, back rounded, back unrounded vowels is strictly adhered to.

   A convenient shorthand for such patterns is the index notation, e.g. *-lVk*^{4} which indicates that the vowel (V) in the suffix *-lVk* has four variants: in Turkish, *lik/lık/luk/lük*.

   Consonantal sandhi at junctures may increase the number of possible permutations to twelve:
3. There are no articles.
4. There is a total absence of grammatical gender.
5. The adjective precedes the noun; there is no concord.
6. Typically, the postposition is preferred to the preposition.
7. Relative clauses are recast as participial constructions and placed to the left of the head-word, i.e. in adjectival position.

8. Typically, verb forms are negated by a negative marker infix, which almost never carries stress.
9. The verb is usually final.

The following specimen of agglutinative build-up shows Kazakh forms, but an equivalent expansion could be provided for any Turkic language:

jaz	'write' (base = second singular imperative)
jaz.u	'letter, writing'
jaz.u.šı	'writer'
jaz.u.šı.lar	'writers'
jaz.u.šı.lar.ım	'my writers'
jaz.u.šı.lar.ım.ız	'our writers'
jaz.u.šı.lar.ım.ız.da	'appertaining to our writers'
jaz.u.šı.lar.ım.ız.da.γı	'that (quality, thing) which our writers have'
jaz.u.šı.lar.ım.ız.da.γı.lar	'those (qualities, things) which our writers have'
jaz.u.šı.lar.ım.ız.da.γı.lar.dan	'from those qualities (etc.) which our writers have'

TYPICAL PARADIGMS

1. Nominal declension: formula + three specific realizations:

	Formula	*Kirgiz*	*Bashkir*	*Turkish*
nominative	-Ø	köz 'eye'	bala 'child'	ev 'house'
genitive	-(d/t/n)V n/n	köz**nün**	bala**nın**	ev**in**
accusative	-(d/n) V	köz**dü**	bala**nı**	ev**i**
dative	-(k/g/γ) V	köz**gö**	bala**γa**	ev**e**
ablative	-d/t/n V n	köz**dön**	bala**nan**	ev**den**
locative	-d/t/C V	köz**dö**	bala**la**	ev**de**

where V depends on vowel harmony

2. Personal pronouns with possessive pronominal endings, front-vowel forms:

	Singular	*Plural*
1	ben ...m	biz ...(i)miz
2	sen ...n/n	siz ...(i)niz
3	o ...(s)i	onlar ...i

3. Verbal system: formulae with Azerbaijani realization in first person singular (root *al-* 'to take, get, buy'):

Infinitive	m + V + k/g	almag
Imperative	Ø	al; alın
Present/aorist	V + r	al.ır.am
Future	acak/ecek	al.aca.γ.am
Past	d-t + V	al.dı.m
Inferential past	miş	al.mış.am
Conditional	sa/se	al.sa.m
Optative	(j) V	al.a.m

Necessitative	malı/meli	al.malı.j.am
Present participle	V n	al.an
Past participle	d V k/g	al.dıγ.ım
Gerund	ıp/ ip	al.ıb
Passive	ı/i l/n	al.ın.mag
Causative	d/t + ı/i + r(t)	al.dırt.mag

4. Personal endings: basic forms: I present, future, aorist; II past, conditional:

	I		*II*	
	Singular	*Plural*	*Singular*	*Plural*
1	-im	-iz	-m	-k
2	-sin	-siniz	-n	-niz
3	-(dir)	-(dir)ler	ø	-ler

All endings are affected by the rules of vowel harmony.

TURKISH

INTRODUCTION

Anatolian Turkish, described here, is classified by Baskakov (1966) as a member of the Oguz group of the Turkic family (*see* **Turkic Languages**); apart from Turkish, this group contains Azerbaijani, Gagauz, and Turkmen (the so-called *s*-group). Turkish is spoken by about 50 million people in Turkey, by about 120,000 in Cyprus, where it is co-official language with Greek, and by an estimated million in large Turkish minority groups in Bulgaria, Greece, and Yugoslavia.

The earliest literary records in Turkish date from the thirteenth century and already show substantial Arabo-Persian influence, a component which was to increase so markedly through following centuries that literary Ottoman Turkish is largely an artificial construct, remote from spoken Turkish. This Classical Turkish literature culminates in two great poets – Bakî and Fuzulî (both in the sixteenth century). In the wake of the political and social reform movement known as the Tanzimat (mid-nineteenth century) Turkish writers were introduced to Western models, a widening of mental and technical horizons which bore fruit most notably in the work of Ekrem Recaizade, Namik Kemal, and Tevkif Fikret. The associated movement for the erosion of the Arabo-Persian element in favour of native Oguz words antedates the switch from Arabic to Roman script by some twenty years. Modern Standard Turkish is based on the Istanbul dialect.

SCRIPT

From the outset until the late 1920s, Turkish was written in the alien and quite unsuitable Arabic script. Since 1928/9 the Roman alphabet has been used, minus *q*, *w*, *x* but with the additional letters *ç*, *ğ*, *ş*, *ı*, *ö*, *ü*. *ç* denotes /tʃ/, *ş* /ʃ/, *c* /dʒ/; *ğ* lengthens a preceding vowel, with attendant reduction of following vowel: e.g. *ağır* = /aː(ɪ)r/ > /aːr/ 'heavy'. Undotted *ı* = /ɪ/, *ö* = /œ/, *ü* = /y/.

The circumflex is found mainly in the loan-words from Arabic and Persian; it serves (a) to indicate a long vowel, and (b) to mark a preceding *l*, *k*, *g* as slightly palatalized.

PHONOLOGY

Consonants

stops: p, b, t, d, k, g; ʔ occurs in Arabic loan-words
affricates: tʃ, dʒ
fricatives: f, v, s, ʃ, z, h
nasals: m, n
lateral and flap: l, r
semi-vowel: j

/k, g, l/, have palatalized values: /k′, g′, l′/.

CONSONANT ASSIMILATION
Example: final /p, tʃ, t/ are voiced at junctures preceding a vowel: e.g. *kitap* 'book', accusative *kitabı*; *ağaç* 'tree', genitive *ağacın*; *gitmek* 'to go', aorist stem *gider*. Final /k/g/ > [ğ] before a vowel: e.g. ***ekmek*** 'bread', accusative *ekmeği*.

Vowel

front: i, ɛ, œ, y
back: ɪ, a, o, u

All are normally short; long vowels appear (a) as lengthened by *-ğ-* (see above) and (b) as reflexes of original long vowels in Arabic or Persian loans.

VOWEL HARMONY
Basically, front vowels are followed by front, back by back. If the vowel initiating a harmonic sequence is unrounded, so are the following vowels; if the leading vowel is rounded, following vowels are rounded or unrounded. Some examples: ***evde*** 'in the house'; ***ormanda*** 'in the forest'. The suffix *lVk*, for example, appears in four forms: *-lik*, *-lık*, *-luk*, *-lük*; e.g. *işçilik* 'workmanship'; *pazarlık* 'bargaining'; *çoğunluk* 'majority'; *ölümsüzlük* 'immortality'. It is convenient to write such a suffix as *-lik*^{4}, indicating that four variants occur.

Stress

In citation form, stress is usually on the final syllable. In connected speech, and especially in the verb, the allocation of stress is complicated; the presence of the negative marker *-me/ma-* fixes stress on the preceding syllable.

MORPHOLOGY AND SYNTAX

Noun

Turkish has no grammatical gender, and there is no definite article. The numeral *bir* 'one', may be used as an indefinite article. A nominal in the accusative case is regarded as definite.

The plural marker *-lar/-ler*, depending on stem vowel: e.g. *elmalar* 'apples'; *dersler* 'lessons'.

DECLENSION
The paradigm is invariable for all Turkish nouns: it is exemplified here by a back-vowel stem, a front-vowel stem, and a vocalic ending:

	Back vowel	*Front vowel*	*Vocalic ending*
nominative	baş 'head'	ev 'house'	oda 'room'
genitive	baş**ın**	ev**in**	oda**nın**
dative	baş**a**	ev**e**	oda**ya**
accusative	baş**ı**	ev**i**	oda**yı**
locative	baş**ta**	ev**de**	oda**da**
ablative	baş**tan**	ev**den**	oda**dan**

Choice of *t/d* initial in the locative/ablative ending depends on word final; the voiced consonant, for example, follows a voiced final or a vowel. In vocalic stems *-y-* and *-n-* are inserted before the affix.

The same paradigm applies to the plural form: the endings follow the plural marker: e.g. *baş.lar.ın* 'of the heads'; *ev.ler.de* 'in the houses'.

POSSESSION
The formula is: possessor in genitive, followed by possessed object with possessive suffix: e.g. *bu adam.**ın** kalem.**i*** 'of this man his-pencil' = 'this man's pencil'; *köpeğ**in** reng**i*** 'the colour of the dog' (*köpek* 'dog' *k* → *g*)

Adjective

As attribute, adjective precedes noun and is invariable. The indefinite article is normally between the adjective and the noun: e.g. *kırmızı bir gül* 'a red rose'; *ünlü bir kahraman* 'a famous warrior/hero'.

COMPARATIVE
Made with *daha* 'more' + ablative case: e.g. *Bu kitap şu kitap**tan** daha iyi* 'This book is better than that one.'

Pronoun

The personal pronouns are:

	Singular	*Plural*
1	ben	biz
2	sen	siz
3	o	onlar

These are fully declined in all cases: e.g. for first person singular: gen. *benim*, dat. *bana*, acc. *beni*, loc. *bende*, abl. *benden*

POSSESSIVE MARKERS
These are affixed to the noun: sing. 1 -(*i*)m^4, 2 -(*i*)n^4, 3 -(*s*)i^4; pl. 1 -(*i*)miz^4,

2 -(*i*)*niz*[4], 3 -*leri*/*ları*: e.g. *lokanta.nız* 'your restaurant'; *lokanta.nız.ın ismi* 'the name of your restaurant'; *Türkiye (bizim) vatan.***ımız** *dir* 'Turkey is our motherland'; *Türkiye toprak.ları.nın büyük bir kısm.ı* 'a large part of Turkey's lands'.

DEMONSTRATIVE PRONOUN/ADJECTIVE
bu 'this'; *şu* 'that'; fully declined.

INTERROGATIVE PRONOUN
kim 'who?'; *ne* 'what?'; declined.

RELATIVE PRONOUN
None; *see* **Verb**, Relative clause, below.

Numerals

1–10: *bir*, *iki*, *üç*, *dört*, *beş*, *altı*, *yedi*, *sekiz*, *dokuz*, *on*; 11 *on.bir*; 12 *on.iki*; 20 *yirmi*; 30 *otuz*; 40 *kırk*; 50 *elli*; 100 *yüz*.

Verb

(*See also* **Turkic Languages**.) A typical Turkish verb form is constructed as follows: stem – aspect and/or tense marker – personal ending: e.g. *gel.i.yor.um* 'I am coming' (where *gel-* is the stem of *gelmek* 'to come': *-i-* is a connective vowel: *-yor-* is the characteristic of the present continuous tense; and *-um* is the first person singular personal marker); *gel.ebil.e.ceğ.im* 'I shall be able to come' (*-ebil-* is the potential aspect marker; *cek-* → *ceğ-* is the characteristic of the future tense).

There are three sets of personal endings, all close to the possessive series set out above. One set provides the endings for the existential verb: sing. 1 *-im*[4], 2 *-sin*[4], 3 *-dir*[4]; pl. 1 *-iz*[4], 2 *-siniz*[4], 3 *-dirler*[4.2]: e.g. *evde.***siniz** 'you are in the house'. With certain exceptions these are also the affixes for the present continuous, the aorist, the future, and the inferential past; the third person marker is Ø: e.g. *gel.i.yor.um* 'I am coming'; *gel.i.yor***Ø** 'he is coming'.

A very similar set of endings used in the past definite and in the conditional mood has one anomalous form: *-k* in the first person, e.g. *geldi***k** 'we came'; *gelsek* 'if we were to come'.

The third set of endings is used with the subjunctive mood: sing. 1 *eyim*, 2 *esin*, 3 *e*; pl. 1 *elim*, 2 *esiniz*, 3 *eler*.

The main tense characteristics are: present *-yor-*; future *-cek*[2]*-*; definite past *-di*[4]*-*; inferential past *-miş*[4]*-*; aorist *-r-*; conditional *-se*[2]*-*. Some examples:

present: *ver.i.yor.sunuz* 'you are giving (pl.)'
future: *ver.e.cek.ler* 'they will give'
past definite: *ver.di.k* 'we gave'
inferential past: *ver.miş.siniz* '(it seems that) you gave'
aorist: *ver.i.r* 'he gives'

conditional: *ver.i.yor.sa.m* 'if I am giving'
subjunctive: *ver.el.im* 'that we may give'

NEGATIVE CONJUGATION

The negative marker *-me/ma-* precedes the tense characteristic; stress is transferred to the syllable immediately preceding this marker. There are specific rules for stress in the aorist negative. Examples:

present: *gör.mü.yor* 'he is not seeing'
future: *gel.mi.ye.cek* 'he will not come'
aorist: *gel.mez* 'he doesn't come'
past definite: *al.ma.dı.m* 'I didn't take'
inferential past: *bul.ma.mış.ım* '(it seems that) I didn't find'

NEGATIVE COPULA

Made with *değil*: e.g. *hasta değil.im/değil.sin* 'I am/you are not ill'. The existential verb is negated by *yok*: e.g. *yok(tur)* 'there is not':

Dedim: bayram mıdır? Söyledi: yok, yok.
'I said: is there a festival? He said: no, there is not.' (Emrah: nineteenth century)

This line of poetry also illustrates the interrogative conjugation; the marker is *mi*^{4}, which follows the focal point in the verbal complex. Again, the preceding syllable is stressed: e.g. *Ver.i.yór* ***mu****.sunuz?* 'Are you giving?'; *Bil.méz* ***mi****.siniz?* 'Don't you know?'; *Bana yardım edér.****mi****.siniz?* 'Will you help me?' (*yardım* 'help'; *bana* 'to me'; *etmek* 'to do').

PASSIVE VOICE

The marker is *-il*^{4}*-/-in*^{4}*-*: e.g. *görmek* 'to see' – *gör****ül****mek* 'to be seen'.

CAUSATIVE

-dir^4*-*: e.g. *ölmek* 'to die' – *öl****dür****mek* 'to kill'.

NECESSITATIVE

-meli^2*-*: e.g. *gel.meli.y.im* 'I ought to come'.

RELATIVE CLAUSE

Various participial forms are used: e.g. with present participle in *-en*^{2}*-*, *gel.en adam* 'the man who is coming'; *gel.e.cek (ol.an) adam* 'the man who will come'; *gel.miş (ol.an) adam* 'the man who is said to have come'.

The participial form made from the past definite tense is in *-dik*; this is very extensively used in all sorts of relative clauses. Some examples: *gel.****diğ****.i zaman* 'when he comes' (*-dik* → *diğ* before third person marker *-i*: *zaman* 'time' → 'when ...'); *ev.e dön.****düğ****.üm zaman* 'when I (*-üm*) reach(ed) home'; *üzerinde yaş.a.****dığ****.ımız topraklar* 'the land(s) on which we live(d)'; *harabeler gör-.ül.****dük****.ten sonra* 'after the ruins have been viewed ...'; *bizim öğrenci vizesi ver.****diğ****.imiz kimselerden iste****diğ****imiz şey* 'what we want from those people to whom we have given student visas'; *hiç bir parti çogunluğu kaza-na.ma.****dığ****.ın.dan sonra* 'since no party won a majority'.

Postpositions

The last example above shows a postposition following the ablative case: *sonra* 'after'. Other postpositions are used with the nominative (e.g. *gibi* 'like', *için* 'for') and the dative (e.g. *göre* 'according to', *kadar* 'as far as', *karşı* 'against').

Word order

SOV is basic; the inverted sentence (*devrik cümle*) is possible, with certain reservations.

1 İptidada Kelâm var idi, ve Kelâm Allahın nez-
2 dinde idi, ve Kelâm Allah idi. O, iptidada Alla-
3 hın nezdinde idi. Her şey onun vasıtasile ol-
du, ve olmuş olanlardan onsuz hiç birşey olmadı.
4 Hayat onda idi, ve hayat insanların nuru idi.
5 Nur karanlıkta parlıyor, ve karanlık onu yenmedi
6 Allah tarafından gönderilmiş bir adam çıktı, onun
7 ismi Yahya[1] idi. Bu adam şehadet için geldi,
ta ki o nur hakkında şehadet etsin de bütün in-
8 sanlar onun vasıtasile iman eylesinler. Kendisi o
nur değildi, ancak o nur hakkında şehadet etmek
için geldi.

TWI

See **Akan**.

UKRAINIAN

INTRODUCTION

The name of this Eastern Slavonic language derives from *ukraina*, the 'border area', the domain of the Cossacks, which lay between the Slav principalities to the north and west, and the Turkish hordes to the south. Today, the language is spoken by about 50 million in the Ukrainian Republic, and by considerable numbers in contiguous areas of Poland, the Czech and Slovak Republics, and Romania, and in Canada, the USA, and Australia. The total number of speakers is probably around 60 million.

Three main dialect areas are distinguished: northern, south-western (including Galicia and Bukovina), and south-eastern. The modern literary language is based on the Middle Dniepr dialect, and Kiev usage. Like Russian and Belorussian, Ukrainian derives from the Slavonic languages spoken in the early Middle Ages in the area between the Black Sea and the Baltic – the Kievan state, or *Rus'*. Specifically Ukrainian features can be detected in documents dating from the twelfth century, and by the fourteenth century the sound shifts and morphological innovations typical of Ukrainian are established. The literary language was, of course, strongly influenced by Old Church Slavonic. Two literary registers can be detected, one largely shared with Russian, the other a specifically Ukrainian variant, with some intake from the spoken Ukrainian language: the so-called *prosta mova*. Translation into *prosta mova* includes the Peresopnitskoe Evangelie (mid-sixteenth century). Towards the end of the sixteenth century the first printed books in Ukrainian appeared. An ever-present source of lexical and morphological enrichment lay in the rich oral literature generated during the struggles for national liberation against the Poles and Turkic invaders.

The consolidation and development of literary Ukrainian in line with the spoken language gathered impetus through the eighteenth century, a process which culminated in the mid-nineteenth century in the impressive figure of Taras Shevchenko (1814–61), whose literary and philological work was of crucial importance for the western Ukraine (i.e. the Austro-Hungarian lands). For the last thirty years of the nineteenth century the use of Ukrainian as a written language was prohibited in the eastern – Russian – part of the Ukraine.

SCRIPT

Cyrillic, with the additional letters є, *і*, *ї*.

PHONOLOGY

Consonants

stops: p, b, t, d, k, g; **t′**, **d′**
affricates: ts, dz, tʃ, dʒ; **ts′**, **dz′**
fricatives: f, (v), s, z, ʃ, ʒ, x, h; **s′**, **z′**
nasals: m, n; ɲ
lateral and flap: l, r; ʎ, **r′**
semi-vowels: **j**, w

The nine consonants and the semi-vowel shown in bold type are invariably soft. /p, b, k, g, tʃ, dʒ, f, v, ʃ, ʒ, m, x, h/ are soft if followed by /i/; i.e. their palatalization is conditional.

Vowels

hard: ɪ, ɛ, a, o, u; /o/ and /u/ are labialized;
soft: i/yi, yɛ, ya, yo, yu

Confusingly, the hard /ɛ/ is notated in the script as *e*; the soft /yɛ/ as є. Hard /ɪ/ is notated in Cyrillic as и; /iː/ as i. Soft /ji/ is notated as ї or и. The other three soft vowels are denoted as я, ьо, ю.

Some notable features of Ukrainian phonology:

1. The presence of long soft consonants: e.g. *žitt′a* 'life', [ʒɪt′t′a]; *znann′a* 'knowledge', [znan′n′a]. A hard consonant may be assimilated to a soft to produce a long soft cluster: e.g. *holosn′išatɪ* 'to get louder' = [holos′n′iʃatɪ].
2. Common Slav. /*ě/ (giving /ě/ in Russian) has an /i/ reflex in Ukrainian: cf. Russ. *leto* 'summer' – Ukr. *lito*; Russ. *les* 'forest' – Ukr. *lis*; Russ. *xleb* 'bread' – Ukr. *xlib*.
3. Vowels in unstressed position are not reduced as in Russian; unstressed /e/, however, tends to [i]: e.g. *selo* 'village', [seilɔ].

Stress

Free, on any syllable. Stress does not always coincide with Russian: cf. Russ. *málуj* 'small' – Ukr. *malíi*.

MORPHOLOGY AND SYNTAX

Noun

As in Russian, there are three genders and two numbers; the noun has six cases plus a vocative.

Nouns are divided into hard and soft declensions. Nouns with a final consonant are mainly masculine; *-a*/*-ya* are typically feminine endings, though many in *-ya* are neuter; *-o* and *-e* are typically neuter. Four declensions are distinguished.

Specimen paradigms: *voda* 'water' (fem. *-a* decl.); *stil* 'table' (masc.)

	Singular	*Plural*	*Singular*	*Plural*
nominative	vodá	vódɪ	stil	stolí
accusative	vódu	vódɪ	stil	stolí
genitive	vodí	vod	stolá	stolíw
locative	vodí	vódax	stolí	stoláx
dative	vodí	vódam	stolú	stolám
instrumental	vodóju	vódami	stolóm	stolámi

The accusative form depends on whether the referent is animate or inanimate; if animate, accusative = genitive as in Russian: e.g. *Ja ne znayu cɪx studentiw* 'I don't know these students'; *Vin zustriw brata* 'He met (his) brother.' In the colloquial language, the use of the genitive form is extending to the inanimate sector.

The genitive is used after negative verbs: e.g. *Ja ne znaju c'ohó učitel'a* 'I don't know this teacher'; *Tut nemaje paperu* 'There's no paper here.'

Adjective

As attribute, adjective precedes noun and agrees with it in gender, number, and case: e.g. the paradigm of *ridne selo* 'native village' (*selo* is neuter):

	Singular	*Plural*
nominative	rídne seló	rídni séla
accusative	ridne selo	ridni sela
genitive	ridnoho sela	ridnix sil
locative	ridnomu seli	ridnix selax
dative	ridnomu selu	ridnim selam
instrumental	ridnim selom	ridnimi selami

The stress in *selo* is on the ending in the singular, on the stem vowel in the plural.

COMPARATIVE

The marker is -(*i*)*š*: e.g. *xolodnɪi* 'cold' – *xolodnišɪi*; *starɪi* 'old' – *staršɪi*. Example with consonant alternation: *vɪsokɪi* 'high' – *vɪščɪi*. Some are suppletive: *velɪkɪi* 'big' – *bil'šɪi*; *dobrɪi* 'good' – *kraššɪi*.

Pronoun

PERSONAL

sing. 1 *ja*, 2 *tɪ*, 3 masc. *vin*, fem. *vona*, nt. *vono*;
pl. 1 *mɪ*, 2 *vɪ*, 3 common, *vonɪ*

These are declined in six cases: e.g. for first person singular: acc. *mene*, gen. *mene*, loc. (*na*) *meni*, dat. *meni*, instr. *mnoju*.

The oblique forms of the third person are based on -(*n*)*jo*-: *joho* 'him', *jii* 'her':

e.g. *ja joho ne znaju* 'I don't know him'. The form *joho* is also the possessive pronoun for third masculine/neuter; *jii*, feminine. These are indeclinable. The possessive pronominal adjectives for the other persons are marked for number and gender: e.g. *miji – moja – moje – moji*.

DEMONSTRATIVE PRONOUN/ADJECTIVE
cei/cja/ce; pl. *c'i* 'this, these'; *toi/ta/te*; pl. *t'i* 'that, those'. Declined in six cases.

INTERROGATIVE PRONOUN
xto 'who?'; *ščo* 'what?'. Declined in six cases.

RELATIVE PRONOUN
kotrii/kotorii; used as in Russian.

Numerals

1–10: the base forms, as used in counting, are *odɪn, dva, trɪ, čotɪrɪ, p'at', šist', sim, visim, dev'at', des'at'*. 11 *odɪnadc'at'*; 12 *dvanadc'at'*, 20 *dvadc'at'*; 30 *trɪdc'at'*; 40 *sorok*; 100 *sto*. All cardinal numbers are declined.

Verb

As in Russian, the distinction between perfective (completed) and imperfective (durative/on-going) action is fundamental: cf.

ja čɪtaw gazetu 'I was reading the paper'

ja **pro**čɪtaw gazetu 'I read the paper (and finished it)'

Formation of perfective:

(a) By prefix: e.g. *pɪsatɪ* 'write' – ***na****pɪsatɪ*; *rozumitɪ* 'understand' – *zrozumitɪ*; *gotuvatɪ* 'prepare, cook' – ***prɪ****gotuvatɪ*.
(b) By change in stem: e.g. *l'agatɪ* 'lie down' – *l'agtɪ*.
(c) By stress change: e.g. *zdɪbátɪ* 'meet' – *zdíbatɪ*.
(d) By means of *-nut'* (giving semelfactive meaning): e.g. *stukatɪ* 'knock' – *stuknutɪ*.
(e) Suppletion: e.g. *bratɪ* 'take' – *uz'atɪ*; *govorɪtɪ* 'speak' – *skazatɪ*.

Voice, mood, and tense are, in general, as in Russian.

There are two conjugations. Conjugation I has a third person singular (present tense) in *-(j)e*, and third plural in *-(j)ut'*; the corresponding forms in conjugation II are *-t'/-jit'* and *-(j)at'*. As example, the present tense of the first conjugation verb *čɪtatɪ* 'to read':

	Singular	*Plural*
1	čɪtaju	čɪtajemo
2	čɪtaješ	čɪtajete
3	čɪtaje	čɪtajut'

Second conjugation: e.g. from *bačɪtɪ* 'to see': 1 *baču*, 2 *bačɪš*, 3 *bačɪt'*.

The past tense is marked for gender and number only, excluding person:

	Singular	*Plural*
masc.	čıtáw	
fem.	čıtála	čıtálı
nt.	čıtálo	

A Ukrainian innovation is the synthetic future made from imperfective verbs, in parallel with the analytical future with the auxiliary *butı*; this synthetic future is unique in the Slavonic group of languages. It is made by adding *-m-* plus the personal endings of the present tense to the infinitive of the sense-verb; e.g. *robıtı* 'to do':

1 *robıtı.mu*, 2 *-meš*, 3 *-me*; pl. 1 *robıtı.memo*, 2 *-mete*, 3 *mut'*

VERBS OF MOTION

As in Russian, there is a basic opposition between (a) determinate (vectorial) motion and (b) indeterminate (random). Both sets are further sub-divided to denote motion on foot or by means of transport. The aspectual distinction cuts across these categories; thus, (b) verbs are imperfective only, the other sets have both aspects: e.g. (a) *pitı* (perf.) – (b) *xodıtı* (imperf.) motion on foot:

Vonı pišlı do mista 'They walked to town'

Vin xodıt' povil'no 'He's a slow walker'

(a) *po-yixatı* (perf.) – (b) *yizdıtı* (imperf.) motion by means of transport:

Vonı po.jixalı do mista 'They drove to town'

Vin jizdıt' povil'no 'He's a slow driver'

Prepositions

Largely as in Russian. *V* 'in, at' and *u* 'at', distinct in Russian, have coalesced in Ukrainian.

Word order

Basically SVO.

У почи́ні було́ Сло́во, и Сло́-
во було́ в Бо́га, и Бог було́
Сло́во.

2. Воно́ було́ в почи́ні у
Бо́га.

3. Все ним ста́лося; и без
не́го не ста́лося нішо́, що
ста́лося.

4. У іо́му житте́ було́: и
житте́ було́ сві́тлом лю́дям.

5. И сві́тло у те́мряві сві́-
тить, и те́мрява іого́ не об-
няла́.

6. Був чолові́к по́сланий від
Бо́га, имя́ іому́ Іоа́н.

7. Сей прийшо́в на сві́д-
кува́ннє, щоб свідкува́ти про
сві́тло, щоб усі́ ві́рували че-
ре́з не́го.

8. Не був він сві́тло, а щоб
свідкува́ти про сві́тло.

URALIC LANGUAGES

The languages belonging to this family lie mainly in a broad band extending across northern Europe and Siberia, from Finland to the Taymyr Peninsula. On both sides of the Urals, the Uralic speech areas centre round the great rivers – the Ob and the Yenisei to the east, the Pechora and the Volga to the west. Still further to the west, a cluster of Uralic languages is found on the north-east Baltic seaboard. Hungarian, isolated from its congeners in central Europe, is the sole outlier.

Though they are structurally heterogeneous, there is no doubt that the Uralic languages are genetically related, and much research has gone towards reconstruction of the parent language and identification of its habitat. The presence of common roots denoting deciduous trees and terms connected with apiculture, suggest an Urheimat to the west, rather than to the east of the Urals. The absence of a common root for 'beech', however, which does not grow east of the Baltic–Black Sea line, may be taken as indicative of a western limit. Other notable lacunae are terms for the sea, rocks, sand, the tundra, and so on. On the whole, the evidence points to an original Uralic habitat between the middle course of the Urals and the Volga.

The first division of the parent language, into Proto-Samoyedic and Proto-Finno-Ugric, has been tentatively dated to the middle of the third millennium BC. A thousand years later, a similar split yielded Proto-Hungarian and Ob-Ugric on the one hand, Permic-Volgaic on the other. The family as it appears at present is internally classified as follows:

1. Samoyedic: Northern: Nenets, Enets, Nganasan;
   Southern: Selkup, Kamassian.
2. Finno-Ugric:
   (a) Ugric: Hungarian;
   (b) Ob-Ugric: Khanty, Mansi;
   (c) Permic-Volgaic: Komi, Udmurt, Mordva, Mari;
   (d) Balto-Finnic: Finnish, Estonian, Karelian, Ingrian, Veps, Vot, Liv;
   (e) Lappish.

Several of these languages were known by other names in the past; e.g. Ostyak (Khanty), Vogul (Mansi), Zyryan (Komi), Votyak (Udmurt), Cheremis (Mari).

Kamassian is now extinct (one speaker was known in 1970), and some of the Balto-Finnic minor languages are moribund. At present, about 23 million people speak Uralic languages, with Hungarian and Finnish accounting for about 80 per cent of this total.

See **Hungarian, Finnish, Estonian, Lappish**.

URDU

Urdu is the official language of Pakistan, where it is spoken by about 10 million people. In India, it is spoken by many millions of people, either as mother tongue or as second language, in the Panjab and in the states of Uttar Pradesh and Andhra Pradesh; about 50 million is a reasonable estimate. Phonologically and morphologically, Urdu and Hindi are virtually one and the same language. For a description of this language, *see* **Hindi**.

Historically, this common language derives from the Khaṛī Bōlī group of dialects centred on Uttar Pradesh and the Delhi area, which served as a lingua franca between the local population and the Moslem invaders from the west. Through the Middle Ages, this lingua franca – known as *zabān-e-urdū*, the 'language of the camp/army' – gradually consolidated its position as the main inter-regional language of north India: a tribute, in a way, to the stability created by the Mughal dynasty. From being no more than a colloquial, it was able to graduate to the status of a literary language, used, along with Persian, in the Moslem courts (sixteenth to eighteenth centuries). Given the cultural affiliations of these courts, it is not surprising to find that large numbers of Arabic and Persian words entered the lexicon. From the late eighteenth century onwards the Farsi–Hindustani of the Mughal courts and their entourages is known simply as Urdu.

In other words, Farsi–Urdu, especially of the southern Indian courts, where it was known as *rextā* 'mixed', was a somewhat artificial product, whose specialized vocabulary hardly reached the Khaṛī Bōlī-speaking masses. In the late eighteenth century Hindu writers and scholars, nourished on native Indian tradition, rather than on Arabo-Persian culture, began to use Khaṛī Bōlī ('Hindustani') as a medium for literary expression in terms of Sanskrit–Hindu culture. This development had two corollaries: the use of the Devanagari script instead of the Arabic, and recourse to Sanskrit for lexical enrichment. By the mid-nineteenth century Hariścandra could use 'Hindi' as an effective and well-equipped vehicle for creative writing in the modern sense: that is, not simply as a vessel for the decanting of received tradition. Urdu and Hindi are, thus, cultural polarizations emanating from a common linguistic core.

Classical Urdu literature of the seventeenth/eighteenth centuries is rich and extensive, and some of it is of superlative quality: e.g. the ghazals of Mīr Taqi Mīr (1722?–1810). Today, Urdu is the vehicle of one of the sub-continent's most prolific and important literatures.

SCRIPT

The Arabic–Persian script is used, with additional letters for the retroflex series.

UZBEK

INTRODUCTION

Baskakov (in *Jazyki Narodov SSSR* 1966) allocates Uzbek to the Karluk-Khoresmian sub-group of the Karluk groups of Western Hunnic (*see* **Turkic Languages**). Old Uzbek or Chagatay (also known simply as Turki) was one of the literary languages used at the Tīmūrid court in Herat in the fifteenth/sixteenth century by such distinguished writers as Alīshīr Navā'ī (1441–1501), the 'father of Uzbek culture'; and, later, by the Emperor Babur, whose delightful autobiography, the *Bāburnāma,* is a classic of world literature. Among outstanding writers and scholars native to the region, though they wrote in Arabic or Persian, is the polymath al-Bīrūni.

With around 12–13 million speakers, Uzbek is the third most widely spoken language of the CIS (after Russian and Ukrainian). Most Uzbeks live in the Uzbek and Tajik Republics, with some spread into the adjacent Kirgiz, and Kazakh Republics. The language is used at all levels of education, and in the local media, with numerous newspapers and periodicals. More books appear in Uzbek than in any other language of the Moslem republics.

SCRIPT

The Arabic script was finally abandoned in 1927. After an experimental period of romanization, Cyrillic with additional letters was adopted in 1940.

PHONOLOGY

Consonants

stops: p, b, t, d, k, g, q
affricates: ts, tʃ, dʒ
fricatives: f, v, s, z, ʃ, ʒ, x, γ, h, j
nasals: m, n, ŋ
lateral and flap: l, r

Vowels

The six letters: *i*, *e*, *a*, *o*, *ŭ*, *u* represent the following sounds:

i, ɪ, ɛ, æ, a, aː, ə, ɔ, u, uː

In contact with a palatalized consonant, /u/→ [y]: e.g. *juda* 'very' = /dʒyda/. The sounds /ya, yo, ye, yu/, are denoted by the equivalent Cyrillic letters. Cyrillic hard sign is used to represent 'ain in Arabic words: the hard sign also lengthens the vowel: e.g. /fɛːl/ = Arabic *fa'ala*. /u/ is lengthened by the addition of Cyrillic в: e.g. *suv* /'water'/ = /suː/.

VOWEL HARMONY

Uzbek has lost the standard Turkic opposition between front/back, rounded/unrounded vowels, which determines the vocalic articulation of words throughout the family. Thus, where Turkish, for example, has *onlardan/sizlerden* Uzbek has back vowels in both: *ulardan/sizl**ar**dan*. The practical result is that, whereas elsewhere in the Turkic family there is at least a dual set of endings displaying concord with front or back stem vowels (and often more than two – e.g. in Altay, which has sixteen possible notations of the plural affix), Uzbek has only one set. Thus the infinitive ending, for example, is always *-moq*: e.g. *yozmoq* 'to write', *bermoq* 'to give'. Similarly, the negative infix remains *-**ma**-* for any root: e.g. *kel**ma**di* 'he didn't come' (contrast Turkish: *gel**me**di*). On the other hand, the notation selected for the past tense, for example, favours a front-vowel spelling: *-dim*, *-ding*, *-di*; pl. *-dik*, *-dingiz*, *-dilar*, though there is a tendency to realize the *-i-* as *-ɪ-* after back vowel stems: e.g. *išladim* → [iʃlad**ɪ**m].

MORPHOLOGY AND SYNTAX

In declension, the predicative personal affixes, the possessive markers, the treatment of the adjective, the pronominal system and the numerals, Uzbek has standard Turkic forms.

Noun

The accusative ending is *-ni*: e.g. *kitoblarni* 'books'. A stem-final /g/γ/ tends to become [k/q] before the dative ending, which then assimilates: e.g. *boγ* 'garden' (Iranian loan-word) – *bo**qq**a* 'to the garden'. Arabic words may take the Uzbek plural marker *-lar* or retain a broken plural: e.g. *taraf* 'side', pl. *taraflar* or *atrof*.

Examples of cases:

genitive: *Toškent – Uzbekiston**ning** eng katta šahari* 'Tashkent is Uzbekistan's biggest town', *Uzbek adabiyot**ning** otasɪ* 'the father of Uzbek culture';
accusative: *biz Tamara**ni** kutubxonda kurdik* 'we saw Tamara in the library';
dative: ... ***menga** xat yozdi* '... wrote me a letter';
ablative: ... *keča Samarqand**dan** keldi* '... came yesterday from Samarkand'

Verb

Like the Uzbek noun, the Uzbek verb has a single set of endings, though here, as pointed out above, this single set often reflects a reductionist orthography rather than actual realization.

Tense structure is standard, as is the formation of the basic tenses: present–future in *-a-*, past in *-di*, future in *-ajak*, conditional in *-sa*. Uzbek, however, has several ways of making a present continuous tense: thus, from *yozmoq* 'to write':

yoz.a.yotir.man	'I am in the process of writing'	(literary style)
yoz.a.yap.man		(spoken language)
yoz.ib.turib.man		(continuity emphasized)
yoz.moqda.man		(not necessarily punctual)

The formation of the passive, reflexive, and causative forms is standard. The perfect marker is *-gan-*: e.g. *yoz.gan.man* 'I have written'.

PARTICIPLES

present: *-yot.gan/di.gan*;
past: *-gan*;
future: *-ar/-a.-jak.*

Examples: *kel.ar* '(he, etc.) who will come'; *iš.lar* (< *iš.la.ar*) '(he, etc.) who will work'. Negated by *mas*: *iš.la.mas* 'who will not work'. The *-jak* form, frequent in Turkish – *gel.e.cek, ol.a.cak* – is less used in Uzbek: *kel.a.**jak** yil* 'next year'.

These are used in the formation of relative clauses: e.g. *kel.a.yot.gan kiši* 'the man who is coming (now)'; *bu kitob.ni uqi.yot.gan bola* 'the boy who is reading this book'.

Rašida.ning kelgan.i.ni bil.a.man
'I know that Rašida has arrived' (*Rašida.ning* 'of R.'; *kel.gan.**i*** 'his coming'; *-ni* acc. ending after *bilaman* 'I know').

The participles are neutral as to voice: e.g. *kitob.ni ol.gan kiši* 'the man who took the book'; *ol.gan pul* 'the money that was taken'; *men borgan yer* 'the place I went to'.

PASSIVE CONSTRUCTION
Example:

*Eski uzbek tili.dan hozirgi zamon tili.ga kučir.**il**.di*
'was translated from old Uzbek into the present-day language'.

Postpositions

Postpositions may follow nominative, genitive, dative, or ablative, and may take cases and possessive markers: e.g. *yoni* 'beside': *mening yoni**m**da* 'beside me'; *sening yoni**ng**da* 'beside you'; *siz**ning** yoni**ngiz**da* 'beside you (pl.)'.

Word order

SOV.

١ اوّل‌ده سوز بار ایردی و سوز خداده ایردی و سوز خدا ایردی۝
٢ ٣ اول سوز اوّل‌ده خداده ایردی۝ بارچه نرسه آنینك برلان بولدی
٤ وهیچ بولغان نرسه آنسیز بولمادی۝ آنینك ایچیده تیریکلیك ایردی
٥ هم تیریکلیك انسانلارنینك نوری ایردی۝ و نور قارانغولیق‌ده
٦ یاقتیرادور لیکن قارانغولیق نورنی قبول قیلمادی۝ خدا یبارکان یحیی
٧ آتلیغ بر کیشی بار ایردی۝ بول شهادت اوچون کیلدی نور
خصوصیده شهادت برکای بارچه‌لار آنینك واسطه‌سی برلان ایمان
٨ کیلتورکای‌لار۝ اول اوزی نور ایماس ایردی لیکن اول نور
خصوصیده شهادت برماککا (کیلیب) ایردی۝

VIETNAMESE

INTRODUCTION

The genetic status of Vietnamese has been the subject of some controversy. For long, it was regarded as a member of the Sino-Tibetan family, and, certainly, there is a very substantial Chinese element in the language, which is hardly surprising, given the decisive influence of Chinese language and culture on Vietnam over some 2,000 years. Research in the nineteenth and twentieth centuries, however, has gone to suggest that this Chinese element is superimposed on a non-Sino-Tibetan substratum. What is controversial is the exact nature of the substratum. According to H. Maspéro (1912, 1916) Modern Vietnamese represents the fusion of a Mon-Khmer language with a Tai language; and, in view of the tonal structure of Vietnamese, the tonal Tai language was taken to be the decisive formant. Accordingly, Vietnamese was classified as a Tai language. In the 1950s, however, A.G. Haudricourt showed that Vietnamese did not acquire its tonal system till comparatively late in its history (probably during the first millennium AD) and that it was basically a Mon-Khmer language, belonging to the Austro-Asiatic phylum. This is now the accepted classification. About 65 million people speak the language in Vietnam, and at least another million speakers are scattered abroad, with large colonies in the USA, in Hong-Kong, Paris, and several Pacific islands.

Typical of Vietnamese classical literature is the *truyện thơ* or verse-novel, the most celebrated example of which is the *Truyện Kiêu* by Vietnam's greatest writer, Nguyễñ Du (1765–1820). Formally, the truyện thơ is composed in alternating six- and eight-syllable strophes, with a musical counterpoint between the two level tones and the four moving tones. The Tang seven-syllable line was also very popular in Vietnamese poetry.

DIALECTS

The main dialectal divisions have always tended to centre round the major cities – Huế, Hã-nôi, and Saigon (now Hô-Chí-Minh City). The modern literary standard combines the consonantal inventory of the central dialect with the tonal system of the northern.

SCRIPT

Diachronically, four main stages can be distinguished in the development of written Vietnamese:

1. Sino-Vietnamese: from BC to the tenth century AD. This period is characterized by the use of the Chinese script, and by Chinese pronunciation of Vietnamese words.

2. The medieval period, fourteenth to seventeenth centuries. In this period the writing system known as chữ nôm was developed by Buddhist scholar–priests. Chinese script continued to be used for Vietnamese pronunciation; and composite graphs were used, in which one component signals the pronunciation, while the other component indicates the meaning: e.g.

至典 = *đến* 'to come',

where

典

in Chinese, *diăn*, suggests the pronunciation, and

至

in Chinese, *zhì* 'to reach, arrive at', indicates the meaning. Again, a Chinese character denoting a semantic equivalent in Vietnamese, may be given a supporting Chinese graph to reinforce the equation; e.g. the non-Chinese graph

𡗶 = *trơi* 'sky'

in which two Chinese characters

天 *tiān* 'sky', and 上 *shàng* 'above, up',

have been superimposed.

3. The Roman script was introduced by Catholic missionaries in the seventeenth century. It is extended by the use of diacritics to mark certain vowels and five of the six tones, and by the use of the letters *ơ*, *ư*, and *đ* = /d/; unbarred *d* = /z/.

4. In the twentieth century, more especially in its second half, this 'national script', quốc ngữ, has helped to extend literacy to all classes of Vietnamese society.

PHONOLOGY

Consonants

stops: p, b, t, d, k; aspirated stops: t', k'
affricate: tʃ
fricatives: f, v, s, z, ʃ, ʒ, x, γ
nasals: m, n, ɲ, ŋ
lateral: l

[g] is an allophone of /γ/. /p, t, k/ are non-aspirates and are unreleased as finals. The sound notated as *tr* in Vietnamese is /ʈ/, tending to retroflex fricative. Final *-ch* is realized as /-ⁱk/, the *-k* being unreleased, tending to /ʔ/.

Vowels

i, ɪ, e, ɛ, ʊ, u, o, ɔ, aː, a, ʌ, ə

Correspondence between sound and symbol is weak; /z/, for example, is variously notated as *d*, *gi*, and *r*. The two most difficult vowel sounds are *ư* which is approximately /ʊ/ and *ơ* which is a wide, unrounded /ə/.

There are over 20 diphthongs and a dozen triphthongs, mostly containing /ʌ/.

Tones

There are six tones in the standard (northern) dialect:

1. mid-level: not marked in script, e.g. *tôi* 'I';
2. low falling: marked by grave accent, e.g. *rồi* (perfective marker);
3. high rising: marked by acute accent, e.g. *cá* 'fish'; *khách* 'guest';
4. low, rising after initial dip: marked by ̉: e.g. *của* (genitive particle);
5. high broken: marked by tilde, e.g. *sẽ* (future particle);
6. low broken: marked by subscript dot, e.g. *lại* 'to come'; *lực* 'strength'.

Tones 5 and 6 are glottalized.

Tone is further modulated by intonation patterns of an affective nature.

MORPHOLOGY AND SYNTAX

As in Chinese, there is no inflection of any kind; meaning in a sentence depends on the due ordering of its components. The Chinese distinction between 'full words' (*shící*) and 'empty words' (*xūcí*) can be usefully applied to Vietnamese: 'full words' include nouns, pronouns, verbs, and quantifiers; 'empty words' are particles, connectives, and interjections.

Noun

Nouns differ grammatically from other words in Vietnamese in that they take classifiers: most importantly, *cái* for inanimate objects, *con* for animates. Other classifiers include: *chiếc* (for vehicles, boats, etc.) *quyển* (books) *người* (people), *vị* (important people), etc. Use of the classifier is obligatory if a numeral is present (apart from *một* '1'). The order is numeral – classifier – nominal: e.g. *hai con cá* 'two fishes'; *năm mươi sáu quyển sách* '56 books'.

NUMBER

Plural markers are *nhiều, nhữ-ng, các,* preceding noun: e.g. *những tiệm tạp-hóa* 'bazaars'. The pronominal plural marker is *chúng*: e.g. *chúng tôi* 'we'.

POSSESSION

The marker is *của: e.g. máy ảnh của tôi* 'my camera'; *Ai là bạn của chúng tôi?* 'Who are our friends?' Simple apposition is valid where possession is self-evident or inalienable: e.g. *cho nhà tôi và các cháu* 'for (*cho*) my wife and children'.

A focusing or topicalizing marker is *thì*.

Adjective

The predicative adjective is a stative verb. Attributively, the adjective follows the noun: e.g. *một lá cờ đỏ* 'a red flag' (*đỏ* 'red'; *cơ* 'flag': *lá* is a classifier); *các nước cộng-sản* 'Communist countries' (*các* is a pluralizing marker).

COMPARATIVE

Made with *hơn*: e.g. *lớn hơn* 'bigger'; *nhỏ hơn* 'smaller'.

Pronoun

Tôi is the usual first person singular form: pl. *chúng-tôi* (excl.), *chúng ta* (incl.). For the second person there is a fairly wide choice of socio-linguistic options, many forms being kinship terms. Generally, *ông* is used to males, *bà* to older women, *cô* to younger women. More familiar modes of address are: *anh* (elder brother), *chị* (elder sister).

Standard third person forms are: *ông ấy* 'he', *cô ấy/bā ấy* 'she': e.g. *Ông ấy nói tiếng gì?* 'What language does he speak?' (*nói* 'to speak').

DEMONSTRATIVE PRONOUNS

này 'this, these'; *ấy* 'that, those': e.g. *hôm này* 'today'; *ba cái bàn này* 'these three tables'.

INTERROGATIVE PRONOUNS

ai 'who?'; (*cái*) *gì* 'what?'. Several interrogative particles serve to round off sentences, e.g. *phải không* is equivalent to French *n'est-ce pas?*: e.g. *Ông muốn mua sách phải không?* 'You want to buy books, don't you?' (*mua* 'buy'; *sách* 'book').

RELATIVE PRONOUN

mà may be used where the referent is specifically identified: e.g. *cái nhà trắng ấy* ***mà*** *ông đứ ng đay thấy...* 'that white (*trắng*) house (*nhà*) which you can see (*thấy*) from this position...'. Where the referent is indefinite, no relative particle is necessary: e.g. *tôi gặp một người bạn* **Ø** *đi...* 'I met (*gặp*) a friend (*bạn*) who was going...'; *tôi có em gái* **Ø** *đang dạy ở...* 'I have a sister who is teaching in...'.

Numerals

1–10: *một, hai, ba, bốn, năm, sáu, bảy, tám, chín, mười*. 11 *mười một*; 20 *hai mươi*; 100 *một trăm*.

Verb

A characteristic of all predicatives in Vietnamese is that they can be negated. The general negating particle is *không*, which precedes the verb: e.g. *tôi không có tiền* 'I have no money'. *đâu* is a final negative particle.

Verbs are divided into active (functional) verbs, stative verbs, and co-verbs. Stative verbs include adjectives. The copula is *là*, which is negated by *không phải là* 'it is not true that...': e.g. *tôi là Mỹ, chứ không phải là người Anh* 'I am American, not British' (*Mỹ* 'American', cf. Chinese *měi*).

The existential verb *ở* is used to mean 'to be located in': e.g. *Ông Nam ở bên Pháp* 'Mr Nam is/lives in France'.

Verbs are not marked in any way for person, number, tense, or aspect. Various particles are used to give a temporal fix: e.g.

đã: past-tense marker, preceding sense-verb, e.g. *chính-phủ Anh đã thay-đổi chính-sách* 'the English government has changed its policy (and will...)' (*chính-phủ* 'government'; *thay-đổi* 'to change');
chưa 'not yet', e.g. *ông ấy chưa đến* 'he has not come yet';
sẽ: future marker, e.g. *ông ấy sẽ đi Mỹ* 'he will be going to America';
sắp: imminent future, e.g. *Chúng tôi sắp đi Hanoi* 'We are just about to go to Hanoi';
rồi: perfective marker; this particle follows the sense-verb, e.g. *ông ấy đến rồi* 'he has already come' (Chinese: *le*);
đang: progressive marker, e.g. *Cô ấy đang học tiếng Việt* 'She is at present studying Vietnamese'.

PASSIVE

Expressed by *bị* or by *được*; *bị* (cf. Chinese *bèi*) retains the true passive sense, suggesting that the patient is being subjected to something he or she cannot help or does not particularly enjoy: e.g. *Ông aý bị vơ bỏ* 'His wife walked out on him.' Contrast: *Ông aý đư ộc thăng chức* 'He was promoted.'

MODAL VERBS

Example: *phải nên* 'should, must'; *đừng* (*nên*) 'should/must not'; *được* 'to be able to/be allowed to' (depending on word order): cf. *bịnh-nhan được ăn* 'the patient was allowed to eat'; *bịnh-nhan ăn được* 'the patient was able to eat'.

Word order

SVO is basic; OSV is common.

[1]Ban đầu trước hết có Ngôi Lời, và Ngôi Lời 1
ở cùng Đức Chúa Trời, mà Ngôi Lời là Đức
Chúa Trời. [2]Ban đầu trước hết ngôi ấy ở cùng 2
Đức Chúa Trời. [3]Mọi vật bởi ngôi ấy mà sanh 3
ra, và chẳng có sự gì đã làm nên, mà chẳng
phải bởi ngôi ấy. [4]Sự sống ở trong ngôi ấy, 4
mà sự sống ấy là sự sáng soi thiên-hạ. [5]Và sự 5
sáng ấy đã soi trong sự tối tăm, mà sự tối tăm
chẳng nhìn lấy sự sáng.

[6]Đức Chúa Trời đã sai một người tên là Jean. 6
[7]Ông ấy đến mà làm người làm chứng, để làm 7
chứng về sự sáng, hầu cho mọi người được tin
bởi ông ấy. [8]Ông ấy chẳng phải là sự sáng ấy, 8
song ông ấy đến để được làm chứng về sự sáng.

WELSH

INTRODUCTION

The Celtic people who colonized the British Isles in the second half of the first millennium BC were speakers of P-Celtic (see Celtic Languages in Campbell 1991). By the time the Romans arrived in Britain, this P-Celtic or Brythonic was the language of 'Britannia' = Brythonia, spoken from the Channel to the Clyde-Forth valley. The Anglo-Saxon invasions followed the Roman occupation, and by the seventh century AD the Celtic-speaking area was halved, with Anglo-Saxon established in a broadening swathe from the Tyne to the Channel coast as far west as Dorset, and Brythonic confined to a shrinking foothold in the western marches. Inherent in this process of break-up and tribal dispersion was the emergence of dialects – the earliest forms of Welsh and Cornish–Breton.

The Brythonic language spoken in what is now the Principality of Wales is usually periodized as follows:

Sixth to eighth centuries: primitive Welsh
Eighth to twelfth centuries: Old Welsh
Twelfth to fifteenth centuries: Middle Welsh
Fifteenth century to present day: Modern Welsh

The oldest text in what is recognizably the Welsh dialect of Brythonic is the *Gododdin*, a heoric lament for the Celtic warriors of the Kingdom of Edinburgh, who fell trying to take Catterick in Yorkshire from the Saxons. The poem has been attributed to Aneirin, one of the two celebrated Welsh bards of the sixth/seventh century. The other is Taliesin, whose figure was to blend in later Welsh literature with that of the mysterious and shadowy seer Merlin (< *Myrddin*).

From the eleventh century onwards Welsh poetry entered upon one of its greatest periods, that of bardic or courtly poetry. The bards – the *gogynfeirdd* – were attached to princely courts where they were organized in hierarchies, ranging from master singers to apprentices or disciples. Subject matter was prescribed and correlated with different grades within the hierarchy: thus, the production of eulogies was obligatory for a master bard, for whom, however, love was an unworthy and therefore taboo subject. A very high degree of technical skill in the handling of complicated prosodies was demanded, and, to ensure that such skills were duly cultivated and transmitted to posterity, a kind of competition – the eisteddfod – was introduced. The supreme master of the bardic style – Dafydd ap Gwilym (fourteenth century) – appeared, in fact, when the cult was well past its heyday; his influence both on the style and content of later Welsh poetry, and on the Welsh language itself, was enormous.

Two fourteenth-century manuscripts, *The White Book of Rhydderch* and *The Red Book of Hergest*, contain the text of the prose masterpiece of early Welsh literature – the *Mabinogion*, a collection of tales reflecting an interweaving of Celtic and Norman-French motifs and beliefs.

In 1547 the first Welsh printed book appeared. The importance of William Morgan's translation of the Bible (1588, revised 1620) for subsequent Welsh prose writing can hardly be overestimated.

Nineteenth-century Welsh literature was closely associated with religious revivals and movements. An outstanding figure is Daniel Owen, the Welsh Dickens.

The twentieth century has seen a remarkable revival in the use of Welsh for prose, poetry, and journalism; since the 1960s the language has enjoyed joint official status in the principality.

DIALECTS

There is a broad division into north and south dialects, which affects for example the pronunciation of certain vowels; the letter *u* is pronounced as /iː/ in South Wales, as /ɪ/, tending to /ʉ/, in North Wales.

SCRIPT

The Roman alphabet minus *k*, *q*, *v*, *x*, *z*. There are eight digraphs for specifically Welsh sounds: *dd* = /ð/, *ff* = /f/, *ng* = /ŋ/, *ll* = /ɬ/, *ph* = /f/, *rh* = /r̥/, *si* = /ʃ/, *th* = /θ/.

PHONOLOGY

Consonants

stops: p, b, t, d, k, g
fricatives: f, v, θ, ð, s, ʃ, x, h
nasals: m, n, ŋ
laterals and flaps: l, ɬ, r, r̥
semi-vowels: j, w

/ɬ/ and /r̥/ are voiceless; the corresponding voiced sounds are /l/ and /r/. The affricate /dʒ/ occurs in loan-words.

Vowels

short: ɪ, i, ɛ, a, ɔ, u
long: i, e, a, o, u
ə

In Welsh orthography, *w*/*ŵ* denotes /u, uː/: e.g. *cwm* 'valley' = /kum/; *y* denotes /ə/, /ɪ/, or /i/.

Diphthongs are rising (consonantal *j*/*w* + vowel) or falling (vowel + consonantal *j*/*w*): e.g. /ia, wo/ are rising; /ai, ey, aw/ are falling.

Stress

Stress is usually on the penultimate in polysyllables, but final stress is common.

Mutation

As in all Celtic languages, consonantal mutation plays a key role in Welsh phonology and morphology. The consonants which undergo mutation are the six stops: *p*, *b*, *t*, *d*, *c* = /k/, and *g*; also *m*, *ll*, and *rh*. Three kinds of mutation are distinguished:

(a) Soft mutation (lenition): /p, t, k/ mutate into their voiced correlatives /b, d, g/; /b, d, g/ become /f, ð, Ø/; *m* → *f*, *ll* → *l*, *rh* → *r*. This is by far the commonest form of mutation; Williams (1980) lists over 40 instances in which it occurs.

(b) Nasal mutation; this affects the stops only; the unvoiced become *mh*, *nh*, *ngh*, the voiced become *m*, *n*, *ng*.

(c) The spirant mutation; only the unvoiced stops are affected: → *ph*, *th*, *ch*.

For example, *pen* 'head': *ei **ben** e* 'his head' (lenition); *'y **mhen** i* 'my head' (nasal mutation); *ei **phen** hi* 'her head' (spirant mutation). Similarly, *gardd* 'garden': *ei **Ø**ardd e* 'his garden'; *'y **ngardd** i* 'my garden'; *ei **gardd** hi* 'her garden'.

MORPHOLOGY AND SYNTAX

Definite article

yr; *'r* after vowel or diphthong, *y* in interconsonantal position; e.g. *yr haf* 'summer'; *yr eira* 'the snow'; *Ble mae 'r tŷ?* 'Where is the house?'; *pen y rhiw* 'the top of the hill'.

The initial of a singular feminine noun mutates after the article: e.g. *pont* 'bridge': *y **bont*** 'the bridge'; *torth* 'loaf': *y **dorth*** 'the loaf'.

The presence or absence of mutation will help to determine gender, if the initial is a mutating consonant. There is no indefinite article.

Noun

Two genders and two numbers. Certain endings of derivative nouns are gender-related; e.g. *-edd*, *-did*, *-ad*, *-iant* are masculine, *-aeth*, *-as*, *-fa* are mostly feminine. In some cases, feminine counterparts may be formed from masculine nouns by the addition of *-es*: e.g. *brenin* 'king'; *brenhines* 'queen' (with stem modification); *llew* 'lion'; *llewes* 'lioness'.

NUMBER

There are several ways of forming the plural:

(a) by vowel change: *gafr* 'goat' – pl. *geifr*;
(b) by suffix: *afal* 'apple' – *afalau*; *esgob* 'bishop' – *esgobion*; *mor* 'sea' – *moroedd*; *llwynog* 'fox' – *llwynogod*;
(c) (a) and (b) combined: *mab* 'son' – *meibion*;
(d) singular ending dropped, with or without ablaut: *eisen* 'rib' – *ais*; *meipen* 'turnip' – *maip*;
(e) many irregular formations; some nouns have more than one plural.

Plural nouns do not show mutation; there are some exceptions to this rule.

POSSESSIVE

By juxtaposition: the noun denoting the possessor does not mutate: e.g. *mab **b**ardd* 'a poet's son'; *drws y **t**y* 'the door of the house'; *pen y **rh**iw* 'the top of the hill'. As in the Semitic languages, the possessed noun does not take the article.

Adjective

Adjective follows noun and mutates after feminine singular. Many adjectives have plural forms, and may also be marked for feminine gender. In literary Welsh, concord between noun and adjective is normal (though a singular adjective may accompany a plural noun). In the colloquial, concord is very rare. Like nouns, adjectives may be pluralized (a) by vowel change; (b) by ending; (c) by a combination of (a) and (b): e.g. *marw* 'dead': pl. *meirw* or *meirwon.*

Masculine adjectival forms with root *w* or *y* change these to *e*/*o* for feminine: e.g. *gwyn* 'white', fem. *gwen*; *hyll* 'ugly', fem. *hell.*

The adjective mutates after a feminine singular noun: e.g. *coch* 'red': *het **g**och* 'red hat'; *het **w**en* 'white hat'.

COMPARATIVE

The ending is *-ach*, which may induce vowel change: e.g. *cryf* 'strong' – comp. *cryfach*; *tlws* 'pretty' – comp. *tlysach*.

Suppletive comparatives: *da* 'good' – *gwell* (with an equative *cystal*, and a superlative *gorau*); *drwg* 'bad' – *gwaeth*.

If the adjective precedes the noun, the noun initial is lenited: *castell* 'castle' – *hen gastell* 'old castle'.

Pronoun

Standard literary forms:

			Independent	*Dependent*		
				Prefixed	*Infixed* (genitive)	*Affixed*
sing.	1		mi/fi	fy	'm	i/fi
	2		ti/di	dy	'th	di/ti
	3	masc.	ef	ei	'i/'w	ef(o)/fo/fe'hi
		fem.	hi			
pl.	1		ni	ein	'n	ni
	2		chwi	eich	'ch	chwi
	3		hwy(nt)	eu	'u/'w	hwy(nt)

The accusative forms are identical to the infixed (genitive) forms, except for *'w* in the third person, which is replaced by *'s*. Examples:

Prefixed: *fy mam* 'my mother'; *fy **mrawd*** 'my brother' (***brawd*** 'brother').
Infixed: *fy mrawd **a'm** chwaer* 'my brother and my sister'; ***o'th** gartref* 'from thy home'; ***i'm** gweld* 'to see me'.
Affixed: used after personal forms of verbs; e.g. the ending *-f* is sufficient to identify a verbal form as 1st person singular but *i/fi* may be added. Similarly, in the possessive formula: e.g. *'y mhen **i*** 'my head'.

In the colloquial language, the possessive forms are as follows:

		Singular	*Plural*
1		'yn...i	ein...ni
(2		dy... di)	eich...chi
3	masc.	ei + soft mutation ... e	eu...nhw
	fem.	ei + aspirate mutation ...hi	

Thus, with the noun *car* 'car': *ei **gar** e* 'his car'; *ei **char** hi* 'her car'.

In the colloquial language, the first person prefixed form *fy* is reduced to *'y*, plus nasal mutation; after a vowel, the *'y* may also be dropped: e.g. *'y **nghar** i* 'my car'; *Mae **Ø nghar** i...* 'My car is...'

The formula for transitive verb + objective pronominal complement is copula + sbj. + *yn* ('in') + possessive adjective in concord with object + sense-verb + personal marker in concord with object: e.g. *mae e yn **'yn** nabod **i*** 'he (*e*) is (*mae*) in (*yn*) knowing (*nabod*) me (*'yn...i*)'; *rydw i yn **ei** nabod **e*** 'I know him'. *See also* **Preposition**, below.

DEMONSTRATIVE PRONOUN/ADJECTIVE

The literary series: masc. *hwn*, fem. *hon*; pl. common: *hyn*.

Colloquial Welsh has three forms for differing degree of distance: *dyma* 'this' – *dyna* 'that' – *dacw* 'that (yonder)'. The formula article + noun (sing. or pl.) + *'ma* (< *yma* 'here') may also be used: e.g. *y stafell 'ma* 'this room'.

INTERROGATIVE PRONOUN

Literary and colloquial: *pwy* 'who?'; literary *pa* 'what?'; colloquial, *beth*.

The interrogative of the copula is formed by dropping initial *r*: e.g. *rydw* 'I am': **ø***ydw* 'am I?'

RELATIVE PRONOUN

In the literary language the relative particle is *a* + lenition for both subject and object. The negative counterpart is *na*(*d*). Since *a* is singular, the verb is third person singular: e.g. *Ef yw'r dyn* ***a dd****aeth* 'This is the man who came' (*daeth* = 'came'). This relative *a* is no longer used in spoken Welsh, but its attendant lenition remains where compatible. In older literary Welsh, the verb was in concord with the antecedent.

In the colloquial language, the relative construction is marked for tense: e.g. *y ferch* ***sy'n*** *canu* 'the girl who is singing'; *y car* ***oedd/fydd*** *o flaen y tŷ* 'the car that was/will be in front of the house', where *fydd*, the mutated form of *bydd*, indicates the former presence of *a*.

Numerals

1–10: *un*, *dau/dwy*, *tri/tair*, *pedwar/pedair*, *pump*, *chwech*, *saith*, *wyth*, *naw*, *deg*. *Dwy*, *tair*, and *pedair* are feminine forms. *Dau* and *dwy* take lenition: e.g. *dau fachgen* 'two boys' (***b****achgen* 'boy'). *Tri* (but not *tair*) takes aspiration: e.g. *tri* ***ch****ae* 'three fields' (***c****ae* 'field').

From 20 upwards, there is a choice between the decimal and the vigesimal systems: 11 *un deg un* (*un ar ddeg*); 12 *un deg dau* (*deuddeg*); 20 *ugain* (vig.) or *dau ddeg* (dec.); 40 *deugain* (vig.) or *pedwar deg* (dec.); 100 *cant*.

Verb

In the literary language there are three moods (indicative, subjunctive, imperative); the indicative has four tenses (present, imperfect, preterite, and pluperfect), the subjunctive has a present and an imperfect. As an example of conjugation in the literary language, here is the paradigm of *canu* 'to sing':

	Present		*Imperfect*		*Preterite*	
	Singular	*Plural*	*Singular*	*Plural*	*Singular*	*Plural*
1	canaf	canwn	canwn	canem	cenais	canasom
2	ceni	cenwch	canit	canech	cenaist	canasoch
3	can	canant	canai	canent	canodd	canasant
Impersonal:	cenir		cenid		canwyd	

Subjunctive mood: present sing. *canwyf*, *cenych*, *cano*; pl. *canom*, *canoch*, *canont*; impersonal: *caner*. The imperfect subjunctive is the same as the imperfect indicative.

THE COLLOQUIAL VERBAL SYSTEM

Tenses are perfective or imperfective. Present affirmative: imperfective: the formula is copula + sbj. + *yn* + sense-verb (+ obj.); the verb does not mutate: e.g. *rydw i'n yfed coffi* 'I am drinking coffee'; *rydyn ni'n yfed coffi* 'we are drinking coffee'; *mae e'n darllen llyfr* 'he is reading a book'. Negative: the *r-* initial of the copula becomes *d*, and *ddim* follows the person marker: e.g. ***dydw** i ddim yn yfed coffi* 'I'm not drinking coffee'. Likewise, the *r-* initial becomes Ø for the interrogative: e.g. ***Ø**ydw i'n yfed coffi?* 'Am I drinking coffee?'

Past imperfect, affirmative: imperfective: the formula is: *roedd* + person marker + sbj. marker (if pronominal) + *yn* + sense-verb: e.g. *roedd-wn i* 'I was'; *roedd-en-ni* 'we were'; *roedd-en-ni yn gweithio* 'we were working'. Negative: *r-* → *d-*: e.g. ***d**oedd-wn i ddim yn gweithio* 'I wasn't working'. Interrogative: *r-* → Ø: e.g. ***Ø**oedd-wn i yn gweithio?* 'Was I working?'

Preterite affirmative: perfective: the formula is: *fe* + stem (with mutation) + personal ending + sbj. pronominal marker: e.g. *fe **w**eles i* 'I saw' (root ***g**weled* 'see'); *fe **b**rynodd hi* 'she bought' (root ***p**rynu* 'buy'). Negative: mutation of stem initial, if possible, + *ddim*: e.g. ***Dd**aeth e ddim i'r dre* 'He didn't come to town.'

Perfect affirmative: perfective: *wedi 'after' replaces yn* in present tense forms: e.g. *mae e wedi darllen* 'he's after reading' = 'he has read'. Negative: *dydy e ddim wedi dod* 'he hasn't come' (root *dod* 'come'; irregular).

Future affirmative: imperfective: the future tense of the verb *bod* 'to be' is *bydda*: preceded by the future marker *fe, bydda* becomes *fydda*: e.g. *fe fydda i* 'I shall be': *fe fydda i'n chwarae* 'I'll be playing'; *fe fyddwn ni'n chwarae* 'we'll be playing'. Negative: ***Ø** fydda i ddim yn chwarae* 'I shan't be playing'.

A perfective plural is made with *wedi* replacing *yn*.

The impersonal forms (see the *canu* paradigm above) are used in the literary language, when the agent of an action is not specifically expressed: e.g. *nid cenir yn i capel* 'it is not sung in the chapel' = 'there is no one singing...' (*nid*, in this example, is the literary negative marker).

Passive: the literary language has no passive construction. In the colloquial, *cael* 'to have', is used as an auxiliary: e.g. *Mae'r ffilm yn cael ei dangos* 'The film is being shown.'

Preposition

In the literary language, prepositions are (a) inflected for person when governing a pronoun, or (b) uninflected. Those in (a) are further sub-divided, with a suggestion of vowel harmony, into three sets: these are classified by first person singular affix: *-af*, *-of*, *-yf*. For example, with

> *ar* 'on': *arn**af*** 'on me', *arn**at*** 'on you', *arno/arni* 'on him/her';
> *o* 'from': *o.hon.**of*** 'from me', *o.hon.**ot*** 'from you';
> *er* 'for': *er**of*** 'for me', *erddo* 'for him', *er**om*** 'for us';
> *tros* 'over': *tros**of***, *tros**och*** 'over you (pl.)', *tros**tynt*** 'over them';
> *gan* 'with': *genn**yf*** 'with me'.

The personal deixis *may* be reinforced by addition of the personal markers: e.g. *arnaf fi*, *arnat ti*. This addition is obligatory in the colloquial language: e.g. *arna/arno **i*** 'on me'; *arno **fe*** 'on him'; *i **ni*** 'for us'; *ynoch **chi*** 'in you'; *ohonot **ti*** 'from you (sing.)'.

Word order

VSO is normal.

YN y dechreuad yr oedd y Gair,
a'r Gair oedd gyd â Duw, a
Duw oedd y Gair.
2 Hwn oedd yn y dechreuad gyd
â Duw.
3 Trwyddo ef y gwnaethpwyd
pob peth; ac hebddo ef ni wnaethpwyd dim a'r a wnaethpwyd.
4 Ynddo ef yr oedd bywyd; a'r
bywyd oedd oleuni dynion.
5 A'r goleuni sydd yn llewyrchu
yn y tywyllwch; a'r tywyllwch nid
oedd yn ei amgyffred.
6 ¶ Yr ydoedd gŵr wedi ei
anfon oddi wrth Dduw, a'i enw
Ioan.
7 Hwn a ddaeth yn dystiolaeth,
fel y tystiolaethai am y Goleuni,
fel y credai pawb trwyddo ef.
8 Nid efe oedd y Goleuni, eithr
efe a anfonasid fel y tystiolaethai
am y Goleuni.

WENLI

See **Chinese, Classical**.

YIDDISH

INTRODUCTION

Half-way through the first millennium of our era, Jewish immigrants began arriving in western Europe, and at once the bilingualism, or even trilingualism, that had been a characteristic feature of diaspora life since the Babylonian Exile, asserted itself in new surroundings. Judaeo-Latin was succeeded by Judaeo-Old French, based on a Frankish dialect, which forms the first *galut* (Hebrew *gālūṯ* 'exile') language in the West.

In this context, bilingualism operated on two planes. The Holy Language, the Hebrew of the Torah, remained the canonical written language of Jewish institutions, *vis-à-vis* the spoken Aramaic of daily life, which, in its turn, entered upon a symbiosis with the language of the host country. By the ninth and tenth centuries the Jews had moved on to the cities along the middle course of the Rhine, and the appropriation process was under way, this time as applied to Middle High German. In the transfer process, the phonological profile of Middle High German was somewhat modified, while the morphological structure was appropriated almost intact. Décsy (1973) describes Yiddish as a co-Sprache, a co-language of German. The earliest documents of the Judaeo-German language as spoken and written in Worms, Speyer, and Mainz, date from the eleventh and twelfth centuries.

Religious persecution in the late Middle Ages led first to an eastwards extension of Yiddish culture, subsequently to its near total transfer to eastern Europe, especially to Poland and Russia; and Yiddish began to assimilate a Slavonic element, which did little, however, to alter its essentially German nature. Large members of Jews settled throughout eastern Europe, spreading into Hungary, Romania, and Lithuania. Two or three hundred years later, faced with religious persecution and intolerance in the East, many Jews started out on the reverse migration to the West. But by then it was too late for Yiddish – particularly a slavicized Yiddish – to re-establish itself in western Europe. The ideas of the Aufklärung had been taken up by the Jewish Haskalah movement (Hebrew root *SXL*: *sāxal* 'to have understanding, insight') whose outstanding protagonist was Moses Mendelssohn, the prototype for Lessing's Nathan der Weise. As an exercise in cultural symbiosis, Mendelssohn translated the Pentateuch into German, using Hebrew script. Part of the price, however, for induction into the economic, political, and cultural mainstream of western Europe was the rejection of Yiddish in favour of Standard High German or other standard host language. Warnings from traditionalist circles that Haskalah spelled the destruction of Yiddish culture in western Europe were not idle. The Netherlands and north Germany became staging posts on the trek to America; those who felt they could integrate stayed. By the early twentieth century, western European Yiddish was virtually extinct, apart from a small enclave in Alsace, where it may still linger on.

In eastern Europe, Yiddish continued to thrive as the language of the *shtetl* or small-town culture. In 1908, at the Czernowitz Conference, it was agreed that Yiddish was *a* national Jewish language.

After the 1917 Revolution in Russia, Yiddish was accorded equal status with the other minority languages of the Soviet Union, and in 1934 the Ievrejskaja Autonomous Region – also known, after its principal town, as Birobidzhan – was established on the middle course of the Amur, close to Khabarovsk. This was supposed to be a 'Sovietisch Heimland' for Jews, with Yiddish as its official language. The experiment was not a great success; urbanized and educated Jews were not drawn to the Middle Amur.

In 1925 the Yiddish Scientific Institute was inaugurated in Berlin, with headquarters in Vilnius (moved subsequently to New York).

When the opportunity finally came for Jews to select a national language for the state of Israel, an updated Hebrew in its Sephardic version was the natural choice. As a co-language of German, Yiddish hardly stood a chance.

Estimates of the number of Yiddish speakers at the present time vary very considerably. Crystal (1988) gives a maximum total of 600,000. The 1970 USSR census lists 379,000 speakers of Yiddish out of a total Jewish population of just over 2 million. As for the USA, Décsy (1973) gives a figure of half a million, while other sources give the following statistics: USA 1 million, USSR slightly under 1 million, Israel 200,000. Finally Solomon Birnbaum (1979) estimates that a figure of 12 million Yiddish speakers before the First World War had been reduced by the 1980s to roughly half.

Eastern Yiddish literature centres round the 'classical triumvirate' of Mendele Mocher Sforim, Sholem Alejchem, and Yitzhak Leibush Peretz, chroniclers and visionaries of the *Shtetl* culture, of Jewish life in the Pale of Settlement (*čerta osedlost'i*, the Russian territory allotted to Jewish settlers). Sholem Ash and David Pinski were products of the Peretz circle. The translation of the Hebrew Bible into Yiddish by Yehoash should also be mentioned.

SCRIPT

Yiddish is written in the Hebrew character (*see* **Hebrew**), with many innovations due to (a) the use of a *scripta plena*, i.e. with certain consonantal signs doing duty for vowels, as inherited from the original *galut* languages; and (b) an imitation of German orthography, particularly widespread in the Haskalah period.

At present, several spelling systems are current. Steps towards a standardization are being taken at the Yiddish Scientific Institute in New York. The transliteration used here is based on Fal'kovič (in *Jazyki Narodov SSSR* 1966).

Some of the more important innovations are: 'aleph with qāmeṣ is generalized as /ɔ/, long or short; 'ayin represents /ɛ/; /ej/ is represented by double yodh, /aj/ by double yodh plus paṯaḥ, /oj/ by waw plus yodh; e.g.

דער מאן *der man*;

די פרוי *di froj*;

דאָס קינד *dos kind*;

beth represents /b/, i.e. the voiced stop only; the correlative fricative /v/ is represented by double waw; zayin + sin = /ʒ/; ṭeth + sin = /tʃ/; initial 'aleph before yodh, waw or a diphthong is silent.

PHONOLOGY

Consonants

stops: p, b, t, d, k, g
affricates: ts, tʃ, (dz, dʒ)
fricatives: f, v, s, z, ʃ, ʒ, x, h
nasals: m, n
lateral and flap: l, r
semi-vowel: j

The palatalized consonants /t′, d′, s′, z′, n′, l′/, the affricates /dz, dʒ/, and the fricative /ʒ/ occur under Slavonic influence. /n/ and /l/ are syllabic. Voiced consonants are not devoiced in final position.

Vowels

i, e, a, o, u

e = [ɛ]; o = [ɔ]. Diphthongs: /ej, aj, oj/

Stress

Stress tends to fall on the first syllable, thus often varying from a German original: e.g. *lébedik* 'alive' < *lebéndig*

MORPHOLOGY AND SYNTAX

Noun

The original gender of German nouns is largely retained, but there are exceptions, e.g. *di shif* (< Gm. *das Schiff*).

The indefinite article is *a*/*an* (invariable); the definite article is marked for gender: e.g. *der man* 'the man'; *di froj* 'the woman'; *dos kind* 'the child'. The plural definite article is *di*.

DECLENSION

The genitive marker *-s* is retained for proper nouns and nouns denoting people: e.g. *šolem-alejxems werk* 'the works of SA'. For the oblique case of inanimate and abstract nouns, the use of the preposition *fun* (< Gm. *von*) plus article is preferred: e.g. *fun der xoxme* 'of (about) wisdom'. The article changes to *des* for masculine/neuter genitive, to *der* for the feminine.

Certain kinship terms take *-n* in the accusative/dative, adding *-s* for the genitive: e.g. *zaidy* 'grandfather', obl. *zaidn*, gen. *zaidns*.

PLURAL

Typical endings are *-s*, *-is*, *-er*, *-(i)n*, *-im*; often with stem mutation in Semitic roots, the original or secondary umlaut in German words: e.g. *der xusn* 'bridegroom' – *di xasanim*; *der con* 'tooth' – *di cejner* (Gm. *Zahn* – *Zähne*); *dos hojz* 'house' – *di hajzer* (Gm. *Haus* – *Häuser*); *der fojgl* 'bird' – *di fejgl* (Gm. *Vogel* – *Vögel*); *der barg* 'mountain' – *di berg* (Gm. *Berg* – *Berge*).

Adjective

The adjective has strong and weak declensions with reduced endings. Birnbaum (1979) gives the following example: *Er vil koifn a groisn suud mit alte bajmer* 'He's going to buy a big garden with old trees' (*suud* < Russ. *sad* 'garden'). In the plural the adjectival endings are reduced to *-e*.

As predicate, the adjective seems to be inflected when reference is to stable, permanent qualities, and invariable for contingent and temporary states, for example: cf. *er iz a gezunter* 'he is a healthy man', *zi iz a gezunte* 'she is a healthy person'; contrasted with *er iz gezunt* 'he's fine (today)'; *zi zajnen gezunt* 'they're fine'.

A remarkable innovation in word order occurs where an adverb modifies an adjective: e.g. *zaier a hojexer bojm* = Gm. *ein sehr hoher Baum* 'a very high tree'.

Pronoun

The personal pronominal grid is a replica of the German, with certain innovations, e.g. first person plural *mir* (< Gm. *wir*); second person plural oblique *ajx* (< *euch*); third person plural *zaj* (< *sie*); first person plural oblique *undz* (< *uns*).

It is noteworthy that the reflexive pronoun *zix* (< Gm. *sich*) has been generalized to refer to all three persons: e.g. *ix vaš zix* 'I wash myself'.

POSSESSIVE PRONOUNS

The pronoun may show concord or take *-s*, and is followed by the indefinite article in, e.g. *majner/majns a bruder* 'a brother of mine'; *majn bruder* 'my brother'. In the plural, only the form *majne brider* is possible.

DEMONSTRATIVE PRONOUNS

The definite article is used.

INTERROGATIVE PRONOUNS

vejer 'who?'; *vos* 'what?'. A yes–no question is introduced by the particle *či* (Polish *czy*).

RELATIVE PRONOUN

vos, e.g. *der man, vos zict bajm tiš* 'the man who is sitting at the table'. Note here, in contrast to German word order, the verb is not in final position.

Numerals

As in German, with adjusted spellings: 1–10: *(a)ejns*, *cvej*, *draj*, *fir*, *finf*, *zeks*, *zibn*, *axt*, *najn*, *cen*; 11 *elf*; 12 *zvelf*; 13 *drajcen*; 20 *cvancik*; 40 *fercik*; 100 *hundert*.

Verb

The Yiddish verb has an inflected present tense, composite general and frequentative past tenses, a composite future, an imperative mood, participial forms, and an infinitive. The composite forms are made with the auxiliaries *hobn* 'to have', *zajn* 'to be', *veln* 'to want to'.

SPECIMEN PARADIGM

hern 'to hear':

	Singular	*Plural*
1	ix her	mir hern
2	du herst	ir hert
3	er, zi, es hert	zi hern

Past general: *ix hob gehert*: The present tense of *hobn* used in this tense is: sing. 1 *hob*, 2 *host*, 3 *hot*; pl. 1 *hobn*, 2 *hot*, 3 *hobn*.

Past frequentative: *ix pleg hern* (Gm. *pflegen* 'to be in the habit of').

Future: e.g. *ix vel hern*, *du velst hern*.

Past participle: *gehert*; gerundive *herndik*.

Imperative mood: sing. *her*; pl. *hert*.

Verbs of motion are conjugated, as in German, with *zajn*; the present tense is: sing. 1 *bin*, 2 *bist*, 3 *iz*; pl. 1 *zajnen*, 2 *zajt*, 3 *zajnen*.

German stems such as *darfen* (< *dürfen*), *weln* (< *wollen*), *zoln* (< *sollen*), *megn* (< *mögen*), etc. have not been levelled; i.e. they follow German in not taking *-t* in the third person singular: *vil*, *darf*, *zol*, etc.

German ablaut series (strong verbs) are reflected in many past participles: e.g. *visn* 'know' – *gev**u**st*; *veln* 'want to' – *gev**o**lt*; *brengen* 'bring' – *gebr**acht***.

As in German, directional prefixes are frequently used: e.g.

fanander	fanander.nemen 'to take apart' (< Gm. voneinander)
mit	mit.filen 'to sympathize with' (< mit)
(a)hin	(a)hin.ton 'to put (there)' (< hin)
anider	anider.lejgn 'to place, put down' (< nieder)
arum	arum.nemen 'to embrace' (< herum)
curik	curik.gejn 'to go back' (< zurück)
arejn	arejn.gejn 'to go in' (< herein)

NEGATION

The particle of negation is *nit/ništ*. Double negatives are used: e.g. *kain menč vajst es ništ* 'no one knows it'.

Prepositions

Both Hebrew and German roots are used: e.g. Hebrew *veroš* 'headed by'; *mixuc* 'outside, out of'. German: *kegniber* (< *gegenüber*) 'opposite'; *cvišn* (< *zwischen*) 'between, among'; *on* (< *ohne*) 'without'; *onštat* (< *anstatt*) 'instead of'.

The prepositions take the dative case, i.e. are followed by the *dem/der* form of the article, with no distinction between motion towards/rest in a place: e.g. *oyf der erd* 'on (the) earth'; *leibn dem bojm* 'beside the tree'; *in der grojser štuut* 'in(to) the big town'.

Article and preposition may fuse: e.g. *inym jam* 'in(to) the sea' (*jam* 'sea'; Hebrew noun). The preposition *fun* (< Gm. *von*) 'of, from', combines with the postposition *veijgn* to denote 'on account of, for': e.g. *fun der zixerkejt veign* 'for (in the interests of) security'.

Semitic roots are not always formally stable in Yiddish usage: e.g. the triliteral *MLX* is stable in *MejLeX* 'emperor', pl. *MeLoXim*, and in *MeLuXe* 'empire'; but *X* > *K* in *MaLKe* 'queen' (cf. Hebrew *MaLXah* /malka/).

Word order

SVO order is adhered to in composite tenses, where German has the non-finite part of the verb following the object; e.g. *ix vel im hajnt šrajbn a briv* = *ich will ihm heute einen Brief schreiben* 'I shall write him a letter today'.

YORUBA

INTRODUCTION

Yoruba belongs to the Kwa group of Niger-Congo languages, and is spoken by about 16 million people in Nigeria and in Dahomey. Standard Yoruba is a blend of two closely similar dialects, Ọyọ and Lagos. There are many other dialectal forms.

Yoruba was one of the earliest west African languages to be codified in the shape of a written grammar and a vocabulary (1843–9), and the credit for this goes to Samuel Crowther, a Yoruba who was sold as a slave in 1821, freed by the British, baptised and ordained to serve as a missionary in the Yoruba country. In 1859 a Yoruba news-sheet began to appear; in 1900 a complete translation of the Bible, initiated and, in part, carried out by Crowther, was published. Original Yoruba writing in both prose and verse dates from the 1920s, when literacy in Yoruba was spreading rapidly. The period 1945–60 produced the four very popular novels by Daniel Fagunwa, and since the 1950s there has been a steady flow of fiction, drama, and verse. Mention should also be made of the Yoruba folk-opera, a genre primarily associated with religious festivals but one which readily lends itself to social criticism – e.g. in the satirical plays of Hubert Ogunde. The fertility of the Yoruba literary scene is matched by the keen critical interest taken by Yoruba scholars in both traditional and modern writing. Albert Gérard (1981) speaks of a stupendous growth in what he calls 'native scholarship'.

SCRIPT

Romanization with diacritics: tone marks (acute, grave) and subscript dot to distinguish open *ẹ* and *ọ*, and the palato-alveolar fricative *ṣ*.

PHONOLOGY

Consonants

stops: b, d, t, g, k; + two labio-velars: kp, gb (non-tense)
affricates: ʤ (ǰ)
fricatives: f, s, ʃ, h
nasals: m, n, ŋ
lateral and flap: l, r
semi-vowels: j, w

/kp/ is notated as *p*.

Vowels

i, e, ɛ, a, ɔ, o, u

/ɛ/ and /ɔ/ are notated as ẹ, ọ.

/e/ and /o/ are not nasalized; all the others are, and nasalization is phonemic. Long vowels are written double: e.g. *déédéé* 'exactly'.

Tones

There are three stative tones – high, mid, and low level – with portamento glides between tones; a low tone following a high tone, has a pronounced downward glide. Stress is evenly distributed on all syllables. Tone is phonemic.

MORPHOLOGY AND SYNTAX

Noun

Yoruba has no grammatical gender, no class system of nouns, and no articles. Nouns share certain formal characteristics, e.g. they are never monosyllabic, and usually have an initial vowel which is never a high tone. Natural gender is distinguished lexically: e.g. *ọmọkọnrin* 'son', *ọmọbinrin* 'daughter'. The plural is not specifically marked: context decides. The word *àwọn* may be used to suggest a plurality of individuals, i.e. not a collective: e.g. *àwọn ọkùnrin* 'the men'.

POSSESSION

Possession is expressed positionally, the possessed object preceding the possessor. This is the normal order for referent plus attribute; cf. *apa òkè Afrika* 'the mountainous (*òkè*) part (*apa*) of Africa'; *ọgbà ọlọ́pa* 'police (*ọlọ́pa*) station'; *aṣọ òyìnbó* 'European clothes'.

Adjective

From stative verbs like *kéré* 'to be small', *dára* 'to be good', an adjectival form can be made by prefixing a high-tone pre-echo of the first syllable: e.g. ***ké****keré* 'small'; ***dí****dára* 'good'. Reduplicative forms, not associated with any Yoruba verb, are also found; Rowlands (1969) calls these 'phonaesthetic' words: e.g. *wúruwùru* 'untidy', *ṣákiṣàki* 'rough'.

Normally, the adjective follows the noun, but may precede it for emphasis; and in many cases Yoruba prefers to use a relative clause; thus, 'a strong man' can be expressed as: *ọkùnrin alágbára, ọkùnrin t' ó lágbára, alágbára ọkùnrin.*

Pronoun

There are two sets of unstressed pronominal markers, subject and object; there is a specific set for use with the negator *ko*, and a nominal emphatic set:

		Subject	*Negative*	*Object*	*Emphatic*
singular	1	mo	ng	mi	èmi
	2	o	o	ọ/ẹ	ìwọ
	3	ó	Ø	repeat of verb vowel	òun
plural	1	a	a	wa	àwa
	2	ẹ	ẹ	nyin	ènyin
	3	nwọ́n	nwọn	wọn	àwọn

The possessive pronoun forms are: sing. 1 *mi*, 2 *rẹ*, *ẹ*, 3 *rẹ̀*, *ẹ̀*; pl. 1 *wa*, 2 *nyín*, 3 *wọn*: e.g. *ilé wa* 'our house'. These are phonotactically linked to the vocalic final of the preceding referent, which then shows tonal and quantitative change.

Examples of repeat of verb vowel in third person objective form: *ó rí **i*** 'he sees him'; *ó rà **a*** 'he buys it'; *mo gbé **e** wá fún **u*** 'I brought it for her' (*gbé...fún* 'lift...give' = 'bring'; *wá* 'come').

DEMONSTRATIVE PRONOUN

èyí 'this'; *nì/náà* 'that'.

INTERROGATIVE PRONOUN

tani/tali 'who?'; *kíni/kílí* 'what?'.

RELATIVE PRONOUN

tí is invariable, and requires pronominal recapitulation if the antecedent is a noun or pronoun: e.g. *ọmọkọnrin tí **ó** rí i* → *ọmọkọnrin t'ó rí i* 'the boy who saw him' (*tí* + *ó* → *t'ó*).

Numerals

The traditional system is based on the use of cowry shells as currency; and in one set of numerals the word *owó* 'money' is present, at least in residual form. There is a 'basic' set of numerals with low-tone initials, and a full set in which the basic numerals receive an initial *m-* and change initial low tone for high. The basic set is as follows: 1–10: *ení*, *èjì*, *ẹ̀ta*, *ẹ̀rin*, *àrún*, *èfà*, *èje*, *ẹ̀jọ*, *ẹ̀sán*, *ẹ̀wá*. From 10 to 20 the formula is 10 + 1, 2, 3, 4, 5: 20 – 4, 3, 2, 1; i.e. at 15, cowries began to be taken from the 20 pile instead of being added from the 10 pile. Similarly, 23 is *mẹ́tà.lé.lógún* (*ogún* '20'), 27 *mẹ́tà.dí.lọ́gbọ̀n* (*ọgbọ̀n* '30'). From 40 upwards the even decades are made by multiplying 20 by 2, 3, etc.; the odd decades involve subtraction from an even decade. In its higher reaches the system is of extreme complexity and has been largely abandoned in favour of the decimal system.

Verb

The Yoruba verb has a consonantal initial. There are accordingly many homonyms distinguished only by tone: *dé* 'to arrive, happen' – *dè* 'to await'; *rò* 'to think, relate' – *ro* 'to till the ground'.

Many compound verbs are formed from simple verb + noun: e.g. *dáhùn* 'to answer', formed from *dá* 'to do' + *ohùn* 'voice'. Transitive verbs formed in this way are separable: e.g. *rígbà* 'to get': *mo rí owó gbà* 'I got the money'.

As the Yoruba verb is marked for neither person nor number, the personal pronouns are required throughout.

TENSE SYSTEM

The only tenses in the strict sense are the present and the future. The present consists of the bare stem: e.g. *mo gbọ́* 'I hear/understand'. This tense is negated by *kò*: ***ng** kò gbọ́* 'I do not hear'. The future is made with the particle *yió* → *ó* + stem; the *ng* series of pronominal markers is used to denote subject: e.g. *ng ó wa lọ́là* 'I'll come tomorrow'. In the spoken language, this form is usually negated by the phrase (*ng*) *kò ní*(*ì*) '(I) do not have a ...'; *ng kò ní ṣe e* 'I shan't do it'.

ASPECT

The imperfective aspect is marked by prefixed *ń-/ḿ-*; negated by *ko/ki*: e.g. *nwọ́n ńjó* 'they are playing'; *ó ńṣiṣẹ́* 'he is working'. The perfective, with reference to both past and future, is made with *ti*: e.g. *mo ti ṣe gbogbo iṣẹ́* 'I have done all the work'. A present perfect (i.e. action begun in the past and still going on) is made by combining the two aspectual markers: e.g. *mo ti ńṣiṣẹ́ lati àárọ̀* 'I've been working since morning'.

The presence of mood in Yoruba is a disputed point.

As in Chinese, many verbs require a supporting directional verb, e.g. *wá* 'come' – *mú...wá, gbé...wá*: both mean 'to bring', literally 'take...come', 'lift...come'.

Prepositions

Prepositions are primary or derived.

Word order

SVO.

LI àtetekọṣe li Ọrọ wà, Ọrọ si wà
pẹlu Ọlọrun, Ọlọrun si li Ọrọ na.
2 On na li o wà li àtetekọṣe pẹlu
Ọlọrun.
3 Nipasẹ̀ rẹ̀ li a ti da ohun gbogbo;
lẹhin rẹ̀ a ko si da ohun kan ninu ohun
ti a da.
4 Ninu rẹ̀ ni ìye wà; ìye na si ni
imọle araiye.
5 Imọlẹ na si nmọlẹ ninu òkunkun;
òkunkun na kò si bori rẹ̀.
6 ¶ Ọkọnrin kan wà ti a rán lati
ọdọ Ọlọrun wá, orukọ ẹniti njẹ
Johannu.
7 On na li a si rán fun ẹri, ki o le ṣe
ẹlẹri fun imọlẹ na, ki gbogbo enia ki o
le gbagbọ nipasẹ rẹ̀.
8 On kì iṣe Imọlẹ na, ṣugbọn a rán
a wá lati ṣe ẹlẹri fun Imọlẹ na.

ZULU

INTRODUCTION

Zulu belongs to the South-Eastern group of Bantu languages (the Nguni group). It is spoken in Natal (into which the Zulu kingdom was incorporated in 1897) and in Transvaal, with some spread into Zimbabwe, Malawi, and Tanzania. Four main dialects are distinguished: Kwabe, Lala, Ndebele, and Nguni. The latter is characteristic of Malawi and Tanzania; Ndebele ('Matabele') is found in the Transvaal and Zimbabwe. Zulu in its original forms is spoken today by about 3½ million people.

The original Zulu homelands seem to have been in the neighbourhood of what is now Tanzania. The Zulu presence in South Africa dates from about the fourteenth century AD. A Zulu independent kingdom was recognized in 1832.

A translation of the Bible into Zulu appeared in 1883. In 1901 the Ohlange Institute – the first native educational institution in South Africa – was founded by John Dube, a Zulu from Natal, who also produced the first native African newspaper, the *Ilanga lase Natal* ('The Natal Sun') from 1903 onwards. Dube is also the author of the first Zulu novel: *Insila ka Chaka* (1933). He was followed by R. Dhlomo, who wrote several novels in Zulu dealing with the rise and fall of Zulu power in the nineteenth century, e.g. *u-Dingane* (1936), *u-Shaka* (1937), *u-Cetshwayo* (1952). The poet Benedict Vilakazi (1906–47) should also be mentioned (*Inkondlo kaZulu* 'Zulu Songs' 1935). There is a rich Zulu folklore.

SCRIPT

A Roman alphabet was first provided for Zulu in the 1830s. To begin with, morphological formants – suffixes, class markers, etc. – were written separately from the roots modified by them, a practice which was later abandoned. The Roman script now in use has the 26 letters of the English alphabet plus *ɓ*, which notates the implosive labial stop. Seventeen digraphs and 1 trigraph represent the 12 clicks, the aspirate stops, and the specifically Zulu laterals. The palatalized dentals are notated as *ch* and *j*; thus *ch* = /ty/ or /thy/. The circumflex is used to notate a falling tone.

The capital initial of a personal name is preceded by the lower-case marker for Class 1a nouns (*see* **Noun**, below); cf. the novels by R. Dhlomo, listed above: *u-Dingane*, etc.

PHONOLOGY

Consonants

stops: k
tense: ḳ, p, t
aspirates: kh, ph, th (k′, p′, t′)
voiced: g, b, d
implosive: ɓ
affricates: tʃ, ʤ
fricatives: f, s, ʃ, h, v, z, hh
nasals: m, n, ɲ
lateral and flap: (r), l, hl, dl
semi-vowels: w, j

/hl/ and /dl/ are specific to Zulu.

The bifocal clicks are an importation into Zulu from the Bushman–Hottentot substratum:

	Labio-velar	*Dental-velar*	*Lateral-velar*
Surd	c	q	x
Aspirate	ch	qh	xh
Voiced	gc	gq	gx
Nasal	nc	nq	nx

Preceding the semi-vowel /w/, labials become homorganic palatals: e.g.

ph > tʃh   p > tʃh   ɓ > tʃh   mp > nytʃ etc.

Thus, in Cetshwayo /tʃw/: *-hlatshwa* 'to be transfixed' /tʃw/

Vowels

i, e, ɛ, a, ɔ, o, u

Vowel sandhi takes place at junctures accompanied by both progressive and retrogressive assimilation. Cf. *u* + *i* > *wi*: *izulu*: locative ***ezulwini*** 'in the sky'. In unstressed position, vowels tend to be reduced.

Stress

Normally on penultimate; the stressed vowel is long: cf. *-ɓo:na/-ɓoni:sa/ -ɓonaka:la*. That is, in agglutinative build-up, stress moves progressively to the right.

Secondary stress may fall on penultimate minus 2, minus 4, and so on. In certain particles and demonstratives the stress falls exceptionally on the final.

Tone

Doke (1950) recognizes even and glide tones in Zulu.

MORPHOLOGY AND SYNTAX

Zulu has thirteen noun classes (*see* **Bantu Languages**). They are:

Class 1: the prefix is *um(u)*: nouns denoting human beings: ***umuntu*** 'man', ***umfazi*** 'woman'.
Class 1a: *u-*: proper names, kinship terms, totemic animals: ***ubaba*** 'my/our father', ***u-Shaka*** 'Shaka'.
Class 2: *aba-abe-*: plurals of nouns in class 1: ***abantu*** 'men', ***abafazi*** 'women', ***abelusi*** 'herdsmen'.
Class 2a: *o-*: plurals of nouns in class 1a: ***o-Zashuke*** 'Zashuke and his people'.
Class 3: *um(u)-* (as in class 1): heterogeneous, trees, rivers: ***umuthi*** 'tree', ***ummfula*** 'river'.
Class 4: *imi-*: plurals of class 3 nouns: ***imithi*** 'trees', ***imimfula*** 'rivers'.
Class 5: *ili-/i-*: heterogeneous, parts of body: ***izwe*** 'country', ***izulu*** 'sky'.
Class 6: *ama-*: plurals of class 5 nouns: ***amazwe*** 'countries', ***amazulu*** 'skies'.
Class 7: *isi-*: heterogeneous; in many Bantu languages, class 7 is 'the class of things': ***isihlalo*** 'chair'. The class includes many nouns which have no plural: ***isizulu*** 'the Zulu language'.
Class 8: *izi-*: plurals of such class 7 nouns as have plurals: ***izihlalo*** 'chairs'.
Class 9: *im-/iny-/in-*, depending on initial of root: animals, etc. ***inkabi*** 'bull', ***inyoka*** 'snake'.
Class 10: *izim-/iziny-/izin-*: plurals of class 9: ***izinkabi*** 'bulls', ***izinyoni*** 'birds'.
Class 11: *ulu-/u-*: extremely heterogeneous, includes many objects whose main characteristic is their length: ***umonya*** 'python', ***uthi*** 'club'.
Class 12: *ubu-/u-*: rare: abstract concepts without number: ***ubuntwana*** 'childhood'.
Class 13: *uku-/ukw-*: deverbatives: *-thanda* 'to love' – ***ukuthanda*** 'love'; ***uku.nga.thanda*** 'hate', (where *-nga-* is the verbal negative marker).

DERIVATORY NOUNS

For example, the formula class prefix + root + *-i* yields a noun denoting the agent of the verbal action: from *-hamba* 'to travel' ***um.hamba.i*** 'traveller'.

AUGMENTATIVE AND DIMINUTIVE

-kazi: *umuthikazi* 'big tree'; *-ana*: *imbuzi* 'goat', *imbuzana* 'kid'.

POSSESSION

The pronominal possessive markers for class 1 are: sing. 1 *-mi*, 2 *-ko*, 3 *-ke*; pl. 1 *-ithu*, 2 *-inu*, 3 *-bo*. For all other classes common third person forms indicating number are used. To these possessive markers, class concord markers are prefixed, e.g. for class 1 *wa-* (< *u-* + *-a-*), class 2 *ba*, class 3 *wa*, class 4 *ya*, and so on. Cf. *umfazi wenkosi* 'the chief's wife', where *wenkosi* < *wa.inkosi*; *inja yami* 'my dog' (*ya-* is the concord marker for class 9 to which *inja* 'dog' belongs); *indoda nezinja zayo* 'the man and his dogs' (literally 'the man with-dogs his-them') *nezinja* < *na.izinja*, *za-* is the concord marker for class 10. Cf. *indoda nenja yayo* 'the man and his dog' (*indoda* 'man' in these examples is class 9). When a noun defines another noun, it takes a defining prefix consisting of the formant *a-*, plus the class marker of the noun defined: e.g. *umuntu oliɓutho* 'man of war', where *o-* represents the fusion of the *a-* formant with the class marker *u-*: literally, 'man – who-warrior'.

A vocative is made by discarding the initial vowel: nkosi! 'Chief!' (< inkosi).

Adjective

The attributive adjective follows the noun. Zulu has a small number of adjectival roots, e.g. *-ɓi* 'bad', *-dala* 'old', *-ningi* 'many', *-ncane* 'small'. Most adjectives are formed by prefixing *a-* plus class marker to a nominal base: *umuntu* ***omkulu*** 'big man' (where *om-* < *a* + *um*). Cf. *izinkabi ezimbi* 'bad oxen'; *abantu abakulu* 'big people'; *izinkabi ezinkulu* 'big oxen'.

Pronoun

There are four promoninal series:

1. Absolute/independent based on *-na*, modulated by class prefix; person and number are marked in class 1/2 only:

Class 1 (sing.)	*Class 2 (pl.)*
1 mina	1 thina
2 wena	2 nina
3 yena	3 bona

Class 3 has a common form: *wona*; its plural counterpart (class 4) is *yona*. Similarly for class 5/6: *lona/wona*.

2. The demonstrative pronouns are based on *la-*. For referents close at hand *la-* takes the class marker, or a reflex thereof; more distant referents are designated by *la-* + final *-o*; very remote but still visible referents by final *-ya*. Thus, for class 2 the series is *laba – labo – labaya*; for class 8 *lezi – lezo – leziya*: e.g. *Ngiɓona labo.bantu boba.ɓili* 'I see (*-ɓona*) both (*-ɓili* 'two') of these people (*-bantu*) some distance away (*labo*).'

3. Enumerative pronouns indicating number, again with class markers: e.g. *sonke si.fikile* 'we all arrived' (*-nke* 'all': *sonke* is the first person plural class 2; *fika* 'to arrive' perfect *fikile*; *si-* is the first person plural subject concord in class 1).

4. Possessive pronouns: *see* **Possession**, above.

INTERROGATIVE PRONOUN

Ubani 'who?', pl. *obani* is a class 1a noun. 'What?' can be expressed by *-njani*, used as a copula: *Indlu yako injani?* 'What is your house (like)?'

RELATIVE PRONOUN

The relative concord markers are largely identical to those used for adjectival concord; e.g. class 1 sing. *o-*, class 2 *aba-*:

> umuntu **o**.hamba.yo 'the man who travels'
> mina **o**.qotho = mina engi-qotho 'I who am honest'
> umuntu engi mɓona yo 'the person whom I see'

The prefix *yi-/i-*, *ngu-/u-* combines with the absolute pronominal series and the verbal markers for person and number (*see* **Verb**, below) to express the copula: *si.yi.bona* 'we are those who ...', where *si-* is the class 1 first person plural verbal marker, and *bona* is the class 2 third person plural absolute pronoun.

Numerals

1 to 5 inclusive take adjectival concord; they are: *nye, -ɓili, -thathu, -ne, -hlanu*: e.g. *abantu aba.ɓili* 'two people'.

6 to 10 inclusive are nouns with relative concord: *isithupha* ('the thumb' 6), *isikombisa* (7), *isi.shiya.galo.m.ɓili* ('leaving two fingers (*galo-*) behind' 8), *isi.shiya.galo.lunye* ('leaving one finger behind' 9), *ishumi* (10).

From 11 onwards, the numerals are compounds: *ishumi na.nye, ishumi na.m.ɓili*, etc.: e.g. *abantu aba.**yi**.sithupha* 'six people'.

Verb

A Zulu verb is a complex consisting typically of (a) subject concord marker, (b) tense marker, (c) object marker, (d) sense-verb root: e.g. *u.ya.gi.thanda* 'he loves it', where *u-* is the class 1 third person subject concord marker, *-ya-* is the present tense marker, *-yi-* is the class 9 object concord marker, and *-thanda* is the root of the verb meaning 'to love'. Cf. *i.ya.m.thanda* 'it loves him', where *i-* is the class 9 subject, and *-m-* the class 1 object marker.

Class 1 alone distinguishes person and number in the verbal prefix system:

	Subject concord		Object concord	
	Singular	*Plural*	*Singular*	*Plural*
1	ngi-	si-	-ngi-	-si-
2	u-	ni-	-ku-	-ni-
3	u-	ba- (class 2)	-m-	-ba- (class 2)

In each of the other 12 classes, one marker, singular or plural depending on class, functions as subject, and one as object. Thus, class 9 has common subject marker *i-*, common object marker *-yi-*; the correlative plural class 10 markers are *zi-* for subject and *-zi-* for object: *si.ya.zi.ɓona* 'we see them'. Similarly, *Si.ya.yi.fuma yona* 'We really do want it', where *yona*, the class 9 absolute pronoun, recapitulates and reinforces *-yi-*. In general, the object markers are very close to, if not identical with, the subject markers.

VERBAL BASES

Zulu has a few monosyllabic bases, e.g. *-dla* 'eat', *-pha* 'give'; but the majority of bases are bisyllabic: *-thanda* 'to love', *-ɓona* 'to see'.

DERIVED STEMS

Passive: The formant is *-wa*: *-ɓonwa* 'to be seen'; *-dliwa* 'be said'. Preceding *-wa*, a labial becomes an unvoiced affricate: *-bopa* 'to tie, bind', *-boshwa* 'be tied'.

Causative: In *-isa*: *-ɓonisa* 'to cause to be seen' i.e. 'to show', *-yisa* 'to send' (from *-ya* 'to go'): *Wa.ngi.ɓonisa mina inyoni* 'He showed me the bird' (where *mina* recapitulates *-ngi-*; *inyoni* 'bird').

Benefactive/terminative: The formant is *-ela*: *hlala* 'to wait', *hlalela* 'to wait for someone'; *Ngi.ya.m.leth.ela umfundisi incwadi* 'I am bringing (*-leth*) the teacher (*umfundisi*) a book (*incwadi*)'. The *-m-* infix refers to *umfundisi* 'teacher'.

Reciprocal: *-ana*: e.g. *-ɓonana* 'to see each other'.

MOOD AND TENSE

Imperative, indicative, optative, stative, potential, and intentional moods are present in Zulu, along with perfective and imperfective aspects. Tense (past, general present, punctual present, imminent future, and distant future) is marked by specific infix following subject marker.

Infinitive (or neutral mode) has *uku-* prefix (cf. noun class 13): *uku.thanda* 'to love'. This form is negated by *-nga-*, with final *-a* > *-i*: *uku.nga.thand.i* 'not to love'.

Indicative mood: The tense markers are illustrated with the root *-hamba* 'to travel': (first person singular) past: *nga.hamba*, neg. *angihambanga*; general present: *ngi.hamba*, neg. *angihambi*; punctual present: *ngi.ya.hamba*, neg. *angihambi*; immediate future: *ngi.za.uku.hamba*, neg. *angizi.ukuhamba* (where *ukuhamba* is the neutral mode); distant future: *ngi.ya.ukuhamba*, neg. *angiyi.kuhamba.*

Other moods are formed in similar fashion: thus, *nga.ngi.nga.hamba* 'I could have travelled' (potential), *nga.ngi.ya.ukuhamba* 'I'd have travelled if ...' (intentional), *nga.hamba* 'I wanted to travel' (optative). The optative forms follow such particles as *ukuba, ukuthi* 'so that ...'. This mood has a future tense. For all of these forms there are correlative negative forms: e.g. *ngi.nga.hambi* 'that I don't want to travel'.

Aspect: a perfective marker is *-ile/-e*: *ngi.za.ukulel.e* 'I'll soon have fallen asleep' (immediate future indicative plus perfective *-e*; *-lel(e)-* is the perfective stem of *lala* 'to sleep').

Particles

These are mainly locational, derived from nouns in the locative case: *pezu kwa-* 'on', *pantsi kwa-* 'under', *emva kwa-* 'after, behind': e.g. *Wa.hlala pezu kwendla* 'He sat on (the roof of) the hut', where *kwendlu* < *kwa indlu*; *pambi kwami* 'in front of me'.

Ideophones

Zulu has hundreds of ideophones – indeclinable words overlapping in part with the interjection. Many represent, at least to the Zulu ear, sounds occurring in nature, warfare, hunting, eating and drinking, etc. Total or partial reduplication is also used to suggest a process or action. Ideophones range from one to five syllables: e.g. *ɓoco* (cracking sound as club strikes skull), *nhlo* (= *xhokolozi*) (jabbing the eyes). A vowel, especially a final vowel, is often overlong: *twi::*, the sound of ripping cloth; *nka::* 'gawping'. Stress in ideophones is free, allowing emotional enhancement. The ideophone may be construed as a verbal base, and conjugated accordingly.

Word order

As shown above, the conceptual order within the verbal complex is SOV(O). On proposition level, SVO is basic: *Izinkomo zi.ya.yi.donsa inqola* 'The cattle (*izinkomo*) are-pulling-it (*zi.ya.yi.donsa*) the wagon (*inqola*)'; *Ngi.yi.ɓulele ingwe isilwane* 'I killed (*-ɓul-* with perfective termination *-(l)ele*) it, the animal (*isilwane*) the leopard (*ingwe*)'. VS occurs in impersonal construction: *Ku.khona izinja emazweni onke* 'There are (*ku.khona*) dogs (*izinja*) in-countries (*amazwe* 'country' with locative circumfix *e- ... eni* > *emazweni*) all-of-them (*onke*).'

EKUQALENI kwakukona uLizwi; uLizwi wab'ekona noNkulu-
nkulu; uLizwi uNkulunkulu. 2Yena wab'ekona ekuqaleni no-
Nkulunkulu. 3Konke kw'enziwa ng'uye; ngapandhle kwake
akwenziwanga'luto olwenziwayo. 4Amandhla aba pakati kwake;
lawo'mandhla aba ukukanya kwabantu. 5Ukukanya kukanya
ebumnyameni; kepa ubumnyama abukuqondanga.

6Kwavela umuntu etunywa ng'uNkulunkulu, ibizo lake ng'u-
Johane. 7Lowo w'eza ngokuqinisa, ukuba aqinise ngokukanya,
kona abantu bonke beya'utemba ngaye. 8Yena wab'engesiko
ukukanya loko; w'eza kambe ukuba aqinise ngako ukukanya.

APPENDIX OF SCRIPTS

ARABIC

THE ALPHABET

Transliteration	*Final*	*Medial*	*Initial*	*Alone*	*Name*
ā	ـا			ا	ʔalif
b	ـب	ـبـ	بـ	ب	bāʔ
t	ـت	ـتـ	تـ	ت	tāʔ
θ	ـث	ـثـ	ثـ	ث	θaʔ
ǰ	ـج	ـجـ	جـ	ج	ǰīm
ħ	ـح	ـحـ	حـ	ح	ħāʔ
x	ـخ	ـخـ	خـ	خ	xāʔ
d	ـد			د	dāl
ð	ـذ			ذ	ðāl
r	ـر			ر	rāʔ
z	ـز			ز	zāy
s	ـس	ـسـ	سـ	س	sīn
š	ـش	ـشـ	شـ	ش	šīn
ṣ	ـص	ـصـ	صـ	ص	ṣād
ḍ	ـض	ـضـ	ضـ	ض	ḍād
ṭ	ـط	ـطـ	طـ	ط	ṭāʔ
ð	ـظ	ـظـ	ظـ	ظ	ðaʔ
ʕ	ـع	ـعـ	عـ	ع	ʕayn
ɣ	ـغ	ـغـ	غـ	غ	ɣayn
f	ـف	ـفـ	فـ	ف	fāʔ
q	ـق	ـقـ	قـ	ق	qāf
k	ـك	ـكـ	كـ	ك	kāf
l	ـل	ـلـ	لـ	ل	lām

Transliteration	*Final*	*Medial*	*Initial*	*Alone*	*Name*
m	ـم	ـمـ	مـ	م	mīm
n	ـن	ـنـ	نـ	ن	nūn
h	ـه	ـهـ	هـ	ه	hāʔ
w	ـو			و	wāw
y	ـى	ـيـ	يـ	ى	yāʔ

The vowel diacritics are: *fatħa* ´ /a/; *ḍamma* ʼ /u/; *kasra* ˏ /i/; and *sukūn* ° for zero (no vowel). Long vowels are represented thus: /ā/ by *ʔalif* or *ʔalif madda* (initially), آ ; /ī/ by *yā* ـى; and /ū/ by *wāw*.

Source: Kaye, A.S. (1987) 'Arabic', in B. Comrie (ed.) *The World's Major Languages*, London, Routledge.

ARMENIAN

THE ALPHABET

Capitals	*Lower case*	*Transliteration*	*Cursive*
Ա	ա	*a*	Ա ա
Բ	բ	*b*	Բ բ
Գ	գ	*g*	Գ գ
Դ	դ	*d*	Դ դ
Ե	ե	*e*	Ե ե
Զ	զ	*z*	Զ զ
Է	է	*ē*	Է է
Ը	ը	*ə*	Ը ը
Թ	թ	*t'*	Թ թ
Ժ	ժ	*ž*	Ժ ժ
Ի	ի	*i*	Ի ի
Լ	լ	*l*	Լ լ
Խ	խ	*x*	Խ խ
Ծ	ծ	*c*	Ծ ծ
Կ	կ	*k*	Կ կ
Հ	հ	*h*	Հ հ
Ձ	ձ	*j*	Ձ ձ
Ղ	ղ	*ł*	Ղ ղ
Ճ	ճ	*č*	Ճ ճ
Մ	մ	*m*	Մ մ
Յ	յ	*y*	Յ յ
Ն	ն	*n*	Ն ն
Շ	շ	*š*	Շ շ
Ո	ո	*o*	Ո ո
Չ	չ	*č'*	Չ չ
Պ	պ	*p*	Պ պ
Ջ	ջ	*ǰ*	Ջ ջ

Capitals	*Lower case*	*Transliteration*	*Cursive*	
Ռ	ռ	*ṙ*	Ռ	ռ
Ս	ս	*s*	Ս	ս
Վ	վ	*v*	Վ	վ
Տ	տ	*t*	Տ	տ
Ր	ր	*r*	Ր	ր
Ց	ց	*c‘*	Ց	ց
Ւ	ւ	*w*	Ւ	ւ
Փ	փ	*p'*	Փ	փ
Ք	ք	*k'*	Ք	ք

Source: Adapted from Minassian, M. (1976) *Manuel pratique d'Arménien ancien,* Paris, Librairie Klincksieck.

BENGALI

CONSONANTS

ক *k*	খ *k*	গ *g*	ঘ *gh*	ঙ *ṅ*		
চ *c*	ছ *ch*	জ *j*	ঝ *jh*	ঞ *ñ*		
ট *ṭ*	ঠ *ṭh*	ড *ḍ*	ঢ *ḍh*	ণ *ṇ*		
ত *t*	থ *th*	দ *d*	ধ *dh*	ন *n*		
প *p*	ফ *ph*	ব *b*	ভ *bh*	ম *m*		
য় *y*	র *r*	ল *l*	ব *v*			
শ *ś*	ষ *ṣ*	স *s*	হ *h*	য *z*	ড় *ṛ*	ঢ় *ṛh*

VOWELS

(a) independent:

অ *a*	আ *ā*	ই *i*	ঈ *ī*	উ *u*	ঊ *ū*	ঋ *ri*
এ *ē*	ঐ *ai*	ও *ō*	ঔ *au*	অং *aṅ*	অঃ *a'*	

(b) in combination with /k/:

কা *kā*	কি *ki*	কী *kī*	কু *ku*	কূ *kū*
কৃ *kri*	কে *kē*	কৈ *kai*	কো *kō*	কৌ *kau*

Conjunct graphs are formed as in Devanagari by juxtaposition, amalgamation or subscript. Cancellation of inherent base vowel (/ɔ/ in Bengali) and nasalization are indicated as in Devanagari.

NUMERALS

১	২	৩	৪	৫	৬	৭	৮	৯	০
1	2	3	4	5	6	7	8	9	0

BERBER

The Tifinagh alphabet (*tifinagh* is a plural form: 'letters'; the singular is *tafineq*), as used for certain forms of Berber, is here reproduced, in amended form, from Hanoteau 1896.

The short vowel, notated as *a*, *i*, *u*, is not normally written.

THE ALPHABET

Tar′erit	·	*a, i, u*	Iel	‖	*l*
Ieb	◫ ⴱ	*b*	Iem	⊐	*m*
Iet	+	*t*	Ien	ǀ	*n*
Ied	⊓ ∧ ⊔	*d*	Iek	·:	*k*
Iej	ⵊ	*j*	Iak′	···	*q*
Iez	#	*z*	Ier′	:	*ɣ*
Iez′	ⵥ ⵥ	*z′*	Iech	ⵛ	*ʃ*
Ier	□ ○	*r*	Iah	⋮	*h*
Ies	⊡ ⊙	*s*	Iadh	∃	*ḍ, ṭ*
Ieg	.!. ·ï·	*g*	Iakh	∷	*χ*
Ieg′	⋈	*g′*	Iaou	:	*ū*
Ief	ⵅ ⵊⵊ	*f*	Iéy	≤	*ī*

COMBINED LETTERS

Iebt	+⊟	*bt*	Ielt	⊢⊣	*lt*
Iezt	⌗	*zt*	Iemt	+∃	*mt*
Iert	⊞	*rt*	Ient	†	*nt*
Iest	+⊡	*st*	Iecht	+ⵛ	*ʃt*
Iegt	ǂ	*gt*	Ienk	·İ·	*nk*
Ieg′t	+⋈	*g′t*			

Source: Hanoteau, A. (1890) *La Langue Tamachek*, Algiers

BUGINESE

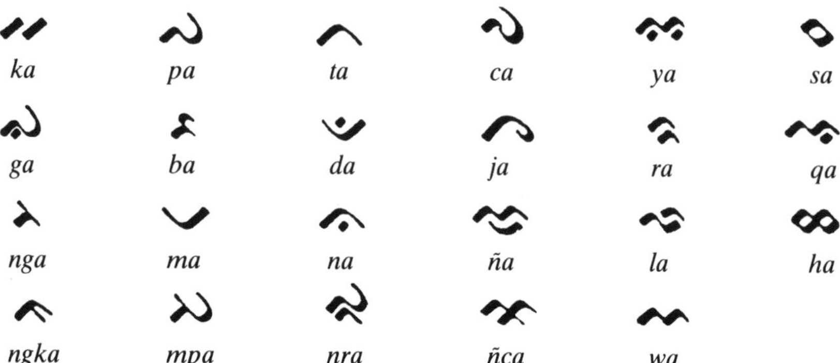

The letter *qa* is used to notate initial ’a/a. There is no separate letter for the glottal stop. *qa* is also used as a base for the diacritics notating the other vowels i, u, e, o, ə, in initial position.

The diacritics are here shown in combination with the consonant *la* :

In Macassarese, which does not have the vowel /ə/, the diacritic is used to indicate that the vowel so marked is followed by a nasal consonant.

BURMESE

CONSONANTS

က	ခ	ဂ	ဃ	င		
ka	*kha*	*ga*	*ga*	*nga*		
စ	ဆ	ဇ	ဈ	ည		
sa	*sa*	*za*	*za*	*nya*		
ဋ	ဌ	ဍ	ဎ	ဏ		
ta	*tha*	*da*	*da*	*na*		
တ	ထ	ဒ	ဓ	န		
ta	*tha*	*da*	*da*	*na*		
ပ	ဖ	ဗ	ဘ	မ		
pa	*pha*	*ba*	*ba*	*ma*		
ယ	ရ	လ	ဝ	သ	ဟ	ဠ
ya	*ya(ra)*	*la*	*wa*	*sa*	*ha*	*la*

VOWELS

(a) independent:

အ	အာ	အား	ဣ(အိ)	ဤ(အီ)	ဥ(အု)
a	*ā*	*ā*	*i*	*ī*	*u*

ဦ(အူ)	အေ့	ဧ(အေ)	အဲ	ဪ(အော်)
ū	*e*	*ē*	*ē*	*ō*

ဩ(အော)	အို	အံ
ō	*ō*	*an*

(b) as used with bearer consonant, represented by ◌ :

◌ *-a* ◌ာ *-ā* ◌ား *-ā* ◌ိ *-i* ◌ီ *-ī*

◌ု (◌ု) *-u* ◌ူ (◌ူ *-ū* ◌ေ့ *-e* ◌ေ *-ē*

◌ဲ *-ē* ◌ော် *-ō* ◌ော *-ō* ◌ို *-ō*

Vowel length is correlated with tone as follows:

(a) short vowels with first tone: e.g. using *ka*:

က *ka,* ကိ *ki,* ကု *ku,* ကေ့ *ke,* ကဲ့ *ke,* ကော့ *ko,* ကို့ *ko.*

(b) long vowels with second tone (long low):

ကာ *kā,* ကီ *kī,* ကူ *kū,* ကေ *kē,* ကယ် *kē,* ကော် *kō,* ကို *kō.*

(c) vowels marked by ◌း, ◌ဲ, ◌ော with third tone (long high):

ကား *kā,* ကီး *kī,* ကူး *kū,* ကေး *kē,* ကဲ *kē,* ကော *kō,* ကိုး *kō.*

CONJUNCT CONSONANTS

As a general rule, conjunct consonants retain their primary form and are written as subscripts, but four – ya, ra, wa, ha – have specific forms, shown here as applied to *ma*:

မ *ma*, မျ *mya*, မြ *mya*, မွ *mwa*, မှ *hma*, မျွ *mywa*, မျှ *hmya*, မြှ *hmya*, မွှ *hmwa*, မြို *myo*.

NUMERALS

၁	၂	၃	၄	၅	၆	၇	၈	၉	၀
1	2	3	4	5	6	7	8	9	0

CAMBODIAN

CONSONANTAL PHONEMES

As in the Devanagari writing system from which it is derived, the Cambodian script arranges the consonantal phonemes of the language in five parallel series: velar, palatal, (retroflex), dental and labial; with a sixth group comprising the sibilants and liquids.

ក	kaa	*k*	ដ	daa	*d*	ប	baa	*b*
ខ	khaa	*kh*	ឋ (ឋ)	thaa	*th*	ផ	phaa	*ph*
គ	kɔɔ	*k*	ឌ	dɔɔ	*d*	ព	pɔɔ	*p*
ឃ	khɔɔ	*kh*	ឍ	thɔɔ	*th*	ភ	phɔɔ	*ph*
ង	ŋɔɔ	*ŋ*	ណ	naa	*n*	ម	mɔɔ	*m*
ច	caa	*c*	ត	taa	*t*	យ	yɔɔ	*y*
ឆ	chaa	*ch*	ថ	thaa	*th*	រ	rɔɔ	*r*
ជ	cɔɔ	*c*	ទ	tɔɔ	*t*	ល	lɔɔ	*l*
ឈ	chɔɔ	*ch*	ធ	thɔɔ	*th*	វ	wɔɔ	*w*
ញ	ñɔɔ	*ñ*	ន	nɔɔ	*n*	ស	saa	*s*
						ហ	haa	*h*
						ឡ	laa	*l*
						អ	qaa	*q*

Note that, as there are no retroflex sounds in Cambodian, the *daa* series, which represents the original *ṭa* series of Devanagari, coincides in point of articulation with the *taa* series of dental consonants.

The phonemic values shown in the above inventory are those of consonants preceding vowels. As first components in clusters, and as finals, the aspirate consonants are reduced to their non-aspirate values: /kh/ > /k/, etc. Consonants with inherent *aa* belong to the First Series, those with inherent *ɔɔ* to the Second. For a note on the two series of consonants, *see* **Cambodian** pp. 255–6.

VOWEL SYMBOLS

Each vowel symbol has either of two values, depending on whether it follows a First or Second Series consonant: thus

Symbol	Name	Values 1st Series	2nd Series
–	sraq qaa	*aa*	*ɔɔ*
–ា	sraq qaa	*aa*	*iə*
–ិ	sraq qeq	*e*	*i*
–ី	sraq qəy	*əy*	*ii*
–ឹ	sraq qəq	*ə*	*ɨ*
–ឺ	sraq qəɨ	*əɨ*	*ɨɨ*
–ុ	sraq qoq	*o*	*u*
–ូ	sraq qou	*ou*	*uu*
–ួ	sraq quə	*uə*	*uə*
េ–ី	sraq qaə	*aə*	*əə*
េ–ឿ	sraq qɨə	*ɨə*	*ɨə*
េ–ៀ	sraq qiə	*iə*	*iə*

Symbol	Name	Values 1st Series	2nd Series
េ–	sraq qei	*ei*	*ee*
ែ–	sraq qae	*ae*	*ɛɛ*
ៃ–	sraq qay	*ay*	*ɨy*
េ–ា	sraq qao	*ao*	*oo*
េ–ៅ	sraq qaw	*aw*	*ɨw*
–ុំ	sraq qom	*om*	*um*
–ំ	sraq qam	*am*	*um*[1]
–ាំ	sraq qam	*am*	*oăm*[1]
–ះ	sraq qah	*ah*	*eăh*

Some examples from the velar, palatal and dental series:

1st Series			2nd Series		
Symbol	Example		Symbol	Example	
ក	ក	/kaa/ neck	គ	គ	/kɔɔ/ mute
ខ	ខាត់	/khat/ to polish	ឃ	ឃាត់	/khoǝ̆t/ to prevent
ច	ចា	/caa/ to inscribe	ជ	ជា	/ciǝ/ be
ឆ	ឆោង	chaoŋ/ interval	ឈ	ឈោង	/chooŋ/ to reach out
ញ៉	ញ៉ាំ	/ñam/ to eat	ញ	ញាំ	/ñoǝ̆m/ meat salad
ដ	ដុន	/don/ elephant command	ឌ	ឌុន	/dun/alike
ត	តា	/taa/ old man	ទ	ទា	/tiǝ/ duck

As will be seen from the consonant chart, certain Cambodian phonemes are not paired, e.g. Second Series *mɔɔ* has no First Series correlative **maa*. Where it is necessary to produce such a correlative, a consonant can be 'converted' by diacritic: ″converts a Second Class into a First Class consonant:

e.g. ម៉ = m*aa*.

Similarly, ៊ converts a First Class into a Second Class consonant.

Conjunct consonants are frequent in Cambodian. The second component is written as a subscript, which is usually a reduced version of the base form. There are, however, several irregularities.

CHINESE

For a general note on the Chinese script and its history, see **Chinese** (Archaic, Classical, Modern Standard) pp. 306–19. Here, the nature of the script, and one standard method of looking up characters in a Chinese dictionary, are illustrated by means of (a) eight full-form characters in bold printed form; (b) the same eight characters in standard written form (not in the so-called 'grass script', *căozi*, which is a highly personalized cursive); (c) stroke order and number; (d) the radical system; (e) search procedure in a Chinese dictionary.

(a) Eight full-form printed characters:

(b) The same characters in standard written form:

(c) Stroke order is illustrated here by means of four of the above characters:

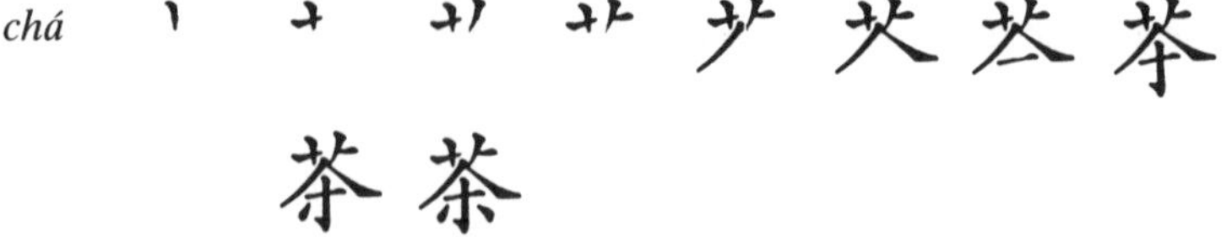

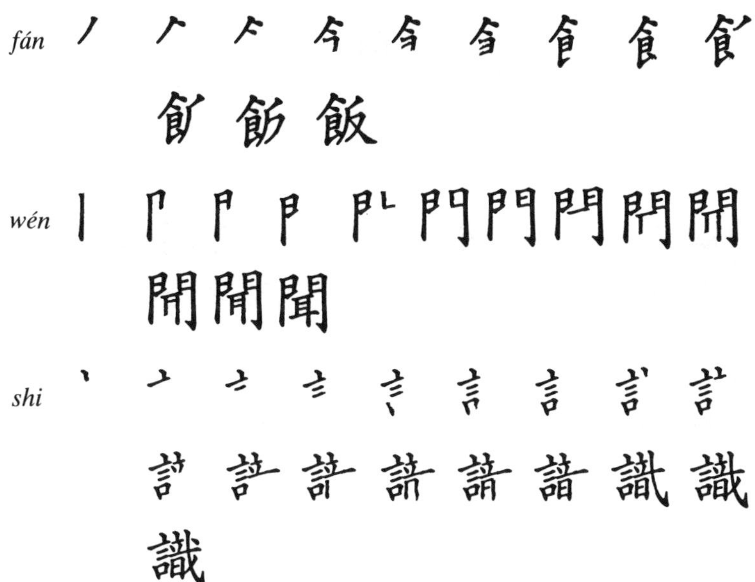

It will be seen that by writing a Chinese character in the correct *order*, we arrive at the correct *number* of component strokes. The number of components underlies both the radical system and the indexing of characters in a Chinese dictionary.

(d) The radical system is now set out (pp. 1512–13) in traditional form, as a table of 214 radicals, beginning with 1 stroke and rising to 17. This is reproduced from Matthews' Chinese–English Dictionary. The radical table is followed by a specific example – the list of all characters having the 7-stroke radical 言 (pp. 1514–15).

1 stroke

1 一
2 丨
3 丶
4 丿
5 乙
6 亅

2 strokes

7 二
8 亠
9 人,亻
10 儿
11 入
12 八
13 冂
14 冖
15 冫
16 几
17 凵

36 夕
37 大
38 女
39 子
40 宀
41 寸
42 小
43 尢,兀,尣
44 尸
45 屮
46 山
47 巛,川,巜
48 工
49 己
50 巾
51 干
52 幺
53 广
54 廴
55 廾
56 弋

74 月
75 木
76 欠
77 止
78 歹,歺
79 殳
80 毋
81 比
82 毛
83 氏
84 气
85 水,氵
86 火,灬
87 爪,爫
88 父
89 爻
90 爿
91 片
92 牙

110 矛
111 矢
112 石
113 示,礻
114 禸
115 禾
116 穴
117 立

6 strokes

118 竹,⺮
119 米
120 糸,糹
121 缶
122 网,罒,罓
123 羊
124 羽
125 老
126 而

7 strokes

147 見
148 角
149 言
150 谷
151 豆
152 豕
153 豸
154 貝
155 赤
156 走
157 足
158 身
159 車
160 辛
161 辰
162 辵,辶
163 邑,阝
164 酉
165 釆

181 頁
182 風
183 飛
184 食
185 首
186 香

10 strokes

187 馬
188 骨
189 高
190 髟
191 鬥
192 鬯
193 鬲
194 鬼

11 strokes

195 魚

14 strokes

209 鼻
210 齊

15 strokes

211 齒

16 strokes

212 龍
213 龜

17 strokes

214 龠

The 214 Radicals

18 刀, 刂
19 力
20 勹
21 匕
22 匚
23 匸
24 十
25 卜
26 卩, 㔾
27 厂
28 厶
29 又

3 strokes

30 口
31 囗
32 土
33 士
34 夂
35 夊

57 弓
58 彐, 彑
59 彡
60 彳

4 strokes

61 心, 忄, 㣺
62 戈
63 戶
64 手, 扌
65 支
66 攴, 攵
67 文
68 斗
69 斤
70 方
71 无, 旡
72 日
73 曰

93 牛, 牜
94 犬, 犭

5 strokes

95 玄
96 玉, 王, 王
97 瓜
98 瓦
99 甘
100 生
101 用
102 田
103 疋
104 疒
105 癶
106 白
107 皮
108 皿
109 目, 罒

127 耒
128 耳
129 聿
130 肉, 月
131 臣
132 自
133 至
134 臼
135 舌
136 舛
137 舟
138 艮
139 色
140 艸, 艹
141 虍
142 虫
143 血
144 行
145 衣, 衤
146 西

166 里

8 strokes

167 金
168 長, 镸
169 門
170 阜, 阝
171 隶
172 隹
173 雨 ⻗
174 青
175 非

9 strokes

176 面
177 革
178 韋
179 韭
180 音

196 鳥
197 鹵
198 鹿
199 麥
200 麻

12 strokes

201 黃
202 黍
203 黑
204 黹

13 strokes

205 黽
206 鼎
207 鼓
208 鼠

148 角
149 言
150 谷

覽 3804
覿 6230
觀 3575

148

角 1174

2-4

觔 1059
觖 1699

5

觜 6856
觝 6194
觚 3473

149

言 7334

2

訂 6386
訇 2391
計 456
訃 1954

3

託 6461
訑 2943
訖 567
訏 2820
訊 2750
訒 3117
訶 5732
訝 7220
訢 2728
訪 1816
設 5711

5

詛 6818
詿 1343
詐 82
詅 4055
診 306
詋 1303
詷 2817
詘 1622
詔 239

6

詵 2273
該 3191
詮 1672
詾 2813
詗 2923
誆 3599
詭 3626
詹 150
詬 3423
詰 783
註 3513
誇 3530
詫 108
詩 5783
誖 5004
誣 7165
誕 6051
誌 973
認 3113
誠 381
誡 628
誓 5803
誨 2338
誑 3602
誦 5567
誘 7538
誚 762
誩 1133

8

諕 2163
誾 7437
誰 5923
請 1172
誹 1833

9

諭 7641
諵 4621
諤 4795
諴 2667
諮 6923
諠 2874
諦 6208
諺 7374
諞 5251
諢 2369
諱 2357
諳 37
諷 1893

10

謙 885
講 645
謏 5476
謌 3364
謑 2428
謇 842
謝 2630
謅 5645
謗 4919
謖 5900
謦 1166
謬 4539
謹 1074
謨 4591
謼 2159

12

譊 4640
譔 1435
譏 416
識 5825
譈 6563
譖 323
譙 758
譌 4789
證 357
護 2190
譴 903

15

讃 877
讀 6521
讁 279

16

讄 4795
讌 7364
變 5245
讆 7091
讎 } 1333
讐 }

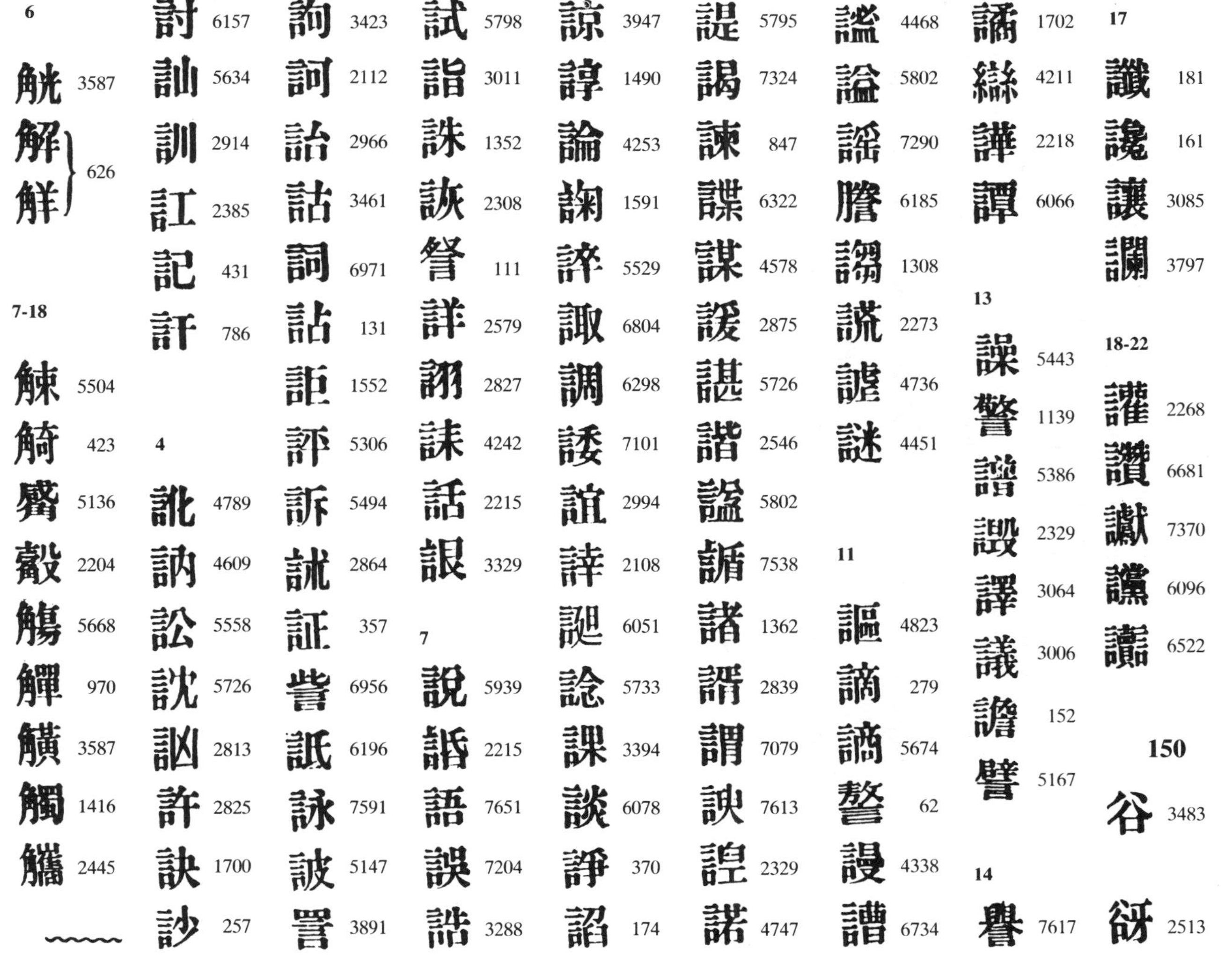

6

觥 3587
解 } 626
觧 }

7-18

觫 5504
觭 423
觱 5136
觳 2204
觴 5668
觶 970
觵 3587
觸 1416
觿 2445

~~~~~

討 6157
訕 5634
訓 2914
訌 2385
記 431
訐 786

4

訛 4789
訥 4609
訟 5558
訦 5726
訩 2813
許 2825
訣 1700
訬 257

詗 3423
訶 2112
詁 2966
詁 3461
詞 6971
詀 131
詎 1552
評 5306
訴 5494
訹 2864
証 357
訾 6956
詆 6196
詠 7591
詖 5147
詈 3891

試 5798
詣 3011
誅 1352
詼 2308
詧 111
詳 2579
詡 2827
誄 4242
話 2215
詪 3329

7

說 5939
[illegible] 2215
語 7651
誤 7204
誥 3288

諒 3947
諄 1490
論 4253
諊 1591
誶 5529
諏 6804
調 6298
諉 7101
誼 2994
[illegible] 2108
[illegible] 6051
諗 5733
課 3394
談 6078
諍 370
諂 174

諟 5795
謁 7324
諫 847
諜 6322
謀 4578
諼 2875
諶 5726
諧 2546
諡 5802
[illegible] 7538
諸 1362
諝 2839
謂 7079
諛 7613
諻 2329
諾 4747

謐 4468
謚 5802
謠 7290
謄 6185
謅 1308
謊 2273
謔 4736
謎 4451

11

謳 4823
謫 279
謪 5674
謷 62
謾 4338
[illegible] 6734

譎 1702
䜌 4211
譁 2218
譚 6066

13

譟 5443
警 1139
譖 5386
譭 2329
譯 3064
議 3006
譫 152
譬 5167

14

譽 7617

17

讖 181
讒 161
讓 3085
讕 3797

18-22

讙 2268
讚 6681
讞 7370
讜 6096
讟 6522

150

谷 3483
谺 2513
~~~~~

(e) To sum up: looking up characters in a Chinese dictionary involves the following steps.

1. Identify the radical; with experience this becomes automatic. The correct radical is usually obvious, but there are many cases where the radical is obscure, or where there is a choice.
2. Count the strokes remaining in the character after the radical has been subtracted.
3. Find the radical in the index of characters. All characters having this radical are listed in order of number of strokes; inspection in correct section yields desired character.

As example, we take the character 識 having the 7-stroke radical 言 . After subtraction of radical 149, the character has 12 strokes. By inspection in the 12-stroke section of radical 149 we find 識 numbered 5825. Turning to 5825 in the body of the dictionary, we find the character with translation and many examples of usage.

CYRILLIC

THE ALPHABET

Printed		*Handwritten*		*Transliteration*
А	а	А	а	a
Б	б	Б	б	b
В	в	В	в	v
Г	г	Г	г	g
Д	д	Д	д	d
Е	е	Е	е	e
Ё	ё	Ё	ё	ë
Ж	ж	Ж	ж	ž
З	з	З	з	z
И	и	И	и	i
Й	й	Й	й	j
К	к	К	к	k
Л	л	Л	л	l
М	м	М	м	m
Н	н	Н	н	n
О	о	О	о	o
П	п	П	п	p
Р	р	Р	р	r
С	с	С	с	s
Т	т	Т	т	t
У	у	У	у	u
Ф	ф	Ф	ф	f
Х	х	Х	х	x
Ц	ц	Ц	ц	c
Ч	ч	Ч	ч	č
Ш	ш	Ш	ш	š
Щ	щ	Щ	щ	šč
	ъ		ъ	”
	ы		ы	y
	ь		ь	’
Э	э	Э	э	e
Ю	ю	Ю	ю	ju
Я	я	Я	я	ja

Source: Comrie, B. (1987) ‘Russian’, in B. Comrie (ed.) *The World’s Major Languages*, London, Routledge

DEVANĀGARĪ

VOWELS (SVARĀH)

अ	आ	इ	ई	उ	ऊ	
a	*ā*	*i*	*ī*	*u*	*ū*	
ऋ	ॠ	ऌ	ए	ऐ	ओ	औ
r̥	*r̥̄*	*l̥*	*e*	*ai*	*o*	*au*

CONSONANTS (VYAÑJANĀNI)

Stops (sparśāḥ)					*Semi-vowels (antaḥsthāḥ)*	*Spirants (ūṣmāṇaḥ)*	*Others*
क	ख	ग	घ	ङ		ह	:
k	*kh*	*g*	*gh*	*ṅ*		h	ḥ
च	छ	ज	झ	ञ	य	श	
c	*ch*	*j*	*jh*	*ñ*	y	ś	
ट	ठ	ड	ढ	ण	र	ष	ळ
ṭ	*ṭh*	*ḍ*	*ḍh*	*ṇ*	r	ṣ	ḷ
त	थ	द	ध	न	ल	स	
t	*th*	*d*	*dh*	*n*	l	s	
प	फ	ब	भ	म	व		
p	*ph*	*b*	*bh*	*m*	v		

Source: Cardona, G. (1987) 'Sanskrit' in B. Comrie (ed.) *The World's Major Languages*, London, Routledge.

EXAMPLES OF COMBINATIONS

का	काँ	कि	की	कु	कू	कृ
kā	*kām̐*	*ki*	*kī*	*ku*	*kū*	*kṛ*
कॄ	कॢ	क्त	क्र	क्ष	ज्ञ	त्र
kṝ	*kḷ*	*kta*	*kra*	*kṣa*	*jña*	*tra*
त्व	द्य	द्र	द्व	प्त	ब्द	र्क
tva	*dya*	*dra*	*dva*	*pta*	*bda*	*rka*
र्कं	श्च	श्र	श्व	स्त	स्य	स्र
rkaṁ	*śca*	*śra*	*śva*	*sta*	*sya*	*sra*
स्व	ह्म	ह्य	ह्र	ह्ल	ह्व	र्त्स्न्य
sva	*hma*	*hya*	*hra*	*hla*	*hva*	*rtsnya*

NUMERALS

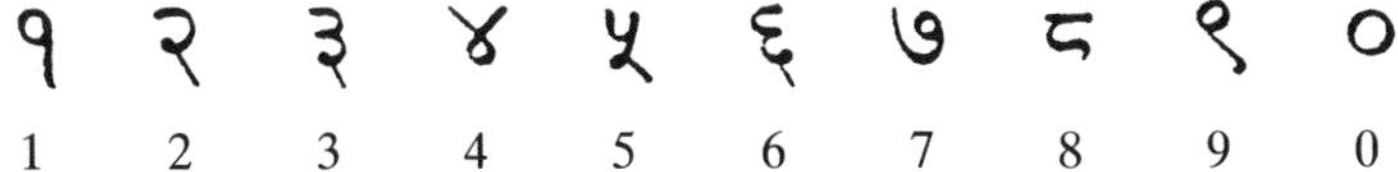

1 2 3 4 5 6 7 8 9 0

The following additional signs are important:

1. virāma: this is a slanting stroke drawn to the bottom right of a consonant to indicate cancellation of the inherent /a/: thus,

   तत् = *tat*

2. anusvāra: a dot over a consonant or vowel indicating nasalization:

   अं = *aṁ*, कं = *kaṁ*

3. pre- and post-consonantal r: r preceding a consonant is written as ॅ above the consonant; thus,

   र्म = *rma*, र्क = *rka*

   r following a consonant is written as a short stroke slanting to the left from the lower part of the consonant:

   क्र = *kra*, प्र = *pra*

These features are reflected more or less completely in all Indian and South-East Asian scripts based on Devanagari.

ETHIOPIC (AMHARIC)

THE SYLLABARY

	a		*ū*		*ī*		*ā*		*ē*		*e*		*ō*
ሀ	*ha*	ሁ	*hū*	ሂ	*hī*	ሃ	*hā*	ሄ	*hē*	ህ	*he*	ሆ	*hō*
ለ	*la*	ሉ	*lū*	ሊ	*lī*	ላ	*lā*	ሌ	*lē*	ል	*le*	ሎ	*lō*
ሐ	*ḥa*	ሑ	*ḥū*	ሒ	*ḥī*	ሓ	*ḥā*	ሔ	*ḥē*	ሕ	*ḥe*	ሖ	*ḥō*
መ	*ma*	ሙ	*mū*	ሚ	*mī*	ማ	*mā*	ሜ	*mē*	ም	*me*	ሞ	*mō*
ሠ	*ša*	ሡ	*šū*	ሢ	*šī*	ሣ	*šā*	ሤ	*šē*	ሥ	*še*	ሦ	*šō*
ረ	*ra*	ሩ	*rū*	ሪ	*rī*	ራ	*rā*	ሬ	*rē*	ር	*re*	ሮ	*rō*
ሰ	*sa*	ሱ	*sū*	ሲ	*sī*	ሳ	*sā*	ሴ	*sē*	ስ	*se*	ሶ	*sō*
ቀ	*qa*	ቁ	*qū*	ቂ	*qī*	ቃ	*qā*	ቄ	*qē*	ቅ	*qe*	ቆ	*qō*
በ	*ba*	ቡ	*bū*	ቢ	*bī*	ባ	*bā*	ቤ	*bē*	ብ	*be*	ቦ	*bō*
ተ	*ta*	ቱ	*tū*	ቲ	*tī*	ታ	*tā*	ቴ	*tē*	ት	*te*	ቶ	*tō*
ኀ	*ḫa*	ኁ	*ḫū*	ኂ	*ḫī*	ኃ	*ḫā*	ኄ	*ḫē*	ኅ	*ḫe*	ኆ	*ḫō*
ነ	*na*	ኑ	*nū*	ኒ	*nī*	ና	*nā’*	ኔ	*nē*	ን	*ne*	ኖ	*nō*
አ	*’a*	ኡ	*’ū*	ኢ	*’ī*	ኣ	*ā*	ኤ	*’ē*	እ	*’e*	ኦ	*’ō*
ከ	*ka*	ኩ	*kū*	ኪ	*kī*	ካ	*kā*	ኬ	*kē*	ክ	*ke*	ኮ	*kō*
ወ	*wa*	ዉ	*wū*	ዊ	*wī*	ዋ	*wā*	ዌ	*wē*	ው	*we*	ዎ	*wō*
ዐ	*ʿa*	ዑ	*ʿū*	ዒ	*ʿī*	ዓ	*ʿā*	ዔ	*ʿē*	ዕ	*ʿe*	ዖ	*ʿō*
ዘ	*za*	ዙ	*zū*	ዚ	*zī*	ዛ	*zā*	ዜ	*zē*	ዝ	*ze*	ዞ	*zō*
የ	*ja*	ዩ	*jū*	ዪ	*jī*	ያ	*jā*	ዬ	*jē*	ይ	*je*	ዮ	*jō*
ደ	*da*	ዱ	*dū*	ዲ	*dī*	ዳ	*dā*	ዴ	*dē*	ድ	*de*	ዶ	*dō*
ገ	*ga*	ጉ	*gū*	ጊ	*gī*	ጋ	*gā*	ጌ	*gē*	ግ	*ge*	ጎ	*gō*
ጠ	*ṭa*	ጡ	*ṭū*	ጢ	*ṭī*	ጣ	*ṭā*	ጤ	*ṭē*	ጥ	*ṭe*	ጦ	*ṭō*
ጰ	*p̣a*	ጱ	*p̣ū*	ጲ	*p̣ī*	ጳ	*p̣ā*	ጴ	*p̣ē*	ጵ	*p̣e*	ጶ	*p̣ō*
ጸ	*ṣa*	ጹ	*ṣū*	ጺ	*ṣī*	ጻ	*ṣā*	ጼ	*ṣē*	ጽ	*ṣe*	ጾ	*ṣō*
ፀ	*ḍa*	ፁ	*ḍū*	ፂ	*ḍī*	ፃ	*ḍā*	ፄ	*ḍē*	ፅ	*ḍe*	ፆ	*ḍō*
ፈ	*fa*	ፉ	*fū*	ፊ	*fī*	ፋ	*fā*	ፌ	*fē*	ፍ	*fe*	ፎ	*fō*
ፐ	*pa*	ፑ	*pū*	ፒ	*pī*	ፓ	*pā*	ፔ	*pē*	ፕ	*pe*	ፖ	*pō*

THE LABIALIZED VELAR SERIES

ኰ	*kua*	ኲ	*kuī*	ኵ	*kue*	ኳ	*kuā*	ኴ	*kuē*
ጐ	*gua*	ጒ	*guī*	ጕ	*gue*	ጓ	*guā*	ጔ	*guē*
ቈ	*qua*	ቊ	*quī*	ቍ	*que*	ቋ	*quā*	ቌ	*quē*
ኈ	*ḫua*	ኊ	*ḫuī*	ኍ	*ḫue*	ኋ	*ḫuā*	ኌ	*ḫuē*

GEORGIAN

Georgian is written in the Mkhedruli script, which had originally 40 letters. Seven of these are now obsolete, or very rarely used. The following 33 are in regular use.

THE ALPHABET

ა	*a*	რ	*r*
ბ	*b*	ს	*s*
გ	*g*	ტ	*ṭ*
დ	*d*	უ	*u*
ე	*e*	ფ	*ph*
ვ	*v*	ქ	*kh*
ზ	*z*	ღ	*γ*
თ	*th*	ყ	*q̣*
ი	*i*	შ	*ʃ*
კ	*ḳ*	ჩ	*čh*
ლ	*l*	ც	*ts*
მ	*m*	ძ	*dz*
ნ	*n*	წ	*ṭs*
ო	*o*	ჭ	*ṭʃ*
პ	*p̣*	ხ	*χ*
ჟ	*ž*	ჯ	*dž*
		ჰ	*h*

The ecclesiastical script known as Khutsuri is no longer in use.

GREEK

THE ALPHABET

Capital letter	*Small Letter*	*Ancient phonetics*	*Usual transliteration*	*Modern pronunciation*	*Usual transliteration*
Α	α	[a]	a	[a]	a
Β	β	[b]	b	[v]	v
Γ	γ	[g]	g	[j] (/—i,e)	y
				[ɣ] (elsewhere)	g(h)
Δ	δ	[d]	d	[ð]	d(h)
Ε	ε	[ɛ]	e	[ɛ]	e
Ζ	ζ	[zd]	z	[z]	z
Η	η	[ɛː]	eː, ē	[i]	i
Θ	θ	[tʰ]	th	[θ]	th
Ι	ι	[i]	i	[i]	i
Κ	ϰ	[k]	k	[k]	k
Λ	λ	[l]	l	[l]	l
Μ	μ	[m]	m	[m]	m
Ν	ν	[n]	n	[n]	n
Ξ	ξ	[ks]	x	[ks]	ks, x (as in *box*)
Ο	ο	[o]	o	[o]	o
Π	π	[p]	p	[p]	p
Ρ	ϱ	[r]	r	[ɾ]	r
Σ	σ (ς)	[s]	s	[s]	s
Τ	τ	[t]	t	[t]	t
Υ	υ	[y]	y, u	[i]	i
Φ	φ	[pʰ]	ph	[f]	f
Χ	χ	[kʰ]	ch, kh	[χ]	h, x (IPA value)
Ψ	ψ	[ps]	ps	[ps]	ps
Ω	ω	[ɔː]	oː, ō	[o]	o

Diphthongs and clusters	*Ancient phonetics*	*Usual transliteration*	*Modern pronunciation*	*Usual transliteration*
αι	[ai̯]	ai	[ε]	e
αυ	[au̯]	au	[av] (/__ + voice)	av
			[af] (/__ − voice)	af
ει	[eː]	ei	[i]	i
ευ	[εu̯]	eu	[ev] (/__ + voice)	ev
			[ef] (/__ − voice)	ef
οι	[oi̯]	oi	[i]	i
ου	[oː]	ou	[u]	u
υι	[yi̯]	yi, ui	[i]	i
γ before γ χ ξ	[ŋ]	n (g, kh, ks)	[ŋ]	n (g, h, ks)
γκ	[ŋk]	nk	[(ŋ)g] (medially)	(n)g
			[g] (initially)	g
μπ/μβ	[mp/mb]	mp/mb	[(m)b] (medially)	(m)b
			[b] (initially)	b
ντ/νδ	[nt/nd]	nt/nd	[(n)d] (medially)	(n)d
			[d] (initially)	d
τζ	-----	-----	[dz]	dz

Source: Joseph, B.D. (1987) 'Greek', in B. Comrie (ed.) *The World's Major Languages*, London, Routledge

GUJARATI

The absence of the horizontal line on top of the letters distinguishes the Gujarati script from the closely connected and very similar Devanagari.

CONSONANTS

ક	ખ	ગ	ઘ	ઙ
ka	*kha*	*ga*	*gha*	*nga*
ચ	છ	જ	ઝ	ઞ
ca	*cha*	*ja*	*jha*	*nya*
ટ	ઠ	ડ	ઢ	ણ
ṭa	*ṭha*	*ḍa*	*ḍha*	*ṇa*
ત	થ	દ	ધ	ન
ta	*tha*	*da*	*dha*	*na*
પ	ફ	બ	ભ	મ
pa	*pha*	*ba*	*bha*	*ma*
ય	ર	લ	વ	
ya	*ra*	*la*	*wa, va*	
શ	ષ	સ	હ	ળ
śa	*ṣa*	*sa*	*ha*	*la*

VOWELS

(a) independent:

અ	આ	ઇ	ઈ	ઉ	ઊ	ઋ
a	*ā*	*i*	*ī*	*u*	*ū*	*ri*
એ	ઐ	ઓ	ઔ			
ē	*ai*	*ō*	*au*			

(b) in combination with the consonant *ba*:

બા	બિ	બી	બુ	બૂ	બૃ
bā	*bi*	*bī*	*bu*	*bū*	*bri*
બે	બૈ	બો	બૌ		
bē	*bai*	*bō*	*bau*		

Conjunct consonants are formed as in Devanagari and Bengali by juxtaposition, amalgamation or subscript.

NUMERALS

૧	૨	૩	૪	૫	૬	૭	૮	૯	૦
1	2	3	4	5	6	7	8	9	0

GURMUKHI (FOR PANJABI)

Panjabi is written in the Gurmukhi script.

CONSONANTS

ਸ	ਹ			
sa	*ha*			
ਕ	ਖ	ਗ	ਘ	ਙ
ka	*kha*	*ga*	*gha*	*nga*
ਚ	ਛ	ਜ	ਝ	ਞ
ca	*cha*	*ja*	*jha*	*nya*
ਟ	ਠ	ਡ	ਢ	ਣ
ṭa	*ṭha*	*ḍa*	*ḍha*	*ṇa*
ਤ	ਥ	ਦ	ਧ	ਨ
ta	*tha*	*da*	*dha*	*na*
ਪ	ਫ	ਬ	ਭ	ਮ
pa	*pha*	*ba*	*bha*	*ma*
ਯ	ਰ	ਲ	ਵ	ੜ
ya	*ra*	*la*	*va*	*ṛa*

VOWELS

Three letters:

ੳ ūṛā ਅ āiṛā ੲ īṛī

are used to provide bases for free-standing vowels. Thus:

ਉ	ਊ	ਓ	ਅ	ਆ	ਐ	ਔ
u	*ū*	*ō*	*a*	*ā*	*ai*	*au*

ਇ	ਈ	ਏ
i	*ī*	*ē*

As illustration, here are the vowel signs in combination with *ka*:

ਕ	ਕਾ	ਕਿ	ਕੀ	ਕੁ	ਕੂ
ka	*kā*	*ki*	*kī*	*ku*	*kū*

ਕੇ	ਕੈ	ਕੋ	ਕੌ
kē	*kai*	*kō*	*kau*

CONJUNCT CONSONANTS

There are very few conjunct consonants in Panjabi. In general, for C_1C_2, C_1 is in base form, C_2 is attached in schematic outline. Specific subscript forms are used for *ra*, *wa*, *ha*.

Tone is indicated by *ha* or by voiced aspirate (*see* **Panjabi**).

HEBREW

CONSONANTS

Phoenician (= Old Hebrew)	*Jewish Square* (modern print)	*Cursive* (modern)	*Name*	*Transcription*
𐤀	א	א	alef	*?*
𐤁	ב	ב	bet	*B; b, ƀ ~ v*
𐤂	ג	ג	g'imel	*G; g, ǥ*
𐤃	ד	ד	d'alet	*D; d, đ*
𐤄	ה	ה	he	*H; h*
𐤅	ו	ו	vav	*W; w ~ v, u, o*
𐤆	ז	ז	z'ayin	*Z; z*
𐤇	ח	ח	xet	*Ḥ; ḥ ~ x*
𐤈	ט	ט	tet	*Ṭ; ṭ ~ t*
𐤉	י	י	yod	*Y; y, i,e*
𐤊	כ (ך)	כ (ך)	kaf	*K; k, ꝁ ~ x*
𐤋	ל	ל	l'amed	*L; l*
𐤌	מ (ם)	מ (ם)	mem	*M; m*
𐤍	נ (ן)	נ (ן)	nun	*N; n*
𐤎	ס	ס	s'amex	*S; s*
𐤏	ע	ע	'ayin	ʿ
𐤐	פ (ף)	פ (ף)	pe	*P; p, ᵽ~f*
𐤑	צ (ץ)	צ (ץ)	tsade	*Ṣ; ṣ~c(=ts)*
𐤒	ק	ק	qof	*Q; q~k*
𐤓	ר	ר	resh	*R; r*
𐤔	ש	ש	shin	*Š; š*
𐤕	ת	ת	tav	*T; t, ŧ~t*

POINTING

A The dot in the consonant (*dagesh*)

(a) Spirantization

ŧ ת *t* תּ *ᵽ* פ(ף) *p* פּ *ꝁ* כ(ךְ) *k* כּ(ךּ)

đ ד *d* דּ *ǥ* ג *g* גּ *ƀ* ב *b* בּ

(b) Gemination

...qq קּ *... mm* מּ *...ww* וּ *...bb* בּ

B The letter *Š*

ś שׂ *š* שׁ

C The vowels (combined with various consonants)

Long	*Short*	*Ultrashort*
ṭå טָ	*ṭa* טַ	*ʿă* עֲ
lē^{y} לֵי *lē* לֵ	*lɛ* לֶ	*ʔɛ̆* אֱ
mō^{w} מוֹ *rō* רֹ	*ṣå* צָ	*ḥå̆* חֳ
tī^{y} תִּי	*si* סִ	*zə, z* זְ
nū^{w} נוּ	*nu* נֻ	

Source: Hetzron, R. (1987) 'Hebrew', in B. Comrie (ed.) *The World's Major Languages*, London, Routledge

JAPANESE

THE SYLLABARIES

HIRAGANA

あ	か	が	さ	ざ	た	だ	な	は	ば	ぱ	ま	ら	わ	ん
a	*ka*	*ga*	*sa*	*za*	*ta*	*da*	*na*	*ha*	*ba*	*pa*	*ma*	*ra*	*wa*	*n*
い	き	ぎ	し	じ	ち	ぢ	に	ひ	び	ぴ	み	り		
i	*ki*	*gi*	*shi*	*ji*	*chi*	*ji*	*ni*	*hi*	*bi*	*pi*	*mi*	*ri*		
う	く	ぐ	す	ず	つ	づ	ぬ	ふ	ぶ	ぷ	む	る		
u	*ku*	*gu*	*su*	*zu*	*tsu*	*zu*	*nu*	*fu*	*bu*	*pu*	*mu*	*ru*		
え	け	げ	せ	ぜ	て	で	ね	へ	べ	ぺ	め	れ		
e	*ke*	*ge*	*se*	*ze*	*te*	*de*	*ne*	*he*	*be*	*pe*	*me*	*re*		
お	こ	ご	そ	ぞ	と	ど	の	ほ	ぼ	ぽ	も	ろ		を
o	*ko*	*go*	*so*	*zo*	*to*	*do*	*no*	*ho*	*bo*	*po*	*mo*	*ro*		*o*
や	きゃ	ぎゃ	しゃ	じゃ	ちゃ	ぢゃ	にゃ	ひゃ	びゃ	ぴゃ	みゃ	りゃ		
ya	*kya*	*gya*	*sha*	*ja*	*cha*	*ja*	*nya*	*hya*	*bya*	*pya*	*mya*	*rya*		
ゆ	きゅ	ぎゅ	しゅ	じゅ	ちゅ	ぢゅ	にゅ	ひゅ	びゅ	ぴゅ	みゅ	りゅ		
yu	*kyu*	*gyu*	*shu*	*ju*	*chu*	*ju*	*nyu*	*hyu*	*byu*	*pyu*	*myu*	*ryu*		
よ	きょ	ぎょ	しょ	じょ	ちょ	ぢょ	にょ	ひょ	びょ	ぴょ	みょ	りょ		
yo	*kyo*	*gyo*	*sho*	*jo*	*cho*	*jo*	*nyo*	*hyo*	*byo*	*pyo*	*myo*	*ryo*		

KATAKANA

ア	カ	ガ	サ	ザ	タ	ダ	ナ	ハ	バ	パ	マ	ラ	ワ	ファ	ン
a	*ka*	*ga*	*sa*	*za*	*ta*	*da*	*na*	*ha*	*ba*	*pa*	*ma*	*ra*	*wa*	*fa*	*n*
イ	キ	ギ	シ	ジ	チ	ヂ	ニ	ヒ	ビ	ピ	ミ	リ		フィ	
i	*ki*	*gi*	*shi*	*ji*	*chi*	*ji*	*ni*	*hi*	*bi*	*pi*	*mi*	*ri*		*fi*	
ウ	ク	グ	ス	ズ	ツ	ヅ	ヌ	フ	ブ	プ	ム	ル			
u	*ku*	*gu*	*su*	*zu*	*tsu*	*zu*	*nu*	*fu*	*bu*	*pu*	*mu*	*ru*			
エ	ケ	ゲ	セ	ゼ	テ	デ	ネ	ヘ	ベ	ペ	メ	レ		フェ	
e	*ke*	*ge*	*se*	*ze*	*te*	*de*	*ne*	*he*	*be*	*pe*	*me*	*re*		*fe*	
オ	コ	ゴ	ソ	ゾ	ト	ド	ノ	ホ	ボ	ポ	モ	ロ		フォ	ヲ
o	*ko*	*go*	*so*	*zo*	*to*	*do*	*no*	*ho*	*bo*	*po*	*mo*	*ro*		*fo*	*o*
ヤ	キャ	ギャ	シャ	ジャ	チャ	ヂャ	ニャ	ヒャ	ビャ	ピャ	ミャ	リャ			
ya	*kya*	*gya*	*sha*	*ja*	*cha*	*ja*	*nya*	*hya*	*bya*	*pya*	*mya*	*rya*			
ユ	キュ	ギュ	シュ	ジュ	チュ	ヂュ	ニュ	ヒュ	ビュ	ピュ	ミュ	リュ			
yu	*kyu*	*gyu*	*shu*	*ju*	*chu*	*ju*	*nyu*	*hyu*	*byu*	*pyu*	*myu*	*ryu*			
ヨ	キョ	ギョ	ショ	ジョ	チョ	ヂョ	ニョ	ヒョ	ビョ	ピョ	ミョ	リョ			
yo	*kyo*	*gyo*	*sho*	*jo*	*cho*	*jo*	*nyo*	*hyo*	*byo*	*pyo*	*myo*	*ryo*			

Long vowels are notated in Hiragana by adding あ, う, え, or お, e.g.

おかあさん *okā-san;*

and in Katakana by adding —, e.g.

テーブル *téburu.*

Syllabic final consonants other than /n/ are notated

by つ in Hiragama

and by ツ in Katakana, e.g.

いった *itta*, and マッチ *matchi.*

JAVANESE

Column 1 shows the *aksara legena* ('bare letters'), the base consonantal forms. Column 2 shows their *pasangan* ('decoration') secondary forms, which figure as the second components of conjuncts, i.e. C_2 in C_1C_2.

1	*2*	*Name*	*Value*
ꦲ ꦲ	꧀ꦲ ꧀ꦲ	hå	h (mute)
ꦤ ꦤ	꧀ꦤ ꧀ꦤ	nå	n
ꦕ ꦕ	꧀ꦕ ꧀ꦕ	cå	tʃ
ꦫ ꦫ	꧀ꦫ ꧀ꦫ	rå	r
ꦏ ꦏ	꧀ꦏ ꧀ꦏ	kå	k (as final > ʔ)
ꦢ ꦢ	꧀ꦢ ꧀ꦢ	då	d
ꦠ ꦠ	꧀ꦠ ꧀ꦠ	tå	t
ꦱ ꦱ	꧀ꦱ ꧀ꦱ	så	s
ꦮ ꦮ	꧀ꦮ ꧀ꦮ	wå	w
ꦭ ꦭ	꧀ꦭ ꧀ꦭ	lå	l
ꦥ ꦥ	꧀ꦥ ꧀ꦥ	på	p
ꦝ ꦝ	꧀ꦝ ꧀ꦝ	ḍå	ɖ
ꦗ ꦗ	꧀ꦗ ꧀ꦗ	jå	dʒ
ꦪ ꦪ	꧀ꦪ ꧀ꦪ	yå	j
ꦚ ꦚ	꧀ꦚ ꧀ꦚ	ñå	ɲ
ꦩ ꦩ	꧀ꦩ ꧀ꦩ	må	m
ꦒ ꦒ	꧀ꦒ ꧀ꦒ	gå	g
ꦧ ꦧ	꧀ꦧ ꧀ꦧ	bå	b
ꦛ ꦛ	꧀ꦛ ꧀ꦛ	ṭå	ʈ
ꦔ ꦔ	꧀ꦔ ꧀ꦔ	ngå	ŋ

a > /ɔ/ is inherent in these consonants. In order to notate the vowels e, i, o, u in post-consonantal position, and other combinations, the following *sandangan* ('clothed') signs are used:

Sign	*Name*	*Value*
	pěpět	ě
	wulu	i
	suku	u
	taling	é/è
	taling-tarung	o (circumfix)
	pangkon Kr., patěn Ng.	cancels inherent vowel; corresponds to Devanagari virāma
	pingkal	marks palatalized consonant
	cåkrå	post-consonantal r
	kěrět	rě following a consonant
	layar	syllabic final r
	wigũan	syllabic final h
	cěcak	syllabic final ŋ
	pa-cěrěk	rě
	ngå-lělět	lě

Vowels in isolation: these occur mainly in foreign words:

a e i

o u

In addition, the classical Javanese script had a series of 'large' letters for use in the names and titles of distinguished personages. Seven Arabic phonemes were represented by placing the diacritic ♣ over the Javanese equivalent; thus, Arabic (ʃ/, for example, is Javanese *så* with ♣ added.

KANNADA

CONSONANTS

ಕ	ಖ	ಗ	ಘ	ಙ
ka	*kha*	*ga*	*gha*	*nga*
ಚ	ಛ	ಜ	ಝ	ಞ
ca	*cha*	*ja*	*jha*	*nya*
ಟ	ಠ	ಡ	ಢ	ಣ
ṭa	*ṭha*	*ḍa*	*ḍha*	*ṇa*
ತ	ಥ	ದ	ಧ	ನ
ta	*tha*	*da*	*dha*	*na*
ಪ	ಫ	ಬ	ಭ	ಮ
pa	*pha*	*ba*	*bha*	*ma*
ಯ	ರ	ಲ	ವ	
ya	*ra*	*la*	*va*	
ಶ	ಷ	ಸ	ಹ	ಳ
śa	*ṣa*	*sa*	*ha*	*ḷa*

VOWELS

ಅ	ಆ	ಇ	ಈ	ಉ	ಊ	ಋ
a	*ā*	*i*	*ī*	*u*	*ū*	*ru*
ಎ	ಏ	ಐ	ಒ	ಓ	ಔ	
e	*ē*	*ai*	*o*	*ō*	*au*	

Vowel signs: here illustrated as applied to *ka*:

ಕಾ *kā*, ಕಿ *ki*, ಕೀ *kī*, ಕು *ku*, ಕೂ *kū*, ಕೃ *kru*, ಕೆ *ke*,

ಕೇ *kē*, ಕೈ *kai*, ಕೊ *ko*, ಕೋ *kō*, ಕೌ *kau*

There are several irregularities in the writing of *-i* and *-u*.

Conjunct consonants in Kannada are generally formed by subscription of the second component, which may be altered in form.

KOREAN

The *Hangul* script, used to write Korean, is a syllabary, in which consonants and vowels combine in their base forms to form syllables. That is to say, vowels following consonants do not assume specific secondary forms as in Devanagari, nor are the consonants themselves amended as in Ethiopic. Pure vowels cannot be written in isolation, i.e. unsupported by a consonant: the bearer ◌ must be used: thus /a/ is notated as ◌ㅏ

The basic forms are given in the following table.

Letter	*Transcription*	*Letter*	*Transcription*
Pure vowels:			
ㅣ	/i/	ㅡ	/ŭ/
ㅔ	/e/	ㅓ	/ə/
ㅐ	/æ/	ㅏ	/a/
ㅟ	/ü/	ㅜ	/u/
ㅚ	/ö/	ㅗ	/o/
Compound vowels:			
ㅑ	/ya/	ㅘ	/wa
ㅒ	/yæ/	ㅙ	/wæ/
ㅕ	/yə/	ㅝ	/wə/
ㅖ	/ye/	ㅞ	/we/
ㅛ	/yo/	ㅢ	/ŭi/
ㅠ	/yu/		
Consonants:			
ㄱ	/k/	ㅇ	/ŋ/
ㄴ	/n/	ㅈ	/c/
ㄷ	/t/	ㅊ	/c^h/
ㄹ	/l/	ㅋ	/k^h/
ㅁ	/m/	ㅌ	/t^h/
ㅂ	/p/	ㅍ	/p^h/
ㅅ	/s/	ㅎ	/h/
Double consonants:			
ㄲ	/k'/	ㅆ	/s'/
ㄸ	/t'/	ㅉ	/c'/
ㅃ	/p'/		

Source: Kim, N. – K. (1987) 'Korean', in B. Comrie (ed.) *The World's Major Languages*, London, Routledge

Two sample rows follow:

(a) C + V

가	갸	거	겨	고	교	구	규	그
ka	*kya*	*kə*	*kyə*	*ko*	*kyo*	*ku*	*kyu*	*kŭ*
기	개	걔	게	계	괴	귀	긔	과
ki	*kæ*	*kyæ*	*ke*	*kye*	*ko*	*ki*	*kwi*	*kwa*
궈	괘	궤						
kwə	*kwæ*	*kwe*						

(b) C + V + C (phonetic realizations)

각	간	갇	갈	감	갑	갓	강
kak	*kan*	*kat*	*kal*	*kam*	*kap*	*kat*	*kang*
갗	갖	같	갚	갛	갉	값	갔
kat	*kat*	*kat*	*kap*	*ka’*	*kak*	*kap*	*kat*

LAO

CONSONANTS

ກ	ຂ	ຄ	ງ	ຈ	ສ	ຊ
ko	*kho*	*kho*	*ngo*	*cho*	*so*	*so*
ຍ	ດ	ຕ	ຖ	ທ	ນ	ບ
nyo	*do*	*to*	*tho*	*tho*	*no*	*bo*
ປ	ຜ	ຝ	ພ	ຟ	ມ	ຢ
po	*pho*	*fo*	*pho*	*fo*	*mo*	*yo*
ຣ	ລ	ວ	ຫ	ອ	ຮ	
ro	*lo*	*wo*	*ho*	*'o*	*ho*	

VOWELS

Notation of the rich vocalic system is virtually identical with that of Thai (q.v.), using superscript, subscript, prefixed and suffixed markers, and circumfix. For example, if C represents a consonant, Cາ = Cā, Cູ = Cū, Cິ = Ci, ເCົາ = Cau, ເCາະ = Co, ໂC = Cō.

NUMERALS

໑	໒	໓	໔	໕	໖	໗	໘	໙	໐
1	2	3	4	5	6	7	8	9	0

MALAYALAM

CONSONANTS

ക	ഖ	ഗ	ഘ	ങ		
ka	*kha*	*ga*	*gha*	*nga*		
ച	ഛ	ജ	ഝ	ഞ		
ca	cha	*ja*	*jha*	*nya*		
ട	ഠ	ഡ	ഢ	ണ		
ṭa	*ṭha*	*ḍa*	*ḍha*	*ṇa*		
ത	ഥ	ദ	ധ	ന		
ta	*tha*	*da*	*dha*	*na*		
പ	ഫ	ബ	ഭ	മ		
pa	*pha*	*ba*	*bha*	*ma*		
യ	ര	ല	വ			
ya	*ra*	*la*	*va*			
ശ	ഷ	സ	ഹ	ള	ഴ	റ
śa	ṣa	*sa*	*ha*	*la*	*ra*	*ra*

VOWELS

(a) independent

അ	ആ	ഇ	ഈ	ഉ	ഊ	ഋ
a	*ā*	*i*	*ī*	*u*	*ū*	*ru*
എ	ഏ	ഐ	ഒ	ഓ	ഔ	
e	*ē*	*ai*	*o*	*ō*	*au*	

(b) as applied to letter *ṭa*:

ടാ *ṭā* ടി *ṭi* ടീ *ṭī* ടു *ṭu* ടൂ *ṭū* ടൃ *ṭru*

ടെ *ṭe* ടേ *ṭē* ടൈ *ṭai* ടൊ *ṭo* ടോ *ṭō* ടൌ *ṭau*

Conjunct consonants are formed by duplication (often vertical) or by fusion, which may involve substantial deformation. Cf. (*6.2*) gga, (*15.18*) lla.

NUMERALS

൧	൨	൩	൪	൫	൬	൭	൮	൯	൦
1	2	3	4	5	6	7	8	9	0

MONGOLIAN

The Classical Mongolian script – now replaced in the MPR for all ordinary purposes by Cyrillic – is written in vertical lines, from left to right. If the letters are viewed horizontally, their derivation (via an Uighur intermediary) from the Syriac Estrangelo script becomes plain.

Initial	*Medial*	*Final*	*Transcription*
ᠠ‍	‍ᠠ‍	‍ᠠ ‍ᠠ	*a*
ᠡ‍	‍ᠡ‍	‍ᠡ ‍ᠡ	*e*
ᠢ‍	‍ᠢ‍	‍ᠢ	*i*
ᠣ‍	‍ᠣ‍	‍ᠣ	*o*
ᠤ‍	‍ᠤ‍	‍ᠤ	*u*
ᠥ‍	‍ᠥ‍ ‍ᠥ‍	‍ᠥ	*ö*
ᠦ‍	‍ᠦ‍ ‍ᠦ‍	‍ᠦ	*ü*
ᠨ‍	‍ᠨ‍	‍ᠨ ‍ᠨ	*n*
ᠪ‍	‍ᠪ‍	‍ᠪ	*b*
ᠬ‍	‍ᠬ‍	–	*ch*
ᠭ‍	‍ᠭ‍	–	*gh*
ᠺ‍	‍ᠺ‍	‍ᠺ ‍ᠺ	*k*
ᠭ‍	‍ᠭ‍	–	*g*
ᠮ‍	‍ᠮ‍	‍ᠮ	*m*
ᠯ‍	‍ᠯ‍	‍ᠯ	*l*
ᠷ‍	‍ᠷ‍	‍ᠷ	*r*

Initial	*Medial*	*Final*	*Transcription*
			t
		—	*d*
		—	*y*
		—	*j, ds*
		—	*ts*
			s
		—	*š*
		—	*w*

As in Semitic scripts generally, letters have different forms depending on whether they are initial, medial or final.

Important ligatures are:

Initial	*Medial*	*Final*	*Transcription*
			ai
			oi

Final		*Medial*	
ba, be		*bi*	*bo, bu*
ke, ge		*ki, gi*	*kö, kü* / *gö, gü*
ng			

SINHALESE

CONSONANTS

ක	ඛ	ග	ඝ	ඞ
ka	*kha*	*ga*	*gha*	*nga*
ච	ඡ	ජ	ඣ	ඤ
ca	*cha*	*ja*	*jha*	*nya*
ට	ඨ	ඩ	ඪ	ණ
ṭa	*ṭha*	*ḍa*	*ḍha*	*ṇa*
ත	ථ	ද	ධ	න
ta	*tha*	*da*	*dha*	*na*
ප	ඵ	බ	භ	ම
pa	*pha*	*ba*	*bha*	*ma*
ය	ර	ල	ව	
ya	*ra*	*la*	*va*	
ශ	ෂ	ස	හ	ළ
śa	*ṣa*	*sa*	*ha*	*la*

VOWELS

(a) independent:

අ	ආ	ඇ	ඈ	ඉ	ඊ	උ	ඌ
a	*ā*	*æ*	*ǣ*	*i*	*ī*	*u*	*ū*
ඍ	එ	ඒ	ඓ	ඔ	ඕ	ඖ	
ri	*e*	*ē*	*ai*	*o*	*ō*	*au*	

(b) as applied to the consonant *na*:

නා	නැ	නෑ	නි	නී	නු	නූ
nā	*næ*	*nǣ*	*ni*	*nī*	*nu*	*nū*
නෘ	නෙ	නේ	නෛ	නො	නෝ	නෞ
nri	*ne*	*nē*	*nai*	*no*	*nō*	*nau*

CONJUNCT CONSONANTS

The subscript model typical of Telugu, for example, is not used in Sinhalese. Instead, there is an extensive repertory of ligatures, many of great complexity.

TAMIL

THE SYLLABARY

–		அ	*a*	ஆ	*ā*	இ	*i*	ஈ	*ī*	உ	*u*	ஊ	*ū*
க்	*k*	க	*ka*	கா	*kā*	கி	*ki*	கீ	*kī*	கு	*ku*	கூ	*kū*
ங்	*ṅ*	ங	*ṅa*	ஙா	*ṅā*	ஙி	*ṅi*	ஙீ	*ṅī*	ஙு	*ṅu*	ஙூ	*ṅū*
ச்	*ç*	ச	*ça*	சா	*çā*	சி	*çi*	சீ	*çī*	சு	*çu*	சூ	*çū*
ஞ்	*ñ*	ஞ	*ña*	ஞா	*ñā*	ஞி	*ñi*	ஞீ	*ñī*	ஞு	*ñu*	ஞூ	*ñū*
ட்	*ḍ*	ட	*ḍa*	டா	*ḍā*	டி	*ḍi*	டீ	*ḍī*	டு	*ḍu*	டூ	*ḍū*
ண்	*ṇ*	ண	*ṇa*	ணா	*ṇā*	ணி	*ṇi*	ணீ	*ṇī*	ணு	*ṇu*	ணூ	*ṇū*
த்	*t*	த	*ta*	தா	*tā*	தி	*ti*	தீ	*tī*	து	*tu*	தூ	*tū*
ந்	*n*	ந	*na*	நா	*nā*	நி	*ni*	நீ	*nī*	நு	*nu*	நூ	*nū*
ப்	*p*	ப	*pa*	பா	*pā*	பி	*pi*	பீ	*pī*	பு	*pu*	பூ	*pū*
ம்	*m*	ம	*ma*	மா	*mā*	மி	*mi*	மீ	*mī*	மு	*mu*	மூ	*mū*
ய்	*y*	ய	*ya*	யா	*yā*	யி	*yi*	யீ	*yī*	யு	*yu*	யூ	*yū*
ர்	*r*	ர	*ra*	ரா	*rā*	ரி	*ri*	ரீ	*rī*	ரு	*ru*	ரூ	*rū*
ல்	*l*	ல	*la*	லா	*lā*	லி	*li*	லீ	*lī*	லு	*lu*	லூ	*lū*
வ்	*v*	வ	*va*	வா	*vā*	வி	*vi*	வீ	*vī*	வு	*vu*	வூ	*vū*
ழ்	*ẓ*	ழ	*ẓa*	ழா	*ẓā*	ழி	*ẓi*	ழீ	*ẓī*	ழு	*ẓu*	ழூ	*ẓū*
ள்	*ḷ*	ள	*ḷa*	ளா	*ḷā*	ளி	*ḷi*	ளீ	*ḷī*	ளு	*ḷu*	ளூ	*ḷū*
ற்	*R*	ற	*Ra*	றா	*Rā*	றி	*Ri*	றீ	*Rī*	று	*Ru*	றூ	*Rū*
ன்	*N*	ன	*Na*	னா	*Nā*	னி	*Ni*	னீ	*Nī*	னு	*Nu*	னூ	*Nū*

எ	*e*	ஏ	*ē*	ஐ	*ai*	ஒ	*o*	ஓ	*ō*	ஔ	*au*
கெ	*ke*	கே	*kē*	கை	*kai*	கொ	*ko*	கோ	*kō*	கௌ	*kau*
ஙெ	*ṅe*	ஙே	*ṅē*	ஙை	*ṅai*	ஙொ	*ṅo*	ஙோ	*ṅō*	ஙௌ	*ṅau*
செ	*çe*	சே	*çē*	சை	*çai*	சொ	*ço*	சோ	*çō*	சௌ	*çau*
ஞெ	*ñe*	ஞே	*ñē*	ஞை	*ñai*	ஞொ	*ño*	ஞோ	*ñō*	ஞௌ	*ñau*
டெ	*ḍe*	டே	*ḍē*	டை	*ḍai*	டொ	*ḍo*	டோ	*ḍō*	டௌ	*ḍau*
ணெ	*ṇe*	ணே	*ṇē*	ணை	*ṇai*	ணொ	*ṇo*	ணோ	*ṇō*	ணௌ	*ṇau*
தெ	*te*	தே	*tē*	தை	*tai*	தொ	*to*	தோ	*tō*	தௌ	*tau*
நெ	*ne*	நே	*nē*	நை	*nai*	நொ	*no*	நோ	*nō*	நௌ	*nau*
பெ	*pe*	பே	*pē*	பை	*pai*	பொ	*po*	போ	*pō*	பௌ	*pau*
மெ	*me*	மே	*mē*	மை	*mai*	மொ	*mo*	மோ	*mō*	மௌ	*mau*
யெ	*ye*	யே	*yē*	யை	*yai*	யொ	*yo*	யோ	*yō*	யௌ	*yau*
ரெ	*re*	ரே	*rē*	ரை	*rai*	ரொ	*ro*	ரோ	*rō*	ரௌ	*rau*
லெ	*le*	லே	*lē*	லை	*lai*	லொ	*lo*	லோ	*lō*	லௌ	*lau*
வெ	*ve*	வே	*vē*	வை	*vai*	வொ	*vo*	வோ	*vō*	வௌ	*vau*
ழெ	*ẓe*	ழே	*ẓē*	ழை	*ẓai*	ழொ	*ẓo*	ழோ	*ẓō*	ழௌ	*ẓau*
ளெ	*ḷe*	ளே	*ḷē*	ளை	*ḷai*	ளொ	*ḷo*	ளோ	*ḷō*	ளௌ	*ḷau*
றெ	*Re*	றே	*Rē*	றை	*Rai*	றொ	*Ro*	றோ	*Rō*	றௌ	*Rau*
னெ	*Ne*	னே	*Nē*	னை	*Nai*	னொ	*No*	னோ	*Nō*	னௌ	*Nau*

Source: Steever, S.B. (1987) 'Tamil and the Dravidian Languages', in B. Comrie (ed.) *The World's Major Languages*, London, Routledge, adapted from Pope, G.U. (1979) *A Handbook of the Tamil Language*, New Delhi, Asian Education Services

TELUGU

CONSONANTS

Traditionally, the Telugu consonantal grid has 34 letters, and is set out, in Devanagari order, as follows:

క	ఖ	గ	ఘ	ఙ
ka	*kha*	*ga*	*gha*	*nga*
చ	ఛ	జ	ఝ	ఞ
ca	*cha*	*ja*	*jha*	*nya*
ట	ఠ	డ	ఢ	ణ
ṭa	*ṭha*	*ḍa*	*ḍha*	*ṇa*
త	థ	ద	ధ	న
ta	*tha*	*da*	*dha*	*na*
ప	ఫ	బ	భ	మ
pa	*pha*	*ba*	*bha*	*ma*
య	ర	ల	ళ	వ
ya	*ra*	*la*	*ḷa*	*va*
శ	ష	స	హ	
śa	*ṣa*	*sa*	*ha*	

However, the ten aspirated consonants occur in only a few Sanskrit borrowings, and *nga* and *nya* are also rare. The great majority of Telugu words can be written in terms of the remaining 22 letters, plus ం , the sign for nasalization.

VOWELS

(a) independent:

అ	ఆ	ఇ	ఈ	ఉ	ఊ	ఋ
a	*ā*	*i*	*ī*	*u*	*ū*	*ru*
ఎ	ఏ	ఐ	ఒ	ఓ	ఔ	
e	*ē*	*ai*	*o*	*ō*	*au*	

(b) as applied to the consonant *ka*:

కా	కి	కీ	కు	కూ	కృ
kā	*ki*	*kī*	*ku*	*kū*	*kru*
కె	కే	కై	కొ	కో	కౌ
ke	*kē*	*kai*	*ko*	*kō*	*kau*

There are many irregularities.

CONJUNCT CONSONANTS

Most conjunct consonants in Telugu are geminates, the second component being subscribed in primary or secondary form.

NUMERALS

౧	౨	౩	౪	౫	౬	౭	౮	౯	౦
1	2	3	4	5	6	7	8	9	0

THAI

CONSONANTS

The five positional series of the Devanagari source (transmitted to Thai via Khmer), have additional letters in the Thai inventory, which has to accommodate a tonal system. The positional grid in Thai is as follows:

Mid	*Mid*	*High*	*High*	*Low*	*Low*	*Low*	*Low*
	ก	ข	ฃ	ค	ฅ	ฆ	ง
	k	*kh*	*kh*	*kh*	*kh*	*kh*	*ŋ*
	จ	ฉ		ช	ซ	ฌ	ญ
	c	*ch*		*ch*	*s*	*ch*	*y*
ฎ	ฏ	ฐ		ฑ		ฒ	ณ
d	*t*	*th*		*th*		*th*	*n*
ด	ต	ถ		ท		ธ	น
d	*t*	*th*		*th*		*th*	*n*
บ	ป	ผ	ฝ	พ	ฟ	ภ	ม
b	*p*	*ph*	*f*	*ph*	*f*	*ph*	*m*

The sixth group in Devanagari, comprising the semi-vowels, and the spirants, is represented in Thai as follows:

(a) the semi-vowels (all low class consonants):

ย ร ล ว
y r l w

(b) the spirants (all high class consonants):

ศ ษ ส
s s s

(c) the mixed group ห h (high), ฬ l (low), อ ʔ (middle), ฮ h (low).

VOWELS

Thai has no forms for independent vowels. The vocalization system is shown here as applied to the low class consonant ค kh:

	Long			*Short*				
	With final		*Without final*	*With final*				*Without final*
	y	*Other*		*y*	*w*	*m*	*Other*	
a	คา			ไค ใค	เคา	คำ	คัน	คะ ค
ə	เคย	เคิน	เคอ					เคอะ
e	เค			เค็น				เคะ
o	โค			คน				โคะ
ua	ควน		คัว	*				คัวะ
ia	เคีย			*				เคียะ
ɨa	เคือ			*				เคือะ
ɛ	แค			แค็น				แคะ
	คอ			คอน				เคาะ
ɨ	คืน		คือ	คึ				
i	คี			คิ				
u	คู			คุ				

Source: Hudak, T.J. (1987) 'Thai', in B. Comrie (ed.) *The World's Major Languages*, London, Routledge, adapted from Brown, J.M. (1967) *A.U.A Center Thai Course*, vol. 3, Bangkok, Social Science Association Press of Thailand, pp. 211–12.

TIBETAN

The *dbu.can* (/u.ceen/) script, consisting of 30 basic letters plus 5 denoting retroflex sounds in Sanskrit words, is shown here, accompanied by a table of conjunct consonants:

ཀ	*ka*	ཀྱ	*kya*	རྗུ	*rju*	བླ	*bla*
ཁ	*kha*	ཀྲ	*kra*	ལྗ	*lja*	རྦ	*rba*
ག	*ga*	ཀླ	*kla*	རྙ	*rña*	ལྦ	*lba*
ང	*ṅa*	ཀྭ	*kva*	སྙ	*sña*	སྦ	*sba*
ཅ	*ca*	རྐ	*rka*	ཏྲ	*tra*	སྦྱ	*sbya*
ཆ	*cha*	རྐྱ	*rkya*	རྟ	*rta*	སྦྲ	*sbra*
ཇ	*ja*	ལྐ	*lka*	ལྟ	*lta*	མུ	*mu*
ཉ	*ña*	སྐ	*ska*	སྟ	*sta*	མྱ	*mya*
ཏ	*ta*	སྐྱ	*skya*	ཐྲ	*thra*	མྲ	*mra*
ཐ	*tha*	སྐྲ	*skra*	དྲ	*dra*	རྨ	*rma*
ད	*da*	ཁྱ	*khya*	དྭ	*dva*	རྨྱ	*rmya*
ན	*na*	ཁྲ	*khra*	རྡ	*rda*	སྨ	*sma*
པ	*pa*	ཁྭ	*khva*	ལྡ	*lda*	སྨྱ	*smya*
ཕ	*pha*	གྱ	*gya*	སྡ	*sda*	སྨྲ	*smra*
བ	*ba*	གྲ	*gra*	སྡུ	*sdu*	ཙུ	*tsu*
མ	*ma*	གླ	*gla*	ནྲ	*nra*	རྩ	*rtsa*
ཙ	*tsa*	གྭ	*gva*	རྣ	*rna*	རྩྭ	*rtsva*
ཚ	*tsha*	རྒ	*rga*	སྣ	*sna*	སྩ	*stsa*
ཛ	*dsa*	རྒྱ	*rgya*	སྣྲ	*snra*	རྫ	*rdsa*
ཝ	*wa*	ལྒ	*lga*	པུ	*pu*	ཞུ	*żu*
ཞ	*ża*	སྒ	*sga*	པྱ	*pya*	ཟུ	*zu*
ཟ	*za*	སྒྱ	*sgya*	པྲ	*pra*	ཟླ	*zla*
འ	*a*, *a̱*	སྒྲ	*sgra*	ལྤ	*lpa*	ཨུ	*u*
ཡ	*ya*	ངུ	*ṅu*	སྤ	*spa*	ཡུ	*yu*
ར	*ra*	རྔ	*rṅa*	སྤྱ	*spya*	རུ	*ru*
ལ	*la*					ལུ	*lu*
ཤ	*śa*						
ས	*sa*						

ཧ	*ha*	སྔ	*sṅa*	སྤྲ	*spra*	རླ	*rla*
ཨ	*'a*	ལྔ	*lṅa*	ཕུ	*phu*	ཤྲ	*śra*
ཊ	*ṭa*	ཅུ	*cu*	ཕྱ	*phya*	སུ	*su*
ཋ	*ṭha*	ལྕ	*lca*	ཕྲ	*phra*	སྲ	*sra*
ཌ	*ḍa*	ཆུ	*chu*	བུ	*bu*	སླ	*sla*
ཎ	*ṇa*	ཇུ	*ju*	བྱ	*bya*	ཧྲ	*hra*
ཥ	*ṣa*	རྗ	*rja*	བྲ	*bra*	ལྷ	*lha*

The Tibetan vowels i, e, o, are notated by superscript signs, the vowel *u* by a subscript. They are shown here as applied to the consonant *ka*:

ཀི	ཀུ	ཀེ	ཀོ
ki	*ku*	*ke*	*ko*

Numerals:

༡	༢	༣	༤	༥	༦	༧	༨	༩	༠
1	2	3	4	5	6	7	8	9	0

BIBLIOGRAPHY

COLLECTIVE WORKS

Campbell, G.L. (1991) *Compendium of the World's Languages*, London.
Comrie, B. (1981) *The Languages of the Soviet Union*, Cambridge.
Comrie, B. (1987) *The World's Major Languages*, London and Sydney.
De Bray, R.G.A. (1980) *Guide to the Slavonic Languages*, 3 vols, Columbus, OH.
Décsy, G. (1973) *Die Linguistische Struktur Europas*, Wiesbaden.
Gérard, A.S. (1981) *African Language Literatures*, Harlow, Essex.
Jazyki Azii i Afriki (1976–9) 3 vols, Moscow.
Jazyki Narodov SSSR (1966–8) 5 vols, Moscow.
Zograph, G.A. (1982) *The Languages of South Asia*, London.

INDIVIDUAL LANGUAGES

Afrikaans

Barnes, A.S.V. (n.d.) *Afrikaanse Grammatika vir Engelssprekende Leerlinge*, Elsiesrivier, Nasou Bepek.
Mironov, S.A. (1969) *Jazyk Afrikaans*, Moscow.
Schalkwyk, H. van (1988) *Teach Yourself Afrikaans*, Johannesburg.

Akan

Christaller, J.G. (1933) *Dictionary of the Asante and Fante Language, called Tshi (Twi)*, Basle.
Redden, J.E. *et al.* (1963) *Twi Basic Course*, Washington, DC.

Albanian

Camaj, M. (1984) *Albanian Grammar*, Wiesbaden.
Hetzer, A. and Z. Finger (1991) *Lehrbuch der vereinheitlichten albanischen Schriftsprache*, Hamburg.
Koçi, R.D., A. Kostallari, and D. Skendi (1951) *Albansko–Ruskij slovar'*, Moscow.
Lambertz, M. (1954–9) *Lehrgang des Albanischen*, 3 vols, Berlin and Halle.
Newmark, L., I. Haznedari, P. Hubbard, and P. Prifti (1980) *Spoken Albanian*, New York.
Radovicka, L., Z. Karapici, and A. Toma (1981) *Gjuha Shqipe*, vol. 3, Tirana.

Amharic

Gankin, E.B. (1969) *Amxarsko–Russkij slovar'*, Moscow.
Gankin, E.B. and Kebbede Desta (1965) *Russko–Amxarskij slovar'*, Moscow.
Kebede, M. and J.D. Murphy (1984) *Amharic Newspaper Reader*, Kensington, MD.
Leslau, L. (1967) *Amharic Textbook*, Wiesbaden.
Leslau, L. (1973) *English–Amharic Context Dictionary*, Wiesbaden.
Leslau, W. (1965) *An Amharic Conversation Book*, Wiesbaden.
Obolensky, S., D. Zelelie, and M. Andualem (1964) *Amharic Basic Course*, Washington DC.
Richter, R. (1987) *Lehrbuch der amharischen Sprache*, Leipzig.
Titov, E.G. (1971) *Sovremennyj Amxarskij jazyk*, Moscow.

Arabic

Beeston, A.F.L. (1970) *The Arabic Language Today*, London.
Cantarino, V. (1974–5) *Syntax of Modern Arabic Prose*, 3 vols, Bloomington, IN, and London.
Haywood, J.A. and H.M. Nahmad (1965) *A New Arabic Grammar*, London.
McCarus, E.N. and A.I. Yacoub (1962) *Newspaper Arabic*, Ann Arbor, MI.
Monteil, V. (1960) *L'Arabe moderne*, Paris.
Pragnell, F.A. (1984) *A Week in the Middle East*, London.
Stetkevych, J. (1970) *The Modern Arabic Literary Language*, Chicago and London.
Tritton, A.S. (1943) *Teach Yourself Arabic*, London.
Wehr, H. (1971) *Dictionary of Modern Written Arabic*, ed. J. Milton Cowan, Wiesbaden and London.
Wright, W. (1951) *A Grammar of the Arabic Language*, 2 vols, Cambridge.

Armenian, Modern Standard

Fairbanks, G.H. and E.W. Stevick (1958) *Spoken East Armenian*, New York.
Garibjan, A.S. and Zh.A. Garibjan (1965) *Kratkij kurs Armjanskogo jazyka*, Erevan.
Kurkjian, H. (1973) *Manuel pratique de la langue Arménienne occidentale*, Beirut.

Assamese

Babakaev, V.D. (1961) *Assamskij jazyk*, Moscow.

Balinese

Kersten, J. (1948) *Balische gramatica*, The Hague.

Bantu Languages

Guthrie, M. (1948) *The Classification of the Bantu Languages*, London.
Meinhof, C. (1906) *Grundzüge einer vegleichenden Grammatik der Bantusprachen*, Berlin.

Basque

Estones Lasa, J. (1972) *Como aprender el vasco facilmente*, San Sebastian.
Ezkila (1963) *Méthode de Basque pour débutants*, Bayonne.
Gereno, X. (1983) *Método fácil para aprender Euskara básico*, Bilbao.
Kintana, X. and J. Tobar (1977) *Euskal Hiztegi modernoa*, Bilbao.
Norbait (n.d.) *Método audio-oral de Euskera básico*, San Sebastian.
Onatibia, J. (1973) *Método de Euskera radiofonico*, San Sebastian.
Saltarelli, M. (1988) *Basque*, London.

Belorussian

De Bray, R.G.A. (1980) *Guide to the Slavonic Languages*, 3 vols, Columbus, OH.
Mayo, P.T. (1976) *A Grammar of Byelorussian*, Sheffield.

Bengali

Bykova, E.M. (1966) *Bengal'skij jazyk*, Moscow.
Hudson, D.F. (1965) *Bengali*, London.
Zbavitel, D. (1953) *Učebnice Bengálštiny*, Prague.

Berber

Ammār ibn Sa'īd (called Bū Līfah) (1910) *Une Première Année de la langue Kabyle*, Algiers.
Basset, A. (1952) *La Langue Berbère*, Oxford.
Cortade, J.-M. (1969) *Essai de grammaire Touareg*, Algiers.
Hanoteau, A. (1896) *La Langue Tamachek*, Algiers.
Harries, J. (1974) *Tamazight Basic Course*, Washington, DC.
Zavadovskij, J.N. (1967) *Berberskij jazyk*, Moscow.

Breton

Desbordes, Y. (1983) *Petite grammaire du Breton moderne*, Lesneven.
Morvannon, F. (1975) *Le Breton sans peine*, London.
Press, I. (1986) *A Grammar of Modern Breton*, The Hague.

Buginese

Matthes, X.X. (1874) *Boegineesche Spraakkunst*, The Hague.
Sirk, J.X. (1975) *Bugijskij jazyk*, Moscow.

Bulgarian

Bödey, J. and T. Nagypál (1963) *Bolgár nyelvkönyv*, Budapest.
De Bray, R.G.A. (1980) *Guide to the Slavonic Languages*, 3 vols, Columbus, OH.

Burmese

Maun Maun N'un *et al.* (1963) *Birmanskij jazyk*, Moscow.
Okell, J. (1969) *Reference Grammar of Colloquial Burmese*, Oxford and London.
Richter, E. (1987) *Lehrbuch des modernen Burmesisch*, Leipzig.

Cambodian

Ehrman, M.E. and Kem Sos (1972) *Contemporary Cambodian*, Washington, DC.
Gorgoniev, J.A. (1961) *Khmerskij jazyk*, Moscow.
Huffman, F.E. (1970a) *Modern Spoken Cambodian*, New Haven and London.
Huffman, F.E. (1970b) *Cambodian System of Writing and Beginning Reader*, New Haven and London.
Jacob, J.M. (1968) *Introduction to Cambodian*, London.
Lim Hak Kheang and D. Purtle (1972) *Contemporary Cambodian*, Washington, DC.
Noss, R.B. and Im Proun (1966–70) *Cambodian Basic Course*, Washington, DC.

Catalan

Yates, A. (1975) *Teach Yourself Catalan*, London.

Chinese, Modern Standard

Chinesisch–Deutsches Wörterbuch (1974), Beijing.
Dow, F.D.M. (1984) *The Pronunciation of Chinese*, Edinburgh.
Kratochvil, P. (1968) *The Chinese Language Today*, London.
Mathews' Chinese–English Dictionary (1969) Cambridge, MA.
Ramsey, S.R. (1987) *The Languages of China*, Princeton.
Simon, W. and T.C. Chao (1945) *Structure Drill in Chinese*, London.
T'ung, P.C. and D.E. Pollard (1982) *Colloquial Chinese*, London.
Wang, F.F. (1967) *Mandarin Chinese Dictionary*, South Orange, NJ.
Yaxontov, S.E. (1965) *Drevne-Kitajskij jazyk*, Moscow.

Czech

De Bray, R.G.A. (1980) *Guide to the Slavonic Languages*, 3 vols, Columbus, OH.
Kopecký, L.V., J. Filipec, and O. Leška (1973) *Česko–Ruský slovník*, 2 vols, Moscow and Prague.
Šára, M., J. Šárová, and A. Bytel (1970) *Čeština pro cizince*, Prague.

Danish

Koefoed, H.A. (1958) *Teach Yourself Danish*, London.

Dutch

Koolhaven, H. (1941) *Teach Yourself Dutch*, London.
Shetter, W.Z. (1984) *Introduction to Dutch*, Leiden.
Weinstein, A.I. and Anny B. De Boeck (1975) *Dutch Reader*, Washington, DC.

English

Blakeley, L. (1964) *Old English*, London.
Quirk, E.G. and C.L. Wrenn (1957) *An Old English Grammar*, London.
Strang, B.M. (1970) *A History of English*, London.
Sweet, H. (1891) *New English Grammar*, Oxford and London.

Estonian

Aben, K. (1960) *Učebnik Estonskogo jazyka*, Tallinn.
Oinas, F.J. (1963) *Estonian General Reader*, Bloomington, IN.
Oinas, F.J. (1966) *Basic Course in Estonian*, Bloomington, IN.
Pjall′, I.E. (1955) *Učebnik Estonskogo jazyka*, Tallinn.

Finnish

Aaltio, M.H. (1963–75) *Finnish for Foreigners*, 3 vols, Helsinki.
Bell, A.R. and A.A. Koski (1968) *Finnish Graded Reader*, Washington, DC.
Englund, R. and W. Wolf (1953) *Finnische Sprachlehre*, Heidelberg.
Papp, I. (1967) *Finn nyelvkönyv*, Budapest.

French

Ferrar, H. (1956) *A French Reference Grammar*, Oxford.
Mansion, J. (1977–81) *Harrap's New Standard French and English Dictionary*, 4 vols, London and Paris.

Fulani

Taylor, F.W. (1953) *A Grammar of Fulani*, Oxford and London.

Georgian

Aronson, H.I. (1982) *Georgian: A Reading Grammar*, Columbus, OH.
Tschenkeli, K. (1958) *Einführung in die Georgische Sprache*, 2 vols, Zurich.

German

Bachmann, Ch.K. (1936) *Mittelhochdeutsches Lesebuch*, Zurich.
Hammer, A.E. (1971) *German Grammar and Usage*, London.

Greek, Modern Standard

Farmakides, A. (1983) *Manual of Modern Greek, and Modern Greek Reader*, 5 vols, New Haven and London.

Guaraní

Guasch, A. (1956) *El idioma Guaraní*, Asunción.

Jover-Peralta, A. and T. Osuna (1951) *Diccionario Guaraní–Español y Español–Guaraní*, Buenos Aires.
Meliá Lliteras, B., A. Pérez Peñasco, and L. Farré Maluquar (1960) *El Guaraní a su alcance*, Asunción.
Saguier, E. (1951) *El idioma Guaraní*, Buenos Aires.

Gujarati

Lambert, H.M. (1971) *Gujarati Language Course*, Cambridge.
Savel'eva, L.V. (1965) *Jazyk Gudzharati*, Moscow.

Hausa

Brauner, S. and M. Ashiwaju (1966) *Lehrbuch der Hausa-Sprache*, Leipzig.
Kraft, C.H. and H.M. Kirk-Greene (1973) *Teach Yourself Hausa*, London.
Smirnova, J.A. (1970) *Jazyk Khausa*, Moscow.

Hebrew

Cohen, A. (ed.) (1947) *The Soncino Chumash*, Hindhead.
Harrison, R.K. (1955) *Biblical Hebrew*, London.
Lambkin, T.O. (1973) *Introduction to Biblical Hebrew*, London.

Hindi

McGregor, R.S. (1972) *Outline of Hindi Grammar*, Oxford and London.
Snell, R. and S. Weightman (1989) *Teach Yourself Hindi*, London.

Hungarian

Koski, A.A. and I. Mihályfy (1962–4) *Hungarian Basic Course*, 2 vols, Washington, DC.
Országh, L. (1969) *Magyar–Angol szótár*, 2 vols, Budapest.

Icelandic

Berkov, V.P. and A. Böðvarssonar (1962) *Islandsko–Ruskij slovar'*, Moscow.
Einarsson, S. (1945) *Icelandic*, Baltimore.
Jonsson, S. (1927) *A Primer of Modern Icelandic*, London.

Igbo

Fixman, B.S. (1975) *Jazyk Igbo*, Moscow.
Green, M.M. and G.E. Igwe (1966) *Introductory Igbo Course*, London.

Indonesian

Clark, S.J. and E. Siahaan (1967) *Structure Drill in Indonesian*, London.
Dardjowidjojo, S. (1978) *Sentence Patterns of Indonesian*, Honolulu.

Harter, J.M., J. Chadran, and A.S. Poeraatmadja (1968) *Indonesian Newspaper Reader*, Washington, DC.
Johns, Y. (1977–81) *Bahasa Indonesia*, 2 vols, Canberra.
Korigodskij, R.N., O.N. Kondraškin, and B.J. Zinov'iev (1961) *Indonezijsko-Russkij slovar'*, Moscow.
Sarumpaet, J.P. and P. Hendrata (1968) *A Modern Reader in Bahasa Indonesia*, Melbourne.
Teselkin, A.S. and N.F. Alieva (1960) *Indonezijskij jazyk*, Moscow.

Italian

Reynolds, B. (1975) *The Concise Cambridge Italian Dictionary*, Harmondsworth.

Japanese, Modern Standard

Clarke, H.D.B. and Motoko Hamamura (1981) *Colloquial Japanese*, London.
Gakken (1973) *Japanese for Today*, Tokyo.
Jelinek, J. (1978) *Reader in Scientific and Technical Japanese*, Sheffield.
McClain, Y.M. (1973) *Intermediate Japanese Reading Aids*, 2 vols, Tokyo.
Martin, S.E. (1954) *Essential Japanese*, Rutland, VT.
Martin, S.E. (1975) *A Reference Grammar of Japanese*, New Haven and London.
Miller, R.A. (1967) *The Japanese Language*, Chicago and London.
O'Neill, P.G. (1966) *Respect Language in Modern Japanese*, London.
Uehara, T. and G.N. Kiyose (1974) *Fundamentals of Japanese*, Bloomington, IN, London, and Tokyo.

Javanese

Bohatta, H. (n.d.) *Praktische Grammatik der Javanischen Sprache*, Vienna.
Teselkin, A.S. (1961) *Javanskij jazyk*, Moscow.

Kannada

Andronov, M.S. (1962) *Jazyk Kannada*, Moscow.
Jensen, H. (1969) *Grammatik der Kanaresischen Schriftsprache*, Leipzig.
Ziegler, F. (1920) *Practical Key to the Kanarese Language*, Mangalore.

Kashmiri

Kachru, B.B. (1969) *A Reference Grammar of Kashmiri*, Urbana, IL.
Zaxar'in, B.A. and D.I. Edel'man (1971) *Jazyk Kašmiri*, Moscow.

Korean

Mazur, J.N. (1960) *Korejskij jazyk*, Moscow.
Park, B. Nam (1968–9) *Korean Basic Course*, 2 vols, Washington, DC.
Usatov, D.M., J.N. Mazur, and V.M. Mozdykov (1954) *Russko-Korejskij slovar'*, Moscow.

Kurdish

Abdulla, J.J. and E.N. McCarus (1967) *Kurdish Basic Course: Dialect of Sulaimania, Iraq*, Ann Arbor, MI.
Bakaev, V.D. (1957) *Kurdsko–Russkij slovar'*, Moscow.
Blau, J. (1980) *Manuel de Kurde (dialecte Sorani)*, Paris.

Lahndá

Smirnov, J.A. (1970) *Jazyk Lendi*, Moscow.
Zograph, G.A. (1982) *The Languages of South Asia*, London.

Lao

Hoshino, T. and R. Marcus (1981) *Lao for Beginners*, Rutland, VT, and Tokyo.
Morev, L.N., A.A. Moskalev, and J.J. Plam (1972) *Laosskij jazyk*, Moscow.
Sobol'eva, V.S. *et al.* (1988) *Russko–Laosskij i Laossko–Russkij razgovornik*, Moscow.

Lappish

Børretzen, J. (1977) *Liten Samsk Grammatik*, Trondheim.
Collinder, B. (1957) *Survey of the Uralic Languages*, Stockholm.
Décsy, G. (1965) *Einführung in die Finnisch-Ugrische Sprachwissenschaft*, Wiesbaden.
Guttorm, I., J. Jernsletten and K.P. Nickel (1984) *Davvin 1: Saamen kielen peruskurssi*, Helsinki.
Miettunen, G. (1968) *Abbes*, Pieksämäki.

Latvian

Budiņa Lazdiņa, T. (1966) *Teach Yourself Latvian*, London.
Fennell, T.G. and H. Gelsen (1980) *A Grammar of Modern Latvian*, 3 vols, The Hague, Paris, and New York.

Lithuanian

Dambriūnas, L., A. Klimas, and W.R. Schmalstieg (1966) *Introduction to Modern Lithuanian*, New York.
Orvidienė, E. (1968) *Lietuvių kalbos vadovėlis*, Vilnius.

Macedonian

De Bray, R.G.A. (1980) *Guide to the Slavonic Languages*, 3 vols, Columbus, OH.

Malayalam

Sekhar, C. and J.J. Glazov (1961) *Jazyk Malayalam*, Moscow.

Maori

Krupa, V. (1967) *Jazyk Maori*, Moscow.

Mapuche (Mapudungu)

Augusta, Felix José de (1903) *Gramatica Araucana*, Valdivia.
Augusta, Felix José de (1916: 1989) *Diccionario Mapuche–Español*, Santiago de Chile.

Marathi

Katenina, T.E. (1963) *Jazyk Marathi*, Moscow.
Lambert, H.M. (1943) *Marathi Language Course*, London.

Mongolian, Modern Standard

Bosson, J.E. (1964) *Modern Mongolian*, Bloomington, IN, and The Hague.
Hangin, J.G. (1968) *Basic Course in Mongolian*, Bloomington, IN, and The Hague.
Hangin, J.G. (1970) *A Concise English–Mongolian Dictionary*, Bloomington, IN, and The Hague.
Hangin, J.G. (1973) *Intermediate Mongolian*, Bloomington, IN, and The Hague.
Rinchin, A.R. (1952) *Učebnik Mongol'skogo jazyka*, Moscow.
Vietze, H.-P. (1963) *Deutsch–Mongolisches Gesprächsbuch*, Leipzig.
Vietze, H.-P. (1969) *Lehrbuch der Mongolischen Sprache*, Leipzig.

Nama

Hagman, R.S. (1977) *Nama Hottentot Grammar*, Bloomington, IN, and The Hague.

Navajo

Diyin God Bizaad: the New Testament, Psalms and Proverbs in Navajo (1975) New York.
Goossen, I.W. (1979) *Navajo Made Easier*, Flagstaff.
Reichard, G.A. (1951) *Navaho Grammar*, New York.
Young, R.W. and W. Morgan (1948) *The Function and Signification of Certain Navaho Particles*, Phoenix, AZ.
Young, R.W. and W. Morgan (1976) *The Navaho Language*, Salt Lake City.

Nepali

Matthews, D. (1984) *A Course in Nepali*, London.

Nivkh

Panfilov, V.Z. (1962–5) *Grammatika Nivkhskogo jazyka*, 2 vols, Moscow and Leningrad.
Savel'eva, L.V. and C.M. Taksami (1965) *Russko-Nivkhskij slovar'*, Moscow.

Norwegian

Haugen, E. and K.G. Chapman (1964) *Spoken Norwegian*, New York.
Sommerfelt, A. (1943) *Norwegian*, London.

Panjabi

Shackle, C. (1972) *Teach Yourself Punjabi*, London.
Tolstaja, N.I. (1960) *Jazyk Pandzabi*, Moscow.

Pashto

Dvorjankov, N.A. (1960) *Jazyk Puštu*, Moscow.
Lorenz, M. (1982) *Lehrbuch des Pashto (Afghanisch)* Leipzig.

Persian

Alavi, B. and M. Lorenz (1988) *Lehrbuch der Persischen Sprache*, Leipzig.
Avery, P.W., M.A. Jazayery, and H.H. Paper (1962–3) *Modern Persian Reader*, 3 vols, Ann Arbor, MI.
Dresden, M.J. (1958) *Reader in Modern Persian*, New York.
Haidari, A.A. (1975) *Modern Persian Reader*, London.
Kamshad, H. (1968) *A Modern Persian Prose Reader*, Cambridge.
Lambton, A.K.S. (1967) *Persian Grammar*, Cambridge.
Miller, B.V. (1953) *Persidsko–Russkij slovar'*, Moscow.
Moshiri, L. (1988) *Colloquial Persian*, London.

Polish

Mazur, B.W. (1983) *Colloquial Polish*, London.
Patkaniowska, M. (1944) *Essentials of Polish Grammar*, Glasgow.
Penny, B. and K.T. Malinowska (1974) *Communicating in Polish*, Washington, DC.
Schenker, A.M. (1970) *Fifteen Modern Polish Short Stories*, New Haven and London.

Polynesian Languages

Krupa, V. (1982) *The Polynesian Languages*, London.

Portuguese

Cunha, C. and L. Cintra (1985) *Breve gramática do Português contemporâneo*, Lisbon.
Willis, R.C. (1971) *An Essential Course in Modern Portuguese*, London.

Quechua

Bills, G.D., B. Vallejo, and R.C. Troike (1969) *Introduction to Spoken Bolivian Quechua*, Austin, TX, and London.
Crapo, R.H. and P. Aitkin (1986) *Bolivian Quechua Reader and Grammar-Dictionary*, Ann Arbor, MI.
Guardia Mayorga, C.A. (1980) *Diccionario Kechwa-Castellano y Castellano-Kechwa*, Lima.
Perroud, C. (1961) *Gramática Quechua*, Lima.
Soto Ruiz, C. (1979) *Quechua: manual de enseñanza*, Lima.
Urioste-Herrero, S.I. (1955) *Gramática y vocabulario de la lengua Quechua*, La Paz and Cochabamba.

Romanian

Deletant, D. (1983) *Colloquial Romanian*, London.
Ştefănescu-Drăgăneşti, V. and M. Murrell (1970) *Teach Yourself Romanian*, London.

Romany

Vencel', T.V. (1964) *Tsyganskij jazyk (severnorusskij dialekt)*, Moscow.

Russian

Borras, F.M. and R.F. Christian (1971) *Russian Syntax*, Oxford and London.
Falla, P.S. (ed.) (1984) *The Oxford English-Russian Dictionary*, Oxford.
Matthews, W.K. (1953) *The Structure and Development of Russian*, Cambridge.
Wheeler, M. (1972) *The Oxford Russian-English Dictionary*, Oxford.

Samoan

Arakin, V.D. (1973) *Samoanskij jazyk*, Moscow.
Churchward, S. (1951) *A New Samoan Grammar*, Melbourne.
Marsack, T.Y. (1962) *Teach Yourself Samoan*, London.

Sanskrit

Antoine, R. (1954–6) *A Sanskrit Manual*, Calcutta.
Coulson, M. (1976) *Teach Yourself Sanskrit*, London.
Ivanov, V.V. and V.N. Toporov (1960) *Sanskrit*, Moscow.
Lanman, C.R. (1947) *A Sanskrit Reader*, Cambridge, MA.

Macdonell, A.A. (1917) *A Vedic Reader for Students*, Oxford and London.
Macdonell, A.A. (1924) *Sanskrit Dictionary*, Oxford and London.
Macdonell, A.A. (1927) *A Sanskrit Grammar for Students*, Oxford.

Semitic Languages

Bergsträsser, G. (1928) *Einführung in die Semitischen Sprachen*, Munich.
D'jakonov, I.M. (1965) *Semito–Xamitskie jazyki*, Moscow.
Moscati, S., A. Spitaler, E. Ullendorff, and W. von Soden (1980) *Introduction to the Comparative Grammar of the Semitic Languages*, Wiesbaden.
Watt, W. Montgomery (1968) *What is Islam?*, London and Beirut.

Serbo-Croat

Hawkesworth, C. (1986) *Colloquial Serbo-Croat*, London.
Hodge, C.T. and J. Jankovic (1965–8) *Serbo-Croatian Basic Course*, 2 vols, Washington, DC.
Schmaus, A. (1964) *Lehrbuch der Serbokroatischen Sprache*, Munich and Belgrade.

Sindhi

Egorova, R.P. (1966) *Jazyk Sindhi*, Moscow.

Sinhalese

Fairbanks, G.H., J.W. Gair, and M.W.S. De Silva (1968) *Colloquial Sinhalese*, Ithaca, NY.
Reynolds, C.H.B. (1980) *Sinhalese*, London.
Vyxuxolev, V.V. (1974) *Singal'skij Jazyk*, Moscow.

Slavonic Languages

Bidwell, C.E. (1963) *Slavic Historical Phonology in Tabular Form*, The Hague.
Braun, M. (n.d.) *Grundzüge der Slawischen Sprachen*, Göttingen.
De Bray, R.G.A. (1980) *Guide to the Slavonic Languages*, Columbus, OH.
Entwistle, W.J. and W.A. Morison (1964) *Russian and the Slavonic Languages*, London.

Slovak

Kollar, D., V. Dorotjakova, M. Filkusová, and E. Vasilievová (1976) *Slovatsko–Russkij slovar'*, Moscow and Bratislava.

Slovene

Nemec, J. (1947) *Grammatica della lingua slovena*, Gorizia.

Somali

Bell, C.R.V. (1953) *The Somali Language*, London.
El-Solami-Mewis, C. (1987) *Lehrbuch des Somali*, Leipzig.
Issa, A.A. and J.D. Murphy (1984) *Somali Newspaper Reader*, Kensington, MD.
Puglielli, A. (ed.) (1981) *Studi Somali*, vol. 2: *Sintassi della lingua Somali*, Rome.

Spanish

Ingamells, L. and P. Standish (1975) *Variedades del Español actual*, London.
Smith, C. (1971, 1984) *Collins Spanish–English, English–Spanish Dictionary*, London and Glasgow.

Sundanese

Pavlenko, A.P. (1965) *Sundanskij jazyk*, Moscow.

Swahili

M'ačina, E.N. (1960) *Jazyk Suahili*, Moscow.
Perrott, D.V. (1951) *Swahili*, London.
Stevick, E.W., M. Lehr, and P.G. Imhof (1966) *Swahili: an Active Introduction*, Washington, DC.
Wilson, P.M. (1985) *Simplified Swahili*, London.
Zawawi, S. (1971) *Kiswahili kwa Kitendo*, New York and London.

Swedish

Hildeman, N.-G. *et al.* (1964) *Practise Swedish*, 2 vols, Stockholm.
Holmes, P. and G. Serin (1990) *Colloquial Swedish*, London.
Milanova, D.E. (1959) *Švedsko–Russkij slovar'*, Moscow.

Tagalog

Aspillera, P.S. (1969) *Basic Tagalog*, Rutland, VT, and Tokyo.
Bowen, J.D. (1965) *Beginning Tagalog*, Berkeley and Los Angeles, CA.
Cruz, M. and S.P. Ignashev (1959) *Tagal'sko–Russkij slovar'*, Moscow.
Cruz, M. and S.P. Ignashev (1965) *Russko–Tagal'skij slovar'*, Moscow.
Cruz, M. and L.T. Skarban (1966) *Tagal'skij jazyk*, Moscow.
Ramos, T.V. (1971) *Tagalog Structures*, Honolulu.

Tamil

Andronov, M.S. (1960) *Tamil'skij jazyk*, Moscow.
Andronov, M.S. (1966) *Grammatika Tamil'skogo jazyka*, Moscow.
Clayton, A.C. (1939) *Introduction to Spoken Tamil*, Madras.
Jothimuththu, P. (1965) *A Guide to Tamil*, Madras.
P'atigorskij, A.M. and S.G. Rudin (1960) *Tamil'sko–Russkij slovar'*, Moscow.

Pope, G.U. (1911) *A Handbook of the Ordinary Dialect of the Tamil Language*, Oxford.

Telugu

Arden, A.H. (1937) *A Progressive Grammar of the Telugu Language*, Madras.
Krishnamurti, B.H. and J.P.L. Gwynn (1985) *A Grammar of Modern Telugu*, Delhi.
Lisker, L. (1963) *Introduction to Spoken Telugu*, New York.
Petruničeva, Z.N. (1960) *Jazyk Telugu*, Moscow.
Šastri, K.M. (1985) *Descriptive Grammar and Handbook of Modern Telugu*, Stuttgart.

Thai

Brown, J.M. (1967–9) *Thai Course*, 3 vols, Bangkok.
Campbell, S. and Ch. Shaweevongse (1957) *The Fundamentals of the Thai Language*, Bangkok.
Eagling, G.G. (1951) *Elementary Thai*, Bangkok.
Haas, M. (1954) *Thai Reader*, Washington, DC.
Haas, M. (1955) *Thai Vocabulary*, Washington, DC.
Haas, M. (1964) *Thai–English Student's Dictionary*, Stanford, CA.
Morev, L.N., A.A. Moskalev, and J.J. Plam (1961) *Tajskij jazyk*, Moscow.

Tibetan

Goldstein, M.C. (1973) *Modern Literary Tibetan*, Urbana, IL.
Goldstein, M.C. (1975) *Tibetan–English Dictionary of Modern Tibetan*, Kathmandu.
Goldstein, M.C. (1984) *English–Tibetan Dictionary of Modern Tibetan*, Berkeley, Los Angeles, CA, and London.
Goldstein, M.C. and Nawang Nornang (1970) *Modern Spoken Tibetan: Lhasa Dialect*, Seattle and London.
Hahn, M. (1971) *Lehrbuch der klassischen Tibetischen Schriftsprache*, Hamburg.
Jäschke, H.A. (1968) *Tibetan–English Dictionary*, London.
Parfinovič, J.M. (1970) *Tibetskij pis'mennyj' jazyk*, Moscow.
Sedláček, K. (1972) *Tibetan Newspaper Reader*, 2 vols, Leipzig.
Tomulić, R. (1984) *Manuel de Tibétain, parler de Lhasa*, Paris.

Turkish

Ağralı, S., L.Y. Fotos, S.S. Demiray, and L.B. Swift (1970) *Turkish Basic Course and Reader*, Washington, DC.
Lewis, G.L. (1967) *Turkish Grammar*, London.
Mardin, Y. (1976) *Colloquial Turkish*, London.

Ukrainian

Humesky, A. (1986) *Modern Ukrainian*, Edmonton and Toronto.
Il'in, V.S. *et al.* (1975) *Ukrains'ko-Rosijs'kij slovnik*, Kiev.
Makarova, H.I., L.M. Palamar, and N.K. Prisjažnjuk (1975) *Learn Ukrainian*, Kiev.

Uralic Languages

Collinder, B. (1957) *Survey of the Uralic Languages*, Stockholm.

Urdu

Bailey, T.G. (1956, 1974) *Urdu*, London.
Russell, R. (1981) *A New Course in Hindustani*, London.

Uzbek

Akabirov, S.F., Z.M. Magrufov, and A.T. Khodzhakhanov (1959) *Uzbeksko–Russkij slovar'*, Moscow.
Mansurov, R.I. and I.A. Kissen (1953) *Uzbek tili*, Tashkent.
Poppe, N. (1962) *Uzbek Newspaper Reader*, Bloomington, IN.
Raun, A. (1969) *Basic Course in Uzbek*, Bloomington, IN.

Vietnamese

Nguyen Dinh Hoa (1966a) *Speak Vietnamese*, Rutland, VT, and Tokyo.
Nguyan Dinh Hoa (1966b) *Read Vietnamese*, Rutland, VT, and Tokyo.
Nguyen Dang Liem (1971) *Intermediate Vietnamese*, South Orange, NJ.
Solntsev, V.M. *et al.* (1960) *V'etnamskij jazyk*, Moscow.
Thompson, L.C. (1965) *A Vietnamese Grammar*, Seattle.

Welsh

King, G. (1993) *Modern Welsh: a Comprehensive Grammar*, London and New York.
Rhys-Jones, J.J. (1977) *Living Welsh*, London.
Williams, S.J. (1980) *A Welsh Grammar*, Cardiff.

Yiddish

Birnbaum, S.A. (1966) *Grammatik der Jiddischen Sprache*, Hamburg.
Birnbaum, S.A. (1979) *Yiddish: a Survey and Grammar*, Toronto and Manchester.

Yoruba

McClure, H.D. and J.O. Oyewale (1967) *Yoruba Intermediate Texts*, Washington, DC.
Rowlands, E.C. (1969) *Teach Yourself Yoruba*, London.

Yakovleva, V.K. (1963) *Jazyk Yoruba*, Moscow.

Zulu

Doke, C.M. (1950) *Text-book of Zulu Grammar*, 2nd edn, London.
Oxotina, N.V. (1961) *Jazyk Zulu*, Moscow.